Please remember that this is a library book,
and that it belongs only temporarily to each
person who uses it. Be considerate. Do
not write in this, or any, library book.

APPROPRIATE TECHNOLOGY SOURCEBOOK

A guide to practical books
for village and small community technology

By
Ken Darrow
Mike Saxenian

WITHDRAWN

Revised and Enlarged Edition
September 1986

A Volunteers in Asia Publication

ABSTRACT

Appropriate Technology Sourcebook, September 1986.

This is the latest edition of the guide to practical books on village and small community technology. Over 50,000 copies of previous editions have been used in more than 130 countries, to find a wide range of published technical information that can be used by individuals and small groups. In the new edition, 1150 publications from international and U.S. sources are reviewed, covering small water supply systems, renewable energy devices such as water-mills and improved cookstoves, agricultural tools and implements, intensive gardening, workshop tools and equipment, crop preservation, housing, health care, forestry, aquaculture, nonformal education, small business management, transportation, small industries and other topics. Extensive index. Price and ordering information are provided for each publication. 500 illustrations. The Sourcebook can also be used as the index for the Appropriate Technology Microfiche Library, which contains the complete text of 1000 books. Complete sets of the microfiche library are also available from the publishers at low cost.

ISBN 0-917704-17-7 (paperback)
ISBN 0-917704-18-5 (hardbound)

First Printing September 1986
Printed in U.S.A.

Cover design by Kathy Barker.
Cover illustration by Rob Colvin.

Additional copies of this book can be ordered from: Appropriate Technology Project, Volunteers in Asia, P.O. Box 4543, Stanford, California 94305, USA. The regular price of the paperback edition is $17.95. For local groups in developing countries, the price is $9.00. Postage costs are $2.00 for domestic U.S. addresses, and $3.00 for foreign addresses. A hardbound edition with a sewn binding is available for $26.95 plus postage ($14.00 plus postage to local groups in developing countries). Discounts are available for purchases of 10 copies or more.

Table of Contents

ACKNOWLEDGEMENTS

This edition of the Appropriate Technology Sourcebook and the September 1986 expansion of the A.T. Microfiche Library were made possible in large part due to the financial support of Church World Service, United Methodist Committee on Relief, and the Atkinson Foundation.

Previous editions of the A.T. Sourcebook were supported by the above organizations and United Church Board of World Ministries, United Presbyterian Church, Maryknoll Fathers, Bishop's Fund for World Relief (Episcopal Church), Catholic Relief Services, CODEL, and Lutheran World Relief.

Financial support for the original creation of the A.T. Microfiche Library was generously provided by The James C. Penney Foundation, The New Land Foundation, and Mr. and Mrs. Warren T. Weber.

Our special thanks go to the hundreds of appropriate technology practitioners, writers and publishers, who have agreed to allow us to include their publications in the microfiche library.

The Appropriate Technology Sourcebook has benefitted from the help of numerous individuals over the years since it first appeared in 1975. Thomas Fricke has been an important contributor to all of the editions. Kent Keller and Rick Pam were co-editors with Ken Darrow for the 1981 and 1976 editions. John Morris, Mike Connor, Bill Bower, David Werner, Mary Pat O'Connell, Cliff Halverson, Bob Huppe, Jim Bateson, Marcus Kauffman, Dick Stanley, Lynne Coen, Charles Kolstad, Martha Lewis, Jim Kalin and Maryanna Maloney also contributed reviews or provided important advice. Others too numerous to name suggested books to be included. Darby Hoover heroically completed the long task of typesetting and provided invaluable help with most aspects of the latest edition. Alison Davis helped greatly with pasteup, and Sarah Whitmore helped in various phases of the production process. Al Fabrizio at Cameragraphics was a regular source of good advice for our graphics needs. Father Patrick Shaules provided seed money when the Sourcebook was only an idea, thereby calling our bluff. James MacCracken saw the initial pilot edition in 1975 and helped to arrange the funding to make the Sourcebook a full-sized book. Dr. W.P. Napitupulu, founder of Indonesia's domestic volunteer service, provided the authors with much of their initial inspiration.

The September 1986 expansion of the A.T. Microfiche Library benefitted from the observations and advice of hundreds of users around the world. Michael Saxenian and Ken Darrow coordinated the expansion project. Darby Hoover helped in all aspects of production.

Many people helped to assemble the original A.T. Microfiche Library. Jonathan Bell came to VIA with information about the very low costs of microfiche reproduction, and a vision of publishers around the world adding low cost microfiche titles to their lists. Ken Darrow conceived of the concept of the A.T. library on microfiche, packaged with a portable microfiche reader, and linked to the A.T. Sourcebook. Ken and Bill Stanley researched the feasibility of the project, did the initial planning, and began the long process of collecting permissions to reproduce materials. Michael Saxenian then took over as project coordinator and supervised the complicated and enormous task of producing the library on microfiche. Management of the permissions, along with that of materials acquisitions and preparation for filming, passed to David Pierce, who also nursed our computer. Buzz Thompson, Matt Lippert, Roger Hart, and Scott Templeton helped with various production related tasks. Special thanks to Robert Lewis, for his advice on microfiche and reader technology, to Thomas Fricke for his enthusiasm and support, and to Ada Jo Mann for her early confidence in the usefulness of the library. Mike Gee, Jean Hilken and their colleagues at Western Microfilm provided important advice on many occasions.

How to Use this Book

This book contains reviews of the best available literature on small-scale technology, especially for use in developing countries. Use the table of contents (on page 3) and the index (beginning on page 726) to find reviews on specific topics of interest.

In most cases, ordering information is provided after the title. In some cases, abbreviations are used for publishers; see the section entitled "Book Ordering" on page 30 for the full addresses of these publishers.

This book can also be used as an index to the Appropriate Technology Microfiche Library, a complete low-cost library that contains most of the books reviewed here. Instructions for use of the microfiche library are on page 670.

Introduction

". . .valuable know-how as well as excellent equipment, fitting into the constraints and limitations of poverty and suitable for genuine development, exist all over the world — in the rich as well as in the poor countries. But it is scattered, hidden, often very poorly documented, and generally inaccessible to those in need, when it is most needed. Countless men and women 'in the field' are trying to solve problems for which solutions have already been found somewhere else; are embarking on experiments which have already been shown to be unfruitful; are trying to find methods of working and items of equipment which may be available, but they do not know where. At this level of know-how and technology there is an almost total lack of effective international communication."

— E.F. Schumacher, **Appropriate Technology Journal**, 1976

This book represents an attempt to improve access to information on small-scale technologies. Our purpose is to present a selection of capital-saving, labor-using tools and techniques that already have proven to be valuable in different circumstances around the world. We do not suggest that any specific technology will always be appropriate. The appropriate technology worker needs options, not a prescribed package of technology.

Appropriate Technology

What is appropriate technology all about? It is a way of thinking about technological change, recognizing that tools and techniques can evolve along different paths toward different ends. It includes the belief that human communities can have a hand in deciding what their future will be like, and that the choice of tools and techniques is an important part of this. It also includes the recognition that technologies can embody cultural biases and sometimes have political and distributional effects that go far beyond a strictly economic evaluation. "A.T." therefore involves a search for technologies that have, for example, beneficial effects on income distribution, human development, environmental quality, and the distribution of political power — as well as productivity — in the context of particular communities and nations.

The appropriate technology movement in rich countries such as the United States got started due to the convergence of a variety of concerns. These included the need to find a more harmonious and sustainable relationship with the environment, identify a way out of the accelerating energy and resource crises, reduce alienating work disconnected from its products and goals, develop more democratic workplaces, bring local economies back to health with diverse locally owned and operated enterprises, and revitalize local communities and cultural traditions.

Thoughtful, careful social choices are needed to correct the excesses and imbalances of an industrial culture driven by endless materialism. An essential quality of the appropriate technology movement in the United States can therefore be expressed by the word "restraint."

The appropriate technology movement in poor countries has, on the other hand, developed in a very different fashion. In the rich countries the investment required to create one new manufacturing job typically is in the range of $20,000-$150,000, and in heavy industry this figure is higher still. In the poor countries the small amounts of capital available have usually been concentrated in a small industrial sector, creating very few jobs due to the high investment required per workplace. The appropriate technology movement in poor countries has come out of the recognition that industrialization strategies have not been successfully solving the problems of poverty and inequality. Indeed, in many cases "modernization" efforts have been massive assaults on local culture. The result for hundreds of millions of people has been the modernization of poverty — the neglect or destruction of traditional crafts occupations, the consolidation of farm lands into fewer and fewer hands, and the division of communities, leaving these people to eke out an existence on the fringe of economic activity. The appropriate technology movement in the Third World has developed as "the art of the possible" among the world's poor, seeking ways to solve pressing basic problems and create jobs with resources consisting of local skills and materials but little surplus cash.

From these different origins, the appropriate technology movements in rich and poor countries have been moving towards each other. The development of renewable energy technologies has long been a chief area of activity among U.S. appropriate technology groups. It moved high on the list of priorities in oil-importing poor countries in the late 1970's, as they faced high prices and scarcity of fuel for buses, tractors, and irrigation pumps. Similarly, environmental protection has gained increased attention in poor countries as pesticides have created major health risks for farmers and farmworkers, and deforestation has reached a critical level.

Criteria for appropriate technology

This book, though primarily oriented towards appropriate technology activities in poor countries, contains relevant materials for North Americans as well. The books and documents reviewed here describe tools and techniques that, in general:

1) require only small amounts of capital;

2) emphasize the use of locally available materials, in order to lower costs and reduce supply problems;

3) are relatively labor-intensive but more productive than many traditional technologies;

4) are small enough in scale to be affordable to individual families or small groups of families;

5) can be understood, controlled and maintained by villagers whenever possible, without a high level of special training;

6) can be produced in villages or small workshops;

7) suppose that people can and will work together to bring improvements to communities;

8) offer opportunities for local people to become involved in the modification and innovation process;

9) are flexible, can be adapted to different places and changing circumstances;

10) can be used in productive ways without doing harm to the environment.

Some of the reasoning that underlies the concept of appropriate technology may be summarized as follows:

1) it permits local needs to be met more effectively, because local people are involved in identifying and working to address these needs; for the same reasons, it is likely to be in harmony with local traditions and values;

2) it means the development of tools that extend human labor and skills, rather than machines that replace human labor and eliminate human skills;

3) it represents a comprehensible and controllable scale of activities, organization and mistakes, at which people without management training can work together and understand what they are doing;

4) it allows a more economical operation by minimizing the transport of goods in an era of expensive energy, allowing greater interaction of local industry and permitting greater use of local resources — both human and material;

5) it makes unnecessary many expensive or unavailable finance, transportation, education, advertising, management, and energy services; and avoids the loss of local control that use of such outside services implies;

6) it helps to establish a self-sustaining and expanding reservoir of skills in the community which begins from already existing skills;

7) it provides a region with a cushion against the effects of outside economic changes (e.g., the collapse of the world sugar market or the sudden unavailability of fertilizer);

8) it helps to reduce economic, social, and political dependency between individuals, between regions, and between nations, by recognizing that people can and will do things for themselves if they can find a way. (See Tom Bender in **Sharing Smaller Pies** on many of the criteria listed here.)

Addressing many obstacles

Appropriate technology has special appeal probably in part because it addresses a number of problems at once. The emphasis on self-reliance and local production for local needs removes from the list of development obstacles many of the inequities of an international system that is dominated by the expensive technology and economic power of the rich countries. At the same time, the lack of a well-developed infrastructure and the shortage of highly-trained humanpower to efficiently run large industrial organizations become much less important when production is decentralized. It is probably for these reasons that the concept of appropriate technology is so popular. Those who believe in small entrepreneurial capitalism, democratic institutions, decentralist Marxism, European socialism, African communalism, Buddhism, and numerous other systems can find much of value in the ideas underlying appropriate technology.

Nicolas Jequier has described the popularity of the appropriate technology approach as evidence of a "cultural revolution" in development thinking. The elements of self-reliance, local initiative, and local control that are essential parts of this approach present a challenge to conventional thinking in the development institutions.

The village perspective

Up to 80% or more of the population in most developing countries lives in rural villages. Many of the people in urban areas fled the stifling lack of opportunities that tends to characterize rural areas. Thus successful rural appropriate technologies might concern some 90% of the population. An important voice in the dialogue about village technology can and should be provided by educated people working in rural areas in small projects. However, many of these people seem hesitant to get involved in experiments with technology, perhaps because this is seen as the work of engineers and scientists, and therefore too difficult for others to undertake. Yet the development of appropriate technology is not solely or even primarily a question of engineering design—it involves a wide range of considerations.

Appropriate technology work cuts across traditional lines of expertise, and benefits from the insights of local farmers, technologists, educated generalists and businesspeople. The small-scale technologies and techniques covered in this book are not particularly difficult to understand. Village problems do not generally require the importation of licensed technology, the intervention of multinational corporations, or the use of computer print-outs for their solutions. These problems are centered around basic needs such as water supply, adequate housing, increased food production and processing, crop storage, and fuel supplies. Many of the people with a generalist background who are now involved in running small village development projects are quite capable of studying, understanding, and effectively using most of the books reviewed here on these subjects. There is a clear need for such people to begin to think of themselves as "village technologists" who support small experiments and tests, and who try to make villagers aware of what has been done elsewhere.

It is increasingly evident that appropriate technology workers should be forging relationships and making alliances with people active in complementary development activities such as community organizers, planners, university students and faculty, staff of small business and cooperatives promotion programs, members of unions and peasant organizations, teachers in technical high schools, and librarians. All have much to share with technologists. For this reason we have added new categories of readings to this book over the years. One section is concerned with strategies for appropriate technology and local self-reliance. Discussed here are the advantages of small scale in community-based efforts, and how government policies can support those efforts. Another section reviews the literature on the successful operation of small businesses and cooperatives—important vehicles for the application of appropriate technologies and the equitable distribution of the benefits. Educational strategies that support local problem-solving are necessary if local knowledge of needs and the power of community action are to be tapped. We have therefore included chapters on science teaching to support local technical innovation, and nonformal education approaches and training techniques.

The theme of people's participation runs through much of what has been said about appropriate technology. This comes in part from a philosophy which measures development in terms of the people's skills and their ability to solve their own problems.

In northern Bali there is a village in which the people have been very active in their own self-help projects for many years. They asked an engineer in a nearby town if it was true that electricity could be produced by harnessing a small stream. They ended up getting all the technical help they needed to design a small water-turbine system, which they proceeded to build and pay for themselves using money from the sale of coffee. They had to buy the generator and they had the simple Banki turbine made in a large city, but the dam construction, the turbine installation, the wiring throughout the village, and all the rest were done by the villagers themselves. This is a dramatic example, which admittedly could not have been completed without the coffee revenues. Yet it demonstrates that remarkable things are possible when villagers are organized and begin to believe that they can work to develop their own village.

The decentralization that should be part of participation also makes a great deal of sense from a technical standpoint:

> "Detailed technological information in terms of local labor conditions, and the resource situation, transport facilities, etc., may

well be more easily accessible to the man on the spot, but does he really know very much about the potentially relevant techniques used in other economies but not yet locally? Certainly, if he learns more about the experiences of other countries, he may well be in a better position than the man at the center to judge the local technological possibilities in the light of rural conditions."

— Amartya Sen, in **Technology and Employment in Industry**

The recent track record

We wish we could report that the purely technological reasons for poverty (inadequate tools and techniques and therefore inefficient use of labor and resources) are well on their way to being eliminated. Unfortunately, this is far from being true. The achievement of some respectability for appropriate technology within both the academic community and the development community over the past ten years does not mean that a major effort to apply A.T. concepts is underway. During the same period the running shoe industry in the United States reached $2.0 billion in annual sales. Shoe designs have improved dramatically, as large sums of money have been devoted to research and development in the race to make better shoes to protect runners from injury. In comparison, progress in appropriate technology efforts have certainly not been as well funded. In 1985, $100 million in talking toy bears were sold to the U.S. public. This exceeded the value of all newly designed equipment promoted as appropriate technology sold in the Third World (though not the value of all equipment that *could* be classified as A.T.).

A general reevaluation of the potential and role of A.T. as an important part of development strategy has been taking place in recent years. Progress has seemed slow to many observers, and aid projects intended to push appropriate technologies have often been ineffective. Yet the experience of the last 15 years, as documented by the books reviewed here and incorporated in the A.T. microfiche library, points to an exciting number of successes, new insights, and advances in technology in almost every field.

Much has been learned from the failures of the past, which deserve some attention. In the first 10 years of widespread, enthusiastic A.T. activity around the globe, the same 15 items were built and rebuilt, and research centers acquired cemetaries of artifacts with which to impress international visitors. Most of this equipment was not very economical or practical. One common reason for failure has been that the economic viability of new technologies was not explored. Technology is fundamentally the application of human knowledge to create a tool or technique *to perform an economic task*. To ignore the economic aspects of a technology is to ignore the main factor determining eventual success or failure of that technology in the outside world. To many readers this linkage between technology and economics is self-evident, yet it is widely ignored by voluntary organizations and R&D institutions in the Third World. A simple economic evaluation is an important first step in considering technology projects. It allows technologies with little or no economic value to be screened out, and those with strong economic advantages (and benefits to the users) to be more readily identified.

There are now many A.T. success stories, typically the result of long-term (5 years or more) programs with strong field testing components.. Hundreds, thousands and tens of thousands of units of these technologies have been sold and installed and are providing good service. Examples include improved cookstoves in Sri Lanka, Nepal, Kenya, Indonesia and elsewhere (more than 25,000 distributed); hand-operated Rower pumps for irrigation in Bangladesh (5000-10,000 distributed); foot operated treadle pumps for irrigation in Bangladesh (20,000 distributed); double-vault water seal latrines in India (60,000 installed); water turbines for mills in Nepal (hundreds installed, providing milling services to hundreds of thousands of people);

oral rehydration mixes to combat infant diarrhea (millions of packets distributed). The World Bank, one of the largest of the international institutions, has made a great contribution in searching for, compiling, evaluating and field testing low-cost water supply and sanitation technologies. They have demonstrated that there are a number of economical, technically proven alternatives to the costly municipal water and sewerage systems seen in rich countries. Thousands of insightful, creative people around the world have become intrigued by the possibilities, and have conducted solid experiments that have led to a variety of maturing technologies. The 350 books added to this edition of the **Sourcebook** document many of these.

Although funds for appropriate technology work are short, the largest single factor preventing more rapid progress is probably the lack of understanding of how organizations can combine funds and human resources to efficiently develop and market technologies. In the case of international aid agencies, the challenge is how to effectively support local groups in their work. There are, for example, a number of communications tasks or "overhead" functions that need attention. These include smoothing the flow of technical documentation, disseminating information on successful policy measures, supporting dialogue between partner institutions, and channeling small amounts of funds to grass-roots technology research and development efforts. Some of these might be tasks that existing international agencies or networks should take on or support others to take on. Other tasks are perhaps best initiated and financed by local networks or individual groups. Yet differing languages and cultural attitudes are barriers to building systems that work; and the differences in organizational forms among cultures make the challenge all the more difficult.

There continue to be well-funded pilot projects demonstrating too-expensive "village" technology. Genuine grass-roots practitioners are scarce at conferences, where sympathetic non-practitioners, unfamiliar with the daily obstacles to technology improvement in the field, have difficulty identifying the truly useful "overhead functions" that coalitions and aid agencies could perform.

Institutional change

Now that "appropriate technology" is being added to the activities of national and international organizations, it is catching the interest of those who would like to use elements from it to repair the creaking, battered bridges of development aid. A.T., however, is an awkward approach to incorporate into large agency planning efforts. The concept of "local self-reliance," for example, is difficult to define or quantify and will vary from place to place. Furthermore, it is a quality that can be either nurtured or destroyed from the outside, but never created. "Self-reliance" also sounds vaguely utopian or ideologically-tainted. To many planners it looks unnecessary, and out it goes.

Equally difficult is the concept of "people's participation." "Participation" is probably the most often invoked and least often attempted aspect of rural development programs. Participation is often interpreted to mean the carrying out of instructions. This kind of interpretation makes participation simply a measure of the degree of local acceptance of a project, not a strategy for success and human development. Nor does this approach to participation contribute at all to an ongoing process of community problem-solving. A higher stage of participation may be reached when community reaction is sought to the activities planned by intervening agencies. Such an approach is sometimes taken in the hope that local enthusiasm will be increased and gross mistakes (due to factors unknown to the planners but evident to the community) can be avoided. Yet even this leaves the community in essentially a passive role, as Denis Goulet aptly points out:

> "One may plausibly argue that to structure feedback is merely to assure that any participation elicited will be a mere 'reaction' to what is proposed. To *propose* is thus, in effect, to *im-*

pose, inasmuch as those who plan initial arrangements do not provide for a *feed-in* at early moments of problem-definition. Feedback prevents non-experts from gaining access to essential parameters of the decision process *before* these are congealed."

— Denis Goulet, **The Uncertain Promise: Value Conflicts in Technology Transfer,** 1977

In true participation, community members are involved from the outset, beginning with the setting of the development priorities. Large development agencies generally lack the local contacts and rapport with community members required for project participation. They may be further constrained by a need to move quickly in project implementation.

Another important concept in the A.T. approach is that development should increase (or at least not reduce) the ability of the poor to cope with their problems. Yet the project designer is hard-pressed to ensure this; no project's consequences can be fully known beforehand. Unpredictability must be kept in mind when evaluating the kinds of activities that are chosen. We should ask ourselves: What new risks come with a proposed activity? Will this project make the poor more or less capable of dealing with unforeseen problems and crises which may arise? These questions are particularly important when we consider projects that tie the poor into the world economy. Planners and decision-makers have pointed to international markets and invoked the benefits of "interdependence," but have neglected the question of who stands to lose out when times are difficult. For it is the poor, in the end, who will be hit by famine when the crop fails, left with their equipment idle when fuel is unavailable, and find themselves on the street without work when fashions change and their exported handicraft product is no longer in vogue.

These, then, are some of the reasons why it is difficult to incorporate A.T. principles into large agency programs of action. Concepts like "local self-reliance" and "people's participation" are difficult to work with and they are therefore not popular with planners. Yet when the small farmer is integrated into the world economy, the roller coaster price cycles of international commodity markets can undercut his or her chances for self-reliant advancement. Unless thoughtful attention is given to these difficult issues, projects and programs will have little about them that is really "appropriate."

Policymakers responsible for the national decisions that influence technological change also need to carefully examine whether their policies are supportive of appropriate technologies. People who work with appropriate technologies at the grassroots levels in many countries consider governmental measures out of touch and ineffectual, and have become thoroughly skeptical of government and international agency activities labeled "A.T." In few countries have the policy makers provided evidence to change this view.

If the world were made up of autonomous communities, people could make their own choices about technological change. But the image of the completely isolated village is an illusion. In Indonesia, for example, where more than 70% of the population lives in rural areas, most have watched television and know of Honda motorcycles and Levi's jeans. The materialism of the West has very nearly reached the farthest corners of the earth, and profoundly affected the aspirations and behavior of much of humanity. In villages in which the largest killer is infant diarrhea, people save from tiny disposable incomes to buy quartz-crystal watches, cameras, and motorcycles while the need for clean water goes unaddressed. Not only the landless but also the young, the bright, and the enterprising people are lured to the city. They leave behind village economies drained of resources by international soft drinks, cigarettes, and consumer goods, and drained of talent by the pull of economic opportunity and "modernization."

Local A.T. workers must consider these powerful forces influencing the communities in which they work. Community-based development strategies will be up against great odds where the vitality of the community has been sapped. It is just as clear that neglect at the national policy level will greatly increase the odds against A.T. development.

The challenge is to devise policy measures and government programs which will support widespread local A.T. efforts — instead of replacing or attempting to direct them. Nicolas Jequier notes that the A.T. movement does

> ". . .not really know how to handle A.T. on the scale that is required by the needs of hundreds of millions of poor people. . .The problem in effect is not to simply to develop more appropriate types of technology, important as this may be, but to start redesigning the existing system of planning, investment, and development. . ."
>
> — "Appropriate Technology: The Second Generation," 1978

Who are the innovators?

There is a widespread misconception that new technologies are produced by large groups of people working in government research centers. In fact, this has rarely been true. The great majority of technological innovations have always been the products of individuals and small groups of people. Small businesses, not government R&D centers or large corporations, are the major source of innovations, even in high technology products such as microcomputers. For example, as this book was going to press, a new world record for longest airplane flight without refueling was set by the Voyager aircraft. This plane was designed by one man and built and flown by his brother and a friend.

What kinds of individuals originate successful technological innovations? The answer to this question is important in choosing a strategy for village technology research and development. It has been commonly recognized that engineers, scientists, and foreigners have made significant innovations in a variety of settings. Each of these sometimes overlapping groups has its own strengths: engineers are versed in the fundamentals of design; scientists have powerful conceptual and methodological skills; foreigners bring ideas from outside and insights from a different way of looking at problems.

It is not as commonly recognized that craftspeople, farmers, and other villagers have been contributing to the village technology innovation process for much longer than the professionals and outsiders. The idea that poor farmers and craftspeople are not inventive is usually built into technology improvement programs. This kind of assumption is an unfortunate misconception held (often unconsciously) by people who have had little direct contact with villagers in their own or other countries. In fact, the poor in both rural and urban areas around the world show considerable ingenuity in using the materials available to them to solve their problems. Recycling industrial materials into shoes and oil lamps, imitating natural ecological interactions in small farming systems, and keeping vehicles running for decades without the proper spare parts are just three of thousands of possible examples.

A person convinced of the existence of lively inventive activity among the people of the rural areas and urban slums of the Third World may still be inclined to dismiss this as too small in magnitude to be relevant to appropriate technology efforts. But is it? Suppose we assume that roughly 2% of any human population acts in ways that deserve the label "inventor." This is the figure used for the San Francisco Bay Area of California by a regional inventor's council. If this is accurate, there would be 1.7 million "inventors" among the 85 million inhabitants of Java! Obviously, these population groups are quite different. The San Francisco Bay Area has a reported 100,000 inventors in a population of 5 million. The Bay Area contains a large number of highly educated people, and is the heart of the rapidly growing electronics industry. On the other hand, the mostly rural population of Java has greater daily involvement with tools and materials, a great range of traditional technologies, and a larger immediate survival problem. Even if the figure of 2% is reduced by a factor of ten, that would leave 170,000 people informally involved in day-to-day village technology adaptation in Java. This figure dwarfs the number of researchers working in formal programs on the same tasks. Appropriate technology efforts should be designed to take advantage of this large and creative group of people and support them, with technical assistance when necessary and with formal and nonformal educational programs, to put such inventive activity on a firmer technical footing and accelerate it.

We must keep in mind the fact that craftspeople and farmers commonly have a knack for devising tools. They also have a firm grasp of acceptability, affordability, and usefulness that is sorely needed in institutional research and development (R&D) programs. The magnitude of the potential contribution by craftspeople and farmers in an innovation process is at least as great as that of the professionals and outsiders. This suggests that programs for the indigenous development of appropriate technologies should draw on the different perspectives and innovative talents of each of these groups, by giving special attention to imaginative ways to directly include the beneficiaries.

The structure of R&D efforts

Most research and development institutions in the Third World today are structured in ways that work against the development of appropriate technologies. This continues to be true even when the content of R&D activities has been changed to "appropriate technology." Most of these institutions have staff from an urban elite, who look to their peers for recognition. Facilities are located far from villages and trials of new technologies are conducted in artificial environments. In this kind of institutional setting, there is generally little place for (or interest in) input from farmers and other villagers.

For years observers from around the world have been pointing to the need for direct involvement of farmers and other villagers in any technological research intended to benefit them:

> "The farmers in a land parcelization project complained of little or no corn response to fertilizer even though it was required in the complete credit package. . . (Subsequent) results from Farm Trials indicated response in some cases, especially in some of the hybrids tested, but in none was it profitable; conventional wisdom, coupled with the natural tendency to consider fertilizer necessary in any complete recommendation, had created a situation in which the farmers were being forced in to unprofitable investments . . ."

> — Peter Hildebrand, "Generating Small Farm Technology," 1977

> "The challenge before us is to establish a system which will produce machines that will make poor people more productive — machines that will work, will last, and are affordable. In developing this system, we must ensure that the villager becomes an active member of the research team. For it is the villager. . .who is the focal point of all this activity, and ultimately it is the villager who will judge if we are making a serious effort to solve his problems, or if we are merely continuing to tinker with his future."

> — David Henry, "Designing for Development: What is A.T. for Rural Water Supply and Sanitation?", 1978

Several of the new books reviewed in this edition discuss and detail the necessary steps for small farmer involvement in R&D work. They provide mounting evidence that successful programs work with users beginning early in the process. Those institutions and programs that remain without user involvement are not succeeding in producing technologies that people want. In industry, the same pattern holds: those companies that work closely with users when developing new products are generally successful, while companies that do not, have poor results.

With the cart still serving as the primary mode of transport of goods in many countries around the world, virtually no systematic design work to improve these carts had taken place until the last few years. (Recently there has been some interesting work on bullock cart design in India; see **The Management of Animal Energy Resources and the Modernization of the Bullock Cart System**, by N.S. Ramaswamy, 1979.) Such neglect is not simply the result of oversight but part of a pattern in which the research content and application of science has been heavily biased toward the needs of industrialized countries. The everyday pressing problems in poor countries have rarely been sufficiently unique or "interesting" to attract the attention of the scientist eager to investigate some phenomenon never before researched. This complaint is a fundamental one, and a major reason for the existence of the appropriate technology movement.

How might research become more responsive and related to everyday problems? One way, mentioned above, is to involve people who will use the fruits of research in the research process itself, and in decisions about research content. An alternative approach to research, already evidenced by some committed scientists and technical people in the Third World, also offers promise. Whereas commercial research and development has responded to the promise of economic gain for the innovative firm (as in the case of the running shoe industry), the "social entrepreneur" identifies needs and organizes responses primarily in hopes of finding a better way to do things that will benefit many people. These investigators choose to study new roofing materials and productive, ecologically sound small farming systems, while their counterparts in the rich countries study such things as the mating behavior of exotic fish.

> "The prime criterion for good research should be that it is likely to mitigate poverty and hardship among rural people, especially the poorer rural people, and to enhance the quality of their lives in ways which they will welcome; that in short, priorities should be arrived at less by an overview than by an underview, grounded in the reality of the rural situation. Starting with rural people, their world view, their problems and their opportunities, will give a different perspective. To be able to capture that perspective requires a revolution in professional values and in working styles; it requires humility and a readiness to innovate which may not come easily in many research establishments."
>
> — Robert Chambers, "Identifying Research Priorities in Water Development," in **The Social and Ecological Effects of Water Development in Developing Countries**, 1978

There is a wide range of very low-cost village technologies that require little more than local materials and labor for adaptation work, which could be carried out by small organizations with few resources but close ties to users. Included here are such important technologies as improved cookstoves and grain storage bins. Moreover, many of the technological improvements involving the lowest cash investments hold the greatest potential for spreading quickly in poor communities.

Science Teaching

The experience and natural inventiveness of local people have been identified as key elements in relevant research and development efforts. Improving basic science education could also strengthen and broaden the local capability to do research and design work, harnessing the systematic methods of scientific inquiry to the creativity and experience which people already possess. Yet science education in developing countries rarely is intended to develop a basic understanding of scientific approaches to problem-solving, nor does it offer students skills that are relevant to their daily lives. This is true in the secondary schools as well as the primary schools which provide the only years of schooling for most rural people. Major problems include the lack of affordable texts and lab equipment, the lack of written or printed materials in the local language, the failure of curricula to show connections between science (with its odd lab apparatus) and the natural world, and meager science background among teachers. Most importantly, the basic purpose and method of science is usually lost in Third World educational systems. With little or no chance to participate in simple experiments, students do not learn to take systematic steps in testing hypotheses and prototypes. Science is presented to them as a set of abstract concepts to be memorized. Educational systems geared to the needs of the few students who pass to subsequent levels (instead of the larger numbers who leave school at the end of each level) make science courses primarily tools for screening students rather than developing a basic scientific literacy throughout the population.

A way out of the dilemma may be found by relating science more directly to the natural processes going on around students in their daily lives, by making low-cost lab equipment (see the SCIENCE TEACHING chapter), and by using devices and materials that are normally found in the community (such as bicycle pumps and market scales). Students could then become directly involved in the systematic procedures of science, learning valuable problem-solving skills. They could begin to escape the deadening effect of rote schooling where memorization rather than skill development and understanding is the goal. Courses on simple machines and agriculture, directly related to farm activities, could be included. This has been tried, with success. Special curriculum development and teacher training are crucial for the success of such efforts.

This kind of shift in science education may be similar to what Albert Baez (director of UNESCO's division of science teaching from 1961 to 1967) had in mind when he observed: "The inquiry mode of science and the design mode of technology should both infuse the science education of the future." ("Curiosity, Creativity, Competence and Compassion — Guidelines for Science Education in the Year 2000," by Albert V. Baez, June 1979.) In that 1979 paper he went on to note that both Einstein and Edison were stifled and powerfully alienated by their early contact with rote schooling. An essential part of a new approach to science education, he argued, is the fostering of creativity. He cited a study which indicated that creative people "challenge assumptions, recognize patterns, see in new ways, make connections, take risks, take advantage of change, and construct networks."

It may be possible to create a corps of people who can use both "the inquiry mode of science and the design mode of technology" to help solve the technological problems of their communities. These people would receive special practical training in addition to the new science courses. They would play a role similar to that of the "barefoot doctors" who have been successful in China and an increasing number of other developing countries. These "barefoot engineers" would not replace other engineers, but would greatly increase the availability of technical skills for problem-solving at the grass-roots level. In rural Colombia, the FUNDAEC program has been training such a corps of "barefoot engineers" (see review of **The Rural University**). These young people, coming from the rural communities with a sixth grade education, go through a three-year training program. A university-based group distills and combines concepts from a variety of technical fields, to arm students with a set of skills relevant to the problems of their communities.

Basic steps for R&D

From this discussion, we can identify at least four basic steps that are likely to increase the relevance and productivity of appropriate technology R&D efforts:

1) Change the criteria for "good" research. Good research should be that which is likely to reduce poverty.

2) Seek to understand the viewpoint of the poor—their perceptions of problems and opportunities.

3) Actively include the poor, especially small farmers and craftspeople, in both decisions about research content, and in the research itself.

4) Offer basic relevant science education geared to the challenges of local problems, with curricula adapted to employ available materials and common devices to illustrate principles, and to provide young people and farmer-inventors with a more scientifically sound basis for their innovation efforts. Offer related courses on simple machines, how they work and how to fix them.

Education and Training

Relevant science education might accelerate the process of generating useful and affordable village technology adaptations. There are other potential links between educational efforts and improved tools and techniques as well.

Increases in the material standard of living come with advances in productivity. This is accomplished through upgraded technologies—which embody human knowledge—and increases in the skills of the people. When better technologies and skill development opportunities are widely available, increases may be seen in the local standard of living.

Conventional development strategies and programs tend to concentrate resources on a narrow range of activities. Scarce capital and R&D funds are channeled to industry, which employs only a very small part of the work force. Costly training programs yield small numbers of graduates for a few sectors of the economy. A high rate of economic growth may occur in these sectors, but most of the benefits reach only a few people. At the same time, the vast majority of economic activities remain stagnant, experiencing no (or very slow) increases in productivity. Important sectors of the economy may decline, as traditional materials become scarce and some of the more capable workers move to the cities.

The appropriate technology approach therefore includes the question, "How can we create conditions in which productivity in most important activities will increase?" With the resources used to train one engineer, it would be possible to train 10-50 or more farmer/inventors who would have incentive to focus their efforts on raising productivity and earnings in the traditional sectors of the economy. Such a shift in the emphasis of technical training could mean that the people would no longer be forced to simply wait for industrialization to make them either prosperous or destitute. Instead, they could become involved in the development of new tools and skills that emerge from the old, setting into motion a dynamic process of productivity increases that actually involves the whole society.

Educational and training opportunities are also more than a strategy for raising the productivity of ordinary people. They have intrinsic value too, in that they broaden the intellectual and technical perspective, widen the horizons of general knowledge, and help liberate individuals from the oppression of meaningless tasks, poverty, and political domination. This "humanistic" perspective, which asserts that relevant learning opportunities are inherently worthwhile, can be seen at work in nonformal education efforts offering reading and vocational skills to groups of out-of-school adults. Such an orientation favors promotion of technologies and programs which have educational consequences for the poor majority. Too often, however, development planners are not interested in the widespread development of skills and knowledge that comes with decentralized technology and participatory community development programs. Any extra effort required to initiate an educational process may be seen as an obstacle to achieving the more measurable goals (e.g., the number of wells and hand pumps installed or the number of patients examined). The disregard of informal training effects when pursuing narrow goals can be seen regularly in the way large programs are organized.

The benefits of informal training, community organization, and an increased level of local experimentation and problem-solving do not show up in the calculations of categorical programs (which focus on one kind of development objective, such as improved health or housing). These benefits are effectively invisible, and they are not taken into account — except by the few categorical programs that focus on these as their own particular objectives.

The example of the 2800 small-scale cement plants operating in the People's Republic of China illustrates how widespread training benefits can follow directly from choice of technology. These cement plants provide cheap cement for local infrastructure construction projects such as irrigation canals; they employ ten times as many people (per unit of output) as the conventional larger rotary kilns; and they provide workers with a range of practical technical and administrative skills which serve as a valuable foundation for other small industry activities. In this case, the skills of the rural population have broadened significantly — more than would have been the case had the centralized "higher technology" rotary kiln been chosen.

Valuable informal training effects can also be seen in a wide variety of private, day-to-day activities. For example, while in most poor countries managerial and entrepreneurial talent is thought to be in short supply, children of the ethnic groups controlling particular economic activities (e.g., shipping or retail sales) become exceptionally talented and successful businesspeople. They do this without enrolling in formal business training programs. Rather, they participate in daily business activities, and have a high motivation to learn. Informal "learning by doing" can also be seen when communities undertake their own development projects. Mistakes are more evident and more likely to occur on a scale which is correctable by the participants. Appropriate technology advocates should be aware of these natural informal educational processes, and should think about ways to open them up to more people.

Local resources

> "Personal and local resources are imagination, initiative, commitment and responsibility, skill and muscle-power; the capability for using specific and often irregular areas of land or locally available materials and tools; the ability to organize enterprises and local institutions; constructive competitiveness and the capacity to co-operate."
>
> — John Turner, **Housing by People**, (1976)

Formal and informal learning opportunities — whether science education offered in the classroom or the chance to acquire managerial skills in a factory or business — are crucial in mobilizing these local human resources. Skilled, creative local people will, in turn, be able to better use local material resources — often the only alternative in poor countries:

> "To construct using renewable resources is not a sentimental fad in an area without exportable products to pay for imports... In a low cash economy it is the interactions of human resources with the immediate materials of the land that provide for the richness and fullness of life."
>
> — Peter van Dresser, **Homegrown Sundwellings**, (1977)

We noted above that learning opportunities are often overlooked in the calculations of development planners. Likewise, local labor and materials are frequently ignored when planners consider the assets of a poor community.

One of the prime considerations in the development of appropriate village technology is to find ways in which people can invest their unemployed labor to produce something of value. If these people are not fully participating in a market economy (which is commonly the case), it is not a question of what manipulations an economist can suggest to maximize the yield on their time and capital; capital in this case is not easily measured because it is in the land and the trees and the bamboo. Conventional economic analysis has little to say in such a situation because such capital is generally ignored.

The investment of cash has the effect of mobilizing the efforts of other, distant people; money for sheet metal, for example, pays for the efforts of the workers in the mill and the miners who extract ore and coal, along with the transport and "middle" workers necessary to bring this material to the community. If we can accomplish the same task by mobilizing our own effort (e.g., building effective grain storage bins using our own labor and locally available basket materials and clay) we can avoid spending cash on sheet metal for bins. In other words, labor and local materials can be converted into capital, without any cash input. Which we choose (or are forced) to do depends on whether we know about alternatives, whether opportunities to earn cash are available, what skills we have, and which use of time and effort will most easily accomplish the task at hand. Wherever jobs that pay cash are few but local materials and labor abundant, a reliance on cash investment poses an unnecessary obstacle to the construction of new more effective grain storage bins, basic houses, or new agricultural tools.

The use of local materials not only offers opportunities for action where money is scarce, but has other advantages as well. Nicolas Jequier has pointed to a distinction between what he calls "systems-dependent" and "systems-independent" technologies (see "Appropriate Technology: Some Criteria" in **Towards Global Action for Appropriate Technology**, 1979). "Systems-dependent" technologies are those which require, for example, a supply line of materials, spare parts, fuel, maintenance and repair skills to be efficiently used. Any break in the chain of related elements results in the idling of a "systems-dependent" technology. "Systems-independent" technologies, on the other hand, can be efficiently used without such supply lines; they include tools, techniques, and structures that are made of local materials.

Local materials are thus often the key to what the members of a poor community can afford to do. "Affordable," in this context, has a very different meaning than "economically competitive." A technology is termed "competitive" if, over time, it is cheaper than the conventional approach used to accomplish the same task. This does not mean, however, that it is cheap enough to be affordable and a better choice for the poor than what they currently use. For example, a windmill designer once told us that he was pleased that windmills were soon going to be economically competitive with diesel-driven pumps for water lifting, since oil prices were going up. To a poor person who couldn't afford to buy or rent the engine-driven pumps when oil was cheap, a steel windmill is equally out of reach. This is not to say that steel windmills do not have a place in appropriate technology efforts; they may be an excellent product with good prospects for replacing engine-driven pumps in some areas. The windmill designs that are most likely to reach the poor, however, are those that emphasize the use of local materials in their construction, and thus minimize the cash investment required.

Similarly, a careful calculation of what constitutes an "affordable alternative" should be made when we look at investments in improved cooking technologies from the point of view of the poor. Because firewood used in cooking is the major form of energy consumed in rural areas, fuel-efficient stoves could be a major tool in the effort to increase available rural energy supplies (and reduce deforestation). Yet most firewood is gathered (not purchased) and traditional cooking stoves usually require little or no cash investment. Therefore, regardless of how fuel-efficient an improved stove may be, it must also be very inexpensive to be attractive and affordable.

A.T. and income distribution

Saving labor serves no purpose if it is your own job that is "saved" and no other real employment — and thus income — opportunities exist. In China, in 19th century England, and in the Third World today, a central question regarding mechanization and industrialization has been: Whose labor will be saved? Who will benefit and who will simply lose any opportunity to earn a living?

In the industrialized countries, new jobs are theoretically created to replace those that are destroyed. The fact that this has been an awkward, unequal and demoralizing process is generally overlooked, while much is made of productivity increases leading to benefits for all. (The stubborn persistence of high unemployment and increasing inequality in wealth and income in industrialized countries like the United States suggest that this process may have finally come to a halt.)

Much mechanization and industrialization in the Third World has simply cut people out of the production process, changing who makes the goods (and thus who ends up with some purchasing power) without changing very much the amount of goods produced or their prices. For example, when aluminum pots replace clay pots made by villagers, the result is a) a marginally better product, b) the same number of pots in use, c) perhaps a lower price when calculated over the life of the pots, d) a lot of unemployed potters who now have no purchasing power, e) a smaller number of new jobs in an urban-based industry, f) an enriched industrialist, and g) a shift away from the products of village industry previously bought by potters (e.g., tools produced by local blacksmiths) towards a smaller number of more highly processed foods, transportation services, and imported goods bought by urban residents. In this example "productivity" (as measured by the amount of product created per worker hour) has gone up, although total product has not. More people are unemployed, income inequality has increased, and village development has been set back. This process of destroying crafts has been repeated all over the world. Without a political commitment to full employment and the sharing of the benefits of technological change, the great technological gap created by the sudden arrival of imported technology can thus quickly increase poverty. It is in grappling with this kind of problem in societies shot through with inequalities that labor-intensive, decentralized, productivity-increasing technologies have a role to play. The need is for both national productivity increases and individual worker participation in production and consumption.

This need is acute in the agricultural sector of poor countries, where most of the people earn their livelihoods. To help the small farm family better use their resources, a program to adapt agricultural tools and equipment could be aimed at several categories of activities. One group of needed technologies are those that speed work at the points in the agricultural calendar when all available person-power is released. Another tactic, one that the Chinese have used effectively in the commune system, is to mechanize the particularly low productivity activities that are major time consumers in the rural sector, and shift this labor to other activities, such as making threshers, pumps, and hand tractors. (The production of agricultural machinery in the rural areas of China has meant that the equipment made is responsive to technology needs and that mechanization does not necessarily replace agricultural jobs with jobs in urban industry. This situation is virtually unique in developing countries (see **Rural Small-Scale Industry in the People's Republic of China**, by Dwight Perkins, et. al., 1977).

When land ownership is heavily concentrated in a few hands, this labor reallocation process is likely to be incomplete, leading to technology choices which may not benefit the majority of the population.

"To maintain. . . a rational growth of capital use in a low-income economy, small farms are better suited than large ones, for the small farmers do not experience the same pressure to substitute capital for labor; *no one wants to mechanize himself out of his job.* Large farms are in fact the least economical, in social account, in the use of scarce capital and underemployed labor. Land reform countries generally exhibit a better record of a resource use that is rational in social account."

— Folke Dovring, "Macro-Economics of Farm Mechanization," 1978, in **Agricultural Technology for Developing Nations: Farm Mechanization Alternatives for 1-10 Acre Farms,** 1978, emphasis added, see review.

Farmers who hire labor to carry out low productivity activities are likely to substitute machines when possible, thereby replacing a number of farm labor jobs with a smaller number of machine operation and maintenance jobs. If farm labor is in short supply, wages may rise with productivity and everyone benefits. This is rarely the case in poor countries, however. More likely, the landowning farmer reaps the benefits and some laborers lose their jobs.

The tenant farm family is less likely to be hiring labor, and has less capital in any case to invest in machines. These families are faced with the possibility that new technologies that raise the productivity of the land may lead to rent increases which capture the gains. There are of course many ways they can invest their own labor, through composting, tree planting, and general soil conservation work that pays off over a long term. But they probably will be unwilling to make this investment, fearing that they will not be around to reap the benefits.

These considerations make it unlikely that improved tools and methods for increased agricultural production can be targetted primarily for the tenant farmer. The landless laborer is even less likely to be able to directly increase his/her income through improved field crop technologies, unless production increases create more work (e.g., at the processing stage). More to the advantage of tenants and laborers would appear to be technologies for small-scale crop processing, drying, and storage; home gardening; and household needs.

Of course in many communities, most of the people own or have guaranteed access to some land, as individuals, through extended family ties, through legislated communal land ownership, or through secure tenant-landlord relationships. In these places there may be great scope for the application of small-scale agricultural technologies which would increase the viability of small farms and result in broadly distributed benefits. In many other communities, however, vigorous land reform efforts may be necessary before much can be accomplished through agricultural technology change.

Systems for renting machinery can be an important means of distributing costs and benefits of new equipment among a large group of farmers. Such systems work best when competition keeps the charges reasonable. Otherwise, rental systems can be a means for owners to make monopoly profits; this is unfortunately quite common. Cooperative ownership, by contrast, usually involves more management problems but ensures broader distribution of benefits. Cooperatives too, however, are frequently taken over by elites.

We cannot automatically assume that new or adapted low-cost technology will be "accessible" to the masses or equitable in its distributional effects. Many small-scale machines imported into poor rural areas (such as Japanese engine-driven rice mills brought to Java) are affordable only to the wealthiest of rural people. Such machines may be accessible and small, but they are not accessible or small enough. Use of such machines can destroy jobs while providing benefits primarily to the owners. On the other hand, such machines may provide a valuable service at a reasonable price, in which case most of the community will benefit.

The foregoing discussion suggests that there can be fundamental political qualities associated with scale and cost of technology. Large-scale expensive technologies and centralized production systems tend to concentrate wealth, and can be vehicles that destroy the livelihoods of the poor majority in developing countries. Conversely, while village elites are quite capable of consolidating their positions with "intermediate" technologies, small-scale tools and techniques are less likely to contribute to the destruction of village economies. This is why technology policy—the set of codes, incentives, and restrictions affecting the direction of technological change—is such an important political matter. In almost all poor countries, government policies are determined primarily by a narrow group of urban-based elites; thus the resolution of this important matter will not necessarily be in the interests of rural people, much less the poor majority of rural people. Those who govern, it seems, may perceive little benefit for themselves in wholeheartedly instituting policy measures needed to support a small-scale technology strategy.

An equally important related political question is whether—with or without substantial policy support—community organizations can exist or be created to serve as mechanisms for technological improvements that benefit everyone. The answer here seems to be a qualified "yes." Community organizers are becoming interested in A.T. because some technologies offer the opportunity for substantial benefits through community action, and thus encourage organization building. Technologists, on the other hand, have become increasingly aware of community organizing as a crucial activity (and even a requirement) for the success of their technology programs; a climate of community awakening, self-respect, and cooperation, and the chance to participate in a two-way dialogue, can have a major effect on whether improved tools and techniques are applied successfully. Thus appropriate technology and community organizing work are seen by many as mutually supportive, each contributing to the progress and growth of the other.

Community organizers, while not seeking conflict for its own sake, recognize that the small communities of the Third World are often riddled with inequalities of wealth and power. An important step in community organizing is to awaken a community to its own political, economic and technological problems and opportunities. Then, the challenge is to find mechanisms which will allow progress for all, and prevent elites from taking over new community institutions. The promotion of small-scale technologies faces the same hurdle—either a strong community organization or a very careful technology group (or both) may be needed to ensure that a new technology will not be controlled by elites. (Elite control is most likely with crop processing equipment, pumps and tillers, vehicles, and equipment for small industry; it is least likely with household technologies—improved stoves, home crop storage units, sanitation systems, and new construction materials.) An important strategy for both appropriate technologists and community organizers may be to concentrate initially on technologies which will benefit all, regardless of differences in wealth and power. On this point, a training team in rural India observes:

> "Today there is much talk about 'total revolution' and radical transformation of society. But what really matters are the changes taking place in the socio-economic reality of the villages where poverty crushes the poor. In this stark reality of life the rural poor can hardly envisage more than creating for themselves some free space in society where they can breathe more freely and begin to stretch themselves. What is crucial at the moment is to create a base for joint action which is relatively free from control of the locally powerful. Wherever this has been achieved, people begin to move."

—**Moving Closer to the Rural Poor**, MOTT, 1979

Crucial "breathing space" for the poor may be created, without local political opposition, through the use of improved stoves which save ⅓ of the fuel normally used in cooking, low-cost grain storage units that can significantly reduce losses of grain stored in the home, or by water supply and sanitation systems that can markedly improve community health. Properly chosen and developed, such very low-cost technologies can provide a crucial entry point for community organizing efforts. At a later stage, great inequalities may have to be confronted directly or neither community organizing nor technological advance can proceed.

Those who have overlooked the importance of community organizing should bear in mind that in addition to helping spread benefits from new technologies, community organizations open up other possibilities. Community technologies, such as water supply and sanitation systems, commonly fail when there is not a high degree of participation (i.e., a local committee for maintenance and repair). Technology adaptation and skills acquisition can also often be effectively pursued by community groups. In addition, cooperative community organizations offer members the chance to share resources and consolidate buying power. These intertwining functions can be seen at times in the more successful farm cooperatives:

> "It was the farm co-op that got America's farmer out from under the oppressive crop-lien system, which kept nineteenth-century farmers in hock [debt] to local merchants and distant brokers. Co-ops gave farmers an equal measure of bargaining power in the marketplace. With co-ops, farmers could market their crops directly, and could also do away with the hated middleman to purchase their supplies."

> —Jerry Hagstrom, "Whose Co-op Bank?", Working Papers, July/August 1980

The links beginning to form between appropriate technology and community organizing should lead to ideas for organized cooperation on higher levels. Community organizing, appropriate technology, and other allied groups from different nations, for example, would find much in common and benefit greatly by learning about each other's experiences. How might this come about?

Communications

The concept that improved village technologies should be based upon local human and material resources, and in harmony with local culture, has gained great acceptance within the appropriate technology movement. As a result, prevailing models of the role of communications in development have become increasingly inadequate for A.T. advocates. The "diffusion of innovations" theories, on which so many extension programs have been based, have assumed that centralized agencies would determine which technologies to promote. For the most part the task of communications has been defined, therefore, as the persuasion of the poor "target" population to accept these solutions. This process has not left room for input from the poor as to what solutions might interest them, nor has it allowed for the fact that some needs are more pressing in one community, while entirely different needs may have priority in nearby communities. The extension agent has typically been assigned to a vast area due to funding shortages, and has found his/her impact seriously diluted. In addition, errors and misunderstandings have been compounded as information passes from trainer to extension agent to "opinion leader" to the rest of the farmers.

Two of the most serious problems with this kind of approach are: 1) there is little room for "participation" by the beneficiaries except in the most minor sense — carrying out instructions; and 2) information flows almost entirely one way, from central agency to the poor. It is therefore essentially impossible for the villager to get technical assistance with anything except what the extension agent is promoting. Not surprisingly, the technologies promoted through this process have not been notably "appropriate," nor have the majority of extension programs achieved the success rate (measured in numbers of people adopting the prescribed technologies) expected.

What are some of the elements that should be incorporated into communications strategies to make them more consistent with A.T. concepts? If we agree that an active level of participation in problem identification and solution by the members of poor communities is highly desirable, this requires that they have:

    a) access to information in a form in which it can be of practical use;

    b) the ability to initiate communications in search of relevant experience and information from other communities, including information on the successful technologies that have been developed nearby, within the region, and around the world;

    c) support from those with more advanced scientific and technical skills, through technical assistance centers that respond to requests.

A key local informal communication mechanism is the network, created by the social ties of a community that lead people to help each other with skills and pass on information. When new skills and information get into such a network they become available for all the members to tap. Car repair, home improvement and many other skills in the U.S. are usually shared this way. Individuals pick up skills and ideas from each other and pass them along to others. An approach designed to take advantage of this phenomenon has been used effectively in teaching people to build solar water heaters in the United States (see review of **A Solar Water Heater Workshop Manual**, by Ecotope Group, 1978). A weekend solar training workshop was regularly offered to members of social clubs — natural networks. Later these people were in a good position to help each other properly complete solar water heater installations for their homes.

On local, national, regional, and international levels, networks of appropriate technology people are exchanging ideas and information in a highly active, decentralized fashion. Mimeographed newsletters can be low-cost vehicles for information exchange among groups across some distance. Grassroots radio programs produced on cassette tapes can be used as a forum for questions and ideas about common problems (see review of **Grass Roots Radio**, by Rex Keating, 1977). In this way, people at the grass-roots level can listen to each other. Some of the other low-cost technologies for horizontal communications strategies, many of them affordable at a village level, are documented in the LOCAL COMMUNICATIONS chapter.

Organizations trying to help the poor find out more about technology options should consider the possibility of producing and distributing catalogs to document widely-relevant technologies that are traditional and efficient, new, or from outside the country. (Many examples of such catalogs are contained within this book, which itself is such a catalog. Perhaps the best examples of catalogs with information selected for a particular developing country are the **Liklik Buk**, from Papua New Guinea, and **The People's Workbook**, from South Africa.) The cost of producing such a catalog is much less than the extremely high cost of operating a technical information data bank that gathers information from all over, stores it for retrieval, and responds to individual requests. Even in developing countries, when the total cost of running a conventional technical information data bank is divided by the number of requests, the cost per request can easily be $100-300 — equal to the annual per capita income in many countries (see Nicolas Jequier's discussion of this in **Appropriate Technology: Problems and Promises**, 1976). Catalogs, by contrast, can be produced at a cost of a few dollars each when several thousand are printed. They should be designed to anticipate and offer answers to many commonly asked questions, in addition to stimulating new thinking. This will not eliminate the need for information banks, but it should reduce the costs of having skilled staff respond to routine questions.

The A.T. microfiche library

An even more powerful tool for A.T. information is the library. If a high-quality technical library is available, A.T. practitioners can find answers to the great majority of technical problems encountered in the field. The possibility of quickly finding a solution to the problem at hand, rather than waiting weeks or months for a book to arrive, means that far more questions will be researched, and fewer opportunities missed. Unfortunately, few A.T. groups have a good library. The cost of purchasing the books ($5,000 to $15,000 or more for a well-rounded collection) and organizing, indexing and housing the collection makes such a library too expensive for most organizations.

With this problem of cost in mind, we took our own A.T. library, upon which the **A.T. Sourcebook** is based, and reproduced the books on microfiche, to form the Appropriate Technology Microfiche Library. Microfiche are plastic cards, 11 cm by 15 cm, which contain very small photographic images of the pages of books. Each microfiche card can hold 100 or more pages of information. A microfiche "reader," which operates much like a slide projector, is then used to view the pages.

By reproducing our 1000-title library in microfiche form, we are able to produce and sell copies for $\frac{1}{20}$ of its paper cost. This has enabled hundreds of development groups with limited resources to have excellent libraries in their offices. Each book included in the A.T. Microfiche Library is reviewed and indexed in this **Sourcebook**.

Another powerful tool for information collection, storage and retrieval is the computer. Unfortunately, computerized systems for controlling and providing access to information are ill-suited to a situation in which end-users are scattered about the globe in remote parts of poor countries. In addition to high cost, the fundamental problem with such systems linking microcomputers to a centralized computer data base is that the information going into the data base has to be screened for relevance and accuracy. Unless this is done well by experienced and knowledgeable people, the computer system will become a processor of "garbage in, garbage out." A related approach is for the local group to tap into international networks of microcomputer users for answers to their information needs. The problem here is that someone at the other end needs to have the time, knowledge, and resources to respond. Unfortunately, few people are in a position to volunteer such assistance, leaving this role to the high-cost technical information data banks mentioned above. Most productive applications of microcomputers in developing countries are going to be for data manipulation, recordkeeping, and wordprocessing, not technical information access. Even here, local groups will face the same obstacles to computerization as small organizations in the industrialized countries. As the purchase price of computers drops, the real cost (in terms of staff time) of learning how to use them efficiently remains high.

Tasks for international efforts in A.T.

By their very nature, appropriate technology organizations working at the community level have few "disposable" resources to spend on anything but their immediate activities. Lower priority is therefore usually given to experimentation that is not linked to direct applications, careful preparation of documentation on successful and unsuccessful work and searches for other groups with relevant experiences. Yet taking the opportunity to innovate at the community level and create a stock of useful information and experiences (including that from other groups), is an important step towards the decentralization of technology choice and the strengthening of community self-reliance.

There seem to be two categories of needs in international A.T. cooperation. One is for grass-roots groups to know more about what other grass-roots groups are doing, both in terms of technology adaptation and strategy within the community. A second need is for large agencies to better understand the aims and activities of grass-roots groups so that assistance to them will be of greater value. One tactic which has been used extensively in attempting to address both of these needs is the international conference. Unfortunately, few if any people with direct experience working at the community level are included in such meetings because they are unknown to funders and conference organizers. Also, in many cases community workers are understandably reluctant to attend meetings at which, all too often, little is accomplished. Those who do attend risk being vacuumed up into a planning, advisory, or administrative role which takes them away from work in their communities. The more common conference-goers are expatriates and Third World officials for whom international travel is (an expensive) part of a way of life.

Regional and international networks and coalitions often suffer from the same problem seen in international conferences. When those involved are a step or two away from the real grass-roots A.T. practitioners, the connection to real problems and needs rapidly dwindles and may disappear altogether. Currently the greatest need appears to be for more decentralized local networks and coalitions, whose members may have more of immediate relevance to share with each other, and who are less likely to face language and cultural barriers. Once local networks are established and healthy, regional and international networks can be strengthened.

A.T. support programs might try to identify and support several kinds of people. One is the "social entrepreneur," a creative individual who can recognize social needs, overcome obstacles, and find ways to perform needed overhead functions. Equally important is the business entrepreneur (and her/his counterparts in cooperatives and worker-owned enterprises) who can create, produce and market needed tools at affordable prices.

The following are examples of specific functions in international cooperation which could be supported by regional, national and international groups.

Communications, documentation and reference functions

1. Compilations of documentation on successful traditional technologies within a country; of interest in the same country, in the region, and in the world; published in book form.

2. Catalog publishing for low-cost dissemination of commonly relevant technical information, and to provide access to additional, more specific assistance (some examples are **Liklik Buk**, **People's Workbook**, **The Whole Earth Catalog**, and the **Sears and Roebuck Catalogs**; the last of these had wide circulation among North American farm families before World War II).

3. Assembly or production of simplified basic technical reference books, translated and adapted where necessary and made available at low cost. **A Farmer's Primer on Growing Rice** and **Where There is No Doctor** have proven the value of this approach.

4. Keeping unique and valuable reference books in print, by acquiring the publishing rights and reprinting books that are out of print due to low commercial sales. (For example, we have produced on microfiche more than 100 out-of-print books.)

5. Library grants — sets of basic books (including those mentioned above) totalling 50-1000 volumes and distributed (for example, through national coalitions of development organizations) directly to small A.T. groups, along with small discretionary accounts through which these groups can pay for additional published items acquired from around the world. (The A.T. Microfiche Library, which includes most of the books reviewed in this sourcebook, is such a low-cost basic library.)

People moving functions

1. Staff exchange programs among appropriate technology groups in different countries to share skills and perspectives.

2. Short-term tours of successful A.T. programs, by groups of A.T. people, including village craftspeople and inventors.

3. International training exchanges of farmers and craftspeople; e.g., tapping Javanese farmers to teach techniques of training and handling water buffaloes for plowing and other field preparation work in areas where these skills are unknown.

4. In-country training exchanges among allied appropriate technology, community organizing, nonformal education, and other groups.

Small grant programs

1. Seed capital to help equip small community-based appropriate technology groups with workshop tools and libraries, involving young people and local craftspeople.

2. Operating funds for the R&D or adaptation activities of small appropriate technology groups.

3. Block grants given to established appropriate technology organizations and coalitions with proven records, distinct from grants for their own use. These groups would identify new appropriate technology groups and pass on this money in small amounts.

4. Small venture capital investments in enterprises to produce and market appropriate technologies.

Funding specific technology research

1. Pilot project testing and accelerated further refinement of specific technologies identified as most urgent by a panel of A.T. activists; carried out whenever possible by those who have done some of the important initial work. Selected would be technologies that are broadly relevant to the daily needs of poor people in developing countries. Where possible, several lines of development would be pursued, so as to generate options that include a maximum of commonly available local materials as well as options that require purchased materials.

2. National and international annual competitions with prizes awarded to the innovations most likely to help alleviate poverty. The best entrants would be documented in a catalog.

Most of the examples listed here have been successfully tried at one time or another. All of them deserve more attention than they are presently receiving.

In the pages that follow, you will find reviews of more than 1000 books and documents, on specific technical subjects as well as on many of the topics discussed in this introduction.

— The Editors

Book Ordering
Information

Book Ordering Information

Prices

The prices listed in this Sourcebook are an approximate guide to what you will have to pay. While these prices were all accurate at one time, fluctuations in the international exchange rates, changes by publishers, rising postal rates, and inflation make it impossible to provide completely accurate price information in a printed book.

Many of these publications are offered by small appropriate technology groups. They are often quite willing to trade publications with other groups, avoiding the problem of acquiring foreign currency, additional bank charges, and so forth. Readers facing problems obtaining foreign exchange can also try to obtain UNESCO coupons from the local UNESCO office. UNESCO coupons can be purchased with local currency, and can be used to buy books from overseas. Most publishers accept UNESCO coupons as payment.

The prices listed here sometimes include surface postage. Airmail postage will often double the cost of a book. Airmail may be necessary, however, when it is important to avoid the delay of 6 weeks to 4 months (depending on location) involved in surface mail.

When ordering publications that require airmail shipping and/or an awkward currency exchange process, we recommend sending an airmail letter of inquiry to obtain the most up to date price information before sending payment.

Some publications have gone out of print since they were first reviewed. These items are noted in the text. They represent less than 10 percent of the books in this collection. These out of print books are reproduced as part of the A.T. Microfiche Library.

Addresses

For most of the more than 1000 publications reviewed in this book, the ordering address has been included with the review. For some organizations that have multiple publications listed, we have used an abbreviated name only. This is not intended to be a list of the "best" publishers and appropriate technology organizations, but merely a means of saving a lot of unnecessary repetition. The addresses are:

BRACE—Brace Research Institute. Their particular focus is on water supply for arid regions. Write to Publications Dept., Brace Research Institute, MacDonald College of McGill University, Ste. Anne de Bellevue, Quebec H0A 1C0, Canada.

CWD—Consultancy Services Wind Energy Developing Countries. CWD tries to help governments, institutes and private parties in the Third World with their efforts to use wind energy. Research institutes in the Third World may ask for one copy of any of their publications free of charge. Other groups wishing to order CWD publications should ask for a publications list with current prices and ordering information. CWD, c/o DHV Consulting Engineers, P.O. Box 85, 3800 AB Amersfoort, The Netherlands.

DWS—Dept. of Works and Supply, Papua New Guinea. They have a limited number of the publications reviewed here, some of them priced and some of them available free to serious groups in developing countries. Expect a small fee to cover postage. Please do not send personal checks on private banks. Department of Works and Supply, P.O. Box 1108, Boroko, Papua New Guinea.

FAO—Food and Agriculture Organization of the United Nations. Many of their publications are available through UNIPUB in the U.S. and FAO book distributors in developing countries. To order directly, write to: Distribution and Sales Section, FAO, Via delle Terme di Caracalla, 00100 Rome, Italy.

GATE—German Appropriate Technology Exchange. Has a variety of English language publications documenting technologies of interest in developing countries. GATE, Dag-Hammarskjold-Weg 1, 6236 Eschborn 1, Federal Republic of Germany.

GRET—Groupe de Recherche et d'Echanges Technologiques. This organization has an extensive set of French language publications on appropriate technologies. GRET, 213, rue La Fayette, 75010 Paris, France.

IDRC—International Development Research Center. This Canadian aid organization has consistently produced valuable books on subjects of interest to village technology workers. Unlike their counterparts to the south, IDRC has people from the developing countries on their board. Their publications are free to local people in developing countries. All of these publications are available in microfiche form for $1.00 from the Communications Division. IDRC has sales agents and regional offices around the world. IDRC, Box 8500, Ottawa, Canada K1G 3H9.

ILO—International Labour Office, 1211 Geneva 22, Switzerland. The U.S. branch office also has most ILO books available for sale: ILO, 1750 New York Ave., N.W., Washington, D.C. 20006, USA.

IRC—International Reference Centre for Community Water Supply and Sanitation. This special unit of the World Health Organization has produced many valuable water supply books in recent years. IRC, P.O. Box 93190, 2509 AD The Hague, The Netherlands.

ITDG—Intermediate Technology Development Group. The organization founded by the late E.F. Schumacher in the 1960's is responsible for the outstanding publishing program in this field. They have produced the largest selection of books on appropriate technology, while setting a standard of quality equaled by few. Their most recent edition of Tools for Agriculture, for example, is an extraordinary resource. Many of ITDG's books can be obtained in the U.S. from their distributor (ITDG of North America, P.O. Box 337, Croton-on-Hudson, New York 10520, USA). For a current publications list, write to Intermediate Technology Publications, 9 King St., London WC2E 8HW, England.

NTIS—National Technical Information Service. This U.S. government organization reprints many of the publications originally produced by other government agencies. For example, this is where things can be found when they have gone out of print at the National Academy of Sciences. Most of this material is available on microfiche ($4-8 per title), but unfortunately the original microfilming of most of these documents was not of high quality. Paper copies are usually reproduced from these microfiche originals, and are therefore both expensive and often not very clear. Prices are high, usually double outside the U.S.. Some documents are now available free or at lower cost through U.S. Agency for International Development missions in Caribbean and Latin American nations, in a special arrangement. NTIS is represented by local sales agents in about 20 different countries. When ordering from NTIS, you must include the "accession number" listed with the review, or they may not be able to find the item you want from among the vast collection of documents they have in storage. Orders from developing countries should be sent to Development Assistance Division, NTIS, Office of International Affairs, 5285 Port Royal Rd., Rm 306 Y, Springfield, Virginia 22161, USA. All other orders should be sent to NTIS, Springfield, Virginia 22161, USA.

Popular Mechanics—Popular Mechanics plans. These are photocopies of articles on homebuilt workshop equipment that originally appeared in Popular Mechanics magazine. The photos do not reproduce very well. The drawings are generally clear, however. Other limitations are that the plans are at times rather brief; it is assumed that the reader has some familiarity with shop power tools. All of the designs include small electric motors. The designs use commonly available materials of standard sizes. Skills required for production are not great. The durability of such homebuilt equipment will vary. Include the reference number of the item when ordering. Popular Mechanics Plans, Dept. 77, Box 1014, Radio City, New York 10101, USA.

RODALE—Rodale Press. The publishing center of the North American organic gardening movement is the Rodale Press, which in recent years has become increasingly active in publishing books about small scale technology and renewable energy systems. Rodale also publishes magazines about health, organic gardening, small farming, and home remodelling/renovation. Rodale Press, 33 E. Minor St., Emmaus, Pennsylvania 18049, USA.

SATA—Swiss Association for Technical Assistance, P.O. Box 113, Kathmandu, Nepal.

SATIS—Socially Appropriate Technology International Information Services. Their catalog of books is $2.50. SATIS, Mauritskade 63, 1092 AD Amsterdam, The Netherlands.

SKAT—Swiss Center for Appropriate Technology. They publish books based on aid projects in various parts of the world. SKAT, Varnbuelstrasse 14, CH-9000 St. Gallen, Switzerland.

TALC—Teaching Aids at Low Cost. An excellent source of low-cost books in the health care field. Write for their catalog and latest price and postage cost information. Teaching Aids at Low Cost, P.O. Box 49, St. Albans, Herts. 4L1 4AX, United Kingdom.

TDRI—Tropical Development and Research Institute. Formerly called the Tropical Products Institute, TDRI produces a variety of publications on tropical agricultural products, and a series of booklets on simple processing tools (Rural Technology Guides). No charge is made for single copies of publications sent to governmental and educational establishments, research institutions and non-profit organizations working in countries eligible for British Aid. All publications are available from

Publications Section, Tropical Development and Research Institute, 127 Clerkenwell Rd., London EC1R 5DB, United Kingdom.

TOOL—The TOOL Foundation for Technical Development in Developing Countries has members on many university campuses in The Netherlands. They offer publications in English, Dutch and French, including some Dutch-only publications that we have not reviewed. They also publish a newsletter in Dutch for people working in developing countries. Catalogs are available on request. Stichting TOOL, Entrepotdok 68A/69A, 1018 AD Amsterdam, The Netherlands.

UNIDO—U.N. Industrial Development Organization. Most of the UNIDO publications reviewed here are available free of charge to readers in developing countries. You must quote the publication number with the title. Write to the Editor, UNIDO Newsletter, P.O. Box 300, A1400 Vienna, Austria.

UNIPUB—This U.S. company handles a large number of United Nations publications, along with those of other international organizations such as FAO and IDRC. UNIPUB, 205 East 42nd St., New York, New York 10017, USA.

USGPO—U.S. Government Printing Office. In contrast to the high prices of NTIS, USGPO has very low prices. Make checks payable to Superintendent of Documents. Write to: USGPO, Washington D.C. 20402, USA.

VITA—Volunteers in Technical Assistance. This group does not send volunteers, but handles requests for technical information, which it forwards to a network of U.S.-based volunteers for response. They have a long publications list, and accept UNESCO coupons in payment. VITA Publications, P.O. Box 12438, Arlington, Virginia 22209, USA.

WEA—Whole Earth Access Co. These people stock books from many of the small U.S. publishers, allowing you to obtain them from a single source. Whole Earth Access, 2990 7th St., Berkeley, California 94710, USA.

Background Reading

Every machine that helps every individual has a place,
but there should be no place for machines
that concentrate power in a few hands
and turn the masses into machine-minders,
if indeed they do not make them unemployed.

—Gandhi

Shall we forever resign the pleasure
of construction to the carpenter?
...Where is this division of labor to end?
and what object does it finally serve?
No doubt another MAY also think for me;
but it is not therefore desirable that he should do so
to the exclusion of my thinking for myself.

—Thoreau

Background Reading

The books reviewed in this chapter offer a variety of views on the cultural and economic aspects of technology choice, some of the political choices reflected in development strategies, and common technology needs in rural areas of the Third World.

E.F. Schumacher's **Small Is Beautiful** *has played a crucial inspirational role for much of the "A.T. movement." For readers interested in the hard economic basis for appropriate technology, there is no better reference than* **Technology and Underdevelopment. Appropriate Technology: Problems and Promises** *gives an historical perspective on factors that have influenced the development of practical technologies in the United States and China, and explores a large number of policy issues that surround appropriate technology. This continues to rank as one of the most insightful books in the A.T. literature.*

The A.T. Reader *assembles in one place a set of the best articles and commentary on the subject from around the world. A thoughtful analysis of the problems and issues involved in transnational "technology transfer" is contained in* **The Uncertain Promise***. This volume is particularly concerned with the impact of alien technology on cultural value systems.*

Coming Full Circle *explores the increasingly accepted view that farmers should be directly involved in technology development — that it is only through this involvement that acceptable innovations can be developed. If local participation in development projects is to be achieved, bureaucracies will have to change; this is the theme of* **Bureaucracy and the Poor***.*

Paper Heroes*, while favorably reviewing several particular tools and techniques, is critical of many of the basic assumptions and perceived benefits associated with appropriate technology. For the most part these are "the excessive claims and unsubstantiated promises of paper heroes," argues the author.*

The World of Appropriate Technology *offers a picture of the institutions involved in this work.* **Stepping Stones** *is a collection of many of the best articles that have contributed to appropriate technology thinking in and for the United States.* **Repairs, Reuse and Recycling** *discusses the technological alternatives in reducing the flow of valuable materials to dumps and landfills, an important step on the road to a more environmentally-sound society.*

The author of **Questioning Development** *suggests that a critically important measuring stick for evaluating the worth of development projects should be their anticipated effects on the distribution of power in the community, the nation, or the world.*

Among the other books included in this chapter are sets of case studies of technologies and projects that offer insights into what has and hasn't succeeded in various circumstances. There are also publications that suggest what kinds of everyday activities in the rural Third World most urgently need improved technologies, and give many examples of tools and techniques that may be appropriate. **Ap-**

propriate Technology for African Women *and* **Rural Women** *are specifically concerned with the effects of technological change on women's lives, and discuss improved technologies that might particularly help women.*

Small is Beautiful, book, 297 pages, by E.F. Schumacher, 1973, £3.70 surface mail, from ITDG; or $3.50 plus postage from WEA.

Schumacher's famous introduction of the concept of "intermediate" (or "appropriate") technology has had a major impact on current thinking in the development field. Schumacher was a founder of the Intermediate Technology Development Group.

For Schumacher, solutions to the world's problems must embody the four qualities of smallness, simplicity, capital-saving, and non-violence. To that end he is a leading advocate of "appropriate technology" as a partial answer to global problems of food and energy shortages, alienation, and poverty. In the developing countries, designed particularly to suit agricultural conditions that are different from those in the industrialized countries, this technology should be superior to the primitive forms of the past. Yet it should also be simpler, cheaper, and all but independent of the energy requirements of today's technology of the rich. "One can also call it 'self-help' or 'people's technology'," says Schumacher.

"The task, then, is to bring into existence millions of new workplaces in the rural areas and small towns. That modern industry, as it has arisen in the developed countries, cannot possibly fulfill this task should be perfectly obvious. It has arisen in societies which are rich in capital and short of labor and therefore cannot possibly be appropriate for societies short of capital and rich in labor. The real task may be formulated in four propositions:

1) Workplaces have to be created in the areas where the people are living now, and not primarily in metropolitan areas into which they tend to migrate.

2) These workplaces must be, on the average, cheap enough so that they can be created in large numbers without this calling for an unattainable level of capital formation and imports.

3) The production methods employed must be relatively simple, so that the demands for high skills are minimized, not only in the production process itself but also in matters of organization, raw material supply, financing, marketing, and so forth.

4) Production should be mainly from local materials and mainly for local use."

Schumacher on technological complexity: "Any third-rate engineer can make a machine or a process more complex; afterwards, it takes a first-rate engineer to make it simple again."

An excellent book.

Appropriate Technology: Problems and Promises, MF 01-2, book, 344 pages, edited by Nicolas Jequier, 1976, $12.50 from OECD Publications, special discount to educational institutes, 2 rue Andre Pascal, 75775 Paris CEDEX 16, France, or 1750 Pennsylvania Avenue N.W., Washington D.C. 20009, USA; Part 1 (100 pages) is available in a special low-cost edition for sale only in the U.S. and developing nations, $2.50 plus $1.00 postage in the U.S., $1.00 plus $0.83 postage to local groups in developing nations, from the A.T. Project, Volunteers in Asia, Box 4543, Stanford, California 94305, USA.

Here is the most significant publication on the subject of appropriate technology since Schumacher's **Small is Beautiful** appeared in 1973. The editor emerges as the most valuable contributor, providing a brilliant 100-page overview of the major policy issues that confront appropriate technology advocates. 19 articles by participants in the 1974 OECD conference on low-cost technology give a backdrop of some of the efforts and perspectives currently found among practitioners in the appropriate technology movement.

Jequier describes appropriate technology as a cultural revolution in the field of development (and spells out implications that virtually no one else was writing about at the time); identifies local people as the primary innovators of appropriate technology; points to the danger that appropriate technology research will be carried out mostly by groups from the rich countries, thereby stifling the development of research groups with this focus from within the developing countries and leading to the same technological dependency that currently exists; discusses the political implications of appropriate technology; poses questions for national government policy and for aid policy; contrasts decentralized with centralized research on appropriate technology; and explores many other "problems and promises" of the appropriate technology movement. In short, Jequier is among the first to try to identify the disagreements and problem areas facing appropriate technology enthusiasts; he draws up an agenda for discussion and action.

Highly recommended.

The A.T. Reader: Theory and Practice in Appropriate Technology, MF 01-20, book, 468 pages, edited by Marilyn Carr, 1985, £9.95 from ITDG.

Marilyn Carr has provided a valuable service by assembling in one place a selection of some of the best thinking on appropriate technology. More than 100 contributors discuss everything from economic theory and the nature of the innovation/product development process to specific experiences with choices of technology in real circumstances around the world. Readers will find this a good exposure to the ferment of ideas and observations that have come out of the A.T. movement over the past 15-20 years. The contributions are generally of a high caliber, and sure to be thought-provoking to even the well-read A.T. enthusiast.

Recommended.

Technology and Underdevelopment, book, 320 pages, by Frances Stewart, 1977, $27.75 (hardback) from Westview Press, 5500 Central Avenue, Boulder, Colorado 80301, USA; or £2.50 (paperback) from ITDG.

Stewart leads the reader through the most comprehensive book to date dealing with the economic theory of appropriate technology and development in the Third World. The book is technical but can be absorbed by anyone with a modest background in economic jargon.

There are two parts: 1) a theoretical discussion of the nature of technology and the social consequences of its use, and 2) a set of case studies. The theoretical discussion is aimed at the reader familiar with conventional economic theory. The author points out precisely where the false assumptions and unwarranted extrapolations are found.

Stewart begins with a discussion of the nature of technology, and the kinds of technical choices open to a developing country. She defines "technological choice" both in terms of product and the technology to create that product. Stewart states that the major reason developing countries are limited in their choice of technology is that technology has evolved to meet the different needs of developed countries. A new technology is more than a purely scientific achievement — it reflects a society's needs, standard of living, tastes, and relative scarcity of labor, capital and resources. Thus it would be purely coincidental that an ideal technology would exist for a specific application in a developing area.

The author notes the usefulness of some but not all technologies used in the evolution of developed countries. If a technology becomes obsolete in the West purely because of changes in the relative prices of capital and labor, or due to shifts in consumer tastes, then that technology may be usable in a developing country. However, technologies that became obsolete due to technical improvements may be obsolete in any context. (The failure to make this distinction underlies much of the debate on the relevance of older industrial technologies.)

Another of Stewart's major themes is that technical choice is not a narrow choice of a particular technique at a particular time. Rather, a national economic system is either oriented towards foreign advanced technology or towards more appropriate technology. If the "modern" approach is emphasized, consumers, infrastructure, and urban concentration tend to lock the country into "foreign" technology. An indigenous technology may not be able to compete in such an environment, despite its overall social desirability. The point is that the national choice of technology and lifestyle is a social choice which will dominate the narrow choice of technology for a specific application.

Highly recommended.

Introduction to Appropriate Technology, MF 01-9, book, 194 pages, 1977, edited by R. Congdon, $9.95 from RODALE.

Most of these lectures were originally given by members of the Intermediate Technology Development Group to a university audience in The Netherlands. "Socially" appropriate technology is the subject, on the assumption that "all development must be for the benefit of as large a section of the population as possible, and not remain the privilege of a small elite."

The 12 lectures provide a range of insights into the nature and definition of appropriate technology, from the perspectives of members of ITDG. George McRobie's lecture, "Approach for Appropriate Technologists," gives a good overview of the rationale and work of ITDG. S.B. Watt's lecture on choosing water technologies is illustrative of some of the best thinking from that group (e.g., "the professionals have become colonials in the sense that they have taken possession of the knowledge of technology—a knowledge that all people should possess to be able to change their own lives.") Other subjects include agricultural tools, pedal power, building, energy, chemicals, education, industrial liaison, social criteria for appropriate technology and production systems.

Harry Dickinson's concluding piece, entitled "The Transfer of Knowledge and the Adoption of Technologies," should be required reading for any person going overseas to do appropriate technology work. "As Westerners and as technologists we have a role to play but we must be self-critical about our own society before we have the wisdom and insight to be of any real value."

A Handbook on Appropriate Technology, MF 01-8, 265 pages, by the Brace Research Institute and the Canadian Hunger Foundation, 1976, $15.65 Canadian surface mail to all countries, from the Canadian Hunger Foundation, 323 Chapel Street, Ottawa, Ontario K1N 7Z2, Canada.

An introduction to the concepts of appropriate technology, this handbook includes case studies and a bibliography of pre-1976 literature. The 12 case studies form the strongest section in this handbook. They include: village-scale iron foundry in Afghanistan; well-drilling bit rebuilding in India; solar distillation in Haiti; solar crop dryers in Colombia; small-scale biogas plants in India; smokeless fuel conserving stoves in Ghana; a pedal thresher and hand weeder in Bangladesh; group credit in community development in the Dominican Republic; and ferrocement boat building in Bangladesh.

High Impact Appropriate Technology Case Studies, MF 01-24, 76 pages, by Thomas Fricke, 1984, available from A.T. International, 1331 H Street N.W., Washington D.C. 20005, USA.

Interesting examples of eight very successful appropriate technology efforts are collected in this book. Each of these technologies has benefitted thousands to hundreds of thousands of people. The author identifies factors which have contributed to the success of each.

The Mark II deep well handpump in India represents an important experience with a simplified unit, in which much of the maintenance and repair can be carried out at the village level.

Oral rehydration therapy has proven to be a very low-cost and simple technique for saving the lives of dehydrated infants suffering from infant diarrhea. UNICEF, WHO and many local organizations have launched programs to reach millions of people with this technology.

Argentina is now the world's leading producer of waterpumping windmills, and has some 60,000 units operating domestically. The design is a reproduction of an Aermotor windmill from the U.S.

Bamboo-reinforced concrete rainwater storage tanks have been built by the thousands in drought-prone northeastern Thailand since 1979. Family members provide their own labor and pay for materials, while obtaining technical assistance from a Thai voluntary agency.

In India, the use of bamboo materials and a technique for well sinking using labor-intensive methods has dramatically lowered the cost of installing tubewells for irrigation pumping. Tens of thousands of bamboo tubewells have been installed throughout India. A major advantage is that they can be used with portable, rented pumps instead of stationary ones.

The rural access roads program in Kenya has demonstrated the cost advantages of both labor-intensive construction techniques and maintenance by local villagers under contract for short road sections. "By early 1984, over 7,000 km of roadway had been completed."

A women's cooperative food processing organization in India has become a very successful business, with sales of more than $4 million annually. Members are partners rather than employees, and produce hand-rolled pappad in their homes.

In Tanzania, the decentralized production of thousands of carts and toolbar plows by two private enterprises is being met with strong market demand from farmers. This equipment has a high financial rate of return for farmers, who use it to put more land into production.

Experiences in Appropriate Technology, MF 01-6, book, 150 pages, edited by Robert Mitchell, 1980, available in English, French, and Spanish, $8.95 from Canadian Hunger Foundation, 323 Chapel Street, Ottawa, Ontario K1N 7Z2, Canada.

Nineteen case studies reveal problems and possibilities encountered in appropriate technology efforts in a variety of countries. Good background reading to stimulate thought and discussion on important issues.

Participatory Approaches to Agricultural Research and Development: A State of the Art Paper, MF 01-22, book, 111 pages, by William F. Whyte, 1981, $5.00 from Rural Development Committee, Center for International Studies, 170 Uris Hall, Cornell University, Ithaca, New York 14853, USA.

The agriculture and rural technology research, development, and extension approaches of the 1960s and 1970s failed to reach the majority of rural poor farmers. This volume summarizes and explains what has been learned from these experiences, and new models of agricultural research and development that are working. These new approaches involve substantial farmer participation and much greater involvement of scientists in on-farm testing of new crops and crop combinations. "This approach focusses on searching out what the small farmer needs and can use. In this process, scientists must and can learn much from the small farmer."

This excellent explanation of the importance and benefits of farmer participation in research and development should be required reading for people doing rural technology development work of all kinds.

Coming Full Circle: Farmer's Participation in the Development of Technology, MF 01-21, publication IDRC-189e, book, 176 pages, edited by Peter Matlon et. al., 1984, $12.00 from IDRC.

The need to include the farmer's perspective in agricultural systems research and technology development is now widely recognized by serious researchers. This book is an excellent collection of insights and observations by a group of 50 scientists with experience in using this approach, which is relevant to all kinds of rural technology development efforts.

"Researchers. . . must learn as fast as possible what the conditions are in the areas where they are working and then get on with the task of doing something about the problems. The farmers have been in the area for years or for decades or for centuries. . .They know what is going on. . . In partnership with the farmers we have to set about to see what can be done to improve conditions, given all the factors that are there. If fertilizer is not available, then researchers should not worry about fertilizer, although they can advise policymakers and infrastructure managers that it should be available. People doing research have got to address the systems that exist and stop finding excuses. They must stop saying they have a perfectly valid technology if only the policymaker would provide a fertilizer market. That does not help farmers."

For readers who are not yet convinced of the need to incorporate farmers' thinking into their work, this volume will provide ample evidence to change that. And readers who are already persuaded will find this a rich source of ideas to make their work more successful.

Strategies for Small Farmer Development Projects, Executive Summary, MF 01-26, revised paper, 34 pages, by Elliot R. Morss et. al., U.S. Agency for International Development, 1975, from Development Alternatives, Inc., 1823 Jefferson Place N.W., Washington, D.C. 20036, USA.

This important summary of a USAID-funded study of strategies for small farmer development finds that overall project success is affected most heavily by local action. The most important components of local action were found to be 1) small farmer involvement in decision-making in the implementation phase of a development project, and 2) small farmer resource commitment (labor and cash) to a development project. Chalk one up for community participation! This is essential reading with implications for all areas of community development.

Bureaucracy and the Poor, book, 258 pages, edited by David Korten and Felipe Alfonso, 1983, $9.95 from Kumarian Press, 630 Oakwood Avenue, Suite 119, West Hartford, Connecticut 06110, USA.

The management of development efforts to successfully incorporate local level needs and priorities is the theme of this volume. Experience from around the world is presented to illuminate the common obstacles that tend to prevent development bureaucracies from achieving their stated goals. Development professionals will find much familiar here, and may also be able to use this material to anticipate likely future difficulties in their own programs.

"This review of obstacles to participation at the agency, community and societal levels shows the difficulties of the participatory approach. Often many of these obstacles are ignored in program design and management; hence it is not surprising that many efforts to evoke participation do not work. Success requires major transformations in the way an agency performs its task, in the way the community relates to the agency, and in the way the society views the poor and their rights. Such transformations are inevitably slow and filled with set-backs. But the reasons for seeking participation are compelling. There are clearly no pat answers to solving the problems, but the struggle to find them evidenced in numerous programs around the world adds a healthy dimension to the world development experience."

An underlying theme is that most of the government agencies now in place were created during a period in which highly centralized decision-making was the expected pattern. Thus the structures of these bureaucracies do not easily lend themselves to greater participation at the local level. A variety of actions to make these organizations more responsive and thus more successful are suggested. The authors concede the uncomfortable truth that politics is an undeniable part of efforts to reach the poor. Some interesting parallels are drawn between the skills needed for entrepreneurial management and those needed in management of development efforts. More evidence is presented that suggests that outstanding managers can often find a way to overcome typical difficulties; yet the need is clearly for programs that will succeed with average managers.

Not surprisingly, the authors go farther in identifying the nature of these problems than in articulating convincing solutions. The stories of a few extraordinarily effective institutions are certainly hopeful. The lessons of this book may be best absorbed by members of nongovernmental organizations not immobilized by inertia, indifference, self-interest, and the sheer enormity of the problems that entangle government bureaucracies.

Readers able to plow through the difficult language and sentence structures, and the partially redundant contributions from different authors, will find valuable thought-provoking insights here, gleaned from many years of experience.

Recommended.

Ecological Principles for Economic Development, book, by Raymond Dasmann, John P. Milton, and Peter H. Freeman, 1973, $8.95, from International Union for the Conservation of Nature and Natural Resources (IUCN), 1110 Morges, Switzerland.

"This book is written from the point of view of the ecologist, for the use of those concerned with development, whether at the purely national level or in connection with specific aid programs of development agencies. It sets out to explore as briefly as possible some of the ecological concepts which have been sufficiently tested in practice to be considered valid and useful in the context of development activities."

This is the basic resource book for planners, students, and activists concerned with the impact of development on the environment. Written by three prominent ecologists, this book identifies specific concepts of ecology (the science of the interrelationship of living things and their environment) which should be incorporated into development activities. The authors argue that developing nations cannot afford to continue repeating costly errors which have brought much unanticipated or unchecked environmental damage and inflicted needless human suffering. Guidelines are presented for the areas most subject to development pressure: tropical rain forests, savannahs, mountains, coastal areas, islands, and other fragile ecosystems. Alternative strategies are proposed for handling problems, e.g., from changes in agricultural practices or tourism.

Ecological Principles for Economic Development was one of the first major expressions of the "ecodevelopment" movement. Concern about environment grew in the late 1960's and early 1970's in response to the negative side effects of large scale development projects such as dams and roads, of industrial growth, and of deforestation. The term "ecodevelopment" was coined in 1972 following the UN Conference on the Environment. "Ecodevelopment" implies a coming together of energy, economics and technology to create a form of development which can improve living conditions and be sustained over time.

People in both rich and poor countries began exploring ways to restructure their societies and avoid wasting energy, raw materials, and human potential. Local self-reliance and decreased dependence on centralized industrial systems became the basis for both the "ecodevelopment" and the "A.T." movements. Principles based upon an appreciation of the potential and the limitations of the environment show the way and appropriate technologies act as the means to achieving this form of development. While "ecodevelopment" is concerned with global problems, the focus is often on local or regional solutions.

Among the leading advocates of "ecodevelopment" are Ray Dasmann, co-author of this book, and Jimoh Omo-Fadakah, who writes frequently in **The Ecologist** magazine and **Ecodevelopment News** (see reviews). Nigerian Omo-Fadakah feels that the cause of poverty and environmental deterioration in the Third World is not a result of "backwardness," but due to the decay of rural structures and the suppression of indigenous cultures in the name of "modernization." He embraces an approach that emphasizes agricultural development over capital-intensive industrialization, based on the principles of self-reliance, grass-roots change, and extension of indigenous practices. For more detailed discussions and practical applications of "ecodevelopment," see **Ecodevelopment News**. The IUCN has produced a set of specific guidelines for regions and environments; see their publications list.

"Technology for the Masses", MF 01-10, January-February 1977 issue of **Invention Intelligence** magazine, National Research Development Corporation of India, out of print in 1985.

This special issue of the magazine **Invention Intelligence** deals with the prospects for affordable technology for rural India. Strategies for rural industry and rural development are discussed. One proposal includes a national upper consumption limit for individuals. In evaluating the role of science and technology, one author states: "We have yet to make properly documented studies on our traditional skills and practices and systematically explore the possibilities of both learning from and contributing to them, in order to evolve appropriate technology for the masses."

Several articles on energy sources describe the progress of the Indian biogas programs, the scope for the use of windpower, possible direct solar devices, the

substitution of organic fertilizers for energy-intensive chemical fertilizers, and the increased use of waterways for transport. Tree-and-pasture plantations are proposed, to make maximum use of solar energy for fuel, food and fodder.

Commenting on the importance of the bullock cart, one author notes that the total investment in carts and animals exceeds the total investment in either the railroad system or the road network in India. He proposes a number of design improvements for the bullock cart.

Low-cost housing, dairy farming, aquaculture and increased water use efficiency in irrigation are among the other topics discussed.

Relevant reading for much of the Third World.

Appropriate Technology for African Women, MF 01-1, report, 101 pages, by Marilyn Carr, 1978, available in English and French, free from the African Training and Research Centre for Women, United Nations Economic Commission for Africa, P.O. Box 3001, Addis Ababa, Ethiopia.

"An increased emphasis on 'intermediate' technologies promises to do much to lessen the inequalities between the urban and rural areas, and between rich and poor families. Its effect, however, will be limited unless increased emphasis is also given to the women who, especially in the rural areas, have the major responsibility for lifting their families out of poverty. Agricultural, rural and national development will be a slow and difficult process if the women, who form half the population and, in some countries, represent up to 80% of the agricultural labor force, continue to be denied access to knowledge, credit, agricultural extension services, consumer and producer cooperatives, labor-saving devices, and income-generating activities."

Extension programs that neglect the roles of women often have disappointing results. "Thus, in one West African country, although extension workers had shown the men the correct depth to dig the holes, coffee continued to die due to bent tap-roots because it was the women who were doing the digging."

Many improved village technologies could distinctly help rural women, "who are the drawers of water, the hewers of wood, the food-producers and often the overall providers for the families of Africa." In the main part of this report, the author identifies some of the activities for which intermediate technologies are needed to ease the burdens of rural women, and some of the possible technologies to choose from. Also included are descriptions of a wide variety of village technology-related programs in Africa, and an annotated bibliography on women and technology in Africa.

Rural Women: Their Integration in Development Programs and How Simple Intermediate Technologies Can Help Them, MF 01-15, booklet, 84 pages, by Elizabeth O'Kelly, 1978, out of print in 1985.

O'Kelly discusses the daily tasks of women in Asia and Africa, the concept of intermediate technology, and particular technologies that would tend to make life easier for rural women without reducing their role and status. She recommends hand-operated seeders, push carts and wheelbarrows, fencing, threshers, winnowers, improved hand-operated rice mills, corn mills, improved grain storage units, heavy gauge black polyethylene sheeting for sun-drying, fuelwood plantations, biogas plants, solar dryers for vegetables and fruits, improved stoves, haybox cookers, rooftop catchment water tanks, pumps, water filters and latrines.

She notes that "the part that women play in village life in general and in agriculture in particular, is consistently underestimated and many programs are drawn up on the assumption that it will be the men who will be carrying them out when, in fact, it will be the women." And when technologies are directed towards women's work, "care needs to be taken that these do not unintentionally reduce their standing."

Organizations for rural women should be created "beginning in a small way in one or two neighboring villages and continuing by working outwards in ever-widening circles." This is more likely to be successful than top-down initiatives which often lose their thrust before they have filtered down through the bureaucracy to the local level. She describes successful efforts of this kind, in the creation of corn mill societies in the Cameroons, and women's groups in Sarawak.

Design for the Real World, MF 01-4, book, 318 pages, by Victor Papanek, 1974, £7.95 from ITDG.

The author is a UNESCO International Design Expert and former Dean of the School of Design at the California Institute of the Arts. His basic thesis is that designers should design for use and address real human needs. Instead, today most design is for style and planned obsolescence. Papanek attacks the wasteful, irresponsible use of design in the industrialized world, and provides hundreds of examples of inexpensive, long-lasting, highly useful products that he and others have "designed for the real world." He is opposed to patents, because he feels ideas should be made freely available.

Although most of the book is directed towards proposed changes in the industrialized world, the author frequently discusses innovative designs that address the needs of the developing world's villagers.

Papanek provides hundreds of ideas and a starting point for responsible, socially useful design. Many photos and illustrations.

Village Technology in Eastern Africa, MF 01-25, book, 60 pages, UNICEF, June 1976 seminar report, free from UNICEF, Eastern Africa Regional Office, P.O. Box 44145, Nairobi, Kenya.

Here is an excellent introductory book, relevant to most Third World countries. It includes a review of the basic concepts of appropriate technology, and an overview of potential A.T. tools and techniques for agriculture, food preservation, preparation of nutritious infant foods from local sources, and water supply. Criteria for evaluating rural energy needs and affordable alternatives are presented.

The Karen Village Technology Unit, a demonstration center with working tools and machines, a workshop, and a simple laboratory for testing A.T. devices is described here. This was one of the first efforts of its kind.

The extension systems discussed in this book differ from the conventional "top-down" approaches. "Thinking based on 'introduction' of appropriate technology tends to foster an attitude that the technology is something brought in from outside. Whereas, it would probably be more useful to think in terms of the 'generation' of the technology within the society."

Radical Technology, MF 01-13, book, 304 pages, by Godfrey Boyle, Peter Harper, and the editors of **Undercurrents Magazine**, 1976, out of print in 1985.

An "extensively illustrated collection of original articles concerning the reorganization of technology along more humane, rational and ecologically sound lines. The many facets of such a reorganization are reflected in the wide variety of contributions to the book. They cover both the 'hardware' — the machines and technical methods themselves — and the 'software' — the social and political structures, the way people relate to each other and to their environment, and how they feel about it all."

Radical Technology gives a thorough treatment of what for many is the logical application of the concept of appropriate technology to the developed countries. Thus, while coming from a different perspective, it does cover nicely (though briefly) such topics as biodynamic agriculture, composting, agribusiness, hydroponics, solar energy, water power, metalworking, and transport, along with the more expensive intermediate technologies of printing and communications. Essays alternate with factual presentations.

Unquestionably the recent popularity of appropriate technology stems at least in part from the energy/environmental/cultural crisis in the West. This book provides a good overview of some of the thinking going on in the West in response.

"**Radical Technology** encompasses much that is meant by 'alternative technology' but sees these new, liberating tools, techniques and sources of energy as part of a restructured social order, and aims to place them directly in the hands of the community."

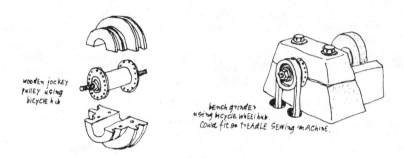

WOODEN JOCKEY
PULLEY USING
BICYCLE HUB

BENCH GRINDER
USING BICYCLE WHEEL HUB.
COULD FIT ON TREADLE SEWING MACHINE.

Repairs, Reuse, Recycling — First Steps Toward a Sustainable Society, Worldwatch Paper 23, MF 01-14, booklet, 45 pages, by Denis Hayes, 1978, $2.00 from Worldwatch Institute, 1776 Massachusetts Avenue N.W., Washington D.C. 20036, USA.

This report critically examines the flow of most materials from their sources (a mine, forest, or crop) to the dump. The imperatives for recycling materials are reviewed: increasing scarcity and energy expense of recovering non-renewable resources; political tensions caused by uneven distribution of resources worldwide; and escalating environmental costs and hazards.

Three basic approaches to sustainable resource use are waste reduction (emphasizing more durable appropriate technologies), waste separation, and waste recovery. Examples of recent recycling programs illustrate the importance of scale for recovery systems. Centralized high technology recovery facilities depend on long-term guarantees of a steady flow of waste materials. Any programs which actually reduce the flow of waste then threaten the financial viability of the high-cost recovery facilities. "A more sensible approach would be to first see how much of the problem could be solved by comprehensive programs for reducing waste, recycling, and composting. Appropriately-scaled resource recovery facilities could then be constructed to process the remaining waste."

A well-documented paper, pointing to the importance of both "technical fixes" and social reorientation.

Stepping Stones: Appropriate Technology and Beyond, large paperback, 204 pages, edited by Lane de Moll and Gigi Coe, 1979, $9.50 postpaid from RAIN, 3116 North Williams, Portland, Oregon 97227, USA; or £4.95 from ITDG.

This is a collection of some of "...the philosophical stepping stones which have helped shape the techniques, values, tools, and politics of appropriate technology" edited by associates of **Rain Magazine** and the California Office of Appropriate Technology. Most of the articles are written by well-known thinkers and practitioners from the U.S. Reprinted pieces cover the tools and approaches of appropriate technology, and application of these in our lives now. A set of mostly new essays examines this for our individual and collective futures.

The writings offer a wide range of opinion on a broad spectrum of issues: restraint and re-evaluation of our lifestyles; small vs. large scale; permanence vs. economic efficiency; and simplicity vs. fashion and convenience. It is important to note that these are not the central issues in appropriate technology for the Third World. In many of these countries, appropriate tools and techniques are playing a role in an ongoing uphill struggle for better livelihoods by enlarging the realm of what is actually possible. Such technologies do reflect concern for ecological principles

and remain at a scale affordable to the poor majority, but they do not usually come as a result of a process of scaling down or cutting back.

For these reasons many of the essays in this book do not address the circumstances faced by appropriate technology groups in poor countries. The essays do offer insights into the North American appropriate technology movement. They show that the philosophical foundations and everyday applications of appropriate technology not only have roots in our past, but also represent a starting point in our work to build a better future.

Tools for Conviviality, book, 119 pages, by Ivan Illich, $4.00 from WEA.

Illich used the unfamiliar term "convivial" in a special way — "as a technical term to designate a modern society of responsibly limited tools. . . People need new tools to work with rather than tools that 'work' for them. They need technology to make the most of the energy and imagination each has. . . A convivial society should be designed to allow all its members the most autonomous action by means of tools least controlled by others. People feel joy, as opposed to mere pleasure, to the extent that their activities are creative. . .We must recognize the nature of desirable limits to specialization and output. . .Common tools would be incomparably more efficient than primitive, and more widely distributed than industrial devices."

The language used in this book is often rather difficult; while the subject matter is theoretical and philosophical. Illich makes an interesting contribution to a philosophy of appropriate technology that would be applicable to both rich and poor countries. The book is a critique of the system of industrialization which destroys people's capacity to do things for themselves. Illich sees "conviviality" as one of the primary treasures still remaining in small communities of developing countries, that has already been tragically lost in the industrialized countries.

Illich comments on the housing industry in Latin America: "Components for new houses and utilities could be made very cheaply and designed for self-assembly. People could build more durable, more comfortable, and more sanitary dwellings as well as learn about new materials and systems. But instead of supporting the ability of people to shape their own environment, the government deposits in these shanty-towns public utilities designed for people who live in standard modern houses. The presence of a new school, a paved road, and a glass and steel police station defines the professionally built house as the functional unit, and stamps the self-built home a shanty."

The Politics of Alternative Technology, book, 204 pages, by David Dickson, 1974, $4.50 from Universe Books, 381 Park Avenue South, New York, New York 10016, USA.

Dickson examines the "modern" technology of the industrialized countries and concludes that "technology, originally developed as a means of raising man above a life of poverty, drudgery and ill health, now shows its other face as a major threat to sanity and survival."

The book includes a summary of the basic principles of "alternative" or "utopian" technology (involving community production and social organization), the characteristics that distinguish it from the dominant technology, and its relationships to the individual, the community, and the environment.

Throughout the book, the author argues that the development of modern industrialized technology has been a reflection of and a reinforcement of existing dominant political interests.

There is a chapter on intermediate technology and the Third World, providing a critique of the view that intermediate technology has no political component. "Political changes will neither flow automatically from, nor be determined by, the technology. They must be introduced separately as part of the general political struggle for emancipation. Truly appropriate technology can only come from the demands of the people by whom and for whom it is to be used, once they have successfully realized their own political and economic strength."

The Uncertain Promise: Value Conflicts in Technology Transfer, MF 01-19, book, 324 pages, by Denis Goulet, 1977, $6.50 from Overseas Development Council, 1717 Massachusetts Avenue N.W., Washington D.C. 20036, USA.

"This study of value conflicts in technology transfer has attempted to peel away the mystifications which veil the true impact of technology on societies nurturing diverse images of development. Technology is revealed herein as a two-edged sword, simultaneously bearer and destroyer of values. Yet technology is not static: it is a dynamic and expansionist social force which provides a 'competitive' edge enabling its possessors to conquer economic, political, and cultural power. Consequently, Third World efforts to harness technology to broader developmental goals are paradigmatic of a still greater task: to create a new world order founded not on elitism, privilege, or force but on effective solidarity in the face of human needs. The gestation of a new world order poses two troubling questions for all societies: Can technology be controlled, and will culture survive?"

"Technology is indispensable in struggles against the miseries of underdevelopment and against the peculiar ills of overdevelopment. Technology can serve these noble purposes, however, only in those societies in which ideology, values, and decisional structures repudiate the tendency of technology to impose its own logic in striving after goals."

"At least three values must now be internalized in any efficiency calculus: the abolition of mass misery, survival of the ecosystem, and defense of the entire human race against technological determinism. . . It is no longer correct to label some procedure efficient if it exacts intolerable social costs, proves grossly wasteful of resources, or imposes its mechanistic rhythms on its operator. . . Firm managers and designers of technology will need to explore ways of becoming integrally efficient — that is, of producing efficiently while optimizing social and human values."

This book offers an insightful examination of the values implicit in technological society; international mechanisms, and high financial and social costs, of transnational transfer of industrial technology; and basic strategies and policies in the Third World to channel technology to serve development goals. For those who can make their way through the difficult (even for native English speakers) language used, this will make excellent background reading for the discussion of appropriate technology policies.

Sharing Smaller Pies, MF 01-16, leaflet, 38 pages, by Tom Bender, 1975, out of print in 1985.

This is the American response to **Small is Beautiful**.

"There is no longer any doubt that our age of affluence based upon depletion of our planet's non-renewable energy and material resources is at an end and that major changes must be made in every aspect of our lives."

"Medicine, architecture, law, education, transportation, social work, and civil engineering have all followed the path of increasingly professionalized, more restricted, and less beneficial application of their skills."

"We need skill-developing rather than labor-saving technologies."

This leaflet includes an excellent 6-page discussion of the meaning of appropriate technology for industrialized nations. A thoughtful look at what has gone wrong in America's high-technology society, and explanations of a new set of values which might help us move toward a society characterized by "stewardship not progress" and "enoughness not moreness."

Paper Heroes: A Review of Appropriate Technology, MF 01-11, paperback book, 181 pages, by Witold Rybczynski, 1980, $4.95 from Doubleday and Company, 245 Park Avenue, New York, New York 10017, USA.

Paper Heroes is an attack on both romantic myths and basic assumptions of the "appropriate technology movement." The author has himself done some very important work on low-cost technologies, co-authoring, for example, the instant classic **Low Cost Technology Options for Sanitation in Developing Countries** (see review in WATER SUPPLY AND SANITATION chapter). Amid a small but growing literature of backlash against appropriate technology values and assumptions, this represents the first lengthy critique of A.T. by an "insider."

Rybczynski begins by attacking Schumacher. "**Small is Beautiful** . . . did not attempt a reasoned argument but appealed directly to the emotions . . . (it) was first and foremost a diatribe against modernization." He deplores a "California youth culture" concept of technology that he attributes to spinoffs from the **Whole Earth Catalog**, in a lengthy digression from his main theme. He claims that Illich, Ellul, and others who have significantly influenced A.T. thinking are "modern Luddites," dismissing the original Luddites of early 19th century England as "a kind of anti-technological Ku Klux Klan."

Rybczynski was probably correct at the time when he claimed that "A.T. could be described as an inverted pyramid—a great deal of verbiage and speculation resting on few accomplishments." The situation has changed since 1980, however, as witnessed by many of the books reviewed here. Having laid waste to what he considers "the excessive claims and unsubstantiated promises of paper heroes," the author switches to a more positive tone, favorably describing several specific technologies that might be called A.T. Readers are warned about the problems of appropriate technology strategies that attempt to use conventional aid mechanisms and institutions as the vehicles for reaching the poor. The author suggests alternatives to aid, with technology choice left to the people in the Third World. "A more successful approach, which is particularly evident in soft tech, is the provision of information on intermediate technologies directly to the individual . . . it permits the individual to decide what is appropriate, it supports decentralization, and, almost by definition, it ensures that the individual establishes a healthier control of his technology . . . It could also be argued that the successful A.T. antecedents such as rural medicine in China, the Vietnamese sanitation program, or Gandhi's hand-spinning campaign, have all been primarily information strategies. The decentralization of technique has been the result of the much more important strategy of the decentralization of knowledge."

An excellent chapter on China takes a hard look at imaginary and real lessons to be learned from that nation's experience.

Rybczynski also reminds us of a distinction between "social change" and "social reform," arguing that technological change always brings some social changes, but no technology, in and of itself, brings social reform. "Better technology (of any kind) can certainly not be a substitute for social reform. Landlordism, powerful rural elites, conservative banks, and rapacious money lenders all conspire to maintain the poverty of the landless peasants."

In the end, Rybczynski has produced a thought-provoking critique. Yet he does not seem to succeed in discrediting the propositions that 1) many technologies contain within them cultural and political biases, and 2) there are other paths to the future than that of the Western industrial model.

Questioning Development: Notes for Volunteers and Others Concerned with the Theory and Practice of Change, MF 01-12, booklet, 48 pages, by Glyn Roberts, 1981, £1.50 (British Sterling only accepted), from ITDG.

A discussion of some philosophies of development currently in practice around the world; "ideas which may be useful to anyone who wonders about the changes he is helping to bring about." The author suggests that "we shall clearly have to come to an agreement as to what we mean by development. Paradoxically, this is something which many 'development' personnel have never faced up to. Despite years in the Aid business, they have always been too busy getting on with the job to worry much about the overall picture." People use the word "development" to describe many different types of activity, many of which do more harm than good to the people affected. "We are all agreed, no doubt, that Development means healthier, happier, fuller and more meaningful lives for everyone. Earlier this was simply rephrased as 'Development = the more equal distribution of power among people.' " As a result of "looking at the development in terms of power, we may gain insight into the cause of poverty in our own countries. We may find that the differences traditionally noted between the 'advanced' and the 'less developed' nations are less important than the similarities."

Technology and Employment in Industry, MF 01-17, book, 389 pages, edited by A.S. Bhalla, revised 1981 edition, 37.50 Swiss Francs (approximately US$21.40), from ILO Publications, CH-1211 Geneva 22, Switzerland; or ILO, 1750 New York Avenue N.W., Washington D.C. 20006, USA.

A collection of case studies: can making in Kenya, Tanzania and Thailand; jute processing in Kenya; textile manufacturing in the United Kingdom; sugar processing in India; manufacturing cement blocks in Kenya; running engineering industries in Colombia; metalworking in Mexico; and extracting and processing copper and aluminum in the United States, Zambia, Zaire, and Chile.

"The studies demonstrate quite clearly that substitution possibilities exist in industry in both core and ancillary operations. This conclusion, based on empirical evidence, is important, since it has often been assumed that there is no choice of techniques in manufacturing industry. Secondly, the range of available techniques can be widened by re-designing or copying older designs and blueprints with local engineering adaptations, or through local manufacture of equipment. Thirdly, quite often the use of capital-intensive techniques, where more labor-intensive ones could have been used equally efficiently, is due not to the fact that there are no other technical possibilities in industry — there are — but to imperfect knowledge and inappropriate selection systems."

This book strays rather far from our focus on home-built and village-level technology, but the conclusions are significant from the point of view of village industries and other small-scale industries to which they may be linked.

Towards Global Action for Appropriate Technology, MF 01-18, book, 220 pages, edited by A.S. Bhalla, 1979, $13.00 from Pergamon Press, Inc., Maxwell House, Fairview Park, Elmsford, New York 10523, USA.

A set of essays examining the need for and nature of national and international mechanisms to support appropriate technology research, development and dissemination. Nicolas Jequier writes about some of the non-economic criteria that should be considered in evaluating possible appropriate technologies. Ajit Bhalla discusses the elements of a basic needs strategy for development, and policy choices to make appropriate technology part of that strategy. Amulya Reddy offers a framework for understanding why existing R&D institutions in developing countries do not generate appropriate technologies, and what shifts in policy and orientation are needed to ensure the development of A.T.s within some of these institutions. Willem Floor describes the activities of the U.N. agencies, and how they do or do not touch on appropriate technology. Paul Marc Henry, Reddy and Stewart present a final 13-page proposal for a "new international mechanism for appropriate technology," a non-governmental organization to be associated with, but outside of, the United Nations.

National policy initiatives and programs, and international institutions can all play a major role in improving the climate for A.T. work. In reality, however, many of the most effective A.T. efforts around the world were initiated without government and international agency support. This volume unfortunately does not discuss the possibilities for in-country and international cooperation among grass-roots appropriate technology groups themselves, often forced to operate without policy support or funding.

The World of Appropriate Technology: A Quantitative Analysis, MF 01-23, book, 210 pages, by Nicolas Jequier and Gerard Blanc, 1983, from OECD, 2 rue Andre Pascal, 75775 Paris Cedex 16, France.

After studying the growth of institutions and activities in the late 1970s, the authors came to the conclusion that appropriate technology thinking had been far more accepted by governments and large institutions than had been previously supposed.

"Governments have become the main source of funds for A.T. activities throughout the world, and their weight tends to be particularly high in the developing countries... Sociologically speaking, the A.T. movement has many features in common with the intellectual elites that brought about political revolutions in other places and other times. Not only because of the educational level of its members, the urban location of its activities or the intensity of its communications networks, but because of a much more subtle phenomenon of termite-like penetration into the decision-making circles of governments, industry, banks, political parties and trade-unions."

The authors illuminate the linkages among groups, the levels of funding and staffing, and the strengths and weaknesses of the A.T. movement as it existed at the time. The concluding remarks provide another set of provocative insights in keeping with the high standards of Jequier's previous book, **Appropriate Technology: Problems and Promises** (see review).

ADDITIONAL REFERENCES FOR BACKGROUND READING

The first books reviewed in each chapter are often background reading for that topic area.

General References

General References

As most of the publications reviewed throughout this book can be considered references, this chapter was created for special kinds of publications. These include books and periodicals that span many topic areas, several bibliographies, and directories of appropriate technology groups. Books that contain information on a number of technologies within a single general subject area have been placed in the corresponding chapters.

Entries in this chapter from Nepal, Bangladesh, France, Peru, Indonesia, Papua New Guinea, India and South Africa each contain information on a variety of technologies relevant to many developing countries. (See especially **People's Workbook** and **Liklik Buk**.)

More Other Homes and Garbage is a valuable textbook and reference for calculations needed for a variety of technologies. **Field Engineering** and the turn-of-the-century **Mechanical Engineer's Pocket-Book** are packed with hard-to-find technical information relevant to the rural areas of developing countries.

Four bibliographies have been included here. **Non-Agricultural Choice of Technique** and **Economically Appropriate Technologies for Developing Countries** lead the reader to the literature on the economic implications of technology choice. **Appropriate Technology Information for Developing Countries** is an attempt to cull and re-evaluate U.S. AID and government research reports for possible relevance to appropriate technology efforts — a difficult task. **Guide to Convivial Tools**, intended for librarians, identifies the books of a new discipline — the study of the cultural, social, and political conditions necessary to allow democratically determined limits to industrial technology.

Rainbook and several other books are concerned with activities in the U.S. The **Foxfire** books document historical technologies once widely used in the rural areas of this country.

Six directories of appropriate technology institutions are included. The most up-to-date is ITDG's aptly named **Appropriate Technology Institutions: A Directory**. Readers operating information services or small libraries will find valuable advice in **Small Technical Libraries** and **How to Build Up a Simple Multidimensional Documentation System**. For those who just want to stir things up a little, two formula manuals contain a number of household product formulas that would also be relevant in the Third World.

Completing this section is the low-cost two-volume **Chambers Dictionary of Science and Technology**, with some 50,000 English technical terms from 100 fields of activity.

More Other Homes and Garbage, MF 02-47, book, 374 pages, by J. Leckie et. al., revised edition 1981, $14.95 plus $1.00 postage (California residents add 6% tax) from Sierra Club Books, Box 3886, Rincon Annex, San Francisco, California 94119, USA.

This valuable, easy-to-read textbook contains well-illustrated presentations that successfully make technical information available to people without formal technical training.

Topics include: alternative architecture, small-scale generation of electricity using wind power and water power, and solar heating of houses and water. The solar section contains useful charts such as the coefficients of transmission of heat for various building materials, and the proper solar collector orientation for different latitudes. Biogas digesters are discussed in the waste systems section, while the

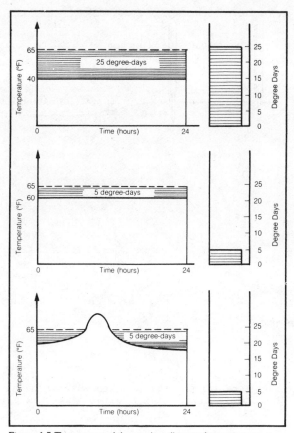

Figure 4.5 The concept of degree-days illustrated in various ways.

water supply chapter covers wells, solar distillation of water, pumps and water purification. Each of the chapters includes many sample calculations to aid the reader in understanding how to solve practical problems. The emphasis is on providing the reader with most of the necessary background information needed to design projects.

The new edition reflects a more sophisticated approach to the economics of alternative technologies, and advances made in commercially available materials. The section on solar thermal applications, in particular, has been thoroughly revised.

While much of the content of this book is U.S. oriented, this can also be a valuable reference in developing countries, especially for understanding basic concepts and doing calculations correctly.

Field Engineering, MF 02-71, book, 251 pages, by Peter Stern, F. Longland, et. al., 1936 original edition, revised 1983, £5.95 from ITDG.

Workers in developing countries have long needed a simplified, small engineering handbook for quick reference. This one was widely used in East Africa from its appearance in 1936 until after its revision in 1952. The current, substantially

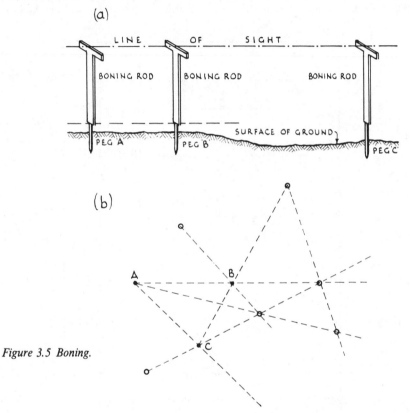

(a)

LINE   OF   SIGHT

BONING ROD   BONING ROD   BONING ROD

SURFACE OF GROUND

PEG A   PEG B   PEG C

(b)

A   B

C

Figure 3.5 Boning.

PEGS A, B & C ARE LEVELLED WITH SPIRIT OR OTHER LEVEL. THE REMAINDER ARE BONED IN.

PLAN OF LEVELLING OPERATIONS

revised 1983 edition contains much basic information on surveying, building construction and water supply. The many illustrations and emphasis on techniques make this a handbook that will be useful to people without any engineering background.

Simple surveying equipment and techniques are described along with how to set out building plots. The characteristics of different building materials are explained (wood beams, thatch roofs, tile roofs, reinforced concrete and more). Pipelines and pumps for water collection and distribution, and basic latrine and privy designs are covered. Earthen road and timber bridge construction are followed by basic formulas for different power sources. Important design considerations, safe loads, etc. are set out for most of these topics.

Readers looking for more extensive engineering reference material should consult **The Mechanical Engineers' Pocket-Book** (1910 edition) included in the microfiche library (paper edition out of print).

The Mechanical Engineers' Pocket-Book, MF 02-74, book, 1461 pages, by William Kent, 1910 edition, paper edition out of print, microfiche edition available for $10.00 from A.T. Microfiche Library, Volunteers in Asia, P.O. Box 4543, Stanford, California 94305, USA.

This long out-of-print engineering handbook contains information on a range of technologies and materials that are still commonly used or that could be used in developing countries, but have disappeared from current engineering handbooks. While most of the information contained within will not prove of use to most readers, the sheer size of this "pocket book" (1461 pages) means that it is peppered with interesting entries. These include, for example: steam engines (140 pages), human and animal power, strength of lime and cement mortar, stresses in framed structures (e.g. timber bridge trusses), pelton wheel sizes and specifications, sugar cane bagasse as a fuel, measuring water flow using "miner's inches," windmill capacity and economy, weight of materials for roofs, characteristics and splicing of wire and hemp ropes for power transmission and haulage, shearing strength of a wide variety of American wood species, and use of belts for power transmission. Introductory and summary material is provided for each section of the handbook: strength of materials, geometry, calculus, mechanics, basic machines, water power, etc.

The reader is to be forewarned that some of the information contained in this book is no longer valid, as the composition of materials has changed over the years. However, for the range of technologies on which it is almost impossible to find any engineering information elsewhere, this is a welcome reference.

The Next Whole Earth Catalog, large paperback book, 608 pages, edited by Stewart Brand, 1981, $16.00 from WEA.

The Whole Earth Catalog was started in an attempt to provide information about where to buy good quality tools (including books as "tools"). The **Catalog** expanded from that vision to include books, products and information on practically everything for the U.S. reader—from environmental law through French cookware to mysticism.

The Whole Earth Catalog represents one of the best models for low-cost information exchange anywhere, but little from the **Catalog** is appropriate to the needs of developing countries. (In Papua New Guinea, development workers have produced a local catalog of information and resources available within the country. This is an excellent example of what can be done with this approach. See review of **Liklik Buk**, MF 02-44).

Liklik Buk—A Rural Development Handbook/Catalogue for Papua New Guinea, MF 02-44, 270 pages, Melanesian Council of Churches, 1977 second edition, $9.95 from VITA.

Liklik Buk contains a wealth of practical information for rural development in Papua New Guinea. Tells a great deal about who's doing what in PNG, and where to go for further information.

There are 120 pages on crops and livestock, with attention to processing and utilization. Some coverage of village industries (good short description of silk-screen printing and soapmaking), food processing, and building and roads construction. 12 pages on health and nutrition.

The Design section includes many photos and drawings that are great sources of ideas; some of the equipment could be built from this information alone. Of particular interest are the pedal-powered thresher, winnowing machine, coconut scraper, oil press, and sugar cane crusher. Some information is presented on alternative sources of energy and water resource development.

An excellent model for what a national catalogue/handbook can be. Highly recommended.

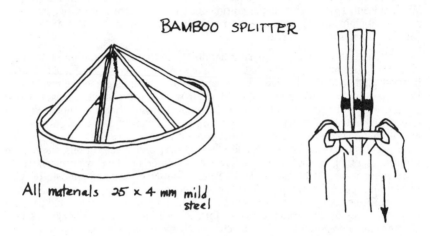

BAMBOO SPLITTER

All materials 25 x 4 mm mild steel

China at Work, MF 02-77, book, 357 pages, by R. Hommel, 1937 (reprinted 1969), out of print in 1985.

The author lived in China between 1921 and 1930. In this remarkable book, he examines "primary tools, those which met people's basic needs: the handcrafting of tools, the providing of food, clothing, shelter, and transportation. The photographs and sketches are thoroughly documented and the various processes explained." There are more than 500 photos and sketches, and a very useful index with several hundred individual items of village technology listed.

Although much of the material in this book is quite dated and primitive, the book is so comprehensive that it undoubtedly includes a few useful items for any village technologist.

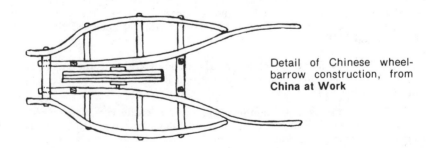

Detail of Chinese wheelbarrow construction, from **China at Work**

Teknologi Kampungan: A Collection of Indigenous Indonesian Technologies,
MF 02-60, book, 154 pages, by Craig Thorburn, June 1982, $6.00 from Volunteers
in Asia, Appropriate Technology Project, P.O. Box 4543, Stanford, California 94305,
USA.

Successful, ingenious traditional technologies are used throughout the world,
and represent an important resource of human knowledge that should be tapped
in appropriate technology development. The people of Indonesia, in the rural areas
and urban "informal sector," employ a great variety of clever, resource-conserving,
low cost tools and techniques. Author Craig Thorburn has added 270 illustrations
to an informative text that will allow readers to make, use or adapt many of the
best of these technologies to fit their own circumstances. Topics include agricultural
hand tools, water lifting devices, metal working tools including a carbide gas
generator for welding, fish traps and nets, crop threshing and processing equipment, stoves, three-wheeled cycles, construction techniques and materials, waterwheels, and a variety of other rural and small industry technologies. Recommended.

Appropriate Technology: Directory of Machines, Tools, Plants, Equipment,
Processes, and Industries, MF 02-23, book, 280 pages, by M.M. Hoda, second
edition 1977, Rp. 60 in India, US$13.00 plus $9.00 postage abroad, from Appropriate
Technology Development Association, Post Box 311, Gandhi Bhawan, Lucknow
226001, U.P., India.

This book exposes the reader to some of the intermediate technologies that are
relevant in Indian circumstances. Subjects include agricultural tools, crop processing
equipment, crafts tools, village and cottage industries, transport, water supply,
biogas, and solar devices.

More than 50 pieces of equipment are presented; the information has been compiled from a variety of sources. There are descriptions, drawings and construction
notes for most of these. For the following items the material included appears to

be sufficient for construction: six agricultural handtools, hand crop duster, earth auger, hand seed drill, plant puller, seed dresser, oil drum forge, metal bending machine, equipment for parboiling rice, hand-operated workshop drilling machine, sugar cane crusher, equipment for making matches, equipment for making candles and soap, three-geared cycle rickshaw, water seal latrine, hand pumps, hydraulic ram pump, hand-operated washing machine, solar cooker, and forms for casting well rings.

Some information, although not enough for construction, is also provided on the following: seed & fertilizer drill, paddy transplanter, ground nut harvester, paddy thresher, grain purifier, mini-sugar mill (very informative on a successful effort to decentralize sugar refining), equipment for red clay pottery, lime kiln, charkha, non-ferrous metal foundry, equipment for making chalk and beekeeping, biogas plants, and designs for one and two room houses.

Techniques Appropriate for the Villages: Some Examples, MF 02-59, booklet, 50 pages, 1977 (revised 1980), Rs. 10 ($1.00) plus shipping, from Director, Centre of Science for Villages, Magan Sangrahalaya, Wardha — 442 001, India.

"Herein are collected some examples of techniques appropriate for the villages which could be tried." This booklet presents 33 short descriptions (no drawings) of tools and techniques for housing, motive power, and small chemical industries currently being developed at several Indian research institutes. Some of the techniques are simple enough to be tried without further information. Many (e.g. mushroom cultivation in paddy straw; chemical treatment of bamboo for handicrafts and bamboo-cement construction; fungi treatment and fire protection for thatch roofs, etc.) are of interest in countries other than India as well.

Traditional Crafts of Persia, MF 02-78, book, 304 pages, by Hans Wulff, 1966, MIT Press, out of print in 1985.

An inventory with photos of the traditional crafts and tools used. Major topics are metalworking, woodworking, building, ceramics, textiles, leather, and agriculture. Descriptive text. Among the most interesting items covered are: flour mills and rice hulling mills driven by wooden water wheels or vertical-axis windmills; the Qanat water supply system; and oil-seed milling.

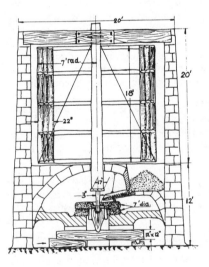
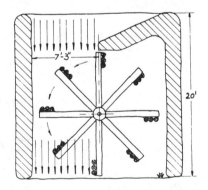

Two views of a Persian vertical-axis windmill that has traditionally been used to grind grain (see grindstones at bottom left).

People's Workbook, MF 02-76, book, 560 pages, by Robert Berold et. al., 1981, $12.75 from Environmental and Development Agency (EDA), Box 62054, Marshalltown, 2107 Johannesburg, South Africa, or TOOL.

A wonderfully-illustrated, large reference book/catalog, this is full of practical information for rural development in South Africa. Major subjects are small farming (crops, animals, tools, draft animal power), water supply, health, building construction, working in groups and legal rights. The book begins with a lengthy comic book story of the history of South Africa.

This is the most extensive book of its kind, and should be of interest in many developing countries.

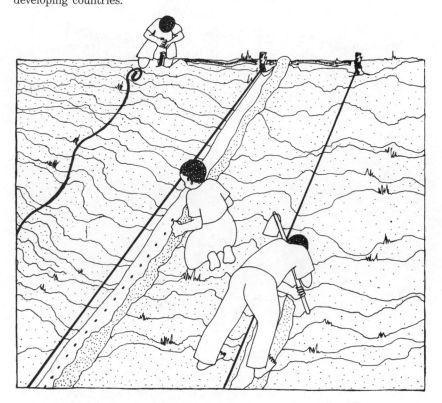

Mini Technology, MF 02-45, booklet, 76 pages, by B.R. Saubolle, S.J., and A. Bachmann, 1978, free from UNICEF, P.O. Box 1187, Kathmandu, Nepal.

"This booklet is based very largely on the experience of the author, who was born and bred in India. It gives mostly Indian solutions to problems encountered in an earlier age before the onrush of modernity. It tells how to cool a house without air-conditioning, how to chill beer without a refrigerator, how to produce gas for cooking and lighting where there is no town supply, a way to make crows trap themselves, several ways of getting hot water at no expense, and so on and so forth." There are, in fact, four ways to cool food and yourself, four solar water heaters, an unusual solar dryer, several cookers and ovens, a self-closing water standpipe, some water filters, a one-person desk fan, a hand-held corn sheller, a fly trap, a fluorescent light insect trap, and an African bee hive.

Delightfully written and full of unusual devices that are otherwise largely undocumented.

Mini Technology II, MF 02-75, booklet, 68 pages, by A. Bachmann and B.R. Saubolle, 1983, free from UNICEF, P.O. Box 1187, Kathmandu, Nepal.

A companion volume to the original **Mini Technology**, this one provides details on more devices and techniques. Included are a water-powered pestle hammer, wooden winnowing fan, fence post driver, techniques for killing rats and repelling mosquitos, and more.

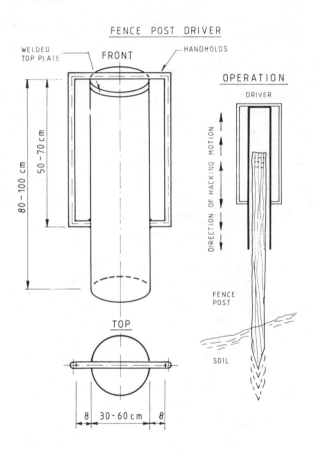

FENCE POST DRIVER

The Journal of the New Alchemists, vol. 1 MF 02-79, vol. 3 MF 02-80, volumes 1-4 out of print in 1981, volume 5 still available, at price listed below, from New Alchemy Institute, 237 Hatchville Road, East Falmouth, Massachusetts 02536, USA.

The journals offer a sampling of the work of the New Alchemy Institute, an organization working with sophisticated appropriate technologies, primarily for temperate climates. The Institute also has a small farm in Costa Rica, at which some of its members spend part of each year. Each journal contains a mix of practical and theoretical articles, some of which are listed below.

Volume 4 (MF 02-81, 148 pages) includes:
  a) description of intensive vegetable gardening activities
  b) solar algae ponds for aquaculture

c) experiments with semi-enclosed fish culture systems
d) cage culture of fish
e) the Ark—a "bioshelter" for Prince Edward Island
f) backyard solar greenhouse
g) "Return to the Feminist Principle"

Volume 5 (MF 02-82, 152 pages, $7.00) includes:
a) New Alchemy sailwing windmill
b) Green Gulch sailwing windmill
c) Hydrowind development program (windgenerator using hydraulic fluid pumped to the base of the tower where it drives a generator)
d) intensive gardening—mulches, bean pests, energy efficiency, earthworms
e) permanent agriculture
f) semi-enclosed aquatic ecosystems
g) small scale trout farm

The Book of the New Alchemists, MF 02-24, 174 pages, edited by Nancy Jack Todd, 1977, $7.00 from New Alchemy Institute, 237 Hatchville Road, East Falmouth, Massachusetts 02536, USA.

A collection of articles on the work of the New Alchemy Institute on Cape Cod, Massachusetts. This group carries out probably the most scientifically sophisticated work of any of the U.S. -based appropriate technology groups. The articles are about gardening and small-scale farming, aquaculture in small ponds, and "bioshelters" (primarily the Ark, a complex unit that combines passive solar heating, greenhouse food production, fish raising and human living quarters). Twenty pages are devoted to strategies for ecological farming in Costa Rica, where some of the Institute members work part of the year. Most of these articles are reprinted from the earlier issues of the annual **Journal of the New Alchemists** (see review).

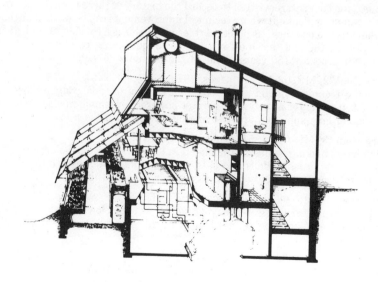

A section through residential greenhouse, heat storage composting toilet, and living areas of the Ark

Pictorial Handbook of Technical Devices, MF 02-50, book, 600 pages, by O. Schwarz and P. Grafstein, 1971, $14.00 from Chemical Publishing Co., Inc., 80 Eighth Avenue, New York, New York 10011, USA.

This is an idea book with 5000 illustrations. Major sections are: machine technology, magnetics and electronics, light and optics, industrial processes, power generation, structural engineering, comfort heating and cooling, and measuring devices. Short descriptions are provided for some of the more complex devices. Materials used and exact dimensions are not given.

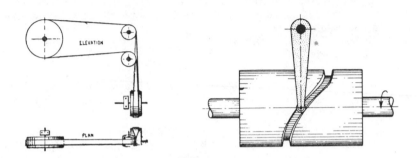

The Foxfire Books, vol. 1, MF 02-32, Elliot Wigginton, advisor, at prices listed below, from Doubleday, 245 Park Avenue, New York, New York 10017 USA.

The Foxfire Books document the daily lives and traditional tools and techniques of the mountain people of the eastern United States. Much of each volume is given to interviews and conversations with old-timers in the region. As an historical record, these books have proved immensely popular, selling over 1 million copies. Photos and drawings are abundant.

Because the books were written to record the history of these rural people, they do not attempt to point out where technical improvements can be made. For those who would like to use these as practical references, this is a considerable obstacle, made worse by the fact that most of these techniques have remained nearly unchanged for probably 150 years. Some of the contents of each:

Foxfire Book 2, MF 02-33, 410 pages, 1973, $5.95.
Beekeeping techniques; wild plant foods; making an ox yoke, wagon wheels, a wagon, a tub wheel for a vertical-axis water-powered grain mill; raising sheep for wool, and carding, spinning, and weaving cloth; how to make a loom.

Foxfire Book 3, MF 02-34, 511 pages, 1975, $4.95.
Tanning hides; making banjos and dulcimers, a lumber kiln, a smokehouse, butter-churns, brooms, brushes, dolls and hats; using an animal-powered mill to crush sorghum for syrup and candy (same as a sugar cane crushing mill).

Foxfire Book 4, MF 02-35, 496 pages, 1977, $5.95.
Making knives and carving wood; making fiddles, wooden plows and sleds, wooden water pipes, traps, and cheese; gardening; building a still furnace (for alcohol production).

Foxfire Book 5, MF 02-36, 511 pages, 1979, $6.95.
Blacksmithing and gun making (flintlock rifles — 230 pages); bear hunting.

Foxfire Book 6, MF 02-37, 507 pages, 1980, $7.95.
Making a gourd banjo and song bow, toys and games (170 pages), shoes and wooden locks; an old water-powered sawmill.

Simple Working Models of Historic Machines (Easily Built by the Reader), MF 02-54, book, 79 pages, by A. Burstall, 1968, MIT Press, out of print in 1985.

35 different machines are presented in the form of drawings of simple working models. The emphasis is on the essential operating features of the machines. Most of the devices can be built with woodworking tools in a small workshop; some of them, however, require machined metal gearing. A description of the origin and use of each is provided.

The drawings include: great wheel lathe, treadle lathe, screw cutters for wooden screws (male and female threads), a variety of pulleys and other lifting devices, Chinese spoon-tilt hammer, escapement mechanisms in clocks, two kinds of bellows, and machines for pumping and raising water (Archimedes' screw, chain pump, suction pump, diaphragm pump, hydraulic ram).

The intent of the author is to "encourage a talent for experimenting and improvising." The drawings illustrate important principles in mechanical engineering. They can either serve as the basis for practical applications of these principles, or as teaching models. "Much appeared to be learned by feeling and touching a working model that otherwise eluded the students when only diagrams, slides, or cinema films were used."

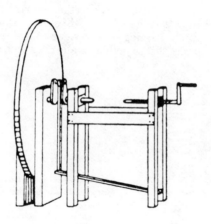

Leonardo's treadle lathe

Village Technology Handbook, MF 02-64, book, 387 pages, VITA, 1970, $13.00 in U.S., $13.75 international surface mail, $18.25 international airmail (free if you live in a developing country and can't afford it), Spanish and French editions also available, from VITA.

"This handbook describes techniques and devices which can be made and used in villages. Hopefully the book will generate new ideas as well as pass on information which has already been tried."

The book "was conceived by VITA volunteers in 1962 as a means of bridging the technical information gap which keeps the world's villages from learning from one another's experience. The book's aim is to gather in one publication information from many sources which has been found helpful in villages."

Subjects covered include:

a) Developing water resources (including basic well-drilling or digging information, such as how to make a hand-operated earth boring machine).

b) Water lifting and transport (chain pump for irrigation, pipelines, hydraulic ram pump).

c) Water storage and water power.

d) Water purification (for example, sand filters).

e) Health and sanitation (principles of latrine building).

f) Agriculture (earth-moving devices for irrigation and road-building, underground irrigation using tiles, tile-making, grain drying, two-person bucket sprayer, back-pack crop duster).

g) Food processing and preservation (for example, iceless refrigerator).

h) Construction (concrete, bamboo, making glues).

i) Miscellaneous (solar water heater, hand-operated washing machines, soap-making, building a kiln for pottery, silk-screen printing, and winding a spring).

j) An appendix with conversion charts for English to metric units.

Due to the great amount of village technology development work that has taken place in the last 15 years, this book is somewhat out of date. It still makes a good introductory book and reference.

Soft Tech, MF 02-56, book, 175 pages, edited by Jay Baldwin and Stewart Brand, 1978, out of print in 1985.

A compendium of the "soft technology" sections — articles and reviews of products and books — from past issues of the **CoEvolution Quarterly** (itself an extension of the **Whole Earth Catalog** — see reviews). What is "soft technology" to the editors? " 'Soft' signifies that something is alive, resilient, adaptive, maybe even lovable."

IT'S A NEW ERA, MAN!

I didn't believe in the alternate-energy future until I saw how dull it was gonna be and how stupid the slogans were gonna be and how much I wasn't gonna like it. Then I knew it would come.

— Steve Baer

The emphasis here is on technologies that can be used in the U.S. Much of this book provides access to products — identifying who is making and selling the best quality and most unusual practical tools — from hand tools to machines and renewable energy measuring devices. In this sense **Soft Tech** is a buyer's guide for a "highly evolved toolbox." You'll also get a look at solar gadgets for U.S. homes, the 1891-1930 California solar water heater boom, energy-efficient cars and mopeds, folding bicycles, wood-burning for space heat, underground buildings, owner-building strategies, passive solar design, and the New Alchemy Ark.

RAINBOOK: Resources for Appropriate Technology, MF 02-51, book, 256 pages, by the editors of **Rain Magazine**, 1977, $7.00 postpaid, from **Rain Magazine**, 3116 North Williams, Portland, Oregon 97227, USA.

A compilation of information that has appeared in **Rain Magazine** (see review) plus a lot of new material. Describes reference materials, activities of U.S. groups, and includes articles on: appropriate technology, place, economics, creating community, communications, transportation, shelter, agriculture, health, waste recycling, and energy. The emphasis is on changing the U.S. towards decentralized, environmentally appropriate technology, and having fun doing it.

Like the journal, **RAINBOOK** is the best single reference for Americans looking for excellent resources for changing lifestyles so that we consume less of the world's resources, while becoming fuller human beings ourselves.

Fichier Encyclopedique du Developpement Rural, MF 02-28, folders of leaflets, available for 130 Francs per year, add 60FF foreign postage, from RESEAUX— La Lettre du GRET, 34, rue Dumont d'Urville, 75116-Paris, France.

These are sets of leaflets, in French, on a wide variety of village technology topics. The information is taken from French sources and international sources such as VITA and Brace Research Institute. References for additional information are given in each case. These leaflets offer an introduction to the concepts and applications of many successful technologies. Some of the topics covered: soil-cement block making, raising grapes and making wine in the tropics, water supply, bamboo construction, and cane crushing for sugar production.

GRET has a large collection of other French language publications on village technologies, and we urge readers in French-speaking countries to write to them for their publications list.

MINKA: A favor de una autentica ciencia campesina, Boletin de la Comision Coordinacion de Tecnologia Andina, MF 02-46, edited by Grupo Talpuy, 4 issues per year, $15.00 individuals and $30.00 institutions per year (international subscription), or exchange, from MINKA, Apartado 222, Huancayo, Peru.

This Spanish-language journal provides the rural people ("campesinos") of Peru with information on locally successful appropriate technologies. MINKA is committed to a search for local solutions to local problems, through the development of a more scientific approach among the campesinos. It emphasizes technologies that have come out of the people's own experiences, such as the waterpumping windmills built at Miramar. An attractive mix of drawings, cartoons, photos and articles present information on a wide variety of subjects. Each issue concludes with a project for children, with simple plans for a working model of a tool or

Operating a chain pump

machine. Past issues have covered topics such as: "Is Mechanization Progress? For Whom?", plans for a locally-designed spade that is easily made and repaired, plans for a chain pump that can be built in a village, and a description of traditional Inca and pre-Inca water technologies. There are also reviews of illustrated manuals that can be of practical use to campesinos.

To the question "Do the campesinos read?", the editors answer that publishing is always done in cities, on topics that city people want to read about. By publishing a journal in a popular format on topics of direct concern to the campesinos and with their input, the editors hope to encourage a wide readership in the rural areas of Peru.

An outstanding example of a local communications resource for the sharing of local ingenuity and information on appropriate technologies.

Simple Technologies for Rural Women in Bangladesh, MF 02-53, book, 70 pages, by Elizabeth O'Kelly, 1983, free from UNICEF, CPO Box 58, Dacca 5, Bangladesh.

This is a compilation of simple equipment that can be made or purchased in Bangladesh and many other developing countries. Only single drawings or photos are included for most examples; for some items this is sufficient information to make them.

The book begins with a description of the activities of rural women in Bangladesh, and the tools and equipment they use. Some employment-generating activities that could benefit rural women are suggested. Potentially relevant technologies presented have been taken from a variety of sources (FAO, ITDG books and equipment catalogs, the **A.T. Sourcebook**); these include vegetable coolers, cooking stoves, threshers, winnowers, and water pumps. Some manufacturers' addresses and a bibliography are included.

The author notes that "the division of labor between the sexes...needs careful study especially as in many countries the women enjoy considerable prestige as

Foot-operated grain huller

the growers of food for their families — which they will lose if the pattern of living is changed too drastically."

Economically Appropriate Technologies for Developing Countries: An Annotated Bibliography, MF 02-27, book, 123 pages, compiled by Marilyn Carr, 1976, revised 1981, £5.95 from ITDG.

This is an annotated list of 308 "reference materials on the economic aspects of intermediate technology and its appropriateness." Studies are of the following categories of technologies: agriculture, housing, manufacturing, power sources, water supplies, health services, and transport. Most of the studies "have been aimed at assessing how 'intermediate' techniques compare in terms of capital and labour productivity, employment generation, cost of production, and generation of surplus with more conventional techniques." Many of the conclusions of the reports are given.

Appropriate Technology for Rural Development: The ITDG Experience, Occasional Papers 2, MF 02-70, booklet, 31 pages, by D.W.J. Miles, 1982, £1.00 from ITDG.

As the best known of all the A.T. organizations, the Intermediate Technology Development Group (ITDG) is contacted by people from all over the world. This short booklet provides a nice summary of the experiences, philosophy and current-strategy of the group. It will aid readers in understanding what ITDG has defined as its primary tasks, and thus what kinds of assistance and collaboration may be possible.

"We see serious 'training gaps' at four levels:
— at the artisanal level, we see a need for practical training for people who will be using appropriate technologies, such as brick-makers...
— at the enabling level of supervisors, foremen and managers of labour-intensive operations...
— at the professional level...for designers and operating staff of institutions and enterprises...
— at the political level, where planners, administrators and decision-makers need exposure to the wide variety of governmental and institutional changes which may support and make more effective implementation and expansion of A.T. programmes."

Intermediate Technology in Ghana: The Experience of Kumasi University's Technology Consultancy Centre, MF 02-40, book, 111 pages, by Sally Holtermann, £7.95 from ITDG.

Case studies are presented which document the Technology Consultancy Centre's experience with projects for manufacturing glue, soap, animal feed, glass beads, brass casting, nuts and bolts, and for broadloom weaving, and the development of a "plant construction unit." Each project is analyzed in the context of the local economy and government policies. Background information on the TCC may be valuable to people wishing to replicate the TCC model.

Guide to Technology Transfer in East, Central, and Southern Africa, MF 02-38, book, 134 pages, by Anthony Ellman, Bruce Mackay, and Tony Moody, Commonwealth Secretariat, 1981, £2.25 from ITDG.

Many people in East, Central, and Southern Africa are dependent upon equipment purchased at high cost from Europe while low-cost, locally-adapted alternatives are available within the region. This guide catalogues a variety of equipment for agriculture and home industry. Good drawings and ordering information. Country guides for Botswana, Kenya, Lesotho, Malawi, Swaziland, Tanzania, Uganda,

Zambia, and Zimbabwe give data on the countries' agriculture, transportation, freight companies, trade regulations, and customs tariffs. This is a good model for catalogues covering other regions, too.

Field Directors' Handbook, MF 02-29, loose-leaf notebook, about 400 pages, 1981, £12.00 from Oxfam, Publications Officer, 274 Banbury Road, Oxford OX2 7DZ, United Kingdom.

This manual, designed as a guide for Oxfam field staff in evaluating, supporting, and advising community development projects, is a survey of key approaches to assessing and approaching rural needs. The **Handbook** includes sections on agriculture, health, social development, humanitarian programs, and disaster relief. It is a good overview of approaches to participatory needs assessment, project planning, and technologies that facilitate high degrees of participation.

Appropriate Technology and Research Projects, MF 02-20, book, 66 pages, by M.M. Hoda (Director of the Appropriate Technology Development Association), $1.00 plus postage from Appropriate Technology Development Association, P.O. Box 311, Gandhi Bhawan, Lucknow 226001, U.P., India.

This is a notable little book because it suggests possible student projects on practical applications of appropriate technology, and lists a large number of such projects currently being undertaken.

"It requires some imagination to conceive and formulate the problems and introduce them in the institutions. Real life problems should be given to the students rather than theoretical problems, if maximum benefit is sought to be derived from them. Before that can be done, the concept of appropriate technology has to be fully understood to apply its principles for the solutions of the problems. There are many constraints and impediments which seriously restrict the scope of working in a rural surrounding, like absence of electricity, lack of communication, unavailability of materials, servicing and repairs. The designer has to keep all these aspects in mind to design equipment suitable for village use."

The author also discusses: the early beginnings of the village technology movement in India, and the important roles polayed by Tagore, Gandhi, and the Sarvodaya movement; the current situation in India; the emergence of the Appropriate Technology Development Association; and the philosophy that underlies appropriate technology.

World Neighbors in Action, quarterly newsletter, $5.00 per year from World Neighbors, 5116 North Portland, Oklahoma City, Oklahoma 73112, USA; also in Spanish, French.

This newsletter sometimes has how-to-do-it information. In particular, the following issues may be of interest ($1.25 each):

Vol. 4, No. 1E: how-to section on visual aids.
Vol. 6, No. 1E: information on soil-testing.
Vol. 6, No. 2E: how-to section on contour ditches for soil conservation (MF 02-67).
Vol. 7, No. 1E: information on growing, pruning, and grafting fruit trees.

Other printed materials from World Neighbors include:

a) **Visual Aids Tracing Manual** (MF 02-65, 20 pages, $2.00): Ideas and step-by-step instructions for making filmstrips by drawing on polyvinyl or acetate plastic. Pages of drawings included to aid an extension worker in making his or her own filmstrips. Available in English, Spanish, and an African edition in French.

b) **The Use of Radio in Family Planning** (MF 02-63, $2.50): 60 pages of text and 100 pages of appendices including family planning radio scripts from 18 countries.

c) **Introducing Family Planning in Your Neighborhood** (MF 02-42, 40 pages, $2.50): Designed to help family planning workers organize their approach in the community, and to enable other community development workers to include family planning motivation in their current extension work. Includes 14 "experience stories" illustrating some of the problems faced and how they have been overcome.

d) There are two catalogs of identical information, one in English and one in Spanish. Both list all the World Neighbors overseas development publications including filmstrips, flipcharts, newsletters and books on agriculture, food production, health care and nutrition, community development, and family planning. Ordering information is included. Catalogs are free. There are now more than 75 filmstrips listed. Prices of the filmstrips start at $10.00. About half of these are on family planning. Other subjects include: rat control, fish farming, mushroom growing, grain storage, taking soil samples, small plot irrigation, rabbit raising, and the proper care of young and sick children.

Small Technical Libraries, MF 31-768, booklet, 40 pages, by D.J. Campbell, 1973, reprinted 1980, UNESCO, out of print in 1984.

In this valuable little book you will find lots of good ideas that will prove very helpful in organizing and effectively operating a small technical library to support the work of a small research institute or a technical information clearinghouse. The author emphasizes frequent meetings with the research staff to better understand and provide for their information needs, and make them aware of newly arrived reference materials of possible interest. Recommended.

How to Build Up a Simple-Multidimensional Documentation System on Appropriate Technology, MF 02-73, paper, 8 pages, by Urs Heierli, 1982, Swiss Francs 3.50 from SKAT.

The addition of a card catalog to a small library allows information to be found more easily, by creating a simple index. This is because several or many cards can be filed on a document, allowing the user to find it when looking at cards for any major topic covered by that document. For example, a paper describing a wind-powered irrigation pump in Thailand might have cards filed under "windpower," "irrigation," "waterpumping," and "Thailand." If shelf placement is the only system of filing, a document can only be found by looking in one place.

This short paper describes a simple card catalog. For a more extensive discussion of how to organize and operate a library for the specific needs and interests of your organization, see **Small Technical Libraries**.

Microcomputers in Development: A Manager's Guide, book, 174 pages, by Marcus D. Ingle, Noel Berge, and Marcia Hamilton, 1983, $12.75 plus postage from Kumarian Press, 630 Oakwood Avenue, Suite 119, West Hartford, Connecticut 06110, USA.

"There is little question that within several years microcomputers will play a substantial role in the less developed countries. At the same time we must recognize the potential for disfunctional as well as beneficial effects of the introduction of microcomputers. Microcomputers can build or *block* the maintenance of a collaborative relationship within working groups. There are many indications that *how* the microcomputer is introduced will influence its success profoundly. For example, the capabilities of microcomputers can give the illusion that centralized control is appropriate for situations that require greater local autonomy for effective performance of tasks. Finally, whatever the potential net advantages of microcomputers in a specific situation, one must reckon with and be prepared to cope with the transitional costs and difficulties involved in the introduction of any new technology."

"This guide is intended for development personnel who are associated with the management of projects or institutions. It focuses on individual managers, management teams, or related support personnel who are likely to purchase a single-user microcomputer or who already have one and are interested in expanding and sustaining its use in a development organization."

Written specifically for use in development work in developing countries, this book provides a solid overview of what the introduction of a microcomputer can mean to a project or institution, examining both positive and negative aspects. A good deal of attention is paid to assessing whether a microcomputer would be of use in a given situation, and how to select the proper equipment and software. Examples are given of how microcomputers have been used in the development context, and several systems which were purchased for work in development are given as examples of complete packages.

Some of the equipment described is no longer available or has been replaced by better alternatives, and some of the experience reported has now become outdated. However, we imagine that these shortcomings will be corrected in a new edition of the book scheduled in 1986.

Appendices include information on how to provide a stable, safe electrical power supply for the computer, and lists of periodicals and names and addresses of computer manufacturers. Very useful.

The Women's Computer Literacy Handbook, book, 254 pages, by Deborah L. Brecher, 1985, $10.00 plus postage from The New American Library, Inc., P.O. Box 999, Bergenfield, New Jersey 07621, USA.

This clearly-written book uses non-technical language to introduce the terminology, hardware (or physical components), and software (or programs) of micro-

Block of
text to be
moved

FIGURE 3-1. To indicate that you marked a block of text, many computers highlight the block using reverse video. Once you've marked the block you can move it.

computers, providing the reader with a solid understanding of the basic concepts. It includes very good explanations of software for word processing and data base management. Although some of the material is quite sophisticated, the text never gets heavy and difficult to read.

For those planning to purchase a computer, there is some discussion of the important categories (IBM-compatible, CP/M, etc.), but no attempt is made to present an exhaustive list of products. Since this book is intended for a U.S. audience, the numerous special considerations for developing countries are not treated. Equally appropriate for women and men.

Dick's Encyclopedia of Practical Receipts and Processes, MF 02-26, book, 607 pages, originally published in 1870, reprinted 1974, out of print in 1985.

This book is from an era when American families were largely self-sufficient. It contains 6400 formulas and recipes for a wide range of household and small workshop processes. It is not a cookbook, but instead covers subjects such as making soap entirely from natural raw materials, waterproofing, making glues and cements for many different applications, and making paints, inks and lacquers. The majority of these recipes will probably not be relevant to appropriate technology practitioners, but there is such an enormous volume of information here that the useful material may still make the book a good purchase.

Some of the terms used are no longer common in English, and a large number of the basic chemicals and substances will be unfamiliar. However, it may be easier to obtain these basic substances in some developing countries that have chemist's shops remaining from colonial times.

We suggest this book for use only by people who understand English well.

The Formula Manual, MF 02-31, by Norman Stark, 1975, 1980; out of print in 1986.

This volume is filled with 558 formulas for household products, many of which are relevant to the Third World. All have been chosen to be made in the home, with simple tools. Thus some of these might be appropriate for production in small-scale industry efforts in the Third World. Equipment needed is very simple: double boilers (one pot sitting on top of a second pot filled with water), wooden spoons, mixing bowls, measuring cups, thermometers.

The author claims that some of the formulas have been "modified from large scale manufacturing quantities to small batches that are suitable for the do-it-yourselfer," and that "all are tested under actual use conditions."

There is a listing of the usual sources of supply for the chemicals used (mostly drugstores, hardware stores and grocery stores in the U.S., though sometimes chemical supply houses). All these chemicals are defined in an appendix.

Some examples: waterproofing mixture for concrete, waterproofing mixture for canvas (using soybean oil and turpentine), mixtures to protect wood from fire and termites, biodegradable laundry detergent, mixture for fireproofing cloth, chimney soot remover, safe cockroach poison, airtight seal for canning, bay leaves used in stored flour and cereals to repel insects, liquid glue, mixtures for the repair of holes in galvanized roofing sheets, automobile radiator leak sealer, and tire leak sealer.

Knots for Mountaineering, Camping, Climbing, Utility, Rescue, Etc., MF 02-43, booklet, 27 pages, by Phil D. Smith, 1975, out of print in 1985.

Fifty-six useful knots are illustrated and briefly described in an informative "how to do it" pamphlet. Includes many variations on the common loops, splices, and hitches which should allow those with some prior experience in utility rope work to apply the most appropriate knot to the job at hand.

Appropriate Technology Institutions: A Review, Occasional Papers 7, MF 02-69, book, 74 pages, by Richard Whitcombe and Marilyn Carr, 1982, £2.50 from ITDG.

"The broad purpose of this study is...to review, classify and analyse the experience gained in the establishment and operation of AT institutions, to identify their purposes and objectives, strengths and weaknesses, achievements, and problems." The discussion is based upon ITDG's familiarity with some 60 appropriate technology institutions. Unlike the other booklets in this series on institutions, this one does not primarily list and describe particular institutions. Instead, the authors have attempted to make some conclusions about A.T. institutions as a group.

"Examples of projects which have taken technologies beyond the pilot stage into widespread production and use are very thin on the ground."

"Non-governmental organizations that concentrate on a few technical subject areas in which their staff have specific expertise have often worked successfully on rural technology programmes, both in establishing small rural industries and in improving living standards in rural communities. Without institutional affiliation they have had to develop a methodology for utilising the research and development facilities and extension services of others, and some have become skillful at this, thus allowing concentration of their own resources on neglected aspects of the implementation process."

A Guide to Appropriate Technology Institutions, MF 02-72, book, 124 pages, by Angela Sinclair, 1984, £4.95 from ITDG.

Here are interesting 2-5 page summaries of the historical evolution and activities of each of some 40 A.T. institutions around the world. This will allow the reader to quickly get a basic understanding of the major players in this field. ITDG has also published in-depth reports on several of these organizations, issued as separate books, and a directory which simply lists addresses of a much larger number of groups (see review of **A.T. Institutions: A Directory**).

Appropriate Technology Institutions: A Directory, MF 02-68, booklet, 36 pages, ITDG, 1985, free from ITDG.

In the interest of creating a low-cost, up-to-date listing of active appropriate technology institutions, ITDG has published this directory of some 180 groups worldwide (addresses only). ITDG intends to regularly update this list.

Appropriate Technology Directory, MF 02-21, book, 361 pages, by Nicolas Jequier and Gerard Blanc of the Development Center of the Organization for Economic Cooperation and Development (OECD), 1979, $22.50 in English or French, from OECD Publications Office, 2 rue Andre Pascal, 75775 Paris Cedex 16, France; or OECD Information and Publications Center, Suite 1207, 1750 Pennsylvania Avenue N.W., Washington D.C. 20006, USA.

"The idea for such a 'Who's doing What' in the field of appropriate technology grew out of hundreds of requests for information addressed to the OECD Development Center...In trying to provide these answers, we soon discovered that the number of organizations involved in developing and diffusing 'appropriate,' 'intermediate,' or 'soft' technologies was considerably larger than anyone had suspected...What we have attempted to do here is to present in a standardized way...all the basic information about organizations involved in the promotion of appropriate technology, both in the industrialized and developing countries."

280 groups and organizations are listed alphabetically by country. Text on each organization includes information about origin, funding, main objectives, examples of technologies worked with, and future plans. Data on scale of activities, budget, and staffing are also given when available.

Directory of Institutions and Individuals Active in Environmentally-Sound and Appropriate Technologies, hardcover book, 152 pages, revised edition 1979, by the United Nations Environment Programme, $25.00 from Pergamon Press Ltd., Headington Hill Hall, Oxford OX3 0BW, England, or Pergamon Press Inc., Maxwell House, Fairview Park, Elmsford, New York 10523, USA.

This directory was compiled as a listing of potential sources for UNEP's International Referral System for environmental information. It contains names and addresses of some 2000 individuals and groups around the world. The project descriptions are brief. The information was compiled from a variety of secondary sources and much of it is unchecked.

While it is much less well-researched than the **Appropriate Technology Directory** published by OECD, this book represents a more extensive listing.

Rural Technology in the Commonwealth: A Directory of Organizations, MF 02-52, 127 pages, 1980, £1.50 from ITDG.

A listing of 118 institutions in 26 Commonwealth countries. Consists of clear short descriptions, giving address, major functions, programs, and specializations of each organization. This directory concentrates on organizations working in agriculture, forestry, and water resources for rural development. A useful index of equipment and processes is included. "We hope that this directory will fill an immediate need for two groups of people. The first group comprises those who are working on appropriate technologies, who we hope will be assisted by the directory to find out less laboriously who is doing what and where. . .the second group which we felt would make use of this directory are the 'travellers' of the development business. . .this directory will, we hope, enable you to make contact with people who share your interests. Equally useful contacts can be made by correspondence."

This Way Out: A Philippine Guide to Alternative Technologies and Those Who Practice Them, MF 02-61, booklet, 48 pages, by Dan Thomas, November 1980, $5.00 postpaid from Secretariat, Association of Foundations, Room 403, Fourth Floor, Yutiro Building, No. 270 Dasmarinas Street, Binondos, Manila, Philippines.

A carefully organized, cross-referenced listing of nearly 100 A.T. groups and their activities in the Philippines, along with selected organizations in Indonesia. Provides names of individuals to contact in each organization and complete addresses. "All those listed here have indicated a willingness to share their knowledge and expertise with others. They are quite varied — from university researchers to village workers, from government agencies to community-based development groups. . . Most favor the direct participation of the people concerned in the development and application of tools and techniques to meet the demands of their situation. Most would prefer using locally-available resources, whether these be human or physical."

Bibliography of Appropriate Technology Information for Developing Countries: Selected Abstracts from the NTIS Data File, MF 02-22, 452 pages, edited by Paul Bundick, domestic $7.50, foreign $15.00, from NTIS.

This bibliography contains 2000 annotated entries, chosen from the materials held by the National Technical Information Service (NTIS). The editor hopes that this information can be adapted for "direct benefits which foster self-reliance and a sense of dignity among the poor." This publication came out of a collaborative effort between NTIS, the U.S. Agency for International Development, and VITA.

Unfortunately, few of the reports included were originally written with any sensitivity to the concept of appropriate technology. These are mostly reports on research projects; there are virtually no practical publications with information that can be directly applied. Recommended only for those willing to work their way through a lot of extraneous information in search of a few valuable items.

To label this collection of government (mostly AID) research papers "appropriate technology" is to ignore the dramatic shift of development strategy represented by the appropriate technology movement. An awkward dilemma facing A.T. supporters is the question of how to extract the valuable technical information from past research efforts which neglected social factors, and which were based on now-discredited assumptions (e.g. about acceptable levels of investment per job created). Because this bibliography does not help the reader to identify the relevant portions of these research papers, we recommend that you handle it with great caution.

Guide to Convivial Tools, Library Journal Special Report #13, 112 pages, by Valentina Borremans, 1979, $5.95 (payment with order), from R.R. Bowker Company, 205 East 42nd Street, New York, New York 10017, USA.

This annotated bibliography was produced by Valentina Borremans, director of the Centro Intercultural de Documentación (CIDOC) in Cuernavaca, and a close associate of Ivan Illich. (It was Illich who coined the term "convivial tool" — see review of **Tools for Conviviality**). The bibliography "lists and describes 858 volumes and articles that, in their turn, list books on alternatives to industrial society or people who write on that subject."

"This new discipline deals with the cultural, social, and political conditions under which use-value oriented modern tools can and will be widely used, and with the renewal of ethics, politics, and aesthetics which is made possible by the democratically decided limitation of the industrial mode of production."

There are three kinds of people in the intended audience: 1) the librarian attempting to create a specialized research library away from the large general libraries; 2) the librarian in the industrialized countries who wishes to expand the reference section on this topic; and 3) the individual researcher without access to a library at all.

Non-Agricultural Choice of Technology: An Annotated Bibliography of Empirical Studies, MF 02-49, book, 84 pages, by Gareth Jenkins with an introduction by Frances Stewart, 1975, Institute of Commonwealth Studies, Oxford University, £4.00 from ITDG.

Provides access to a fascinating list of studies on technology choice, with implications for many of the debated economic aspects of appropriate technology theory. The annotations make very interesting and valuable reading even without going to the original articles.

Chambers Dictionary of Science and Technology, Volumes 1 (A-K) and 2 (L-Z), books, a total of 1300 pages, edited by T.C. Collocott and A.B. Dobson, 1974, $10.95 for the set of two volumes, from The Two Continents Publishing Group, 30 East 42nd Street, New York, New York 10017, USA.

This dictionary contains "50,000 entries from 100 fields of activity covering every aspect of scientific and technological knowledge, all carefully integrated into a single alphabetical list." It may not cover every aspect but it sure comes close. Definition and field of use are given for each word. This two-volume set would be of great use to anyone trying to read, understand and use books printed in English on science and technology topics. The fields covered include forestry, botany, chemistry, plumbing, printing, veterinary medicine, textiles, architecture, fuels, surveying, and many others.

Highly recommended.

Appropriate Technology and Local Self-Reliance

Appropriate Technology and Local Self-Reliance

Many of the publications reviewed in this book contain evidence that community involvement and increased self-reliance in problem-solving go hand in hand with appropriate technologies. Together they can make a large contribution in solving the problems of poverty, particularly in the Third World. But one should not forget that the community exists within the political and economic confines of the nation-state. Because of the great economic and coercive power of these states, national decisions about development strategy and allocation of resources will deeply affect all the choices open to communities.

This fact of life—that decisions and choices made "at the top" crucially affect what is possible "at the bottom"—is the focus of this section. **Appropriate Technology: Problems and Promises, Part I** *(see review in the BACKGROUND READING chapter) provides an insightful examination of what this means for the development of technologies. Many other publications reviewed here give concrete evidence of the importance of integrating high-level development policy with locally-based decision-making if a project is to be successful (see, for example,* **Participation and Education in Community Water Supply and Sanitation Programmes***).*

If a genuine effort is to be made to support community-based development of skills, problem-solving capabilities, and institutions, it will be necessary to reorient current structures that channel technical information and assistance, training and education, capital, government revenues, research and development work, and political power. If the point of initiative and problem-solving is to be at the community level, then the community must have access to these supportive systems that make it possible for things to happen. The writings in this chapter address these issues by discussing the most practical sizes of political and economic units and illustrating how the level at which initiatives are taken is a determining aspect of any development strategy.

Leopold Kohr has done some of the pioneering thinking on the differential nature and functioning of social organizations—communities, cities, nations—as they grow larger and larger. In **The Breakdown of Nations** *he argues that as social units increase in size, social problems increase faster, until these problems reach a magnitude and complexity at which they can no longer be understood and controlled by human beings. He urges a return to small political states, small cities, and small communities, in which problems can be broken down to a manageable size.* **Rural University** *describes an exciting program in which a university in rural Venezuela has had success in addressing local needs.*

Some of the environmental benefits of smaller states are suggested in **A Landscape For Humans**, *which examines the potential for "ecologically guided development" in a region of the southwestern United States.* **Local Responses to Global Problems: A Key to Meeting Basic Human Needs** *describes many local initiatives that are being undertaken around the world to solve what are often described as being primarily global problems.*

Appropriate Technology in Social Context *is an annotated bibliography that reviews the literature on the socio-cultural aspects of technological choice. The author concludes that to ensure that socially appropriate technology is chosen, it is necessary to involve "the community itself in the mechanics of technology choice, even if new procedures and institutions have to be created for this purpose."*

Three books reviewed here reveal the importance of rural self-reliance in increasing agricultural production and developing rural small-scale industry in China. The decentralized production of cement has been an important factor in enabling the Chinese communes to carry out at reasonable cost a wide range of public works projects such as irrigation canals and building construction. Small cement plants also employ 10 times as many people as modern large-scale plants. (See **Small Scale Cement Plants: A Study in Economics.***)* **Rural Small Scale Industry in the People's Republic of China** *reports on the decision-making process which has supported the remarkable growth of rural industries. These industries have brought with them the development of valuable technical and managerial skills among the rural population, and allow better support of agriculture and more productive use of rural personpower when it is not needed in agricultural activities.* **Learning from China: A Report on Agriculture and the Chinese People's Communes** *examines the participatory structures (such as research and development teams that include farmers as members) that have been keys to the advances of Chinese rural development.*

The possibilities and potential pitfalls that surround intermediate technology when applied in the context of Tanzanian ujamaa villages are explored in **Technology for Ujamaa Village Development in Tanzania.** *A look at the many and complicated factors likely to affect the success of appropriate technologies at the local level is provided in* **Soft Technologies, Hard Choices.**

The last three entries in this chapter are concerned with the identification of policy measures that can foster the development of appropriate technologies and support alternative, people-centered development strategies. Conventional development strategies are criticized and the assumptions underlying a different approach are described in **Alternative Development Strategies and Appropriate Technology: Science Policy for an Equitable World Order.** *Need-oriented, culturally-linked development that aims at liberation is the topic of* **Another Development: Approaches and Strategies.** *The ILO volume* **Technologies for Basic Needs** *notes that decentralization has particular advantages in carrying out basic needs strategies, and points to lack of contact with the real problems and experiences of farmers as a major reason for the disappointing contribution of R and D institutions in the Third World.*

There are a number of particularly relevant entries that have been placed in other chapters. Many of the entries in the NONFORMAL EDUCATION AND TRAINING chapter provide insights into effective roles and strategies for outside groups that wish to support the growth of community-based concientizacion and problem-solving. •

The Breakdown of Nations, MF 03-71, book, 250 pages, by Leopold Kohr, 1957, reprinted 1978, out of print in 1985.

It is in this volume that Kohr first develops, and in delightful fashion, his theories of scale. Despite his unconvincing attempt to explain away all social problems as due to bigness, he ably defends his thesis that scale is an important variable and that systems and institutions that are too large inevitably fail to function properly. The author's humorous tone at times distracts the reader from the seriousness of his points, but makes for a book that is hard to put down.

"If the great powers had at least produced superior leadership in their process of growing so that they could have matched the magnitude of the problems which they produced! But here, too, they failed because, as Gulliver observed, 'Reason did not extend itself with the Bulk of the Body.' "

"Neither the problems of war nor those relating to the purely internal criminality of societies disappear in a small-state world; they are merely reduced to bearable proportions. Instead of hopelessly trying to blow up man's limited talents to a magnitude that could cope with hugeness, hugeness is cut down to a size where it can be managed even with man's limited talents."

Rural University: Learning about Education and Development, MF 03-80, book, 71 pages, by Farzam Arbab, 1984, $8.00 from IDRC.

"A population must contain proper institutions that can lead the search, without losing touch with the realities of the region or the state of scientific and technological progress worldwide. In most rural populations, such institutions do not exist; the rural university, as a learning institution of the region, was a logical candidate to assume the responsibility and face the challenge."

"Early — with the first project on domestic water — the FUNDAEC group realized that access to information worldwide was indispensable if the rural university was to become an efficient agent of technological change. Many groups reinvent what is already known by others, and much energy is lost in working with solutions that have already proven worthless elsewhere. A most important element of the 3-year plan, then, was to develop a documentation centre and incorporate it fully into technological change."

A Landscape for Humans, MF 03-72, book, 149 pages, by Peter van Dresser, 1972, $12.00 postpaid from The Lightning Tree, P.O. Box 1837, Santa Fe, New Mexico 87501, USA.

Here is "a case study of the potentials for ecologically guided development in an uplands region." Chosen was an area in the northern part of the state of New Mexico, USA, long a secluded zone of Spanish culture. "It is no longer possible to 'solve the problems' of such a regional community by expediting wholesale out-migration and assimilation of its population into the urban, metropolitan, or industrial areas of the nation. . . Neither is it possible to rehabilitate provincial regions such as the uplands by importing big industry and its works. The dominant characteristic of modern primary and extractive industry (including 'agribusiness'), geared to the national market, is labor-conservative, machine-intensive, and moving towards maximum automation. Very large investments are required per job created (e.g., $175,000 for a modern pulp mill). Regions dominated by such industries tend to depopulate except for company towns of varying degrees of cultural and social impoverishment."

Van Dresser suggests a variety of environmentally-sound, community-supportive economic activities that could be carried on or expanded within the region, to fill the needs for goods, services, and employment. He notes, for example, that a decentralized timber industry would be well suited to the existing distribution of timber resources and population. It might be possible to "vertically-integrate" such a timber industry, so that more employment and value-added would remain in the region, when processed timber products are sold outside the region.

". . .The bulk of the livelihood needs of such a region must be met within the region itself by skilled, scientific, intensive, and conservative use of the lands, waters, and renewable biotic and environmental resources of the region. The long-term strategy for economic development should be gradual de-involvement from the mass logistic machinery of the continental economy, with its enormous and ever-increasing consumption of energy and irreplaceable natural resources."

The author's recommendation of gradual de-involvement from the national economy is contrary to the thinking of most economic development institutions. The conventional wisdom of the latter is that increased trade is primarily beneficial.

Van Dresser makes a persuasive case that the recent effects of such economic ties have been, on balance, quite negative.

"Such an evolution calls for a new technological, agricultural, and industrial orientation, stressing small-scaled and diversified primary production, adapted to the land and natural resource patterns of the region, to the ecologic balance and health of the total biotic community, and to the needs of a decentralized and dispersed population of effective and vital small communities. This type of productive economy will be manpower- , skill- , and science-intensive, rather than capital- , energy- , and machine-intensive."

Van Dresser argues that an important part of the foundation for building such an economy is the high level of non-commercial "primary production" already taking place in the region. This is particularly strong in the growing and processing of foodstuffs and in the construction of homes and farm buildings. The author's observations about road building, education, and other aspects of a practical plan for ecologically-guided development would be relevant in many rich and poor countries. This short book offers a remarkably broad and stimulating introduction to these issues that affect appropriate technology efforts. Highly recommended.

Local Responses to Global Problems: A Key to Meeting Basic Human Needs, Worldwatch Paper 17, MF 03-74, booklet, 64 pages, by Bruce Stokes, 1978, $2.00 from Worldwatch Institute, 1776 Massachusetts Avenue N.W., Washington D.C. 20036, USA.

Self-help and self-reliance are the important keys to better living conditions and broader opportunity for people the world over. This paper shows how individuals and communities are meeting their basic needs with little or no help from outside institutions.

In housing, carpentry, plumbing, and bricklaying, skills shared at the neighborhood level provide the technical basis for self-help homebuilding in urban slums around the world. Successful projects have often involved the government providing land, credit, and basic services to poor families who can then build their own dwellings.

For food production: "Whether judged by yield per acre or by the cost of production, small farms compare favorably with large farms on all continents. Most of the economies of scale associated with size can be achieved in units small enough to be farmed by a family. . . A 1970 survey for the United States Agency for International Development (USAID) showed that small farms in India, Japan, Taiwan, the Philippines, Mexico, Brazil, Colombia, and Guatemala had higher productivity per acre than large farms."

Energy conservation and examples of self-reliance in small-scale energy production and consumption are also discussed.

The author concludes that while foreign aid and other forms of international cooperation can be constructive, problems of basic needs must be addressed at the local level. "In 1975, public and private official development assistance. . .totaled $18.4 billion, not even enough to meet yearly basic housing needs according to the (World Bank's) estimate. The political will does not exist to solve problems through large transfer of resources. Any development strategy based on the assumption that the rich will more than double their foreign aid is doomed to failure. This does not mean that foreign aid should be abandoned. But if the resources to fully meet basic needs are not forthcoming from national and international sources, then they must come from communities and individuals. While ready capital is scarce at this level, there is a reserve of labor and ingenuity that money cannot buy."

Appropriate Technology in Social Context: An Annotated Bibliography, MF 03-70, 33 pages, by David French, 1977, $2.95 from VITA.

Lists 180 books, articles and papers, with short paragraph annotations. Many case studies are identified, and a number of important issues are raised. This is not a review of the technical literature.

"Harmony between technology and social context is important. Abundant evidence shows that implanting a socially 'inappropriate' technology in a village has the same result as implanting a foreign object in a person: either the technology is rejected or the village may 'die' as a social organism. . .novelists and anthropologists have long recorded the disruption of traditional societies by new technologies."

"To take full account of context implies involving the community itself in the mechanics of technological choice, even if new procedures and institutions have to be created for the purpose."

The materials in the bibliography are "abstracted from four separate literatures, those of development agencies, the applied social sciences, village-oriented programs, and sources of technical information. . .There is a need to break down the walls (between these groups) if appropriate technology is to be kept in social context. . .Perhaps the first job here should be design of an appropriate institutional technology for 'technology' transfer."

The author uses a relatively full definition of appropriate technology, noting the importance of people's participation, low costs, and use of local resources; thus, his reviews are more interesting and valuable than those in many other bibliographies.

Recommended.

Small Scale Cement Plants: A Study in Economics, MF 03-76, booklet, 28 pages, by Jon Sigurdson, 1977, £2.50 from ITDG.

"Small scale cement plants have recently been attracting more and more attention from international agencies and industrial economists concerned with rural development. In China there are more than 2800 active small scale plants and more than 200 in Europe (Spain, Yugoslavia, France, Germany and Italy). This booklet examines the criteria which would justify the establishment of mini cement plants in developing countries and specifically compares the situation in India with that

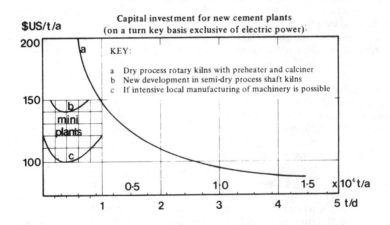

in China, where more than 57% of cement is produced in small plants. . .A short bibliography is provided as well as designs of vertical shaft kilns taken from a Chinese book on small scale cement plants."

In China, "the initial smallness of a plant enables the capacity of the plant to grow with the local demand. This may make overall costs lower than if a large capacity plant had been set up from the very beginning."

"When deciding location, size and technology for the cement plants it appears that in China transportation costs are much more important than investments costs per ton of finished product." (Other studies of the Chinese rural development effort indicate that the savings to a public works program can more than offset the investment in a small kiln within a year or two.) Sigurdson notes that the freight policy in India makes cement the same price at all rail depots. (Transport costs are "pooled" and assigned equally to all cement sold in the country.) This eliminates the advantage that small kilns would have in local marketing areas, as the substantial costs of transport are not reflected in the price of cement produced by distant large kilns.

"The viability of small cement plants is at least partly a reflection of demand created through substantial public works programs and other construction activities in rural areas." (Conversely, it must be noted, in many countries the high cost of cement prevents the undertaking of rural public works programs.)

The author raises the question of "appropriateness of product." The Chinese small vertical shaft kilns apparently do not produce cement of Portland Cement quality (in strength and uniformity). However, for most rural area uses, higher quality is not needed.

The small rural cement plants employ at least 250,000 people directly. "This number is at least 10 times higher than employment would be in a small number of modern large scale cement plants producing the same quantity of cement."

A short but important case study that illustrates many of the issues surrounding appropriate technology.

Rural Small-Scale Industry in the People's Republic of China, MF 03-75, book, 310 pages, by Dwight Perkins et. al., September 1977, $7.95 from University of California Press, 2120 Berkeley Way, Berkeley, California 94720, USA.

Much can be learned from the remarkable success of the Chinese efforts to develop grassroots skills and innovative capability, and improve the standard of living through promotion of rural small-scale industry. This report of a distinguished group of American visitors in 1975 offers many valuable insights into the successes and problems of these efforts.

The authors discuss the administrative systems, worker incentives, economies associated with small-scale industries, the relationship between these industries and agriculture, and their impact on Chinese society. Special treatment is given to agricultural machinery, chemical fertilizer technology, and small-scale cement plants.

"First and foremost, China is developing a rural small-scale industry because this strategy is believed to be doing a better job of supporting agriculture than did the large-scale strategies of the past."

"The rationale for the use of small-scale factories in rural areas begins with a recognition of the inadequacies of China's rural transport and marketing systems. . . Reinforcing the effects of high transport costs is the nature of China's rural commercial system. Even when communes are prepared to pay the going price for some desired item, it won't necessarily be available. . . it may get it faster if it builds one on its own."

"The planning system seems to be in part a nested or hierarchical system of rationing of technically advanced products in such a way that the demand for scarce, high-technology products in the production of products for rural life is minimized." To the extent that rural production units can meet their own equipment and other capital needs, the Chinese can avoid "wasting Shanghai talent producing small threshers for the whole country."

"No research institute in Peking will be able to design machines suitable for all environments and conditions. Local production facilities coupled with design inputs from two directions have largely alleviated this problem. Assistance from above is readily available — e.g., for 12 h.p. diesel engines — or for electric motors and pumps. From below comes a flow of comments and suggestions as to how trial machines perform and what tasks need to be mechanized. The local factories, especially the commune level machine shops, seem ideally suited to wed these two inputs into locally adapted machines.

"Instead of leaving innovations to technicians alone, 'three-in-one' groups consisting of administrators, technicians, and senior workers are organized to attack technical problems and produce innovations in factory technology."

"A reasonably strong argument can be made that the major contribution of the agricultural machinery industry. . .has been through an indirect process of 'scientification' of the rural masses. A hand tractor imported from Japan would have the same physical productivity as one made in China, but it would certainly not have the same impact as one made in a brigade or commune machine shop where every peasant knows someone who helped build it."

The Chinese have deliberately followed a strategy of starting rural industries small and gradually making them bigger and more modern. The larger, more modern stage could not be reached "without the industrial experience, the chance to mobilize the masses in technical renovation, and the capital funds from profits in the meantime, that are the products of its first period."

The demand for electricity that has accompanied the spread of rural small-scale industries has led to the construction of a very large number of small hydroelectric plants, some 60,000 in south China alone.

"It is not the techniques themselves that the Chinese are adding to the world's storehouse of knowledge, but the fact that these techniques can be adapted to rural conditions on a widespread scale."

Highly recommended.

Towards Village Industry: A Strategy for Development, MF 03-81, book, 100 pages, by Berg, Nimpuno, and Van Zwanenberg, 1976 (revised edition 1979), £3.25 from ITDG.

This book supplies the contemporary appropriate technology enthusiast with a whole new perspective — one which can be a good deal more valuable than other contemporary approaches. By analysis of what existed in the past (pre-colonial Tanzania is the example), the whole picture of a well-integrated naturally flowing economic order emerges — an order which is precisely what so many developing nations have intended to retain, but have lost due to colonization or media and physical exposure to Western societies. The authors state that one must have a genuine reverence for the technological and cultural history of the population — and give it at least as much emphasis as is placed on current economic and technical analyses. Completely local production in a labor-intensive process is stressed.

This book cites Tanzania's pre-colonial industrial/agrarian specialized technologies and local trading patterns, to develop a historical basis for appropriate technology. Western appropriate technology development specialists often seem to introduce, the authors claim, a technically and even economically suitable technology, but a technology out of context with the culture and history of the people — which is often a reason for its failure to spread. The implication is that economic interdependence existed among the Tanzanian people before the colonial period, and that by reinvestigating the period important considerations for A.T. will be found.

Examining the products of East African village craftspeople today, the authors note the effect of the introduction of city-trained craftspeople into the villages. These people are commonly producing copies of devices they were trained to make in Western-oriented technical schools. Where mass-produced items are copied by craftspeople, the product is usually inferior in quality to the original. Superior products can be made through the craft processes, but only when following the methods that correspond to these processes and materials. The authors assert that the craftsperson should once again become a creator or innovator of technology responding to the needs of the rural people — which implies a major overhaul of the selection and training process. Ways in which this overhaul could be accomplished are suggested. Strong emphasis is placed on the development of useful village workshops. Equipment, workshop requirements, and types of training are identified.

This perspective could be valuable to many people working in the field today.

Technology for Ujamaa Village Development in Tanzania, MF 03-79, book, 64 pages, by Donald Vail, $6.00 from FACS Publications, 119 College Place, Syracuse, New York 13210, USA.

A thoughtful discussion of the social/political/economic circumstances that affect intermediate technology in one country of Africa attempting to develop a decentralized, self-reliant village socialism.

There is an interesting look at the potential for creative exchange between a testing unit and both 1) international sources of ideas and information, and 2) local people using adapted tools in real farming activities. How can a testing unit learn from both the enormous variety of small tools already in existence worldwide and from the farmers themselves? (Learning from the farmers ensures their participation and greatly increases the chances that the equipment developed will be relevant.)

The relationship between intermediate technology and the strengthening — or undermining — of Ujamaa village development is explored. The author argues that without policy backing for Ujamaa as the dynamic mechanism for A.T. development, new small-scale technology seems likely to strengthen private enterprise at the expense of the cooperative Ujamaa villages. This in turn would have the effect of a concentration of land holdings and stratification into a relatively small group of haves and a much larger group of have-nots.

Soft Technologies, Hard Choices, Worldwatch Paper 21, MF 03-77, booklet, 41 pages, by Colin Norman, 1978, $2.00 from Worldwatch Institute, 1776 Massachusetts Avenue N.W., Washington D.C. 20036, USA.

A good overview of the arguments in favor of the development of appropriate technology. Full of sensible observations such as: "Skewed income distribution leads to the development and adoption of technologies that meet the demands of the privileged. . .Without social and political changes that redistribute income, overhaul inequitable land ownership patterns, reform credit systems, and provide support for small farmers and manufacturers, appropriate technologies will be difficult to introduce. Powerful vested interests support large-scale manufacturing, mechanized farming and other symbols of modernity. . .By stimulating local innovation and reinforcing other development efforts, simple technologies can lead to self-sustaining development. . .No technology — however appropriate — will solve social problems by itself. . .Nevertheless, the choice of inappropriate technologies can only exacerbate social, economic, and environmental problems. . .The entire innovation process, from basic research to the production of a new technology, is conditioned by such factors as the profit motive, prestige, national defense needs, and social and economic policies. Those forces must be understood in any discussion of appropriate technology. . .The unfettered workings of the market system cannot be relied upon to promote the development and adoption of appropriate technologies."

Learning from China: A Report on Agriculture and the Chinese People's Communes, MF 03-73, book, 112 pages, by a U.N. Food and Agriculture Study Mission, 1977, available from FAO, Director, Publications Division, Via delle Terme di Caracalla, 00100 Rome, Italy.

"This is a nation that, within the short span of 27 years, has succeeded in banishing starvation. It is now providing food, clothing, shelter and reasonable security for over 800 million people. It has mobilized the world's largest agricultural labour force, reversed the flood of people into cities and kept people on the land." A multi-disciplinary team of FAO officers compiled this report, which is focused on the participatory structures that have enabled China's dramatic achievements in meeting basic human needs. Present-day organization of production along commune, brigade, and production team lines is presented as part of the history of traditional and revolutionary Chinese collectivism.

Much of the report is devoted to the educational, research, and mechanization strategies employed by the collectives to boost agricultural output. Mobilization of the productive workforce is key to this strategy: "Most other developing countries. . .are impaled on the horns of a cruel dilemma: there is massive unemployment precisely at a time when so much needs to be done. China has largely solved this dilemma through a development approach that, among other things, designed the commune. In the process, it unleashed a tremendous force for development."

An important conclusion emerging from this report is that technological changes cannot substantially change the position of the small farmer unless they are part of a genuine structural or organizational reform in the countryside. "The Chinese experience suggests that developing countries should consider a temporary and selective moratorium on current plans for comprehensive diffusion or 'transfer' of technology, among these most disadvantaged farmers. These farmers need instead more intensive policies of tenurial improvement and selective, if not widescale, measures of land reform; progressive upgrading of traditional tools and equipment; more intensive use of local resources such as organic manure, and compost and small bio-gas plants; and the mobilization of traditional forms of peasant cooperation and mutual aid for both production and rural capital formation."

Alternative Development Strategies and Appropriate Technology: Science Policy for an Equitable World Order, MF 03-68, book, 255 pages, by Romesh K. Diwan and Dennis Livingston, 1979, $25.00 from Pergamon Press, Maxwell House, Fairview Park, Elmsford, New York 10523, USA.

Here is a summary of the criticisms of the conventional industrialization-led, GNP-measured development strategies, and a description of the elements of emerging alternative development strategies. Despite the subtitle, the authors do not really explore science policy except in the broadest sense, arguing for the development of indigenous capabilities to generate environmentally-sound, culture-linked appropriate technologies for the poor. Some science policy issues and other political and economic issues are identified, but specific policies are not proposed. Nicolas Jequier's **Appropriate Technology: Problems and Promises** (see review) gives the policy issues associated with appropriate technology a deeper look.

The authors draw from a broad relevant literature, touching on so many problems and issues that many sections seem too brief. (An extensive bibliography is included.) Useful distinctions are made between high-income developing countries, high-technology developing countries, and the rest of the developing countries. Insights into the behavior of the international organizations will be of particular interest to many readers.

Because the authors have taken a broad view of the concepts of "development" and "appropriate technology," their conclusions are not crippled by the timid definitions that tend to emerge in international conferences and the publications of U.N. agencies, where polite fictions must be observed. "In the literature on international science and policy, there is a tendency to confuse the 'interests' of the governments with the 'appropriateness' of technology. . .However, the concept of 'appropriateness' as discussed in A.T. literature is quite different, and may even be poles apart."

"The conventional development strategy. . . leaves the bulk of Third World peoples dependent on institutions and forces, within their countries and abroad, that are unreachable and unaccountable." The authors recommend "delinking of developing countries from debilitating global networks dominated by the affluent." They observe that much of the international debate on codes for technology transfer and the New International Economic Order are simply part of the failing conventional development strategy; unless domestic structural change takes place the elite will reap all of the benefits.

A basic assumption of the authors, which lies at the heart of the emerging human-centered concepts of development and appropriate technology, is that "people, even those who are poor, illiterate, and unemployed, are intelligent. They are capable of defining their own needs and given opportunities, they can and will solve their own problems."

This is an inherently optimistic book. Diwan and Livingston identify areas for cooperation where many might see inevitable, tragic, sources of conflict. "It is. . . in the self-interests of the governments and elites of both developed and developing countries to work cooperatively towards the formulation of an alternative international order which reduces and eventually eliminates inequalities, armaments, biases in the price system, and technological inappropriateness, both nationally and internationally."

Another Development: Approaches and Strategies, MF 03-69, book, 265 pages, edited by Marc Nerfin, 1977, $19.00 surface mail or $21.00 airmail, from the Dag Hammarskjold Foundation, Ovre Slottsgaten 2, S-752 20 Uppsala, Sweden.

Here can be found some interesting thinking on new development goals and strategies for the rest of this century, in a collection of 10 articles by well-known writers.

"Another Development would be need-oriented (geared to meeting human needs, both material and non-material). . . endogenous (stemming from the heart of each society, its values). . . self-reliant. . . ecologically sound. . . based on structural transformations (in social relations, in economic activities, and in the power structure, so as to realize the conditions of self-management and participation in decision-making by all those affected by it, from the rural or urban community to the world as a whole). . . These five points are organically linked. . . For development is seen as a whole, as an integral cultural process. . . Another Development means liberation."

Part One begins with the concept of Another Development, and examines the positions of peasants and women, alienation in industrial societies, and emerging simpler alternative life styles in those societies. In Part Two, national case studies and proposed strategies include: a look at growth and poverty in Brazil, the history of achievements and backsliding following the Mexican Revolution, an alternative framework for rural development in India, a strategy for Another Development in Chile (requiring major political change and based on the lessons of the early '70s), and a discussion of structural transformation in Tunisia.

"The New International Economic Order. . . makes full sense only if it supports another development. . . If it lacks a development content, it is bound to result simply in strengthening the regional or national subcenters of power and exploitation."

"Resources to meet human needs are available. The question is that of their distribution and utilization. . . The organization of those who are the principal victims of the current state of affairs is the key to any improvement. Whether governments are enlightened or not, there is no substitute for the people's own, truly democratic organization if there is to be a need-oriented, endogenous, self-reliant, ecologically-minded development."

Technologies for Basic Needs, MF 03-78, book, 158 pages, by Hans Singer, ILO, 1977, Swiss Francs 20.00 from International Labor Office, CH-1211 Geneva 22, Switzerland.

This book was inspired by discussions held at the World Employment Conference in Geneva in 1976. It is largely concerned with top-down national planning for "appropriate technology," covering national policy, programs and institutions that might be able to contribute. The suggestions made are mostly aimed at the large-scale and small-scale industrial sector. While mention is made of the informal and rural small farm sectors, the assumption seems to be that technology will be created for the people in these sectors without their real participation. The author sees no potential conflict of interest between government-determined priorities and those that might most benefit the largest number of poor people. He is relatively un-critical of the possible role of multinational corporations in developing A.T., impressed by the strong research and development capabilities of these institutions. He claims that beneficial effects such as reduction in transfer payments for technology and the spread of the results of MNC-financed technology research among indigenous producers would be forthcoming — without seeing that such actions are simply not in the interests of the multinational corporations.

There are, however, a few points made that would have relevance in rural grassroots development strategies. Some of them are:

"The experience of countries which have tried to implement a basic needs strategy (e.g., China, Cuba, Tanzania) suggests that the improvement of simple village technologies is the only feasible approach to the gradual modernization of the rural economy."

There is "growing evidence. . .that formal technical training plays a smaller part than was previously assumed and that experience and on-the-job training are the main vehicles for implanting new skills."

"A major reason for the disappointing contribution of R and D institutions to the creation of appropriate new technology is the lack of contact" with real problems and actual experience. The R and D institution itself is a modern import from the rich countries, "and disregards past experience. . .(when) the bulk of technological innovation arose directly from within the production plant" or workshop in response to needs and opportunities perceived there.

"Decentralization has obvious advantages, to help to eliminate the communications gap. . .This is particularly so in the context of a basic needs strategy, when local needs and the nature of local poverty problems may differ greatly in different regions of a country, when the use of appropriate technology involves the participation of innumerable small production units, and in the context of rural development generally (when the obvious need for community involvement and grassroots identification of problems has led to many variations of decentralized administration)."

The Workshop

The Workshop

Tools and techniques for small workshops are the subjects of this chapter. The use of tools, and the ability to make them using local resources and equipment, are certainly very important in any appropriate technology effort. In some areas where small blacksmith shops, foundries, woodworking or machine tool workshops exist, many of the tools and processes covered in these books may have been in use for many years. In other areas, most of these crafts and skills are unknown. Therefore, the tools found in this section are of many different types, from simple hand tools to wood-turning lathes to metalworking equipment. Some may be made at the village level, others may require metalworking shop facilities.

The first several books offer illustrated inventories of a great variety of tools. Other books describe the proper uses of a wide range of hand tools and machine tools for both wood and metal work. The crafts and skills covered include woodworking, blacksmithing, general metalworking, forging and casting, sharpening, sheet metal working, designing bearings and springs, working with metal tubing and copper piping, and others. There are also plans for workshop equipment: lightweight power tools, sheet metal bending tools, and more.

These reference books, containing thousands of ideas, should be valuable to an appropriate technology group in its own workshop. They are also a source of learning materials for improving skills, increasing versatility, and expanding available tools and equipment among local craftspeople. It should be remembered that many workshop crafts, such as blacksmithing, cannot be easily learned from a book; these reference materials can only supplement skilled instructors. However, even the most experienced blacksmith will find many unusual and valuable ideas in a reference such as **Practical Blacksmithing**.

Tools and How to Use Them: An Illustrated Encyclopedia, MF 04-122, book, 352 pages, by Albert Jackson and David Day, 1978, $9.95 from Alfred A. Knopf, Inc., 201 East 50th Street, New York, New York 10022, USA.

This beautifully illustrated book is the best one available for descriptions of the wide range of useful hand woodworking tools. It also covers a few gardening tools,

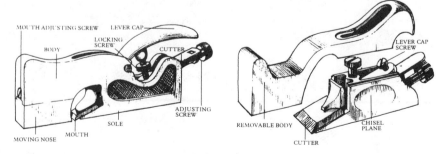

power tools, plumbing tools, and includes more than 1500 excellent drawings. For each tool the authors list other commonly used names, size, the material it is made from, and its purpose; this is followed by a short but valuable description of how it is used. Most of these tools originated in Europe or North America, but many are in common use all over the world. A good source of ideas for local adaptation.

Highly recommended.

Tools and their Uses, MF 04-123, book, 186 pages, by the U.S. Navy Bureau of Naval Personnel, 1973, $2.75 from Dover Publications, Inc., 31 East 2nd Street, Mineola, New York 11501, USA.

This book covers a very wide selection of common hand and power tools. The purpose is to "identify tools and fastening devices by their correct names; cite the specific purposes and uses of each tool; describe the correct operation, care and maintenance required to keep the tools in proper operating condition; and finally, perform accurate measurements." This book will not substitute for books covering in detail the techniques and equipment used in woodworking and soldering, for example. It is just a general introduction, but one that would be useful to any workshop education program using common tools. Safety information is included throughout.

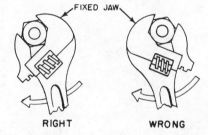

*Proper procedure for
pulling adjustable wrenches*

Basic Machines and How They Work, MF 04-81, book, 161 pages, prepared by the U.S. Navy Bureau of Naval Personnel, 1971, $4.50 from Dover Publications, 31 East 2nd Street, Mineola, New York 11501, USA.

Written as a reference manual for sailors in the U.S. Navy, this book explains basic mechanical principles and their applications in simple and complex machines. Illustrated examples are used to show how these principles work in common devices. For example, oars, wheelbarrows, handpump handles, and the block and tackle are forms of the lever; the brace and bit, wrench, and winch are forms of the wheel and axle. Many of the examples include explanations of how mechanical advantage is obtained, and how to calculate that advantage using simple arithmetic. Later

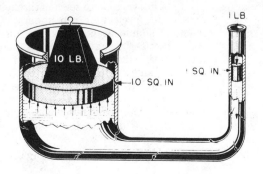

*Mechanical advantage
in a hydraulic system*

chapters explain the uses and combinations of basic machine elements (like bearings, linkages, cams) in machines such as the typewriter and automobile engine.

Useful as a reference and as a practical way to study the physics of mechanical devices. Slang and sailing terminology may sometimes be difficult for the non-native speaker of English.

Equipment for Rural Workshops, MF 04-92, book, 94 pages, by John Boyd, 1978, ITDG, out of print in 1985.

This book "is intended to help people choose appropriate tools and equipment. It is not an instructional textbook on workshop technology."

Shows workshop building layout and basic sets of tools (primarily hand tools) for 1-6 person workshops, without and with power supply, for woodworking or metalworking. The simplest level of powered equipment requires an electric drill with attachments to convert it into a circular saw, grinding wheel, jig saw, and power hacksaw. Machine tools are shown for the larger, powered, 4-6 person workshops.

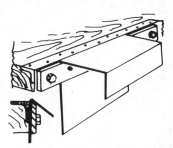

Simple bench fitting
for folding sheet metal

The author notes that "the hand tools in the lists of basic equipment can be used to do the same work as the much more costly power tools... Power tools only speed up the work and are not economic unless there is enough work to keep them in use for a substantial part of each day."

Includes mid-1977 prices of tools. Lists suppliers in Asia/Africa/Latin America. Many illustrations and photos.

Shop Tactics, MF 04-118, book, 114 pages, by B. Abler, 1973, $3.95 from WEA or Running Press, 125 South 22nd Street, Philadelphia, Pennsylvania 19103, USA.

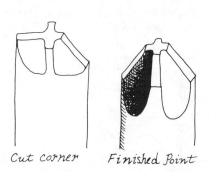

Cut corner   Finished Point

"**Shop Tactics** is a guide to tools, materials, and procedures that are within the reach of a small basement shop. The beginner and amateur (and low-budget) tinkerer, artist or scientist will find here plenty of information to see him through almost any project he can undertake, whether simple or complex. Because **Shop Tactics** begins with simple tools and materials (hammer, nails, wood, file, drill, saw, and wrench) the beginner can use it as an introduction to manual techniques. He will find step-by-step instruction leading him through the motions for using these and other basic tools and materials."

"After familiarizing you with basics, this book describes the use of abrasives, adhesives (solder, glues), plastics (plexiglas, epoxy), and finally molds and casting. The last chapter concerns efficiency and effectiveness in the use of manual techniques. An appendix of basic devices, a bibliography and an index are included.

"The description for each tool and material is presented with concrete examples (the section on sheet metal describes how to make a ring) so that when you work through the example to learn the procedures you will have a completed piece of work. But this is not a how-to book presenting instructions for the completion of a few projects; instead it gives you skill and insight into tools and materials so that you can plan and complete your own projects. The home tinkerer who wants to build a mold, or the scientist who wants to build a specialized gas burner will all find here not specific instructions, but plenty of information to guide the project to completion."

This book is "directed at your imagination in the hope that, when you know what is already known, you will be able to think of new things (that you would never have been able to think of otherwise) by recombining processes and extending materials to satisfy each new demand you make of them."

Illustrations (literally hundreds of them) are included to accompany each step in the text, and ensure that the text will be understood by any reader. Each presentation is very clear and easily understandable. In particular, there is a valuable discussion of a variety of casting methods. The "Devices" section gives illustrations and simple explanations of 12 simple devices (solar still, bicycle sprocket drive, set screw).

This is an excellent book, both because of the clarity of presentation of the material, and the regular use of illustrations. Perhaps of greatest value is that the author seeks to develop basic skills and an experimental approach that is fundamental to future development of appropriate technology devices.

The Use of Hand Woodworking Tools, MF 04-125, book, 273 pages, by Leo McDonnel and Alson Kaumeheiwa, 1978, $11.20 ($8.40 to schools), from Delmar Publishers, 2 Computer Drive West, Box 15-015, Albany, New York 12212, USA.

This introductory book presents only the basic hand tools used in carpentry, and most of the book is devoted to explaining how to properly use them. No previous knowledge is assumed. Designed for use in teaching, the book contains questions at the end of each section.

Chamfering an edge with the work held in a clamp

The author begins with measuring tools (from the T-square to the builder's transit level — the only rather complicated tool presented), and continues with saws, planes, edge cutting tools, and boring tools. Sharpening is discussed in detail for each of the cutting tools. Also covered are nails, screws, and dowels. Well-illustrated.

Handtool Handbook for Woodworking, MF 04-97, book, 184 pages, by R.J. DeCristoforo, 1977, out of print in 1985.

This book shows how to use woodworking tools commonly found around the world. These include measuring devices, saws, hammers, drills, screwdrivers, chisels and planes. The author also discusses safety, sharpening, shop math and how to choose good tools.

"You won't find this (a crown) on all saws, but many experts look for it as an indication of careful designing and superior quality. A crowned saw is one where the silhouette of the toothed edge shows a gentle arc rather than a straight line from the heel to the toe. The reason for the shape is to obtain maximum cutting effect with minimum drag. The arc brings fewer teeth into contact with the wood fibers. While you don't have as many teeth in full contact, those that are cut deeper, faster, and easier."

This book is full of tricks and tips for woodworkers, and the 400 illustrations make it easy to understand. Safety measures are very well covered.

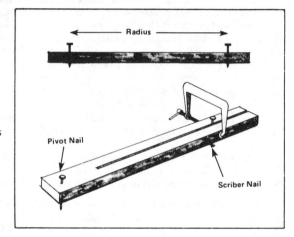

Trammels you can make: Fixed trammels can be made by driving two nails through a strip of wood. A variable type shown at bottom has a fixed pivot nail and an adjustable scriber nail held by a small C-clamp in a saw-cut groove.

Woodwork Joints, book, 176 pages, by Charles Hayward, 1974, $6.95 from WEA.

"The craft of woodwork consists largely of joining pieces of wood together. In this book we have taken the basic joints, given their chief variations, and shown how to cut them. It is not suggested that the methods of cutting described are the only ones possible...but it can be taken that the way described is useful and has been proven by experience to be reliable."

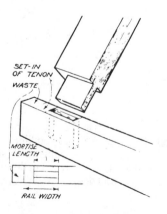

This book is suitable for anyone experienced in working with wood who wants to learn different methods of making joints.

The Making of Tools, MF 04-103, book, 93 pages, by Alexander Weygers, 1973, $8.25 from WEA.

"This book teaches the artist and craftsman how to make his own handtools: how to design, sharpen, and temper them, using only basic shop equipment and scrap steel." There are many illustrative drawings on each page that show the "step-by-step progression from the raw material to the finished product — the handmade tool."

Raw material is usually high-carbon steel — from steel scrapyards and auto junkyards (U.S.). Hardwood is used for the handles.

Contents include: tempering steel; sharpening tools; making a screwdriver, cold chisel and other simple tools; stonecarving tools; cutting tools; eyebolts and hooks, tool handles, hammers, gouges, seating cutter and hinge joints, tinsnips, wire and nail cutters, large shears, and pliers; applying color patina to steel surfaces. There is also a glossary of tool-making terms (useful to non-native English speakers).

The author was born in Java, educated in Holland as an engineer, and has worked in Java and the U.S. before concentrating on art. This book, based on his teaching experience, is designed for the artist and craftsperson who is interested in making (or forced to make) his or her own tools.

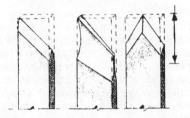

wood lathe-turning tools made from old files

The Modern Blacksmith, MF 04-108, book, 96 pages, Alexander Weygers, 1974, $9.30 from WEA.

This book is very similar to Weygers' previous book **The Making of Tools**, but the focus is on things that can be made with hammer, anvil and forge. The basic skills of blacksmithing are covered in detail.

There is an initial chapter on elementary blacksmithing exercises: squaring and straightening a round bar, and shaping the end of a square rod. Further chapters include: tempering and hardening high carbon steel, making a small anvil from

anvil made from scrap railroad rail

a railroad rail (see drawing), and upsetting steel (making a bolt head). There is a glossary of blacksmithing terms.

This is a very good introduction to the skills of blacksmithing, with many drawings and examples.

The Recycling, Use and Repair of Tools, MF 04-116, book, 112 pages, by Alexander Weygers, 1979, $6.95 from Van Nostrand Reinhold, 135 West 50th Street, New York, New York 10020, USA.

"The scrap steel yards across the country are full of every conceivable metal object discarded for reasons of wear, obsolescence, or damage. Much of this material can become useful stock for the beginner, as well as the skilled metal craftsman, who intends to 'make do' with what can be gleaned from this so-called junk."

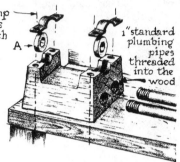

4 bolts & 2 forged straps clamp ball bearings in seat grooves of hardwood headstock to bench

A →

1" standard plumbing pipes threaded into the wood

a wood-turning lathe made from salvaged materials & inexpensive surplus items

In this book the author uses more than 600 drawings to show how to make useful woodworking and metalworking tools and other implements from steel scrap and discarded machine parts. Punches, chisels and gouges can be shaped and forged from steel tubing, automotive shafts, and spring steel. Files, rasps, fireplace tools, candlesticks, and other decorative implements can be made from mild and high-carbon steel scrap. Detailed perspective drawings show how to make a wood-turning lathe from salvaged materials, and adjustable bearings from fruitwood. The final third of the book discusses rehabilitating and operating metal-turning lathes, and how to use and make inserts for a trip-hammer. A short section on how to temper high-carbon steel is included, but in general it is assumed that the reader has basic blacksmithing skills. The author's previous book **The Modern Blacksmith** (see review) provides a good introduction to the use of the hammer, anvil, and forge.

"It is through actual demonstration, seeing how to manipulate tools to make tools, that I believe the student benefits most. But short of that one can learn from books in which the illustrations come as near as possible to live demonstrations. I have tried to present the information in such a way that the reader can imagine he is watching me making things in the shop."

A practical book illustrating a creative craftsman's approach to repair and re-use.

The Blacksmith's Craft: An Introduction to Smithing for Apprentices and Craftsmen, book, 116 pages, by Council for Small Industries in Rural Areas, 1955, £5.10 surface mail from Information and Publications Section, CoSIRA, 141 Castle Street, Salisbury, Wiltshire SP1 3TP, England.

This well-written book is divided into 37 lessons to teach people the basic skills of blacksmithing. These sections cover the tools and techniques very thoroughly,

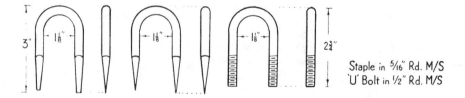

3"　1⅛"　←1⅛"→　←1⅛"→　2¾"

Staple in ⁵⁄₁₆" Rd. M/S
'U' Bolt in ½" Rd. M/S

and the many photos show each step in making chain links, u-bolts, harrow bars, and many other things. There is a list of books recommended for further reading. This is possibly the best introduction to blacksmithing available.

Practical Blacksmithing, MF 04-114, book, 1089 pages, compiled and edited by M.T. Richardson, originally published 1889, reprinted 1978, $10.00 plus $1.50 postage and handling, from Outlet Book Co., Crown Publishers, 34 Engelhard Avenue, Avenel, New Jersey 07001, USA.

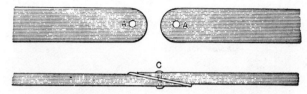

Fig. 97—Welding Springs by the Method of " W. B."

Originally published in 1889, **Practical Blacksmithing** is a compilation of a great variety of articles on different aspects of the craft. These articles, originally printed in the 19th century journal **The Blacksmith and Wheelwright**, were submitted by hundreds of blacksmiths from all over the United States. This book thus represents an extraordinary attempt to collect, preserve, and make available common "hands-on" wisdom about a critically important craft. Hundreds of drawings show tools, layout of blacksmiths' shops, and methods of working steel and iron which had previously been passed from individual smiths to a few apprentices.

This is an outstanding reference book, to go with the teaching books **The Modern Blacksmith** and **The Blacksmith's Craft** (see reviews).

Blacksmithing, MF 04-85, book, 109 pages, by James Drew, 1943, out of print in 1985.

This book covers most simple blacksmithing skills for forging metal parts— especially useful in making and repairing agricultural implements. The chapters include: forging iron and steel, simple exercises in blacksmithing, forging and tempering steel tools, plow work, soldering and brazing. The chapter on forging steel tools covers chisels, drills, and knives. The explanations are clear, although there are only a few drawings.

This book would be a useful introductory book in an area where blacksmith facilities are desired. Experienced blacksmiths, however, will probably find the information too elementary.

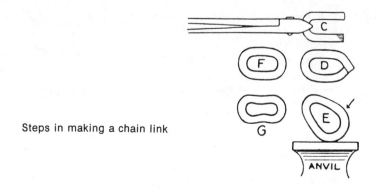

Steps in making a chain link

Hardening and Tempering Engineers' Tools, MF 04-98, 89 pages, by G. Gentry, 1950, revised by E. Westbury and reprinted 1985, £6.50 plus £0.65 shipping from Model and Allied Publications, Argus Books Ltd., P.O. Box 35, Wolsey House, Wolsey Road, Hemel Hempstead, Hertfordshire HP2 4SS, England.

"The efficiency of cutting tools employed in engineering and other crafts depends very largely on their correct heat treatment. In the past, the methods employed

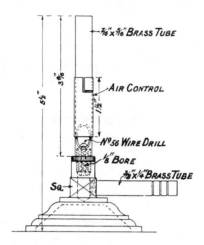

An easily made Bunsen burner for hardening and tempering small tools

in these processes have often evolved individual methods which have been in some cases closely guarded as trade secrets. There is, however, no reason why even the novice should not be able to harden and temper tools quite successfully by adopting simple methods which can be applied without the need for elaborate equipment."

This book contains all the relevant information on simplified processes available to craftspeople with small workshops to maintain their tools in proper working strength for a long lifetime. Detailed descriptions of case hardening and the latest processes, materials and equipment are included, plus valuable information on gas hardening, nitriding, and flame hardening. Although emphasizing modern appliances and conveniences such as welding torches and gas and electric furnaces, a very helpful chapter on forging reminds toolmakers of the importance of shaping steel by hot working under the hammer. This is precisely the state of the art for most traditional blacksmiths in developing countries, for whom the tempering suggestions should prove valuable.

Good illustrations with clear text.

Oil Drum Forges, MF 04-110, dimensional drawings, 40 pages, £1.50 or US$3.00 surface mail from ITDG.

Making these forges requires no welding or brazing. One forge is bellows-operated, the other is fan-operated. Both are made from old oil drums. The plans are very simple — numbered drawings (with separate text, to simplify translation) with English and metric measurements.

These can be used by one person for any kind of blacksmith work. The author

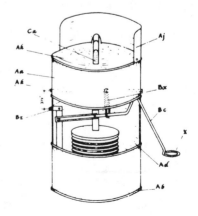

notes that these devices are also "suitable as engineering exercises, as rural crafts-men must be able to make their own tools."

A Blacksmith's Bellows, MF 04-84, plans, 23 pages, by A.R. Inversin and D. Sanguine, 1977, K4.00 in South Pacific region, K9.00 to rest of the world, from South Pacific Appropriate Technology Foundation, P.O. Box 6937, Boroko, Papua New Guinea.

The South Pacific Appropriate Technology Foundation (SPATF) has been organized by the government of Papua New Guinea to develop and promote the use of technologies encouraging in-dividual and village self-help and self-reliance. This booklet, one of SPATF's "how-to-do-it" publications, shows how to construct a hand-operated double-action bellows. Rubber from old inner tubes is used for the flap-valves as well as for the bellows themselves. The simple step-by-step instructions are accompanied by large, clear drawings and an explanation of how the finished mechanism works.

The design in this booklet could be built or adapted at very low cost for any kind of blacksmithing.

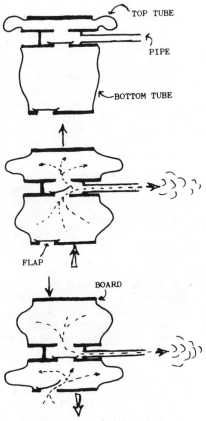

Metals for Engineering Craftsmen, book, 69 pages, CoSIRA, 1964, £6.00 by International Money Order from Information and Publications Section, CoSIRA, 141 Castle Street, Salisbury, Wiltshire SP1 3TP, England.

This book is designed to be a simple guide to the properties of a wide range of metals, and be a useful alternative to very large technical books on metallurgy. The characteristics of most useful metals are all included, along with information such as the welding and casting properties of each.

This is not a how-to book, but it is very informative.

Metallurgy, MF 04-106, book, 472 pages, by Carl G. Johnson and William R. Weeks, 1977, $15.75 from American Technical Publishers Inc., Alsip, Illinois, USA, 25% discount to LDCs.

Intended for those who require cast metals of high strength and durability, this book is biased towards the high-technology metals industries. There is, however, plenty of background information that could be useful to small-scale operations. A general introduction to the science of metals, the book covers the properties and testing of materials, and treatment and production of a variety of ferrous and non-ferrous metals and alloys. There is a glossary of terms used in the metals sciences.

This book could be useful as a reference in a large blacksmithing, casting, or smelting operation. Some basic knowledge of chemistry is required.

Lost-Wax Casting: A Practitioner's Manual, MF 04-130, book, 73 pages, by Wilburt Feinberg, 1983, £5.95 from ITDG.

"The successful endurance of any technology over thousands of years is an impressive feat; for such a technology to find applications in our modern industrial world is a phenomenon." Metal casting of objects is practiced throughout the world,

Fig. 41 The moulds are filled with molten metal.

often using techniques that are centuries old. Despite the rudimentary and unlikely nature of the technology often employed, village craftspeople regularly achieve good results. This book aims to inspire simple, basic improvements and encourage further resourcefulness among practitioners in Africa, Asia, and Latin America, and anyone working with limited resources. Following a discussion of basic techniques the author presents a number of practical, low-cost suggestions to enhance quality and productivity. The emphasis is on attainable improvements based on the realities of village foundries.

These improvements include mold and pattern-making for low-cost duplication, use of scrap material, formulas for compounds used in modeling, mold-making, kiln construction, and even the production of crucibles in which the metal is melted. Metal casting (for machine parts, tools, hardware, and so on) is a technology with great potential for local employment generation and enhanced self-reliance. Though somewhat brief, this book could contribute greatly to the quality of production and economic viability of village-level foundries. Includes case studies and technical appendices.

Foundrywork for the Amateur, MF 04-94, book, 108 pages, by B. Aspin, 1954 (revised 1986), £5.50 plus £0.55 shipping from Model and Allied Publications, Argus Books Ltd., P.O. Box 35, Wolsey House, Wolsey Road, Hemel Hempstead, Hertfordshire, HP2 4SS, England.

A basic skills book for making metal castings, describing the tools and techniques needed. The requirements are simple, although some of the tools described may not be locally available (such as a ceramic crucible). A foundry can be very useful for producing metal tools and replacement parts. Scrap metal can often be used, and the tools can often be made.

The book covers subjects such as furnaces, sand, molding boxes, how to make and ram a mold, and melting iron and aluminum. Illustrations of the tools used and the steps in the casting process are included. Useful examples are given, such as the casting design for an engine crankcase. Some of the English is a little complex.

Although this book was written for use in Britain, it should be valuable in rural areas where foundry skills are needed to produce things locally.

Small Scale Foundries for Developing Countries: A Guide to Process Selection, MF 04-127, by J.D. Harper, 1981, 66 pages, £4.95 from ITDG.

"This book is not intended as a textbook of foundry practice. The purpose is rather to assist anyone about to start or to expand a small scale foundry to consider the various available processes, and to select the most appropriate for the circumstances. An indication is given of the type of raw materials and equipment which will be needed, and the degree of training or skill which is likely to be required."

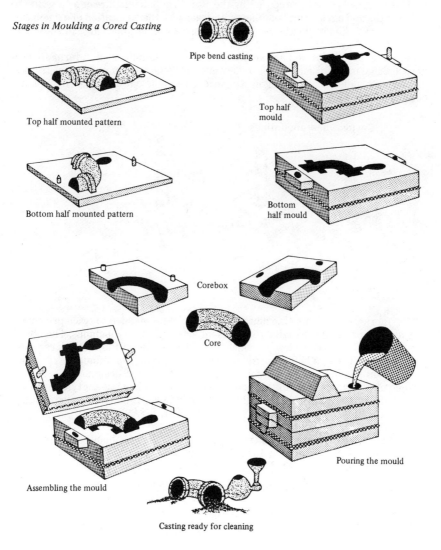

Stages in Moulding a Cored Casting

Pipe bend casting

Top half mounted pattern

Top half mould

Bottom half mounted pattern

Bottom half mould

Corebox

Core

Assembling the mould

Pouring the mould

Casting ready for cleaning

Smelting Furnace, Popular Mechanics Plan X297, MF 04-113, 5 pages, by E.R. Haan, 1964, $2.50 from Popular Mechanics.

"With this small furnace you can smelt aluminum, brass and copper; preheat small, thick pieces of iron and steel for brazing or forging; caseharden soft steel; make up alloys...You can use either LP or city gas. The cost is about $25 (1964 prices)." The furnace is about 17 inches high and 12 inches in diameter; it holds a 3-inch diameter crucible. Clear photos and drawings with the text show how to make and operate the smelting furnace. A vacuum cleaner is needed to supply forced air.

This might be of use in a small workshop where casting work is occasionally done.

Fabricating Simple Structures in Agricultural Engineering, book, 68 pages, 1955 (reprinted recently), Information Section, Council for Small Industries in Rural Areas, 141 Castle Street, Salisbury, Wiltshire SP1 3TP, England.

"This volume has been prepared by the Rural Industries Bureau as a guide to blacksmiths and agricultural engineers. It deals with the application of oxygen cutting and arc welding fabrications and therefore assumes knowledge of these two processes."

The structures described are all metal, and are generally used in farm applications: linkage mechanisms, wheels, rollers and brackets, bearing mountings, trusses, gates and a trailer chassis design. All pieces are made out of angle, channel and plate iron.

Castor wheel mountings

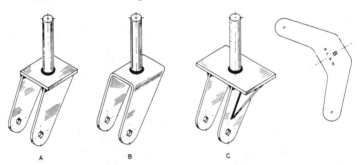

A   B   C

"The fabricated parts used to illustrate this book are intended to teach principles; they are not primarily intended to represent actual parts of machines. The object is not to show the precise way in which an exact number of fabrications can best be made, but rather to help the reader to become 'fabrication minded.' " The emphasis is on helping the reader fabricate parts of his own design.

Some of the same topics in this book are covered in **The Oxy-Acetylene Handbook**, 300 pages, 1976, $9.00 from Union Carbide Corp., Linde Reference Library, 47-36 36th St., Long Island City, New York 11101, USA.

The Procedure Handbook of Arc Welding, MF 04-115, book, 630 pages, by The Lincoln Electric Company, 1973, $5.00 plus $1.00 postage, from The Lincoln Electric Company, 22801 St. Clair Ave., Cleveland, Ohio 44117, USA.

This remarkably thorough and detailed book tells you probably everything you would ever want to know about small- and large-scale electric arc welding. It "is directed toward those people who have day-by-day working interest in arc welding — to the supervisory and management personnel of fabrication shops and steel erection firms; to welders and welding operators; to engineers and designers; and to owners of welding shops. The editorial aim has been to be practical — to present information that is usable to those on the job." The authors have also attempted to make the text as understandable as possible to the beginner.

Following an introduction to the fundamental principles of electric arc welding, the topics covered include preheating, relieving stress, welding different types of metals, safety, and welding underwater, in addition to power sources, equipment and supplies for arc welding.

There is an extensive reference section containing data on weights, hardness of different materials, and etching methods. There are many illustrations and a good index. Readers should have some understanding of basic welding methods.

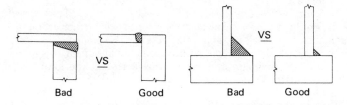

Size of weld should be determined with reference to thinner member

Welding Craft Practices, Volumes 1 and 2, MF 04-126, books, 159 pages (Volume 1), 182 pages (Volume 2), by N. Parkin and C. Flood, 1969, $9.50 for Volume 1 and $9.00 for Volume 2, from Pergamon Press, Maxwell House, Fairview Park, Elmsford, New York 10523, USA.

"The two volumes of this book cover the ground necessary for the acquisition of the essential basic skills and safe working methods in welding, sufficient technology and related studies being included to provide a suitable background to the practical work and form a basis for further, more advanced studies. It is intended for all who wish to learn to weld and the ground covered will enable the beginner to obtain a sound knowledge of the equipment, an appreciation of safety and, by means of a graduated series of practical exercises, a good standard of skill.

"Volume 1 deals with Oxygen-Acetylene Processes and Weld Defects, Testing of Welds, and Welding Science; Volume 2 with Electric Arc Processes and Elemen-

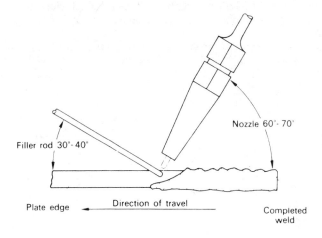

tary Electricity, Classification of Electrodes, Welding Symbols, Engineering Drawing, Metal Plate Surface Development and Workshop Calculations." These latter
sections on drawing and welding symbols could be useful references for those who
work with dimensional/mechanical drawings.

The two volumes can be bought separately; both have drawings and a few
photographs. While welding is a skill that must be learned by practice, usually with
the help of an experienced welder, these two books are well suited to library or
textbook use.

3 Welding Jigs, ITDG Complete Technical Drawings #19, MF 04-121, 3 large
sheets, by R. Mann, £1.50 from ITDG.

Welding jigs are used to hold parts in place and facilitate the repetition of a
welding task during the fabrication of identical steel items. These drawings provide details on three jigs: a "plow share" jig for repair or fabrication of irregular
sections, a shift and stock jig, and a universal jig. Exploded views are included,
along with materials lists. Although measurements are given, it is noted that the
dimensions are approximate and can be varied to suit the local availability of
materials and particular jig requirements.

Farm Shop and Equipment, MF 04-93, booklet, 16 pages, 1953 (reprinted 1975),
$1.50 from the Cumberland General Store, Rt. 3, Box 479, Crossville, Tennessee
38555 USA.

"Farm machinery is important to self-sufficiency. Effective care and repair of
farm machinery requires an organized farm shop, as well-equipped as possible."

This booklet was originally written for small American farmers. It discusses the
kind of work that can be done, desirable building features, and a simple equipment
list for making repairs, in a farm shop. It shows how to sharpen and grind drill
bits, and how to make a chisel. One of the unique features of this booklet is a full-
page table in which the following are listed: major kinds of metals used in farm
machinery, how to identify them, why the manufacturer used the particular metal,
common causes of failures, and recommended method of repair. There are numerous
diagrams and photos, including a farm-made substitute for a drill press that uses
a hand electric drill and simple plumbing parts, and dimensional drawings for a
medium-sized brick forge.

Sheet Metal Former, Plan No. X609, MF 04-112, 7 pages, 1966, $3.50 from
Popular Mechanics.

This hand-operated tool allows you to make perfect cylinders in any diameter
from 1⅝" up. It will handle 20-gauge sheet iron up to 12" wide, and thicker pieces
of softer metals.

Two important pieces are cut from aluminum alloy plate; production will be more
difficult if steel is used. This tool will require a lot of precision metal work to make.

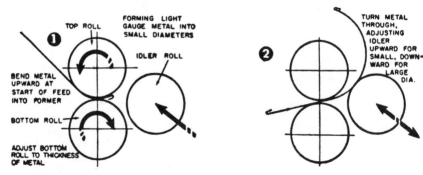

How to Work Sheet Metal, MF 04-100, book, 142 pages, by Herbert J. Dyer, 1963, Model and Allied Publications, U.K., out of print in 1986.

This book outlines methods of sheet metal working using techniques and equipment that stress low-cost efficiency. Riveting, soldering, brazing, and other metal joining techniques are discussed as well as sheet edging and shaping methods. Includes sections on equipment, materials, and metalworking machines. Also included are dimensional drawings of a few basic sheet metal tools and equipment.

A beginner may at times have difficulty following the text; but, on the whole, an excellent book.

HOLLOWING AND BLOCKING

A typical block

Start about ¼ in. from edge and work inwards

Ease out crinkles and carry on in circles

Raise the angle and hit square

Work the bottom right in to centre

Change ends with hammer and block all over again to final shape

Work all over with mallet, using domed stake

Repeat previous operation, using flat faced hammer rubbed clean on emery cloth

Unless hammer is clean every little dust particle on it will be shown with each blow

How to Make a Folding Machine for Sheet Metal Work, MF 04-99, booklet, 32 pages, by Rob Hitchings, 1981, $3.75 from ITDG.

Clear text and drawings distinguish this guide to building a simple yet effective and versatile tool for sheet metal work. The required materials and equipment should be available in most rural or semi-rural locations and the resulting machine will produce superior quality work with a great savings in time when compared with hand materials.

Sheet Metal Brake, Plan No. X606, MF 04-112, 8 pages, 1964, $4.00 from Popular Mechanics.

This is a valuable, versatile, simple workshop tool for quickly and accurately bending sheet metal. For use in workshops where a lot of sheet metal bending is done, or where precision is important. Hand-operated. The tool is 18 inches wide and can bend up to 20-gauge sheet metal the full width, or thicker narrower pieces.

"By using the proper forming block or mold, you can bend sheet metal to any angle, make radius bends, reverse bends, and seams." Part II describes techniques for the effective use of the tool.

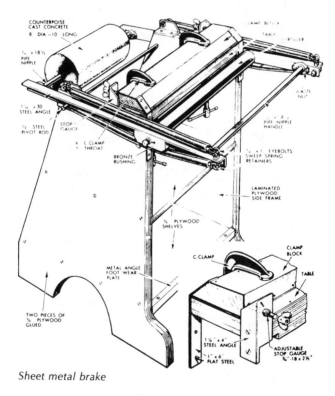

Sheet metal brake

Metal Bending Machine, MF 04-105, dimensional drawings and photos, 24 pages, ITDG, out of print in 1985.

This remarkably simple machine can be used to bend thin strips of metal (the width can be varied), from right angle bends to circular rims for cart wheels. It is hand-operated by two people, and has very few parts.

The booklet has very detailed drawings with English and metric measurements. It also includes instructions and photos on how to make cart wheels with an axle jig assembly. Several ITDG designs use wheels fabricated with this machine (see the agricultural leaflet entitled **Carts**). An ingenious piece of intermediate technology.

Try Your Hand at Metal Spinning, Popular Mechanics Plan X420A, MF 04-111, 5 pages, by Sam Brown, 1954, $2.50 from Popular Mechanics.

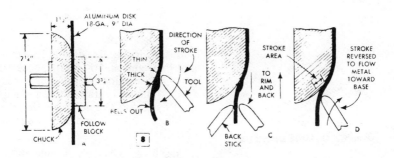

Spinning aluminum bowls on a lathe

This is a set of directions for making bowls out of aluminum by bending it into the proper shape on a lathe. No cutting is involved. "If you begin with soft aluminum and work it over a simple form you can spin a bowl in less than five minutes after the job is set up. Aluminum spins very easily and does not tend to score or buckle under the forming tools." Drawings and photos illustrate the techniques and special tools needed (simple to make). Requires 16- to 22-gauge aluminum. The lathe has to operate at about 900 rpm.

DeCristoforo's Book of Power Tools, Both Stationary and Portable, MF 04-88, book, 434 pages, by R. DeCristoforo, 1972, $14.95 from Book Division, Times Mirror Magazines, 380 Madison Avenue, New York, New York 10017, USA.

A clearly-written, extensively illustrated guide to the use of power woodworking tools, both stationary and hand-held. Includes table saws, drill presses, lathes, band saws, belt sanders and more. Each chapter describes the safe operation of a tool, and standard techniques, as well as many innovative applications of that

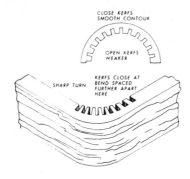

Bending wood

particular machine. Most useful are photos and plans for simple jigs and accessories which increase the versatility of the power tools and allow the production of many identical pieces. For example, there are plans for an adjustable wooden frame for cutting large panels easily with a power hand saw.

This book only provides instruction in the proper use of commercially available machines. No design and construction details for such machines are provided. The greatest weakness of this book is that it includes almost no information about repair or even routine maintenance of the power tools. May be useful to those wishing to teach themselves wood shop techniques, especially for small industry furniture production.

TURNING OUTSIDE DIAMETER

CUTTING THREADS

TURNING INSIDE DIAMETER

FACING

DRILLING

Metalworking Handbook: Principles and Procedures, MF 04-107, book, 480 pages, by Jeannette T. Adams, 1976, $12.95 (plus 75 cents postage and handling) from ARCO Publishing Company, 219 Park Avenue South, New York, New York 10003, USA.

This book is both a manual for the beginner and a reference book for the skilled craftsperson. For example, you'll find an introduction to working with sheet metal, soldering, rivetting and metal spinning. A variety of machine tools are discussed: drilling machines, milling machines, shapers, planers, lathes, and grinding machines.

The appendix offers many useful tables.

Principal
lathe operations

Workshop Exercises Metal, Part A, Fundamental Skills, MF 04-129, book, 90 pages, and **Technology Metal 1, Part A, Fundamental Skills**, MF 04-128, book, 90 pages; 1982, edited by H.N.C. Stam, Dfl. 27.50 and 34.50 from TOOL, Entrepot-dok 68a/69a, 1018 AD Amsterdam, The Netherlands.

Technical and vocational education in developing countries can benefit from clear and easy-to-understand texts on workshop skills. The pictorial system and straightforward language of this pair of workbooks make them appropriate for beginning shop classes anywhere metalworking tools are available. The exercises require the production of practical objects that develop skills in layout, measurement, metal-cutting, forming and fastening. The tools required may be somewhat sophisticated for typical rural workshops and schools. But where the resources are available, and a curriculum for enhanced industrial capability is desired, these books will be useful.

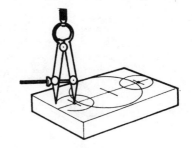

The Beginner's Workshop, MF 04-83, book, 244 pages, by Ian Bradley, 1975, Model and Allied Publications, U.K., out of print in 1986.

This book will introduce you to the basic tools and machines in a metalworking workshop. The author provides suggestions on buying tools and building some small items. The basic uses of the tools and machines are very well described.

Recommended for the reader wishing to develop basic workshop skills. Readers who already have such skills may find some new information here too.

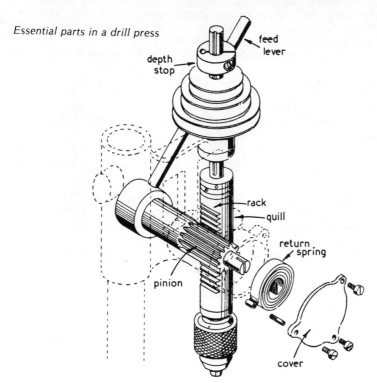

Essential parts in a drill press

Amateur's Workshop, MF 04-80, book, 256 pages, by Ian Bradley, 1976, revised edition 1986, £7.95 plus £0.80 shipping from Model and Allied Publications, Argus Books Ltd., P.O. Box 35, Wolsey House, Wolsey Road, Hemel Hempstead, Hertfordshire HP2 4SS, England.

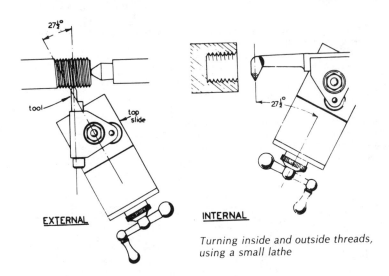

Turning inside and outside threads, using a small lathe

This book is intended for people who already possess at least the basic skills of metalworking using hand and power tools. Despite the use of the term "amateur" in the title, this book contains an enormous amount of useful information. The text is clear and well-illustrated. Workshop skills are thoroughly covered. There are many detailed plans for tools and attachments to tools; many of these are complex devices.

Amateur's Workshop will help someone with basic skills become a skilled craftsperson, after lots of practice. The book would be especially useful in programs for training metal workers. There is no glossary.

This is a step beyond **The Beginner's Workshop**, by the same author. An excellent book.

Heavy Duty Drill Press, Plan No. X245, MF 04-111, 4 pages, $2.00 from Popular Mechanics.

This appears to be a very sturdy, powerful drill press for heavy drilling in wood and metals. An imaginative design, yet reasonably simple to make. A small amount of machine shop work would be needed on a few minor parts. A small electric motor is used, but a geared-up pedal-power unit would work also. The drawings are quite clear and sufficiently detailed. This is a possible substitute for expensive heavy duty imported drill presses for many circumstances.

How to Mill on a Drill Press, Plan No. X422A, MF 04-111, 5 pages, 1969, $2.50 from Popular Mechanics.

This article includes plans for cutting attachments that can be added to a metalworking drill press to enable you to do milling work. It also describes the techniques to use.

Gear Wheels and Gear Cutting, MF 04-95, paperback book, 92 pages, by Alfred W. Marshall, 1984, £3.50 plus £0.35 shipping from Model and Allied Publications, Argus Books Ltd., P.O. Box 35, Wolsey House, Wolsey Road, Hemel Hempstead, Hertfordshire HP2 4SS, England.

"An elementary handbook on the principles and methods of production of toothed gearing." The author tells why and how to design and make gears. He discusses gear principles and tooth shapes, a wide variety of gears (including bevel and chain gears), and cutting gears on standard metalworking machine-tools. A knowledge of basic geometry is necessary in order to use this book.

Making gears is a complex task that requires a workshop with at least a metalworking lathe and drill press. This is a good guide to the process.

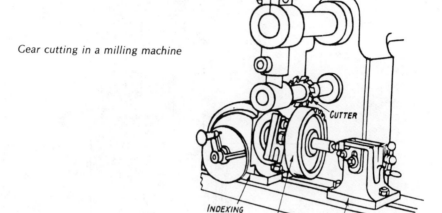

Gear cutting in a milling machine

10-inch Table Saw, Plan No. X585, MF 04-111, 10 pages, $5.00 from Popular Mechanics.

This unit would involve quite a bit of machine shop metal work, but the plans are quite clear, and the final product would be a solid, versatile table saw. The 10-inch circular blade can be raised, lowered, or tilted. The electric motor would be difficult to replace with another power source.

4-Wheel Band Saw, Plan No. X245, MF 04-111, 4 pages, $2.00 from Popular Mechanics.

"Except for ball bearings and retainers, metal yokes, sheet-metal cover, and such shafts and bolts as are necessary in the assembly, the machine is entirely made out of wood. Most of the parts are cut from a single piece of ⅝" plywood." The four wheels are made of plywood, and covered with pieces of inner tube to provide a surface against which the blade rubs as it rotates. A pulley can be changed to allow a second speed. Uses blades 10 feet long and up to ½-inch wide. The small electric motor could be replaced by a 1–2 person pedal-power unit with a flywheel. Will cut wood and light metals (this requires changing to a metal-cutting blade and operating at a lower speed). Clear drawings, sufficient for construction.

Two Speed Bandsaw Cuts Wood and Metal, Plan No. X37, MF 04-112, 7 pages, 1951, $2.50 from Popular Mechanics.

This machine can be used to cut wood or metal, by shifting v-belts between pulleys to change the speed of the blade. "It has every essential feature of the average dual purpose type machine." The frame is made of water pipe and fittings, while the band wheels are made of hardwood.

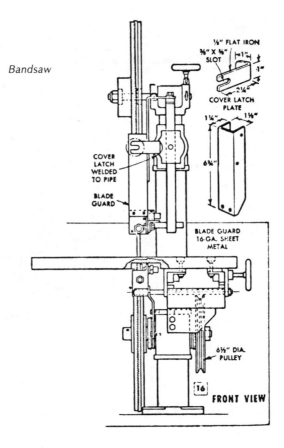

Bandsaw

Gilliom Build-It-Yourself Power Tool Plans, several large sheets with drawings and photos, $5.00 surface mail ($6.00 airmail) for each tool, $2.00 for a catalog; from Gilliom Manufacturing Inc., 1700 Scherer Parkway, St. Charles, Missouri 63303, USA.

These plans are all designed to accompany low-cost build-it-yourself kits that Gilliom sells; they are sold separately, however. Gilliom's kits include a number of useful castings that will have to be made if plans only are purchased. This should not be too difficult. Photos and drawings are included, along with full-scale patterns for cutting plywood parts. All of these plans use electric motors, but pedal-power or waterpower could be used (except to operate the two tilt saws). The plans are a good value; excellent for ideas.

Such kits (consisting of well-illustrated plans along with a small number of critical castings so that the buyer need only do woodwork and assembly) could represent an innovative distribution approach if imitated in developing countries using local designs.

Gilliom plans include:

No. 481 10-inch tilt/arbor floorsaw (10″ diameter blade)
No. 461 9-inch tilt/table bench saw
No. 431 6-inch belt sander
No. 771 12-inch band saw (12″ refers to distance from back to blade)
No. 451 18-inch band saw
No. 421 drill press/lathe (a multiple use tool)

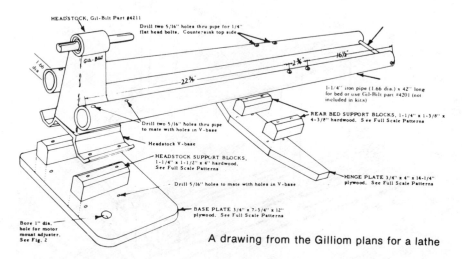

A drawing from the Gilliom plans for a lathe

Motorize Your Hacksaw, Plan No. X334, MF 04-112, 2 pages, 1952, $1.00 from Popular Mechanics.

"If you have a small metal working shop or use steel bar or shafting to some extent in your home workshop, motorizing a hand hacksaw will save hours of work and can be done at a fraction of the cost of a commercial power hacksaw. The inexpensive drive unit consists of an 8- or 10-inch v-pulley and shaft, a connecting rod and a guide rod, a vise or clamping arrangement to hold the work and a suitable wooden base. When needed for handwork, the saw can be removed from the unit in a few minutes." Uses a ¼ hp electric motor.

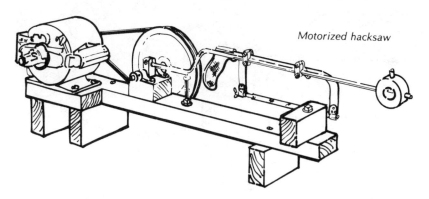

Motorized hacksaw

Scroll Saw, Plan No. X594, MF 04-112, 5 pages, 1945, $2.50 from Popular Mechanics.

This saw is similar to a jig saw, with a narrow, reciprocating blade. The plans have to be studied carefully to be fully understood. This design is made of hardwood and a variety of small metal parts from old automobiles. Some cutting, drilling and tapping steel is required. Uses a ¼ hp electric motor. Appears to be a sturdy machine.

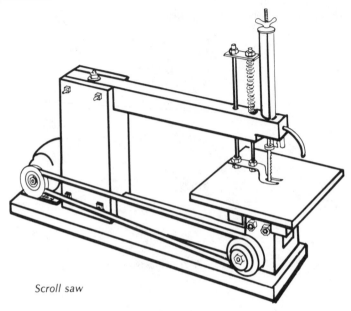

Scroll saw

Metal Turning Lathe Built from Stock Parts, Plan No. X387, MF 04-113, 4 pages, 1959, $2.00 from Popular Mechanics.

This metalworking lathe is not a precision tool. It can accept work up to 4½″ in diameter and 10″ long. Standard pipe and fittings are used to form a frame on which the rest of the lathe is fitted. Precision metal work is required to make this lathe.

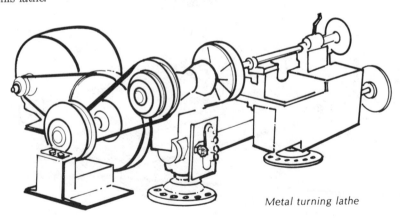

Metal turning lathe

Lathe Sanders, Plan No. X388, MF 04-112, 2 pages, 1949, $1.00 from Popular Mechanics.

This article provides ideas for making simple disc and drum sanding attachments for use with a woodshop lathe. Also shows another drum sander powered by an electric drill.

Sanding on a lathe

Wood Planer for $100, Plan No. 802B, MF 04-112, 9 pages, 1970, $4.50 from Popular Mechanics.

This is a workshop machine for planing wood to a specified thickness. Metalworking tools are needed to do a lot of precision work to make this machine. Cost $100 for materials in 1970. Useful in converting scrap, low-grade, or recycled lumber into more valuable boards.

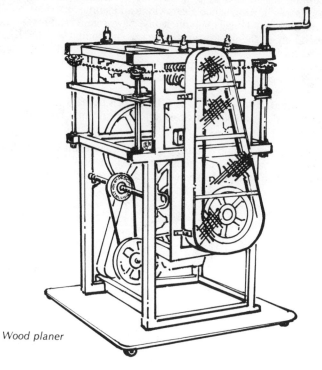

Wood planer

A Manual on Sharpening Hand Woodworking Tools, MF 04-104, large booklet, 48 pages, by J.K. Coggin, L.O. Armstrong, and G.W. Giles, $2.60 from The Interstate Printers and Publishers, Inc., Danville, Illinois 61832, USA.

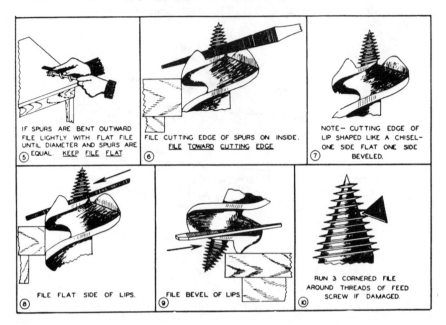

Written and published as a shop manual for students in woodworking and industrial arts classes in rural schools. Drawings and simple instructions show how to grind and sharpen chisels, plane irons, saws, augers, knives, axes, and screwdrivers. Many of the illustrations are clear and complete enough to be used without the text. Includes simple explanations of types of steel used in hand tools, and an illustrated glossary of sharpening terms.

An excellent low-cost teaching tool and reference.

Sharpening Small Tools, MF 04-117, book, 128 pages, by Ian Bradley, 1980, MAP Publications (UK), $5.95 from Sterling, 2 Park Avenue, New York, New York 10016, USA.

"In this book the sharpening of tools in general use is dealt with, and, whenever possible, simple and well-tried methods have been adopted, bearing in mind that usually the aim when sharpening a tool should be to restore, as accurately and

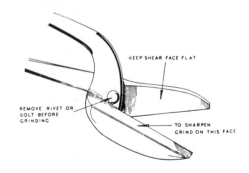

Sharpening metal shears

as consistently as possible, the original form of the cutting edge."

Bradley begins with an introduction to the materials and equipment used in sharpening. Then he explains (with illustrations) the proper sharpening techniques to use with metalworking tools—lathe cutting tools, shears, drill bits, and other tools used in boring. This is followed by sharpening techniques for woodworking tools—planes, saws, chisels, and drill bits—and some common household tools such as knives and scissors.

When a sharpening "stone is used dry, it will soon become filled with metal particles and...have little abrasive action...water or oil is applied to the stone to enable the metal dust to be carried away..."

"The four common forms of cold chisels...are generally sharpened on the grinding wheel, [although] when the edge is but little blunted it can readily be restored on a coarse emery bench stone."

Bearing Design & Fitting, MF 04-82, paperback book, 80 pages, by Ian Bradley, 1979, Model and Allied Publications, U.K., out of print in 1986.

"Although the subject of this book is complex and covers a very wide field, an attempt has, nevertheless, been made to deal with the main principles involved and, at the same time, to furnish examples of bearing design and application that may be found of use particularly in the small workshop."

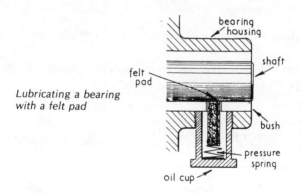

*Lubricating a bearing
with a felt pad*

Bearings are used whenever something rotates or slides against something else and it is desirable to reduce friction and wear. This book is good on the design and production of metal bearings. Many of the ideas could be applied to other materials, such as wood, of which bearings are often made in developing countries. The book covers casting of bearings from metals and plastics, machining bearings, design, lubrication, different types, and maintenance and repair. See also **Oil Soaked Wood Bearings** , reviewed on page 221.

Spring Design and Calculation, MF 04-119, book, 37 pages, by R.H. Warring, 1973, Model and Allied Publications, U.K., out of print in 1986.

This book tells you how to make metal springs. Topics covered include spring materials and the following kinds of springs: flat, helical, tapered helical, torsion, clock, constant force, and multiple leaf. Wire sizes and other details of spring construction are also discussed. Simple algebra is needed to design springs using this book.

"Spring design proportions are not something that can be 'guesstimated' with any degree of accuracy—and trial-and-error design can produce a succession of failures. Thus this book on spring design is full of formulas, as the only accurate

largest active coil
bottoms first

solid height

TAPERED HELICAL SPRINGS

method of predicting spring performance. However, all are practical working formulas; and all are quite straightforward to use."

This is not a book that shows specific spring making procedures — it just covers the designing of springs. Once you master the simple math you should have no problem using this book to design springs of good quality. There are numerous illustrations and charts that will help the reader more fully understand the methods and principles described.

How to Work With Copper Piping, Plan No. X198C, MF 04-111, 4 pages, 1974, $2.00 from Popular Mechanics.

Good illustrations and text for "sweat" soldering copper pipe joints. Notes on tools and techniques for cutting copper pipe.

How to Use Metal Tubing, Plan No. X422, MF 04-111, 4 pages, 1956, $2.00 from Popular Mechanics.

This article contains lots of valuable hints with drawings, on how to bend, cut, connect, solder, enlarge and generally handle metal tubing. There is a good description of soldering copper tubing joints. Relevant for plumbing, solar water heaters, steam engines, and other uses.

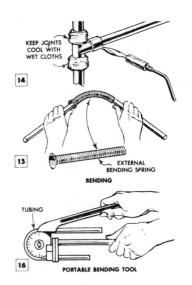

KEEP JOINTS COOL WITH WET CLOTHS

14

15

EXTERNAL BENDING SPRING

BENDING

TUBING

16

PORTABLE BENDING TOOL

Electroplating for the Amateur, MF 04-91, book, 106 pages, by L. Warburton, 1963, Model and Allied Publications, U.K., out of print in 1986.

Electroplating is a process in which electricity is used to produce a protective coating on metal parts. The author attempts "to provide the amateur engineer with what is hoped will be sufficient data, not only to carry out successful electroplating in the small workshop, but also to provide himself with the essential tools of the trade, i.e., the electrical equipment and plating tanks. . . reduced to their simplest forms without serious loss of efficiency. . . The only plating plant obtainable is on a far bigger scale than anything required by even the most enthusiastic amateur." Thus, there is "a detailed discussion of a suitable size of plant, together with details as to how such a plant can be assembled in the small workshop."

The book covers electrical principles and procedures; the plating tank; chemicals; preparation of surfaces to be plated; electrolytes; chromium, copper, nickel and silver plating; anodizing aluminum; and some other techniques.

Electric Motor Test and Repair, MF 04-90, book, 168 pages, by Jack Beater, 1966, $8.65 from TAB Books, Blue Ridge Summit, Pennsylvania 17214, USA.

This is a guide to rewinding and testing single and poly-phase, plain and split-loop small-horsepower electric motors. Winding diagrams show the sequence and number of coils to be wound into armature and stator slots, and simple schematics show electrical connections to commutator and field windings. Accompanying text gives full instructions: ". . . any armature with an even number of slots can be wound in the same general manner. The first coil is started in the slot selected as number 1 and comes back in slot 7, then back through slot 1 and so on around until the correct number of turns have been placed. The wire is now cut at the commutator end, leaving ample length to reach the proper commutator bar with an inch or two left over. . ."

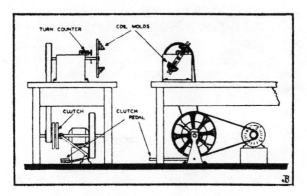

Two views of a coil group winding machine;
construction described in the text

Testing and winding equipment, expensive or unavailable in many areas, can be made by the person doing repairs. The author explains how to build a motortest panel, simple hand-operated armature and stator coil winding machines, devices for taping and packing coils, and gear and pulley puller plates. He also discusses the use of small lamps, hand compasses, and homemade induction devices to test armatures and stators. Other useful ideas and information: reversing motor rotation direction; rewinding automobile generator armatures; building a dipping tank and baking hood for application of coil insulating varnish.

This book requires a basic understanding of electric motors. Bound with a durable cover and packed with ideas for improvising equipment, it could be used wherever motors are being repaired.

LeJay Manual, MF 04-102, booklet, 44 pages, 1945 (reprinted many times since), $3.50 postpaid from LeJay Manufacturing Co., Belle Plaine, Minnesota 56011, USA.

This is an illustrated manual on how to rewind automobile generators for all kinds of uses: from direct drive windgenerators and waterwheels to arc welders and soldering irons. For windgenerators, rewinding is done so that the generator will begin charging at a lower rpm, thus avoiding the need for gearing. This allows the propeller to directly drive the generator shaft. The specific generators referred to have mostly disappeared; however, the principles remain the same.

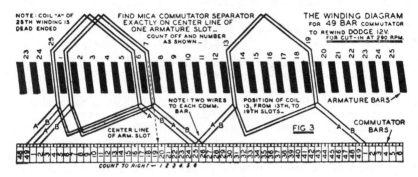

The winding diagram for rewinding an old Dodge 12-volt generator

A Museum of Early American Tools, MF 04-109, book, 108 pages, by E. Sloane, 1964 (fourth edition 1974), $4.95 from Ballantine Cash Sales, Box 505, Westminster, Maryland 21157, USA.

"Covers building tools and methods, farm and kitchen implements, and the tools of curriers, farriers, wheelwrights, coopers, blacksmiths, coachmakers, sawyers, loggers, tanners," and others. The tools were generally made from wood and iron.

This book was written by a collector of early tools, with the philosophy that tools represent extensions of the human hand. The book includes drawings of the tools, descriptions of their uses, and some production sketches. These are tools that were produced by blacksmiths and farmers — from an era when most rural Americans made many of their own tools out of local materials.

Interesting items include: making barrel staves, reaming, nail-making; and complete drawings of a boring machine, wooden jacks and lifts, and smithy tools.

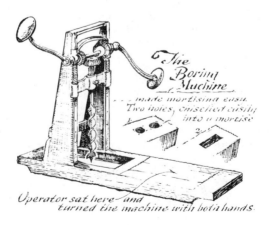

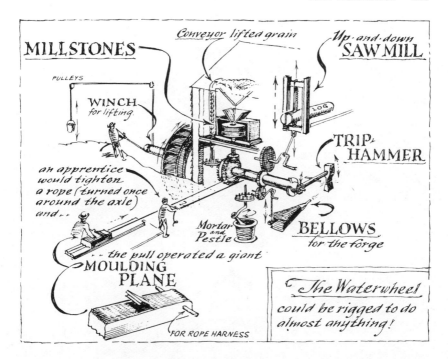

Diary of an Early American Boy, MF 04-89, book, 108 pages, by Eric Sloane, 1965, $4.95 from Ballantine Books, 400 Hahn Road, Westminster, Maryland 21157, USA.

The A.T. value of this book is in about 10 drawings: a simple bridge building technique, a water hammer, a pole saw, bow saw and crank saw, a diagram which illustrates the multiple uses of a waterwheel (above), and a beam drill (in which a weighted bar replaces the lever of a hand-operated drill press). These are simple but useful do-it-yourself devices made of wood.

Stocking Spare Parts for a Small Repair Shop, VITA Technical Bulletin No. 2, MF 04-120, 4 pages, by Phil Cady, P.E., out of print in 1985.

Basic good advice for systematic stocking and record-keeping for parts.

Hard-to-Find Tools and Other Fine Things, catalog, 70 pages average length, published quarterly, free (overseas shipping postage charge only) from Brookstone Company, 127 Vose Farm Road, Peterborough, New Hampshire 03458, USA.

A commercial catalog, with photos, offering a wide variety of unusual tools. Although some of the listings are expensive gimmicks, most of the tools are of high quality.

ADDITIONAL REFERENCES ON THE WORKSHOP

Simple Working Models of Historic Machines includes drawings of two different lathes, screw cutters for wooden screws, a variety of pulleys and other lifting devices, the Chinese spoon tilt hammer (which can be used by a blacksmith), and two kinds of bellows; see GENERAL REFERENCE.

Construction Manual for a Cretan Windmill contains plans for a pedal-powered turning lathe; see ENERGY: WIND.

Agriculture

Agriculture

Productive agricultural land is the most fundamental resource of all rural communities and nations. An agriculture which forms a basis for rural and national self-reliance in food production depends upon equitable distribution of this resource. Without secure access to land, the tenant farm family is not in a position to carry out many of the long-term improvements (such as terracing, composting and tree planting) that may be needed, nor are they in a position to benefit from the multitude of small farm programs sponsored by national agriculture departments and international and bilateral aid agencies. The landless farm laborer is often ignored entirely, though he or she is most vulnerable to unemployment from mechanization. Participation in agricultural production, it has been repeatedly demonstrated, is the only clear guarantee of participation in food consumption.

The concentration of land holdings in a few hands appears to be a major engine of environmental destruction as well, forcing subsistence cultivators onto marginal lands and hillsides. The loss of topsoil that follows is swift and often irreversible. Deforestation becomes a way of life as existence is scratched from land in a capital-consuming, desperate process.

The amount of productive land lost to deforestation and desertification is staggering, and the rate of loss is increasing. A central concern of agriculture must therefore be a sustainable resource base — soil conservation, an assured supply of nutrients, and a buffer from the inflationary costs of inputs that accompany the oil-based agriculture of the rich countries. The elements needed for ecologically responsible agricultural systems exist in most parts of the world. In developing such approaches, indigenous agricultural systems deserve special attention, for they often reflect important ecological interactions and yield a variety of crops.

In any agricultural system, crop diversity is usually a key to sustainability. There must be a balance between production of cash crops for income, and production of subsistence crops for direct consumption. Cash crops can allow a greater flexibility and access to crucial tools and inputs that would otherwise be unobtainable, and they usually mean a higher value production from a particular piece of land. Yet cash crops often bring with them dependency on global market forces for the sale of produce and for the supply of fertilizers. They also tend to bring a reduction in crop diversity. All of these factors significantly increase the risks facing farmers. Cash crops can lead to mining of agricultural soils for short-term gain, reducing both short-term food supplies and long-term productivity of the land. Cash cropping also contributes to the concentration of landholdings, displacement of tenant farmers, and abandonment of traditional social mechanisms of redistribution and collective welfare.

The social aspects of the organization of agriculture are major considerations in the search for appropriate agricultural strategies. What does a new agricultural system do to social relations, the extent to which extended families continue to take responsibility for all their members? What does a new agricultural system do to the composition and character of rural communities?

In recent years there has been a rethinking of the role of the small farmer in agricultural research. There is now strong evidence that to be successful, research programs must include small farmers in thinking about what changes might be tried, and in testing and evaluating proposed improvements in the farming system before widespread dissemination is attempted. When typical farmers are partners in the research teams, experience has shown that innovations coming out of the research program are far more likely to be acceptable.

When all of these concerns are taken into account, several avenues for appropriate technologies seem evident. There is a need for increased emphasis on intensive food production. Growing fruits and vegetables in home gardens can be done by nearly every family. Relatively high production can be obtained from a small area, and the increased variety in the family diet has clear nutritional advantages.

Farming systems that combine agriculture with forestry bring a varied and higher total production from multiple tiers of plants and trees. Reduced pest problems result, as a more diverse plant environment offers less shelter to pests and more to their predators. More stability over time is also assured as differing crops provide protection from weather and market fluctuations. Alternating tree crops with row crops enables a sustainable productive agriculture as protected topsoil and variety of plant life mean that soil fertility can be maintained. The addition of animals, including livestock, fish and bees, into these farming systems can also be important in providing additional food, income and fertilizer.

These complementary themes can be found throughout the entries included in this chapter; more synthesis needs to be done in actual programs.

The first books consider the social, political and economic sides to agriculture, criticizing the conventional narrowly-technical approach in rich and poor countries. **Food First** *is a broad-ranging critique that seeks to explode many of the myths about world hunger, while perpetrating a few of its own.* **As You Sow** *paints a saddening picture of the negative social consequences in small communities that have accompanied the transition from family farms to huge agribusiness operations in California. This process of decay through growth in landholdings involves a substantial reduction in the number of opportunities for rural people to develop basic business, managerial, and entrepreneurial skills.*

Small Farm Development *is an exceptionally valuable and highly readable book. It illuminates the dynamics, characteristics, and constraints of small farms in the tropics. It should be required reading for those working on farming systems, tools and equipment, and related activities such as farm co-ops.*

Two Ears of Corn *is filled with valuable advice on how to successfully work with a local community to improve agricultural practices.* **Training and Visit Extension** *documents a low-cost extension approach which can help farmers improve their basic practices with almost no cash investment, yet with a high chance of achieving higher production. This approach relies heavily on village-level workers with a low educational background, a strategy somewhat similar to the use of "barefoot doctor" health workers.*

Many of the publications included offer insights and practical considerations relevant to the creation of sustainable agricultural systems and agro-forestry combinations. The journals also provide contact with the worldwide network of enthusiastic and imaginative people working in this field.

Reference books on soils, seeds, crops and fertilizers are reviewed. Soil testing, seed production, composting and soil conservation (controlling erosion and gully formation) are some of the topics covered here. The proper protection of workers from pesticides is addressed by several books, while **Integrated Pest Management** *reviews the techniques used to control pests while minimizing pesticide use.*

Three volumes introduce the technical considerations for small-scale irrigation efforts. Irrigation is the biggest single factor in raising farm yields. As its proper planning from a technical and environmental viewpoint can be quite complicated, these are welcome references.

Intensive gardening is the topic of ten entries. The manuals from Bangladesh, Peru, Jamaica and the Philippines are highly recommended references, to go with **How to Grow More Vegetables** *from the United States.*

The last section includes a number of books on raising animals under various climatic conditions. The final entry in this group is the encyclopedic **Tropical Feeds**, *a unique reference covering nutritional content and uses of 650 tropical feeds, most of them plants.*

Small Farm Development: Understanding and Improving Farming Systems in the Humid Tropics, MF 05-214, book, 160 pages, by Richard Harwood, 1979, $10.50 plus $1.50 postage and handling from Westview Press, 5500 Central Avenue, Boulder, Colorado 80301, USA.

The author states, "In our impatience with 'backward' small farmers and in our haste to rapidly 'commercialize' them, we have overlooked key aspects of their farming systems that could enhance efforts to increase food production and improve rural well-being. To accomplish the development of a greater number of the world's small farms, shifts in emphasis must be made in our thinking, in our technological research, and in our communications with farmers."

Better understanding and analysis of the bulk of the Third World's small farm production systems is the theme of this important book. The author discusses with great depth and sensitivity the issues and options facing resource-limited small farmers in the tropics. He suggests that a "purposeful blending of traditional and modern technologies may well prove the key to starting the most disadvantaged farmers along a more rapid development path."

In the first part of his book, Harwood presents an overview of small farms from subsistence hunting-gathering to primary mechanized operations. He endorses a development approach of scientists, extension workers, and farmers working in close cooperation in farming areas. "The agricultural development specialist must remain constantly aware of — and on guard against — the natural tendency to superimpose his own values on those of the farmer. The reality that faces the farmer who ekes out his existence from a mere half-hectare of poor land can only be understood — if it is seen as he sees it."

The second part of the book reviews critical factors in small farm development which are often overlooked or given little emphasis in development programs. Some examples of these factors include:

Animals in Mixed Farming Systems:
"Despite the almost universal interest of farmers in mixed crop-animal systems, professionals in both crop and animal production commonly pursue research in pure crop systems or pure animal systems, without reference to the interactions between the two that increase the productivity of both. Fortunately, most farmers have no such inhibitions or prejudices. Science should do more for them."

Noncommercial Farm Activities:
"Fencerows are often used for noncommercial plantings as well as for their primary functions as field boundaries, enclosures for containment or exclusion of grazing animals, and erosion controls. There is evidence to indicate that the plant diversity and permanence of the fencerow makes it a refuge for beneficial insects and predators. The relative rarity of pest outbreaks in highly diversified small farm areas where hedgerows and farmyard plantings are extensively used may be due to the net benefits of these traditional features."

Other chapters deal with resource and economic limitations of intensive and multiple cropping systems; economic determinants and resource optimization of micro-enterprises; farm mechanization requirements; and stability in farming systems. An excellent annotated bibliography is also included.

Technical charts and graphs are balanced by photographs of farm families at work. All in all, this book is a fine blending of reasoned arguments for new directions in agricultural development projects. It should receive wide circulation among agriculturalists and development workers concerned with agriculture in the humid tropics of the Third World.

Two Ears of Corn: A Guide to People-Centered Agricultural Improvement, MF 05-224, book, 264 pages, by Roland Bunch, 1982, $7.95 from World Neighbors, 5116 North Portland Avenue, Oklahoma City, Oklahoma 73112, USA.

A program beginning with a redefined goal of agricultural improvement which emphasizes the development of indigenous participation and capability rather than simply introducing production-raising techniques is more likely to yield long-term benefits, according to this guide for village-level program leaders. The importance of small scale, local cultural values, feedback, and non-paternal methods of leadership is established in an informative, insightful text which draws from examples of both failures and successes throughout the world's villages. Includes advice for program planning, encouraging participation, technology choice, employee policy, socio-cultural surveys, marketing, and eventual phase-out of outside assistance. Applicable to non-agricultural programs also. Highly recommended.

Understanding Small Farmers: Sociocultural Perspectives on Experimental Farm Trials, MF 05-258, paper, 9 pages, by Robert Rhoades, 1982, from International Potato Center, Aptdo. 5969, Lima, Peru; or order publication no. PNAAN869, $1.17 from AID Document and Information Handling Facility, 7222 47th St., Suite 100, Chevy Chase, Maryland 20815, USA.

This is a good quick introduction to the reasons why understanding the farmer's perspective is vitally important to the success of efforts to develop improved agricultural practices through farm trials. The author points to seven essential questions: "1. Is the problem to be solved important to farmers? 2. Do farmers understand the trials? 3. Do farmers have time, inputs, and labor required by the improved technology? 4. Does the proposed technology make sense within the present farming system? 5. Is the mood favorable for investing in certain crops in a region? 6. Is the proposed change compatible with local preferences, beliefs, or community sanctions? 7. Do farmers believe the technology will hold up over the long term?"

"In the end, the acceptability of a technology depends on what the farmers actually do. This may not, as we have stressed, be the same as what they have told us. We can discover this only in a final stage of farmer testing where farmers themselves take over the new technology and incur all risks, costs, and benefits. Until this final step is taken, all other evaluations remain only suggestive of the technology's potential."

Insights of Outstanding Farmers, MF 05-238, book, 114 pages, IRRI, 1985, $8.30 to highly developed countries, $2.50 to Third World countries, plus $1.00 surface mail or $3.00 airmail postage, from Publications Office, International Rice Research Institute, P.O. Box 933, Manila, Philippines.

IRRI has brought together the stories of 14 outstanding rice farmers from different countries in this excellent book. These people provided their own background information and were interviewed for additional details. The result is a fascinating view of the circumstances, thinking and decision-making of these farmers. Many of them are very systematic in experimenting in their own fields. While these people are more representative of "leading" farmers than "average" farmers, their stories give the reader a better understanding of the small rice farmer and the technological changes that may benefit her or him.

Readers with varied interests in rural development will find this a revealing book.

Farm Management Research for Small Farmer Development, FAO Agricultural Services Bulletin 41, book, 145 pages, by John I. Dillon and J. Brian Hardaker, 1980, $11.50 from UNIPUB.

Persons working on the improvement of small farm equipment, the development and introduction of new varieties and techniques, and any other innovations that affect the small farm as an enterprise will find this a valuable reference. The reader is reminded that small farmers usually make efficient use of their available resources, that important crop-crop and crop-animal interactions exist on most small farms, and that a good understanding of existing farming systems is necessary before potentially useful improvements can be identified. Most of the manual explains the elements essential to good survey strategies and techniques, interpretation of data, modelling of farm activities, and economic/financial evaluations of alternative choices.

This book should help the reader to systematically identify research project possibilities that are likely to lead to useful and economically viable technologies. This approach is far more likely to succeed than the common practice of choosing topics based on incomplete information and incorrect assumptions about what farmers are actually doing.

Agricultural Extension: The Training and Visit System, MF 05-127, booklet, 55 pages, by Daniel Benor and James Harrison, 1977, $5.00 from Publications, World Bank, 1818 H Street N.W., Washington D.C. 20433, USA.

The System "has been put into operation in areas where the need is to improve the level of agricultural production by large numbers of farmers cultivating mostly small farms using low-level technology and usually traditional methods. . .The cost to farmers is very small. . .The smaller cultivators, who have an abundant supply of labor, may benefit at least as much as the larger farmers."

This low-cost extension system "uses village-level workers with comparatively low educational standards supported by subject matter specialists. . ."

"In the Seyhan project in Turkey, farmers increased cotton yields from 1.7 tons to over 3 tons per hectare in three years. In Chambal, Rajasthan (India), farmers increased paddy yields from about 2.1 tons to over 3 tons per hectare in two years. Combined irrigated and unirrigated wheat yields in Chambal, Madhya Pradesh (India), rose from 1.3 tons to nearly 2 tons per hectare after one season and have since risen higher."

The author describes the common problems with extension programs: multiple roles (not just agricultural) expected of the extension worker, excessively large area of assignment for each worker, and theoretical pre-service training with no in-service training.

For a reformed extension service, the author recommends that extension workers report directly and only to the agricultural department, spend full time on agriculture, and make regular visits to farmers. "Contact farmers must be willing to try out practices recommended by the extension workers and be prepared to have other farmers visit their fields. But they should not be the community's most progressive farmers who are usually regarded as exceptional" and are not often followed by their neighbors.

After the simpler field management practices have led to higher incomes, extension workers should recommend to farmers "the minimum quantity of fertilizer which would noticeably increase their net yields and incomes, and teach the farmers how to make the best use of this amount—for example, when and how to apply it, and how to combine it with organic fertilizers."

"To remain effective, extension must be linked to a vigorous research program, well-tuned to the needs of the farmers. Without a network of field trials upon which new recommendations can be based and without continuous feedback to research from the fields, the extension service will soon have nothing to offer farmers, and the research institutions will lose touch with the problems real farmers face."

Training and Visit Extension, MF 05-256, book, 202 pages, by Daniel Benor and Michael Baxter, 1984, $5.00 from World Bank Publications, 1818 H Street N.W., Washington D.C. 20433, USA.

This volume contains a more complete description of the extension system presented in **Agricultural Extension: The Training and Visit System**. The T&V system is essentially an intelligent simplification of conventional extension structures to create closer links between farmers and researchers, and, in particular, to make better use of farmers' resources with basic agricultural practices that require little or no investment of cash but some additional labor (e.g. "better seed, seedbed preparation, cultivation and weeding").

The initial dramatic success of this system in Turkey and India has led to a great deal of interest in applying it elsewhere. In some countries a tendency to adopt the name and some of the form, but not the substance of the system, has meant disappointing results.

The successful functioning of an extension system requires more than simply a good organizational structure. In apparent recognition of the many forces that affect and hamper the effective functioning of the T&V system, in this volume the authors give considerable attention to the essential elements of the system that cannot be changed without diminishing its effectiveness. "Leadership of the extension service must be strong, active, innovative, and field oriented. . . For T&V extension to have an impact, research must support it strongly, coordinate with extension, and tackle farmers' immediate problems; production recommendations taught to farmers must be relevant to their needs and resource conditions, be economically viable, and require only inputs that are actually available; and regular and special training of extension staff must be timely and specific to their needs. Most importantly, hard decisions have to be made in setting priorities, requiring concentration of efforts on a small number of feasible goals and a commitment to this system of professional agricultural extension. If any one of these requirements (or any of a number of other basic features of the system) is ignored, or is weak relative to others, the impact of the entire system is compromised."

There is much good advice here that is relevant to all kinds of appropriate technology development and extension activities.

Agricultural Extension, MF 05-230, book, 308 pages, by Michael Gibbons and Richard Schroeder, 1984, available to fieldworkers from Peace Corps, Information Collection and Exchange, Room 701, 806 Connecticut Avenue N.W., Washington D.C. 20526, USA.

Agricultural extension used to be conceived of as a one-way flow of technical information from a central source to the farmer to encourage him or her to undertake "correct" agricultural practices. This volume provides convincing evidence and examples of why it is important to understand the farmer's position and viewpoint, and work with the farmer to identify priorities for improvements, before any "answers" are proposed. Emphasizes that small farmers are expert at what they do, and are very familiar with the micro-environmental details of their land. Full of good advice based on long experience, this book should help new fieldworkers avoid many of the mistakes that have bedeviled agricultural extension programs in the past.

Losing Ground, MF 05-197, book, 223 pages, by Erik Eckholm, 1976, $5.95 from W. Norton & Co., 500 5th Avenue, New York, New York 10110, USA, or WEA; also in French, Spanish, Japanese.

Losing Ground is at once a disturbing and exciting book. It brings into sharp focus the struggle for survival of a large portion of the world's people — their immediate need for fuel and food has led to actions with potentially disastrous human and ecological consequences. The author thoughtfully analyzes the global extent of human-made environmental stress, and shifts attention from the pollution and inflation of industrial countries to the concerns of the world's poor, whose "energy crisis" has largely gone unnoticed.

Eckholm sees the shortage of firewood as a central feature of this crisis. The uncontrolled clearing of remaining or replanted trees has its severe ramifications: precious topsoil erodes not in centuries as in the past, but practically overnight; a disastrous increase in flooding occurs on lowland plains; and new deserts and grass wildernesses are created in drier zones by inhabitants removing the remaining ground cover.

Economic development prospects in Africa, Asia and Latin America are now dimmed by accelerating destruction of the land's productivity. Slash and burn shifting cultivation has in many places increased beyond the ability of the sensitive forest to recover. Massive forest-clearing operations by governments and corporations in places such as the Amazon river basin and Borneo are often followed by heavy grazing, which completes the land's destruction.

Eckholm calls for massive tree-planting campaigns, agricultural reforms to benefit peasant farmers, and reduced world population growth.

"People hungry for land are not apt to leave forest or pasture lands unplowed, regardless of what ecological soundness dictates. Farmers hungry for bread are not likely to defer production this year to enhance soil quality for the next generation. Those with no other means than wood to cook their dinner cannot be expected to leave nearby trees unmolested even if they are labeled 'reserved' by the government. And people brutalized by exploitive economic and social systems will probably not treat the land any more gently and respectfully than they are treated themselves."

"Measures will never succeed until the populace has the technical and financial means to cooperate, and this means reaching the masses with ecologically-sound agricultural advice and with credit facilities; maximizing rural employment on farms and in small-scale industries; and breaking down the social, legal, and economic structures that deny the poor basic opportunities for advancement. It means creating participatory institutions, whether through local government, cooperatives, or communes, that give the poor a sense of responsibility for and control over their own destiny. That these prerequisites of ecological recovery are identical to the tactics of a more general war against poverty and hunger should come as no surprise."

Highly recommended.

Food First: Beyond the Myth of Scarcity, MF 05-177, book, 412 pages, by Frances Moore Lappe and Joseph Collins, with Cary Fowler, 1977, $2.95 plus postage from Institute for Food and Development Policy, 2588 Mission Street, San Francisco, California 94110, USA.

"Every country in the world has the capacity to feed itself. . . food self-reliance is the cornerstone of genuine self-determination." This is the thesis of **Food First**, an extraordinary book that examines the constraints and opportunities facing agriculture in developing countries. Citing case studies and statistics from all over the world, the authors assert that hunger is not caused by too many people, too little arable land, lack of technology, or overconsumption by greedy Americans. "Inequality in control over productive resources is the primary constraint — on food production and on equitable distribution."

The authors claim that ecological destruction is more closely related to economic exploitation than population pressure. "Soil erosion occurs largely because fertile land is monopolized by a few, forcing the majority of farmers to overuse vulnerable soils."

"Food self-reliance depends on mass initiative, not on government directives . . . Self-reliance is not the 'project approach' to hunger," state the authors. They recommend that food aid, controlled by multilateral organizations, "be used as payment for work that directly contributes to creating the preconditions for food self-reliance."

The export of cash crops is attacked as a practice that leaves hunger among the producing population. And the plight of the landless is noted: "being excluded from production means being excluded from consumption . . . People will escape from hunger only when policies are pursued that allow them to grow food and to eat the food they grow."

The authors are not believers in "appropriate technology," claiming that "there can be no separation between technical innovation and social change. Whether promotion of the wealthier class of farmers is deliberate government policy or not, inserting any profitable technology into a society shot through with power inequalities (money, land ownership, access to credit, privilege) sets off the disastrous retrogression of the less powerful majority."

Although the authors are given to repeated rhetorical excesses, readers who can overlook this will find some interesting challenges to many of the assumptions of the general public regarding hunger, food production and development.

As You Sow: Three Studies in the Social Consequences of Agribusiness, MF 05-131, book, 560 pages, by Walter Goldschmidt, 1978, $7.95 from Allanheld, Osmun and Co., Publishers, 81 Adams Drive, Totowa, New Jersey 07512, USA.

For the past several decades, American agriculture has been held up as a model for poor countries. This approach has been criticized for many different reasons. **As You Sow** documents the negative social consequences, within the U.S., of an agriculture that increasingly depends on large-scale farms. Goldschmidt notes, for example, that the number of skilled people in communities with small farms is much higher than in communities with a few large farms. Small farms allow the widespread development of entrepreneurial and management skills that are essential to the development of other rural enterprises. Large farms restrict this process, concentrating management and business learning opportunities in the hands of a few.

Interesting documentation of the relationship between patterns of land ownership and the vitality of rural communities.

Women and Food: An Annotated Bibliography on Food Production, Preservation, and Improved Nutrition, MF 05-229, 47 pages, by Martha W. Lewis, 1979, free to serious groups and individuals concerned with women's development issues, from Office of Women in Development, Room 2720, New State, Agency for International Development, Washington D.C. 20523, USA, limited number of copies available.

This annotated bibliography "was prepared for program planners working to help women in small scale agriculture and family food production. It describes material that should help raise the level of understanding of the crucial role women play in food producing and gathering. It is directed to encourage rural development workers to appreciate the job that home gardening can do to improve the nutrition of the family and the economy of the community. And it presents information on practical and useful manuals and guides."

"Some of the materials are unpublished papers or publications no longer in print. Sources for publications available and suggestions of resources for additional materials and information are provided."

The author of this directory, Martha Lewis, is a "hands-on" horticulturalist and educator, who has served as a consultant to small-scale gardening projects in Jamaica, Somalia and elsewhere, where she has worked directly with rural women. In this directory, she has thoughtfully compiled practically all the information available specifically on women and food from around the world. It is a document which deserves wide circulation.

Historically in the Third World, "women have been responsible for nearly all stages of food raising and preparation while dominating marketing and processing as well." Yet new agricultural technologies and cash crops have mostly been directed towards, and later controlled by, men. "In countries such as Jamaica, with severe unemployment, low wages for semi- or unskilled labor, a great deal of untilled land, and a high percentage of women-headed households, the answer to survival for these families must lie in subsistence food production, small animals, and the family vegetable garden...Greater attention to garden crops and to marketing of fresh vegetables and fruits should be a priority in any planning for rural development."

Environmentally-Sound Small Scale Agricultural Projects: Guidelines for Planning, MF 05-170, book, 103 pages, by the Mohonk Trust and VITA, 1979, $5.75 in U.S., $10.00 international surface mail, $13.25 international air mail, from VITA, also available in French and Spanish.

A sustainable agriculture must be ecologically sound. Practices that are not will degrade and consume the natural basis of agriculture. This book explains why this is true, discussing basic ecological principles and the implications of human alterations of naturally stable systems. Much of the book shows the importance of water supply, soil, and pest management in good planning.

"What are the effects of using groundwater for irrigation?" "What is pesticide persistence?" These are examples of questions posed and answered, with clear text and line drawings. Questions aimed at the effects of different alternatives are especially useful. For example, when considering chemical pesticides and/or Integrated Pest Management techniques: "Can a species-specific pesticide be used?...Does the project design recognize the possibility that the target species

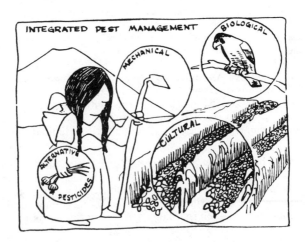

will develop resistance to the pesticide?. . . Are similar pesticides being used locally for health purposes, such as malaria control?. . . Are there plants with pesticidal properties which could be used?"

Also included is an "easy-to-use-in-the-field" methodology for planning and benefits/costs analysis of small-scale projects." This chapter emphasizes the importance of intelligent questions, readiness to learn from local experience, and flexibility.

However, this book does not focus on the tropical and semi-arid conditions which are found in most developing countries; and it does not provide specific details on any techniques suggested (such as building terraces for erosion control, or monitoring local conditions).

One Straw Revolution, book, 224 pages, by Masanobu Fukuoka, 1978, $9.95 from RODALE.

This thought-provoking book is considered a classic text for advocates of what has been called "natural farming" or "permaculture" (see review of **Permaculture II** in this section). The author was trained in microbiology, specializing in plant disease, in industrializing pre-World War II Japan. His studies stressed high inputs of energy, capital, and chemicals to control and, if necessary, combat natural forces. He began to question the wisdom of these practices, and returned to his village to try an alternative approach. Over the years, Fukuoka, through painstaking observation and experimentation, developed a method of farming which mimics the natural succession of plant communities and the self-regenerating aspects of ecosystems. He claims that farming units can produce food and fiber in an almost effortless fashion without chemicals or cultivation.

This low-energy system of agriculture contains the following four principles:

No cultivation—do not turn the soil over, and so avoid injuries that divert productive activity;

No chemical fertilizer or prepared compost—let the plants and animals that make the soil go to work on the soil;

No weeding by tillage or herbicide—use the weeds; control them by natural means or occasional cutting;

No dependence on chemicals—insects and disease, weeds and pests, have their own controls—let these operate, and assist them.

One Straw Revolution is a very readable book, with photos of the author practicing his techniques in the fields. While it is inspirational, some caution should be used in considering its relevance to tropical and Third World countries. First, Fukuoka has successfully practiced his "natural farming" only in temperate climate Japan. Attempts to make the system work in North America are as yet inconclusive. We have heard of no attempts to promote Fukuoka's system in the tropics.

Second, the system requires a great deal of patience, perseverance, and knowledge, possibly only gained by years of experience. Most traditional Third

World farmers do not have the margin of error for experimentation available to nonconformists in developed countries. The immediate problem for most farmers is one of survival, not sustained yields. However, these farmers often do have highly evolved systems of cultivation and extensive traditional knowledge about soils, plants, and local ecology. Quite often they do practice minimum tillage and marginal use of chemicals. Perhaps a dialogue between concerned scientists, development field workers, small farmers, and natural farming advocates could lead to further refinements and broader applications for farming systems such as this one.

Ideas such as those proposed in this book may be seen by many today as wild and unrealistic. Still, Fukuoka's methods may yet prove to be the last straw if the world's heavily subsidized and centralized food and energy systems were to crumble.

Permaculture II: Practical Design for Town and Country in Permanent Agriculture, MF 05-201, book, 150 pages, by Bill Mollison, 1980, Australian $12.00 plus postage from Tagari Books, P.O. Box 96, Stanley, Tasmania, 7331, Australia.

Permaculture II is the second, more practical volume, in a series of two fascinating publications that present an approach to permanent agriculture. These books are based on the author's experience in rural Tasmania and the semi-arid areas of Australia. He and his family are part of an intentional community practicing self-reliance in food, energy, and shelter. "Permaculture" is "primarily a consciously designed agricultural system...a system that combines landscape design with perennial plants and animals to make a safe and sustainable resource for town and country. A truly appropriate technology giving high yields for low energy inputs, and using only human skill and intellect to achieve a stable resource of great complexity and stability."

The author argues for species-diversity in combined agricultural-forestry systems, in place of the energy-intensive mechanized monocultures that are standard in developed countries (and increasingly in developing countries). His book is an impassioned appeal, with numerous design sketches, references, and anecdotes to back up his points. "Without permanent agriculture there is no possibility of a stable social order. We can see the departure from productive permanent systems, where the land is held in common, to annual, commercial agricultures where land is regarded as a commodity. This involves a departure from a low to a high-energy

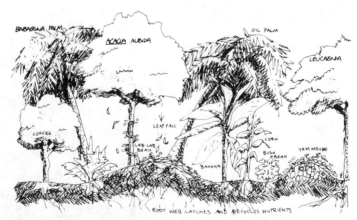

FIG. 5-26: TROPICAL STRATEGIES OF PLANT STACKING AND NUTRIENT RECYCLING. CROPS ARE MULCHED FROM LEAVES AND BRANCHES OF TREES, WHICH HOLD THE LEACHED NUTRIENTS IN AN UNDERGROUND ROOT WEB.

society, the use of land in an exploitive way, and a demand for external energy sources, mostly provided by the Third World."

Permaculture II builds upon the philosophy of Fukuoka and his book **One Straw Revolution** (see review in this section): "of working with, rather than against nature; of protracted and thoughtful observation rather than protracted and thoughtless labor; of looking at plants and animals in all their function, rather than treating any area as a single-product system."

This is essentially a design and planning workbook which provides practical details of how plant, animal, and human communities can be organized as a unit. **Permaculture II** claims to be a realistic and optimistic, yet not utopian book.

A strong emphasis is given to water resource management and homesite integration into the overall plan. Mollison's group employs a method of soil and water conservation known as the Keyline System, with which unproductive and sterile soils can be rehabilitated. Soils are reconditioned by the use of chisel plows and no-tillage implements where tractors or animal traction are available (since these may have been the cause of compacted conditions), or with deep-rooted plants. These efforts, combined with innovative rainwater catchments, contour irrigation dams, ditches, wells, and fishponds, help to provide adequate irrigation water for the next phase of development. Mixed tree crops and field crops are planted successively, as gardens are laid out and kept nourished by plant litter. Planted and built shelters are devised for humans and livestock, and are incorporated into the perennial-based plant community.

This is, of course, an oversimplified account of the Permaculture system, which becomes increasingly complex and organized over time. The author provides only brief overviews of how a Permaculture system might operate in semi-arid and humid areas of the tropics. Since the species selected are applicable to the southern hemisphere and Tasmania specifically, many adaptations would be required before this system could be attempted in other areas. For its insight and inspiration, however, this book deserves wide circulation.

Recommended.

The Future is Abundant: A Guide to Sustainable Agriculture, book, 192 pages, by Tilth, 1982, available for $11.95 plus $1.00 shipping in North America, $2.00 shipping overseas, from Tilth, 13217 Mattson Road, Arlington, Washington 98223, USA.

This book presents a practical inventory for North Americans seeking regional self-reliance in agriculture. It combines agriculture, aquaculture, and forestry to promote more permanent and environmentally-sound approaches to the production of fuel, food, fiber, and shelter. The book consists largely of concise articles, bibliographies, and excellent resource directories. The chapters summarize the various components of what is being called "sustainable agriculture": principles and practices of agricultural ecology, farm and garden management, tree cropping and nursery maintenance, animal husbandry, and community land use.

Although much of the material is geared to the northwestern United States and is somewhat dated, many of the principles and two very useful reference tools can be applied to other regions with proper adjustment for crops, soils, climate and socio-economic factors. The latter refers to two inventories which merit consideration and emulation by those wishing to support small-scale agriculture in other parts of the world: a detailed guide to more than 350 important plant species, and a listing of over 130 sources of seeds, plants, and tools.

The Farmer's Guide, MF 05-171, book, 1053 pages, by the Jamaica Agriculture Society, 1962, out of print.

Written for use on the Caribbean island of Jamaica, the **Guide** contains more than 1000 pages of text on topics of interest to farmers in tropical regions, including soil maintenance, irrigation, animal husbandry, a wide variety of field crops, pest control, and much more. Some of the material is now dated. Recommended.

Agro-Forestry Systems for the Humid Tropics East of the Andes, MF 05-128, booklet, 25 pages, by John P. Bishop, 1980, available from the author (donations for postage or exchanges suggested), at Estacion Experimental Napo/Centro Amazonico Limoncocha, Instituto Nacional de Investigaciones Agropecurias, Apartado 2600, Quito, Ecuador.

This is a set of two papers by Dr. John P. Bishop, an agricultural researcher located in Ecuador. Bishop works with traditional farmers, who are called "colonists," "uncontrolled migrants," "shifting cultivators," and other less favorable things. Bishop is convinced that traditional farmers have an understanding of species, soils and ecology that can be put to use in modified "permanent agriculture" models (see review of **Permaculture II**).

The papers are entitled "Integrated Foodcrop, Swine, Chicken and Fuelwood Production," and "Integrated Timber and Cattle Production." The first covers small farmholdings of 1 to 10 hectares. The second describes a supplemental scheme requiring an additional 30-40 hectares. Included are charts of cropping system timelines and systems models.

Since this information comes from monitoring real farms, it could be directly relevant to conditions in the delicate humid American tropics, and of interest to people in other regions of the world.

Microbial Processes, MF 05-198, book, 198 pages, by National Academy of Sciences, 1979, free from Commission on International Relations (JH 215), National Academy of Sciences — National Research Council, 2101 Constitution Avenue, Washington D.C. 20418, USA.

"Microbes can be marshalled to aid in solving many important global problems including food shortages, resource recovery and reuse, energy shortages, and pollution. Microbiology is particularly suited to make important contributions to human needs in developing countries, yet it has received comparatively little attention. The range of possible applications covers uses by individuals and industries in rural settings, villages, and cities."

This volume contains information on microbial processes within ten subject areas, chosen by a National Academy of Sciences panel. Topic areas include food, animal feed, soil microbes, nitrogen fixation, insect control agents, waste treatment, and antibiotics and vaccines. From each topic area, a small number of examples of the uses of microbes that could be valuable in many developing countries were chosen. These examples include Indonesian tempeh (a high-protein fermented soybean food), and the freshwater fern Azolla pinnata (which harbors a blue-green nitrogen-fixing alga), commonly used to supply nitrogen in the rice paddies of Southeast Asia. For each example, the value, limitations, R&D requirements, suggested readings, and sources of micro-organisms are listed.

How to Perform an Agricultural Experiment, MF 05-188, book, 30 pages, by G. Pettygrove of VITA, 1971, $7.25 in U.S., $7.50 international surface mail, $9.75 international air mail, from VITA, also available in Spanish and French.

"Improved varieties, new fertilizer practices, irrigation, pesticides, new feed mixtures, and improved harvest procedures are just a few of the more important innovations which must be thoroughly tested at the local level before they are passed on to the farmer by extension methods. . .The purpose of this paper is to provide local agriculturalists with an understanding of the basic considerations in the design, execution, and measurement procedure of an agricultural experiment."

Quarterly Review of The Soil Association, MF 05-206, quarterly newsletter, £8/year from The Soil Association, 65 Mortimer Road, Mitcham, Surrey, CR4 3AS, United Kingdom.

This is the newsletter of a worldwide charitable organization dedicated to the promotion of a fuller understanding of the vital relationship between soil, plants, animals, and humans. From the newsletter's worldwide contributors, a subscriber gains the insights and contact with prominent pioneers and advocates of permanent, biological agriculture. Recommended for agriculturalists and students interested in ecology, organic farming & gardening, and nutrition & health. The reviews of books, abstracts and articles are excellent, and not as technical as the **IFOAM Newsletter**. Some excerpts:

"Known to many as 'The Mother of Mulch,' Ruth Stout is now 93 years old and continues to garden the way she has for more than 30 years—with time left over to write and lecture about her methods. What's her secret? By using a year-round mulch on her garden she avoids the laborious ploughing, harrowing, hoeing, weeding, watering, fertilizing, composting, poisoning and cultivating that other gardeners spend their time and energy on."

"Nowhere is the neglect of poor man's crops greater than in the tropics—the very area where food is most desperately needed. The wealth and variety of tropical plant species is staggering, but most agricultural scientists are unaware of their potential. This neglect...occurs largely because the major scientific research centres are located in temperate zones."

IFOAM Bulletin, MF 05-190, journal, 4 times each year, $7.00 domestic, $9.50 foreign from Rodale Research Center, RD1, Box 323, Kutztown, Pennsylvania 19530, USA.

This is the technical bulletin of a very effective organization linking scientists, farmers, students and supporters of what is called "organic, biological, sustainable, permanent, or ecological" agriculture. This group does reputable research on various agriculture topics such as integrated pest management, humus and soil fertility, and lunar influences on plants. They combine this with practical outreach and communication with successful groups and individuals worldwide. Inspiring ideas and individuals abound in IFOAM's ranks.

The Spring 1978 issue contained the following articles: "Ecofarming in Rwanda and Tanzania," "Third World Technology for the United States," and "Organic Farming Research in Europe: Effects of Agricultural Practice on Soil and Plant Quality."

Organic Gardening magazine, MF 05-262, monthly, $12.00 for one year for U.S. residents, $12.00 for one year for foreign residents, from Organic Gardening, Rodale Press, 33 East Minor Street, Emmaus, Pennsylvania 18409, USA; also available as of 1981 is **New Farm** magazine, 7 issues per year, same prices.

This is a magazine on small-scale agricultural techniques that do not use chemical fertilizers or pesticides. Also includes information on appropriate technology tools for agriculture and home use. They have begun to include articles on pedal-powered equipment and other alternative energy sources in recent years.

Handbook of Tropical and Subtropical Horticulture, MF 05-185, book, 186 pages, by E. Mortensen and E. Bullard, 1964, USGPO Stock No. 044-001-00022-5, out of print in 1981; see reviews of **Guide for Field Crops in the Tropics and Subtropics** and the intensive gardening manuals.

"Based upon an extensive survey of available literature...(this manual) is written in layman's terms so that it may be understood by the non-specialist who is called upon to work with farm families in solving their agricultural problems. It also serves as a reference and guide for teaching courses."

"Major tropical fruit, nut, and tree crops are discussed in the second chapter with emphasis on such important points as spacing, pruning, fertilizing, budding, and disease and insect control. A few temperate zone fruits are included to stress that they can be grown only at higher elevations in the tropics, due to chilling requirements. Crops are listed alphabetically and scientific names are given for reference purposes."

"The Handbook continues with a description of all major vegetable crops. Information is presented on seed storage, vegetable varieties, fertilizer recommendations, plant spacing, temperature requirements, soil and cultivation. Major diseases with their controls are presented in a table for easy reference."

This handbook is heavily slanted toward row-cropping, the use of synthetic fertilizers and toxic chemicals, and a highly technical approach to agricultural development. The information it provides, however, on plant varieties, nutrient needs, and nutritional content is very helpful to anyone working in the field. To people seeking locally-available organic resources and techniques, a great deal of this book must be disregarded. Recommended as a secondary reference resource.

Guide for Field Crops in the Tropics and Subtropics, MF 05-184, book, 321 pages, edited by Samuel Litzenberger, reprinted by Peace Corps in 1976, free to Peace Corps volunteers and development organizations in developing countries, from Peace Corps, Information Collection and Exchange, Room 701, 806 Connecticut Avenue N.W., Washington D.C. 20525, USA.

"In the tropical and subtropical areas of the world, food grains make up the bulk of the diet for most people. Food grains together with fiber and specialty crops are also principal cash producers. It is with these commodities that this Guide concerns itself. . .The Guide is designed for use by foreign assistance personnel and cooperators. . .The text (composed of 40 chapters) is written in layman's language. . .The first four are general introductory chapters, and treat rather extensively the important subjects of climate, soil, cropping, and farming systems as related to the tropics and subtropics. The other 36 chapters are divided as follows: 6 on cereal crops, 9 on food legumes, 6 on oil crops, 7 on root or tuber crops and bananas, 6 on major fiber crops and 2 on other cash crops. These chapters do not attempt to deal with the factors of providing inputs such as national supplies of fertilizer, insecticides and fungicides."

This manual is quite a balanced textbook for development workers with interests or skills in agriculture. Of special interest are the chapters entitled "The Tropical Environment for Crop Production" and "Farming Systems for the Tropics and Subtropics," which provide useful information on traditional farming models and tropical ecology.

"There is a possibility that the functions of the slow restoration of soil productivity by native vegetation can be duplicated by man's management of soils without removing them from continued farming. The first step should be to extend the years of continued crop production, by the adoption of technology for individual crops. Such technology is outlined in the 36 chapters on the different crops. An important feature is the addition to soil organic matter by the return of crop residues to the soil, and by the use of manures and compost for producing crops. Adequate fertilization will certainly increase substantially the annual addition of crop roots to the total soil organic matter. . .A second step when feasible may be to grow green manure crops to restore soil organic matter. These may follow a regular crop, or replace a year of crop production. The green manure crops may be utilized for feeding livestock, but the green manure should be plowed under, so that decaying roots and tops will add to fertility. Small farmers are usually not in a position to grow green manure crops. More appropriate would be for them to produce an economic crop as recent research has shown that with the use of soil amendments most soils can be maintained in food production returning only crop residues to the soil."

This book clearly favors field crops and makes little mention of perennials and agroforestry. We do feel that it can be a helpful supplemental handbook for agricultural students, rural development volunteers and extension agents.

Soils, Crops & Fertilizer Use, MF 05-218, book, 103 pages, by Dave Leonard, 1969, free to PC volunteers and development organizations in developing countries, from Peace Corps, Information Collection and Exchange, Room 701, 806 Connecticut Avenue N.W., Washington D.C. 20525, USA.

Developed for Latin America-based volunteers, this book presents basic information on the physical and chemical characteristics of soils, plant nutrition, and soil fertility. The author is openly skeptical about the practicality of organic fertilizers. He emphasizes the use of chemical fertilizers and soil amendments, such as lime, as a means of achieving higher yields in agricultural development projects.

This book should be used along with a training program consisting of actual field analysis of soil structure and texture, chemical soil tests, and pot or plot trials. This will help avoid wasteful use of chemical fertilizers where no net benefits are likely. Although no previous agricultural education is necessary, the reader should have at least a secondary school command of English.

This manual is way over on the chemical side of the chemical fertilizer/organic fertilizer debate. It should be used as a reference if balanced by other publications that describe the advantages of and techniques for organic fertilizers.

Soil Tillage in the Tropics and Subtropics, MF 05-255, paperback book, 310 pages, by R. Krause, F. Lorenz, and W.B. Hoogmoed, 1984, DM 33.50 plus postage from GTZ, Dag-Hammarskjold-Weg 1-2, D-6236 Eschborn 1, West Germany.

"This book is intended primarily for agricultural specialists and their colleagues, extension workers and farmers and also for teachers and students of agricultural engineering and agronomy in the tropics and subtropics. Part I deals with the objectives, principles, and problems of soil tillage in different climatic zones while Part II examines the main implements and systems from the point of view of their purpose, limitations, method of operation and technical data on such topics as linkage and drive systems, etc."

"In many cases the results of subsoiling are scarcely positive and may even be detrimental as regards not only the soil structure but also the financial benefits. The operation requires a high energy consumption and is effective only when there is a genuine hardpan which can be shattered under dry soil conditions. Subsoiling operations must be given careful consideration, especially in developing countries where only limited energy and equipment are available."

This book provides very comprehensive coverage of the various aspects of soil tillage — the preparation, maintenance, and ideally, the enhancement of soils for effective crop production and other agricultural uses. The specific implements and practices for primary and secondary tillage, seed preparation, weeding and other related operations are discussed in great detail, with clear illustrations. The book focuses on the delicate and diverse soils of the tropics and subtropics, and primarily features mechanical means to increase cropping intensity. Handtools and draft animal implements are not reviewed, except for a brief discussion of the rice paddy tools. Despite higher investment costs and potential social problems, mechanical tillage is considered a suitable alternative to handtools and animal power by many agronomists when used in areas where land is extensive and/or labor is not readily available during critical periods. This book is a very helpful addition to the literature on agricultural mechanization, providing a balanced review of environmental impacts and good insights and design criteria for the development of new tools.

Intercropping in Tropical Smallholder Agriculture with Special Reference to West Africa, MF 05-240, paperback book, 312 pages, by Kurt R. Steiner, 1982, DM 41.50 plus postage from GTZ, Dag-Hammarskjold-Weg 1-2, D-6236 Eschborn 1, West Germany.

"There are many advantages of intercropping for smallholdings, and this is obviously the reason why farmers have not abandoned their traditional systems in spite of the efforts of extension services to introduce sole cropping.

"The main advantages of intercropping can be summarized as follows:

— better use of limited resources (light, water, nutrients) resulting in higher yields per unit area and unit of time;

— increased yield stability and reduced probability of incomes falling below the subsistence level;

— reduced crop losses due to weeds, pests and diseases;

— contribution towards soil fertility maintenance through reduced erosion and nutrient leaching; and,

— more balanced distribution of labour requirements throughout the season, as labour peaks for land preparation and weeding are reduced."

This is a valuable reference book for agronomists, extension agents, and agricultural policymakers, on the practice of growing several crops on the same piece of land at the same time. The very scientific language and technical illustrations (particularly of the sections reviewing currently available research and literature) make it less appropriate for use by local development workers of farmers. More information on intercropping in West Africa is contained here than has previously been assembled. The author has effectively organized a large body of data and information to make a persuasive case that traditional and improved intercropping systems are a viable approach to optimizing crop production in West Africa. The book includes an overview of intercropping in smallholder agriculture

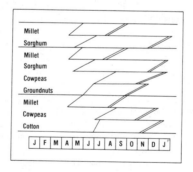

Cropping calendar of sorghum-based cropping
systems in the Sudan Savanna of Nigeria (Norman, 1973).

in tropical Africa, detailed descriptions of the agronomic and socio-economic aspects of this approach, and conclusions and recommendations for further research and extension. This last section is excellent, though lamentably too brief. An appendix contains a number of very useful maps and tables, such as good crop combinations for specific countries and the region. Hopefully, this publication may provide stimulus and helpful guidelines for the compilation of similar information for other countries and regions of the world.

East African Crops, book, 252 pages, by J.D. Acland, 1971, £4.20 plus postage, from ITDG.

The FAO sponsored this reference book on common field and plantation crops in Tanzania, Kenya and Uganda. Horticultural and fodder crops are not covered. Plant characteristics, ecology, field operations, harvesting, pests and diseases are each discussed for each crop. The length of the text varies, presumably with the crop's economic importance, from 30 pages for Arabica coffee to 2 pages for pigeon peas. The importance of some of these crops has likely changed significantly since this book was published in 1971.

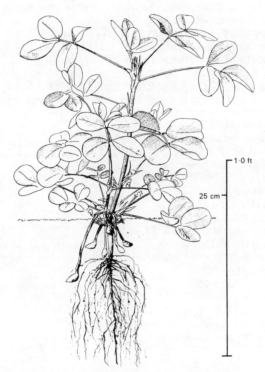

Fig. 74: A groundnut plant of a bunch variety with pods in an early stage of development.

Five Acres and Independence, book, 397 pages, by M.G. Kains, 1973 (reprinted 1935 edition), $3.95 plus postage from Dover Publications, 31 East 2nd Street, Mineola, New York 11601, USA.

Five Acres and Independence is a text on farming for self-sufficiency, emphasizing intensive cultivation techniques on small, diversified farms which depend on legumes, crop rotations and organic manures to supply nutrient needs and maintain fertility. These were the ideas typical of American agriculture before large mechanized farms.

This book should be read as a sourcebook of key knowledge on which to build a self-contained agricultural unit. It is an excellent companion to **The Samaka Guide**, although of less use to tropical countries. The sections on water supply and sanitation, organic crop production and orcharding are highly recommended.

Better Farming Series, booklets, 29 to 63 pages each, 1977 FAO English edition, $3.00-$6.00 each from UNIPUB.

Twenty-six titles have been published in this series of handbooks for a two-year agricultural training course. In each case the text is very simple, containing only basic but useful information, and many drawings. The United Nations Food and Agriculture Organization (FAO) has published this English set. These booklets were originally produced by the Institut africain pour le developpement economique et social (INADES) in French, for use in Africa. (French language editions are available from INADES Formation, 08 B.P. 8, Abidjan, Ivory Coast.)

1. The plant: the living plant; the root (MF 05-137, $4.50)
2. The plant: the stem; the buds; the leaves (MF 05-138, $4.50)
3. The plant: the flower (MF 05-139, $4.50)
4. The soil: how the soil is made up (MF 05-140, $4.50)
5. The soil: how to conserve the soil (MF 05-141, $4.50)
6. The soil: how to improve the soil (MF 05-142, $4.50)
7. Crop farming (MF 05-143, $4.50)
8. Animal husbandry: feeding and care of animals (MF 05-144, $3.00)
9. Animal husbandry: animal diseases; how animals reproduce (MF 05-145, $3.00)
10. The farm business survey (MF 05-146, $4.50)
11. Cattle breeding (MF 05-147, $4.50)
12. Sheep and goat breeding (MF 05-148, $6.00)
13. Keeping chickens (MF 05-149, $4.50)
14. Farming with animal power (MF 05-150, $4.50)
15. Cereals (MF 05-151, $4.50)
16. Roots and tubers (MF 05-152, $4.50)
17. Groundnuts (MF 05-153, $3.00)
18. Bananas (MF 05-154, $4.50)
19. Market gardening (MF 05-155, $4.50)
20. Upland rice (MF 05-156, $3.00)
21. Wet paddy or swamp rice (MF 05-157, $3.00)
22. Cocoa (MF 05-158, $4.50)
23. Coffee (MF 05-159, $4.50)
24. The oil palm (MF 05-160, $4.50)
25. The rubber tree (MF 05-161, $4.50)
26. The modern farm business (MF 05-162, $4.50)
27. Freshwater fish farming ($5.00)

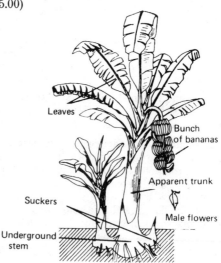

Banana plant

Leaves

Bunch of bananas

Apparent trunk

Male flowers

Suckers

Underground stem

Guide for Small-Holder Coffee Farmers, book, 38 pages, by Dept. of Agriculture, Zambia, 1983, available free from FAO, Via delle Terme di Caracalla, 00100 Rome, Italy.

A set of simple, illustrated instructions showing recommended steps in planting, growing and harvesting coffee. Prepared for small-holder farmers in Zambia; reproduced by FAO.

CAP AT KNEE HEIGHT 45cms-50cm
TO PRODUCE 2 STEMS

Underexploited Tropical Plants with Promising Economic Value, MF 05-225, book, 188 pages, National Academy of Sciences panel report, 1975, $12.00 in United States, $24.00 for foreign orders, quote accession number PB-251 656/5 when ordering from NTIS.

This is a remarkable survey of rarely utilized or underexploited plants which offer promise as sources of food, forage, or industrial raw materials for developing countries. Compiled by a panel of international agricultural experts. 37 species of cereals, tubers, vegetables, fruits, oilseeds, forage, and miscellaneous crops are presented.

What makes this book especially valuable is the inclusion of selected readings on each crop and personal contacts for research and seed sources. The reader can immediately put the information to use. A sampling of the entries:

Grain Amaranths (Amaranthus species): The seeds of these almost totally neglected Central American grain crops have extremely high levels of protein and of the nutritionally essential amino acid lysine, which is usually deficient in plant protein.

Wax Gourd (Benicasa hispida): This large, melon-like vegetable is easy to grow and can yield three crops per year. Its outstanding feature is that the fruit can be kept without refrigeration for as long as 12 months.

Durian (Durio): The common durian is a large, spiny fruit that is enjoyed by many for its taste and disliked by others for its odor. Newly discovered odorless species might be more aesthetically acceptable and could open a world market for this crop.

Jojoba (Simmondsia chinensis): This subtropical, North American desert plant is unique in the vegetable kingdom; it secretes liquid wax in its seeds instead of the glyceride oils secreted by other plants. Liquid waxes are important in industry. They are difficult to synthesize, and the only other source is the sperm whale. The development of jojoba as a crop promises to provide important economic benefits to arid tropical and subtropical regions.

Tamarugo (Prosopis tamarugo): A hardy, leguminous tree, native to the forbidding Atacama Desert in Chile, tamarugo grows through a layer of salt sometimes 1 meter thick. The nutritional quality of its pods and leaves allows sheep to be stocked at rates approaching those of the best forage areas of the world.

Spirulina (Spirulina platensis and Spirulina maxima): These high-protein algae grow in brackish and alkaline waters. Unlike some other algae, spirulina's large clumps make it easy to harvest by net or other simple means. It is palatable and is already eaten in Chad and Mexico.

The Winged Bean: A High-Protein Crop for the Tropics, MF 05-228, booklet, 27 pages, 1975, report of a National Academy of Sciences panel, $8.50 in U.S., $17.00 for overseas orders, quote accession number PB-243 442/1 when ordering from NTIS.

Edible legumes are excellent sources of dietary protein and oils. This report focuses on the exceptional promise offered by a minor tropical legume that has received little scientific attention. The panel that produced this booklet consisted of people who are familiar with this bean. They are convinced that "with research the winged bean can become a significant food crop in the humid tropics," and that this bean may be as important as the soybean in the future. Currently the winged bean is eaten throughout Southeast Asia, although it is not nearly as important a food source there as it could be.

This booklet represents an overview of what is known about the winged bean, its potential and research needs. The booklet is intended for development assistance agencies and institutions concerned with agriculture in tropical countries. A list of researchers who might supply seeds or advice is included.

The winged bean has these characteristics: 1) it grows in humid zones but can also be grown in drier or higher altitude zones (up to 7000 feet); 2) the entire plant is rich in protein and the tuberous roots have ten times the protein concentration of cassava, potatoes, sweet potatoes, or yams; 3) its nitrogen-fixing capacity enables it to grow in poor soils; 4) the whole plant can be eaten and it does not have the bitter beany flavor of the soybean, but is quite tasty; and 5) it is suited to the small farm, requiring staking and harvesting over many months instead of all at one time.

Tropical Legumes: Resources for the Future, MF 05-223, book, 331 pages, by the National Academy of Sciences, 1979, free from Commission on International Relations, JH 215, National Academy of Sciences, 2101 Constitution Avenue N.W., Washington D.C. 20418, USA.

This book features over 30 members of the Leguminosae family of plants, commonly known in English as legumes. These highly valued plants can improve soil conditions and are excellent sources of protein. Rhizobium bacteria attached to growths (nodules) on certain legume roots capture nitrogen from the air, which gives the plants the power to grow in areas subject to erosion, low fertility, and other adverse conditions. Root crops, pulses (beans), fruits, forage crops, fast-growing trees, luxury timbers, ornamentals, and miscellaneous species from within this vast plant group are discussed in this well-documented and illustrated text. Brief descriptions of each species — advantages, limitations, and research needs — are provided. There is a very good chapter that illustrates how legumes can be used for green manures, soil reclamation, and erosion control. Also included are charts of comparative nutritional values for the various species; address lists for seed and germplasm sources; and listings of research correspondents around the world.

A National Academy Sciences panel selected each plant on the basis of:
1. Its potential to help improve the quality of life in developing countries;
2. The present lack of recognition of this potential;
3. Its need for greater attention from researchers and farmers, and increased investment by organizations that fund research and development projects.

Some of the more remarkable species include:

African Yam Bean. "This root crop from Africa produces a nutritious seed, as well as edible tubers and leaves. It can be grown in inherently infertile, weathered soils where the rainfall is extremely high. Although highly regarded among people of tropical Africa, the crop is virtually unknown elsewhere. It has received essentially no research attention or recognition from agriculture researchers."

Moth Bean. "An exceptionally hardy South Asian legume that thrives in hot, dry, tropical conditions, the moth bean produces nutritious seeds and green pods, leafy forage for hay or pasture, and a soil-building 'living mulch' to complement orchard crops and to protect and improve fallow land. Nonetheless, the moth bean remains virtually untouched by modern science and unknown outside the Indian subcontinent. It has characteristics that could make it valuable for torrid, semiarid regions throughout the tropics. It is likely to prove very useful in extending agricultural production into marginal regions — especially those bordering tropical arid zones."

Carob. "The sugar-rich, mealy pulp contained in carob pods has for millenia been a favorite of people in hot, dry areas of the Mediterranean basin. The handsome, drought-tolerant carob tree deserves more research and widespread exploitation in semiarid areas, for in addition to pulp it provides a chocolate substitute, high-protein flour, and an industrial gum, as well as shade, beautification, erosion control, and forage."

Sesbania grandiflora. "This Southeast Asian tree grows exceptionally fast and provides an amazing range of products: edible leaves, flowers, and gum, as well as forage, firewood, pulp and paper, and green manure. It is also used as a shade tree, ornamental, nurse crop, and living fence. It has extraordinarily prolific nodulation and could become valuable for village use and for large-scale reforestation throughout much of the tropics."

Root Crops, Crop and Product Digest No. 2, book, 280 pages, by Mrs. D.E. Kay, 1973 edition out of print, revised edition due in 1985, free to U.K. aid recipients, from TDRI.

This book contains the same kind of information as in **Oils and Oilseeds** (see review), except that this book covers 40 varieties of root crops.

One underexploited root crop is the Jerusalem artichoke. It is "relatively free from serious attacks of pests and disease in the field, although if grown where the drainage is poor, root rot, Sclerotium rolfsii can be troublesome. . .The tubers are ready for harvesting when the leaves begin to wither and die and are usually lifted manually with a fork as required, since they can be 'field-stored' without any deterioration in their quality or flavor. When grown for pig feed the animals are often turned loose on the plot and root out the tubers."

Oils and Oilseeds, Crop and Product Digest No. 1, book, 202 pages, by Mrs. V.J. Godin and Dr. P.C. Spensley, 1971 edition out of print, new edition due in 1985, free to U.K. aid recipients, from TDRI.

Here is information on 36 plants which produce oil and oilseeds. Growth requirements, planting and harvesting procedures, products and their uses, yields and trends in world supplies are noted. The book also contains information that can help in "making a first, tentative selection of possible crops for cultivation in a given set of geographic and economic circumstances."

There are indexes of botanical names, common names, sources of common oils and fats, and an extensive list of sources for further information.

A Farmer's Primer on Growing Rice, MF 05-236, book, 221 pages, by Benito S. Vergara, 1979, from IRRI, P.O. Box 933, Manila, Philippines.

"A progressive rice farmer should understand *why* and *how* the improved rice varieties and farm technology increase production. But recommendations given to farmers often fail to answer questions such as why a farmer incubates seed, why he or she applies fertilizer, or how and when that fertilizer should be incorporated.

"The farmer needs this knowledge to adjust his practices to suit his own unique farm situation."

More than 150 full-page line drawings illustrate the important basic concepts

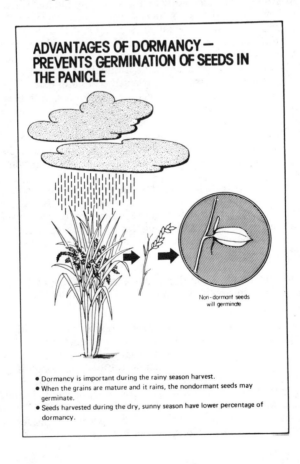

ADVANTAGES OF DORMANCY— PREVENTS GERMINATION OF SEEDS IN THE PANICLE

Non-dormant seeds will germinate

- Dormancy is important during the rainy season harvest.
- When the grains are mature and it rains, the nondormant seeds may germinate.
- Seeds harvested during the dry, sunny season have lower percentage of dormancy.

surrounding rice production, particularly production with the new high yield varieties. Text is limited to a few sentences explaining each illustration. This makes the book accessible to those who don't read well. Non-literates will be able to use the book with the help of a fieldworker who can explain the illustrations. The limited text also makes it easy to produce translations of the English version, and a number of such translations have already been published. The illustrations can also be enlarged, and used as training aids in a poster format.

This book has proven popular in the field, and we recommend it.

Guayule: An Alternative Source of Natural Rubber, MF 05-183, book, 90 pages, by National Academy of Sciences, 1977, free from Commission on International Relations, JH 215, National Academy of Sciences, 2101 Constitution Avenue N.W., Washington D.C. 20418, USA.

"This report examines the state of knowledge and the future promise of guayule Parthenium argentatum Gray, a little-known shrub native to the desert of southwest Texas and northern Mexico that was a commercial source of natural rubber during the first half of this century."

This perennial shrub thrives in arid conditions and can survive heavy frosts. Guayule, after thorough drying, has been found to contain as much as 26% rubber. This rubber can be used to make vehicle tires or any other item currently made with natural rubber. It is a promising plant for use in reforestation of desert fringe lands and is easy to grow. Extraction of the rubber is not technically difficult; in fact, small-scale household extraction is possible. The plant can be cut down to the ground and will grow again from the roots.

The book covers: background and history, botanical information, rubber extraction, agricultural production, rubber quality, economics, research needs, selected readings and recommendations. There are no lists of sources for seeds.

"When guayule grows actively, it produces little or no rubber. If the plant is stressed, growth slows and the products from photosynthesis are diverted into rubber production. Thus when growth slows during cold weather or because of reduced moisture supply the rubber content begins to increase."

Jojoba Publications, from the Office of Arid Lands Studies, University of Arizona, 845 North Park Avenue, Tucson, Arizona 85719, USA.

Jojoba, a plant native to the Sonoran desert in North America, produces a liquid wax with a wide variety of potential uses. This liquid wax possesses "qualities not to be found in any other vegetable oil." One major use is to replace sperm whale oil as a lubricant for high-speed machinery. Historically, the plant has had a wide range of uses among the native American populations in the area.

Much recent research has focussed on plantation cultivation of jojoba. **Jojoba and Its Uses** (MF 05-193, Hease and McGinnies, eds., 81 pages, $5.00 plus $3.00 overseas postage) is a 1972 conference report, including a paper on the potential of using rainstorm runoff farming techniques to increase jojoba yields. A major drawback of plantation cultivation of jojoba is the length of time needed before significant production can be achieved—up to 10 years. Some recent developments indicate that it may be possible to greatly reduce this gap between planting and full production.

Several bibliographies, with over 750 entries, were incorporated into one volume (**Jojoba: A Guide to the Literature**, MF 05-195, by A. Elias-Cesnik, $15.00) in 1982. The Office of Arid Lands Studies acts as a clearinghouse for this and other information on jojoba activity, and arranges for distribution of jojoba seed. **Jojoba Happenings** (MF 05-194) is now published by the Jojoba Growers Association (805 North 4th Avenue, #404, Phoenix, Arizona 85003, USA) six times a year ($15.00 USA, $20.00 foreign, add $6.00 for airmail).

The Nursery Manual, MF 05-245, book, 456 pages, by L.H. Bailey, 1922, out of print.

This out-of-print classic, first published in 1891, is still an authoritative reference on the propagation of plants by means of seeds, layers, cuttings, buds, grafts, and other techniques. The manual was part of a set of one-volume encyclopedias (known as "The Rural Manuals") edited by Dr. Bailey for small farmers and agricultural extensionists. The various means of multiplication are defined and described in detail, with excellent line illustrations. Also included is an illustrated account of the main diseases and insects of nursery stock, which would be most useful to commercial growers. In this case, the remedies for specific infestations need to be reevaluated in light of the current understanding and practice in integrated pest management. For example, some of the milder controls such as applying soap or tobacco solution (nicotine sulphate) may well be worth using, while extremely toxic pesticides such as lead arsenic should be avoided. One third of the book contains an alphabetic list of plants with full directions for propagation of each of them. Unfortunately, given the book's intended North American audience, crops from other climates are inadequately covered here.

Growing Garden Seeds: A Manual for Gardeners and Small Farmers, MF 05-182, booklet, 30 pages, by Robert Johnson, Jr., 1976, $2.30 plus $1.25 postage and handling from Johnny's Selected Seeds, Organic Seed and Crop Research, Albion, Maine 04910, USA.

The author of this booklet is the founder of a successful small-scale vegetable seed production and distribution company. The booklet is informative and easy to understand and apply. A brief description of the process of selecting, harvesting, and storing seeds is followed by instructions for producing seeds from 33 of the most common vegetables grown in North America and Europe. No special tools, expensive facilities, nor education are necessary to master the techniques described.

"Adaptation, usefulness, and quality characteristics of a vegetable variety can be improved...by selection. The basic type is 'Natural Selection,' caused by environmental pressures. For example, in the North in a given year, perhaps only half of the plants of a corn crop will produce mature ears and kernels. Naturally, the ears selected for seed would be chosen from these earlier maturing ears. In this way, Nature forces a crop to either adapt or perish."

"The other type of selection is accomplished by the gardener. For instance, not only would one choose for seed ears of corn which did mature well, but further select the most desirable ear types from what are considered to be the best corn plants." This is of course what traditional farmers have done for centuries in most places.

The main drawback to using this booklet in other parts of the world is that the vegetable varieties are from temperate zones, and many can't be grown in tropical regions except in highland areas. Groups in developing tropical countries could adapt this information to suit their own conditions, by including other crops and consulting with local farmers and extension agents about the best local practices.

Vegetable Seeds for the Tropics, Bulletin 301, MF 05-259, by G.J.H. Grubben, 1978, Department of Agricultural Research of the Royal Tropical Institute Amsterdam, 40 pages, Swiss Francs 12.00 from SKAT.

"This bulletin is meant to give guidelines for local seed growers, for extension workers and for vegetable growers, both commercial and non-commercial, to obtain...the best quality imported seeds and how to improve the quality of the locally produced seeds. It is not a guide for large scale commercial seed production...Bad seed gives an irregular stand, weak seedlings, a low yield and an inferior product. Good seed means a good start for a high yield of good quality vegetables." Climate, day length, seed drying and storage, seed testing, and recommended varieties are discussed. A list of sources is provided.

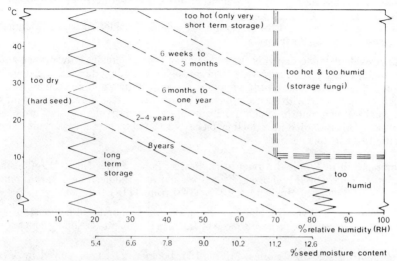

Figure 3. *Schematic diagram illustrating the safe storage period for vegetable seed under various conditions.*

Small Farm Weed Control: An Annotated Bibliography, MF 05-215, book, 175 pages, by J.A.F. Compton, $10.00 from ITDG.

Weed control can play an important role in raising the productivity of small farms. This bibliography surveys literature on weed control tools and techniques for use in rice paddy, highland and temperate zones, humid tropics, and the semiarid tropics. A useful "Overview" introduces the reader to the options available and provides references to specific reviews within the bibliography. Ordering addresses for copies of the reviewed papers are given for readers who are unable to obtain the documents locally.

Simple Assessment Techniques for Soil and Water, MF 05-213, booklet, 37 pages, $3.00 from Coordination in Development, Environment and Development Program, 79 Madison Avenue, New York, New York 10016, USA; available in Spanish.

This fine booklet presents procedures for six simple soil and water tests using mostly locally-available materials such as tin cans and glass jars. The tests include: soil pH, soil texture, percolation, dissolved minerals (in water), sodium in water, and coliform bacteria. Each test is followed by interpretations of the results. "What is surprising is how much useful information can be gained with so little equipment. These tests deal with significant features of soil and water and with reasonable care the results can be meaningful and reliable." Recommended for people doing farming, irrigation, and water supply work. Also good for science teaching.

Test the Soil First, Popular Mechanics Plan No. X630, MF 05-221, 4 pages, 1957, $2.00 from Popular Mechanics.

This article provides a good basic explanation of soil testing, including the preparation of chemical solutions to do the tests and evaluating test results.

No mention is made of local plants which can often be used to measure pH. The author recommends adding chemical fertilizers even when tests for phosphorus, potassium and nitrogen indicate very high levels are already present — a wasteful recommendation. There is also no mention of natural fertilizers or composting.

Basic Soil Improvement for Everyone, MF 05-136, booklet, 31 pages, by James M. Corven, 1983, $5.95 from VITA.

This excellent guide explains the basics of soil management. Advantages and disadvantages are given for various forms of tillage, including u-bar tillage, double digging, chisel plow, and low-till cropping. The importance and methods of composting are presented with special reference to sugarcane trash, forest leaves, paddy husk, and water hyacinth. Mulch, fertilizer and nitrogen-fixing legumes are also discussed. This is a good introductory piece, but it will be useful to consult more specific texts in this section.

Composting in Tropical Agriculture, Review Paper Series No. 2, MF 05-165, booklet, 36 pages, by H.W. Dalzell, K.R. Gray, and A.J. Biddlestone, International Institute of Biological Husbandry, 1979, £1.20 from ITDG.

This book looks at the principles, techniques, and economics of composting as they apply to the specific problems faced by farmers in tropical developing countries.

Composting for the Tropics, MF 05-164, booklet, 27 pages, edited by V.L. Leroux, 1963, Henry Doubleday Research Association, out of print in 1985.

Dating from British colonial days in Eastern and Southern Africa, this booklet describes three successful composting methods developed in present-day Kenya, Malawi and Zimbabwe. The simple but effective methods of three former market gardeners and farmers are presented by the Henry Doubleday Research Association in the hope of sharing practical experience with farmers in other tropical countries.

Perhaps the greatest challenge to tropical agriculture is to maintain soil fertility and productivity at the same time. Often the value of both natural and chemical fertilizers is lost, due to rapid processes of decay and leaching. Using sawdust-based composts, these farmers were able to take advantage of the long decay period of sawdust to slow the breakdown and loss of plant nutrients. Thus, these nutrients remained available for food crops.

The information is valuable but may be of limited use in developing countries because sawdust may not be a material readily available to the rural farm population. Also, available sawdust and wood shavings are often used for fuel.

No illustrations are included, but the written descriptions of the processes are easy to understand, if the reader has a basic knowledge of agriculture.

Backyard Composting, MF 05-134, booklet, 17 pages, by Helga Olkowski, 1975, $1.00 inside U.S., $1.95 outside U.S., from Berkeley Ecology Center, 1403 Addison Street, Berkeley, California 94702, USA.

This is a brief summary of the Berkeley Fast Composting Method, where organic wastes can yield a nitrogen-rich humus in just 14-21 days. The technique covered in this booklet takes attention and human energy, but its high quality and quick results warrant the effort.

"This compost will provide a plant fertilizer as well as act as a soil amendment and mulch; fly and rodent problems will be kept to minimums; high temperatures will be reached that will kill most plant pathogens, and even take apart pesticides."

The drawings depict the tools needed for this method: a system of bins (at least 3), simply constructed of wood, bamboo, or other available materials, to facilitate storing and turning the organic matter; a pitchfork; and a tool to chop, shred, or otherwise reduce the size of organic wastes for easier decomposition. The raw materials are leafy vegetable material, animal manure, kitchen scraps (or market refuse), and a high carbon substance such as sawdust, rice straw, corn husks, etc. Often animals kept in cages prove to be the most effective "compost shredders," and a chopping tool made of a long-handled blade hinged to a block of wood can be very useful. Pitchforks can be manufactured by local blacksmiths.

We recommend this method and booklet to anyone interested in efficient village or city-based compost production.

Composting: Sanitary Disposal and Reclamation of Organic Wastes, WHO Monograph #31, MF 05-166, book, 200 pages, 1956 (reprinted 1971), by H. Gotaas, $17.50 from World Health Organization, Distribution and Sales Service, 1211 Geneva 27, Switzerland; or World Health Organization regional distributors.

This is a solid, important reference book for anyone seriously interested in composting as part of fertilizer policy. Most of the book deals with fundamentals of composting: decomposition, raw materials, sanitary importance, etc. There are 26 pages on composting methods for villages and small towns. The book also includes a chapter on methods and planning for cities. The facts, figures, and illustrations are comprehensive. Coverage of continuous operation low-impact techniques suitable for developing countries such as the Bangalore/Indore method (see illustration) for handling assorted wastes is outstanding.

One feature of this recommended manual is a 23-page chapter on methane gas recovery in farms and villages. It contains important information on gas pressure and the biological composition of waste input into digesters, as well as a good general introduction. However, the design itself is an unproven one, and from our experience not very workable in practice.

How to Make Fertilizers, Technical Bulletin No. 8, MF 05-187, 8 pages, by Harlan Attfield, illustrated by Marina Maspero, also available in Spanish and French, $2.50 from VITA.

Drawings and simple text on composting crop residues and manure, adapted fom a Bangladesh booklet. Uses bamboo bins.

Organic Recycling in Asia, FAO Soils Bulletin No. 36, MF 05-200, book, 397 pages, 1978, from FAO or $23.00 from UNIPUB.

This collection of papers from a 1976 workshop provides a look at the use of crop residues, animal manures and green manures in agriculture in the region. Brief country papers are included, along with working papers on specific topics (such as the relationship of soil fertility to organic matter, composting of municipal wastes, and economics of sewage sludge composting).

"During the period 1973/74, as a consequence of the energy crisis, mineral fertilizers became very scarce and expensive and, because of this, were out of reach of many farmers particularly in developing countries... For many of these farmers organic sources of fertilization are the only means available and may remain so for a long time to come."

In the early part of this century, night soil and straw supplied 70% of the nitrogen needs of Japanese farms. Rice production at the time was 3300 kg per hectare, "higher than the present-day production of rice in any country in South and Southeast Asia."

Where artificial fertilizers are now used, several of the authors note that simultaneous application of organic fertilizers tends to increase the percentage of artificial fertilizers available to the plants.

China: Recycling of Organic Wastes in Agriculture, FAO Soils Bulletin No. 40, MF 05-163, book, 107 pages, 1977, $5.00 from UNIPUB.

This valuable resource book surveys the use and re-use in present-day China of substances such as night soil (human waste), city garbage, and water weeds — which are often ignored or disposed of in both developed and developing countries alike. Good quality photographs, charts, working drawings, and systems diagrams are used to explain the various methods and installations found in China by an FAO/UNDP study team.

Techniques of special interest include:

— The seeding and inoculation of rice paddies with Azolla Pinnata, a small aquatic plant which harbors nitrogen-fixing blue-green algae. These biological fertilizers are cultivated and stored by simple methods.

— The production of fertilizer directly in the fields in silt-grass manure pits. River silt, rice straw, animal dung, aquatic plants, and small quantities of chemical fertilizers (such as superphosphate) are built up in layers in round or rectangular pits and covered by a sealing layer of soil.

— The composting of night soil and city garbage in concrete tanks and mud-plastered piles. High temperatures, conscientious maintenance, and scientific controls assure that disease-causing organisms are kept under control.

— Extensive use of "green manures," crops which are not harvested for animal or human consumption. These are plowed under to add organic matter, improve soil structure, prevent nutrient leaching, and, in the case of leguminous crops, add nitrogen to the soil.

— The widespread use of biogas technology to convert human and animal wastes into fuel and fertilizer. (This topic is covered more fully by other books reviewed in the biogas chapter of the **A.T. Sourcebook.**)

The information presented in this book is easily understandable. It should be remembered that the cost and production figures cited are as reported by the Chinese themselves. It is doubtful that the virtually complete recycling of organic matter as practiced in China can be adopted in many other countries. Incentives may be lacking, and there are often cultural inhibitions against waste handling. Nevertheless, this book identifies effective and proven options which could be attempted throughout the world. Highly recommended.

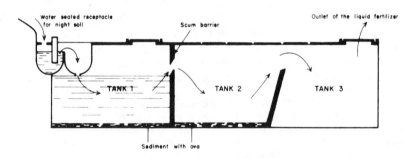

Three-tank fermentation system for treatment of night soil

Small Plastic Greenhouses, Publication No. 2387, MF 05-216, leaflet, 12 pages, by Robert Parsons, 1974, single copies free to serious groups from Publications, University of California, Division of Agricultural Sciences, 1422 Harbor Way South, Richmond, California 94804, USA.

This set of 5 plans for plastic-covered light frame greenhouses can serve as a practical counterpart to **A Global Review of Greenhouse Food Production** (see review). Unlike glass-covered greenhouses, which require expensive glass and heavy wood beams for support, these structures are simply built, low-cost, and lightweight. The plastic film covering, where obtainable, is easily installed and unbreakable. There would be a need to periodically change the worn-out plastic. It is unclear whether the plastic film could withstand heavy tropical monsoon winds and rains.

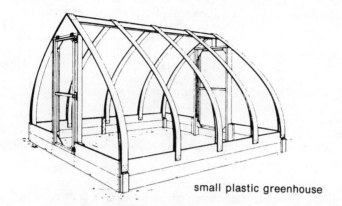

small plastic greenhouse

A Global Review of Greenhouse Food Production, MF 05-181, book, 150 pages, by Dana Dalrymple, 1973, Stock No. 0119-00285, U.S. Government Printing Office, out of print in June 1978, will not be reprinted.

This is an excellent overview of past and recent developments in the field of greenhouse agricultural technology. Although a bit lengthy on statistics, good coverage is given to the important aspects of environmental control: ventilation, carbon dioxide enrichment, the use of evaporative coolers, heating techniques, artificial soil, and the possibility of using distilled sea water in arid nations.

The book is divided into categories of crops, designs, economics and country by country analyses, with distinctions made between the needs in developed and developing nations. With the new potential brought by alternative energy sources, greenhouse agriculture may provide benefits over conventional cultivation under special circumstances. Although capital costs are higher, yields are also greatly increased.

"The Philippines is the only tropical country in the world where greenhouse food production is known to be carried out commercially. The main reason is for protection from heavy summer rains, but the warming effect can also be important at higher altitudes. In addition to physically protecting the plant from the force of the rain, the structure provides other benefits of water control such as reduced leaching of fertilizer, less washing of insecticides, and reduction of disease incidence. Weed control is also made easier. And the harvesting period may be prolonged.

"In 1967, a variation of the high tunnel type, consisting of plastic over bamboo, was tested and found to be suitable for the heavy rains and high winds of the region...The Philippine experience in using simple greenhouses for rainy season fruit production could well be instructive for other tropical nations."

Integrated Pest Management, MF 05-239, book, 120 pages, by Dale Bottrell, 1979, from Consortium for International Crop Protection, 2888 Fulton Street, Suite 310, Berkeley, California 94704, USA.

"Chemical pesticides are — and will continue to be — of considerable importance in food and fiber production, forest management, and public health and urban pest control programs. However, in addition to continuing concern about their environmental and health effects, other disadvantages of heavy dependence on chemical pesticides have become increasingly apparent. The price of synthetic organic pesticides has risen significantly. . .Groups of pests have developed strains that are genetically resistant to the pesticides. . .The resistant groups include some of the world's most serious insect pests affecting agriculture and public health."

"Integrated Pest Management (IPM) seeks maximum use of naturally occurring pest controls including weather, disease agents, predators, and parasites. In addition, IPM utilizes various biological, physical, and chemical control and habitat modification techniques. Artificial controls are imposed only as required to keep a pest from surpassing intolerable population levels predetermined from accurate assessments of the pest damage potential and the ecological, sociological and economic costs of the control measures."

"The presence of a pest species does not necessarily justify action for its control, and in fact tolerable infestations may be desirable, providing food for beneficial insects, for example."

Whereas important advances have been made since this study was done, it provides a good introduction to the subject, with examples of control techniques and strategies.

Large-scale programs of the U.S. Cooperative Extension Service show "the feasibility of IPM on major agricultural crops such as cotton, corn, tobacco, apples, grain sorghum, soybeans, peanuts, and citrus — with little or no reduction in yields and higher net profits than with conventional programs."

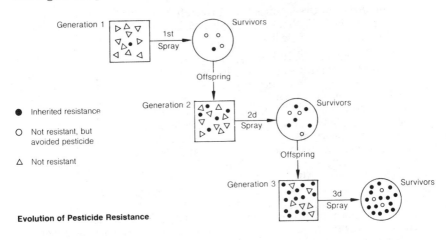

Evolution of Pesticide Resistance

Code of Practice for Safe Use of Pesticides, MF 05-235, booklet, 28 pages, CSIRO, 1976, $6.00 from UNIPUB.

Pesticides are now widely used in developing countries, and farmers and farm workers are often being exposed to great health hazards as a result. While substantially reducing or stopping the use of pesticides may be possible in the long term, protection and handling precautions deserve immediate emphasis. This booklet summarizes the basic steps to minimize the health risks during field application.

"Although any given amount of pesticide is more rapidly and more completely absorbed if inhaled or ingested. . .the most likely route of pesticides into the body is through the skin. . .Most of the pesticides in common use can be absorbed through the skin; this fact is particularly significant when handling the concentrated material. . .More pesticide applications take place in warmer weather, thus giving potentially greater hazard through skin exposure, but in addition, pesticides are absorbed through the skin more rapidly and more completely at higher temperatures...Overalls buttoned at the wrist and neck and a cloth hat should be worn."

The health risks from pesticide use could be greatly reduced by following the no-cost and low-cost recommendations made here. However, the high cost of respirators and the cost and inconvenience of full protective clothing in hot climates mean that substantial risks will remain for pesticide users in developing countries.

SOME EXAMPLES OF BASIC PRECAUTIONS IN THE HANDLING OF PESTICIDES

Protect skin when handling concentrates

Full protection is necessary when using concentrate sprays

Before eating, drinking, or smoking, wash thoroughly and move away from sources of contamination

Bash and bury empty containers to prevent re-use

Stand upwind if burning pesticide cartons

An Agromedical Approach to Pesticide Management, MF 05-231, book, 320 pages, edited by John Davies et. al., from the Consortium for International Crop Protection, 2888 Fulton Street, Suite 310, Berkeley, California 94704, USA.

Safety practices and first-aid for pesticide poisoning victims are treated here. The discussion of how pesticide poisoning commonly occurs is based on experiences in developing countries.

"Past experience has shown that whenever there is increased use of agricultural chemicals human pesticide poisoning soon becomes a major public health problem."

Approved Practices in Soil Conservation, MF 05-130, book, 497 pages, by Albert B. Foster, 1955, $17.35 from The Interstate Printers & Publishers, Inc., 19-27 North Jackson Street, Danville, Illinois 61832, USA.

Written for use in North America, this book sometimes assumes the use of mechanized equipment and chemical inputs not readily available for the local Third World farmer. However, it contains much information which the small farmer and resource management planner would find useful. Emphasis is upon conservation of land cultivated for field crops. Management of woodlands and pastures is also discussed.

Introduction to Soil and Water Conservation Practices, MF 05-241, booklet, 33 pages, 1985, free from World Neighbors, P.O. Box 471, Denpasar, Bali, Indonesia; or CARE-NTB, Jalan Suprapto 37, Mataram, Lombok, NTB, Indonesia.

This comic-book style booklet illustrates simple methods for reducing soil erosion and water runoff on sloping farm land. These methods include erecting barriers or dikes along contour lines and constructing drainage ditches with check dams. All materials used are locally available, usually at no cost.

Barriers may be constructed of wood or bamboo, rocks, or soil. Sometimes certain fast-growing trees, grasses, or pineapple plants are used to strengthen the barriers. They may also provide firewood, fodder, and green manure to increase the fertility of the soil.

Clear illustrations and explanation of basic concepts make this a valuable booklet for fieldworkers and farmers. This is the first book in a series on the topic. For more information on the use of leucaena for soil conservation, see **Leucaena Based Farming**. A number of other booklets on dryland agriculture will be available in the future. Recommended.

Grasses used along the contour dikes or above the rock walls should be cut close to the ground, at a height of about 2 - 3 cm. (about the length of a thumb).

Leucaena Based Farming, MF 05-243, booklet, 29 pages, 1985, free from World Neighbors, P.O. Box 471, Denpasar, Bali, Indonesia; or CARE-NTB, Jalan Suprapto 37, Mataram, Lombok, NTB, Indonesia.

Some farmers in the dry hilly eastern islands of Indonesia have begun to control erosion by planting leucaena trees along the contour lines of their sloping fields. The leucaena trees grow very quickly. When planted closely together in a row along the contour line, they create a live barrier and network of roots which hold soil in place. They also provide firewood, and the leaves can be worked back into the soil to provide a "green manure" rich in nutrients, or used as a feed supplement

In Leucaena-based farming, Leucaena trees are planted in rows between food crops. This system both reduces erosion and helps keep the soil fertile year after year.

for livestock. Other grasses and trees suitable for soil erosion control are also mentioned.

While local farmers have been very happy with the results of this approach, the authors have pointed out to us that it may be wise to avoid exclusive dependence upon leucaena in applying these soil conservation methods. This seems particularly true now, as a leucaena pest has been moving across the Pacific Ocean from Latin America, damaging leucaena trees.

This is the second in the comic-book style series which begins with **Introduction to Soil and Water Conservation Practices**. Recommended.

Guidelines for Watershed Management, FAO Conservation Guide #1, book, 293 pages, 1977, $20.25 from FAO.

A collection of articles and case studies, relevant to conditions in developing countries, including measuring and monitoring of erosion, basic watershed management principles, erosion control methods, terracing, landslide problems, and remote sensing for watershed management.

1. LEVEL BENCH TERRACES

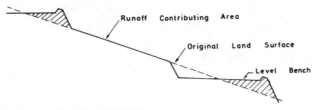

2. OUTWARD SLOPED TERRACES

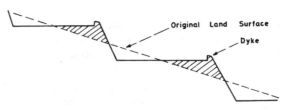

3. CONSERVATION BENCH TERRACES

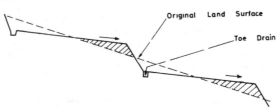

4. REVERSE SLOPED TERRACES

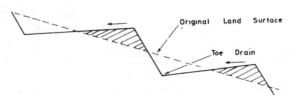

Gully Control and Reclamation, VITA Technical Bulletin 51057-BK, MF 05-260, booklet, 26 pages, by Robert Flannery, 1981, $4.25 in U.S., $4.75 international surface mail, $6.00 international air mail, from VITA.

This manual describes how erosion causes gullies, what can be done to stop gullies from deepening, and how to reclaim eroded soil. Written for South Africa, but useful elsewhere as well. Recommended.

Manual for Calculation of Check Dams, MF 05-244, by Bernhard Hiller, 1979, 85 pages, from Swiss Association for Technical Assistance.

This manual was written for engineers "to calculate and to design check dams for torrent control to prevent erosion under Nepalese conditions. Locally available construction material, the lack of contractors' skill and know-how and the total absence of machinery require a special type of structure: the gravity check dam. This manual shows step by step how to proceed in the construction of such a check dam." Dry masonry and gabion (wire-surrounded) check dams only. Includes detailed information on how to calculate the likely amount of runoff water under extreme conditions.

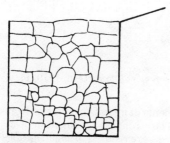

Gabion filled with large material, front side riprapped

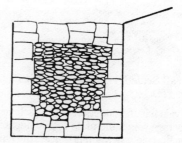

Gabion filled with bigger material at the outside, finer material in the middle

Fig.   21   Filling of a Gabion

Conservation Farming for Small Farmers in the Humid Tropics: Techniques and Tools, MF 05-167, booklet, 19 pages, by Ray Wijewardene, $1.00 from International Institute of Tropical Agriculture/Sri Lanka Program, 133 Dharmapala Mawatha, Colombo 7, Sri Lanka.

A discussion of techniques of no-till agriculture applied to major tropical row crops (maize, rice, grain-legume, etc.) which includes recommendations for planting, weed control and herbicide safety. While providing an introduction to the technology and practices developed by IITA Sri Lanka Program, a strong case is made for the benefits of no-till agriculture (water retention, reduced soil erosion, lowered production costs).

Surface Irrigation, FAO Agricultural Development Paper No. 95, MF 05-219, book, 160 pages, by L.J. Booher, FAO, 1974, $7.25 from Distribution and Sales Section, United Nations Food and Agriculture Organization (FAO); U.S. sales: UNIPUB.

Relevant to both small and large farming units, this is a good introductory reference book on surface irrigation. No special technical background is necessary, although general knowledge of agriculture and basic mathematics is required. This volume is more in-depth than **Small Scale Irrigation**, but it does not cover micro-irrigation with catchments, or runoff irrigation techniques.

The sections on soils, land preparation, ditches, and pipeline distribution systems offer good background material for the later chapters on basin, border, wild flooding, furrow, corrugation and drop irrigation. There are helpful guidelines for choosing an irrigation system based on crop, slope, soil, and available water. Charts and tables show how to plan irrigation systems to suit varying conditions (for example, recommended length and spacing of furrows based on soil type and land slope). Photographs and drawings show both mechanized and low-technology tools and equipment for land preparation and water control.

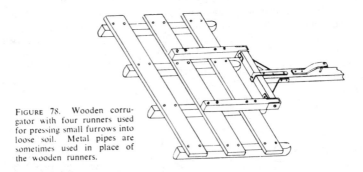

FIGURE 78. Wooden corrugator with four runners used for pressing small furrows into loose soil. Metal pipes are sometimes used in place of the wooden runners.

Small Scale Irrigation, MF 05-217, book, 152 pages, by Peter Stern, 1979, £4.95 from ITDG.

A valuable introduction to the technical requirements of irrigation on farms from .1 hectare vegetable plots to 100 hectare units. "The strongest argument in favor of small scale irrigation is that. . .the human problems are reduced to a manageable scale."

Often people underestimate the quantity of water needed for irrigation. "If all the water consumed in a month by a rural community of 100 people with 250 cattle and 500 sheep and goats were used for irrigation, this would provide two irrigations a month to an area of about a quarter of a hectare."

The author begins with a discussion of moisture conservation techniques, and maximum use of runoff water. He introduces seven principal surface irrigation methods: basin, border, furrow, corrugation, wild flooding, spate and trickle irrigation. Also mentioned are sprinkler systems (too expensive for most uses in developing countries). To calculate water quantities needed, he discusses crop water re-

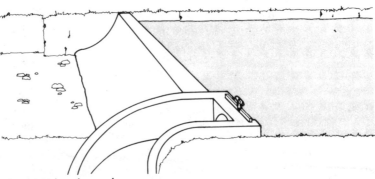

Fig.30 Diversion weir

quirements and soil infiltration rates. The slopes required for different systems and soils are noted. Other topics include design of drainage systems, channels and pipelines, hand- and animal-powered water lifting systems, and measurement of rainfall and water flow in streams. This book gives a basic background, but the reader is expected to get more detailed information either from local agricultural officers or by trial and error.

In areas with very little annual rainfall, micro-irrigation systems can be used. The author gives an example of a farm with annual rainfall of 500 mm, insufficient to produce vegetables. A farmer "could set aside 1000 square meters of his land for catchment irrigation. Of this 1000 square meters, 700 square meters would be prepared as a catchment apron, from which runoff would be fed into a catchment tank, and 300 square meters would be used as a vegetable garden, irrigated by watering can from the tank. In a dry year, with 300 mm of rain, the catchment tank would receive 210 cubic meters of water. . .(and allowing for losses) the garden would then receive 300 mm of direct rainfall plus 330 mm from the tank." Recommended.

Irrigation Principles and Practices, Peace Corps Program and Training Journal reprint series number 5, MF 05-192, book, 112 pages, 1978, available to Peace Corps volunteers and development workers from Peace Corps, Information Collection and Exchange, Room 701, 806 Connecticut Avenue N.W., Washington D.C. 20525, USA.

Clearly written and easily understood, this manual covers water measurement, irrigation water control, drainage, and planning related to irrigation. The appendix includes diagrams for easily-built low-cost tools, and tables for calculating water flow through a weir.

More Water for Arid Lands (Promising Technologies and Research Opportunities), MF 05-199, book, 137 pages, report of a National Academy of Sciences panel, 1974, $11.00 in U.S., $22.00 overseas, Accession No. PB-239 472/4, from NTIS.

"Little-known but promising technologies for the use and conservation of scarce water supplies in arid areas are the subject of this report. Not a technical handbook, it aims to draw the attention of agricultural and community officials and researchers to opportunities for development projects with probable high social value.

"The technologies discussed should, at present, be seen as supplements to, not substitutes for, standard large-scale water supply and management methods. But many have immediate local value for small-scale water development and conservation, especially in remote areas with intermittent rainfall. With further research and adaptation, some of the technologies may prove to be economically competitive with standard methods of increasing the water supply or reducing the demand."

This report attempts to address the need for "fresh innovative approaches to water technologies, particularly those designed to meet the needs of arid regions in the less developed world, where there has often been improper application of practices developed in regions with higher rainfall or more abundant water supplies. Also, we need to reconsider practices developed in arid regions by ancient agriculturalists."

The report is divided into two parts: water supply and water conservation. It includes the following subjects: rainwater harvesting, runoff agriculture, irrigation with saline water, wells, reducing evaporation from water sources, trickle irrigation, use of greenhouses, and other innovative irrigation and water collection methods. For each subject, methods, advantages, limitations, stage of development, and needed research and development are briefly covered.

Although some of the techniques mentioned are high-technology, most of them are simple, low-cost methods gathered from all over the world. Photos and diagrams abound. This booklet has more immediately useful techniques and technology than most of the other NAS reports.

Fields and Pastures in Deserts: A Low Cost Method for Agriculture in Semi-Arid Lands, MF 05-174, large book, 37 pages, 1976, $4.00 (25% discount to readers in developing countries), from Information and Consultation, Wadi Mashash, Bodenacker 10, D-6114 Gross Umstadt/Wiebelsbach, Federal Republic of Germany.

This is a report from an experimental farm, Wadi Mashash, in the Negev desert. The average annual rainfall is about 110 mm, most of which falls within a few hours during the occasional heavy rains. The farm uses simple techniques to trap rainwater; these were developed thousands of years ago, and recently rediscovered through archaeological evidence. The loess soil of the area (often found in other arid regions as well) leads to a high percentage of runoff whenever there is rainfall. Trees are planted in basins, each located at the lowest point of a 250-square-meter micro-catchment area. When there is rain, all of the water runoff from this larger area goes to the tree basins and soaks in — providing all the water the tree needs, even during long periods without rain. Forage crops for sheep are also grown. This technique has been successfully tried in other places. Forty-five drawings and photos are included. This is a fascinating, low-cost method for making productive use of arid land without the use of costly and energy-intensive irrigation canal systems or other expensive technologies.

How to Grow More Vegetables (Than You Ever Thought Possible on Less Land Than You Can Imagine), MF 05-186, large paperback, 150 pages, by John Jeavons, 1982, $10.00 from Ecology Action, 5798 Ridgewood Road, Willits, California 95490, USA (add $3.00 for airmail worldwide). A Spanish translation of the first edition, 88 pages, is available for $5.00 (add $3.00 for airmail); a French translation of the new edition, 159 pages, is available for $8.50.

Ecology Action is devoted to education and research on bio-dynamic/French intensive horticulture. Their gardening classes for the public began on small plots

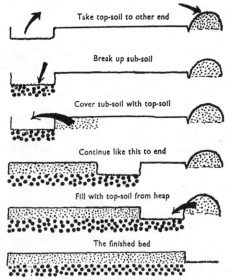

Take top-soil to other end

Break up sub-soil

Cover sub-soil with top-soil

Continue like this to end

Fill with top-soil from heap

The finished bed

An illustration of double-digging (from a different source)

of donated land in 1972. "The series of classes led to the development of information sheets on topics such as vegetable spacings and composting techniques. Many people asked for a book which contains all the information we have gathered. . .This book is the result."

Ten years of research have shown that, as compared to U.S. commercial agriculture, intensive gardening can produce yields that average 4-6 times as much, require ½ (or less) of the quantity of water, and consume only about 1% of the energy. The garden consists of a series of raised planting beds, with heavy additions of organic fertilizers such as manure and compost, prepared by a technique known as "double-digging." "The crops are grown so close to each other that when the plants are mature, their leaves barely touch. The close spacing provides a mini-climate and a living mulch which reduces weed growth and helps hold moisture in the soil."

This edition includes sections on garden planning and fertilization as well as chapters on history and philosophy, preparation of the double-dug raised beds, compost, seed propagation, and companion planting/backyard ecosystems.

An attractive, easy-to-read book with many good illustrations and a great deal of tabular information on seeds, yields, spacings, time to maturity, fertilizing, and insect pests and their plant controls. While successful gardening relies on experience, this book is probably the most useful single reference for getting started in temperate climates. In tropical and subtropical developing countries, the **Samaka Guide** (see review) remains the most directly useful manual on intensive gardening. Simple English and clear drawings make **How to Grow More Vegetables** a useful secondary reference book in the tropics, but the important plant species combinations and soil conditions will be different.

Highly recommended.

The Backyard Homestead Mini-Farm and Garden Log Book, paperback book, 196 pages, by John Jeavons, J. Mogador Griffin and Robin Leler, 1983, $8.95 from Ten Speed Press, P.O. Box 7123, Berkeley, California 94707, USA.

"It is a good idea for all gardeners to keep records of what happens throughout the year in their gardens — what fertilizers have been added, when seeds were planted, what yields were, problems that have come up, and so on. For the mini-farmer, keeping good records is almost essential. To be economically successful, you cannot rely on memory or guesswork. You need to know what worked and what did not so you can plan ahead, and avoid misfortune."

This is a companion volume to the well-known and widely-distributed **How to Grow More Vegetables**, which is considered by many to be the bible of the Bio-dynamic French Intensive Method of intensive horticulture. While it is embraced by many home gardeners and food activists as a means to alleviating world hunger and generating income, this method also has its critics. Some friendly critics see it as one of a number of alternative approaches to conventional chemical-based food production, rather than *the* alternative. Less sympathetic reviewers consider this method's applicability limited to more temperate micro-climates, and its vast economic and agronomic claims as yet unproven on a broader scale.

The authors have sought to provide more technical details and some very useful intensive gardening management techniques and tools. While some of this book's charts and contents are also contained in the earlier reference, it succeeds in filling in some major gaps for prospective "mini-farmers," agricultural extensionists, and development workers. The crops, climates, measurement units, and agricultural assumptions covered in the book are most relevant to temperate regions or uplands in the tropics, and the measurements are in English rather than metric units. Nevertheless, the garden planning maps and guidelines, data logs, and calendars should prove to be very useful references well worth adapting to local crops and circumstances around the world.

The Samaka Guide to Homesite Farming, MF 05-211, book, 173 pages, by Colin Hoskins, 1973, Samaka Service Center, Philippines, out of print in 1981.

The Samaka Guide is an excellent introduction to homesite farming, encompassing the vital skills of homesteading from seed-sprouting to goat-skinning. The **Guide** is closest to the needs and socio-economic level of the bulk of the people in developing countries; the emphasis on village self-reliance, cooperation and respect for traditional methods make it widely applicable outside its Philippine setting.

A summary of the **Guide**'s contents: well drilling, composting, special directions for growing various indigenous vegetables and fruits, building plans for livestock pens, operation of a family fishpond, and care of assorted animals such as rabbits, chickens and water buffaloes. Also briefly covered are home industries, sanitation, tenant rights and barrio fiestas (neighborhood parties). This wealth of information is presented systematically, for an integrated model homestead of 600 to 1000 square meters (⅙ acre). The book is well illustrated and detailed for widespread use.

The Samaka Guide is immediately applicable at the village level (the English used is simple and non-technical). An Indonesian/Malay edition is available from Percetakan Arnoldus, Penerbitan Nusah-Indah, Ende, Flores, Nusah Tenggara Timur, Indonesia for Rp. 250 (1976 price).

Cultivo de Hortalizas en la Huerta Familiar, book, 69 pages, by Hans Carlier, 1978, available from Instituto de Estudios Andinos, Apartado 289, Huancavo, Peru.

Beautifully illustrated, this practical guide to intensive home vegetable gardening was written for the highlands of Peru. All the basics of improved local food production are covered, in simple and straightforward Spanish. Nutritional value of vegetables, varieties, plant propagation, crop rotation, fertilizers, pest management, and simple hand tools are all presented in a systematic and enjoyable format.

This book was written for the direct use of rural people. The safe use of chemical pesticides and fertilizers is stressed, while natural or less dangerous methods of

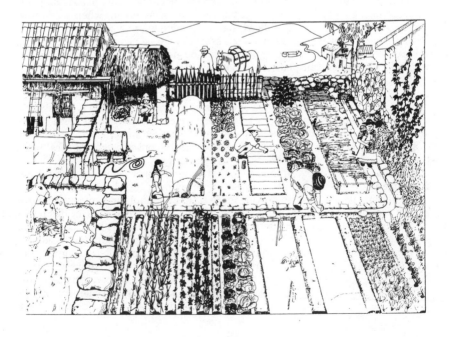

pest control and fertilizer production are preferred. Technically, this is one of the most complete and compact publications on the subject anywhere.

Highly recommended.

Terracing

• Primero separar la tierra buena.
• Hacer los muros con piedras grandes.
• Nivelar el terreno.
• Rellenar con tierra buena.

Gardening for Better Nutrition, MF 05-179, booklet, 64 pages, by Arnold Pacey, 1978, special edition for developing countries is £0.50, price to others is £3.95, from ITDG.

"The subject of this particular manual is the basic technology of horticulture and vegetable growing, as it applies mainly to family gardens."

This is a thought-provoking overview of the practice of nutrition-oriented agriculture for tropical and developing countries. It summarizes the lessons learned

in various projects ranging from Bangladesh to Brazil, and provides a detailed reference bibliography with emphasis on specific regions.

"Although it may include economic activity (such as selling produce at local markets), nutrition-oriented agriculture differs from commercial agriculture in a number of ways:

a. In growing crops because of their nutritional value rather than because of their market value.

b. In concentrating on gardens of a size which most families can cultivate.

c. In appealing primarily to those who produce the family's food — in many communities, the women.

d. In linking agricultural extension work to health education, social education, and community development."

All aspects of gardening vital to the successful implementation of local programs are touched upon, including crop selection, vegetable agronomy, and problems and techniques. The photos and drawings are excellent, the text clear. Highly recommended as a basic resource book, to be complemented by local technical manuals such as Papua New Guinea's **Liklik Buk**, **The Samaka Guide** from the Philippines, **Gardening for All Seasons** from Bangladesh, and **Cultivo de Hortalizas en la Huerta Familiar** from Peru (see reviews).

The Postage Stamp Garden Book, MF 05-204, paperback book, 150 pages, by Duane Newcomb, 1975, J.P. Tarcher, $5.95 from St. Martin's Press, 175 Fifth Avenue, New York, New York 10010, USA.

Subtitled "how to grow all the food you can eat in very little space by intensive gardening techniques," this book covers the same material as **How to Grow More Vegetables** (see listing) in more pages and at a slightly higher price. The emphasis is also on the Biodynamic French Intensive method, although more attention is given to individual vegetable varieties.

If the funds are available, buying and comparing both this book and **How to Grow More Vegetables** would be useful. If not, we recommend Jeavons' book.

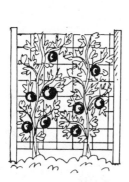 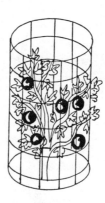 

Gardening with the Seasons, Technical Bulletin No. 46, MF 05-180, 72 pages, by Harlan Attfield, 1979, $7.25 in U.S., $7.50 international surface mail, $10.25 international air mail, from VITA.

Similar in intent to **The Samaka Guide** and **Cultivo do Hortalizas en la Huerta Familiar** (see reviews), this practical booklet describes gardening techniques and vegetable varieties for Bangladesh. **Gardening with the Seasons** is briefer than the others, though it also is well-illustrated and based on extensive field experience. The author has worked on grass-roots rural development projects for 8 years in West Africa, South America and Bangladesh. The Bangladesh gardening project has been a key component of that country's Integrated Rural Development Program.

This booklet contains general guidelines for soil preparation using raised beds, seed germination, transplanting, and companion plants. Brief specific information—when to plant, the best soil conditions, spacing, and care—is provided for 36 vegetables grown in Bangladesh.

"Generally people plant the vegetable they like to eat. But good gardeners should also consider food value because some vegetables are richer in value than others. Vegetables should be selected that are easy to grow under local soil conditions, add richness to the soil, and are resistant to insects and disease. Fresh vegetables are an excellent source of minerals and vitamins. They contain many of the minerals, such as calcium and iron, which the body utilizes to make bone, teeth and blood. They also provide important vitamins, mainly Vitamin A, the B vitamins, and Vitamin C."

Highly recommended.

Intensive Gardening for Profit and Self-Sufficiency, MF 05-191, 159 pages, written and illustrated by Deborah and James Vickery, 1977, from Peace Corps, Information Collection and Exchange, Room 701, 806 Connecticut Avenue N.W., Washington D.C. 20525, USA.

This gardening manual was prepared for use in Jamaican projects but is useful in any area. It starts with simple botany, soils analysis, components of fertility and methods for soil management and improvement. Instruction concentrates on intensive gardening systems, and describes simple tools, composting, irrigation, rotation and companion planting. Useful charts and illustrations.

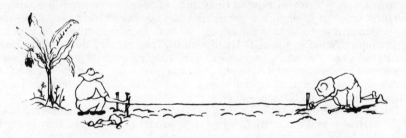

Measure and mark planting beds before working the soil.

The UNICEF Home Gardens Handbook: For People Promoting Mixed Gardening in the Humid Tropics, MF 05-226, book, 55 pages, by Paul Sommers, 1982, $2.00 from UNICEF, Room A-1031, 866 U.N. Plaza, New York, New York 10017, USA.

"Mixed gardens are the result of centuries of trial and error and have evolved into a self-sustaining system that can provide rural households with most of their basic dietary needs and perform many other useful functions." Based upon the author's experience in the Philippines, this fine manual was written to help fieldworkers and planners to establish home garden programs in lowland humid tropical areas. The gardens described are much larger than the yards of some households in developing countries, but the mixed garden approach can be easily modified for smaller holdings. Includes a table of plants and household sprays which repel insects. Highly recommended.

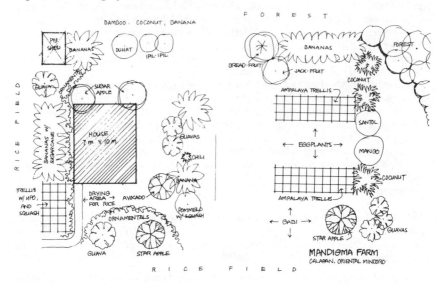

The Basic Book of Organic Gardening, MF 05-135, book, 377 pages, edited by Robert Rodale, 1971, $2.95 from RODALE.

A basic introductory text, this book compresses the essentials of organic gardening into a readable, practical format. For its low price, compact size, and detailed information, it deserves widespread circulation. Although without any illustrations, the book redeems itself with a common-sense approach to plant protection and other standard techniques in the organic arsenal. Organic fertilizer equivalents of the figures cited in the AID **Handbook of Tropical and Subtropical Horticulture** (see review) can be easily calculated — simply substitute ground fish heads or seaweed for urea and superphosphate, for example. Although some of the information applies to temperate climates only, the philosophy and methods are easily adaptable to all conditions.

This book "tells you what soil is, how to create good soil, the fundamental rules about mulching and composting, why you need birds and insects, how to grow marvelous tasting and nutritious fruits and vegetables: it is packed with information about organic materials and foods — and where to get them."

Rodale Press is the foremost publishing and research organization dealing with organic gardening in the world today. Their information, however, is most immediately applicable to temperate climates, and that of the eastern region of the United States in particular. Outstanding and comprehensive Rodale books which deserve mention here are: **How to Grow Vegetables and Fruits by the Organic Method** (1961, 926 pages, $11.95). This book thoroughly covers soils, compost, mulch, and plant varieties (again, mainly from North America) and is well-illustrated. A more advanced treatment intended for experienced gardeners is Rodale's **Encyclopedia of Organic Gardening** (1968, 1145 pages, $12.95). **The Organic Way to Plant Protection** (1966, 355 pages, $8.95) is the best treatment on biological plant pest controls available with specific information on which beneficial bird, insect, companion herb or plant, barrier, decoy, trap or organic pesticide to use with the particular disease or pest invading a particular plant. Those people wanting further information can write Rodale Press for a list of their publications. A series of reprints from their monthly magazine **Organic Gardening** is also available.

The Self-Sufficient Gardener, MF 05-212, book, 256 pages, by John Seymour, 1979, Faber & Faber (London), U.S. edition $10.95 from Doubleday & Co., 501 Franklin Avenue, Garden City, New York 11530, USA.

This large, beautifully-illustrated book was intended as a companion to the author's **The Complete Book of Self-Sufficiency**, which it surpasses. As a practical manual of planting, growing, storing, and preserving home-grown produce in temperate or sub-tropical regions it ranks as one of the clearest and most concise available. Especially useful are diagrams showing how to convert a conventional row-crop garden into an intensive deep digging bed garden. This book covers practically everything under the sun except pest management, and in a most entertaining and informative way.

In developing countries an indigenous gardening resource manual like **The Samaka Guide** (see review) will be much more useful than this book. However, we do recommend it as a supplementary reference in developing countries, and a primary resource in industrialized countries.

Tropical Vegetables, MF 05-257, book, 112 pages, by G.J.A. Terra, Royal Tropical Institute, The Netherlands, 1966, Swiss Francs 12.00 from SKAT.

This volume contains primarily "information on original vegetables of equatorial and subtropical regions. These are more adapted to local soil and climate: leached soils, humidity, temperature, day length, etc., and therefore they can be grown more easily and more cheaply. Moreover, propagation is fairly easy. They offer vast resources for further selection, which has been insufficient until now. Many of them are only found in the wild or half-wild state. They are only locally grown or even locally known as vegetables, and sources of information are few and far between."

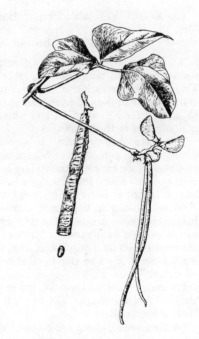

Each plant is identified by Latin name and some English, French, and Spanish common names. Very brief descriptions indicate which part of the plant is eaten, and under what climatic conditions it can be grown.

Vegetables for the Hot, Humid Tropics, annual newsletter, edited by Franklin W. Martin and Ruth Ruberte, Mayaquez Institute of Tropical Agriculture, Puerto Rico; $11.50 for 8 past issues, Accession No. PB 84-112010 from NTIS.

"Within the tropics a relatively few major vegetables are emphasized while the majority of minor vegetables are not well investigated nor even well distributed. It is difficult to get reliable information about varieties and culture of many of these. This annual newsletter. . .is designed to fill a special need through emphasizing the lesser known vegetables and making them available throughout the tropics."

The editors of this newsletter are Dr. Franklin W. Martin and Ruth Ruberte, co-authors of **Edible Leaves of the Tropics** (see review). The newsletter is intended as a means of generating exchanges of seeds and propagating material.

Articles from the 1977 newsletter include: "The Utilization of the Potato in the Tropics," "A Preliminary Checklist of Diseases of Some Local Vegetables in Nigeria," and "Traditional Vegetables of Papua New Guinea."

This newsletter contains moderately technical language. Readers will need to have minimal training in agriculture to appreciate its contents.

Edible Leaves of the Tropics, MF 05-169, book, 240 pages, by Franklin W. Martin and Ruth M. Ruberte, 1975, Mayaguez Institute of Tropical Agriculture, Puerto Rico; available in English (Accession No. PB 84-112531) or Spanish (Accession No. PB 84-112549), $11.50 microfiche, higher for paper copy, from NTIS.

"Green leaves are the most physiologically active parts of the living plant, and as such are usually rich in vitamins and minerals...some contain sufficient protein to supplement an otherwise inadequate starchy diet." The authors discuss green leaves for direct consumption, use of leaves as spices and teas, poisonous tropical leaves, and culture of green leafy vegetables. A lengthy list of tropical plants with edible leaves, giving present geographic distribution, is included.

The AVDRC Vegetable Preparation Manual, MF 05-133, book, 103 pages, by Mrs. T.H. Menegay, 1977, free to Third World countries, from Office of Information Services, AVDRC, P.O. Box 42, Shanhua, Tainan 741, Taiwan.

"Our purpose is to produce a manual for use by field workers such as home economics agents, rural teachers, and public health workers throughout the tropics. Thus, the recipes included here should be simple, tasty, and nutritious. We envision that this project, if given your encouragement, may offer one practical means of uniting food production and nutrition specialists in a concerted attack on malnutrition in the tropics."

This cookbook is an attempt to introduce the soybean, mung bean, tomato, chinese cabbage, sweet potato, and white potato to peoples who have not been exposed to them before, or have not known how to use them in enjoyable meals suited to their culture. The idea of introducing a good crop along with suitable recipes for the local culture has been too often ignored.

"Besides being an important source of protein meal and vegetable oil, the immature soybeans can be eaten as a green vegetable, and the dried beans can be consumed in a wide variety of forms...Fresh green soybeans are a good source of protein, calcium, phosphorus, iron, vitamin A, thiamin, and riboflavin. The dry, mature beans are also rich in all these nutrients, except vitamin A, and contain oil as well."

The recipes are inexpensive and are intended to fit into the cooking habits of many different cultures. There is a list of further sources of information at the back of the book.

"White potato has been referred to as a well balanced, well packaged food. Nutritionally, it is close to sweet potato in calorie production per hectare per day and second only to soybean in protein production per hectare. In addition, white potato is an excellent source of vitamin C and vitamin B."

Hydroponics: The Bengal System, MF 05-189, clothbound book, 185 pages, by J. Sholto Douglas, 1975, $7.95 from Oxford University Press, 16-00 Pollitt Drive, Fair Lawn, New Jersey 07410, USA.

This highly-regarded book, in its 5th printing since its original issue in 1951, is the most complete and comprehensive to be found, incorporating innovations, designs and methods in the field of hydroponics, the science of soil-less cultivation of plants. The author is the originator of the Bengal System of hydroponics, which is suited to developing countries and can be used successfully in areas where normal soil cultivation is impossible, such as in Sahel savannahs or crowded urban areas.

The author is careful to give the reader a solid foundation in the theory of hydroponics. The system uses watertight containers filled with materials such as sand and gravel. This is continuously recharged with a nutrient solution with proper aeration and drainage. Douglas provides many ideas for low-cost systems, including detailed data and types of organic non-chemical fertilizers (the Sharder process) and such construction materials as erosion-resistant mud plaster and alkali-puddled clay.

The systems described are low in capital costs and are labor-intensive, employing existing resources and materials. They are characterized by a high immediate rate of return. Well-illustrated, supported with vital statistics, construction details and maintenance information, **The Bengal System** is a definitive book.

Animal Husbandry in the Tropics, MF 05-232, book, 755 pages, by G. Williamson and W.J.A. Payne, 1980, from Longman Group Limited, Longman House, Burnt Mill, Harlow, Essex CM20 2JE, England.

Here is a reference text which includes brief discussion of some unusual tropical animals such as camels, llamoids (llamas and alpaca), and wild game, as well as the more conventional cattle (200 pages), sheep, goats, pigs, poultry, and buffalo.

Characteristics of common tropical breeds of the economically more important animals are discussed and illustrated with photographs. A section on animal products includes processing of milk and milk products, meat and carcass by-products, and wool production.

The presentation tends to be more academic than many of the practical books reviewed here; background information on climate, health, nutrition, reproduction, species distribution, physiology, and behavior receive relatively more emphasis, while practical management techniques for the low-capital farmer receive less.

Still, there is some discussion of management techniques for the village setting, and we would recommend this book as a solid reference to supplement a more practice-oriented text.

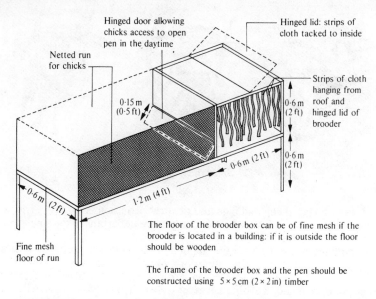

Fig. 13.1 A schematic design of an inexpensive cold brooder suitable for use in the tropics.

A Livestock Manual for the Tropics, book, 406 pages, 1983, $23.00 plus $4.00 postage, from The Jamaica Livestock Association, Newport East, P.O. Box 36, Kingston, Jamaica, West Indies.

This is a solid reference on cattle, goats, sheep, horses, pigs, poultry, rabbits, and bees. Based on experience in Jamaica, the book is intended for use in other tropical areas as well. Sections on pasture and fodder management, and animal diseases, are included, but information on buffalo, ducks and geese is not.

There are two major limitations of this book. The first is that much of the material is oriented towards large-scale commercial producers, with techniques such as artificial insemination, embryo transplant, and the use of milking machines, which are not appropriate for backyard or small commercial operations. The second limitation is the rather hefty price.

Still, there is much good material here, and we would recommend this book for those needing a general livestock text, particularly those in commercial production. The backyard producer will do better to start with one of the books written specifically for small-scale, low-capital operation.

Keeping Livestock Healthy, MF 05-242, book, 322 pages, by N. Bruce Haynes, revised 1985, $15.00 plus postage from Storey Communications, Inc., Schoolhouse Road, Pownal, Vermont 05261.

This is a very good book for those who want to gain a more thorough understanding of animal health and disease. The first 135 pages cover disease prevention, including nutrition, housing, reproduction, animal restraint, and techniques for examination, while the next 170 pages cover various categories of disease (bacterial, viral, parasitic, metabolic, deficient, etc.). Clear explanations of basic concepts such as disease resistance and immunization, and of disease types, set this book apart from other books (or chapters of books) on the topic.

For the small operation in the tropics, however, this book also has several substantial drawbacks. These are primarily due to its U.S. orientation. While the book covers

Figure 2. Steps in tying a rope halter.

cattle, horses, goats, sheep and pigs, the greatest attention is paid to cattle, while pigs, goats and sheep, which are economically more important to the small tropical farmer, get less attention.

A second limitation is that several important diseases foreign to the U.S., such as foot and mouth disease, gain only brief mention. Similarly, special considerations for raising livestock in the tropics are not discussed. Because access to a veterinarian is assumed, **Keeping Livestock Healthy** provides less specific information of medications and dosages than is found in **Goat Health Handbook**, **Sheep Health Handbook**, and **Raising Healthy Pigs Under Primitive Conditions**.

A Planning Guide for Small Scale Livestock Projects, MF 05-246, book, 80 pages, by Gordon Hatcher, from Heifer Project International, P.O. Box 808, Little Rock, Arkansas 72203, USA.

Here is an essential primer for those with limited experience who are considering launching a livestock project. This is not a text on how to raise livestock. Rather, it is a book which outlines the important considerations for project planners. It is packed with useful advice, and warnings, based upon years of experience with community livestock projects in the tropics.

The book discusses cattle, buffalo, sheep, goats, swine, poultry, rabbits, bees and fish, but the general planning approaches can be applied to other species as well. The advantages of local vs. imported animals is discussed, with advice for those who must import animals. Approaches to project monitoring and farmer education are also presented. A good bibliography and list of publishers is included. Highly recommended.

Goat Health Handbook, MF 05-237, spiral bound book, 123 pages, by Thomas R. Thedford, 1983, $4.25 plus $0.95 shipping (overseas airmail postage is $3.40) from Winrock International, Route 3, Morrilton, Arkansas 72110, USA.

The **Goat Health Handbook** will help people raising goats to diagnose and treat their sick animals. A large amount of information is presented in a small amount of space. While the book is generally easy to use, some explanations are so brief that they may be confusing. Often, missing information is presented elsewhere in the book, so a thorough familiarity with the book will reduce this problem.

Because of the complexity of the topic, the author recommends consulting a veterinarian whenever possible. "Remember that diagnosis and treatment are extremely complex tasks...The information in this guide will not allow you to make a specific diagnosis in most cases. However, it can help you to identify symptoms and narrow the range of diseases for treatment.

"The handbook is divided into five major sections:

1. The **Diagnostic Guides** will help you to easily identify a small number of diseases that are the most probable cause of the symptoms that you have observed.

2. The detailed **Disease Descriptions** will allow you to reduce the number of potential diseases even further, provide appropriate treatment, and take preventive measures to avoid further spread of the disease.

3. The section on **Therapy** describes many of the antibiotics and other drugs that are used in the treatment of goat diseases. It provides information on dosage and administration. In addition, this section includes some formulas that are useful in treating sick goats.

4. **Techniques** of treatment are described and illustrated. This section covers tech-

niques of treatment such as the sterilization of instruments and oral administration of medicine, and techniques of normal health care such as castration and foot trimming.

5. The section on **Birth and the Newborn** describes the procedures for both normal and difficult delivery, with illustrations. It also covers pre- and post-delivery care."

An important book for those raising goats, particularly in remote areas.

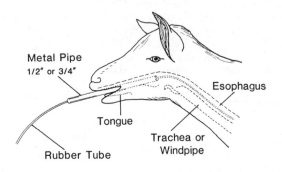

Metal Pipe
1/2" or 3/4"

Esophagus

Tongue

Trachea or
Windpipe

Rubber Tube

Figure 7.   Stomach Tube Technique

Raising Goats for Milk and Meat, MF 05-249, book, 110 pages, by Rosalee Sinn, revised 1985, from Heifer Project International, Box 808, Little Rock, Arkansas 72203, USA.

Goats are an important source of meat and milk in many developing countries. They are well adapted to a wide variety of climates, and can live mainly on a diet

HELPING WITH A DIFFICULT BIRTH

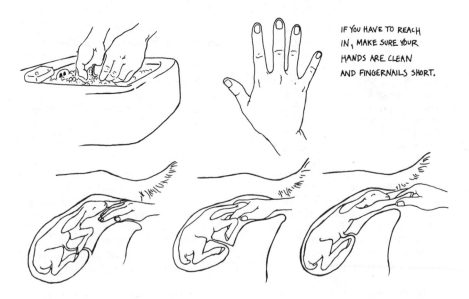

IF YOU HAVE TO REACH
IN, MAKE SURE YOUR
HANDS ARE CLEAN
AND FINGERNAILS SHORT.

of grass and waste plant residue. Due to their small size, goats can be raised on small land holdings, and an entire goat can be eaten by a family before the unrefrigerated carcass spoils in the tropics.

This clearly-presented, comprehensive training manual on the basics of goat raising includes sections on housing, feeding, breeding, kidding (bearing young), milking, slaughtering for meat, record-keeping, and health care. This training course was developed in West Africa, but has been adapted for more general use. The author notes that trainers may wish to supplement it with information on local techniques, when appropriate.

The orientation of the manual is towards small holdings with little capital. It includes instructions for building a disbudding box, and recipes for a variety of cheeses. A filmstrip to accompany this course is also available from the Heifer Project.

Sheep Health Handbook, MF 05-253, spiral bound book, 132 pages, by Thomas R. Thedford, 1983, $4.65 plus $1.25 (overseas airmail postage is $3.40) from Winrock International, Route 3, Morrilton, Arkansas 72110, USA.

This is essentially the same manual as **Goat Health Handbook** (see review above), except that it is written for sheep rather than goats.

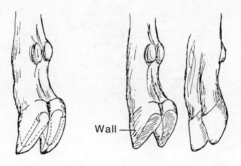

OVERGROWN
Trim to dotted line

PROPERLY TRIMMED

The Homesteader's Handbook for Raising Small Livestock, MF 05-261, book, 256 pages, by J. Belanger, 1974, $12.95 from RODALE.

This is a handbook on raising small livestock on a small scale. Easy to understand, non-technical language. Many drawings and photos, often of build-it-yourself cages, pens, water devices, etc. Covers goats, rabbits, chickens, sheep, geese, hogs, turkeys, guinea fowl, ducks, and pigeons. Written for North Americans moving from the cities back to small farms. No information on vaccinations or shots. Does include a list of further references.

There is a good section on rabbits. Rabbit meat tastes like chicken. France and Italy together produce 200 million pounds of rabbits each year. Rabbits reproduce quickly and have high labor and small space requirements. The fur can be used (tanning instructions are given). Hutches (rabbit cages, usually raised off the ground) can be easily built out of bamboo. This chapter also tells how to make a well-balanced rabbit feed.

Raising Healthy Pigs Under Primitive Conditions, MF 05-250, book, 83 pages, by Dr. D.E. Goodman, from Christian Veterinary Mission, c/o World Concern, Box 33000, Seattle, Washington 98133, USA.

This well-written book is most valuable for its extensive chapter on nutrition. The nutritional value and preparation of a wide variety of possible foods are discussed. Health care, reproduction, and baby pig management are also well covered. The health care section includes short descriptions of the most important diseases, and steps for their prevention and cure.

Non-intensive, low-capital management systems are assumed. Various low-cost feeders, waterers, and houses are illustrated. Information on available breeds of pigs is not given, since it is assumed that most primitive operations will be using locally-available varieties.

Christian Veterinary Mission will provide additional information to pig farmers who are having problems. An outline in the back of the book shows what information is needed.

A FEED MIXER

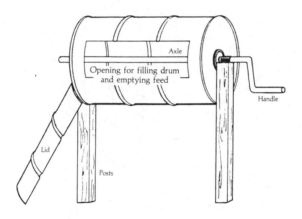

The 200 lb. mixer
made from a 44 gallon drum

Small-Scale Pig Raising, MF 05-254, book, 263 pages, by Dirk van Loon, 1978, $9.95 plus postage from Storey Communications, Inc., Schoolhouse Road, Pownal, Vermont 05261, USA.

This is a complete, well-written, and humorous guide for the backyard pig raiser in the U.S. The book is written for people without prior experience raising pigs, and the author provides a good deal more background information than is usual in a manual of this sort.

This book does not discuss special considerations for raising pigs in the tropics, or with very limited resources. The health section lists common problems, but doesn't provide very much information on treatment, as access to a veterinarian is assumed.

Housing, nutrition, and management are well covered, as are slaughtering and butchering. Good illustrations and numerous useful tips make this a good book for the small pig operation, despite its U.S. orientation, particularly if used in conjunction with **Raising Healthy Pigs Under Primitive Conditions** or **Pigs and Poultry in the South Pacific**.

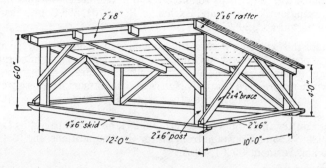

Pig hutches should be moveable. A simple frame with roof (above) may suffice for warm weather, while a four-sided hutch with hinged sides, floor and door (below) is good for winter. Both are built on skids.

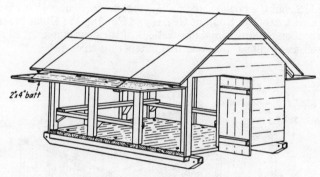

Pigs and Poultry in the South Pacific, MF 05-203, book, 93 pages, by Ian Watt and Frank Michell, 1975, Australian $2.95 from Sorrett Publishing Pty. Ltd., P.O. Box 94, Malvern, Victoria 3144, Australia.

"This book sets out in simple language the information required by extension workers and others responsible for helping the farmer. It deals with all levels, from simple improvisation in a village to semi-intensive and intensive type production."

Two-thirds of the book is on raising pigs. This section covers management systems, pig nutrition, housing, breeds, and diseases. The poultry section covers raising and feeding young chickens, management and feeding of laying hens, timing of replacement of stock, deep litter bedding, ducks, and diseases. Both sections discuss the costs/benefits of home-grown versus commercial feeds. The nutritional needs of the animals are described and some sample home-grown foods are mentioned that will meet these needs.

"By delaying maturity, the bird will produce larger eggs when it starts to lay. If a bird is made to lay eggs at too young an age, most of the eggs it will produce during its life will be small eggs... Lowering the protein content of the feed from 21% to 15% for the actual growing period of the bird is probably the easiest way of delaying maturity. So for the first six weeks a layer chicken is fed a 20-21% protein medicated feed, but at the end of six weeks it is changed over to a grower feed which is also medicated (against Coccidiosis), until the bird is about 24 weeks of age when it begins to lay."

The clear, illustrated presentation should make this book valuable to anyone considering pig or poultry raising in the tropics.

Practical Poultry Raising, Peace Corps Appropriate Technology for Development Series Manual M-11, MF 05-205, book, 225 pages, by Kenneth M. French, 1981, available to Peace Corps volunteers and development workers from Peace Corps, Information Collection and Exchange, Room 701, 806 Connecticut Avenue N.W., Washington D.C. 20525, USA.

Written for the extension worker, this manual focuses on chicken, the most common type of poultry. No fowl knowledge is assumed. Options presented range from "free range" (chickens run free and essentially take care of themselves) to cage systems which may require relatively high capital investment. Marketing considerations are briefly discussed, as are other types of poultry.

Raising Poultry the Modern Way, MF 05-251, book, 220 pages, by Leonard S. Mercia, 1983, $8.95 plus postage from Storey Communications, Inc., Schoolhouse Road, Pownal, Vermont 05261, USA.

Written primarily for small commercial operations in the U.S., this book covers chickens, turkeys, ducks and geese, with more than half of the book devoted to raising chickens for meat and eggs. No consideration is given to conditions outside of the U.S., but the book is otherwise complete, particularly for chickens (for geese and ducks, see **The Book of Geese**, and **Raising the Home Duck Flock**). Includes a section on health, and illustrations of various equipment which can be built, as well as of killing, plucking and butchering chickens.

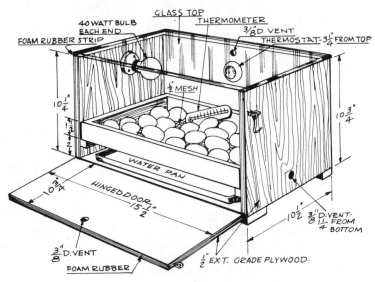

(Figure 17. Homemade incubator.)

Raising the Home Duck Flock, MF 05-252, book, 192 pages, by Dave Holderread, 1978, $7.95 plus postage from Storey Communications, Inc., Schoolhouse Road, Pownal, Vermont 05261, USA.

Ducks are efficient producers of meat and eggs. They are highly resistant to disease and wet weather (both are problems for chickens), and they can tolerate a wide range of temperatures. Ducks are also better at finding their own food, such as snails, insects and weeds, than chickens, and they have a longer productive life for laying eggs than chickens do.

Raising the Home Duck Flock covers all aspects of raising ducks, from selecting stock through incubation, rearing of ducklings, managing adult ducks, and butchering, as well as health care of ducks. The author's experience is mostly in the U.S., and parts of the book reflect this. For example, discussion of the availability of specific breeds in other parts of the world, and special considerations for raising ducks under tropical conditions, are not given much attention. However, the book is very readable, and otherwise complete.

Spraddled legs

Hobbled legs

The Book of Geese, MF 05-234, book, 209 pages, by Dave Holderread, 1981, from The Hen House, P.O. Box 492, Corvallis, Oregon 97330, USA.

"In areas where green grass is available during a good portion of the year, geese can be raised on less grain or concentrated feed than any other domestic fowl, with the possible exception of guinea fowl. Along with being great foragers, geese re-

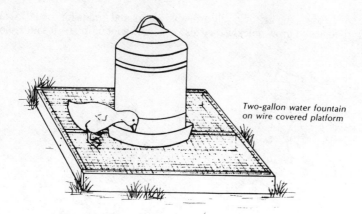

Two-gallon water fountain
on wire covered platform

Adequate receptacles should be provided so their contents are not quickly exhausted and the goslings left without water. Placing water containers on screen-covered platforms is helpful in keeping the watering area dry and sanitary. Waterers should be rinsed out daily and occasionally disinfected.

quire little or no housing in most climates, and, if protected from predators and given reasonably good care, they have an extremely low mortality rate...Along with ducks, they seem to be the most resistant of all poultry to disease, parasites and cold or wet weather."

While geese do not lay as many eggs as chickens or ducks, they grow very quickly and are efficient producers of meat.

This book is similar in organization and completeness to **Raising the Home Duck Flock**, by the same author. The emphasis of the book is upon raising geese in the U.S., and treatment of special considerations for other climates and conditions is limited. Otherwise, all aspects of small-scale goose flock management are covered in this well-written, well-illustrated text.

Poultry Feeding in Tropical and Subtropical Countries, book, 96 pages, FAO, 1965, $10.00 from FAO.

"The importance of poultry (chickens and similar birds) in the production of human food and income is frequently overlooked by leaders and promoters of rural development. Poultry populations can be increased more rapidly than the numbers of other farm animals and therefore poultry raising offers an opportunity for rapid development in countries where a higher standard of human nutrition is being encouraged."

Poultry nutrition and related potential problem areas are covered. The language is technical; this is an academic publication. There are no illustrations. Rather than being a how-to guide, "perhaps the greatest value of this publication will be to point out the wide variety of ingredients which can and are being used for poultry feeding in some of the tropical countries and to review feeding tests and research which have been conducted on these ingredients."

Raising Rabbits, MF 05-208, book, 82 pages, by Harlan Attfield, 1977, $7.25 in U.S., $7.50 international surface mail, $5.75 international air mail, from VITA.

"A rabbit raiser can start with two females and one male and produce fifty, or more, rabbits in one year." This rapid reproduction rate and the rapid growth rate of these animals have made rabbit-raising schemes popular in small development projects. Here is a manual that offers good basic advice for most aspects of rabbit raising.

The author stresses the use of locally-available plants and grains for food. Because rabbits reproduce and grow quickly, they also consume a lot of food — it takes about

*How to hold
an adult rabbit*

*How to hold
a small rabbit*

4 pounds of grain to produce 1 pound of rabbit meat (which tastes much like chicken). Record-keeping to aid in breeding, symptoms and treatment of common diseases, skinning and tanning are all discussed. There is no mention of special problems affecting rabbit raising in the tropics. Cages of bamboo, wood, and wire are shown. In all, a well-illustrated, easy to understand manual.

Rabbit Production, MF 05-247, book, 328 pages, by Cheeke, Patton and Templeton, fifth edition 1982, $12.50 (orders from outside USA add $1.50 handling plus postage), from The Interstate Printers & Publishers, 19-27 North Jackson Street, Danville, Illinois 61832, USA.

This book contains a wealth of good information on most aspects of raising rabbits. Extensive chapters on breed selection, handling and management of rabbits, rabbit nutrition, feeds and feeding, toxins found in feeds, and rabbit diseases make this an excellent reference. For those interested in selective breeding to improve herd quality, there is a section on rabbit breeding and genetics.

Rabbit Production is written primarily for a U.S. audience, and lacks substantial discussion of special considerations for the tropics, or of low-cost techniques.

This is a valuable book for the rabbit raiser, but beginners will find **Raising Rabbits** to be an easier book to start with.

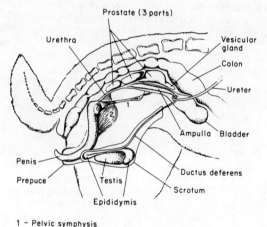

1 – Pelvic symphysis
2 – Ischiocavernosus muscle

Fig. 9-1. The reproductive system of the male rabbit.

The Rabbit as a Producer of Meat and Skins in Developing Countries, MF 05-248, book, 36 pages, by J.E. Owen, D.J. Morgan and J. Barlow, 1977, free to U.K. aid recipients, £0.90 to others from TDRI.

This is a brief discussion of rabbit raising in the tropics, not a how-to manual. "Rabbit production on a relatively small scale, involving minimal inputs, could make a substantial contribution to the supply of animal protein for human consumption in tropical developing countries."

The authors discuss the effects of heat and humidity on rabbits, housing, diseases, feeding, breeds and breeding, slaughter and processing, rabbit skins, and problems with escaped rabbits.

"Heat is one of the most important environmental factors which may affect rabbits in tropical developing countries. At ambient temperatures above approximately

30 degrees Centigrade rabbits suffer increasing discomfort and physiological stress...(these effects) can be greatly reduced by the construction of suitably designed housing...using locally available materials."

A nice introduction to rabbit raising, with a lot of facts and illustrations.

The Water Buffalo, Animal Production and Health Series #4, MF 05-227, book, 283 pages, FAO, 1977, $18.50 from UNIPUB.

This book seems to cover everything one might want to know about water buffaloes, including the types, reproduction, nutrition, diseases, parasites, management, training, and milk and meat production.

Tropical Pastures and Fodder Crops, book, 135 pages, by L.R. Humphreys, £4.20 from Longman Group Limited, Longman House, Burnt Mill, Harlow, Essex, CM20 2JE, England.

Pasture improvement offers the possibility, in some cases, of raising the output and profitability of livestock operations. This text begins with a brief discussion of factors controlling the development of natural grassland, and the philosophy of pasture improvement. It then presents a variety of new and improved pasture plants, discusses pasture establishment, soil fertility and fertilizer, and pasture management practices.

This book was written to be used as a college or university level text. Readers without any botanical background will have to translate from scientific plant species names to the locally-used names.

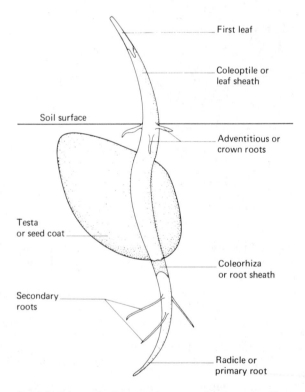

First leaf

Coleoptile or leaf sheath

Soil surface

Adventitious or crown roots

Testa or seed coat

Coleorhiza or root sheath

Secondary roots

Radicle or primary root

fig. 4.1 Schematic diagram of an emerging grass seedling

Tropical Feeds: Feeds Information Summaries and Nutritive Values, MF 05-222 (1975 edition), book, 529 pages, by Bo Gohl, FAO Feeds Information Centre, 1981, $80.50 from UNIPUB.

"Published information on the nutritive value of feeds in general is scanty and when it comes to tropical feeds, it is almost non-existent. Correct data on the nutritive value of local feedstuffs are essential for the expansion of the livestock industry in the developing countries." This enormous reference book covers 650 tropical feeds, most of them tropical plants. "The summaries include short descriptions of the feeds and the more important points in their use." Many references for additional information on specific feeds are provided.

General considerations for use are given at the beginning of each feed group (e.g., grasses, legumes, root crops, oil cakes). In the miscellaneous categories, feeds such as grain distillers' byproducts (left over when alcohol fuels are produced from grain) are discussed. At the end of the book, charts offer such information as crude protein content, metabolizable energy per kilogram, and mineral & vitamin content of the feeds. The index allows the reader to look up plants under either their botanical or English names.

ADDITIONAL REFERENCES ON AGRICULTURE

Liklik Buk has information on a large number of tropical plants; see GENERAL REFERENCE.

People's Workbook covers crops and animals for South Africa; see GENERAL REFERENCE.

Aspects of Irrigation with Windmills and **Syllabus for Irrigation with Windmills** are in ENERGY: WIND.

Food or Fuel: New Competition for the World's Cropland examines the potential effects of large-scale alcohol fuel production on the world food supply; see ENERGY: GENERAL.

Agricultural Tools

Agricultural Tools

There are a number of appropriate technology principles that specifically concern agricultural tools. Such tools should be produced within the country, in part simply because of the large numbers involved. They must be repairable at the local level. With much of agriculture characterized by short intense periods of activity, farmers cannot afford delays caused by equipment failures.

The FAO book **Farm Implements for Arid and Tropical Regions** *includes a list of important general principles for appropriate agricultural tools, some of which go beyond the general criteria for appropriate technology.*

"Such tools should be:
a) adapted to allow efficient and speedy work with the minimum of fatigue;
b) not injurious to man or animal;
c) of simple design, so that they can be made locally;
d) light in weight, for easy transportation (there are also considerable advantages when threshers, winnowers, and machines such as coffee hullers can be easily moved to where they are needed);
e) ready for immediate use without loss of time for preparatory adjustments;
f) made of easily available materials."

Appropriate agricultural tools and equipment should contribute to the broad objective of increasing the viability of the small farm. Where small farmers are currently employing traditional technologies that are inefficient, they often cannot improve this technology because of the leap in scale and capital cost to commercially available equipment. It is therefore the goal of intermediate technology proponents to help fill this gap with good quality tools and equipment that are affordable and suited to the scale of operations of the small farmers.

There is a tendency for equipment development programs and commercial firms to concentrate their energies on tools that are affordable only to the wealthier farmers. This happens in part because of a focus on what technically could be done, without enough attention to the financial constraints faced by the typical small farmer. Contributing factors include the inappropriate application of industrialized, extensive farming strategies to small intensive farming communities, and the failure to include the small farmer in the process of identifying helpful new technologies that can truly fit into the existing farming system. The result is usually either outright failure of innovations to attract interest, or the consolidation of landholdings by wealthier farmers taking advantage of the technology newly available. The position of tenant farmers may become worse, and that of small farmers in general is not improved. Appropriate technology advocates must be careful to avoid repeating these mistakes.

The degree of concentration of land ownership is a key factor in determining if there are opportunities available for appropriate technology strategies in a community. Agricultural technologies developed with and for the smallest farmers can certainly strengthen the viability of their farms. But if most families have no land at all, land reform and the establishment of rural industries may be far more important steps in a positive community development program than the improvement of agricultural tools and equipment.

In most of Asia and much of Latin America, farms are quite small. Under these conditions, most mechanized equipment will not increase the amount of food produced, but will only decrease the amount of labor required. Productivity per acre or hectare may in fact decline, if these large tools require extra space to maneuver and wide lanes to drive or roll over. The appropriate tools under such circumstances, even if supported by unlimited resources, would be very different than those used in most parts of the United States, where the amount of cultivated land per capita is relatively large.

From the national perspective, support for communities of small farms should bring significant benefits. Whereas it has been widely assumed that only the large farm could effectively increase national food production in the struggle against hunger, mounting evidence from many countries indicates that the small farm has higher yields per acre and plays a crucial role in the distribution of food. Small farms also make best use of national capital resources:

"To maintain... a rational growth of capital in a low-income economy, small farms are better suited than large ones, for the small farmers do not experience the same pressure to substitute capital for labor; no one wants to mechanize himself out of a job." (Folke Dovring, in **Agricultural Technology for Developing Nations**).

People interested in improving local agricultural equipment should be looking for technologies that accomplish one or more of the following:

1) Remove labor bottlenecks in the agricultural calendar that are limiting production (e.g., short periods of time when all available labor is fully employed, such as during planting or harvesting).

2) Replace or speed up activities that are extremely inefficient in the use of time (e.g., traditional handmilling). This can free time for more productive activities.

3) Increase the productivity of land (e.g., with irrigation, weeding, natural fertilizers).

The effectiveness of efforts to create relevant new tools can be increased by concentrating on some key agricultural activities. Irrigation is the biggest single factor in increasing crop yields. The successful widespread use of simple hand pumps for small plot irrigation in Bangladesh is a very interesting development. Water-conserving irrigation methods in arid lands have similar potential benefits. Animal-drawn plows, cultivators and carts tend to satisfy the equipment needs of small farms using both intensive and extensive techniques. Good quality hand tools should not be overlooked. Equipment that helps to conserve expensive fertilizers and pesticides will reduce cash costs and have beneficial environmental effects. Greenhouses can conserve water, and in temperate climates offer an early start on the growing season. Crop processing equipment, including threshers and mills, can reduce losses caused by traditional techniques and save much low productivity labor time. Very small-scale equipment of this kind could allow the small farmer to retain full crop production instead of paying 10% or more to the mill owner. Crop storage is a prime area for improvement, as a significant percentage of food produced on small farms may be lost due to poor drying and storage. Low-cost small-scale storage bins are particularly promising (see CROP DRYING AND STORAGE chapter). In many areas it is difficult to move agricultural inputs to the farm, harvested crops from the fields to storage, and surpluses from the farm to markets. Appropriate transportation technologies are thus of great importance to the farmer (see TRANSPORTATION chapter).

In this chapter, the first two entries look at the historical evolution of farm equipment and the effects on labor requirements for different tasks in the United States. They provide some interesting insights. The next three books make recommenda-

tions as to the kinds of agricultural tools and equipment most needed by small farmers in developing countries. Encyclopedic listings of commercially available equipment are contained in **Tools for Agriculture** *and two other books. These and the books documenting older small-scale equipment contain a wealth of ideas that may stimulate the imagination of readers.* **Rural Africa Development Project: An Example of a Farm Level Survey Technique Using Local Resources** *describes a method of identifying labor bottlenecks in the agricultural calendar.*

Eight books on the use of draft animals are reviewed. Animal-drawn equipment and carts are covered in these and subsequent publications, including the ITDG **Agricultural Green Leaflets.**

Hand-operated and solar photovoltaic irrigation pumps are discussed in several entries. Windpowered irrigation pumps are found in the ENERGY: WIND chapter.

On North American family farms, the farmer is often expected to act as mechanic and handyperson during daily farming activities. The well-equipped farm workshop and multiple skills of the farmer have continued to play a powerful role in generating farm equipment innovations. **Mechanics in Agriculture** *is a text for vocational courses teaching the skills commonly required on these farms.*

A large number of small engines are used in the Third World for power tillers, irrigation pumps, crop processing and other applications. The two books on small engines should be helpful references for maintenance and repair of many of these power units.

Most of the remaining entries are plans for threshers, winnowers, corn shellers and so forth, all of them hand or foot-operated, that can be produced in small workshops by local craftspeople. (Three publications reviewed in the ENERGY: GENERAL chapter also discuss pedal-powered agricultural equipment.)

Tools for Agriculture: A Buyer's Guide to Appropriate Equipment, MF 06-256, book, ITDG, 1985, £15.00 from ITDG.

The 1985 edition of **Tools for Agriculture** is an impressive compilation of small-scale equipment and tools from all over the world. Compared with past editions and with the now out-of-print **Tools for Homesteaders** (see next review), there is much more information here from manufacturers based in developing countries.

Each category of tool is introduced with a discussion of key considerations for its use and production. Advantages, costs and benefits, and alternatives are explored. Line drawings of individual items are accompanied by information on capacity and manufacturers' addresses. Many hundreds of items are covered. The careful reader will find that this book alone can provide a considerable education on the topic.

This is the best book available on agricultural tools for developing countries. Highly recommended.

Tools for Homesteaders, Gardeners, and Small-Scale Farmers (A Catalogue of Hard-to-Find Implements and Equipment), MF 06-257, book, 512 pages, edited by Diana S. Branch, 1978, Rodale Press, out of print in 1985.

"Finding the right tools can be the most critical need for a small-scale farmer or a large-scale gardener. It can mean the difference between staying on or leaving the land, between a sense of drudgery or a sense of fulfillment, between a successful harvest or a meager crop, between profit or loss."

"This catalogue will help you to find and use the tools you need to produce food. The tools and equipment described in its pages were selected primarily for their value to the homesteader, truck farmer, and the small-scale organic farmer, but backyard gardeners should also find things of interest."

This very welcome book is the result of a cooperative effort between the London-based Intermediate Technology Development Group and Rodale Press, an American group which researches and publishes many other titles in the fields of alternative energy sources, organic gardening, and waste recycling. "The idea for this book grew out of the ITDG book, **Tools for Agriculture: A Buyer's Guide to Low Cost Agriculture Implements**" (see review).

Thoroughly illustrated and referenced, this catalog of over 700 implements from around the world is an impressive accomplishment. Included are tools for cultivation and plowing; implements for draft animals; tractors and accessories; seeders; planters; harvesting implements; threshing and cleaning tools; processing equipment; tools for composting, mulching and handling sludge; woodlot and orchard equipment; livestock and fish-farming equipment.

The sources for these tools are primarily in industrial countries, although this reflects current manufacturing realities more than any bias on the part of the authors. Most of the best hand tools and animal-drawn equipment for developing countries are included: the Grelinette/U-bar digger, IRRI's push-type paddy weeder, Jean Nolle's various tropical cultivators, the Mochudi toolbar, hand corn shellers, CeCoCo pedal threshers and winnowers, etc. Also featured are interesting articles on topics such as renovating old equipment and experimental stationary winch systems for pulling farm implements.

A minor shortcoming of this book is the lack of price information. Even though inflation would make such prices quickly out-of-date, this would be valuable for comparative purposes.

"There is a strong heritage, especially in the United States but elsewhere too, of the farmer as inventor. A large percentage of our inventors came from rural communities, and virtually all the industries which grew up in the United States in the 1800s started on a very small scale, often as one-man operations. Cyrus McCormick, Oliver Evans, Eli Whitney, even Henry Ford—each grew up on a farm. The inventors of tools we still need will most likely come from the ranks of today's small farmers—and their children."

A very valuable book. Highly recommended.

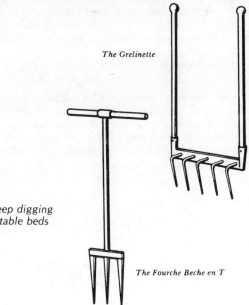

The Grelinette

Hand tools for deep digging
of intensive vegetable beds

The Fourche Beche en T

Guide Book for Rural Cottage and Small & Medium Industries: Paddy Rice Cultivation, MF 06-245, illustrated catalog, 158 pages, by CeCoCo (Central Commercial Company), 1965 (revised 1975), US$15.00 airmail from CeCoCo, Chuo Boeki Goshi Kaisha, P.O. Box 8, Ibaraki City, Osaka, Japan.

CeCoCo is a unique business enterprise. The main interest of this Japanese firm is promoting food production and employment opportunities in developing countries. This "Guide Book" is a catalogue of the hand and machine implements marketed by CeCoCo for the cottage and small industry sector.

A sample of the contents: rice plant cutter, hand seeder and planter, bird and animal scarer & bang (!), noodle making machine, tapioca & fish processing machinery, peanut digger, coconut husk processing machinery, rattan and bamboo weavers, and hydraulic ram pump.

The catalogue includes a wealth of ideas and implements. CeCoCo has drawn heavily fromn the Japanese historical experience, in which a feudal agricultural economy was gradually converted into a mixed modernizing one. The Japanese were able to control their own pace of development and filter Western technologies to suit their own needs. There is much of interest in these examples of ingenious labor-intensive, locally-manufactured agricultural equipment marketed by CeCoCo, many of which contributed significantly to Japan's economic development in the first half of this century.

The Introduction of Farm Machinery in its Relation to the Productivity of Labor in the Agriculture of the United States During the Nineteenth Century, book, 260 pages, by Leo Rogin, 1931, Univ. of California Press, 1966 reprint $20.00 from Johnson Reprint Corp., 111 Fifth Ave., New York, NY 10003, USA.

This 1931 study provides a look at the impact of new agricultural machines on labor requirements for grain production in the 19th century United States. Plowing, harvesting, threshing, winnowing, and seeding operations are discussed in turn. For example, a hand-operated winnower increased tenfold the quantity of grain that a 3-person team could clean and sack in a ten-hour day (400-600 bushels vs. 37.5-45 bushels). Key design features that particularly saved time are identified. This volume is perhaps most relevant for some parts of Africa where extensive farming can still be carried out. The experience described here is not as relevant where intensive farming is practiced, but there are still valuable insights to be had.

American Farm Tools, MF 06-262, book, 121 pages, by R. Douglas Hurt, 1982, $9.95 from Sunflower University Press, Box 1009, Manhattan, Kansas 66502, USA.

Covering nearly the same ground as **The Introduction of Farm Machinery**, this more readable volume has many more photos and drawings of the equipment, but less information on the labor requirements and savings.

The details on plow and harrow design in both books should be valuable to designers of improved small farm implements for better seedbed preparation (for higher production per unit of land area).

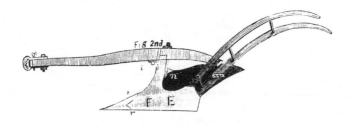

Appropriate Industrial Technology for Agricultural Machinery and Implements, MF 06-237, book, 159 pages, UNIDO, 1979, Document No. ID/232/4, available from Editor, UNIDO Newsletter, Industrial Information Section, UNIDO, P.O. Box 300, A-1400 Vienna, Austria.

This publication is for policymakers and planners, offering a systematic look at the kinds of farm equipment needed for different sizes of farms, and the levels at which the different ranges of farm equipment can be produced. Some examples are given of production facilities for both simple and complex agricultural tools and equipment, including lists of necessary workshop equipment and anticipated operating costs.

There is no mention of the tradeoffs between employment and mechanization, no effort to examine agricultural equipment that would especially support organic agriculture (e.g., manure spreaders and bug light traps), and no concern with participation of the rural people in the design of equipment.

The authors recognize the importance of good quality tools and implements for the very small farms that predominate in much of the Third World. They suggest that "in farms below 2 ha, where farming is carried out in a traditional way, using hand tools and animal-drawn equipment with little or no purchase of inputs...the mechanization policy should be based on: improved supplies of high-yield seeds and fertilizers and single or double cropping; high-quality hand tools such as spades, spading forks, digging hooks and hoes, shovels, ploughs, and singlewheel hoes; animal-drawn ridgers, cultivator ploughs and seed drills; low-cost simple power tillers; effective irrigation and water supply by means of windmills with up to 5 ft (1.5 m) lift or small electric or diesel pumps of up to 15 ft (4.5 m) lift; hand-drills, sickles, scythes, forks, and rakes; hand-operated threshers, crushers, etc.; storage bins of up to 3 ton capacity."

The authors also support the concept of local production of basic tools by rural artisans, with the more complicated equipment to be produced by urban or rural industrial establishments. They note that "government policies must be reoriented to assist artisans in the rural areas. Major efforts are needed to encourage and revive production of hand tools by village artisans through provision of loans at concessional rates, technical assistance, provision of simple design and marketing assistance."

Agricultural Technology for Developing Nations: Farm Mechanization Alternatives for 1-10 Acre Farms, Proceedings of a Conference, MF 06-234, May 1978, limited number of copies remain, from Roy Harrington, Product Planning Department, Deere & Company, John Deere Road, Moline, Illinois 61265, USA.

This collection of papers and panel discussions presents the perspectives of a range of people: World Bankers, multinational agricultural machinery manufacturers, agricultural economists, agricultural engineers and others. Useful as background reading on some of the most promising types of mechanization (broadly interpreted to include animal-drawn equipment) and some of the problems that either prevent or follow mechanization.

For mechanization: "When we began to look at agriculture in other parts of the world, we began to realize that the classic notion that labor is displaced when you increase the number of tractors does not show up in the statistics in a number of countries."

Against mechanization: "...although mechanization raises the productivity of labor, in the conditions prevailing in most Latin American countries its benefits have gone mainly to swell the profits and rents of the large landlords and the wages of the few tractor drivers and other machinery operators...it may be roughly estimated that about three workers are displaced by each tractor in Chile, and about four in Colombia and Guatemala."

What to mechanize: "Mechanization seldom contributes much to the level of crop yields, except in the form of pumps for irrigation." "In Japan...the thresher was more beneficial to farmers than the power tiller."

Ensuring socially useful mechanization: "To maintain...a rational growth of capital in a low-income economy, small farms are better suited than large ones, for the small farmers do not experience the same pressure to substitute capital for labor; no one wants to mechanize himself out of a job."

Farm Implements for Arid and Tropical Regions, U.N. Food and Agriculture Organization Development Paper No. 91, MF 06-242, book, 159 pages, by H. Hopfen, 2nd edition 1981, $12.25 from UNIPUB.

This is a significant resource book. The more important hand tools and animal-drawn machinery suitable for arid and tropical regions in developing countries are presented in clear descriptions and illustrations. Excellent coverage of the historical development of specific tools, such as the evolution of the moldboard plow from ancient to modern times. Included are tillage implements (from simple hand spades to water buffalo-powered cultivators), seeders, sprayers, harvesters, threshers, winnowers, handling and transport equipment, and workshop/maintenance tools.

The author stresses: "A great variety of implements has been developed indigenously all over the world, reflecting the experience handed down for many generations. The introduction of new techniques has the best chance for success when there is a full appreciation of local conditions and traditions before and during the process of introducing new ideas and improvements on the old ones."

"While this publication doesn't claim to be exhaustive, it aims to show how improvement in output can be obtained in areas where it is most needed. It is in fact oriented toward dry-farming tools, rice-growing implements and those used for row crop planting in tropical areas. The implements discussed are not necessarily representative of those found in all areas, but have been chosen because they are common in certain countries; some show how simple modifications can be made to improve performance; others provide examples of the more effective types which have been developed and which could profitably be introduced into areas where they are unknown."

Highly recommended.

Japanese pedal-operated rice thresher: foot action at the pedal drives a rotating wooden drum which knocks the grain loose from the straw held by the farmer; behind the thresher is a cloth screen which prevents the rice and straw from scattering over a wide area.

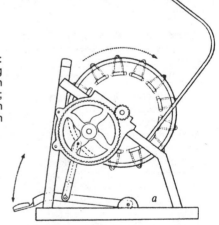

Rural Africa Development Project: An Example of a Farm Level Survey Technique Using Local Resources, MF 06-285, handbook, 26 pages of text and 19 pages of sample charts, by R. Mann, 1974, $11.95 from ITDG.

Report by an ITDG joint project in Zambia. Presents a technique that uses local people without special agricultural training to determine the details of the farming calendar, including the cropping sequence and labor bottlenecks.

"Development plans are missing a link with the dominant type of production unit in agriculture, the smallholder." The author attempts to develop a methodology for determining the needs and circumstances facing the small farmer. He notes that the small farmer "himself is the key to essential information about his activities and his whole environment. His short term and long term memory are excellent, and the data gathered will be meaningless if put through a computer."

The report includes a method for the production of charts which enable the survey team to combine the variables of climatic patterns, crop planting and harvesting, livestock enterprises, off-farm equipment, and more on a single calendar chart. This makes the labor bottlenecks quite evident. Sample questionnaires and charts are included.

A farm-machinery-needs survey system is then described, which is used in combination with the labor chart, to provide "guidelines on which action is taken in engineering development, farm-level testing and modification of equipment, and training procedures for initiating rural craftsmanship and small-scale local manufacture in rural areas" (see following entry).

Expensive, but an interesting model of a low-cost survey technique.

Report on the Farm Equipment Development Project, Daudawa, Nigeria, MF 06-286, report with some dimensional drawings for some of the equipment developed, 111 pages, by John Boyd, 1974, $13.95 from ITDG.

The project objectives were to "study the pattern of local agriculture, assess which labor bottlenecks limit production and introduce appropriate machinery to alleviate bottlenecks." The project itself was in an area with an average farm of 9 acres. The goal was to systematically develop equipment that could be produced locally to meet local requirements. Weeding was identified as a labor bottleneck, and improvements in methods of weed control became a primary objective.

The report includes a description of the farm equipment development project, objectives, obstacles, and results. There are sample questionnaires presented, used to determine the results and local reactions to the project. Dimensional drawings with production and assembly information are included for the following: granule applicator, high-clearance rotary hoe, groundnut lifter, rotary rice weeder, expandable cultivator, and a number of drawings for various attachments. There are photos of much of the equipment built. All of these dimensional drawings are available separately.

Low Cost Rural Equipment Suitable for Manufacture in East Africa, booklet, 82 pages, prepared by S. Minto and S. Westley, sponsored by the East African Agriculture and Forestry Research Organization, 1975, $2.50 from Research Documentalist, Institute for Development Studies, P.O. Box 30197, University of Nairobi, Nairobi, Kenya.

"The purpose of this booklet is to share information about some of the equipment which has been designed and tested for small-scale farmers with the wider audience of those engaged in rural development...The booklet describes, with simple working drawings, illustrations and details of required materials, 23 items of equipment which have been thoroughly tested for their suitability in East Africa." Many of these pieces of equipment have been presented in detail by other organizations, such as the Intermediate Technology Development Group (see reviews of their **Agricultural Green Leaflets**).

Equipment presented: Kabanyolo ox toolframe with plow and cultivator, adjustable inter-row cultivator, Kabanyolo seeder/planter unit, hand-operated seed planter, oxcart frames/wheels/axles/bearings, bicycle trailer, wheelbarrow, water cart, groundnut sheller, hand maize sheller, rotating maize sheller, flap valve pump, IRRI bellows pump, evaporative charcoal cooler, solar dryer, grain storage crib, feed mixer drum, seed dressing drum, ram for building blocks, post hole auger, oil drum bellows forge, anvil, and hydraulic bender.

Animal-Drawn Agricultural Implements, Hand-Operated Machines and Simple Power Equipment in the Least Developed and Other Developing Countries, MF 06-236, report, 45 pages, March 1975, Publication ID/148, free to serious groups, from United Nations Industrial Development Organization (UNIDO), P.O. Box 300, A-1400, Vienna, Austria.

This is a report of a Manufacturing Development Clinic (conference) held in New Delhi, India during October 1974. There were participants from 22 developing countries. One of the valuable parts of the report is 49 photos of agricultural tools.

Farm Tools, book, 235 pages, by Michael Partridge, 1974, $8.95 from New York Graphic Society Ltd., 34 Beacon Street, Boston, Massachusetts 02106, USA.

This is a verbal and pictorial description of the evolution, use and construction of the tools and machines used by farmers in Europe and America during the 18th, 19th, and early 20th centuries. The book doesn't quite reach modern times.

Interesting drawings include a hand-cranked thresher, straw-cutting machine, animal power gear, broadcast sower, metered corn sower attached to a plow, seed drills, harrows, plows and cultivators, mole plow (for drainage) and all kinds of specialized hand tools; over 200 illustrations.

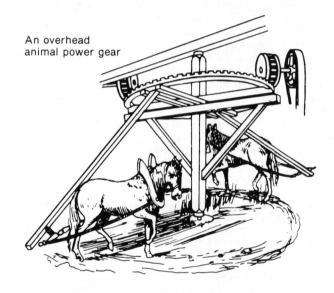

An overhead
animal power gear

There is an interesting but too brief section on power: animal power gears, windmills, water wheels, steam engines. The animal power gear "provided a cheap portable source of power, well within the range of the ordinary farmer's pocket...By about 1860, (this unit) had reached the peak of mechanical efficiency, and most farmers owned one..." Straw-burning steam engines involved the use of "an enlarged firebox with belt-driven rollers at the door for conveying straw into the flames. The compression of the rollers caused the material to 'fan-out' as it entered the firebox, so that each straw caught fire instantly...3½ to 4 lbs. of dry straw would produce the same amount of steam as 1 lb. of the best coal in a well constructed boiler."

Horse-Drawn Farm Implements, Part II: Preparing the Soil, MF 06-271, book, 84 pages, by John Thompson, 1979, $3.00 from John Thompson, 1 Fieldway, Fleet, Hants, United Kingdom.

Each of John Thompson's books on historical agricultural implements gives a sense of the many variations once used. **Preparing the Soil** is a look at animal-drawn cultivators, harrows and rollers. Readers interested in ideas for low-cost harrows and rollers in particular will find them here. Old illustrations are combined with text from agricultural handbooks and encyclopedias of the last century.

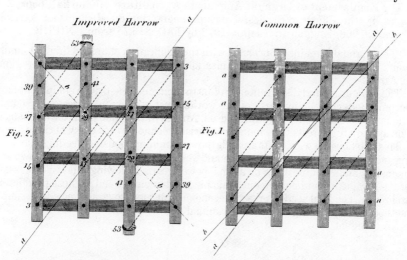

Old Farm Tools and Machinery: An Illustrated History, MF 06-250, book, 188 pages, by Percy Blandford, 1976, $36.00 from Gale Research Co., Book Tower, Detroit, Michigan 48226, USA.

This book is by the author of **Country Craft Tools** (see review). It covers tools and machinery from small farms in Great Britain, Europe, and the United States from the past hundred years. The author briefly looks at animal power gears, carts, steam engines, and the early tractors. Of greater interest, and complete with illustrations, are the chapters on agricultural equipment, most of it capable of being animal-drawn. These include a variety of plows, a cable plow pulled by a stationary

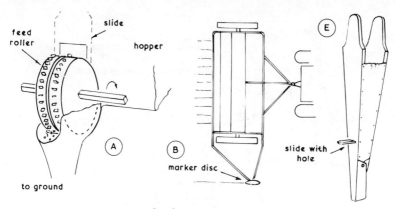

Seeding mechanisms

steam engine, an excellent collection of seeding devices, manure and fertilizer spreaders, spades, forks, rakes, hoes, harrows, cultivators, reaping machines, hand harvesting tools, mowing machines, and tools related to dairy production. There are 30 photographs and more than 150 simple line drawings. The brief text and drawings are usually enough to communicate the basic ideas and principles used, but you wouldn't be able to make any of this equipment from this information alone. Nevertheless, the book is a great source of ideas.

The Employment of Draught Animals in Agriculture, MF 06-241, book, 249 pages, by the Centre d'Etudes et d'Experimentation du Machinisme Agricole Tropical, 1968, English translation 1972 by FAO, $16.75 from UNIPUB.

"This manual is mainly concerned with the application of animal draught equipment, a form of agricultural mechanization predominant in the tropical regions of Africa."

The difficulties and disadvantages of introducing engine-driven equipment have become evident in many parts of the world, most notably in Africa, where draft animals historically have been rarely used. Animal-drawn equipment for mechanization appears to represent the more appropriate technology for many of these areas.

This book begins with draft animals (power, training, housing, feeding, harnessing methods). There is an extensive and very good section on animal-drawn implements, and valuable notes on animal power gears. Following this is a discussion of the rural skills and equipment available for implement and harness production and repair. The final section presents economic considerations, and includes a simple method for calculating the costs of animal power.

An excellent book.

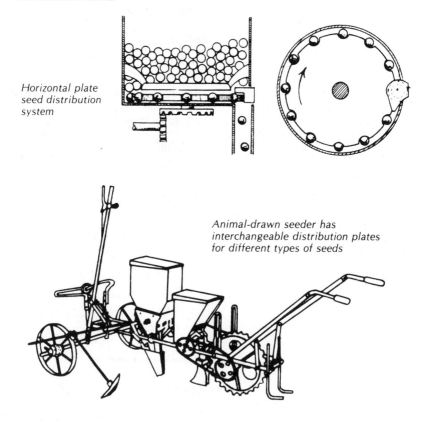

Horizontal plate seed distribution system

Animal-drawn seeder has interchangeable distribution plates for different types of seeds

Animal Traction, MF 06-287, Peace Corps Appropriate Technology for Development Series Manual M-12, book, 244 pages, by Peter R. Watson, 1981, available to Peace Corps volunteers from Peace Corps, Information Collection and Exchange, 806 Connecticut Avenue N.W., Washington D.C. 20525, USA.

"This manual is a practical guide to the selection, care, and training of draft animals, and to the equipment and field techniques used in animal powered farming systems...It is also a guide to animal traction extension, describing how instructors can teach these skills to farmers and other agents." No prior experience with draft animals is assumed in this clearly written and comprehensive book. Includes a brief discussion of some of the possible drawbacks to introducing animal traction to new areas.

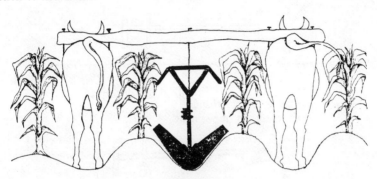

Animal Traction in Africa, MF 06-265, book, 490 pages, by Peter Munzinger, 1982, DM60 (approximately US$22.50) from GTZ (German Agency for Technical Cooperation), Dag-Hammarskjold-Weg 1, D-6236 Eschborn, Federal Republic of Germany.

This lengthy volume contains a thorough compilation of facts, some of them surprising, on draft animals as they are currently used in Africa. "The situation of dairy cows in Africa differs so fundamentally from that of dairy cows in Europe that values determined in Europe can only be applied to Africa with extreme caution. The milk yield of the African cows is considerably lower, with an average of between 2 and 5 liters per day...With an additional supply of nutrients for the animals' working requirements there is no reason to assume that there may be a milk loss, given the relatively low yields. Investigations in Senegal revealed that the weight development of Djakore calves whose mothers were used for draught work and received a working ration was significantly better than that of calves whose mothers did not work."

The equipment section offers some new insights as well. Chapters on crop growing, economic aspects, and sociology round out the general treatment of the material. These are followed by four case studies of draft animal use in different African countries.

Most of the material here is relevant anywhere draft animals are now or may be used in the future.

Draught Animal Power, Renewable Sources of Energy Volume V, MF 06-266, book, 116 pages, ESCAP, 1983, $5.00 from ECDC-TCDC Services, ESCAP Secretariat, United Nations Building, Rajadamnern Avenue, Bangkok 10200, Thailand.

The brief overview of draft animal power as it is found in Asia will be mainly of interest only to people working in the region. This is followed by a listing of institutions involved in related work.

Farming with Work Oxen in Sierra Leone, book, 77 pages, by P.H. Starkey, 1981, Swiss Francs 15.00 from SKAT.

In Sierra Leone, trials of the use of work oxen for plowing and cultivating small farms have shown this technology to be economically superior to the use of tractors. This well-illustrated and detailed description of the project will be of great interest both to readers considering the introduction of draft animals in places where they are not currently used, and to those interested in improving draft animal technology already in use.

The oxen training program is described in some detail, and general conclusions on the applicability of a variety of pieces of equipment are provided.

Recommended.

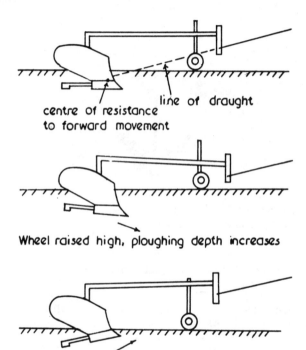

centre of resistance to forward movement

line of draught

Wheel raised high, ploughing depth increases

Wheel lowered. ploughing depth decreases

The Draft Horse Primer: A Guide to the Care and Use of Work Horses and Mules, MF 06-240, book, 400 pages, by Maurice Telleen, 1977, $14.95 from RODALE.

The work horse "is a source of power that reproduces itself, with good care is self-repairing, consumes home-grown fuel, and contributes to the fertility of the soil. Horse farming and organic farming are very comfortable with one another."

This book is interesting for several reasons. First, it shows that some North Americans have either stayed with horse-drawn farming equipment (e.g., the Amish) or are now going back to it. (In the United States, "the demand for draft horses has risen significantly since 1960.") Secondly, it captures some of this practical wisdom which normally passed from farmer to farmer. The author draws from his own experience and brings together "material from booklets published by our

land grant schools during the twenties and thirties when they had an active interest in heavy horses as a major source of agricultural power."

Telleen discusses the breeds of draft horses used in the United States, what to look for when buying, and basic care of these animals. He presents 70 pages on animal-drawn machinery, 50 pages on harnesses and hitches, and 22 pages on logging with horses. Because horse-drawn equipment has historically been far cheaper than mechanized equipment, a smaller farm can finance it.

A thoughtful book that illuminates the potential role of the draft horse in a small-scale, ecologically-sound agriculture.

The Harnessing of Draught Animals, MF 06-270, 92 pages, by Ian Barwell and Michael Ayre, 1982, $5.00 from ITDG.

The type of harness used has a significant effect on the useful power that can be obtained from a draft animal (oxen, horses, donkeys, mules). This volume summarizes what is known about different improved harnesses, in basic principles and in a variety of design examples. Improved harnesses could mean that a single animal could accomplish the job now performed by two animals, in certain situations, or that a single animal or team of animals could cover a larger area, travel a longer distance, or pull a heavier load than was previously possible.

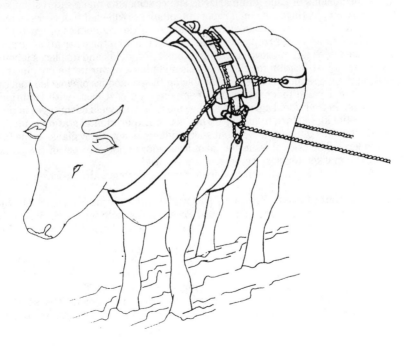

The Harness Maker's Illustrated Manual, MF 06-246, book, 333 pages, 1974, $20.00 from North River Press, Box 241, Croton-on-Hudson, New York 10520, USA.

This is a reprint of a book first published in 1875, when animal-powered transport was normal in the United States. It describes how to make harnesses for horses and mules.

"This book originated from a desire to furnish harness makers with a condensed practical guide suited to the workshop, office, salesroom and stable. It treats of leather as furnished to the harness maker by the currier, its texture, strength, adaptability for specific uses; how to cut, fit, and finish; measuring for a harness; complete tables for lengths and widths for cutting the various classes in use, whether for carriage, farm, or road; bridles, halters, horse-boots, mountings, bits, etc."

The language used is slightly out-of-date and may at times present trouble to the reader. The instructions on horse harness construction and design are excellent.

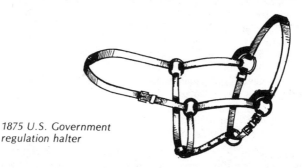

*1875 U.S. Government
regulation halter*

Animal Draught Technology: An Annotated Bibliography, MF 06-263, book, 90 pages, by Jane Bartlett and David Gibbon, 1984, $4.95 from ITDG.

This bibliography begins with a general review of the major topics and issues within this field. Several hundred papers, books, and articles are described and the conclusions of each summarized. The conclusions make interesting reading.

For example, the entry on a report on bullocks, wheeled tool carriers and tractors: "Reviews the available survey evidence on the economics of tractor cultivation for the semi-arid tropics of India. Found that tractor cultivation as generally practised does not improve cropping intensity or yields and displaces labour. This provides a justification for the emphasis on bullock power in the farming systems research programme. Evidence available on the economics of wheeled tool carriers is reviewed. Such machines cannot compete on a cost basis with traditional implements in traditional agriculture. They must provide yield advantages in the order of 200-400 kg/hectare to justify higher costs. Experimental station evidence suggests that this can be achieved, but such evidence is not yet available at the farmer's field level. The critical issue for farm level adoption is the cost of the equipment and the market for service or cooperative use."

For most of the entries in this bibliography, ordering addresses are not provided.

The Animal-Drawn Wheeled Tool Carrier, Information Bulletin 8, MF 06-264, booklet, 13 pages, International Crops Research Institute for the Semi-Arid Tropics (ICRISAT), 1983, available from ICRISAT, Patancheru P.O., Andhra Pradesh 502 324, India.

Wheeled tool carriers represent an important innovation in equipment for use with draft animals. Different attachments are fitted to the basic unit for the different operations of plowing, harrowing, cultivating, etc. The major drawback of the tool carrier is that it costs too much for most small farmers. This short booklet nicely introduces this tool, with many photos to illustrate the many applications.

The Tropicultor Operator's Manual: Field Operations, MF 06-278, booklet, 62 pages, by R.K. Bansal, 1985, available from ICRISAT, Patancheru P.O., Andhra Pradesh 502 324, India.

The most famous wheeled tool carrier is probably the tropicultor, developed by Jean Nolle. This booklet of photographs with English instructions shows the operator how to attach the various tools and use the unit to perform all needed field operations.

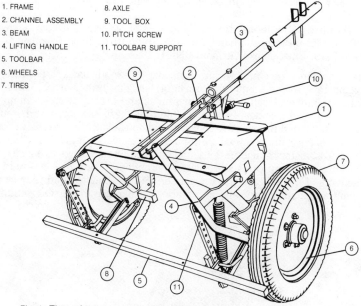

1. FRAME
2. CHANNEL ASSEMBLY
3. BEAM
4. LIFTING HANDLE
5. TOOLBAR
6. WHEELS
7. TIRES
8. AXLE
9. TOOL BOX
10. PITCH SCREW
11. TOOLBAR SUPPORT

Fig. 1. The major components of the Tropicultor.

Carts, AGL No. 44, MF 06-233, dimensional drawings, 8 pages, 1973, ITDG, out of print in 1985.

Detailed drawings are given for 3 different cart designs. The method of fabrication is clear from the drawings. The first two designs require the use of the ITDG Metal Bending Machine (see review) for fabrication of the wheels; the third design uses old car wheels. The first two designs use wood block bearings. The bodies of all 3 carts are made of wood.

Carrying capacity is given as 700 and 1400 lbs. (318 and 636 kg.) for the first two carts; no capacity information is given for the cart that uses old car wheels.

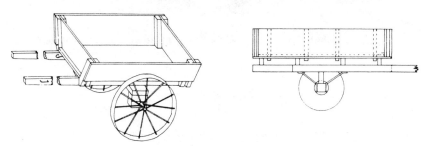

Dahomey Ox-Cart, MF06-239, drawings, 15 pages, free (Reference No. CL/AT/3) from Commission on the Churches' Participation in Development, World Council of Churches, 150 Route de Ferney, 1211 Geneva 20, Switzerland.

This is a very simple ox-cart with a 700 liter or 1000 kg capacity. Frame and body are made of wood. Very detailed information is provided on an ingenious method of wheel manufacture. Hoop iron rims with 16 mm rod spokes riveted in place form the outer part of the wheel; the axle is welded to hub plates. Wood block bearings are made using a piece of axle pipe filed to form a hole saw.
Produced in series of ten in Dahomey beginning in 1968.

The Handcart Handbook, MF 06-269, booklet, 48 pages, by David Tresemer, 1985, $4.50 plus postage and handling from Green River Tools, 5 Cotton Mill Hill, P.O. Box 1919, Brattleboro, Vermont 05301, USA.

"Use it to move dirt and rocks; transport firewood; harvest produce, carry transplant trays, soil and compost; move light, bulky loads (hay, brush, leaves); heavy bulky loads (lumber, trash, ladders, furniture); and transport small animals and feed. This cart can also serve as a portable tool chest, sawhorse, and stepstool."
This is a small and informative report based on the author's extensive research and testing of specially-designed multi-purpose handcarts. It is filled with contemporary photos, historical illustrations, and detailed line drawings to enable readers to construct their own carts and related equipment. The topics covered include the elements of a good cart, using a cart effectively, how to build your own cart, improving an existing cart, and accessories to increase the cart's usefulness.

The author is co-founder of Green River Tools, a trading company based in Brattleboro, Vermont, which specializes in manufacturing quality handtools from all over the world. This company is dedicated to providing durable tools which increase productivity, improve and maintain the user's health, and enhance the environment. They also distribute a number of provocative research reports (many written by David Tresemer) on a variety of topics, including acid rain, tropical deforestation, beneficial birds, tool design to fit the human hand, and natural growing media. A catalogue and publication list is available from the address listed above.

Agricultural Green Leaflets, MF 06-230 to MF 06-233, plans for agricultural equipment, ITDG.

The following plans were offered by ITDG, but are out of print in 1985. Most of these tools were designed for agricultural conditions in Africa.

These leaflets were originally intended for distribution to experienced agricultural engineers in the field, and the descriptive text is often brief. This is unimportant in most cases, but for some of the equipment the precise use is unclear to anyone unfamiliar with African agricultural practices. Construction details are quite easy for anyone to understand.

4 — Kabanyalo Toolbar, MF 06-230, dimensional drawings, 5 pages.

This is a locally-built (and locally repairable) steel plow that also functions as a cultivator/weeder. A simple skid is used instead of a depth wheel.

5 — Chitedze Ridgemaster Toolbar, MF 06-230, dimensional drawings, 6 pages, origin: Malawi.

This is a locally-built and repairable combination steel plow, ridger, and cultivator. "The unique design of this toolbar is that it combines lightness with adequate structural strength, the main parts being fabricated from rectangular hollow section mild steel."

6 — Prototype Multi-Purpose Ox-Drawn Tool, MF 06-230, dimensional drawings, 3 pages, origin: Nigeria.

This is a prototype of a tool to be used for ridging, splitting ridges, cross-tying, weeding, and breaking capped soil in the furrows. The tool frame was designed with an offset beam to avoid blockage when lifting groundnuts. The share is adjustable to allow these different operations to be carried out.

10 — Clod Crushers, Two Designs, MF 06-230, dimensional drawings, 3 pages, origin: Malawi.

"These two simple and cheaply-constructed implements are used for reducing the size of dirt clods in cultivated land prior to ridging up the soil." They are both animal-drawn, and use wooden pegs on rollers to break up the clods as the implement rolls over them.

11 — Ox-Drawn Tie-Ridger/Weeder Implement, MF 06-230, dimensional drawings, 3 pages, origin: Malawi.

"This implement is an attachment only, designed for use with the 'EMCOT' ox-drawn ridging plow." It can be used for cross-tying during ridging, and for both cross-tying and weeding after ridging. Precisely what "cross-tying" means is not made clear for anyone unfamiliar with the technique. Ridging and cross-tying, it is claimed, have resulted in substantial crop yield gains on certain free-draining soils in Africa. This attachment (with the EMCOT plow) cut the labor requirement for use of this technique in land preparation and weeding by an estimated "60% when compared with cultivation by hand."

Fabrication is straightforward, and uncomplicated, requiring some welding. The instructions for field use are vague.

12 — IDC Weeding Attachment for EMCOT Plow, MF 06-230, dimensional drawings, 3 pages, origin: Nigeria.

"This attachment enables weeding in ridged row crops to be carried out by animal power instead of by hand." However, this is only an attachment, to be used with the EMCOT plow. "The tool. . .can be adjusted for height, and also for width according to the row spacing. The sides of the ridges are remade by the ridger body following behind." Essentially, the attachment consists of two steel blades that are pulled along through the earth on the sides of the ridges.

13 — Adjustable Width V-Drag Ditcher/Bund Former, MF 06-230, dimensional drawings, 3 pages, origin: U.S. Dept. of Agriculture.

"This implement is used for making irrigation ditches, and can also be used to construct low-height contour embankments for border irrigation. When making earth ditches for conveying water to crops or drainage channels, a furrow is first opened with a plow (running down and back the required number of times according to the depth required) along the line of the ditch. The V-Drag is then used with the runner board riding in the furrow bottom, the crowder board deflecting the soil sideways. Weight can be added by the operator standing on the runner board. The depth of cut can be increased by placing additional weight towards the front of the implement and/or lengthening the hitch." Animal-drawn.

14 — Sled-Type Corrugator Irrigation-Furrow Former, MF 06-231, dimensional drawings, 3 pages, origin: U.S. Dept. of Agriculture.

"The function of this implement is to make small furrows, or corrugations, for distributing water over a field. The corrugations are run down the slope of the land. This implement can be used after the field has been broadcast seeded or before row-crop planting. The implement design shown can be modified in size to suit animal-draught or tractor-hitching as required." This tool is essentially a sled with four runners that is dragged (loaded) over a field.

15 — Single-Row and Three-Row Rice Seeders, MF 06-231, photoprints, 3 pages, origin: Zambia.

Photoprints only. Two pages on the single-row seeder and one page on the triple-row seeder. This set of plans asks for more local imagination and ingenuity than most ITDG plans do — somewhat hard to understand.

These implements carry out direct seeding of rice fields. They have probably little or no application to Southeast Asia, for example, because they were designed to allow a person to cultivate a larger area (such as in sparsely populated areas of Africa). Where available land is already under intensive cultivation, such equipment would probably lower the total production per unit of land.

16 — Rotary Weeder for Row-Planted Rice, MF 06-231, photoprints, 1 page.

A single page with four photos. The rotary weeder is a very simple piece of equipment, only about 1½ feet long at the base, with a long handle. Measurements are English units only. Two rotary, star-blade clusters are pushed along between two rows. A blade follows the two clusters.

17 — Multi-Action Paddy Field Puddling Tool, MF 06-231, photoprints, 1 page, origin: Japan.

Photoprints with English units only. Some imagination would have to be used by whomever would build from such plans. However, the basic principles are quite clear from the photoprints. Ox-drawn. Apparently, the farmer simply follows along behind, controlling the animal only. Some weights may need to be attached for effective use.

27 — Cassava Grinder, MF 06-231, dimensional drawings, 10 pages, origin: Nigeria.

The exact application of the cassava grinder is not made explicit. No text is included, only assembly instructions. This is a bicycle-pedal, chain-driven grinder. Production is straightforward; certainly possible on a local level.

28 — Rotary Corn (Sorghum) Thresher, MF 06-231, dimensional drawings, 10 pages, origin: Nigeria.

This set of plans has no real text, only a few words with each drawing. Harder

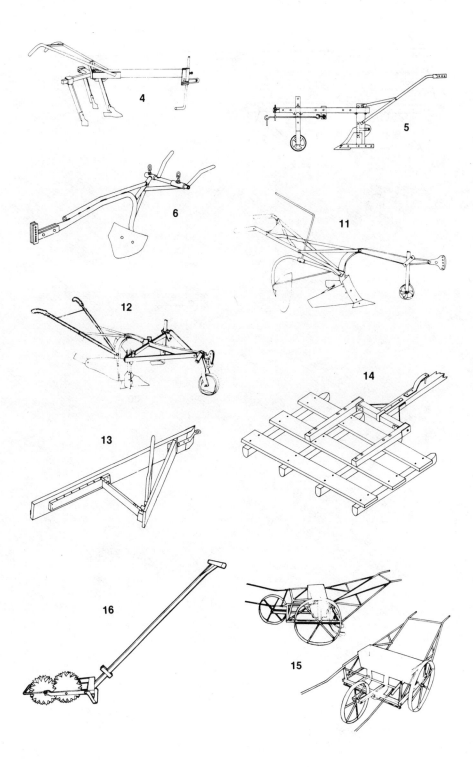

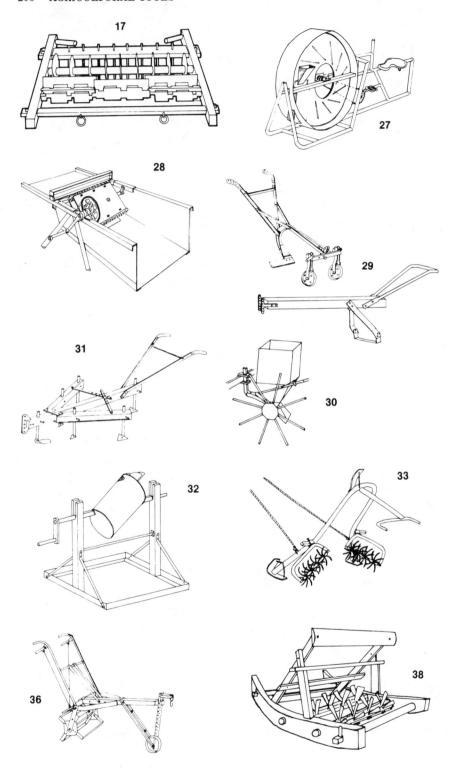

to understand than most ITDG plans. This unit, operated with a hand-crank, is actually for guineacorn (sorghum). Probably operated by two people.

29—IDC-Bornu Groundnut Lifter and IT Groundnut Lifter, MF 06-231, dimensional drawings, 8 pages, origin: Zambia and Nigeria.

This set of dimensional drawings has two items. The IDC-Bornu groundnut lifter is only an attachment for an EMCOT plow. It is pulled by a draft animal, with two depth wheels and a plow-like bar for lifting up the groundnuts.

The IT groundnut lifter is a complete piece of equipment in itself. "A lightweight lifter suitable for groundnuts grown on 75 cm spaced ridges in sandy soils. Suitable for manufacture by village blacksmiths." The minimum equipment required would be a forge, anvil, hammer, tongs, chisel, and punch. This groundnut lifter has no wheels. A flat bar is dragged across the ground, with a person steering it from behind. Animal-drawn.

30—IT Granule Applicator, MF 06-232, dimensional drawings, 14 pages, origin: Nigeria.

This fertilizer applicator fits on a toolbar in place of a mechanical weeder. These plans include a calibration chart for the applicator at various flows and row spacings.

Some of the drawings are not very clear, but the unit should be reproducible. The materials and dimensions can be altered to fit local conditions.

31—IT Expandable Cultivator, MF 06-232, dimensional drawings, 7 pages, origin: Nigeria.

"A lightweight cultivator designed for weeding of crops planted in 70-90 cm spaced rows in sandy soils, to be pulled by one or two oxen or donkeys. Tines are individually adjustable for depth, making the implement suitable for flat or ridge cultivation." The width is also adjustable for the unit as a whole.

This design requires a lot of hole drilling or punching, and thus accuracy in measurement.

32—Seed Dressing Drum (Hand-Operated), MF 06-232, dimensional drawings, 5 pages, origin: Malawi.

Fertilizer and seed are poured into the top of the drum; it is rotated 20-40 times; and the mixture is poured out from the bottom. "It was found that this drum had a capacity of 30 lbs. (13.6 kg) of soya beans or maize, and 38 lbs. (17.2 kg) of fertilizer when filled correctly. In a durability test, a total of 1½ tons of fertilizer was mixed without signs of damage. The drum was also used for seed-dressing of groundnuts and maize with satisfactory coverage performance and no apparent adverse effect on germination."

The fairly simple design can certainly be made by local craftspersons with very few tools.

33—IT High-Clearance Rotary Hoe, MF 06-232, dimensional drawings, 7 pages.

"This animal-drawn implement is designed for seeding of crops grown on ridges at 75-90 cm spacing. It cultivates both sides of one ridge at a time and therefore, unlike cultivators drawn between the ridges, does not require straight and parallel ridges for efficient weeding. . .This implement is not suitable for use in very hard soil conditions. It can be used in wet soil and has been used successfully for weeding cotton while water was standing in the furrows."

36—The Weeder-Mulcher, MF 06-232, dimensional drawings, 8 pages, origin: India.

"This animal-drawn self-cleaning weeder was originally developed for use in sugarcane plantations (by the Indian Institute of Sugarcane Research). It is designed to destroy weeds, leave a mulch on the soil surface to conserve moisture and give a high work output per day (up to 5 or 6 acres of row crop work per 8 hour day). It can be used on most row crops with a spacing of 30 inches (75 cm) or more. . .The blades can easily be replaced by a village blacksmith."

37 — Foot-Powered Thresher, MF 06-232, drawings, 5 pages.

This treadle-operated thresher was designed for rice. Five workers and a thresher can handle 1000 kg of dry paddy or 500 kg of wet paddy daily. The plans are easy to understand. "A bit complex for manufacture at the village level, but easy enough for a simple machine shop."

38 — The "Rasulia" Bladed Roller Thresher, MF 06-233, dimensional drawings, 4 pages, origin: India and Iran.

This implement was seen in use in Iran, and subsequently built in India by Ed Abbot at the Friends' Rural Development Centre in Rasulia. It is pulled by a draft animal, with the driver seated on the unit. It is estimated to be 60% more efficient than the traditional Indian method of using bullocks to trample the harvested crops.

Uses wooden bearings which are not described.

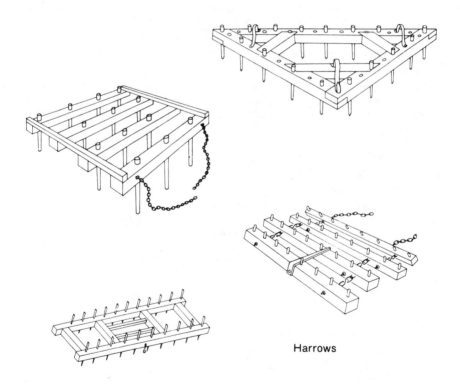

Harrows

41 — Harrows: High-Clearance Peg Tooth (East Africa), Triangular Spike Tooth (India), Flexible Peg Tooth (Iran), and Japanese Harrow, MF 06-233, drawings, 8 pages.

These harrows can all be pulled by animals. The function of a harrow is to prepare seed beds by breaking soil clods, cover seeds after broadcast seeding, and control weeds. Several of these harrows are designed to leave weed residue on the soil surface to conserve moisture.

The Scythe Book, MF 06-273, book, 128 pages, by David Tresemer, 1982, $6.95 plus postage and handling from Green River Tools, 5 Cotton Mill Hill, P.O. Box 1919, Brattleboro, Vermont 05301, USA.

This is a detailed guidebook for the scythe, a traditional cutting tool for moving hay, cutting weeds, and harvesting small grains. The author presents his extensive research on European and North American designs, and covers the equipment, sharpening, techniques, uses, and accessories in detail. The book is loaded with illustrations, historical references, and anecdotes encouraging a resurgence in popular understanding and use of this versatile tool. The lightweight "Austrian-style" version, with a straight snath (or handle) and razor-sharp hammered blade, is favored over the "American" version, with its curved snath and stamped blade. For parts of the world where increased productivity in agricultural operations such

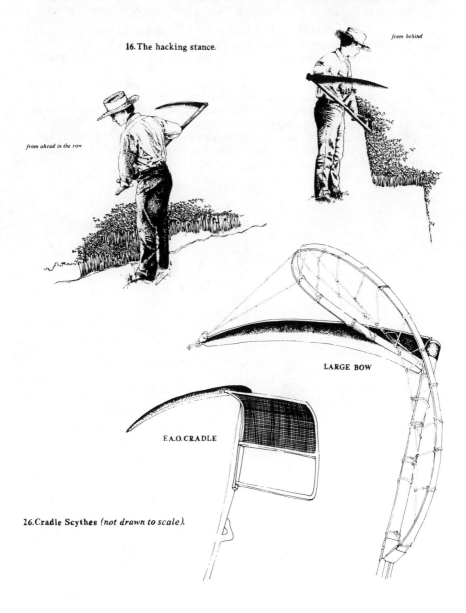

16. The hacking stance.

from behind

from ahead in the row

LARGE BOW

F.A.O. CRADLE

26. Cradle Scythes (not drawn to scale).

as grain harvesting, forage cutting, or composting is called for without resorting to power equipment, the scythe may become a valuable intermediate technology option.

"The most elaborate and most beautiful invention for laying out grain more neatly to the side in scything is the grain cradle. . .It was really a different tool, quite like a scythe in principle, but with a rack of three to five wooden tines curved to follow the shape of the blade. At the end of the stroke, the straws would be bunched together and supported by the tines. The cradler would then tilt the whole thing to the left and let the cut grain slide out in a neat bundle. In the middle of the nineteenth century there were a million cradle scythes being used in the northeast United States alone. . ."

Rice: Postharvest Technology, MF 06-253, book, 394 pages, edited by E. Arguello, D. De Padua, and M. Graham, 1976, IDRC, out of print in 1985.

This large volume covers all the technical aspects of rice postharvest technology: harvesting, threshing, drying, storage, parboiling, milling, and handling. It also describes "some of the anatomical and biochemical properties of the rice grain in relation to postharvest processing problems."

This book was compiled from material used in a training course on postharvest technology in the Philippines. It is not an appropriate technology manual, but rather a reference book on the current state-of-the-art equipment for rice processing operations. It could be useful to small independent groups and university-based organizations that need to know as much as possible about the principles used in the standard commercial designs while working to develop lower-cost alternatives that will benefit even the smallest farmers.

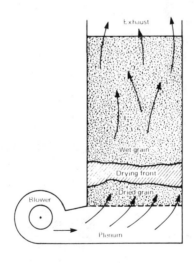

Deep-bed grain drier

The Winnower, MF 06-261, booklet with dimensional drawings and assembly information, 35 pages, 1984, US$2.25 from TOOL.

The authors claim the winnower is easily produced, operated, and maintained. It is operated with a hand crank, but could certainly be adapted to use a pedal-powered chain-drive system. Dimensions and materials are given for each part of the winnower. This unit was designed from an earlier prototype with consideration given to conditions in developing countries.

Winnowing Fan, VITA Technical Bulletin No. 39, MF 06-260, 4 pages, out of print in 1985.

A portable machine from the Philippines for winnowing rice. This design is hand-operated, but it could be adapted to use pedal power or a small engine. The drawings and text are easy to understand.

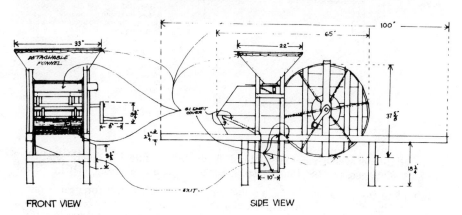

FRONT VIEW   SIDE VIEW

Hand-operated winnowing fan

A Hand-Operated Winnower, Rural Technology Guide No. 11, MF 06-281, booklet, 26 pages, by J. Beaumont, 1981, free to public bodies in countries eligible for British aid, $1.62 to others, from TDRI.

This design for a simple enclosed winnowing fan for separating grain from chaff can be made of wood or sheet metal with simple tools. "This winnower was designed for use with the hand-operated sunflower seed decorticators developed by TPI but it can be used for a wide variety of materials." Photos, drawings, and step-by-step instuctions are provided.

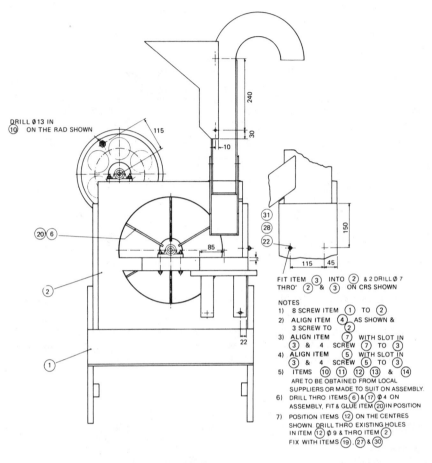

DRILL Ø 13 IN
⑩   ON THE RAD SHOWN

FIT ITEM ③ INTO ② & 2 DRILL Ø 7
THRO' ② & ③ ON CRS SHOWN

NOTES
1)   8 SCREW ITEM ① TO ②
2)   ALIGN ITEM ④ AS SHOWN &
     3 SCREW TO ②
3)   ALIGN ITEM ⑦ WITH SLOT IN
     ③ & 4 SCREW ⑦ TO ③
4)   ALIGN ITEM ⑤ WITH SLOT IN
     ③ & 4 SCREW ⑤ TO ③
5)   ITEMS ⑩ ⑪ ⑫ ⑬ & ⑭
     ARE TO BE OBTAINED FROM LOCAL
     SUPPLIERS OR MADE TO SUIT ON ASSEMBLY.
6)   DRILL THRO ITEMS ⑥ & ⑰ Ø 4 ON
     ASSEMBLY, FIT & GLUE ITEM ⑳ IN POSITION
7)   POSITION ITEMS ⑫ ON THE CENTRES
     SHOWN. DRILL THRO EXISTING HOLES
     IN ITEM ⑫ Ø 9 & THRO ITEM ②
     FIX WITH ITEMS ⑲ , ㉗ & ㉚

Figure 1
Winnower assembly

A Pedal-Operated Grain Mill, Rural Technology Guide No. 5, MF 06-272, booklet, 32 pages, by G.S. Pinson, 1979, $0.80 (surface mail) from TDRI.

Complete instructions for the production of a grinding mill for grains and legumes. The mill and supporting stand are used with an ordinary bicycle which can be quickly connected and disconnected. The rear bicycle wheel drives a rotor at about 5000 rpm to break up the grain. Wire mesh controls the size of the flour product. "The mill works best on hard, brittle grains such as maize (corn), millet and sorghum and on legumes such as soya beans."

Although the mill is of steel construction, it is intended for use over brief periods to meet the daily needs of individual households. It is not designed for continual, intensive use. No cost estimates are provided. An alternative wooden frame using some bicycle parts is shown. Design modifications could eliminate the more difficult metalworking tasks (lathe and milling work), and also reduce some of the other costs. Some field reports indicate excessive tire wear is a problem with the bicycle-attached version.

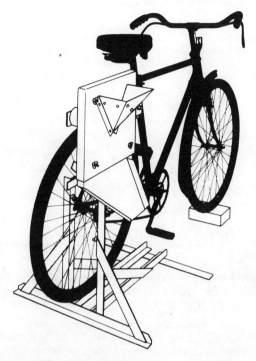

Grain Mills and Flour in Classical Antiquity, book, 230 pages, by L.A. Moritz, 1958, reprinted 1979, $24.50 from The Ayer Co., P.O. Box 958, Salem, New Hampshire 03079, USA.

Himalayan village women spend a great amount of time grinding grain in small stone handmills. A beginning understanding of what design modifications might be possible can be obtained by reading the handmill chapter of this book. There is revealing information on the evolution of handmill design in Europe and the Middle East. The drawings and photos of adjustable handmills are valuable. Most of the rest of the book is of historical interest only.

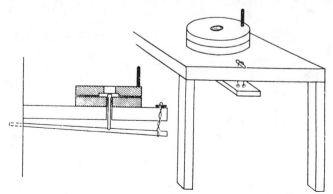

FIG. 11. Diagram showing view of and section through adjustable Scottish quern

Bell Alarms and Sack Hoists in Windmills, MF 06-238, booklet, 16 pages, by H. Clark and R. Wailes, 1973, 45 pence including postage, from The Society for the Protection of Ancient Buildings, 58 Great Ormond Street, London WC1, England.

This is a study of the clever ways in which two important functions were accomplished in windmills and watermills: 1) warning the miller when the grain was low (using bells); and 2) lifting the heavy sacks of grain and flour inside the mill (using hoists that took power off of the windmill or watermill via a drive shaft).

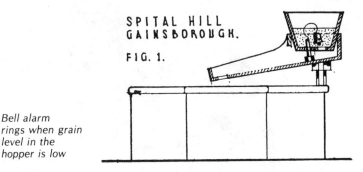

SPITAL HILL GAINSBOROUGH.

FIG. 1.

Bell alarm rings when grain level in the hopper is low

Treadle Operated Peanut Thresher—Complete Technical Drawing No. 20, MF 06-258, (5) 24″ × 36″ sheets of technical drawings with 3 pages of instructions, £3.25 surface mail from ITDG.

This is a simple piece of equipment, but the tolerances are small enough to require relatively accurate crafting. Probably best if built by a small workshop that would produce dozens of units. Standard sizes of lumber are used (English measurements only). The plans may need to be adapted for the use of materials locally available.

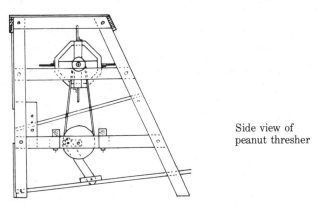

Side view of peanut thresher

A Feeder to Improve the Performance of a Hand-Operated Groundnut Sheller, Rural Technology Guide No. 4, MF 06-267, booklet, 17 pages, by G.A. Collins, L.D.G. Coward and G. Pinson, 1977, $1.00 (surface mail), free to U.K. aid recipients, from TDRI.

This is a construction manual for a device that controls the number of groundnuts (peanuts) dropped (fed) into a hand-operated groundnut sheller. The result is less effort in use and fewer broken kernels. Drawings and instructions are clear, and the feeder should be easy to make if the metalworking tools are available. Wood could be substituted for many of the steel parts, but the authors do not discuss this. The feeder is designed to be attached to existing models of groundnut shellers.

Small Scale Oil Extraction from Groundnuts and Copra, ILO Technical Memorandum No. 5, MF 06-274, book, 111 pages, 1983, $8.55 from International Labor Office, 1750 New York Avenue N.W., Washington D.C. 20006, USA.

A look at the steps involved in removing oil from peanuts (groundnuts) and dried coconut (copra) using small-scale mechanized equipment, this volume should be helpful in either starting a business or in identifying where in the process technical improvements may be made. "It provides detailed technical and economic information on small-scale oil extraction mills using either small expellers or power ghanis, and processing between 100 tonnes and 220 tonnes of materials per year. An economic comparison between these small-scale plants and medium- to large-scale plants is provided."

The traditional technologies of rural areas are either ignored or only briefly mentioned. "An animal-powered ghani (oil press) can process 5 to 15 kg of seeds at a time. An improved version of the ghani has been developed in India. Known as the Wardha ghani, it is larger and more efficient than the traditional ghani, and can crush charges of seed of up to 15 kg in approximately 1.5 hours or close to 100 kg per day."

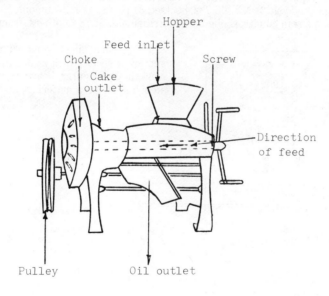

Sketch of a low-pressure expeller   (2 hp)

A Wooden Hand-Held Maize Sheller, Rural Technology Guide No. 1, MF 06-280, booklet, 8 pages, by G.S. Pinson, 1977, $1.05 (surface mail) from TDRI.

This booklet shows how to make a low-cost, simple wooden hand-held tool to remove the grains from maize (corn) cobs when they are hard and dry. The tool can be easily made out of hard wood, using hand tools (including a hand drill). The drawings are clear and easy to understand.

Potentially a very useful tool in many parts of the world where corn kernels are still removed by hand, often without any tool at all, using only the thumbs or another corn cob to pry the kernels loose.

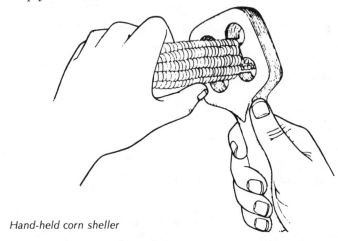

Hand-held corn sheller

A Hand-Operated Bar Mill for Decorticating Sunflower Seed, Rural Technology Guide No. 9, MF 06-282, booklet, 31 pages, by J. Beaumont, 1981, free to public bodies in countries eligible for British aid, $1.78 to others, from TDRI.

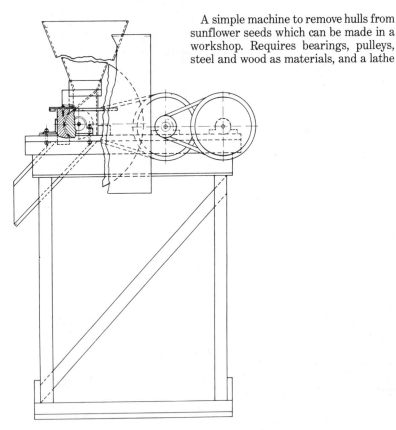

A simple machine to remove hulls from sunflower seeds which can be made in a workshop. Requires bearings, pulleys, steel and wood as materials, and a lathe and welding set as tools. Drawings, photos, and step-by-step instructions are included.

"This type of decorticator is suitable for removing the husk from the smaller, high oil-bearing types of sunflower seed. It will process about 20 kg (40 lbs.) of seed per hour." To be operated by 1-2 persons.

Mechanics in Agriculture, MF 06-249, book, 702 pages, by Lloyd J. Phipps, 1967, third edition 1983, $23.65 (educational discounts may be available) from The Interstate Printers and Publishers, Inc., Danville, Illinois 61832, USA.

This is a comprehensive text for courses in vocational agriculture, divided into five parts: equipping and using a farm workshop, engines and implements, buildings, electrification, and soil and water management. Illustrations and excellent instructions on the use of all kinds of hand and power tools make this an encyclopedia of modern American farm mechanics. The text is particularly strong on explanation of principles of operation, maintenance, repair, and safety, for tools and implements. Though it was compiled for use by American secondary school students entering a capital- and energy-intensive agriculture, the book covers many topics of interest to agriculturalists everywhere. Examples include repairing and sharpening hand tools; making sketches and reading blueprints; understanding concrete; soldering and oxy-acetylene welding; blacksmithing and working sheet metal; using rope and leather; and fundamentals of engines and electric motors.

A good reference book.

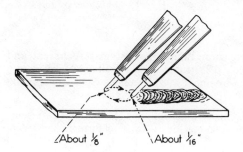

Welding: practicing circular motion with a torch—flame is lifted at the front edge of the circle

/About ⅛"   \About 1/16"

Small Gas Engines, MF 06-255, book, 256 pages, by James Gray and Richard Barrow, 1976, $15.95 from Prentice-Hall, Inc., Englewood Cliffs, New Jersey, USA.

Small gas engines are very common in most parts of the world. They are used in motorcycles, electric generators, water pumps, rototillers, winnowers, boats and many other devices.

This book introduces the theory of small gas engine operation. It does a detailed and thorough job of presenting the basics of repair and maintenance. Understandable to the beginner, and also valuable to those who already know something about the subject.

Recommended.

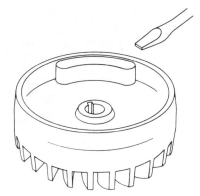

Check condition of flywheel magnet with an unmagnetized screwdriver

How to Repair Briggs and Stratton Engines, MF 06-247, paperback book, 182 pages, by Paul Dempsey, 1984, $8.95 from TAB Books, Blue Ridge Summit, Pennsylvania 17214, USA.

Briggs and Stratton engines power small pumps and agricultural implements all over the Third World. Though it is written for North Americans, this book could be valuable wherever these small engines are being used.

The author "describes repair and maintenance procedures for all current and many older Briggs and Stratton engines. These procedures extend to all phases of the work, from simple tune-up and carburetor repairs to the serious business of replacing main bearings and resizing cylinder bores. The material is organized by subject and by engine model, and as much as possible, divided into steps that are easy to follow." Clear line drawings and text explain the basics of four-cycle internal combustion engines and the adjustment and repair of ignition systems, carburetors, and pull-starters. The section on engine disassembly and overhaul includes standard machining clearances and dimensions as well as replacement part identification numbers.

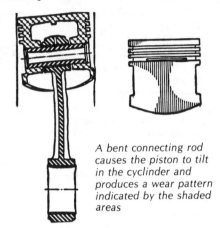

A bent connecting rod causes the piston to tilt in the cyclinder and produces a wear pattern indicated by the shaded areas

Small-Scale Solar-Powered Irrigation Pumping Systems: Technical and Economic Review, MF 06-275, book, 188 pages, by Sir William Halcrow and Partners in association with ITDG, September 1981, available from World Bank, 1818 H Street N.W., Washington D.C. 20433, USA.

An extensive examination of the technical and economic feasibility of both solar photovoltaic and solar thermal irrigation pumps for use by small farmers in develop-

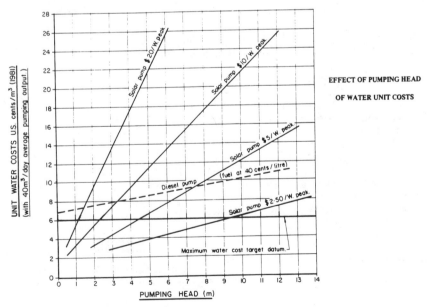

ing countries. Equipment options and performance are discussed. With the conclusion that these pumps are much too expensive at present, attention is given to exploring various assumptions about future costs of solar pumps vs. engine-driven pumps.

A shorter, easier to read summary of the issue that draws on much of the same material is contained in **Solar Photovoltaics for Irrigation Water Pumping** (see review).

The Potential for Small Scale Solar Powered Irrigation in Pakistan, MF 06-283, 41 pages, by Michael Howes, December 1982, $2.85 from Publications Office, Institute of Development Studies, University of Sussex, Brighton BN1 9RE, England.

This report on 14 solar irrigation pumps in Pakistan concludes that significant price reductions (from 1982 levels) will be necessary before such pumps can be expected to be economically competitive with other high-cost alternatives currently in use (animal-powered Persian wheels, diesel deep tubewell pumps) in Pakistan.

Solar Photovoltaics for Irrigation Water Pumping, MF 06-276, paper, 17 pages, by Urs Rentsch, 1982, Swiss Francs 4.50 from SKAT.

This is a good summary of the equipment-matching necessary and the financial requirements for irrigation pumps driven by solar electric cells. The author concludes that with liquid fuel cost increases and dramatic solar cell cost declines, photovoltaic pumps would become competitive with small engine-driven pumps for small plots with low pumping heads. This combination of circumstances is still many years away, however. If solar cell costs dropped to zero, the costs of solar pumps would be at a minimum of about $3/peak watt due to the costs of the structure, wiring, motor, pump, transportation and installation. The capital costs of the solar pump even under these favorable assumptions would be as much as 50 times as great as those of a manually-operated pump. "The Rower pump for example costs about US$10-13, while a corresponding solar pump would cost at least US$600" (at $3/peak watt). Credit and subsidies would be required for small farmers to be able to afford the pumps.

Plans for Low-Cost Farming Implements: Groundnut Sheller, Platform Carts with Drying Pans, Hay Press, MF 06-251, leaflet, 13 pages, 1974, $5.00 airmail, $2.00 surface mail, Agricultural Research Organization, Institute of Agricultural Engineering, The Volcani Centre, Bet Dagan 50-200, Israel.

The pamphlet includes dimensional drawings (metric units) for 3 different agricultural implements developed by a Laos-Israeli team in 1973.

The groundnut (peanut) sheller is made of wood and a metal barrel. It is hand-cranked. Capacity is 80-100 kg per hour with 3 workers. The product has to be cleaned and sized using hand sieves.

Platform carts with drying pans are made almost entirely of wood. They are for crop drying in areas with frequent rains, so that the crops can be brought in under a protective roof easily.

The hay press is a simple device made of wood. It enables workers to easily produce baled hay, which maintains its quality longer than stacked hay.

Polyrow Peristaltic Pump Sprayer, ITDG Complete Technical Drawings No. 23, MF 06-252, dimensional drawings, no text, 3 large sheets, 1972, $2.25 surface mail from ITDG.

Dimensional drawings with English units. This hand-pushed unit is designed so that the single large wheel pumps the liquid by means of rollers that compress a plastic hose. This action takes place only while the unit is actually moving. The drawings are clear enough, but the lack of any explanatory text is a limitation. Great if you already understand the principle of the peristaltic pump. Some substitution of materials would be possible.

Lightweight Seeder/Spreader, Plan No. 596, MF 06-248, 2 pages, $1.00 from Popular Mechanics.

These are brief but complete plans for the standard American lawn seeder/fertilizer spreader. It may have some value with modifications for seeding grasses in small farming operations or for other seeding activities. The distribution and rate of seed flow could be modified for other seeding needs.

The seeder is made of 18-gauge aluminum, bent, drilled, and screwed together. Uses two small wheels.

Grass seeder/fertilizer spreader

Chain Link Fence Making Machine, VITA Technical Bulletin No. 25, MF 06-259, 20 pages, $4.25 in U.S., $4.75 international surface mail, $6.00 international air mail, from VITA.

These are step-by-step instructions for making and using a hand-operated machine to make chain link fencing. There are drawings and photos. "The machine here

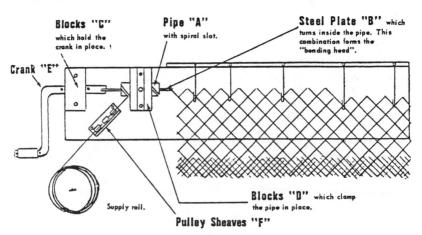

Blocks "C" which hold the crank in place.

Pipe "A" with spiral slot.

Steel Plate "B" which turns inside the pipe. This combination forms the "bending head".

Crank "E"

Supply roll.

Blocks "D" which clamp the pipe in place.

Pulley Sheaves "F"

is designed to produce fencing up to 244 cm (96 ") but can be varied to produce fencing of any height. The size of the openings (can be varied)...The machine described here requires number 12 or 14 wire, but could be modified to take larger wire." A very clever, easily made device.

"In Botswana, the machine has become the basis of a small fence manufacturing business which serves as a source of employment and produces fencing which is far more affordable locally than is the imported fencing which was the only material previously available."

Of course this unit requires the use of wire (probably imported in most countries). For most fencing needs, traditional alternatives exist and are probably more appropriate. Barbed wire should also be cheaper as it uses much less wire per linear foot of fence.

Oil Soaked Wood Bearings: How to Make Them and How They Perform, MF 06-233, leaflet with drawings and text, 10 pages, information from tests done in Zambia; $1.00 from ITDG.

The authors consider the characteristics of wood to be used, how to determine the size of the bearing required, and oil-soaking in the case of high-moisture content of the wood to be used. The oil used was groundnut (peanut) oil or discarded engine oil. Three types of wood bearings are presented and evaluated: solid block, split block, and bush bearings. "The drilling of radial holes for lubrication purposes is only recommended by Pearson for the bush type of bearing. He found that if lubrication holes were drilled in block bearings not only were the bearings weakened but also the holes acted as dirt traps."

Hardwood is required. The bearings are well-suited to low-speed applications such as in carts and water wheels.

Highly recommended.

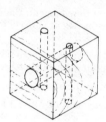

Making Coir Rope, Technical Bulletin No. 44, MF 06-260, leaflet, 8 pages, VITA, out of print in 1985.

A step-by-step presentation of the process of making coir rope from coconut husks. The necessary equipment can be made out of wood, and most of this is shown: a fiber combing board for separating fibers, hand-cranked single and multiple twisting reels, and a strand block and strand guide for the final steps in rope making. The text is at times confusing and misleading, and the reader will have to be careful.

Some of the basic concepts can also be applied in making wire rope.

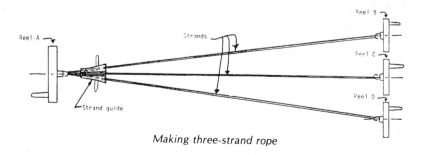

Making three-strand rope

Eight Simple Surveying Levels, Agricultural Green Leaflet #42, MF 06-233, drawings with text, 17 pages, ITDG, out of print in 1985.

These levels, made of wood and rubber or clear plastic tubing, were built and evaluated by an ITDG team. Details are given on the construction, accuracy, and usefulness of each device. All the levels are made using simple hand tools, and are cheap and easy to construct. These levels are quite sufficient for most rural drainage, irrigation, roadmaking, building and other earthmoving work, where extreme accuracy is not needed.

ADDITIONAL REFERENCES ON AGRICULTURAL TOOLS

The Rower Pump describes a low-cost hand-operated pump that is used very successfully in small plot irrigation in Bangladesh; see the pumps section of WATER SUPPLY.

Fichier Encyclopedique du Developpement Rural contains leaflets in French on agricultural tools, such as a sugar cane crusher; see GENERAL REFERENCE.

The Book of the New Alchemists describes the greenhouse and fish tanks combination used in the Ark; see GENERAL REFERENCES.

Greenhouses used for both food production and home heating are described in ENERGY: SOLAR.

Rural Small Scale Industry in the People's Republic of China discusses the relationship between the decentralized agricultural machinery industry and farming; see LOCAL SELF-RELIANCE.

Small Farm Development: Understanding and Improving Farming Systems in the Humid Tropics estimates the effects of various small-scale power sources added to small farms; see AGRICULTURE.

Surface Irrigation contains drawings and photographs of low technology and mechanized equipment for use in land preparation for irrigation and water control; see AGRICULTURE.

Grain storage bins and dryers are shown in CROP STORAGE.

The Management of Animal Energy Resources and the Modernization of the Bullock Cart System includes a discussion of needed cart and harness improvements for these farm vehicles; see TRANSPORTATION.

The Use of Pedal Power for Agriculture and Transport in Developing Countries examines the potential applications of pedal power for driving agricultural equipment; see ENERGY: GENERAL.

Design for a Pedal Driven Power Unit for Transport and Machine Uses in Developing Countries lists crop processing equipment suitable for pedal power; see TRANSPORTATION.

TRANSPORTATION examines small vehicles, wheelbarrows, and carts, many of them important in small farm operations.

Small-scale milling equipment driven by waterpower is described in many of the entries in ENERGY: WATER.

Aspects of Irrigation with Windmills and **Syllabus for Irrigation with Windmills** are in ENERGY: WIND.

Manege: Animal-Driven Power Gear is well-suited to driving most post-harvest processing machinery; see ENERGY: GENERAL.

Liklik Buk has numerous drawings and photos of agricultural tools; see GENERAL REFERENCE.

Crop Drying, Preservation
and Storage

Crop Drying, Preservation and Storage

"Experience has taught the small grower in the developing countries that, if produce is stored, it goes bad. This has two effects: a sufficient quantity is grown to feed the family for about three or four months; immediately after harvest (sometimes before it has been dried thoroughly), when there may be a temporary glut of food and prices are low, produce is sold to traders; moreover, in many areas the farmers are in debt to the traders and any produce surplus beyond their own food requirements is immediately sold to meet accumulated debts. Thus one of the major contributory factors responsible for the economic nonviability of farming areas is the farmer's inability to handle and store food efficiently so that he can sell good quality produce when it is scarce and commands a high price. The standard of living in a rural community depends not only upon the range of foods grown, the capacity to grow in quantity, but also upon the facilities for efficient handling, drying, storage and marketing. . .

"In Latin America it has been estimated that there is a loss of 25 to 50 percent of harvested cereals and pulses; in certain African countries about 30 percent of the total subsistence agricultural production is lost annually, and in areas of Southeast Asia some crops suffer losses of up to 50 percent."
— **Handling and Storage of Food Grains in Tropical and Subtropical Areas,**
FAO

Many observers view effective farm level grain storage as an opportunity to reduce food losses and increase farm family income and security at the same time. Landless laborers may also benefit from good storage, as grain prices flatten out and in-kind wages can be protected from losses in their homes. Centralized government grain storage facilities frequently have proven to be a disappointment, suffering from poor quality control on incoming grain (with resulting high in-storage loss rates) that leads to low prices paid to the farmers. Even with smoothly functioning large-scale grain storage facilities, substantial losses may have already taken place at the farm level before the grain ever reaches the centers.

Several studies of farm level grain storage losses in recent years have concluded that losses in the areas studied were much lower than previously supposed. Studies of this sort have some difficult methodological challenges to overcome, and the complete picture is not yet clear. Certainly there are farmers in some places with particular crops that are experiencing very low storage losses, while some farmers in other places are having high losses with other crops. People interested in this topic should carefully investigate the extent of local losses before launching programs.

Readers who are in a position to help develop or implement appropriate technology solutions in their communities should turn first to two excellent books that detail for different crops the points in the harvest, handling, and storage sequence where losses are most likely to occur. **Post Harvest Food Losses in Developing Countries** *takes a look at the potential for reducing losses of a wide variety* *of foods, while* **Handling and Storage of Foodgrains in Tropical and Subtropical Areas** *is the better technical reference book, concentrating on grain storage. Another valuable source of ideas on how to approach storage problems is* **Appropriate Technology for Grain Storage,** *which describes a successful effort to pool community knowledge of grain storage problems and apply it to develop several solutions tailored to local circumstances.*

Proper drying is considered the biggest single factor in determining whether grain will be effectively stored without damage. Simple direct solar drying already plays a major role in preserving a large portion of Third World production. Usually grain is dried while it stands in the fields, or it is spread out on concrete surfaces, roads, baskets, plastic sheets, or the ground itself.

The standard alternative to such methods has been the fuel-burning artificial dryer. In these units, large quantities of grain can be dried with greater speed and greater control over drying rate and product quality. These dryers require a high capital investment and ever-increasing operating expenditures for fuel, but have relatively low labor costs. There are also a number of small artificial dryers that depend on wood, rice straw, or rice hulls for fuel (see **Drying Equipment for Cereal Grains and Other Agricultural Produce,** **Simple Grain Dryer,** *and* **Small Farm Grain Storage***).*

Solar agricultural dryers have received much attention in recent years. (See **A Survey of Solar Agricultural Dryers** *for a collection of different designs.) They are cheaper to operate than fossil-fueled dryers, requiring no fuel, and they are more easily made with low-cost local materials. There are two general varieties of solar dryers. The simplest (for certain crops such as corn) are raised bins with roofs, that protect the grain from rain and attack by small animals and rodents. They allow air to flow through wire mesh or woven walls to slowly dry the grain. These are "indirect" dryers that depend on air heated by the sun rather than direct exposure to the sun. They are widely used, low-cost, and effective for corn (maize). Much work has been done recently on different dryers that are enclosed with glass or plastic coverings to trap the sun's heat, raising the temperature and lowering the humidity of the air which passes over the crops. Such dryers have a higher cost per unit of drying surface area than the other simpler systems. They offer some protection from dirt, insects, animals and rain (an advantage over ground-spread systems in which the grain must be quickly gathered up whenever rain threatens). For grain drying, however, enclosed solar dryers have a very small capacity compared to what is usually needed, and cost much more than a basic flat surface.*

For fruits and vegetables, the temperatures achieved in an enclosed solar dryer make thorough drying possible when open air drying may not be rapid enough. Drying could extend the low-cost availability of a number of tropical fruits such as mangoes. In many countries these fruits ripen during a very short period, creating a temporary glut.

The appeal of solar dryers in the Third World will depend very much on the local situation — traditional drying practices, crops produced, food price fluctuations over the year, and weather during the harvest season. (No solar drying system works well under continuously cloudy, humid conditions. When harvests coincide with the beginning of a rainy season, a fueled dryer may be necessary.) In many areas, flat drying surfaces may be better investments than solar dryers. On the other hand, dryers made of local materials (e.g. bamboo, wood, adobe) and clear plastic sheeting or low-cost glass need not be very expensive.

In the United States, solar grain drying systems at the farm level are under active testing, and the results to date suggest that they will soon be widely used. These dryers are replacing expensive fossil-fuel burning dryers, and the costs of converting to solar drying can be balanced against reduced fuel bills. Most of these U.S. solar drying systems use large electric fans to circulate air. Two of the publications in this chapter describe these systems.

There are many good quality storage bins that can be made out of locally available, low-cost materials, that will successfully protect properly dried stored grain from moisture, mold, insects, rodents and birds. One such bin is the bissa, which appears to be well suited to storage requirements in Sri Lanka (see **Evaluation of the Bissa***). Lightweight metal bins have proven effective in Guatemala, India, and other countries (see* **Guide to the Manufacture of Metal Bins***). Other traditional and low-cost storage bins are described in* **Post Harvest Food Losses** *and* **Handling and Storage of Food Grains**.

In certain climates, some fruits and vegetables can be stored in underground structures and pits. Canning, drying and pickling are other options for fruit and vegetable preservation. The capital costs of containers and the energy requirements for canning make this option out of reach for family level food preservation in most cases, but canning can still be the basis for successful small industries. Drying may be the lowest-cost, most widely relevant strategy, especially for fruit preservation. Publications on all of these topics are included in this chapter.

Post Harvest Food Losses in Developing Countries, MF 07-276, book, 202 pages, National Academy of Sciences, 1978, free from BOSTID, JH 217D, National Academy of Sciences, 2101 Constitution Avenue N.W., Washington D.C. 20418, USA.

This valuable, informative book examines the potential of food loss reduction for each of the major food crops, on the small farm or small operator level. Includes cereal grains (e.g. rice, maize, millet, sorghum, wheat), grain legumes (e.g. beans, peanuts, soybeans), perishables (e.g. cassava, yams, bananas, potatoes) and fish. Losses are identified at each step of harvesting, processing and storage, and low-cost technology options for reducing these losses are discussed.

For the world as a whole, attention to food losses affecting small farmers holds the greatest potential for benefitting the largest numbers of people. The authors note that improvements must take into account social and cultural factors. Increased losses are often associated with the new high yielding varieties, as they overwhelm traditional processing and storage systems.

Education, training and extension are only briefly discussed. Some important issues are raised, such as the need for improved communication between policymakers and village leadership to insure the development of programs in harmony with village needs.

Highly recommended for the general reader involved in rural development work. Very helpful in understanding the factors affecting food losses, and the opportunities for low-cost technology solutions. The technical vocabulary is not difficult, but the language used may still present problems to the non-native English speaker.

Handling and Storage of Food Grains in Tropical and Subtropical Areas, FAO Agricultural Paper No. 90, MF 07-269, book, 350 pages, by D.W. Hall, United Nations Food and Agriculture Organization (FAO), 1970, second edition 1975, $7.25 from FAO booksellers, or from Distribution and Sales Section, FAO, Via delle Terme di Caracalla, 00100 Rome, Italy.

This is the best technical reference book on grain storage, providing a good summary of the relevant scientific work up to 1970. It will be valuable for anyone working on grain drying and grain storage problems. The text is in readable (not too technical) English.

"This manual describes the causes of grain loss, deterioration and contamination, methods of drying and storage, the design of small and large storage facilities, and also methods of fungus, insect and rodent control." For all of these topics, the author notes traditional local practices which should be more widely encouraged, in addition to relatively simple improved practices.

"Current knowledge of modern handling and storage techniques is derived from industrial counties, which are mainly in the temperate regions of the world. This knowledge has only limited application under the climatic conditions of tropical countries."

"Indigenous farmers always have their own methods for assessing the amount of moisture in grain. Some of these provide a fairly reliable estimate of the grain's suitability for safe storage. These methods include pressing the grain with the thumb nail; crushing the grains between the fingers; biting the grain; rattling a number of grains in a tin; obtaining the 'feel' of the grain by smelling a handful and shaking it; or by plunging the hand (fingers extended) into. . .a sack or heap. With long experience a man can judge whether the grain or kernel is suitable for storage. . .However. . .inconsistency can arise due to differences of opinion when the person concerned feels ill."

"The mixture of wood ash or sand wih food grains is carried out in many areas. . .This method appears to rely for its effectiveness upon the fact that the materials used fill the intergranular spaces and thereby restrict insect movement. . .Mineral dusts. . .scratch the thin waterproofing layer of wax which exists on the outside surface of the insect cutical, allowing loss of water which leads to death."

"Condensation problems, especially in metal silos, occur in the tropics particularly in areas where the sky is clear during both day and night. . .Metal silos should be light in color to reflect most of the incoming radiation during the day. The major temperature changes normally required to cause condensation can be avoided by providing adequate shade to prevent large gains of energy in the grain."

The author does support the use of some insecticides which are now known to be more dangerous and undesirable than previously supposed in 1970.

Highly recommended.

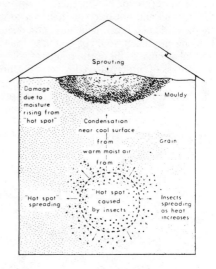

Spoilage of grain in a small storage bin due to temperature differences, movement of moisture, and localized multiplication of fungi and insects

Appropriate Technology for Grain Storage, MF 07-262, book, 94 pages, by the Community Development Trust Fund of Tanzania, out of print in 1985.

This report documents a very important example of a successful strategy to stimulate villagers to create their own appropriate technologies for grain storage. The wealth of knowledge held by the Tanzanian villagers about their own specific local problems in grain storage emerged from dialogues with a team of outsiders (Tanzanians and foreigners). Potentially relevant experience from external sources was made known to the villagers, who criticized, modified and added to this store of possibilities. The villagers then designed three sets of improvements that matched different needs within the village. The outsiders thus served as resource people and facilitators, yet left the choice of actions to the very people who would best know what constraints they faced and what they could realistically afford to do. The entire process stimulated an awareness among the villagers of the high level of their own collective knowledge and capability of solving their own problems.

"The team aimed not to impose an alien analysis of the problem on the villagers but to work from the basis of their perceived and understood reality. . .The villagers already had 'parts' of solutions to their storage problems. It was the aim of this project to reinforce these existing solutions so that they would be more effective, not to replace them with new solutions."

"Villagers found it hard to understand that the team had not brought a solution to the storage problem, that it did not want simply to convince or force them to do something, and it did not have some gift for them. . . It was only after having carried a certain line of design (the Nigerian crib) forward in discussions for several weeks only to drop it when the villagers brought up serious criticisms, that the team's credibility was finally established. It was then clear that the team did not have a vested interest in any particular design."

Village discussion groups told the visiting team that home-drying of grain was an essential element of any improved storage system. The grain could not be dried in the fields because the farmers could not prevent the destruction of the crops by wild pigs. Preventing the pigs from entering the fields would require a level of cooperation that the villagers said they realistically did not yet have. "Such an example highlights three important reasons why the dialogue approach places such a problem area as grain storage in the context of the total village reality. 1) The significance of some seemingly technical detail of a development problem can easily be misunderstood. For instance, a well-meaning expert might have argued that farmers should not harvest their maize while moist; they should let it dry in the fields, and then store it in such and such a way. Such an unfortunately common 'outside' approach would be bound to fail because it lays down rules for the farmers and takes no account of the reality of wild pigs. 2) The dialogue approach generates awareness of interrelated development problems that can be taken up in turn. For instance, the planning committee of the project village has already discussed block farming in relation to the problem of protection against pigs. . .3) By pursuing problems back to their origins, discussion groups confront what are sometimes called 'limit situations', that is, points where they quite genuinely say, 'Tumeshindwa!' ('We have failed!'). By defining and objectifying limit situations and then by focus-

Factors affecting grain storage in a Tanzanian village

ing human energy on them, they are ultimately overcome. It is the experience of bursting through a previously limiting situation that constitutes the liberating effect of adult education."

An excellent example of technical assistance in the context of real community participation. Highly recommended.

An improved 2-ton storage bin with rat-guards

Small Farm Grain Storage, MF 07-278, set of three volumes, "Preparing Grain for Storage," "Enemies of Stored Grain," and "Storage Techniques and Models," 500 pages total, by Carl Lindblad and Laurel Druben, 1976, prices of single volumes: $8.50 in U.S., $9.50 international surface mail, $14.50 international air mail; prices of three-volume set: $18.00 in U.S., $19.00 international surface mail, $32.50 international air mail; prices of single volumes in Spanish: $12.00 in U.S., $12.75 international surface mail, $18.00 international air mail; from VITA.

This three-volume set of books was prepared to be used by local development workers, based on materials developed by the Peace Corps and other organizations. It is simpler but not as comprehensive as (and much more expensive than) **Post Harvest Food Losses in Developing Countries** (1978) by the National Academy of Sciences, and **Handling and Storage of Food Grains in Tropical and Subtropical Areas** (1975) by the U.N. Food and Agriculture Organization (FAO).

"Using a format of plain language and informative illustrations, the handbook gives some background to the world's grain storage problem; presents construction plans for grain dryer and storage facilities; offers information on insect and rodent control (with and without the use of poisons); provides shortened, illustrated versions of text material to serve as guidelines for extension agents who wish to prepare their own materials.

"A main aim of the manual is to present its material in a form as close as possible to the way in which the extension agent needs the information in order to pass it on successfully. Ideally, the only adaptations an extension agent should have to make using the material are to translate it (not in all cases) and/or to add culturally specific illustrations or photos. Or the manual material can be used as a base for audio-visual presentations. The idea is for the manual to serve as an idea facilitator and communication link between the development worker and his audience."

The authors explain the storage problem; the characteristics of grain and how these affect grain storage considerations; grain, moisture and air and the interaction between these; and important notes on the preparation of grain for storage.

There is a major section on grain dryers (95 pages) which includes complete production and operating instructions for 3 different solar dryers, pit & above-ground oil barrel dryers, and improved traditional units such as the maize (corn) drying and storage crib (made of bamboo). Instructions for sun-drying using plastic sheets, and descriptions of the University of the Philippines and International Rice Research Institute (IRRI) rice dryers are provided.

Storage methods are covered in 150 pages, including use of the following: baskets, cloth or burlap sacks, airtight structures, underground pits, plastic sacks, metal drums and bins, earthen structures, cement and concrete structures, and ferrocement pits and bins.

Manual of Improved Farm and Village-Level Grain Storage Methods, MF 07-274, book, 243 pages, by David Dichter and Associates, 1978, DM16 ($9.00) plus postage from TZ-Verlagsgesellschaft mbH, Bruchwiesenweg 19, D-6101 Rossdorf 1, Federal Republic of Germany.

This handbook provides a good explanation of the important considerations that are keys to better grain storage. The introduction also describes the grain storage problem quite well. Photos and text for the construction of 4 different small storage containers are provided. The descriptions, however, are too wordy and not always well matched with the drawings. Standard designs for sun dryers are also shown, but no cost or output figures are given. As a resource for equipment, this handbook is not as complete as we'd like to see.

The text, which could be shortened considerably, takes the form of lectures with questions and answers. It is intended to be used as a training manual for extension workers in a standard extension effort (in which grain storage designs are chosen by a central agency for dissemination). The book does emphasize the importance of understanding the principles of good grain storage and basing improvements on traditional techniques, rather than the transfer of an alien grain storage technology.

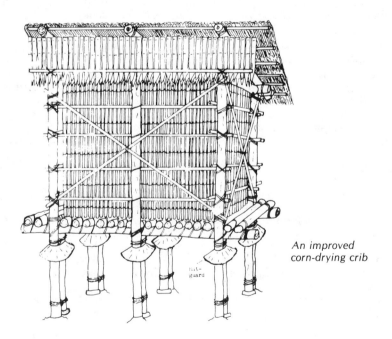

*An improved
corn-drying crib*

Storage of Food Grain: A Guide for Extension Workers, MF 06-281, book, 33 pages, by Abdel-Hamid F. Abdel-Aziz, FAO, 1975, $6.00 from UNIPUB.

Based on an FAO farm and community grain storage project and the Save Grain Campaign in India, this short book is intended to help extension personnel in planning and implementing extension programs for improved grain storage at the farm level. (Some 70% of India's grain is consumed at the farm level, never entering urban markets.) There is little technical information presented; rather, the material covered is the organization rather than the content of an extension effort.

The author takes a conventional information transfer extension approach, but he is sensitive to the value of traditional techniques. He urges creation of a range of storage options for farmers of different income levels, including full use of traditional systems with any necessary improvements. The author stresses practical skills training over scientific explanations; he may even be underestimating the importance of understanding principles. A variety of helpful communication aids and strategies are presented.

Guide to the Manufacture of Metal Bins, plans, 17 pages, and **Domestic Grain Storage Bins**, MF 07-285, booklet, 25 pages, Save Grain Campaign, India, out of print in 1985.

Complete technical drawings for making four sizes of sheet metal grain storage bins. The booklet gives step by step instructions to be used with the plans. Capacity of the bins ranges from .4 cubic meters (230 kgs of paddy or 300 kgs of wheat) to 1.35 cubic meters (750 kgs of paddy or 1000 kgs of wheat). The lightweight bins are easily transported when empty, and can be lifted by one person. These bins were developed by the Indian Grain Storage Institute as part of the nationwide Save Grain Campaign.

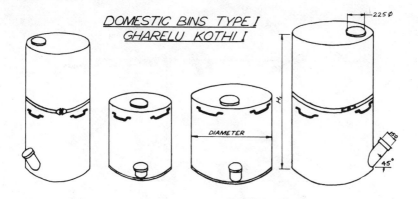

DOMESTIC BINS TYPE I
GHARELU KOTHI I

China: Grain Storage Structures, book, 127 pages, FAO, 1982, $14.50 from UNIPUB.

This is a review of storage structures visited by an FAO study group in 1979. The primary type is a unique clay/straw silo based on a traditional Chinese building technique, in which bundles of straw soaked in wet clay are worked together to form solid, well-insulated walls. Originally built in small sizes (e.g. 4m diameter, 2m high, 25 cubic meter capacity), these were later built in much larger sizes (260 cubic meter average capacity). 70,000 large units were built during the 20 years prior to 1979.

The advantages of these silos are claimed to be:

" — low cost per ton stored grain (usually half the cost of warehouses);

—locally available material (no steel, cement, etc.);
—no specialized labour required (regular labour of a grain depot can build);
—earthquake resistance (claimed, to some extent);
—lot sizes convenient (50-250 tons/silo normally);
—protection of stored grain is good."

Details of this construction technique are described, along with photos and drawings.

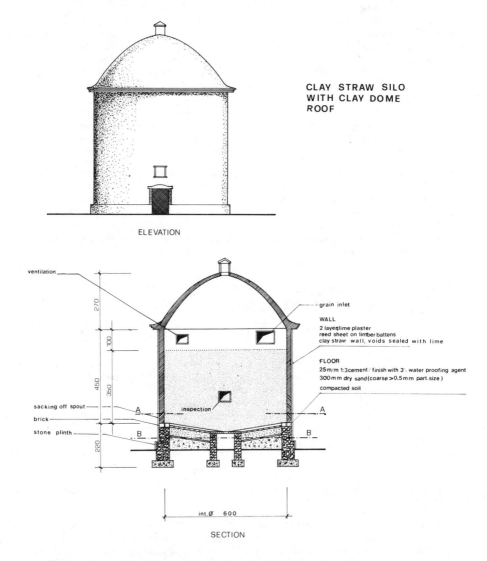

CLAY STRAW SILO
WITH CLAY DOME
ROOF

ELEVATION

SECTION

Evaluation of the Bissa—An Indigenous Storage Bin, MF 07-266, paper, 38 pages, by K. Pallpane, Rice Processing Centre, 1978, available on request from Paddy Marketing Board, Colombo, Sri Lanka.

This paper describes and evaluates the traditional Bissa rice storage bin used by farmers in Sri Lanka. Results of a careful test of the structure are presented.

Drawings for construction are included. The bin is made of woven sticks plastered with clay, with a thatched roof.

In Sri Lanka, only 40% of the total rice production is marketed; consequently, there is a high level of on-farm storage for seeds and family consumption. "In improving farm level storage, it is always better to improve and popularize the already existing permanent storage structures, which can be fabricated from material easily available at farm level at a low cost and also whose design and operation is known."

The Bissa is a permanent structure with a capacity from ½ ton to 10 tons. A 5-ton Bissa is estimated to require 164 person-hours for construction, plus the use of local materials, for a total cost in Sri Lanka of $50. The total maintenance, depreciation, and loading/unloading costs for 1 year are about $1.75 per ton. Properly dried paddy (rice) is generally stored for 6 months without any significant loss of quality or quantity.

"The majority of the farmers do not adopt any pest controlling practices because according to them, the damage due to insect attack is negligible if clean dry paddy is stored in the structure... A main defect of this structure is that it has no facilities for aeration to bring down temperature rises." Some minor changes are proposed.

"According to the farmers, a properly maintained Bissa will last for over fifty years."

A good example of a successful, low-cost traditional grain storage bin that could be relevant in many other countries.

Storage Management, MF 07-293, book, approximately 100 pages, by Malcolm Harper, 1982, $19.95 from International Labor Office, 1750 New York Avenue N.W., Washington D.C. 20006, USA.

These materials are intended for use in training managers of agricultural cooperatives, with 35-40 hours (6-7 days) of instruction. Participants are expected to gain an understanding of how to evaluate costs, benefits and risks of storage; estimate the amount of space needed; choose between storage methods; keep good records; measure grain moisture content and temperature; and control pests. Includes a good collection of common problems and typical tasks for students to perform.

Storing Vegetables and Fruits in Basements, Cellars, Outbuildings and Pits, Home and Garden Bulletin No. 119, MF 07-294, 17 pages, U.S. Dept. of Agriculture, revised September 1973, $2.25 from USGPO.

An introduction to storage cellars and pits, for use in vegetable and fruit storage in areas where the winter temperatures average 30 degrees Fahrenheit or less (-1°C).

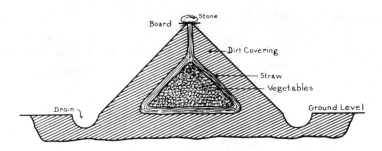

FIGURE 3.—Cone-shaped pit showing details of construction.

Principles of Potato Storage, MF 07-290, book, 105 pages, by Robert Booth and Roy Shaw, International Potato Center, Swiss Francs 16.00 from SKAT; or $5.45 plus postage from Agribookstore, 1611 North Kent Street, Arlington, Virginia 22209, USA.

A thorough reference book on storage from the main international center devoted to the study of the potato, this is the place to look first on this topic. The principles are explained, and the technologies embodying these principles range from very simple and low cost to complicated and more expensive. Management and economics are also discussed.

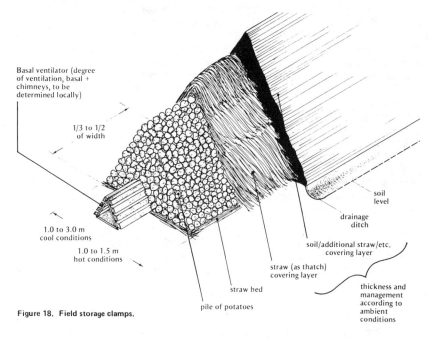

Basal ventilator (degree of ventilation, basal + chimneys, to be determined locally)

1/3 to 1/2 of width

1.0 to 3.0 m cool conditions

1.0 to 1.5 m hot conditions

soil level

drainage ditch

soil/additional straw/etc. covering layer

straw (as thatch) covering layer

straw bed

pile of potatoes

thickness and management according to ambient conditions

Figure 18. Field storage clamps.

Barns, Sheds and Outbuildings, book, 240 pages, by Byron Halsted, 1881, reprinted 1985 by Stephen Greene Press, $7.95 plus postage from Viking Penguin Inc., 299 Murray Hill Parkway, East Rutherford, New Jersey 07073, USA.

The icehouses and cool chambers, including ones using spring water, are the unusual items here that are otherwise hard to find in the literature. The root cellar

Fig. 164.—SECTION OF ICE HOUSE AND DAIRY.

information is also of interest. The rest of the book consists of undistinguished farm structures, primarily for animals.

Home-Scale Processing and Preservation of Fruits and Vegetables, MF 07-270, booklet, 68 pages, Central Food Technological Research Institute, 1977 (7th edition), Rs. 4.50 (English edition) or Rs. 1.00 (Hindi edition) from Director, Central Food Technological Research Institute, Mysore 570013, India.

This Indian publication is a very useful one, both for the material it contains and for the model it presents to other countries. A basic introduction of home-scale food processing technologies (canning, drying, and pickling) is combined with specific fruit and vegetable recipes, a detailed glossary in several important Indian languages, and access information for equipment and supplies.

The wide array of preserved food options is designed to be tasty, reduce produce losses, and improve nutritional levels. Products include: cashew apple extract, mango leather, jackfruit nectar, guava cheese, papaya pickles, and bamboo chutney. Processing time adjustments for higher altitudes are included in the detailed processing charts. The authors also describe a low-cost, complete community canning unit.

"An effort has been made to present information in a simple and comprehensive manner, so that an average housewife can use it without any difficulty. It can be used by home science and catering institutions as well as agricultural extension agencies."

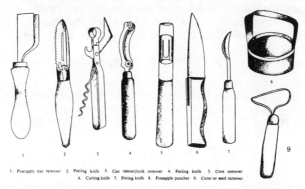

1. Pineapple eye remover 2. Peeling knife 3. Can opener/cork remover 4. Peeling knife 5. Core remover
6. Cutting knife 7. Pitting knife 8. Pineapple puncher 9. Corer or seed remover

Hand tools for home preservation of fruits and vegetables

Stocking Up: How to Preserve the Foods You Grow Naturally, MF 07-292, book, 532 pages, edited by Carol Hupping Stoner, 1977, $19.95 from Rodale.

Rodale Press's bestseller, written for U.S. readers, nevertheless has some information relevant to developing countries. Drying of fruits and the production of fruit leathers, underground storage of fruits and vegetables (in cold areas), pickling, making jams and jellies, making fruit and vegetable juices, the production of cheese and yogurt, and the smoking of meat and fish are covered. The varieties of fruits and vegetables are only those common to the U.S. Although limited by the absence of much of the equipment used in the examples, alert readers in developing countries will find some hints and nuggets of information not found in the other books on these subjects.

Putting Food By, book, 565 pages, by Ruth Hertzberg, Beatrice Vaughn, and Janet Greene, 1975, $4.00 from WEA.

Here is a basic food preservation manual for the U.S. reader, with information on canning, freezing, drying and curing of fruits, vegetables, meats and fish.

Although freezing equipment and canning supplies (especially lids and jars) are relatively more expensive in developing countries (and thus impractical in most places), some of the other techniques are widely relevant. Root cellars, for example, are of interest in mountainous regions such as Nepal and the Andes. Some but not all of the fruits and vegetables covered are found in developing countries. The final section includes recipes for making soap, sausages, cottage cheese and many meals that use the foods preserved with the methods in the book.

Preservation of Foods, MF 07-289, book, 86 pages, by Agromisa, DFl3.50 from TOOL.

A review of techniques for long term food preservation, including canning with glass jars or tins, drying, salting, pickling, jam and juice making, and smoking (meat and fish). The varieties of fruits and vegetables covered are those common to Western countries.

Food Drying, publication IDRC-195e, MF 07-287, book, 104 pages, edited by Gordon Yaciuk, 1981, free to local groups in developing countries, others $8.00, from IDRC; also available in French.

These conference papers examine a variety of traditional and improved technologies for drying rice, potatoes, vegetables, fish and coffee.

The Indonesian paper comes to the interesting conclusion that additional investment in concrete floors for sun drying of rice is superior to investment in artificial dryers. Authors from Thailand and the Philippines, in contrast, support some specific artificial dryer designs that they believe to be advantageous.

Dry It, You'll Like It, MF 07-264, book, 74 pages, by G. MacManiman, $5.00 from WEA.

This book covers drying for food preservation. Dried food is nutritionally better than canned food. No preservatives, chemicals or electricity (freezer) are required. Dried food takes up ⅙ or less of the usual storage space required, and can usually be stored a couple of years.

This is a simple little book with general instructions for all food drying. Specific information is given for most American fruits, vegetables, and some herbs. Two pages on meat and fish are included, along with recipes.

Plans for a food dehydrator using simple tools and made largely of wood are complete and easy to follow. It does require some source of low heat that remains constant near 100 degrees Fahrenheit—the dehydrator could possibly be suspended over a wood-burning stove while other cooking is taking place.

How to Dry Fruits and Vegetables, MF 07-272, leaflet, 12 pages, 1976, free to serious groups, from Action for Food Production (AFPRO), Technical Information Service, Community Centre, C-17, Safdarjung Develop. Area, New Delhi-11 00 16, India.

The purpose of this booklet is to give practical information to people in the rural areas of India "on how to dry fruits and vegetables, which can then be preserved from times of plenty to be used in the lean seasons of the year. It can also be used as a handbook to teach village level Community Development workers."

The information is comprehensive, with tables on preparation hints, treatment before dehydration, dehydrated product yields, description of dried condition, and specific fruit and vegetable refreshing data. Heavy emphasis is given to treatment of various fruits with sulphur, which prevents discoloration during the drying process and provides some protection against insects in storage. (We however do not feel that it is yet clear whether the widespread use of sulphur is justified, due to the added expense and potential health side effects of this preservative — editors.)

Drying and Processing Tree Fruits, publication C040, MF 07-286, booklet, 20 pages, by D. McG. McBean, CSIRO, 1976, $6.00 from UNIPUB.

This describes the important considerations in the sundrying of apricots, peaches, nectarines, pears and prunes during hot dry weather on open wooden trays, as is done in Australia. The use of sulphur is expected and described.

"Halved fruits are placed close together and one layer thick on self-stacking wooden trays...They should be made of relatively knot-free softwood which has been smooth sawn or dressed so as to prevent particles of wood from becoming embedded in the soft fruit tissue. The use of hardwood results in staining of the fruit...The drying-yard should be established where fruit is exposed to direct sunlight for as long as possible during the day and where prevailing winds blow directly across the trays. It should not be near roads or pathways used by wheeled vehicles as this will result in dusty and dirty dried fruit...Trays of fruit are generally placed directly on the ground but it has been shown that fruit dries a little faster if it is suspended up to one metre above ground level...probably due to convective wind currents carrying moisture away from the drying surface of the fruit. Elevation of trays results in cleaner dried fruit and also appreciably reduces back-breaking labour during spreading and picking up...If heavy dews are likely (particularly if associated with poor drying conditions during the day) trays should be stacked at night."

It is recommended that only properly ripe fruit of the same size be dried together, so that a full tray will be dry at the same time. Bruised, damaged, and over-ripe fruit, if included, will reduce the quality of the product, increase the chance of insect infestation, and be likely to stick to the wooden trays.

Sun Dry Your Fruits and Vegetables, MF 07-282, booklet, 26 pages, U.S. Dept. of Agriculture, 1958, out of print in 1985.

This illustrated step-by-step guide was written for extension workers in simple English. Other than simple household equipment, the only items required are wooden trays, and for some fruits, a large box to cover the trays while sulphur is burned inside. The booklet emphasizes the need for cleanliness and hot, dry air that circulates freely. A chart gives directions for many different fruits and vegetables. Steaming is recommended prior to drying for most vegetables. A step-by-step description of the use of sulphur when drying some fruits is provided, as are notes on the preparation of dried food for use.

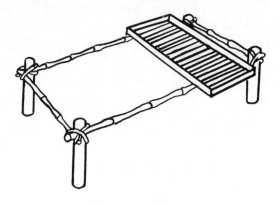

An outdoor drying rack

A Survey of Solar Agricultural Dryers, Technical Report T99, MF 07-283, book, 144 pages, December 1975, $9.00 from BRACE.

This book focuses on experiments with the use of small-scale agricultural dryers in rural areas of developing nations. Includes a representative sample of different types of dryers; emphasizes local improvements and adaptation. There are 24 case studies of different dryers in a variety of countries; each one has photos, full construction drawings, and the address of the people involved.

The dryers included are used for: coffee, grapes, fruits, vegetables, cereals, grains, herbs, flowers, and lumber. They are divided into natural and sun dryers, direct solar dryers, mixed mode solar dryers, and indirect solar dryers.

Highly recommended.

Potential of Solar Agricultural Dryers in Developing Areas, paper, 8 pages, by T.A. Lawand, 1977, included in **Technology for Solar Energy Utilization**, MF 23-563, UNIDO, 1978 (see review).

This paper, presented to a UNIDO conference in 1977, summarizes the principles of solar dryers, as well as surveying various types of dryers from around the world. Some of the examples: a grape drying rack from Australia, a cabinet dryer from Syria, a glass-roof greenhouse dryer from Brazil, a wind-ventilated dryer from Syria, and a lumber-seasoning kiln from India. There is also a bibliography.

This is a condensation of the information contained in the more complete **Survey of Solar Agricultural Dryers** from Brace Research Institute (see review). Lawand hopes to stimulate people to adapt these designs and develop their own to fit local conditions.

A good introduction to the subject.

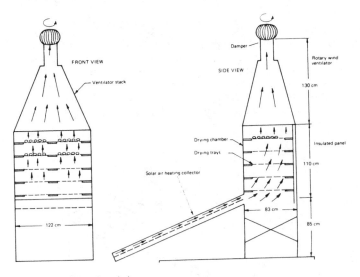

Solar wind-ventilated dryer

How to Make a Solar Cabinet Dryer for Agricultural Produce, MF 07-273, booklet (#L-6), 11 pages of text, diagrams and charts, 1965 (revised 1973), $1.75 from BRACE.

"The dryer is essentially a solar hot box, in which fruit, vegetables or other matter can be dehydrated." It dries produce cheaply for storage, without insect or dust contamination, and reduces moisture content to the lowest necessary level. The dryer is a rectangular container, insulated at the base and sides, with a transparent roof and circular air flow. The framework can be made of virtually any material — woven bamboo, metal, plywood, adobe, or brick. Insulation can consist of "locally available materials such as wood shavings, sawdust, bagasse, coconut fiber, reject wool, or animal hair."

The capacity of the dryer is 7.5 kg per square meter of drying area. Brace's prototype units have dried 3 kgs of onions or okra in 2 days. A model in Syria cost $14.00; one in Barbados cost $23.00 to build. Brace estimates the annual operating cost at $6.89. The temperatures inside reach 70-80 degrees Centigrade, so the dryer can also be used for warming foods and other materials.

A production drawing for this dryer can also be obtained from Brace (see below).

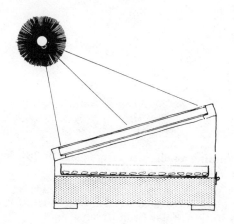

Production Drawing for a Solar Cabinet Dryer, MF 07-273, 1972, 1 large sheet, $2.50 from BRACE.

This is drawing #T-85 from Brace, designed for use with the booklet listed above.

Solar Dryers, Periodical Note No. 3, MF 07-279, 16 pages, 1978, free to individuals and groups involved in development and A.T. work, from Shri A.M.M. Murugappa Chettier Research Center, Photosynthesis and Energy Division, Tharamani, Madras-600 042, India.

Translated from the original Tamil, this report presents 4 very simple solar dryer designs used in rural India for drying paddy (rice), vegetables and fish. All use materials such as bamboo, sand and cement; glazing is provided by a polythene sheet. All were built for Rs. 100-400 (US$12-50) including labor. These dryers were not extensively field tested.

Drawings and descriptions of each dryer are given; these are sometimes hard to follow. This booklet is valuable primarily as a source of ideas on low-cost materials that can be tried.

How to Build a Solar Crop Dryer, MF 07-271, plans, 9 pages, $2.50 from New Mexico Solar Energy Association, P.O. Box 2004, Santa Fe, New Mexico 87504, USA.

Detailed plans for building a crop dryer. Air is drawn in at the bottom, heated by a collector, and then sent up through the drying chamber. An adjustable vent allows control of temperature (which may reach 120 degrees Fahrenheit). The unit

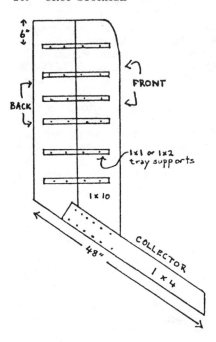

is 4 feet wide and has 36 square feet of drying area, enough for almost 2 bushels of food.

Although the cost is estimated at $60.00, the design can be varied to use cheaper local materials. It is suitable for drying small amounts of fruits and vegetables. Very simple.

Cookbook for Building a Solar Crop Dryer, MF 07-284, booklet, 18 pages, by Arnold and Maria Valdez, 1977, out of print.

A short set of plans with instructions for making a solar fruit and vegetable dryer out of wood, glass, corrugated metal and metal lathe. The design is similar to that in **How to Build a Solar Crop Dryer**.

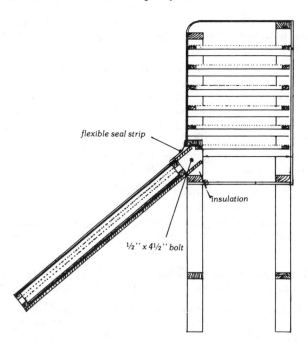

Construction of a Brick Hot Air Copra Dryer, Technical Bulletin #9, MF 07-263, booklet, 29 pages, by S. Mason, 1972, Papua New Guinea, limited supply available, include return postage, from DWS.

"The purpose of this bulletin is to assist the indigenous copra owner who has had no experience in construction work, to construct his own drier, so that a better quality copra can be produced more economically."

"The drier consists of a brick building with a minimum of timber exposed in areas subject to the heated air flow from the firebox. Fuel such as wood or coconut shells is fed into the firebox at the front of the drier. The heat from the fire warms a mild steel radiating plate on the hot air chamber which in turn heats the air within the drier."

This dryer was designed to have an output of six 155-pound bags of copra per week. Construction details, materials list, glossary of technical terms, drawings of the dryer, and drawings of a wooden mold for making individual bricks are all provided. This manual does not tell you how to make the bricks. "**Selection of Materials for Stabilized Brick Manufacture** Technical Bulletin #5 should be studied to assist in selecting materials suitable to make bricks" (see review).

One limitation of this leaflet is that the assembly drawings are hard to read. However, this appears to be a sound design, one that the author claims prevents accidental fires.

Solar Grain Drying: Progress and Potential, MF 07-280, booklet, 14 pages, by G. Foster and R. Peart, 1976, free from Office of Communication, USDA, Washington D.C. 20250, USA.

This booklet describes studies of solar grain dryers, particularly for rice and corn, from the midwestern United States. The dryers were made of inflated polyethylene

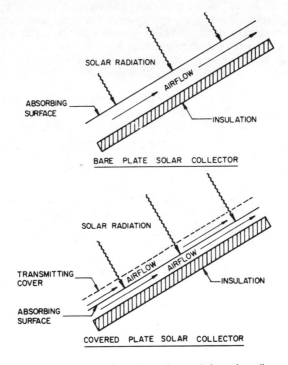

SOLAR RADIATION

AIRFLOW

ABSORBING SURFACE

INSULATION

BARE PLATE SOLAR COLLECTOR

SOLAR RADIATION

AIRFLOW   AIRFLOW

TRANSMITTING COVER

INSULATION

ABSORBING SURFACE

COVERED PLATE SOLAR COLLECTOR

Figure 2.—Schematic of bare-plate and covered-plate solar collector for heating air.

(soft plastic) shells to heat air as in a greenhouse; the air was then pumped through the grain.

These tests were primarily to determine the feasibility of solar grain drying. Details of the designs are not given. The booklet does offer general descriptions of grain drying systems.

The Performance and Economic Feasibility of Solar Grain Drying Systems, Agricultural Economic Report No. 396, MF 07-275, booklet, 33 pages, by Walter G. Heid, February 1978, available from Commodity Economics Division, Economics, Statistics and Cooperatives Service, U.S. Dept. of Agriculture, Washington D.C. 20250, USA.

This is a summary of the performance of various types of solar grain drying systems from the midwestern U.S. All are for large-scale, temperate climate agriculture. Some of these dryers use electric air blowers and/or auxiliary electric heating. There is a short explanation of the various parts of a crop drying system. Tables compare size, capacity, performance from tests, and costs of 8 different systems now in use.

The emphasis in this paper is on economic evaluation (rapidly becoming more favorable to solar drying since this report was published), rather than on the principles of operation.

Drying Equipment for Cereal Grains and Other Agricultural Produce, MF 07-265, plans, 11 pages, by Keith Markwardt, $1.60 from CARE Philippines, P.O. Box 2052, Manila, Philippines.

The agricultural dryer described in these plans was built by a Peace Corps volunteer in the Philippines. It consists of three components: 1) a concrete and brick furnace 48" by 24" which uses rice hulls for fuel; 2) an 8' by 16' drying bed; and 3) a gasoline, diesel, or electric powered fan which blows heated air from the furnace through the perforated floor of the drying bed. The dryer has been used for fish, copra, and a variety of grains and vegetables. Drying capacity varies with type of produce. One batch (50 cavan, or 2500 kg) of paddy dries in approximately 6-8 hours at an operating cost (including engine fuel, maintenance, and depreciation) of about $3.00.

The advantage of this design is the use of rice hulls (plentiful in many rural areas)

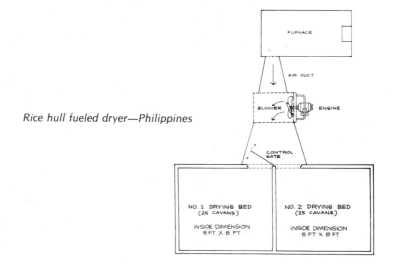

Rice hull fueled dryer—Philippines

to cheaply fuel the furnace. The builders estimate that this dryer can be constructed for about $500 in the Philippines. Such a dryer might best be used by a cooperative, allowing farmers to collectively meet this initial investment and take advantage of the high capacity and low operating costs.

Simple Grain Drier, MF 07-277, 2 descriptive articles plus complete dimensional drawings and photos, 15 pages total, by W. Chancellor, U.C. Davis, out of print in 1985.

This information includes clear production drawings and a report from field tests in Asia.

"Local availability of drying facilities not only can reduce spoilage losses in storage but can also promote increased production through strengthening the practicality of double cropping in irrigated areas where the offseason crop is harvested in humid weather."

This dryer has the following elements: "a horizontal metal surface placed over a fire pit; use of animal power to stir the shallow layer of grain placed on the metal

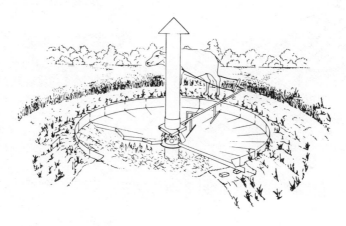

An animal stirring the drier

surface; grain temperature, and thus the rate of moisture evaporation, controlled by adjusting the rate of fuel use."

The dryer is made mostly of sheet metal, and is of simple design. It is easy to build and requires no special skills to operate. It can be disassembled for easy transport and storage. The stirring blade is attached to the smoke stack base with a wooden bearing. A durable thermometer is needed, but the operator can estimate temperatures from the smell and feel of the grain. Cost of all materials was approximately $160.

This unit is for use in humid or rainy conditions when sun drying would not be effective. "In tests using rice straw as the fuel, it was determined that the straw contained in the grain bundles brought to the threshing site would provide enough fuel to complete the drying operation." Grain dried by this process did not germinate, however, so this should not be used for seed.

More than one animal is needed, to allow the animals to rest alternately. Two persons are required. The 16-foot diameter design is capable of drying 1000 lbs. of rice at a time, reducing moisture from 24% to 14% in 4 hours. 160 lbs. of moderately dry straw was used as the fuel.

Small-Scale Processing of Fish, MF 07-291, book, 118 pages, ILO, 1982, $8.55 from International Labor Office, Washington Branch, 1750 New York Avenue N.W., Washington D.C. 20006, USA.

People involved in technical support to small fisheries may find this a useful reference. It covers a spectrum of techniques and technologies that range from virtually no-cost procedures to substantial investment in equipment. Salting, drying, fermenting, smoking, boiling and canning are discussed, along with general guidelines to reduce spoilage before, during and after processing. A variety of simple smoking kilns is shown. An attempt is made to assess the costs of the various processing techniques and technologies.

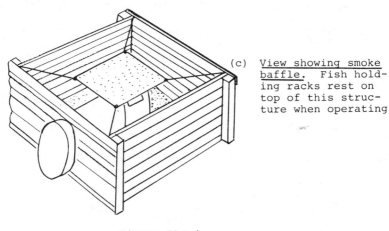

(c) <u>View showing smoke baffle.</u> Fish holding racks rest on top of this structure when operating

Figure III.4
Modified version of traditional oven - Ivory Coast kiln

How to Salt Fish, MF 07-288, pamphlet, 9 pages, by D. Casper, VITA, reprinted in **Village Technology Handbook**.

"The process of salting fish is influenced by weather, size and species of fish and the quality of the salt used. Therefore, experience is needed to adapt the process outlined here to your situation... Salted fish, if properly packed to protect it from excessive moisture, will not spoil."

This article covers the complete process—preparing the fish, salting, washing and drying to remove excess salt, and air drying. It is a simple process requiring only knives, waterproof vats, and large amounts of salt. Curing in the brine takes 12-15 days in warm weather, up to 21 in cold weather. Six days of warm weather are required for drying.

Rural Home Techniques—Volume 1: Food Preservation, FAO Economic and Social Development Series #51, MF 07-267, leaflets, total of 60 pages, 1976, from Dr. Ludmilla A. Marin, Home Economics and Social Programmes Service, FAO, Via delle Terme di Caracella, 00100-Rome, Italy; or $9.50 from UNIPUB.

This is the first of a planned series of Food and Agriculture Organization (FAO) publications on equipment and techniques related to food preparation, handling, and storage. Drawings illustrating the steps in the preservation of fish and meat are presented, with text in English, Spanish, and French. Includes cleaning, filleting, splitting, dry salting, wet salting, smoke drying, sun drying, and storage of fish;

and salting, salt-drying, rendering fat, and storage of meat. Drawings of all the tools needed include 10 different simple designs for smoking ovens made of commonly available materials.

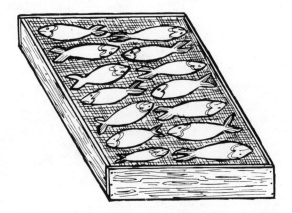

ADDITIONAL REFERENCES ON CROP STORAGE

Village Technology in Eastern Africa reviews some of the simple food preservation and storage technologies affordable at the village level; see BACKGROUND READING.

Rural Women: Their Integration in Development Programs and How Simple Intermediate Technologies Can Help Them suggests the use of enclosed solar dryers, black plastic sheets for direct drying, and improved grain storage units; see BACKGROUND READING.

Low Cost Rural Equipment Suitable for Manufacture in East Africa includes designs for a solar dryer and a grain storage crib; see AGRICULTURAL TOOLS.

Rice: Post Harvest Technology describes the technical requirements for rice drying and storage; see AGRICULTURAL TOOLS.

Plans for Low-Cost Farming Implements includes drawings of platform carts with drying pans for crop drying in areas of frequent rains; crops can be brought in under a protective roof quickly; see AGRICULTURAL TOOLS.

Forestry

Forestry

"The challenge to forestry of contributing to bettering the condition of the rural poor is. . .likely to entail a radical reorientation extending from policy all the way through to its technical foundations."
— **Forestry for Local Community Development**, FAO

Wood is a basic resource for meeting human needs. It has always been important as a cooking fuel and building material. But throughout history, expanding human settlements have threatened and eventually destroyed forests. To the individual farmer, the forest is often a nuisance to be cleared away so that the land can be farmed. To the villager, the forest is the provider of plentiful cooking fuel. And to the industrialist, the forest is the source of plywood, paper, cardboard, and lumber to meet the enormous demands of industrial societies. The result has been that a potentially renewable resource has generally been exploited as a one-time boon for the first to arrive.

The consequences of unrestrained deforestation are many. The cultivation of hillsides generally leads to rapid erosion of topsoil and loss of productive potential. The removal of trees reduces the soil's ability to retain water, leading to ever-increasing cycles of flood and drought in the lands below. Inefficient cooking methods and a lack of deliberate replanting of fuelwood trees have forced millions of the poor to spend a large part of each day hunting for fuel and carrying it long distances on their backs. This time-consuming, exhausting work further guarantees their poverty. In search of maximum immediate production from a piece of land, lumbering companies around the world have clear-cut the forests, leaving a devastated landscape vulnerable to erosion, and destroying any potential for sustained production.

"The humid forests of the tropics once occupied at least 1600 million hectares (4000 million acres), and have not only been the main centers for living species on earth, but have held the lands together, moderated and modified world climates, and helped to maintain a desirable balance of atmospheric gasses. Now they are vanishing at an incredible rate. There are reported to be 935 million hectares in actual humid tropical forest, a 40% reduction in total area. They are disappearing at a rate of sixteen million hectares per year. . ."
— Ray Dasmann, "Planet Earth — 1980", 1980

Some observers are convinced that the considerable local, national and international problems associated with deforestation will be followed by global climatic shifts if deforestation is not brought under control within the next ten years. World food production is thus directly threatened by local soil erosion, floods and droughts, and climatic changes that mean shifting rainfall patterns and expanding deserts.

As the problems caused by deforestation are becoming better understood, development planners are scrambling to find temporary and long-term solutions. The skills of the forestry profession are in great demand. Yet on closer examination it becomes clear that more and better-funded forestry programs alone will not be enough. Major changes in attitude and strategy will also be required. In particular, foresters and planners cannot continue forest management focussed largely on production for industry. Just as important, forestry programs can no longer be based on the strategy of preventing the community from gaining access to the forest. The FAO book **Forestry for Local Community Development** *marks an historical shift in consciousness, as it describes the strategies and programs that can mean successful sustainable production of forest resources through community involvement. But for the most part,*

"In precious few countries have the energies of the foresters been bent upon helping the peasant to develop the kind of forestry that would serve his material welfare. This is why there are so few village woodlots and fuel plantations. This is why so little work has been done on forage trees, fruit and nut orchards. This is why so few shelterbelts have been created. . .This is why forestry has been invoked so rarely to reclaim or rehabilitate land. This is why so few of the many possible agro-forestry combinations have been established which are specifically geared to meeting real local needs. . .

"Agriculture-supportive forestry does not by any means exclude forest industries. Small rural industries are an integral part of agriculture-supportive forestry: fuelwood, charcoal, poles, stakes, fencing, hurdles, screens, farm tools and implements, building materials, simple furniture. But these activities, like all other agriculture-supportive activities, are activities that cannot be carried out on the required scale and in the required manner by a conventionally oriented and conventionally organized forest service. They will only be effective, and will only make sense, if they are carried out by the peasants themselves, for themselves. The role of the forester, wherever he may sit in the organizational structure, can only be to stimulate, offer guidance and suggestions, impart techniques and carry out training."

— "Forest Industries for Socio-Economic Development", by Jack Westoby, 1978, formerly Director, Programme Coordination and Operations, Forestry Department, FAO

The first books in this chapter discuss the extent of the deforestation problem, along with conclusions about sound practices to protect the forests while using them to satisfy human needs. **China: Forestry Support for Agriculture** *offers a fascinating national case study of successful reforestation for maximum agricultural benefit, while* **Reforestation in Arid Lands** *represents a general practical manual.* **Forestry for Local Community Development** *and* **Community Participation in African Fuelwood Production** *shed light on the requirements for successful village woodlots and other fuelwood replanting projects.* **Tree Crops: A Permanent Agriculture** *notes that trees conserve soil far better than row crops on hilly terrain, and argues that conversion to tree crops is the only choice that will maintain the long-term productivity of agriculture in these areas.*

As firewood use continues to be a contributing factor in deforestation, the promotion of efficient low-cost locally-built cooking stoves appears to be a cost-effective first step towards conservation in many areas (see the chapter ENERGY: COOKSTOVES). Fast-growing tree species are also getting a great deal of attention. The National Academy of Sciences book **Firewood Crops** *is one new inventory of fast-growing species, and other books reviewed here cover particular species and growing techniques.*

Village forest industries are the final topic in this chapter. Timber drying, through both regular kilns and solar dryers, is an important step in the production of good quality hardwood for tool handles and furniture. The use and repair of chainsaws, and chainsaw attachments for board production, are covered in the last few entries.

Planting for the Future: Forestry for Human Needs, Worldwatch Paper 26, MF 08-299, booklet, 64 pages, by Erik Eckholm, 1979, $2.00 from Worldwatch Institute, 1776 Massachusetts Avenue N.W., Washington D.C. 20036, USA.

Eckholm describes how the world's most extensive and productive forests (in the humid tropics) are severely threatened. "There are currently about 75 cubic meters of wood in the world's dense forests for every person. By the end of the century, however, the per capita amount of exploitable timber will be nearly cut in half if the current deforestation rate is maintained . . ." Furthermore, these patterns of exploitation are of little benefit to those most dependent on wood in the poorer countries, which export most of their commercial timber as unsawn logs. "Though developing countries contain three-fourths of the world's people and more than half of its forest, they account for just 13 percent of global consumption of industrial wood . . . in fact, each year the average American consumes about as much wood — one cubic meter — in the form of paper as the average resident in many Third World countries burns as cooking fuel."

The author examines the interlocking causes of deforestation, as well as the economic and ecological implications of continued deforestation. "By the turn of the century, at least a further 250 million people will be without wood fuel for their minimum cooking and heating needs and will be forced to burn dried animal dung and agricultural residues, thereby further decreasing crop yields." China and South Korea, however, seem to have reversed serious deforestation trends with aggressive nationwide programs for community tree planting and management. Such strong political commitment to conservation at the top, with broad participation and shared benefits at the bottom, could be keys to successful reforestation in other countries as well.

A timely, provocative view of world forestry problems and possible solutions.

Environmentally Sound Small-Scale Forestry Projects, MF 08-289, book, 109 pages, by Peter F. Folliot and John L. Thames, Codel/VITA, 1983, $6.95 from VITA.

"This manual has been written for community development workers in Third World countries who are not technicians in the area of forestry, but who want some general guidelines for planning environmentally sound small-scale forestry projects." The book opens with a discussion of process for project planning, and the relationship of forestry to the environment. Background for planning is given for multiple-use forestry, harvesting trees for wood products, fuelwood management programs, agro-forestry projects, shelterbelt or windbreak plantings, reforestation and afforestation. We recommend this book as an introduction to forestry principles. Project planners will likely wish to refer to more specific and detailed texts once the material in this book has been covered.

Forestry Case Studies, Peace Corps Case Study CS-3, MF 08-292, booklet, 102 pages, 1982, available to Peace Corps volunteers and development workers from Peace Corps, Information Collection and Exchange, Room 701, 806 Connecticut Avenue N.W., Washington D.C. 20525, USA.

Case studies can be valuable tools to help project planners learn from others' experiences and their mistakes. Case studies from Peace Corps projects in eight countries are presented, each one ending with a section which evaluates the success of the project and restates factors which seemed beneficial or detrimental. The last chapter is a summary of the factors which seem most important to success.

Forest Farming, MF 08-307, book, 197 pages, by J. Sholto Douglas and Robert de J. Hart, 1984 edition, £7.20 from ITDG.

Forest Farming, co-authored by J. Sholto Douglas (who wrote **Hydroponics: The Bengal Method**), updates and expands J. Russell Smith's classic **Tree Crops:**

A Permanent Agriculture (see review). The authors show that "in food productivity alone tree crops can produce 10 to 15 times as much food per acre as field crops." With **Tree Crops** now back in print, the interested reader now has available a good set of introductory books on this extremely important subject.

The authors discuss the role of forests and tree crops in farming and offer detailed advice and information on various economic species, the use of their products for food and raw materials, planting techniques and suggestions, and guidance for the layout and operation of schemes of forest farming.

Douglas and Hart state: "The 'tool' with the greatest potential for feeding people and animals, for regenerating the soil, for restoring water-systems, for controlling floods and droughts, for creating more benevolent micro-climates and more comfortable and stimulating living conditions for humanity, is the tree."

Tree Crops: A Permanent Agriculture, MF 08-302, book, 408 pages, by J. Russell Smith, 1953, reprinted 1978, Harper and Row, out of print in 1985.

"Forest — field — plow — desert — that is the cycle of the hills under most plow agriculture. . .Field wash, in the United States, Latin America, Africa and many other parts of the world, is the greatest and most menacing of all resource wastes. . .We are today destroying our soil. . .faster and in greater quantity than has ever been done by any group of people at any time in the history of the world."

Written over 25 years ago, this is still considered one of the most important texts on the agricultural potential of tree crops. "Agriculturalists have completely overlooked the abundant food produced by such trees as the oaks, honey locust, persimmon, and walnut, which. . .can outproduce, acre for acre, the best efforts of the grass family (corn, wheat, oats) on most lands in formerly forested areas. Moreover, tree crops require less care, bind and improve instead of depleting the soil, and provide a permanent source of income which increases annually."

"If much of the tropic forest is to be preserved, we must make use of tree crops. Tree crops will safeguard fertility while producing food for man. In most cases there can be an undergrowth of leguminous nurse crops of small tree and bush to catch nitrogen, hold the soil, make humus and feed the crop trees — nuts, oils, fruits, gums, fibers, even choice weeds."

"The crop-yielding tree offers the best medium for extending agriculture to hills, to steep places, to rocky places, and to the lands where rainfall is deficient."

"Experiments with trees can be on almost any scale. Two trees, for example, might produce great (hybrid) results. There are thousands of individuals who can experiment and perhaps do something of great value."

Most of this extraordinary book consists of descriptions of the characteristics and uses of what Smith felt were the 35 most promising tree types for temperate and tropical climates. His photos and personal observations from years of traveling throughout the world add considerably to the impact of the book.

Forestry for Local Community Development, FAO Forestry Paper No. 7, MF 08-293, book, 114 pages, prepared by an FAO panel, 1978, available in English, Spanish and French, from FAO.

Here is a summary of what is known about constraints facing the rural poor that affect forestry, programs that address these constraints, and policy measures that have succeeded in different places. The study concentrates on programs in which rural communities process and use the forest products themselves; it excludes large-scale industrial forestry.

"Forestry for community development must. . . be forestry for the people and involving the people. It must be forestry which starts at the 'grass roots.' "

"The core of the problem for forest communities is. . .usually that they derive insufficient benefits from the forest. . .This. . .is often attributable to conventional forest management objectives and administrative practices, an orientation towards conservation, wood production, revenue collection, and regulation through punitive legislation. . . The task of forestry for the development of such communities is consequently to engage them more fully, positively, and beneficially in its utilization, management and protection. This may take the form of. . . logging or sawmilling cooperatives. . . production of honey. . . the concurrent production of forestry and agricultural crops, or. . . grazing of animals. . . This can require quite radical reorientation of traditional forestry concepts and practices."

"A feature of most successful recent community forestry endeavours has been a strong, sustained technical support system, capable of providing advice and essential inputs such as planting stock, and of maintaining such support through the period necessary to generate forestry as a self-sustaining activity in a particular area."

Key factors affecting success or failure of forestry programs are identified and summarized in seventeen brief case studies.

Highly recommended.

China: Forestry Support for Agriculture, FAO Forestry Paper No. 12, MF 08-286, book, 103 pages, FAO, 1978, $6.50 from UNIPUB.

This is the report of an FAO/UNDP-sponsored study tour in 1977, "to observe and analyse the Chinese approach to forestry development whereby it is integrated into and supports agriculture."

"Stricken by a series of natural calamities throughout history, China appears determined to tame rivers, regulate water systems, reverse soil erosion, establish a favorable climatological balance and thus banish the feeling of helplessness against natural disasters. Forestry has played a major role in achieving these objectives."

The participation of the people has been a central concept in China's forestry efforts. Research activities concentrate on practical problems, and include commune members; much is learned from the practical experiences of fieldworkers. Education of the people is seen as a requirement for successful tree planting programs. As a result the average Chinese is "much more knowledgeable about forestry than the average person in any other country," and protection of reforested areas is not a problem. Forested lands have doubled since 1949.

Tree planting has had direct economic benefits in the form of timber, fuelwood, livestock fodder, fruit and other products. In some areas shelterbelt forestry is considered the primary factor in dramatic agricultural gains, ahead of irrigation, fertilization, and improved seeds.

"The team left with the impression that the achievement of the PRC in environmental treeplanting would lie beyond the capacity of any organized forest service if such work were to be carried out in a system where labor had to be compensated directly by money wages. In every commune, 'four around' tree planting is an integral part of the commune's economic activity and tree planting is everybody's business."

The authors give particular attention to the organizational framework within which forestry work is conducted, the major kinds of forestry programs (shelterbelts, "four around" tree plantations, afforestation of bare land, intercropping) and fast-growing tree species commonly planted. The report concludes with notes of possibilities for adaptation of Chinese practices in other countries.

Community Participation in African Fuelwood Production, Transformation, and Utilization, MF 08-287, xeroxed paper, 108 pages, by Marilyn W. Hoskins, November 1979, available from AID Documentation and Handling Facility, 7222 47th Street, Suite 100, Chevy Chase, Maryland 20815, USA.

Drawing from actual case studies, this discussion paper reviews the role of the community development approach in fulfilling fuelwood energy needs. Hoskins acknowledges that there have been many failures in fuelwood projects, and that the time has come to learn from these efforts.

Two very interesting concepts described in this paper are the "Project Package Approach" and the "Management Plan Agreement." The first means that a given fuelwood project will be integrated into larger ongoing community projects. The second concept is unique. It requires that all parties to a project actively participate in design, negotiation and agreement to terms of a particular fuelwood scheme. This should involve donors or project initiators (local, private voluntary, national, or international groups), national government adminstrators, and representatives of the local people. The application of this concept may not assure good projects or prevent bad ones, but it at least makes clear what responsibilities each actor is to assume.

Manual of Reforestation and Erosion Control for the Philippines, MF 08-313, book, 569 pages, compiled by H.J. Weidelt, 1976, DM18 plus postage from GTZ, Dag-Hammarskjold-Weg 1, D-6236 Eschborn 1, Federal Republic of Germany.

Despite its title, only the first 33 pages of this book are specifically for the Philippines. The remaining 500 pages form a general textbook on reforestation and erosion control, most of which is applicable to other tropical countries.

The main topics covered are establishment, maintenance and protection of forest plantations, compass surveying and mapping, nursery techniques, erosion control, and forest tree seed. Techniques and tools presented are simple and low-cost. Management of natural forests is considered to be outside the scope of this book, and gains only brief mention.

A great deal of good information.

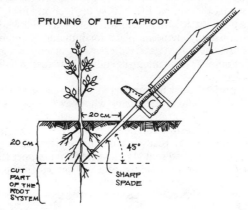

PRUNING OF THE TAPROOT

Tree Planting in Africa South of the Sahara, MF 08-312, booklet, 75 pages, by David Kamweti, 1982, $5.00 from The Environmental Liaison Centre, P.O. Box 72461, Nairobi, Kenya.

This introductory booklet provides enough general information for someone without prior forestry experience to understand and carry out small tree planting projects. Simple techniques using hand tools are described and illustrated. The tree species and climates described are those of Africa, but people new to the topic of forestry in other areas may wish to use this as an introduction to the topic. The treatment of individual species is limited, so the reader will want to refer to other sources for further details.

Recommended as an introduction to this topic.

Reforestation in Arid Lands, MF 08-300, book, 248 pages, by Fred R. Weber, 1977, $10.75 in U.S., $11.75 international surface mail, $17.25 international air mail, from VITA; also available in French.

Though designed for use by people working on reforestation programs in sub-Saharan West Africa, this book would be useful in other arid areas. There are special sections on windbreaks, fire protection and sand dune stabilization.

Half of the book contains a directory of 165 tree varieties found in West Africa, and an expanded look at 30 of these, covering details on such topics as seeds, germination techniques, transplanting, protection and uses.

"This manual assumes basic familiarity with reforestation terms and methods: for example, it takes for granted that the reader will be familiar with laterite soils and with the use of such forestry tools as climate maps and vegetation charts."

"Reforestation programs are part of larger conservation efforts. Increasingly they are being conducted with the realization that it is very difficult to separate reforestation from other revegetation efforts — range management, sand stabilization and similar activities. So while reforestation deals mainly with planting trees in locations able to support at least some species, it is important to think broadly of revegetation — planting trees, shrubs, bushes, grasses, and other ground cover in areas which do not have sufficient vegetation."

Revegetation is a concept that needs wider circulation. The planting of many different suitable types and sizes of vegetation makes the widest possible use of the capacity of a landscape to support plant life. A wide range of plant life also further expands the amount and diversity of animal life that the area can support, and this includes the human animal. A community of plants composed almost solely of trees ignores the potential that shrubs and ground covers can contribute to the productivity of a landscape: animal life, both wild (deer and fowl, for instance) and domestic (such as pigs, cattle and geese) will not do as well when there are only trees. Reforestation usually creates a place for humans to come and get lumber and firewood and little else. Revegetation creates a place for a greater variety of plants and a larger number of animals, including humans, to live...and provides lumber and firewood too.

"A conservation project must be supported by the people living in an area, or it will not work. Local people are the ones who may be asked to give land for a project, or to work on it. And often a reforestation effort will have to be supported by people for years before results can be seen. Therefore, a project should not be started before communities are ready to sustain the effort. And to make this commitment, residents must believe that (1) the project will affect their environment and their lives positively, and (2) the results will be worth the effort."

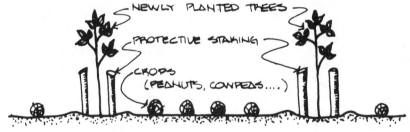

Intercropping trees and row crops

Savanna Afforestation in Africa, book, 312 pages, FAO, 1976, $22.75 plus $1.15 from UNIPUB.

This is a collection of lecture notes and brief papers for a symposium on the planting of trees in African grasslands. Topics covered include a general discussion of African savanna, species introduction and seed handling, nursery practice, plantation establishment and maintenance, techniques for problem areas, plantation protection, and planning for plantations.

The presentation is academic in style, so that the reader will have to work to get practical information from the text. Still, for those working in forestry projects in tropical and subtropical grassland areas, this may prove a worthwhile book.

Firewood Crops: Shrub and Tree Species for Energy Production, MF 08-290, book, 237 pages, by National Academy of Sciences, 1980, free from BOSTID, JH 217D, National Academy of Sciences, 2101 Constitution Avenue N.W., Washington D.C. 20418, USA.

"To alleviate the growing shortage of wood fuel is one of mankind's major challenges. In this connection, firewood research is vital and deserves concentrated financial support. It will take the combined efforts of government, industry, landowners, villagers, researchers, philanthropic institutions and development assistance agencies. Some activities that must be undertaken include:
— Preventing the extinction of existing forests;
— Instituting policies to relieve the often wasteful use of the firewood now available;
— Testing and developing fuel-efficient stoves;
— Instituting policies and programs to encourage the use of alternative energy sources such as biogas and solar heat;
— Testing the cultivation of native tree species for firewood; and
— Testing appropriate new species such as those identified in this report."

Firewood Crops describes woody species suited for use as fuelwood or charcoal in rural developing areas where firewood shortages are reaching a crisis point.

An introduction by Erik Eckholm points out the urgent need for fuelwood programs throughout the world — and the considerable difficulties in actually implementing them. A chapter entitled "Wood as Fuel" presents an overview of wood energy uses, firewood plantation, fuelwood management, harvesting techniques, species selection, and appropriate research methodologies. The intent throughout is to provide options, not specific recommended solutions.

Approximately 60 species for use in the wet-dry lowland tropics, savannah regions, arid areas, and tropical highlands are presented in the main body of the report. There are extensive photographs, references, seed and germplasm sources, and research contacts. For each species listed, other uses besides fuel are also cited.

"Woody plants...can also be sources of: vegetable oil and fruits and nuts for food; edible leaves and shoots for sauces, curries, salads, and beverages; forage for livestock and silkworms; green manure for fertilizing soil; medicines and pharmaceuticals; extractives such as resins, rubber, gums, and dyes...In times of hardship, (the tree owner) may sacrifice some tree growth to feed his family or animals with the foliage. In some cases, dense forests can produce a great deal of burnable materials without a living tree being felled. In others, the owner may sell the best-farmed trees for timber or pulp and use the remainder as fuel. Having such options is important to a rural farmer, and in this report we note the main alternative uses for the species selected, even if they conflict with firewood use."

The technical appendices include a master list of firewood species, and firewood success stories from Ethiopia and South Korea.

Tropical Moist Forests Conservation Bulletins 1 and 2, MF 08-305, booklets, 51 and 29 pages, edited by C. Mackie, G. Ledec, and L. Williamson, 1978 and 1979, available from International Project, Natural Resources Defense Council, 1725 I Street N.W., Washington D.C. 20006, USA.

These bulletins "describe briefly some of the major international and national institutions and programs which contribute to the protection and wise use of the tropical moist forests," including efforts to stop deforestation, and programs of reforestation. Full addresses are provided.

Leucaena: Promising Forage and Tree Crop for the Tropics, MF 08-296, book, 121 pages, by the National Academy of Sciences, 1977, free from BOSTID, JH 217D, National Academy of Sciences, 2101 Constitution Avenue N.W., Washington D.C. 20418, USA.

"Of all tropical legumes, leucaena probably offers the widest assortment of uses. Through its many varieties, leucaena can produce nutritious forage, firewood, timber, and rich organic fertilizer. Its diverse uses include revegetating tropical hillslopes and providing windbreaks, firebreaks, shade, and ornamentation. Although individual leucaena trees have yielded extraordinary amounts of wood — indeed, among the highest annual totals ever recorded — and although the plant is respon-

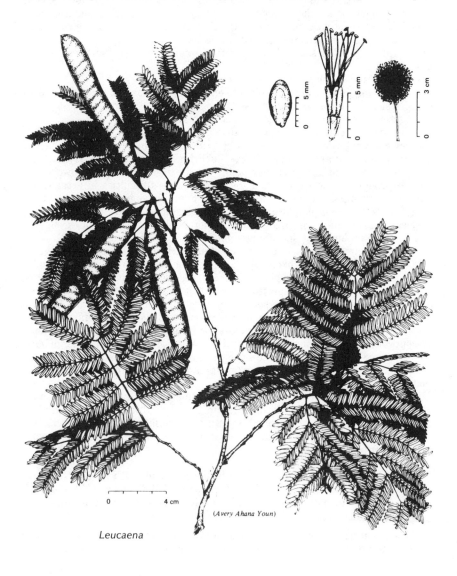

(*Avery Ahana Youn*)

Leucaena

sible for some of the highest weight gains measured in cattle feeding on forage, it remains a neglected crop, its full potential largely unrealized."

Leucaena varieties can grow in arid areas (though they do best in moist conditions) and can tolerate periods of frost and high winds. It is especially useful in reforestation efforts where it is important to get quick results for ecological or economic reasons.

"There is a rising belief among agronomists and foresters that tree growing, crop production and/or animal raising should be combined to best preserve structure and fertility of fragile tropical soils. Trees provide the ecosystem, and an agricultural crop, livestock rearing, or fish culture can provide income while the trees are maturing. Combinations of many different plant and animal species seem possible, but versatile leucaena appears to be an outstanding candidate."

"Leucaena helps to enrich soil and aid neighboring plants because its foliage rivals manure in nitrogen content, and natural leaf-drop returns this to the soil beneath the shrubs. Recent experiments in Hawaii have shown that if the foliage is harvested and placed around nearby crop plants they can respond with yield increases approaching those affected by commercial fertilizer."

The book covers the following topic areas: leucaena botany and cultivation; animal feed; wood products; fuelwood; soil improvement and reforestation; recommendations and research needs; sources of additional information; a list of leucaena researchers; and sources of leucaena seeds, nitrogen-fixing inoculant bacteria, and wood samples. An excellent general survey of the potential of leucaena in tropical, sub-tropical and mild temperate climates.

Natural Durability and Preservation of One Hundred Tropical African Woods, MF 08-298, book, 131 pages, by Yves Fortin and Jean Poliquin, 1974, out of print in 1985.

This is a report on the preservation requirements of 100 different tropical African woods. "Natural durability" refers to the ability of the wood to resist attack by biological agents — fungi, insects, and marine borers were chosen as specific cases. Many woods have certain uses which require little or no preservative treatment, due to this natural durability.

"The protection obtained from a preservative treatment is determined by the effectiveness of the preservative as well as the method of its application. The choice of a suitable preservative is mainly based on the conditions to which the wood is to be exposed. For example, before the wood is utilized, preservatives made of chemicals dissolved in organic solvents, and non-leachable salt preservatives usually give satisfactory protection."

The authors mention the hazards of use of some of the chemical preservatives, plus some safety instructions. Non-commercial preservation techniques are aimed at medium- to large-scale operations, but small-scale operations will also find the book very useful.

Anyone using common African woods will find material of interest in this book. There is an extensive list of sources for further information.

The Propagation of Tropical Fruit Trees, MF 08-310, book, 566 pages, by R.J. Garner, Saeed Ahmed Chaudhri and the staff of the Commonwealth Bureau of Horticulture and Plantation Crops, 1976, available from the Commonwealth Agricultural Bureau, Central Sales, Farnham Royal, Slough, SL2 3BN, England; or UNIPUB.

This is a very welcome addition to the literature on tropical horticulture. This book contains a comprehensive review of the various techniques for the propagation (multiplication) of selected tropical fruit tree species of high economic and nutritional value. The book is divided into two parts — an overview and detailed description of the materials and methods used in tree propagation, and a review of propagation techniques for specific tree species. The book primarily covers simple, low-technology techniques which are easily understood by farmers given adequate training. The text is supplemented by basic line illustrations which are generally adequate for explaining the techniques covered. The book could have been improved by the inclusion of illustrations of the fruit species (i.e. tree profile, fruit sections, etc.) covered in the second section and the addition of a simple glossary of horticultural terms. Nevertheless, this publication should be of value to agricultural researchers, fieldworkers, and trainers throughout the tropics.

"Many different kinds of intimate protection are used in nurseries. Glass structures, so widely used in temperate zones, quickly overheat in hot sun and are generally unsuitable for use in the tropic. Structures which have proved more useful have been a combination of partial shading overhead with moisture-retaining covers below to provide the desired ecoclimate in the immediate vicinity of the plant. . .Various materials serve for shading, including lathes, bamboo, banana leaves and palm branches. A favourite use in Malawi is composed of grass woven into two-inch (5-cm) chicken wire."

"Grafting with detached scions requires extra care in maintaining life in both scion and rootstock throughout the grafting process and until the composite plant is well established. Though it is thus more hazardous than approach grafting it demands less labour per graft and, by its relative simplicity lends itself to standardization essential in the exploitation of mass production techniques. The aim must be simplicity with efficiency. . ."

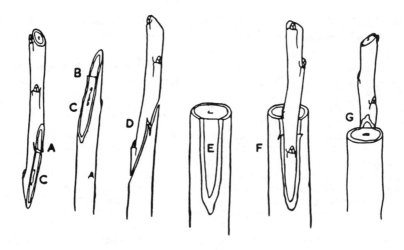

FIGURE 26

Whip and tongue graft

A Forest Tree Seed Directory, MF 08-291, book, 283 pages, by FAO, 1975, $24.00 from UNIPUB.

This is a directory of sources of tree seeds of many varieties. It includes an enormous amount of information on tree seeds, including the number of seeds per kg, germination percentage, and seed treatment applied.

A special remarks section covers such things as germination techniques, ordering delays to be expected, quantities available, and rarity of the seed.

All of the text is in English, French and Spanish.

A Pocket Directory of Trees and Seeds in Kenya, MF 08-309, book, 151 pages, by Wayne Teel, 1984, from KENGO, P.O. Box 48197, Nairobi, Kenya.

The author has geared this book to those people with limited tree planting experience. The opening 15 pages of general information in a question/answer format provide a good introduction to the topic. The book goes on to list local names, uses, preferred climate, information about the seeds, and sources of seeds in Kenya for 90 tree species. The trees and seeds of each species are clearly illustrated. With its focus on Kenya, this book will be most useful in that country. However, it may be useful to groups in other areas with similar climatic conditions.

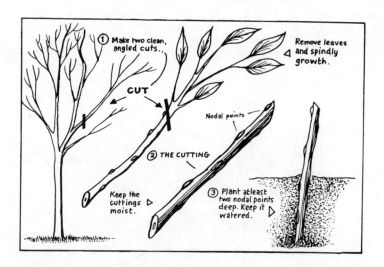

Agroforestry Species: A Crop Sheets Manual, book, 336 pages, by P.K.R. Nair, 1980, from ICRAF, P.O. Box 30677, Nairobi, Kenya.

This is a good reference for those seeking information on the specifics of various crops suited to agroforestry. "Crop sheets" for each of 40 of the most important species provide information on such characteristics as uses and economic role, distribution, plant characteristics, climate and soil requirements, nutritional composition, and diseases, as well as further sources of information.

The manual also presents "short notes" on about 50 underutilized and localized species of food crops, fruits and nuts, spices and condiments, beverages, medicinal and aromatic plants, and others. Tree species are also covered, except for tree crops, which will be the focus of a future publication from ICRAF.

Much of the language used is technical, but a good glossary is provided.

Agroforestry Review, quarterly journal, 25 pages average length, subscriptions $8.00 per year in the U.S., $10.00 airmail postage in other countries, from International Tree Crops Institute USA, Route 1, Gravel Switch, Kentucky 40328, USA.

"**Agroforestry Review** contains articles related to the multiple utilization of trees and shrubs for human food, livestock feed, fuel, conservation purposes, etc." Articles examine specific tree species, relate original research findings, and report on applications of tree croppings in the USA and other countries. Also includes reviews and abstracts of books.

Good material on trees for community self-reliance. Probably most useful to researchers and experimenters in the temperate zones.

Short-Rotation Forestry, MF 08-301, report, 36 pages, by Dr. Geoffrey Stanford, 1976, $5.00 from Greenhills Environmental Center, 7575 Wheatland Road, Dallas, Texas 75249, USA.

"Coppicing" has a long history in Europe. It consists of growing young trees very close together, and harvesting the growth after 3-5 years during the winter season. New growth comes up from the stump and the cycle is repeated.

This report contains an overview of coppicing history, principles, and yields. Coppicing "was not just a way of increasing the yield of fuelwood from stumps near to the village, it was a means for securing construction timber of the right size other than by selection from a natural mixed forest. These coppices also furnished the wood for the enormous quantity of baskets, barrels, tubs, and pails."

"Coppicing has two important advantages over mature timber: firstly, the yield/hectare/year can be many times greater; and secondly, repeated harvestings at intervals of 3-7 years provide a much shorter-term return on invested capital."

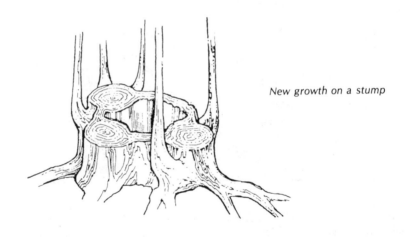

New growth on a stump

Land Clearance: Alternative Techniques for Removing Trees & Bushes, MF 08-295, book, 66 pages, 1981, ITDG, out of print in 1985.

This thorough review of the options available for land clearance could be a model text for matching technology to task in a rational manner. Includes labor and capital requirements (in 1981 prices), ecological and safety considerations, clear illustrations of all tools considered, and a brief bibliography. Recommended.

Chain Saw Service Manual, book, 336 pages, by Technical Publications Division, Intertec Publishing Corp., 1985, $10.95 from Technical Publications, Intertec Publishing Corp., P.O. Box 12901, Overland Park, Kansas 66212, USA.

If you're interested in learning how to repair and maintain chainsaws, this is the book for you. The first section (37 pages) covers chainsaw engine principles, troubleshooting, maintenance and repair of all the parts of a chainsaw.

"Small kinks or bends in guide bars can be removed by laying the bar on a large true (flat) anvil or other similar work surface and using light hammer blows to bring the bar back into shape. The technique is very similar to straightening other flat metal pieces."

The second section covers, in detail, how to service and repair specific chainsaws available from these firms: Advances, Allis-Chalmers, Clinton, Danarm, John Deere, Dolmar, Echo, Ford, Frontier, Homelite, Husqvarna, Jonsereds, Lancaster,

Lombard, McCulloch, Mono, Partner, Pioneer, Poulan, Remington, Roper, Skil, Solo, Stihl, Tecumseh and Wright.

This book covers repair but not use of chainsaws.

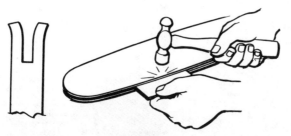

Closing spread bar rails: use steel shim .004" thicker than drive link tangs

Crosscut Saw Manual, MF 08-306, booklet, 27 pages, by Warren Miller, 1978, U.S. Dept. of Agriculture Equipment Development Center, $4.50 from USGPO.

The large hand-operated crosscut saw is still commonly used in developing countries. A well-filed and cared-for saw can perform remarkably well. "Only in recent years was a chainsaw developed that could beat a topnotch bucker in a contest. There is a record of a 32-inch Douglas fir log cut in 1 minute 27 seconds by one bucker." This manual will show you how to properly straighten, set, and file a large saw to make it operate smoothly and effectively.

How a Saw Cuts

The cutting teeth of a crosscut saw sever the fibers on each side of the kerf. The raker teeth, cutting like a plane bit, peel the cut fibers and collect them in the sawdust gullets between the cutting teeth and the raker teeth and carry them out of the cut. A properly sharpened crosscut saw cuts deep and makes thick shavings. For large timber, where the amount of shavings accumulated per stroke is considerable, a large gullet is necessary to carry out the shavings to prevent the saw from binding.

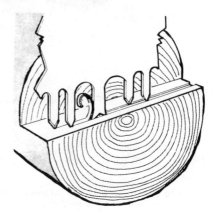

Barnacle Parp's Chain Saw Guide, MF 08-284, book, 281 pages, by Walter Hall, 1977, Rodale, out of print in 1985.

The subtitle accurately states that this book helps you in "buying, using, and maintaining gas and electric chain saws." These are very useful tools where large amounts of timber need to be felled, rapid cutting and processing is important, and a shortage of labor exists.

Basic parts, accessories, safety, and sharpening are presented. Manufacturers' addresses, specifications of currently available chainsaws, and periodicals are listed.

A very good section on the use of chainsaws is matched with clear descriptions of repair procedures. These make this book a good companion to the **Chain Saw Service Manual** (which presents repair details for specific models).

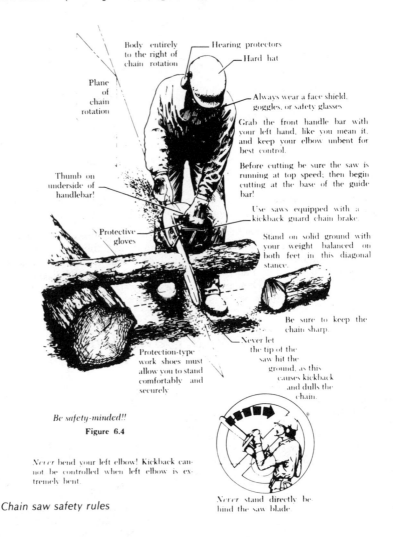

Body entirely to the right of chain rotation

Hearing protectors

Hard hat

Plane of chain rotation

Always wear a face shield, goggles, or safety glasses

Grab the front handle bar with your left hand, like you mean it, and keep your elbow unbent for best control.

Before cutting be sure the saw is running at top speed; then begin cutting at the base of the guide bar!

Thumb on underside of handlebar!

Use saws equipped with a kickback guard chain brake.

Protective gloves

Stand on solid ground with your weight balanced on both feet in this diagonal stance.

Be sure to keep the chain sharp.

Protection-type work shoes must allow you to stand comfortably and securely

Never let the tip of the saw hit the ground, as this causes kickback and dulls the chain.

Be safety-minded!!

Figure 6.4

Never bend your left elbow! Kickback cannot be controlled when left elbow is extremely bent.

Never stand directly behind the saw blade.

Chain saw safety rules

The Chainsaw and the Lumbermaker, MF 08-285, booklet, 28 pages, $1.00 from Haddon Tool, 4719 West Elm Street, McHenry, Illinois 60050, USA.

In the few rural parts of the temperate zones where forests are extensive, trees can be cut or bought and used as a low-cost construction material. While trees are usually sawn at a mill, a tool like the "Lumbermaker" described in this booklet can be used with a chainsaw to produce rough-cut lumber. The "Lumbermaker" allows one person to make straight cuts for boards by guiding the chainsaw along a piece of milled lumber (standard two-by-four) which is nailed to the log. The booklet shows how to use the "Lumbermaker" to saw boards of various sizes using different methods of attaching the guide board to the log. Also included are suggestions on sawing angles, braces, making a jig for cross-cutting, and simple log cabin construction. The "Lumbermaker" is a simpler attachment than that used for the Alaskan sawmill (see next review).

The price of the "Lumbermaker" in January of 1980 was $45.00. Matched with a chainsaw, it may have a place in the Third World, between the two-person hand pit saw and the small motorized sawmill. Easily transported, it would seem most applicable in areas where transport of logs to a small mill is impractical. Chainsaws, however, make a wider cut and thus waste more wood than either of the other alternatives. The "Lumbermaker" will certainly be most widely used in parts of the U.S. and Canada where wood is still abundant and chainsaws have bacome widely-owned tools in an affluent consumer society.

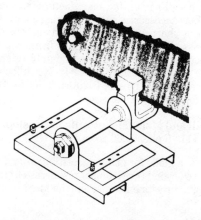

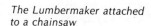
The Lumbermaker attached
to a chainsaw

Make Your Own Precision Milled Lumber from Logs and Trees: Alaskan MKII, MF 08-314, promotional literature (leaflets and booklets), 1976, free from Granberg/Firmont Inc., 244 South 24th Street, Richmond, California 94804, USA.

The Alaskan Mill is a marvelous tool for accelerating forestry operations in developing countries, allowing for intermediate level, small-scale wood processing and lumber production. This device consists of an attachment to a standard gasoline-

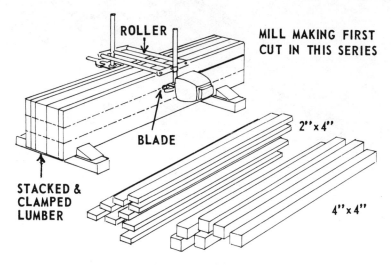

ROLLER

MILL MAKING FIRST
CUT IN THIS SERIES

BLADE

2" x 4"

STACKED &
CLAMPED
LUMBER

4" x 4"

MAKING DIMENSION LUMBER FROM SAWN PLANKS

powered chainsaw (6 horsepower minimum gear drive, with 2:1 gear ratio), which enables the users to cut lumber of any assortment of sizes from rough timber. 1-person to 3-person mills are available. According to reliable estimates, an average of 1000 board feet (approximately 2.25 cubic meters) of finished lumber can be achieved daily with the 1-person operation.

In all areas where an alternative to the extremes of the inexact, time-consuming 2-person handsaw or the high-technology sawmill is sought, the Alaskan Mill is a sound option. The Mill utilizes indigenous labor to a much greater extent than large lumber mills, and can encourage self-reliance, release materials for low-cost housing and other national building priorities, and encourage more prudent forestry practices.

Granberg/Firmont Inc. manufactures various models of these clamp-on chain saw mills, plus accessories such as ripping chains and precision file guides to keep saws uniformly sharp and effective. They will send detailed information free; some people may wish to build their own mills from this. Granberg/Firmont Inc. does not sell chainsaws themselves. The commonly referred-to American sources (from **The Whole Earth Catalog**) are: 1) McCulloch Corporation, 6101 West Century Boulevard, Los Angeles, California 90045, USA; and 2) Homelite, Port Chester, New York 10573, USA.

Small and Medium Sawmills in Developing Countries, book, 149 pages, FAO, 1981, $11.75 plus $0.60 from UNIPUB.

This is a guide for planning, setting up, and running saw mills. The mills described here are beyond the financial resources of most Sourcebook users, involving start-up capital investments of several hundred thousand dollars. However, the framework

A semi—permanent circular sawmill set directly on the ground

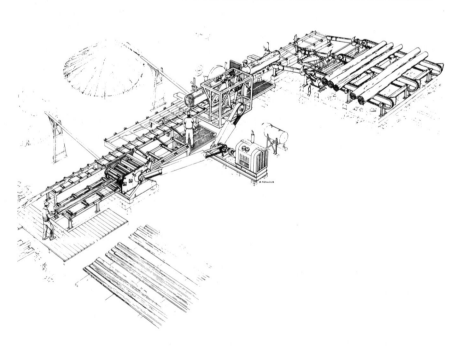

for analysis and planning presented here can be applied to much smaller sawmilling operations.

Part I covers sources of raw materials, marketing, industrial machinery and processing, cost estimates, financial projections and analysis, financing, and other factors relevant to sawmill start-up and operation. Part II presents three sawmill case studies.

Timber Drying Manual, MF 08-311, book, 159 pages, by G.H. Pratt, 1974, second edition, from Her Majesty's Stationery Office Bookshop, P.O. Box 569, London SE1 9NH, England.

This book is a ". . .complete guide to all methods of drying timber. With a total of more than sixty illustrations, this book represents the culmination of nearly fifty years of research on timber drying at the Princes Risborough Laboratory."

It covers such topics as timber moisture, kiln operation, drying damage, air drying timber, kiln types, drying various types and loads of timber, and other drying methods (including vacuum, steam, vapour, and press methods, plus solvent and salt seasoning) for both small- and large-scale drying operations.

"Experience has shown that satisfactory kiln drying can usually be best accomplished by gradually raising the temperature and lowering the humidity of the circulating air as drying proceeds. . . It has already been indicated that the rates at which different timber species can safely be dried, and the air conditions to which they can be subjected without suffering damage, vary very considerably, and the treatment should, therefore, depend to a large extent on the species that is being dried." The appendices cover most of the woods of the world and describe in detail the proper drying procedures for each type of wood. Other technical sections give specific details on testing humidity of wood and air, and redrying timber treated with chemical preservatives. There is an excellent section on troubleshooting timber drying problems, complete with tables of symptoms and cures.

The basic principles of kiln drying described here apply to small- and large-scale operations, solar and traditional heating systems, and community or commercial undertakings. Highly recommended.

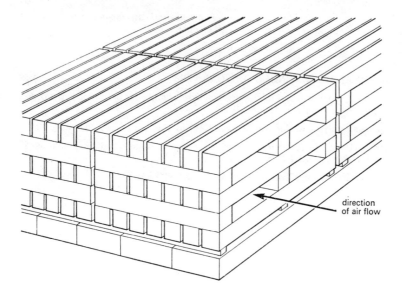

Cross-piling of dimension stock

Constructing and Operating a Small Solar Heated Lumber Dryer, Forest Products Utilization Report 77, MF 08-288, report, 12 pages, by Paul Bois, 1977, free single copies from Forest Products Laboratory, Box 5130, Madison, Wisconsin 53705, USA.

This report briefly describes the construction and operation of a small solar lumber dryer, designed for cold and temperate latitudes (modifications may be required for tropical operation). The advantage of this solar dryer is that hardwood lumber can be dried in it to a significantly lower moisture content than by air drying alone. Very dry wood is important for uses such as furniture.

Three photos and three small sketches of construction details are provided. The dryer uses an air collector and a fan to circulate the air.

Not intended for large, high-speed drying operations. The dryer has a capacity of 750-850 board feet of 8-foot lengths of hardwoods, requiring about 80 days to dry.

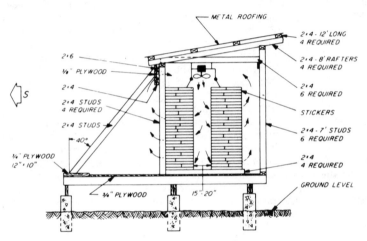

Solar heated lumber dryer: arrows indicate movement of air driven by overhead electric fans

ADDITIONAL REFERENCES ON FORESTRY

Fuel-efficient cooking stoves and improved charcoal kilns can both reduce the pressure on remaining trees; see ENERGY: STOVES.

Agro-Forestry Systems for the Tropics East of the Andes; see AGRICULTURE.

The Draft Horse Primer contains 22 pages on the techniques and equipment used in logging with horses; see AGRICULTURAL TOOLS.

Drying and Processing Tree Fruits; see CROP STORAGE.

Aquaculture

Aquaculture

Many people are now pointing to the farming of fish, shellfish and aquatic plants as the solution to the world's food problems. These people note that there are several advantages of water as a growth medium. For instance, aquatic animals can convert more of their food into growth since most of them do not need to support their weight. Most fish don't spend energy to regulate their body temperature. In addition, water is a three-dimensional growing space, so yields per unit area can be quite high when compared to land-based farming.

These advantages have given aquaculture the label of an "appropriate technology." But just as solar energy technology can include solar-panelled satellites beaming microwave energy to the earth, so aquaculture can be approached from a number of technological starting points. Many appropriate technology aquaculture groups in the United States are working with extremely high densities of organisms in recirculating water systems. Some examples of these "intensive" designs are basement fish tanks, backyard fish farms, dome ponds aand greenhouse ponds. Most of these require careful biological monitoring and management (because a small problem in the system can kill all the fish) and the economics are not yet acceptable.

While this work is certainly important to our urban areas where little space is available, the high capital and material requirements of such aquaculture strategies make them much less relevant to the developing countries. In fact, many people are convinced that the key to large-scale aquaculture development in the United States as well lies in the enormous potential of farm ponds and reservoirs used for irrigation, fire protection, recreation, livestock watering, etc. Throughout the world these unused or poorly managed lakes, ponds, streams and rivers represent a vast resource of harvestable waters. At the same time they are subject to a wide variety of other potential uses. As we manage these water resources, our goal must be expanded from short-term production to long-term stewardship which integrates all potential needs. There are many examples of aquaculture which include sewage treatment, mosquito control, and aquatic weed control. And aquaculture can play a major role in the maximization of traditional fisheries through spawning and ranching techniques — many coastal and inland fisheries are the best producers of cheap protein because the fish raiser does not have to supply the feed.

The following selections partially reflect these views. Much work remains to be done. As an overall source of information to have at your side for constant study during the planning of a fish raising project, start with **Aquaculture: The Farming and Husbandry of Freshwater and Marine Organisms**, and then use Hickling's **Fish Culture** for practical techniques. If you are trying to decide what growing fish might be like, choose between **Fish Culture in Central East Africa** (the most extensive), **Freshwater Fish Pond Culture and Management**, and **Elementary Guide to Fish Culture in Nepal**. The remainder of the selections cover specific topics in aquaculture. (Mike Connor)

Aquaculture: The Farming and Husbandry of Freshwater and Marine Organisms, book, 868 pages, by J. Bardach, J. Ryther, and W. McLarney, 1972, $19.00 from Wiley-Interscience, John Wiley and Sons, Inc., 605 Third Avenue, New York, New York 10016, USA.

Despite its expense, semi-technical approach and encyclopedic nature, this book is the best investment for any group seriously considering starting an aquaculture project. It is the only place where information about aquaculture in every part of the world, including a multitude of species and methods, can be found. The book thoroughly discusses the energy-intensive culture methods used in American catfish, trout and lobster farming, in addition to providing a state-of-the-art treatment of fish culture in Africa, South America and Asia. In many cases this comprehensive coverage, illustrating various approaches to solving particular problems, allows the fieldworker to combine several different solutions in developing a response to the local situation. The value of this book as a reference guide will be well worth any difficulties encountered with the biological terms.

The book is organized into chapters on each of the various species groups of fish, shellfish, other invertebrates, seaweeds and freshwater plants. Where appropriate, the chapters are subdivided into the different parts of the world where these animals are grown. At the end of each chapter there is an extensive list of reference and/or personal contacts.

"In the developing world the predominant problem is one of producing additional animal proteins, which may be so scarce that any meat, unless excessively cheap, is a luxury commodity available only to the wealthy few. The corollary here is that

FIG. 3. Habitat and feeding niches of the principal species in classical Chinese carp culture. (1) Grass carp (*Ctenopharyngodon idellus*) feeding on vegetable tops. (2) Big head (*Aristichtys nobilis*) feeding on zooplankton in midwater. (3) Silver carp (*Hypophthalmichtys molitrix*) feeding on phytoplankton in midwater. (4) Mud carp (*Cirrhinus molitorella*) feeding on benthic animals and detritus, including grass carp feces. (5) Common carp (*Cyprinus carpio*) feeding on benthic animals and detritus, including grass carp feces. (6) Black carp (*Mylopharyngodon piceus*) feeding on mollusks.

especially in developing nations herbivores or plankton filter feeders are most suitable for aquaculture, producing the most per surface or volume of water from the more-or-less natural amenities, such as solar energy, existing standing or flowing waters, and natural or man-enhanced fertility."

Fish Culture, book, 317 pages, by C.F. Hickling, 1971, Faber & Faber, U.K., out of print in June 1980, try to see a copy owned by another fish culturist or a library.

The information in this book is particularly suited to tropical climates, where the biology and chemistry of fish ponds requires different management from that usually recommended in the literature by Americans and Europeans. It is based on conditions at Malacca, Malaysia, where the author did much valuable research with minimum dependence on sophisticated technology. Hickling presents the biological basis for pondfish culture clearly, and in terms broad enough to be useful in other locations and with other fish than those he studies. His approach to fish culture emphasizes locally available natural materials, and assumes that abundant labor but little equipment is available. He expects the reader to know some general biology as he considers the ecological and chemical relationships of the soil, water, plants and animals in a pond that affect fish production.

The most valuable aspect of this book for the user might be the orientation toward nutritious natural fish foods made of wild or easily-cultured plants. Nutritional data on many tropical plants and agricultural wastes, such as rice hulls, are presented. The fish genetics chapter is somewhat obsolete, but there is good treatment of biologically-significant aspects of water, soil, fertilizers (both natural and synthetic) and feeding. Hickling stresses low-cost methods (where appropriate) throughout the rest of the book as well, in chapters on pond construction, pond management, stocking rates, fish diseases, use of brackish and flowing water, mixed rice-fish culture, and public health. There is an excellent bibliography and index.

Highly recommended.

Freshwater Fish Pond Culture and Management, MF 09-313, book, 191 pages, by Marilyn Chakroff, 1976, free to Peace Corps volunteers and development organizations, from Office of Information Collection and Exchange, Peace Corps, 806 Connecticut Avenue N.W., Washington D.C. 20525, USA; others may obtain it for $5.00 in U.S., $9.25 international surface mail, $12.50 international air mail, from VITA.

The Peace Corps has done a lot of aquaculture work in different parts of the world. Several good local manuals were written in the past by their Indian branch. This latest publication integrates all the freshwater aquaculture projects, with the emphasis on warmwater species of fish. It is introductory in nature, aimed at an audience which did not like math or science in high school. Good illustrations com-

Pushing eggs or sperm out of a fish, to be mixed in a dish

plement the clearly written text. The contents cover the basic subjects important to a fish farmer: why grow fish, pond site selection, planning, construction and sealing, water chemistry and fertilization, fish spawning, stocking, feeding, harvesting, preserving and diseases.

"**Freshwater Fish Pond Culture and Management** is a how-to manual. It is designed as a working and teaching tool for extension agents. It is for their use as they establish and/or maintain local fish pond operations. The information is presented here to 1) facilitate technology transfer and 2) provide a clear guide for warmwater fish pond construction and management. A valuable listing of resources at the end of this manual will give further direction for those wishing more information on various aspects of fish pond operation." In fact, the resources section is practically impossible to use. It is not at all integrated into the subjects in the text, and most of the references are only available to those with access to excellent libraries. But this is the only failing of an otherwise good book.

Fish Culture in Central East Africa, MF 09-312, book, 158 pages, by A. Marr, M.A.E. Mortimer and I. Van der Lingen, 1966, $16.25 from UNIPUB.

Of these general "how-to" manuals, this is our favorite. More than any of the other manuals it emphasizes the economic and ecological constraints which demand flexibility by fish farmers. Besides a good summary of the essentials of fish pond management, there is an excellent chapter on growing fish in lakes, reservoirs and seasonal farm ponds. Combining fish farming with other branches of agriculture is also stressed.

The book has a definite regional focus. Tilapias native to Africa are the only fish considered. Nevertheless, many of the ideas would be applicable in other areas. For instance, three aquacultural practices of wide interest are discussed: the polyculture of ducks and fish, the use of other animal manures as fish food and fertilizer, and the culture of fish in irrigated paddies. Fish such as carp or non-herbivorous tilapia can be stocked any time after the rice has rooted in paddies which have a water depth of 30-40 cm, or in paddies with 10-15 cm of water over the central rice growing area surrounded by a 1½ m-wide trench, 70 cm deep.

A glossary and 73 illustrations make the text easier to follow, but the last two chapters on biological production and fish biology are a bit dense.

DIGGING SOIL FROM
FROM THE TOP PART
OF THE POND

TAMPING DOWN
THE SOIL

FIGURE 21.   Making the walls of a contour pond. Soil to make the walls is dug first from the top of the pond. It is dug to a depth of 1 ft. Nearer the bottom wall, soil is dug less and less deep. As the walls are built up, the width is made less and less so that when the top of the posts is reached, the width is only 2 or 3 ft.

Elementary Guide to Fish Culture in Nepal, MF 09-310, book, 131 pages, by E. Woynarovich, 1976, FAO, $8.50 from UNIPUB.

"**Elementary Guide to Fish Culture in Nepal** is designed for practical use in the training of extension workers and progressive fish farmers in the techniques of fish culture." This FAO publication emphasizes the culture and polyculture of the common carp, Cyprinus carpio, Chinese carps and Indian carps. In addition to the usual discussion of pond construction, management and harvest, there is a chapter on the biological background to fish production which includes information more sophisticated than is necessary for the successful management of a pond. There is also a good section on the food value of various feeds made from agricultural by-products.

Don't be fooled by the word "elementary." While the book includes many simple illustrations, the author's attempt to cover all ecological processes very briefly can be confusing to someone who does not already know about them.

Freshwater Fisheries and Aquaculture in China, MF 09-314, book, 84 pages, by D.D. Tapiador, H.F. Henderson, M.N. Delmendo, H. Tsutsui, 1977, $6.00 from UNIPUB.

China accounts for more than half the world's fish production, yet very little was known about its aquaculture efforts until the visit of the FAO mission in 1976. "The particular forms of fish culture practised in China may not be directly applicable in many countries, particularly outside Asia. But the perspectives of Chinese fish farmers on self-reliance and on the interdependence of aquaculture, agriculture and animal husbandry, and their familiarity with fish and fish behavior under conditions of intensive culture, make their experience most valuable elsewhere."

"It seemed particularly significant that all of the major inputs, such as feed, fertiliser and fish seed, are produced within the farm...The use of organic fertilisers and locally-produced feed materials is especially to be recommended for most of the developing countries. Unfortunately, the latter have often elected to adopt commercial fertilisers and feeds simply because it is the practice in the developed countries."

Many people talk about making full use of water resources, recycling wastes and decentralizing planning decisions. In China they do it, and on a scale that produces four million tons of fish annually.

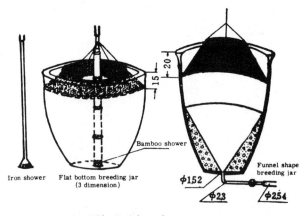

Chinese breeding jars

Freshwater Fish Farming: How to Begin, booklet, 43 pages, FAO, 1979, $1.00 from FAO.

This is a good, simple introduction to fish farming. Rudimentary information is given on building, filling, fertilizing and stocking the fish pond, care of fish and pond, and harvesting. Those undertaking fish culture will need to consult an extension agent or other publications listed in the **Sourcebook** for further details on many of these topics. Written in easy English with good illustrations.

Better Freshwater Fish Farming: The Pond, booklet, 43 pages, FAO, 1981, $1.00 from FAO.

This book is written for fish farmers with simple operations who wish to expand their fish ponds. It is assumed that the farmer has built his or her first pond using **Freshwater Fish Farming: How to Begin** (from this series). However, we feel this would be a good book for the beginner to read before building the first pond. Includes information on site selection and construction details. Clearly written in simple English, and well-illustrated.

Fish in Ponded Areas, MF 09-321, leaflet, 9 pages, free to serious groups, from Action for Food Production (AFPRO), Technical Information Service, Community Centre, C-17, Safdarjung Development Area, New Delhi-11 00 16, India.

An excellent, compact introduction to fishpond construction and maintenance, presented by AFPRO, a grass-roots technical information service for village development. Very practical schemes with simple drawings are described, with consideration given to problem areas in pond aquaculture (including lining, stocking rates, fertilization, and induced breeding).

The authors point out that ponds can be hurt by an overabundance of algae which uses up the oxygen in the water that the fish need to survive. "In such cases, continuous circulation of water through the pond is very helpful (because it provides the needed oxygen and discourages algae growth). Poisoning due to collection of noxious gases is immediately diluted by addition of aerated water...Raking the pond bottom also prevents collection of poisonous gases...To kill parasites and control excessive bacterial growth, ordinary washing soda, wood ash and potassium carbonate are also useful though the required strength has not been worked out. Banana leaf juice or leaves floated on the pond surface help stabilize pond pH...Preventing the spread of a disease by removal and destruction of infected fish is by far the most effective method of control."

Making Aquatic Weeds Useful: Some Perspectives for Developing Countries, MF 09-315, book, 175 pages, National Academy of Sciences, 1976, free from BOSTID, JH 217D, National Academy of Sciences, 2101 Constitution Avenue N.W., Washington D.C. 20418, USA.

Aquatic weeds present serious problems to public health, fisheries production, water quality and navigation in the tropics where they grow most prolifically. "This report examines methods for controlling aquatic weeds and using them to best advantage, especially those methods that show promise for less-developed countries. It emphasizes techniques for converting weeds for feed, food, fertilizer and energy production. It examines, for example, biological control techniques in which herbivorous tropical animals (fish, waterfowl, rodents and other mammals) convert the troublesome plants directly to meat."

The major sections of this book focus on harvesting aquatic weeds either by herbivores which themselves can be harvested (e.g. grass carp, manatees, crayfish, ducks and geese) or by machines with additional treatment and processing. Throughout the book, the emphasis is on aquatic weeds as a resource rather than a nuisance.

Profitable Cage Culture, MF 09-317, booklet, 30 pages, by Gregor Neff and Paul Barrett, 1979, $3.00 to U.S., Canada or Mexico, $4.00 elsewhere, from Inqua Corporation, P.O. Box 86, Dobbs Ferry, New York 10522, USA.

This is the most in-depth summary of the hows and whys of cage culture available — in part a publicity promotion for their brand of plastic mesh cages. If you keep in mind that indigenous materials can be used for the cage mesh and framing, and you have access to alternative feeds, then cage culture can add to your fish raising options. **Profitable Cage Culture** can give you hints on stocking, harvesting and managing your cages.

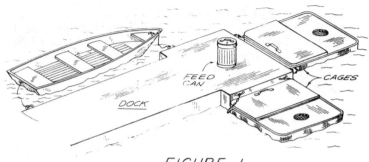

FIGURE I
CAGES TIED TO DOCK.

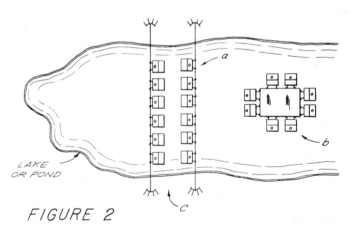

FIGURE 2

(a) CAGES FASTENED TO CABLE ANCHORED AT BOTH ENDS TO OPPOSITE SHORES.

(b) CAGES FASTENED TO FLOATING RAFT.

(c) CAGES CONNECTED IN PARALLEL TO CABLES.

Aquaculture publications from New Alchemy Institute, P.O. Box 432, Woods Hole, Massachusetts 02543, USA. While this group's publications are reviewed elsewhere, certain articles merit special attention by prospective fish farmers. Journals 1-4 are out of print.

1) "Midge Culture," by W. McLarney, J. Levine and M. Sherman, Journal 3 (MF 02-80), on pages 80-84.

Providing cheap sources of natural protein for fish feed is one way to speed their growth. Bug lights will collect protein-rich insects. An alternative is to raise the larvae yourself. This article tells you how.

2) "A New Low-Cost Method of Sealing Fish Pond Bottoms," by W. McLarney and R. Hunter, Journal 3 (MF 02-80), on page 85. Also found in **Book of the New Alchemists** (see review).

Various methods have been used to seal the bottoms of ponds to allow them to hold water, but most methods are expensive. Here the authors describe a virtually cost-free method using layers of manure and other farm wastes to create an anaerobic zone impenetrable to water.

3) "Cultivo Experimental de Peces en Estanques," Journal 3 (MF 02-80), on pages 86-90. Also reprinted in **Book of the New Alchemists**.

This is a translated excerpt from a paper by Professor Anibal Patino R. which presents a plan for tropical aquaculture. For information on obtaining the original paper (in Spanish), write Cespedesia, Jardin Botanica del Valle, Apartado Aereo 5660, Cali, Colombia.

4) "Cage Culture," by William McLarney, Journal 4 (MF 02-81), on pages 77-82.

Growing fish in floating cages is a traditional technique in Southeast Asia and of recent interest in the U.S. This article describes the reasons and methods for building and stocking cages. It also describes some of the pitfalls.

Raising Fresh Fish in Your Home Waters, MF 09-318, pamphlet, 34 pages, by B. Bortz, J. Ruttle and M. Podems, 1977, $1.50 from Barebo, Inc., Box 217, Emmaus, Pennsylvania 18049, USA.

For the reader new to the idea of raising fish, this booklet is useful as a brief introduction to many of the topics of concern to a fish farmer. The central section, "A Catalog of Fish," is a nice collection of the water quality tolerances and preferences of the major fish cultured in the U.S. While the pamphlet is written for the North American fish farmer, the sections on pond management are of general interest.

Position the net so that it covers the pond from bank to bank and crosses the very bottom.

Fish Catching Methods of the World, MF 09-311, book, 432 pages, by Andres von Brandt, 1984, £30.25 from Fishing News Books Ltd., 1 Long Garden Walk, Farnham, Surrey, England.

This book is a testimony to the ingenuity of fishers in their invention of an astounding variety of fishing gear and techniques to meet different environmental, economic and social requirements. While basically a scholarly treatment of the principles of fishing technology, its comprehensive discussions of both commercial and subsistence technologies present a fascinating tale to the lay reader. Of particular interest are the chapters on fish hooks, traps and nets. The potential utility of this book lies in the large number and variety of methods it presents.

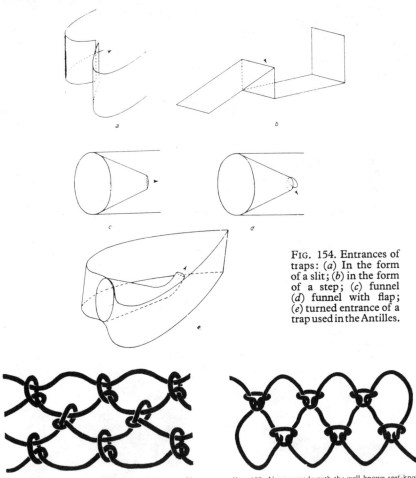

FIG. 154. Entrances of traps: (*a*) In the form of a slit; (*b*) in the form of a step; (*c*) funnel (*d*) funnel with flap; (*e*) turned entrance of a trap used in the Antilles.

FIG. 196. This illustrates the net-making technique used by lake-dwelling fishermen in Switzerland.

FIG. 198. Netting made with the well-known reef-knot.

Practical Shellfish Farming, MF 09-316, book, 91 pages, by Phil Schwind, 1977, $8.95 from International Marine Publishing Company, Camden, Maine 04843, USA.

This easy-to-read book tells how to grow shellfish along the northeast coast of the United States. Consequently, it looks at the question of local regulations more deeply than would be appreciated by those living in other areas. The lively writing makes these few dull pages barely noticeable. The book's strength is its discussion of the management of bottom areas or rafts for maximizing shellfish growth. It lacks a good review of the physical characteristics which influence where shellfish larvae will settle and imaginative ways to collect these settled larvae.

Tropical Oysters: Culture and Methods, MF 09-320, book, 80 pages, by D.B. Quayle, 1980, $6.00 from IDRC.

"Bivalve shellfish such as oysters, mussels, and clams are very widely distributed throughout the world and have long enjoyed a high consumer preference and market value in temperate climates. The change of techniques from bottom cultivation to off-bottom or suspended cultures has contributed to considerably increased production in many countries. However, in general, production from tropical countries has been traditionally very limited even though bivalves flourish and reproduce abundantly in warmer climates. In such tropical countries native oysters are often harvested for subsistence and rural fisheries. They are not a luxury item.

"Only comparatively recently have there been serious attempts at oyster cultivation, but where favourable conditions exist rapid growth has been observed and marketable oysters are obtained in nine months."

This book provides a good introduction to the methods and considerations for raising oysters in the tropics.

Aquaculture Practices in Taiwan, MF 09-308, book, 146 pages, by T.P. Chen, 1976, £6.75 from Fishing News Books Ltd., 1 Long Garden Walk, Farnham, Surrey, England.

T.P. Chen has provided a sampling of Taiwan's aquacultural practices for 29 species of animals including turtles, frogs, fresh and saltwater clams, shrimps and eighteen species of fish. The major emphasis is on milkfish, eels and Chinese carps with a wealth of production statistics and economics. This book is the best source of information on the culture of snakehead (Ophiocephalus), walking catfish (Clarias), mud skipper (Boleophthalmus), Corbicula clams, and the seaweed, Gracilaria.

U.S. Government Publications on Aquaculture, order by title and number, from U.S. Government Printing Office, Superintendent of Documents, Washington D.C. 20402, USA.

A great deal of aquacultural work has been done by a few universities and the government. While the focus is often towards large-scale, labor-extensive productions, much of the biological information is of great value to fish farmers of all types. This information comes in the form of technical papers, popular articles, how-to pamphlets, manuals, etc.

The following are available from the U.S. Government Printing Office for $2.00 domestic and $2.50 foreign: **Trout Ponds for Recreation**, Farmers' Bulletin No. 2249 (SN001-000-01455-2); **Warm Water Fish Ponds**, Farmers' Bulletin No. 2250 (SN001-000-01533-8); and **Ponds for Water Supply and Recreation**, Agricultural Handbook No. 387 (good construction hints).

Publications, Department of Fisheries and Allied Aquacultures, Swingle Hall, Auburn University, Auburn, Alabama 36830, USA.

This is the most comprehensive collection of publications concerning the culture of freshwater, warmwater fishes. While many of these articles have appeared in scientific or trade journals, most of them would not be difficult for the non-professional to understand. Topics include aquatic ecology and marine biology, aquatic plants, baits and minnows, commercial fish production and aquaculture, farm pond management, fishery biology and population dynamics, fish feeds, fish food habits and nutrition, and water quality and waste management.

Foremost among the 300 available papers is H.S. Swingle's classic "Biological Means of Increasing Productivity in Ponds," in which he discusses use of efficient pond fish, polyculture species combinations and stocking rates, control of reproduction, and increasing production of fish food organisms. Swingle's successful combination of pond ecology with aquaculture has been unmatched and will be the key to future development of appropriate technology in aquaculture.

Auburn also has an international branch for aquacultural development in conjunction with USAID. Some of the publications from these groups would be of local interest to those people living near the various projects in El Salvador, Brazil, Colombia and the Philippines.

Bamidgeh, quarterly magazine, since 1948, $12.00 per year (surface mail), make checks payable to The Fish Breeders Association in Israel, from Bamidgeh Editorial Office, Nir-David 19150, Israel.

Now published in a separate English edition, **Bamidgeh** presents the results of Israeli research in pondfish culture. In recent years, their semitropical systems have centered on carp, mullet and tilapia. Although some of the articles are extremely complex, using sophisticated engineering and ecological analysis, many show practical techniques and equipment that can be useful in other countries. The Israeli communes have never been wealthy, so the scientific approach is based on intermediate-level technology, using a maximum of ingenuity and energetic labor.

The topics covered in this magazine are usually strategies for efficient fish production, such as pest control, safe use of manure fertilizers/feeds, and various species combinations in ponds. This is a magazine for those actually engaged in fish culture, who may want to use agricultural wastes for fish food, culture insect larvae for the same purpose, or start a selective-breeding program to reduce the number of bones in a fish. Particularly interesting recent research has been in all-male hybrids of tilapia, cage culture of carp, and comparison of low-cost aeration systems. If for no other reason, practicing fish culturists might consult **Bamidgeh** to appreciate the value of good recordkeeping journals. Subject indexes are published each year for easy reference.

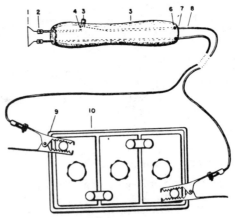

Electric fish brander
connected to a car battery

Aquaculture and Related Publications, of the School of Forestry and Wildlife Management, Publications Clerk, 249 Ag Center, Louisiana State University, Baton Rouge, Louisiana 70803, USA.

These reprints are divided into four major categories: crawfish, catfish, frogs and mariculture. Within these categories, most of the emphasis is on pond management and pond ecology. These are folksier than the Auburn reprints. A sample of some of the 100 plus titles: "Agricultural By-Products as Supplemental Feed for Crawfish," "How to Keep 'em Alive in a Pond," "Polyculture of Channel Catfish and Hybrid Grass Carp."

Salmon Rancher's Manual, MF 09-319, book, 95 pages, by William McNeil and Jack Bailey, 1975, free from Alaska Sea Program, University of Alaska, Fairbanks, Alaska 99701, USA.

"The North Pacific Ocean is a vast nursery ground for the Pacific salmon that spawn in streams and lakes in North America and Asia. These salmon reproduce in fresh water, but most of their growth occurs at sea. When mature they return to their freshwater ancestral spawning grounds, where tens of thousands of genetically-separate stocks segregate for reproduction."

In the past, growing salmonid fishes has required a capital investment beyond the means and interests of most groups. But the chemical imprinting of young fish so that they will return to the hatchery area to spawn after several years in the wild reduces the obstacle of their carnivorous habits. Fish can be spawned, hatched, raised and released from a hatchery to increase their chances of survival. While feeding at sea (or, in the case of steelhead rainbow trout, in a lake), the fish convert protein unavailable to humans into animal flesh; hence the comparison to range cattle and the term "ocean ranching."

"Production of healthy fry is the 'core' of any salmon aquaculture system because the success of ocean ranching will depend largely upon the quality of juvenile fish released into the ocean. The primary purpose of this manual is to assist salmon ranchers with planning, constructing, and operating systems for artificial propagation of salmon fry."

Artificial Salmon Spawning, MF 09-309, pamphlet, 21 pages, by William Smoker and Curtis Kerns, 1978, free from Marine Advisory Program, University of Alaska, 3211 Providence Avenue, Anchorage, Alaska 99504, USA.

"This manual is designed primarily for the aquaculturalist who is just getting started...(It includes) procedures that are least likely to go wrong for the novice egg-taker. Not all have been scientifically tested. But where they have been used, incubators have been filled with live eggs."

ADDITIONAL REFERENCES ON AQUACULTURE

The Book of the New Alchemists describes the Ark, with its indoor fish tanks; see GENERAL REFERENCE.

Permaculture II includes fish ponds in its plan for ecologically-sound development; see AGRICULTURE.

How to Salt Fish and **Small Scale Processing of Fish**; see CROP STORAGE.

Aquaculture: A Component of Low-Cost Sanitation Technology can be found in the sanitation section of WATER SUPPLY AND SANITATION.

Books on small boat design and construction are found in TRANSPORTATION.

Water Supply and
Sanitation

Water Supply and Sanitation

After sufficient food, a good clean water supply and adequate sanitation system are considered to be the most important factors in ensuring good health in a community. Improved water supply and sanitation systems were major elements of the public health measures that drastically cut death rates and improved health levels in the industrialized countries. Though it is not generally appreciated, these measures have been considerably more important than curative medicine in contributing to good health, long life expectancy and low infant mortality. Infant diarrhea, the largest killer in developing countries, is closely related to poor water quality.

The first books in this section provide a context for discussion of water supplies — the social and ecological effects of water systems (including large dams and irrigation projects in addition to community water supplies), and the nature of water supply needs, constraints, and possibilities for Third World communities.

Due to their great potential benefits, village water supply systems have been favorite development projects of government and international agencies for several decades. They make a revealing topic of study for appropriate technology advocates, as they represent one task for which small scale technology has been widely promoted. A basic conclusion: a water supply or sanitation project that is imposed on a community, without community involvement in determining the need for and nature of the system, or without an effort to train some community members to do maintenance and repair, is very likely to fail. **Participation and Education in Community Water Supply and Sanitation Programmes: A Literature Review** offers valuable insights into the requirements for successful programs that fully involve the community. With 20-50% of handpumps in rural areas of the Third World broken down at any one time, the appropriate technology solutions seem to depend on local people and institutional arrangements that can ensure good maintenance and rapid repair. This also implies the use of equipment that can be repaired at the local level.

More than 20 of the entries in this section are manuals on the various aspects of the planning and installation of small water supply systems, including wells, pipelines, storage tanks, and drainage. Another thirteen publications on pumps and water lifters range from broad inventories of water lifting devices to construction plans for particular pumps. **Laboratory Testing of Handpumps for Developing Countries** presents the results of extensive testing of 18 widely-used handpumps. Four additional entries describe the construction and use of ferrocement and bamboo-reinforced tanks (sometimes used in roof rainwater catchment). These are followed by seven publications on water filtration and treatment. In sand filtration, water is passed slowly through a tank filled with sand. The sand traps large particles, and it holds the bacteria that digest fecal matter naturally so that it will be harmless to humans. Solar distillation is another option for water treatment; this is covered by five entries.

The bibliography **Low Cost Technology Options for Sanitation: A State of the Art Review** *offers an excellent summary of the sanitation technologies relevant to urban and rural settings in developing countries, and is a guide to the technical literature (mostly hard-to-get research reports).* **Small Excreta Disposal** *is a valuable small reference manual on the range of waste disposal alternatives that can be used in small communities. The next books describe dry composting toilets and ventilated pit latrines as alternatives to expensive water-borne sewage systems. Many variations have been tried in many different countries; some have been built by the tens of thousands. Most of these books are primarily relevant to Third World conditions, while* **Compost Toilets: A Guide for Owner-Builders** *and several others were written for North American audiences. Natural treatment of waterborne sewage in a marsh pond is a relatively low technology approach that seems to have potential for some communities in North America.* **Natural Sewage Recycling Systems** *describes work done on this technique in the United States. This type of system is now being used by the city of San Diego in southern California. A similar system using fish ponds in cities of China and India is described in* **Aquaculture: A Component of Low Cost Sanitation Technology**.

With several drought years and greater demands on existing water supplies in the western United States, there has been much recent interest in the reuse of household wash water in gardens and yards. **Residential Water Re-Use** *is an excellent compendium of technology ideas and the basic technical considerations of such greywater systems. The last entry in this section,* **Management of Solid Wastes in Developing Countries**, *discusses refuse collection and transport, sanitary landfills, and composting of urban wastes.*

A. Water Supply: General Considerations

The Social and Ecological Effects of Water Development in Developing Countries, book, 127 pages, edited by Carl Widstrand, 1978, $32.00 from Pergamon Press Ltd., Headington Hill Hall, Oxford, OX3 0BW, England; or Pergamon Press Inc., Maxwell House, Fairview Park, Elmsford, New York 10523, USA.

"During recent years it has been shown quite clearly that the expected social benefits from drinking water supplies have not been realized and that irrigation projects have created more problems than they solve. None has fulfilled the expectations of planners and government and most projects are used only to 50% of their capacity. This means that 100 million ha. of land with available irrigation are not used and that millions of rural people who are provided with pumps, pipes and installations cannot get any water out of them. This book is concerned with why this has happened and what can be done about it." These articles are by 10 people experienced in water systems work in developing countries.

Most irrigation schemes "appear to create subsidized income elites; contribute to food production only at high cost; facilitate preconditions for inappropriate mechanization and thus a disappointing employment creation record; and they lead to various aspects of environmental degradation. Public health considerations are typically ignored."

Much of the poor performance of water development schemes is attributed by two of the authors to structural problems in the way research and planning are conducted. David Henry notes that a poor learning situation for planners has prevented them from learning from the mistakes of the past two decades. Robert Chambers points to the problem of research priorities that are determined more by the need for recognition among professional colleagues than by the real needs of rural people: ". . .the primary criterion for good research should be that it is likely to mitigate poverty and hardship among rural people, especially the poorer rural people, and to enhance the quality of their lives in ways which they will welcome; that in short, priorities should be. . . grounded in the reality of the rural situation. Starting with rural people, their world view, their problems and their opportunities, will give a different perspective. To be able to capture that perspective requires a revolution in professional values and in working styles; it requires humility and a readiness to innovate which may not come easily in many research establishments."

Some of the lessons for planners and donors: "more funds and more resources into public health training and education (with local teachers), more funds into training programs for operators and maintenance personnel — not producing full-scale engineers, but, instead, small-scale mechanics with some basic skills directly applicable to the water system — and more thought about the involvement of locals in the planning of water schemes."

Highly recommended.

Environmentally Sound Small-Scale Water Projects, MF 10-320, book, 142 pages, by Gus Tillman, CODEL/VITA, 1981, $9.75 in U.S., $10.00 international surface mail, $13.25 international air mail, from VITA.

"This booklet has been written for community development workers in developing countries who are not technicians in the area of water resources. It is meant to serve as a general guide when planning environmentally sound small-scale water projects — that is, projects which protect and conserve natural resources in a manner which allows sustainable development to take place." Material covered includes a general introduction to ecological principles, the water cycle in the environment, disease control and sanitation, water resources development, and project planning. It is intended that more specific manuals will be consulted for technical details when needed. Recommended as an introduction.

Drawers of Water, book, 306 pages, by Gilbert White, David Bradley and Anne White, 1972, $20.00 from University of Chicago Press, 11030 South Langley, Chicago, Illinois 60628, USA.

Combining engineering, economics, health and sociology, **Drawers of Water** is "a broad view of domestic water supply in the developing tropics." Using examples and studies from East Africa, the authors discuss: traditional water supplies and use in urban and rural communities; the range of attempted and possible improvements; the health costs and benefits of improved water systems; individual and social "costs"; and the successes and problems of standard economic and technical planning methods.

Drawers of Water is intended for "decision-makers" in developing countries — much of the book contains technical discussions of data from sociological and economic studies. The book's strength, however, is that it recognizes that "accepted" planning methods must be altered to account for local physical and social conditions.

Guidelines on Health Aspects of Plumbing, MF 10-322, book, 168 pages, by Floyd Taylor and William Wood, 1982, $10.00 from IRC.

Water and sewage systems installed by public authorities must interact with privately constructed systems at individual buildings. Bad design or faulty installation of the private systems can result in pollution (e.g. through back-siphoning), damage or overload to the public systems, with accompanying health risks to the rest of the community and higher costs to the system. This book attempts to lay out a basic plumbing code of practice to minimize these risks, to be enforced by local authorities.

The problem is a real one, primarily occurring in urban systems. The difficulty of coming up with a generalized code of practice and a set of controls is that it necessarily requires certain assumptions about risk and cost tradeoffs that certainly vary from one place to another. Who is to say that the ad hoc water systems that dot slum communities, certainly in violation of any code of practice, are creating more risks than benefits? In particular, experience has shown that building codes in developing countries tend to set standards that are unaffordable for the poor majority, and that ignore the piecemeal, self-help, make-do-with-the-materials-at-hand approaches these people are forced to use. This book is an interesting attempt to deal with a thorny problem.

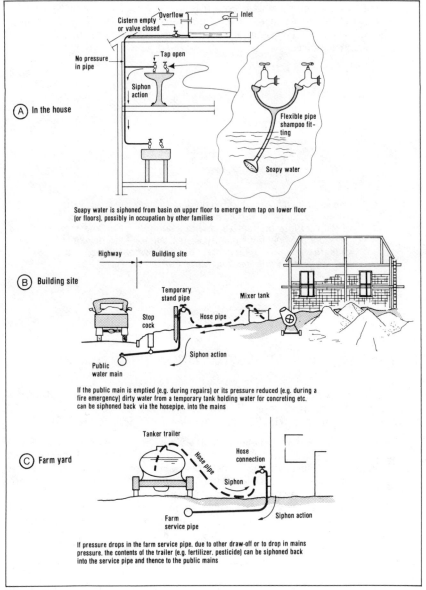

Figure 9.
Ways in which back siphonage can occur.

Water for the Thousand Millions, MF 10-321, book, 58 pages, edited by Arnold Pacey, written by the Water Panel of ITDG, 1977, out of print in 1985.

This short volume differs from the other general water supply books in that it is explicitly about "appropriate water supplies," including the consideration of economic, social, environmental and health factors in determining "appropriateness." The authors have concentrated on how these factors are combined in a variety of low-cost water systems that could be used by the thousand million people currently without clean drinking water.

"Water supplies are not an all-or-nothing phenomenon. Almost every situation lends itself to some improvement, even if funds and skills are severely limited." The key is matching people's needs and cultural patterns with the given water supply potential and much broader technical choice than is usually offered by governments or development agencies.

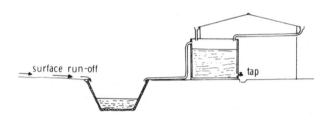

Rainwater catchment from roof and ground surface. With precautions to prevent dust and bird droppings being washed off the roof into the tank, and with a suitable cover, the roof tank can provide high quality water suitable for drinking, while the excavated tank may provide water suitable for washing or watering gardens (after Farrar, 1974).

B. Participation: A Key to Successful Systems

Participation and Education in Community Water Supply and Sanitation Programmes: A Literature Review, Technical Paper No. 12, MF 11-323, book, 204 pages, by Christine Van Wijk-Sijbesma, revised 1981, $10.00 from IRC.

An extraordinary review of conclusions from a wide literature on the participation of communities in water supply and sanitation programs, this should be required reading for people working in these fields. For more information on specific concepts, the reader can refer to the original studies. This volume offers planners and community organizers the opportunity to avoid many of the common mistakes of the past, and create programs with a maximum of community participation. It is also a good general guide for involving the community in any kind of appropriate technology activity, stressing their own perceptions of problems and solutions. An annotated bibliography, published as No. 13 in the Technical Papers Series, contains detailed abstracts of the 145 most relevant works on which the literature review is based.

Community participation in decisionmaking and implementation brings a number of rewards. It is a more democratic approach than imposition of projects from outside. It provides good opportunities for the growth of skills and competence at the grass-roots level — increasingly recognized as the most central goal of development. And it is more likely to be successful in solving problems.

Some of the authors have noted that handpumps are broken down 20 to 70 percent of the time, and that in some countries village water systems are breaking down faster than they are being built. "A community is more likely to cooperate in the implementation, operation and maintenance of new systems if it has had a say in the preparation of plans."

In some countries, water supply programs have been divided into three categories. In communities where water supply and sanitation problems are felt by the entire population, the government agency offers assistance with forming a local committee and planning a work program. If problems are felt only by the village leadership, these people are supported with media and locally-planned primary school education programs to generate broader motivation to solve the problems. If problems are felt only by the water supply specialist, "various surveys are carried out with the involvement of the villagers, a motivation and education campaign is set up, and assistance is provided in solving other, more deeply felt village problems."

Many observers have "stressed the importance of presenting the community with the various technological solutions which are feasible, ranging from simple source protection and pit latrines to multiple house connections...Community choice should include the possibility of rejection of any immediate source improvement...Although this may seem a negative outcome...each community has its own criteria for calculating sets of trade-offs, so that their perceptions of the usefulness and effects of improvements may differ considerably from those of the agency. Besides, self-made choices will ensure a greater commitment than solutions presented from outside."

Recently, some authors have emphasized the need for participatory research, "because it is a process which is part of the total educational experience, serving to identify community needs and to effect increased awareness and commitment." Two of the more innovative information-gathering and educational approaches briefly discussed are the "environmental sanitation walk" with a group of villagers, and the "community self-survey."

Highly recommended.

Hand Pump Maintenance, MF 11-322, booklet, 43 pages, by Arnold Pacey, 1977, revised 1980, £2.50 from ITDG.

This booklet is part of an Oxfam series on socially appropriate technology. The author looks at community well projects in developing countries, and examines why over 60% of these break down and/or are not used. The reason for this is not due to faulty design of the pumps themselves, but because "...the community or village has not been adequately involved in the project in the first place, and has not accepted the social responsibility for the task of maintaining the pump."

"An effective pump system is not simply a technological object but a conglomerate of technology, institutions and people." With this in mind, three approaches are possible: 1) total village self-reliance, where a pump is manufactured using only those materials and skills available locally, 2) partial self-reliance, where a pump may be made outside the village, but the responsibility for maintenance lies within the village, and 3) elimination of village responsibility, usually by use of a manufactured imported pump which requires no maintenance (the most expensive option).

The conclusion is that the partial self-reliance path is most applicable in a variety of situations. Locally-made pumps will also work for low-lift applications.

This booklet is most valuable as a reminder that local people and their institutions are at least as important as the hardware in the introduction of any community-level technology.

Recommended.

C. References

Using Water Resources, MF 12-327, book, 143 pages, VITA, 1970 (reprinted 1977), $8.25 in U.S., $8.75 international surface mail, $11.75 international air mail, from VITA.

Due to the international demand for information on water supplies, VITA has reprinted this from its **Village Technology Handbook** (see review). Subjects are:
  a) Developing water resources: basic well-drilling and digging information, including how to make various hand drilling tools;
  b) Water lifting and transport: measuring water flows, bamboo piping systems, chain pump and inertia pump for irrigation, hydraulic ram pump;
  c) Water storage and water power: springs, cisterns (tanks), dams, power transmission;
  d) Water purification: boiler for drinking water, chlorination methods, sand filter.

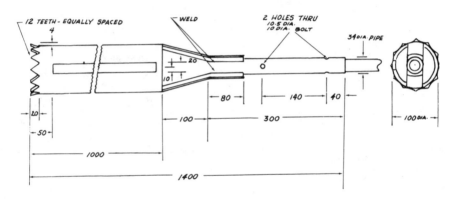

Cutting head, well drilling auger

Practical Solutions in Drinking Water Supply and Waste Disposal for Developing Countries, MF 12-325, book, 124 pages, revised 1982, $10.00 from IRC.

This valuable book supplements other reference books (such as **Water Supply for Rural Areas**, by Wagner and Lanoix, see review) which are becoming very expensive. It is a "picture bibliography" of rural technology. The 150 entries were gathered from healthworkers around the world.

The entries are indexed according to subject, including: rainwater collection; wells; surface water; treatment, filtration and disinfection; pumps and hydraulic rams; solar and wind energy; waste collection and disposal. Among the interesting entries are: a rotary filter with bamboo strainers from Japan; a simple disinfectant device from India; a bamboo water pump from Laos; and a "comfort station" from Nigeria, with a combined unit providing toilet, bathing and washing facilities for groups of families (200-600 people) which can be constructed on a self-help basis.

The first section illustrates designs with brief descriptions, and lists contact people for further details. The second section provides references and contacts for more detailed information without illustrations. The use of pictures makes this a valuable source of ideas.

D. Small Water Supply Systems

Manual for Rural Water Supply, MF 13-333, book, 175 pages plus fold out drawings, by Swiss Center for Appropriate Technology, 1980, Swiss Francs 34 from SKAT.

A very thorough book on small community water supply systems based on 15 years experience of the Swiss Association for Technical Assistance and the Community Development Dept. in Cameroun. The basic elements of a distribution system are presented — wells, springs, stream diversions, storage tanks, distribution pipelines and standpipes. There is a brief maintenance checklist.

This book is unusually broad in scope, beginning with the yearly water cycle (rain to groundwater) and then discussing standards for water quality that are realistic and affordable in rural Cameroun. Also unusual: coverage of the corrosive effects of water flowing through a variety of piping materials, and what can be done about this. Emphasizes the planning of distribution systems for expansion with expected population growth.

Widely relevant.

Water Supply for Rural Areas and Small Communities, WHO Monograph #42, MF 13-346, book, 327 pages, by E. Wagner and J. Lanoix, 1959, out of print in 1985.

This important reference work on water supply deals with both supply systems and sanitation considerations. It focuses on the development of a water supply program, including installation, operation, maintenance, and management of water supply programs.

Besides thorough coverage of rural sanitation, a significant part of the book is devoted to guidelines for effective management of water supply systems after their installation, and efforts to create and sustain community awareness and participation. Most importantly, an entire small community's water supply can be thoroughly planned with the use of this book — taking into consideration all major aspects such as geological formations, topography, needs analyses, flow, distribution, storage systems, and the vital human component — what happens when people accustomed to crossing ravines and climbing down steep slopes have potable water flowing from a tap.

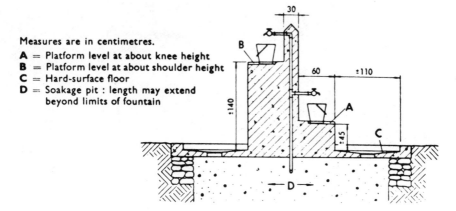

Measures are in centimetres.
A = Platform level at about knee height
B = Platform level at about shoulder height
C = Hard-surface floor
D = Soakage pit : length may extend beyond limits of fountain

Public fountains should be constructed of the most durable materials possible because no other part of the water system will be required to take so much abuse. The weakest part is the faucet itself. This should be the strongest available.

Small Water Supplies, book, 78 pages, by S. Cairncross and R. Feachem, 1978, £2.50 from The Ross Institute, London School of Hygiene and Tropical Medicine, Keppel Street (Gower Street), London WC1E 7HT, England; or ITDG.

This handbook is for "someone who wishes to build only a few water supplies (systems) using simple equipment easily available to him; typically a rural health worker." It is not intended for those working with large-scale water supply systems. All aspects of designing a water supply system are presented for the novice. The subjects include preliminary design, water sources (wells and boreholes), raising water (how to choose pumps of all types), water treatment, storage (dams and tanks), pipes, and distribution. There is an extra chapter on purification on an individual scale.

An appendix describes bacterial analysis of water using simple equipment and MacConkey broth (available from Oxoid Ltd., Wade Road, Basingstoke, Hampshire, England; or Difco Laboratories, Detroit, Michigan 48201, USA.)

This book covers material similar to that in **Water Supply for Rural Areas** by WHO (see review). **Small Water Supplies** is significantly less expensive, and while less detailed it does include a wide range of material on water purification and general aspects of small water systems. For these reasons, we highly recommend it.

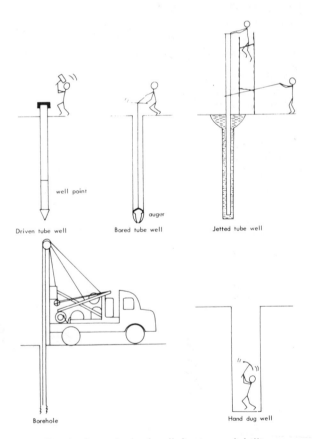

Five basic methods of well digging and drilling

Small Community Water Supplies, Technical Paper No. 18, MF 13-344, book, 415 pages, 1981, $20.00 from IRC.

Covers technology of small community water supply systems including: planning and management, water quantity and quality, water sources, rainwater harvesting, springwater tapping, groundwater withdrawal, surface water intake, artificial recharge, pumping, water treatment, aeration, coagulation and flocculation, sedimentation, slow sand filtration, rapid filtration, disinfection, water transmission, and water distribution.

Rural Water Supply in Developing Countries, MF 13-337, book, 144 pages, 1981, Publication IDRC-167e, $9.00 from IDRC.

This collection of papers presented at a regional workshop on water supply held in Malawi provides a profile of low-cost water supply options for rural Africa. It includes a wide selection of designs and technologies while emphasizing local participation, planning, and training to upgrade water supply in the difficult circumstances found in this region. Recommended.

Rural Water Supply in Nepal: Technical Training Manuals 1-5, 5 short booklets, 1978, by Local Development Department of Nepal, free in limited quantities only, from UNICEF, Box 1187, Kathmandu, Nepal.

These five manuals are very simple training materials for those working in rural water supply development in Nepal. They range from 13 to 30 pages in length and give brief introductions in the following areas:
1) **Hydrology and Water Cycle** (MF 13-340) — the climatology and general water availability in Nepal.
2) **Stone Masonry** (MF 13-342) — how to build tanks and basins for water storage, using stones and cement.
3) **Concrete** (MF 13-338) — mixing and using concrete; also for water storage.
4) **Pipes and Fittings** (MF 13-341) — an introduction to pipes and fittings commonly used in Nepal; both galvanized iron and HDP (high density polyethylene). This manual is useful in showing welding techniques for joining pipes. The advantages and disadvantages of each material are presented: iron is heavier but stronger and easily available; HDP is an easily damaged synthetic that is cheaper, easily connected, and doesn't require special joints.
5) **Construction Design Course** (MF 13-339) — source protection, water treatment, storage tanks, pressure-reducing unit pipelines, and public water tanks.
These manuals are useful examples of how simple but necessary skills for a set of local conditions can be communicated.

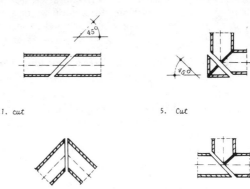

Making a 90-degree branch from PVC pipe

Rural Water Supply in China, MF 13-336, book, 92 pages, 1981, Publication IDRC-TS25e, $7.00 from IDRC.

Water supply solutions for the range of conditions found in the People's Republic of China are presented in a thorough and informative manner. The pragmatic text and clear drawings should allow any of the techniques to be replicated in a rural situation at reasonable cost. Includes information on well location, drilling, casing, and repair. Also covers water lifting, filtering, treatment, storage, distribution, etc. Very useful. Highly recommended.

Rainwater Harvesting for Domestic Water Supply in Developing Countries: A Literature Survey, MF 13-335, WASH C-252, paper, 103 pages, by Kent Keller, from the U.S. Agency for International Development, Water and Sanitation for Health Project, 1611 North Kent Street, Room 1002, Arlington, Virginia 22209, USA.

Rainwater harvesting systems offer many advantages for water collection. Systems can often be adapted to fit locally available skills, materials, patterns of rainfall, and water consumption. Costs of catchment systems are often low relative to other alternatives, and catchment systems can be installed incrementally, reducing high initial costs. Discussion focusing on systems for family and small-scale community water supply are presented in three main sections: "Broad Concerns and Basic Constraints in Rainwater Catchment," "Catchment Technologies," and "Storage Technologies of 'Tanks'. " Each section finishes with a list of published references and ordering information (a number of the referenced materials are included in this microfiche library). Finally, brief technical notes are presented for planning and construction of a few promising rooftop catchment designs. Lucid and comprehensive.

Village Water Systems, MF 13-345, book, 100 pages, by Carl Johnson, UNICEF, Nepal, out of print in 1985.

This is written as a reference for designing water distribution systems, with an emphasis on conditions found in the mountain regions of Nepal.
"Design criteria are presented where standard designs cannot be practically used, while the standard designs that are included are for guide purposes only... "
With charts and sample calculations, the author covers initial surveys, intake works, pipeline sizing, break pressure and reservoir tanks, and public taps. Water quality and/or treatment, windmills and hydraulic rams are mentioned briefly, and the reader is referred to other publications in the bibliography (the book assumes you have access to the UNICEF or WHO libraries in Nepal). An appendix presents a sample design, with calculations, for a rural water supply system, and the cable suspension of a flexible pipe (a frequent need in mountainous areas).

Handbook of Gravity-Flow Water Systems for Small Communities, MF 13-332, book, 242 pages, by Thomas D. Jordan, Jr., UNICEF, Nepal, 1984, £4.95 from ITDG.

This book replaces **Village Water Systems**. Like its predecessor, it is written as a reference for designing water distribution systems, with an emphasis on the conditions found in the mountain regions of Nepal. Topics covered include village evaluation and feasibility studies, topographic surveying, design period, population and water demands, hydraulic theory, air-blocks and washouts, pipeline design, system design and estimates, piping construction, intake works, sedimentation tanks, break-pressure tanks, reservoir tanks, public tapstands, valve boxes, water quality, hydraulic rams, concrete, cement, and masonry. Recommended.

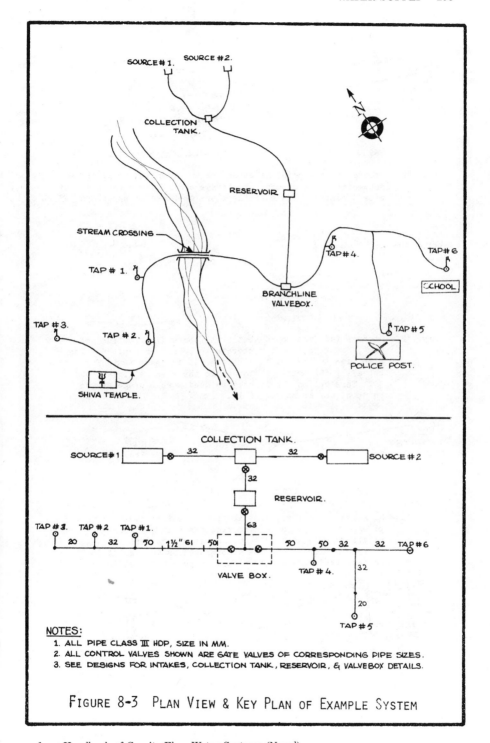

NOTES:

1. ALL PIPE CLASS III HDP, SIZE IN MM.
2. ALL CONTROL VALVES SHOWN ARE GATE VALVES OF CORRESPONDING PIPE SIZES.
3. SEE DESIGNS FOR INTAKES, COLLECTION TANK, RESERVOIR, & VALVEBOX DETAILS.

FIGURE 8-3   PLAN VIEW & KEY PLAN OF EXAMPLE SYSTEM

from Handbook of Gravity-Flow Water Systems (Nepal)

Choices for placement of water storage tanks

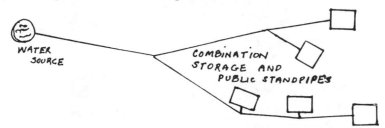

Fig. 1A – Storage at the point of water usage. This is the preferred
schematic for placement of storage and requires the smallest
pipe diameter. Its advantages are outlined in paragraph 3.3.2.

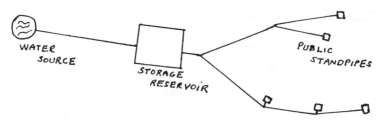

Fig. 1B – Storage far from source but still above distribution network, distribution from storage to public standpipes. The
pipe line to the point of storage is the same as in Fig. 1A
but after the point of storage is the same as Fig. 1C and
1D. This option should only be used when storage at the
point of use is not possible.

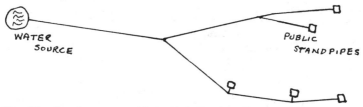

Fig. 1C – No storage provided, distribution direct to public standpipes. This type of system requires a larger diameter
pipeline. The cost is sometimes less than that of the
system in Fig. 1A but use of storage as in Fig. 1A is
preferable for reasons outlined in paragraph 3.3.2.

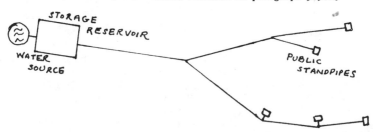

Fig. 1D – Storage provided at or near the water source then distribution
direct to public standpipes. The pipeline diameter is the
same as in Fig. 1C and this is the most expensive option.

from Gravity Flow Water Systems (Indonesia)

Design Problems for a Simple Rural Supply System, MF 13-328, 37 pages, and **Gravity Flow Water Systems**, MF 13-330, 48 pages, by A. Scott Faiia, out of print in 1985.

The author wrote these manuals in response to the great number of gravity-fed water systems which he found not working. They do not attempt to be comprehensive in coverage, and are still in draft form. Nonetheless, they are useful in that they clarify some basic proven design approaches. "The theory of water system design is extensively covered in other publications. The emphasis here is placed on practical methods that have been tested in the field and have given acceptable results...The notes are based on several years' experience in Indonesia and have been used for training of field staff responsible for site selection, design, and implementation." **Design Problems** is a workbook with problems based upon the material presented in **Gravity Flow Water Systems**.

Public Standpost Water Supplies, Technical Paper #13, MF 13-349, book, 104 pages, November 1979; and **Public Standpost Water Supplies: A Design Manual**, Technical Paper #14, MF 13-350, book, 91 pages, December 1979; $10.00 each from IRC.

Most village and town water supply systems in developing countries include public standposts, to allow many different users to draw water from each tap. The proper design of such standposts is therefore quite important to the overall success of the water system. These two volumes review the general considerations and design details that should be incorporated into well-planned public taps.

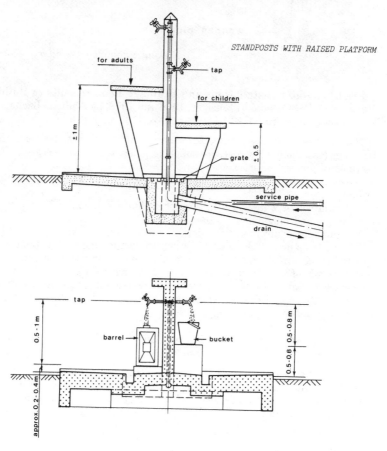

STANDPOSTS WITH RAISED PLATFORM

Manual for Water Systems and Pipe Work, MF 13-334, 37 pages, by Andreas Bachmann and Nir Man Joshi, 1977, free to serious groups from SATA-Director, Box 113, Kathmandu, Nepal.

Subtitled "A Brief Introductory Course for the Establishment of Rural Water Supplies in Nepal," this engineering manual is for those involved in design, construction and plumbing of water supplies in rural areas. The concepts are presented with dimensional drawings and simple English explanations.

The first section provides introductory design information for natural gravity and hydraulic ram distribution systems and water conduits (pipes and valves). The rest of the manual covers the use of the three types of pipe available in Nepal: galvanized iron, HDP (high density polyethylene) and PVC (polyvinylchloride). Included is information on laying pipe and making many different kinds of joints.

Excellent as a field training manual; some of the information is contained in **Rural Water Supply in Nepal: Technical Training**, Manual #4 (see review). Highly recommended.

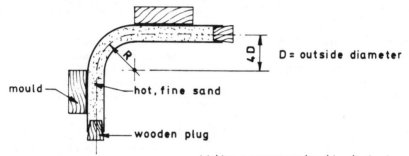

Making a permanent bend in plastic pipe

Drinking Water Installations and Drainage Requirements in Buildings in Nepal, MF 13-329, book, 141 pages, 1976 and 1978, by Andreas Bachmann, free to serious groups from SATA-Director, Box 113, Kathmandu, Nepal.

This is an engineering handbook for designing water installations in Nepalese buildings (assuming a low-pressure supply of piped water already exists). The three sections of general interest are:

1) Design criteria and tables for making design calculations for low pressure systems,

2) Examples of water system designs, including several solar water heating, natural gas and biogas installations, and

3) Drainage requirements for drains and sewers.

There are many detailed system design drawings and design tables included. This reference is meant for buildings in a city like Kathmandu, where water distribution systems already exist, or will exist in the near future.

The special value of this manual is that it represents an adaptation of standard plumbing design and practice to some of the materials, tools, and building construction practices found locally in Nepal.

Hand Dug Wells and Their Construction, MF 13-331, book, 234 pages, by S. Watt and W. Wood, 1977, £4.95 from ITDG.

"This manual describes hand dug shaft wells and their construction by relatively unskilled villagers. Modern concepts, methods and designs are incorporated, but in such a way that those who will carry out the actual work do not require a high degree of education, training or supervision. Much of the equipment can be made locally and costs (especially the cost of imported materials) can be kept to a minimum. The simple directions are based upon proven methods and satisfactory results gathered from various parts of the world. Wells constructed by the methods indicated need be in no way inferior to those produced by mechanical equipment at many times the expense."

"The first part of the book deals with the general principles of ground water storage, hygienic sources, and some notes on the preparatory work. Part II deals with the actual construction, and Part III with alternative methods and techniques. Part IV details the standard equipment and materials used, and Part V provides additional information and sources." There are many drawings and photographs.

The best book on low-cost wells. Highly recommended.

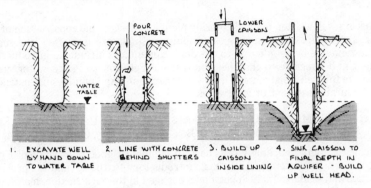

1. EXCAVATE WELL BY HAND DOWN TO WATER TABLE   2. LINE WITH CONCRETE BEHIND SHUTTERS   3. BUILD UP CAISSON INSIDE LINING   4. SINK CAISSON TO FINAL DEPTH IN AQUIFER · BUILD UP WELL HEAD.

Construction of shallow hand dug well.

Self-Help Wells, FAO Irrigation and Drainage Paper #30, MF 13-343, 78 pages, 1978, by R.G. Koegel, from FAO.

This is a good survey of self-help well drilling and digging techniques. The emphasis is on local materials and labor, not on imported technologies. Techniques are described for both small (15 cm) and large diameter wells. Drilling methods discussed include boring, percussion and rotary drilling for small diameter wells. Excavation techniques for larger diameter wells are presented.

The amount of detail in descriptions varies, but there are many good drawings. Even though this is not a construction manual, these drawings are very useful in

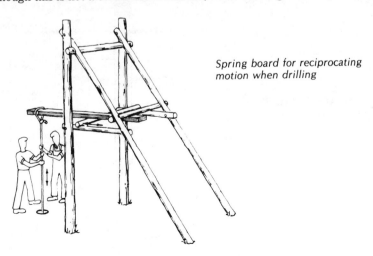

Spring board for reciprocating motion when drilling

explaining the ideas. The materials range from simple wooden tools to metal drill bits, making these techniques adaptable to a wide variety of local conditions. Labor-intensive techniques are emphasized.

Also included are sections on health aspects of drilling, how to find water that is likely to be uncontaminated, safety precautions while drilling, and non-vertical wells (e.g. Qanats — horizontal tunnels that intercept a sloping water table).

Wells Construction, Peace Corps Appropriate Technology for Development Series, MF 13-348, book, 282 pages, by Richard E. Brush, available to Peace Corps volunteers and development workers from Peace Corps, Information Collection and Exchange, Room 701, 806 Connecticut Avenue N.W., Washington D.C. 20525, USA.

This is a well-written manual covering planning, design, and construction of small wells. Both hand-dug and low-cost drilling methods are discussed in a manner understandable by people new to the field. Appendices include an introduction to cement and concrete, techniques for using vegetation to locate water, uses of dynamite for well construction, a survey of common hand pumps, and instructions for chemical treatment of well water.

Water Wells Manual, MF 13-347, book, 156 pages, by U. Gibson and R. Singer, 1971, $13.00 from Premier Press, P.O. Box 4428, Berkeley, California 94704, USA.

This is a "simplified, small wells how-to" manual. A good knowledge of English is necessary. It is intended as a "basic introductory textbook" and to "provide instruction and guidance to field personnel engaged in the construction, maintenance, and operation of small diameter, relatively shallow wells used primarily for individual and small community water supplies. ("Small" used here means up to 4″ in diameter.)

Topics include: background information on water cycles, geologic formations, water quality, ground water exploration, well design, well construction and maintenance, sanitation and wells, and a review of various types of pumping equipment and energy sources including a discussion of the advantages and disadvantages of each.

This book would be useful for a community development worker who reads English well but has no formal training in water supply and/or well design. It is, however, oriented toward more technically-minded people, even though it is described as "simplified."

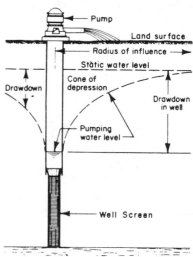

CONE OF DEPRESSION IN VICINITY OF PUMPED WELL.

E. Pumps and Water Lifters

Hand Pumps for Use in Drinking Water Supplies in Developing Countries,
MF 14-355, 230 pages, by F. Eugene McJunkin, 1977, revised 1983, $10.00 from
IRC.

This is the basic reference book on handpumps, describing various types of pumps
and principles of pump operation. It is "intended to serve public health officials,
engineers and field staff who are planning and implementing water supply programs with hand pumps." Fewer pump types are described than in **Pumps and
Water Lifters** (see review). The section on pump principles is detailed and technical,
and includes design principles for each part of a pump assembly (plunger, stand,
suction pipe, seals, valves, cylinders). It is a necessary reference for someone interested in detailed engineering design of simple pumps; many examples are given.
There are two sections describing recent research in handpumps, using wood, bamboo, plastic and steel, and local manufacturing methods for steel parts (such as
casting, machining and welding).
A very complete, detailed handbook. Highly recommended.

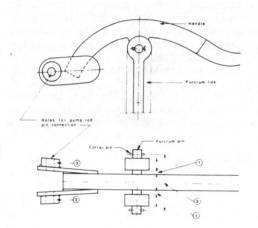

*Examples of common defects
in pump handle link assembly:*

1. *Excessive tolerance between
   fulcrum link and handle*
2. *Distance between cotter pins
   too great*
3. *Misaligned bushings*

**Handpumps Testing and Development: Progress Report on Field and
Laboratory Testing,** World Bank Technical Paper No. 29, MF 14-365, book, 399
pages, by Saul Arlosoroff et. al., 1984, $5.00 from World Bank Publications, 1818
H Street N.W., Washington D.C. 20433, USA.

The UNDP/World Bank project for handpump testing has laboratory- and field-
tested a large number of handpumps. A major purpose of the project has been
to identify and help develop pumps that are "suitable for village level operation
and maintenance (VLOM)."
This report summarizes the fieldtesting results on 2860 pumps of 76 pump types
in 17 countries.
Also included is a 15-page description of the pvc Rower pump, a very low-cost
pump used especially for small plot irrigation in Bangladesh, that has proved very
popular.
"In order to achieve widespread, sustained coverage of the rural and urban fringe
population, pump designs must be based on the VLOM principle. Only then will

FIGURE 3–7   LOOSE NUTS AND BOLTS VS. PUMP AGE

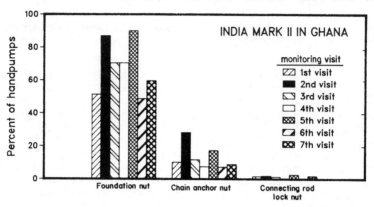

it be feasible to transform the maintenance system practiced in developing countries from a reliance on expensive motorized mobile teams of skilled mechanics paid with government funds to one where the village or a group of villages carries out and pays for pump maintenance and repair. Significant improvements in pump design have been made in this direction over the last few years, but no VLOM pump has reached the stage where it has become a production model with proven successful performance in field trials of adequate duration.

"Each country using handpumps will at some time have to decide which pump types to use. This choice will rarely be a single pump type. Nonetheless, standardization on a small set of pump types must be achieved for the sake of facilitating the distribution of spare parts, exercising stringent quality control of manufacturing, and training installers and village repairers. The ease with which pumps

Handpump Nomenclature

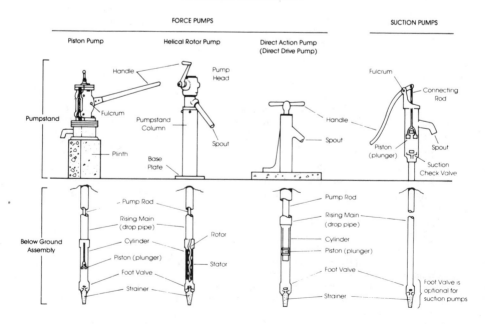

can be locally manufactured (including joint ventures) will be an important consideration in this process.

"The country-wide pump choice will depend on a variety of factors determined by local conditions, such as the range of water table depths, availability of alternative water sources, in-country manufacturing capability, self-help potential in villages, and user acceptability of pump types. To arrive at a selection, the performance of different handpumps must be evaluated in relation to local requirements. Future Project reports will present laboratory and field test results in a manner which will help the concerned organizations to make this choice."

See also the two books that follow, from the same series.

Highly recommended.

Laboratory Testing of Handpumps for Developing Countries, World Bank Technical Paper #19, MF 14-366, Rural Water Supply Handpumps Project, book, 267 pages, $5.00 from World Bank Publications, 1818 H Street N.W., Washington D.C. 20433, USA.

The results of extensive laboratory testing of 18 handpumps from around the world are presented. The tests included an endurance test of 4000 hours of operation, and performance tests (of volume lifted, work input, leakage, and efficiency). Also included are user comments and an engineering assessment of the design and materials used.

This will be valuable reading to anyone designing pumps, as it identifies the failure points and problem areas in each design, as well as the successful features. Recommendations for improvements are also included.

Many of these pumps are being made in developing countries.

Highly recommended.

Handpump Testing Tower

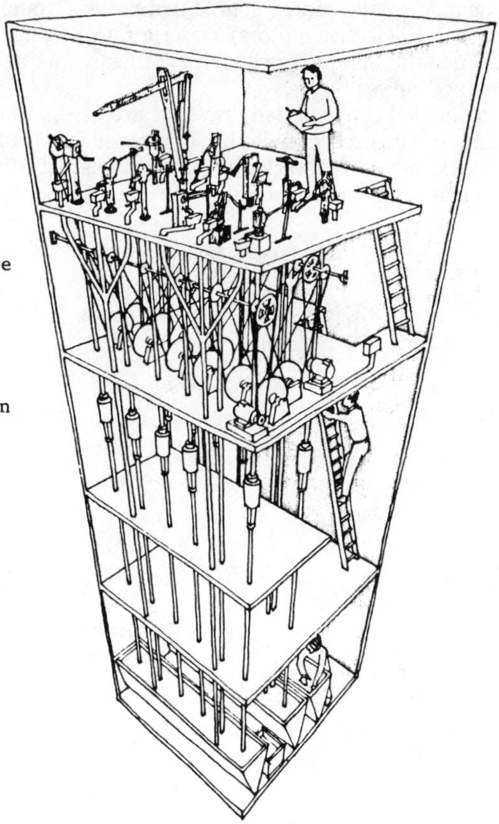

Pumps on Test

Endurance drive mechanism

Head simulation valves

Water tanks

Handpumps Testing and Development: Proceedings of a Workshop in China, World Bank Technical Paper Number 48, MF 14-364, book, 240 pages, edited by Gerhard Tschannerl and Kedar Bryan, November 1985, $5.00 from Publications Office, World Bank, 1818 H Street N.W., Washington D.C. 20433, USA.

The Chinese contributions to these workshop proceedings indicate that they have been producing a surprising number of innovative and unique human- and animal-powered pumps. Many of these pumps have been made in large numbers. In Hebei province alone, it is stated that there were "2,700,000 human and animal operated pumps, of which most were tube-chain water wheels" (also called "chain pumps"). Also unusual are a pedal-operated centrifugal pump and two designs of diaphragm pump (10,000 units sold in one year). These and other more conventional pumps are to be tested as part of the UNDP/World Bank project for laboratory testing of handpumps.

The remainder of this book describes activities of international agencies and work in other countries; most of this material can be found in other sources.

Pumps and Water Lifters for Rural Development, MF 14-363, book, 317 pages, by Alan Wood, revised 1977, $11.50 postpaid in U.S., $13.00 postpaid elsewhere, from Civil Engineering Department, Engineering Research Center Publications, Foothills Campus, Colorado State University, Fort Collins, Colorado 80523, USA.

A survey of water-lifting mechanisms in use around the world, from simple buckets to hydraulic rams and centrifugal pumps. The emphasis is on those that are built locally in developing areas, using local materials.

For each type of device, drawings, operating principles, and most appropriate conditions are given. Also included: discussions of historical uses of water pumps, prime movers (the energy source that powers a pump, from animal power and falling water to electric motors), criteria for choosing pumps for particular applications, general pumping principles with sample calculations, and how to read performance curves.

No detailed construction drawings are given. There are 123 clear illustrations, making this an excellent idea book for those who want to know what types of pumps are in use all over the world. It could serve as a starting point for someone to design and build his or her own pump for a particular application.

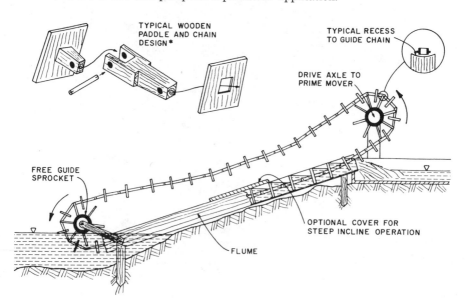

The Rower Pump, MF 14-368, reports and brochures, 1984 and later, available from Mirpur Agricultural Workshop and Training School (MAWTS), Mirpur Section 12, Pallabi, Dacca-16, Bangladesh; or Mennonite Central Committee, 1/1, Block "A" Mohammadpur, Dacca, Bangladesh.

Thousands of low-cost direct action handpumps made of pvc pipe are being used in Bangladesh for low-lift irrigation of small plots. The Rower pump can be easily made in developing countries, and the farmer can do his/her own simple repairs. The pump pays for itself in one crop.

The extremely low cost of the handpump (approximately US$15) and pvc tubewell

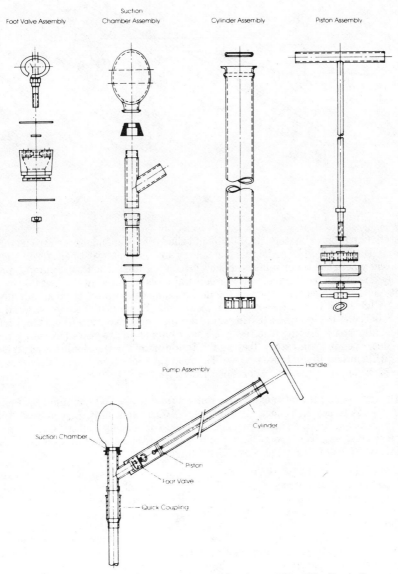

Sub-Assemblies of the Rower Pump

Rower Pump Installation for Irrigation

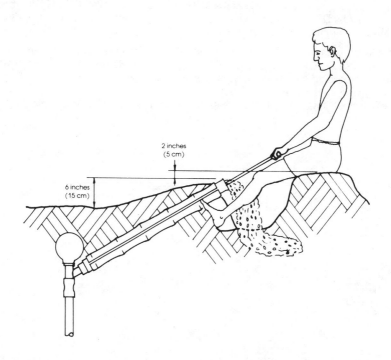

installation (approximately US$30-45) and the large economic return from small plot irrigation together make this technology an excellent investment for farmers in areas where the water table is shallow (15 feet or less). The Rower pump is probably one of the most important agricultural tools invented in the last 20 years.

Readers seeking information on the Rower pump can write to the manufacturer (MAWTS) for a brochure with technical details. Some of the same material is reproduced in **Handpumps Testing and Development: Progress Report on Field and Laboratory Testing** (see review). The results of an extensive laboratory test are described in **Laboratory Testing of Handpumps for Developing Countries: Final Technical Report** (see review). The relevant pages from both of these books are reproduced in the A.T. Microfiche Library as MF 14-368.

Design of Simple and Inexpensive Pumps for Village Water Supply Systems, MF 14-351, research report, 41 pages, by N.C. Thanh, M.B. Pescod, and T.H. Venkitachalam, 1977, $8.00 in Thailand, $10.00 to developing countries, and $15.00 to developed countries, from Library and Regional Documentation Center, Asian Institute of Technology, P.O. Box 2754, Bangkok, Thailand.

The final report of a project to develop two pumps intended to be built and maintained locally describes the design and testing of a bicycle-driven inertia pump and a bellows pump (also foot-powered). The bellows design achieved a pumping rate of 89 liters/minute with a 1.5 meter lift, and the inertia pump in some cases pumped as much as 300 liters/minute with the same lift. No tests were made to determine how much water could be lifted over a longer period of time, considering the pedalling endurance of one person. Construction details are not given but dimensional drawings illustrate the pumping principles adequately.

A large diameter Rower pump appears to be a significantly better choice than either of the pumps described in this report. The IRRI bellows pump has proved disappointing, and the inertia style of pump has never achieved widespread use anywhere, to the best of our knowledge.

Hand Pumps for Village Wells, MF 14-354, booklet, 14 pages, by C. Spangler, 1975, $3.25 from VITA.

This publication reviews the principles of operation of piston and diaphragm hand pumps used in many parts of the world. Deep and shallow well types are included. There are clear drawings of the various types that show the general features and method of operation. Although detailed designs are not given, the design principles are simple and clear.

Materials such as metal castings and PVC pipes are recommended, but simpler locally available materials such as wood could be used. Adaptation to fit local conditions will be necessary.

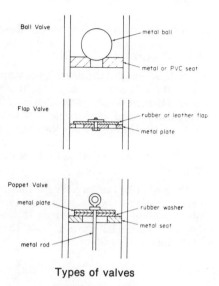

Types of valves

Chinese Chain and Washer Pumps, MF 14-349, booklet, 49 pages, by S. Watt, 1976, out of print in 1985.

"This publication contains 21 versions of the chain and washer water lifting device, displayed at the 1958 Peking Agricultural Exhibition, in China. Each version of the pump was designed and built by separate communes, using local materials, skills and tools. A description of each pump with performance figures was written up in the simple information sheets that have been literally translated for this publication. The drawings presented are on the information sheets, and have been copied to allow anyone with a basic understanding of mechanics to build one of

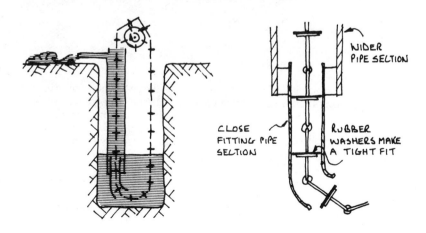

the devices; construction details are not included in this publication."

Each pump design listed has information on the rate of pumping and a summary of the construction method and materials. The introduction describes the principles of operation of chain and washer pumps, components of the pumps, design factors, and power sources available for water pumping (human, animal, wind, solar, and electric). The appendix includes 5 more pump designs, from India, France and Britain.

Village Handpump Technology: Research and Evaluation in Asia, MF 14-367, book, 72 pages, edited by Donald Sharp and Michael Graham, 1982, Publication IDRC-204e, $4.00 from IDRC.

IDRC sponsored the development and testing of an innovative handpump using low-cost PVC plastic materials for most of the parts. The above-ground components were different in each of the four countries in which testing was conducted, while the below-ground components were the same. This volume summarizes the results of the field testing during the early 1980s.

A Manual on the Hydraulic Ram Pump, MF 14-358, booklet, 37 pages, by S.B. Watt, £2.50 from ITDG.

The hydraulic ram is a device that makes water pump itself. It pumps only a small percentage of the water that flows through it, but it does so to a level that is much higher than the source. It can, for example, be used to pump water to a house on a small hill above a creek. The power source is the water moving through the pump.

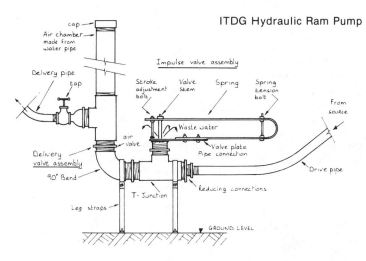

ITDG Hydraulic Ram Pump

"We have written this manual primarily to show field workers how they can design and construct a simple ram pump from commercial pipe fittings, how to choose a suitable site for the ram, how to install and adjust the ram, and the sort of maintenance the pump will need during its working life. We have tried to write the manual in non-technical language so that it can be used by people with little or no technical training; this information makes up Part I. In Part II, we describe in greater detail the range of operation of ram pumps, and the different materials that have been used to make them." This part of the manual explains the calculations necessary to design a ram.

"In places where this ram can be used, it has many advantages over other pumps

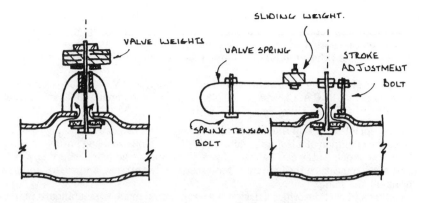

a) SIMPLE CLACK VALVE   b) CLACK VALVE WITH SPRING

Two designs for the impulse valve on a hydraulic ram pump

powered by hand, animal, wind or motors, despite the fact that a lot of water passes through it without being pumped:

a) it does not need an additional power source and there are no running costs,
b) it has only two moving parts, and these are very simple and cheap to maintain,
c) it works efficiently over a wide range of flows, provided it is tuned correctly,
d) it can be made using simple workshop equipment."

This design is an improvement on the original **VITA Hydraulic Ram** design (see review) — it is described more thoroughly and is adaptable to different water flows and heads. There appears to be no way to avoid the necessity for pipe fitting equipment, drilling, and a little welding in any good ram design.

A Hydraulic Ram for Village Use, MF 14-356, booklet, 11 pages, by Ersal Kindel, 1975, VITA, out of print in 1985.

This manual consists of "working instructions and drawings on how to construct a small, simple hydraulic ram from commercially available water pipe fittings. The ram described has a supply head of 6.5 meters, a delivery head of 14 meters, with

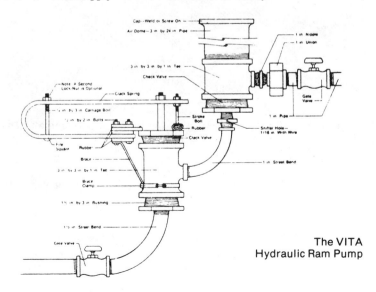

The VITA
Hydraulic Ram Pump

a delivery of 7 liters/minute. It is thus only used for small water supplies."

Although less detailed and thorough than the **Popular Mechanics** article, this information is more adapted to village resources. The operating mechanism is a bit simpler than the **Popular Mechanics** designs.

Popular Mechanics Hydraulic Ram, Reprint No. X346, MF 14-360, article with plans, 11 pages, by C.A. Crowley, $3.50 plus postage from Popular Mechanics, Dept. 77, Box 1014, Radio City, New York 10101, USA.

This reprint from **Popular Mechanics**, a magazine, has two parts. The first explains the operation of a hydraulic ram, simplified methods enabling anyone to determine how much water can be lifted from a stream to the place where it will be used, how to measure the amount of water flow in the stream, and where and how to install the pump.

The second part describes a design for a ram pump made from standard plumbing parts. The drawings and construction are clear. The materials and production processes required may not be locally available everywhere.

Manual of Information — Rife Hydraulic Rams, MF 14-357, booklet, 15 pages, 1985, 25 cents from Rife Hydraulic Engine Manufacturing Co., P.O. Box 790, Norristown, Pennsylvania 19401, USA.

This pamphlet covers the information you need to install a ram: where to place it, how to estimate the water output, how to measure the flow, choosing the size for the drive and delivery pipes. Describes the operation of a ram, but does not describe a ram design. The information is for use with rams manufactured by Rife; other ram designs will have somewhat different performance.

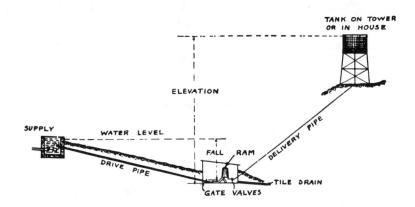

Use of Hydraulic Rams in Nepal: A Guide to Manufacturing and Installation, MF 14-362, booklet, 46 pages, by Mitchell Silver, free to serious users from UNICEF, Box 1187, Kathmandu, Nepal.

This book includes what **Construction of a Hydraulic Ram Pump** (see review) does not: how to install, use and maintain a hydraulic ram after you've built or bought one. It is written in plain English.

Although aimed at local conditions in Nepal (for example, the availability of supplies in Kathmandu hardware stores is discussed), this book is useful for anyone with little mechanical background who wants to use a hydraulic ram in any location.

Included are chapters on: how a hydraulic ram works, surveying a site, descriptions and design considerations for intake tanks, reservoirs, operating a ram pump, maintenance and repair. Conversion tables are included.

There are 14 pages on building a ram pump using standard pipe fittings. The valves can be either bought or made. The instructions and drawings are not as detailed as in other hydraulic ram publications, but they could be used by someone with mechanical experience. The most useful part of this booklet, however, is that it shows how hydraulic rams can be simply adapted for use in differing local conditions.

Recommended for use with a hydraulic ram construction manual.

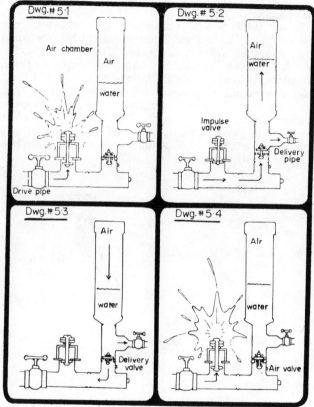

Opening and closing of the valves and the flow of water during one pumping cycle of a hydraulic ram (Nepal)

The Construction of a Hydraulic Ram Pump, MF 14-350, booklet, 36 pages, by Allen Inversin, 1978, Appropriate Technology Development Unit, Papua New Guinea, out of print in 1985.

Allen Inversin has designed and tested the first working hydraulic ram design we've seen that requires no welding or special skills. "Both VITA and ITDG have long had available designs for a low-cost ram pump. These designs, however, require special skills and tools to construct, have not been tested to any extent over a range of operating conditions, and consequently provide little data on the performance of the actual rams described."

Starting from the basic ITDG ram design, Inversin has redesigned the parts so that studs, nuts and bolts carry the loads, using epoxy adhesive only as a sealant. The valves have been simplified, eliminating much of the machining and/or special tools that are required in the ITDG and VITA designs (see reviews).

The author intends this to be built by someone with very little machining experience; however, ". . . it is quite probable that those who have had machine shop experience will prefer alternative means of construction (rather than the simple ones described in the manual)." Very simple yet detailed instructions, easily the clearest we've seen, are given, along with clear illustrations. Construction is simple, as only handtools and a drill press are necessary. In addition to commercially available pipe fittings, small strips of scrap steel, nuts, bolts and epoxy are the only materials required.

A significant part of this manual is the 8 pages devoted to performance information, based on a year of testing and improvement in PNG. The pump has been tested at drive heads (heights) of .5 to 4 meters. For delivery heads of 10 times the drive head, it can deliver 3600 liters of water/day. Graphs for predicting performance at various operating heads are included.

There is purposely no information provided on how a hydraulic ram works, or how to install, operate and maintain a ram, since these subjects are adequately covered in other publications, such as the ITDG and VITA booklets, or the UNICEF/Nepal booklet (see review). However, this manual is a welcome improvement in simple ram design, and would be valuable to use in combination with any of the three books mentioned above.

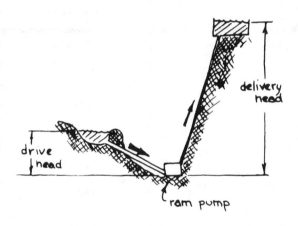

F. Storage Tanks

Ferrocement Water Tanks and Their Construction, MF 15-365, book, 118 pages, by S.B. Watt, 1978, £3.95 from ITDG.

The book covers a number of different ways to use ferrocement (wire-reinforced cement mortar) to construct water storage tanks and jars of many shapes and sizes. The author has worked with ITDG for years and has written a book that thoroughly covers design, construction and use of ferrocement water storage containers. The book is an excellent construction manual, but it also covers catching and using rainwater from roofs and land surfaces, health aspects of water storage, use of ferrocement linings for earthen tanks, and sources of further ferrocement information. There are many detailed photos and illustrations.

"The Dogon people of Mali, living in the Sahelian drought zone with a rainfall of only about 40 cm (16 in.) per year, suffer greatly from water shortages during the dry season. The method of storing water described in this chapter was devised to provide a cheap tank for water collected from the flat roofs of the houses. The water tanks, which consist of traditional (adobe) grain bins, lined with a thin layer of reinforced (ferrocement) mortar, are readily acceptable to the users and fit well into their social and cultural visions of life."

This book seems to contain all the information one would need to build ferrocement water storage tanks. The water tank construction techniques would also be useful to someone building other types of ferrocement structures such as grain bins or houses.

An excellent book, highly recommended.

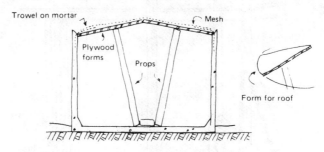

Constructing the roof of a ferrocement water tank

Construction Manual for 3500 gal. Ferrocement Water Tank, MF 15-364, pamphlet, 19 pages, by E.H. Robinson, $2.50 from Caribbean Appropriate Technology Center, Caribbean Council of Churches, P.O. Box 616, Bridgetown, Barbados.

This construction manual is best suited for people who have had experience working with ferrocement, as the instructions and illustrations are sparse, although generally quite clear. People without prior experience in this area should check more detailed references on the topic (see, for example, **Ferrocement Water Tanks and Their Construction**).

Bamboo-Reinforced Concrete Rainwater Collection Tanks, booklet, 50 pages, by Thomas Fricke, ATI, 1982, available from A.T. International, 1331 H Street N.W., Washington D.C. 20005, USA.

Rainwater catchment tanks are proving to be a popular, affordable technology in Northeastern Thailand, where some 2500 11-cubic meter tanks have been constructed between 1978 and 1982. Villagers are paying for these tanks through loans provided by the implementing agency, and by providing some of the construction labor themselves. The loans are being repaid on time. The unusual organizational structures involved and some interesting conclusions and implications for other technology dissemination programs are described. Some construction details are provided, but this is primarily a review of the program and the process, rather than a how-to-do-it manual.

From Ferro to Bamboo: A Case Study and Technical Manual to a Rain Water Catchment Project, MF 15-366, booklet, 48 pages, by Marcus Kaufman, 1983, $5.50 postpaid from Publication Section, Yayasan Dian Desa, P.O. Box 19, Bulaksumur, Yogyakarta, Indonesia.

Finding that the high cost of materials for ferrocement water catchment tanks in Central Java was limiting the tank's dissemination to projects with outside funding, Yayasan Dian Desa developed a bamboo-reinforced tank which is based on technologies already in use locally. Although the design proved to be popular and technically suitable, Dian Desa's evaluation team found that many tank owners would exhaust their convenient supply of tank water soon after the rainy season, when other sources of water were still available. This left the tanks empty through the critical summer months of water scarcity, defeating the major purpose of the tank building program. Clear instructions and drawings show how to build the 4.5 cubic meter "single family" bamboo cement water catchment tank described in the case study. Highly recommended.

G. Filtration and Treatment

Water Treatment and Sanitation: Simple Methods for Rural Areas, MF 16-381, book, 96 pages, by H. Mann and D. Williamson, 1973, revised edition 1982, £3.95 from ITDG.

This is still a good introductory book on these subjects, but many of the newer books reviewed here go into much greater depth on narrower topics. Includes chapters on selection of source and simple water testing, water supply, water treatment, excreta disposal, sewage treatment, temporary and emergency treatment. Charts, graphs and simple methods for roughly calculating water demand, flow measurement, and pump heads are included, as are simple drawings of a variety of water system equipment: sand filters, pumps, privies, water seal toilets, and simple sludge treatment ponds. A glossary of technical terms is included, as are drawings and a bibliography.

Slow Sand Filtration, MF 16-376, book, 115 pages, by L. Huisman and W. Wood, 1974, $8.00 from World Health Organization, Distribution and Sales Service, 1211 Geneva 27, Switzerland.

The slow sand filter is one of the best means of treating a raw water supply where specialized chemical technology is not available. Far from being an old-fashioned technology, the authors feel that the slow sand method can be the cheapest, simplest and most efficient method of water treatment.

Several scales of design are discussed and illustrated, although knowledge of basic engineering mathematics would be helpful. The last part of the book discusses the use of sand filters for recharging groundwater, an important consideration for arid areas. In areas of known biological contamination, however, the use of chemical treatment (chlorine or preferably iodine) along with sand filtration would provide a very safe water supply.

Slow sand filtration methods are also very simple to operate: "Provided that a plant has been well designed and constructed there is little that can go wrong as long as the simple routine of operation is carried out."

A very valuable book for those involved with planning water supplies for small to medium size communities.

FIG. 1. DIAGRAM OF A SLOW SAND FILTER

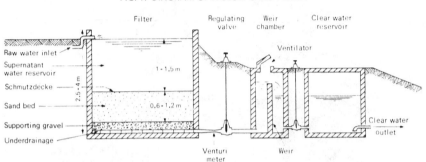

Slow Sand Filtration for Community Water Supply in Developing Countries: A Design and Construction Manual, Technical Paper No. 11, MF 16-378, book, 178 pages, by J.C. Van Dijk and J.H.C.M. Oomen, 1978, $10.00 from IRC.

"Although the field of water treatment offers a variety of technological choices, only a few of them can in principle fully meet the specific requirements of developing countries. One such method is slow sand filtration — a simple, efficient and reliable technique for the treatment of water. Its costs generally lie within the resources of the community and/or country and the skills for design, construction, operation, and maintenance are usually available locally or can be fairly easily acquired."

Slow Sand Filtration for Community Water Supply in Developing Countries, Bulletin No. 9, MF 16-377, annotated bibliography, 61 pages, by H. Hartong, 1978, $5.00 from IRC.

Slow sand filters have been in use for almost 150 years in public water supplies. Even though some European cities use them on a large scale, they tend to be dismissed as old-fashioned or out of date. However, many people are once again concluding that slow sand filtration for purifying drinking water is very effective, and deserves more widespread use, particularly in rural and urban fringe areas of developing countries.

This bibliography contains 79 entries on the technical aspects of slow sand filtration. Each entry is summarized and indexed according to author and keywords. Included is a list of institutions around the world active in developing low-cost slow sand filtration methods.

L. Huisman notes in the preface: "In developing countries...slow sand filtration is often applied as a single treatment process, only where necessary preceded by a simple pre-treatment for turbidity removal. Optimal use can be made of locally available materials such as bricks, mudblocks and mass concrete, while also filter sand of good specifications is readily available in most countries. Operation and maintenance are relatively easy and can be done by semi-skilled operators. Operational costs are minimal, the more so as no chemicals are required. Slow sand filtration may be regarded as an appropriate water treatment process and its wider application may considerably contribute to an improved provision of safe drinking water in developing countries."

An extensive, excellent bibliography.

Application of Slow Filtration for Surface Water Treatment in Tropical Developing Countries, MF 16-368, technical report, 75 pages, by N.C. Thanh and M.B. Pescod, 1976, $8.00 in Thailand, $10.00 to developing countries, $15.00 to developed countries, from Library and Regional Documentation Center, Asian Institute of Technology, P.O. Box 2754, Bangkok, Thailand.

This is a report on performance tests of 3 different slow filtration systems for purifying water using various combinations of sand, burnt rice husks, and coconut fibers. Data are given on the influence of turbidity (cloudiness) and filtration rates on the quality of filtered water.

The goal of these studies is to provide relatively inexpensive treatment for surface waters, using materials common to Southeast Asia. The systems tested are for a village water supply, and would require an operator. The construction cost of such a system is estimated at 15,000-20,000 Baht ($750-$1000).

Very technical; useful primarily for researchers in slow sand filtration techniques. For a study of prefilters to be used with slow sand filters, see review below.

Horizontal-Flow Coarse-Material Prefiltration, MF 16-369, research report, 46 pages, by N.C. Thanh and E.A.R. Ouano, 1977, $8.00 in Thailand, $10.00 to developing countries, $15.00 to developed countries, from Library and Regional Documentation Center, Asian Institute of Technology, P.O. Box 2754, Bangkok, Thailand.

Slow sand filters are accepted means of treating water for drinking; they can, however, be clogged by inorganic materials. The authors have been working at the Asian Institute of Technology on prefilters which are horizontal and use coarse crushed stone and gravity to help settle out the suspended inorganic and large organic materials.

This report describes and gives results from research on coarse prefilters used with both sand filters and burnt rice husk filters. The authors found that the horizontal prefilter was effective, removing up to 60-70% of the solid matter in water before it reached the regular filter. It was found that the sand filter produced a better tasting water, although the rice husk filter performed better in terms of water flow. The filter/prefilter combinations also removed much, but not all, of the non-fecal coliform organisms present in the unfiltered water. This indicates that a high degree of health protection is possible with such filter combinations.

Simplified Procedures for Water Examination, Manual M12, MF 16-375, laboratory manual, 190 pages, 1978, $20.40 ($19.20 for Spanish edition) from American Water Works Association, 6666 West Quincy Avenue, Denver, Colorado 80235, USA.

A detailed, step-by-step laboratory manual for testing water quality, using modern laboratory equipment. Chemical, bacteriological and biological (microscope) examinations are all discussed.

Chemical tests can be used to determine whether too much or too little disinfectant is being added to water. Bacteriological tests determine the presence of coli-

form bacteria, which can make drinking water unsafe.
Useful only in areas where laboratory facilities already exist.

The Purification of Water on a Small Scale, Technical Paper #3, MF 16-373, booklet, 19 pages, 1973, IRC, out of print in 1985.

This short booklet contains practical instructions for water purification by boiling, chemical disinfection and filtration. Chemical disinfection includes chlorine, iodine and potassium permanganate (not recommended). Filtration methods include sand filters for coarse filtration, and ceramic filters for finer filtration. A simple filter design is given. This sand filter removes visible dirt and particles such as ova and cysts; the authors say it won't remove bacteria. The importance of storage in preventing re-contamination of water is emphasized.
Recommended.

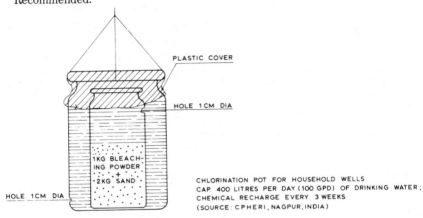

PLASTIC COVER

HOLE 1 CM DIA

1KG BLEACH- ING POWDER + 2KG SAND

HOLE 1 CM DIA

CHLORINATION POT FOR HOUSEHOLD WELLS
CAP. 400 LITRES PER DAY (100 GPD) OF DRINKING WATER ;
CHEMICAL RECHARGE EVERY 3 WEEKS
(SOURCE : C P H E R I , NAGPUR, INDIA)

Solar Distillation as a Means of Meeting Small Scale Water Demands, MF 16-379, book, 86 pages, 1970, reprinted 1977, pub. no. 70.11.B.1, $7.00 from UNIPUB.

Solar distillation is an elementary process: salt water or polluted water is placed in a container under a transparent cover. This cover traps solar energy which heats the water. The water evaporates and then condenses on the inside of the cover, and the impurities are left behind. This condensed water can be collected and used for drinking and cooking. However, only small quantities of water are produced (about 25-30 gallons per square foot of still per year). Solar distillation is therefore an expensive technology in terms of cost per gallon of water. It is a real option primarily in island and arid coastal locations where surface or groundwater sources of fresh water are not available. In many of these places, rainfall is significant during part of the year, and rainwater catchment systems may be a more economical alternative to provide at least part of the water needed.

This is an excellent manual on all sizes of solar distribution plants, for providing fresh water in small communities. The purposes of the manual are: "to review the current status of solar distillation, outline the general situations where it may be the best solution to water supply problems, provide a method for potential users to estimate performance and costs of current still designs in their area, to note practical problems of solar still design and operation, and to recognize possible changes in solar distillation technology and economics which may affect the applicability of the process in the future."

Very good information on the design of stills is included, requiring a knowledge of basic mathematics. There is a lack of detailed plans, but construction of stills using the ideas and drawings in the book is possible. The major requirements for a solar still are simply a basin of cement or other material to catch water, and a clear covering of glass or plastic.

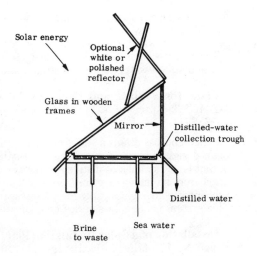

How to Make a Solar Still (plastic covered), MF 16-370, dimensional drawings with text, 13 pages, Brace Research Institute, 1965 (revised 1973), $1.75 from BRACE.

"This leaflet permits the user to make a relatively inexpensive solar still, primarily out of plastic sheets and bricks. It is not what might be recommended for a long-term installation. However, this plastic covered unit can certainly be adequately used for temporary installation."

"It has the advantage of being suitable for units producing anywhere from 1 gallon to 1000 gallons per day, and will operate for long periods in isolated locations without attention. No auxiliary power source is needed, other than means for feeding water into the unit...12 square feet of solar still area are needed to produce one gallon of water daily." A 400 square foot still in the West Indies cost US$228.00 for materials.

To really use this leaflet well, one would have to improvise considerably. The size they chose is 100 feet long, with a concrete base — hardly a temporary enterprise — yet the plastic sheeting will last only 6 months to 2 years even though it represents ½ the cost of the materials. The task of replacing it is easy.

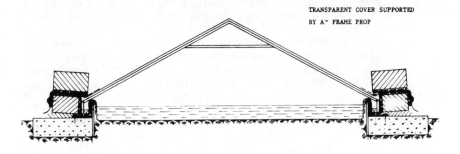

Simple Solar Still for the Production of Distilled Water, Technical Report No. T17, MF 16-374, 6 pages, by T.A. Lawand, 1965 (revised 1967), also available in French and Arabic, $1.75 from BRACE.

This unit was "designed primarily for use in service stations with the object of providing distilled water for automobile batteries." Distilled water is very necessary for battery maintenance, especially in arid regions. This still will produce an average of 3 liters per day.

Clean fresh water (can be collected on roof during rainy season) is added to the still each day — distilled water is drained off. Users must be careful with the storage of the distilled water to avoid contamination.

Plans for a Glass and Concrete Solar Still, Technical Report No. T58, MF 16-372, 8 pages of text plus 2 large blueprints, by T.A. Lawand and R. Alward, 1972, $4.50 from BRACE.

"This report contains a series of plans and specifications for a solar distillation plant designed by the Brace Research Institute for a site in Haiti." The average output is 200 gallons of distilled water per day. "The units are simply built and, apart from plumbing, are composed of four components: concrete curbs, a butyl rubber basin liner, glass panes for the transparent cover and a silicone glass sealant." This system is actually a series of solar stills connected together.

Installation of a Solar Distillation Plant on Ile de la Gonave, Haiti, Internal Report No. 167, MF 16-371, 10 pages plus 10 photos, by R. Alward, 1970, BRACE, out of print in 1985.

This report covers the actual installation of the glass and concrete solar still for which plans are given in the above Technical Report No. T58. Illustrates point by point the problems encountered in the actual construction, and the solutions that were found. There are 10 excellent photographs showing the method and stages of construction.

H. Sanitation

Low-Cost Technology Options for Sanitation: A State-of-the-Art Review and Annotated Bibliography, Appropriate Technology for Water Supply and Sanitation Vol. 4, MF 17-387, book, 184 pages, by Witold Rybczynski, Chongrak Polprasert, and Michael McGarry, 1978, from Publications Unit, World Bank, 1818 H Street N.W., Washington D.C. 20433, USA.

This is a sourcebook on sanitation alternatives. The first quarter of the book is a review of the existing methods for collection, treatment, reuse and disposal of human wastes.

"There exists a wide range of effective alternatives between the unhygienic pit privy and the Western waterborne sewerage system. These systems are generally far cheaper. Most of them do not demand a heavy use of water. And many make creative use of the nutrients in human waste to fertilize fields and fish ponds or to contribute to biogas production — and they can do this without serious risk of returning pathogens to human food or drinking water."

The bibliography fills the rest of the book. Thousands of pieces of literature were examined in the process of choosing 530 documents summarized here. "Emphasis has been placed on technological issues, but institutional, behavioural, and health-related aspects of excreta disposal were also considered." Most of this literature is available only in English, but some of it is also available in Spanish, French, Norwegian or Swedish.

Very little documentation of indigenous excreta disposal practices exists, the authors note. "It has been assumed that these (practices) are of little importance as they will eventually be replaced by sewerage. As a result, the potential for upgrading existing practices has been largely ignored. . . Once existing conditions are understood as a starting point, certain solutions will be more compatible with resources available. Particular options will integrate reuse possibilities that reflect energy, food, or agricultural needs of the particular community. Whether such solutions lead to waterborne sanitation is less important than the fact that they will be the beginning of a dynamic process of development."

Unfortunately there are no prices listed, and most source addresses given are incomplete. This will make acquisition of the documents difficult.

There is a thorough index and an excellent glossary of sanitation terms. Highly recommended.

Small Excreta Disposal Systems, booklet, 54 pages, by R. Feachem and S. Cairncross, 1978, £2.00 from The Ross Institute, London School of Hygiene and Tropical Medicine, Keppel Street (Gower Street), London WC1E 7HT, England; or ITDG.

This booklet presents "the range of technologies available for excreta disposal in small communities and describes each system in simple terms. Design formulas are included where appropriate and (for experienced people) it is possible using this booklet to design the main elements of the systems."

Two chapters cover individual components and complete waste systems, from bucket latrines to water seal privies and septic tanks. The information here is largely descriptive. A third chapter covers the design and construction of squatting slabs,

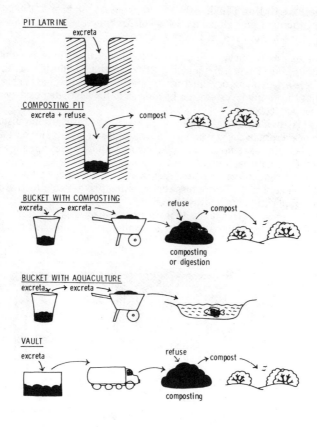

A variety of excreta disposal systems

pit latrines, water privies, septic tanks, soakways (leachlines or drainfields), and waste stabilization ponds.

A good mix of description and design details is presented. The book's strongest point is that it concentrates on rural, tropical areas in developing countries, analyzing what is and what isn't appropriate. (For example: the Clivus Multrum self-composting toilet "has not yet proved its worth in the tropics or among low income communities.")

Recommended.

Excreta Disposal for Rural Areas and Small Communities, World Health Organization Monograph #39, MF 17-392, book, 176 pages, by E. Wagner and J. Lanoix, 1958 (reprinted 1971), $14.00 from World Health Organization, Distribution and Sales Service, 1211 Geneva 27, Switzerland.

This is a solid reference work on the disposal of human wastes. 100 pages are given to various privy methods of waste disposal; advantages and disadvantages are given for each method considered. Water-carried methods and considerations are similarly treated with 35 pages. The many drawings generally include enough information for local construction.

Much of the material presented in this excellent but high-priced manual is covered by other sources (**Village Technology Handbook**, **Stop the Five Gallon Flush**, **Septic Tank Practices**) which cumulatively give more information.

Stop the Five Gallon Flush, MF 17-399, booklet, 88 pages, 1980, $4.00 from Center for Minimum Cost Housing, School of Architecture, McGill University, 3480 University Street, Montreal H3A 2A7, Canada.

This is an extensive survey of human waste disposal systems, ranging from the $7.50 Chiang Mai (Thailand) squatting plate, to the $7,000 high-tech Cycle-Let system. There are explanatory illustrations and text, which would enable the reader to construct the simpler systems on his/her own. 66 waste disposal systems from 14 countries are covered.

Systems are divided into the following categories: Infiltration (absorption and dispersion of excreta in the soil and groundwater, as in pit latrines or aqua privies); Manual or mechanical removal (buckets, vacuum units, or sewage pipe networks); Destruction (incinerating toilets); and Decomposition (where microbiological action destroys pathogens and creates fertilizer, as in compost privies or methane digesters). Included is the Vietnamese composting privy — an effective device with widespread applications (see drawing above).

"It should be clear, at this point, that water-borne waste represents a (relatively recent) answer within a particular set of economic and physical conditions, and

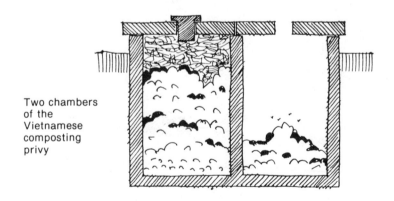

Two chambers
of the
Vietnamese
composting
privy

not clearly the least wasteful answer at that. Flush toilets should not be considered as 'advanced' compared to the pit latrine. Under certain conditions the latter is ecologically sound, cheap and quite safe."

Goodbye to the Flush Toilet, MF 17-393, book, 296 pages, edited by Carol Hupping Stoner, 1977, $10.95 from RODALE.

"A waste is a resource out of place." This book describes the best biological systems developed during the early 1970s in North America for on-site recycling of human wastes and waste water (greywater). Numerous designs are presented, with text and drawings that would allow readers to build or maintain such devices. The Farallones Institute vault and drum privies, Ken Kern's solar shower and privy, the Clivus Multrum and other manufactured units are featured. This book is written primarily from a North American context, and is probably most valuable in temperate regions and industrialized countries.

An essay by Witold Rybczynski describes an experimental dry toilet design tested in the Third World: "The Minimus chamber is built out of cement blocks, plastered inside, and has a concrete bottom. The vent pipe is galvanized metal, and the air ducts are PVC. The total material costs (not including labor) was US$55. The construction time was six man-days."

"It should be stressed that there is no one 'design' for the Minimus. It must be adapted to meet local climatic conditions, available building materials, local skills, and conditions. The application of composting sanitation technology to developing countries cannot be on a piecemeal basis. It must be done on a community (not individual) scale and integrated with social and education development. It was precisely in such a way that rural composting toilets were introduced to North Vietnam during the years 1961-1965."

Sanitation in Developing Countries, MF 17-396, book, 172 pages, 1981, Publication IDRC-168e, $9.00 from IDRC.

Experience with many levels of sanitation technology in a variety of African nations is presented in this record of the proceedings of a regional workshop held in Botswana in 1980. Notable for the clear-sighted appraisal of what works and what doesn't in a given cultural, technical and economic setting, the papers draw well-considered conclusions that are applicable to a broad range of village improvement efforts, especially those that require community cooperation. Recommended.

Sanitation Without Water, MF 17-397, book, 133 pages, by Uno Winblad and Wen Kilama, revised 1985, free from Swedish International Development Authority, S 105 25, Stockholm, Sweden.

"The flush toilet cannot solve the problems of excreta disposal in the poor countries. Nor has it indeed solved those problems in the rich part of the world." To document some alternatives, the authors have written this practical manual on waterless waste treatment systems, primarily compost privies and pit latrines for individual households. These units do not require waterborne sewage disposal lines, and are thus less expensive and complex.

The information presented here is intended for health officers, medical workers, and village technicians in East Africa, although the authors feel the information is adaptable elsewhere. The book should also be useful as a guide in training programs. There are four parts:

1) The relationship between sanitation and disease; the digestion and composting processes; 2) a description of 10 dry sanitation systems around the world (for a more extensive summary, see **Stop the Five Gallon Flush**); 3) a latrine manual, including explanations of latrine components, design information, operating in-

structions, and proper location for latrines; 4) appendix: fly control in dry latrines.

The authors also add a note of caution: "There are no miracle solutions to the problem of excreta disposal...The methods and systems described can work and some do work very well indeed. But when not fully understood by the users or constructed in the wrong way or in the wrong place, they may fail completely."

The best (and only) book we've seen that covers all aspects of dry sanitation systems on an easily understood level. The 97 drawings are very helpful in understanding these simple methods of sanitation that can be applied with limited resources.

Highly recommended.

Appropriate Technology for Water Supply and Sanitation, series of books published by The World Bank, available from Publications Unit, World Bank, 1818 H Street N.W., Washington D.C. 20433, USA.

This series reports the findings of a two-year World Bank study on appropriate technology for water supply and waste disposal in developing countries. "The objective of the project was to identify and evaluate sanitation technologies for their potential to meet the needs and match the resources of project beneficiaries." Consideration is given to a wide range of technical, economic, and social factors relevant to a choice of traditional or "improved" technologies. The series will eventually include 14 volumes.

Vol. 1: **Technical and Economic Options** (MF 17-382)

Vol. 1a: **A Summary of Technical and Economic Options** (MF 17-383)

Vol. 1b: **Sanitation Alternatives for Low-Income Communities — A Brief Introduction** (MF 17-384)

Vol. 2: **A Planner's Guide** (MF 17-385)

Vol. 3: **Health Aspects of Excreta and Sullage Management — A State-of-the-Art Review** (MF 17-386)

Vol. 4: **Low-Cost Technology Options for Sanitation — A State-of-the-Art Review and Annotated Bibliography** (MF 17-387, see separate review)

Vol. 5: **Sociocultural Aspects of Water Supply and Excreta Disposal** (MF 17-388)

Vol. 10: **Night Soil Composting** (MF 17-389).

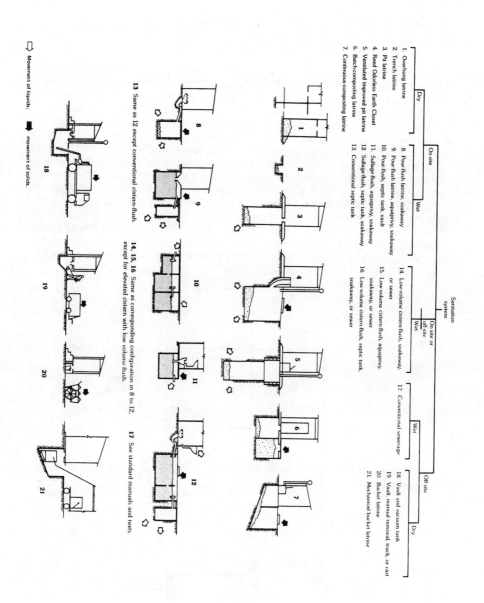

1. Overhung latrine
2. Trench latrine
3. Pit latrine
4. Reed Odorless Earth Closet
5. Ventilated improved pit latrine
6. Batch-composting latrine
7. Continuous-composting latrine

8. Pour-flush latrine; soakaway
9. Pour-flush latrine, aquaprivy, soakaway
10. Pour-flush, septic tank; vault
11. Sullage-flush, aquaprivy, soakaway
12. Sullage-flush, septic tank; soakaway
13. Conventional septic tank

14. Low-volume cistern-flush, soakaway, or sewer
15. Low volume cistern-flush, aquaprivy, soakaway, or sewer
16. Low volume cistern-flush, septic tank, soakaway, or sewer

17. Conventional sewerage

18. Vault and vacuum tank
19. Vault, manual removal, truck, or cart
20. Bucket latrine
21. Mechanical bucket latrine

Sanitation system

Dry | On-site | Wet | On-site or off-site | Wet | Off-site | Dry

13 Same as 12 except conventional cistern-flush.

14, 15, 16 Same as corresponding configuration in 8 to 12, except for elevated cistern with low volume-flush.

17 See standard manuals and texts.

⇨ Movement of liquids;   ⬛ movement of solids.

Generic Classification of Sanitation Systems

Source: The World Bank, Water Supply and Waste Disposal, Poverty and Basic Needs Series (Washington, D.C., September 1980).

Double Vault Composting Toilets: A State-of-the-Art Review, MF 17-403, by Witold Rybczynski, in Environmental Sanitation Reviews, No. 6, December 1981, journal, 27 pages plus appendix, Swiss Francs 18.00 from SKAT or approximately $8.00 from Environmental Sanitation Information Center, Asian Institute of Technology, P.O. Box 2754, Bangkok, Thailand.

Double vault composting toilets are attracting considerable attention due to their low cost, simplicity, and large-scale successes reported from India and North Vietnam. The author of this review provides an enlightening and entertaining review of the history and variations among the major design options.

"The necessity for constructing a slab to span the composting vaults, which is both expensive and complicated (as well as using reinforced concrete), is neatly avoided in the sopa sandas (simple latrine). The pits are offset from the squatting plate and an inclined chute connects the two. . . installations have used baked earthen pans and chutes, as well as more expensive glazed ceramic. . .The organic refuse is added to the vault all at once, before it is used, rather than continuously. When the vault is filled it is sealed, organic refuse added to the adjoining vault, and the adjoining pan is used. The vaults have no bottoms and excess liquid is infiltrated into the ground. No vent pipes are required. The sopa sandas has a number of advantages: extremely low cost through offsetting the vaults and eliminating vent pipes; simple operation since organic waste is only added once every six months;

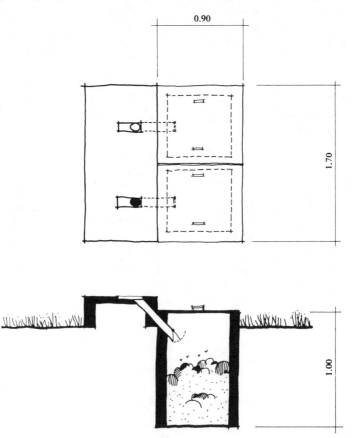

Fig. 7   Sopa Sandas (after Maharashtra Gandhi Smarak Nidhi)

it easily accepts anal cleansing water since the floor of the vaults is permeable. The sopa sandas DVC toilet has been in continual use in India for the last 20 years, and has been popularized by such volunteer organizations as Maharashtra Gandhi Smarak Nidhi, which... by 1980 had built 60,000 latrines in Maharashtra state."

Dry Composting Latrines in Guatemala, MF 17-404, paper, 15 pages, by A. van Buren, J. McMichael, A. Caceres, and R. Caceres, CEMAT, 1982, $4.00 from CEMAT, Apartado Postal 1160, Guatemala City, Guatemala; or SKAT.

Double vault dry composting latrines reached widespread acceptance in North Vietnam during the period 1958-78, and reportedly greatly reduced the incidence of intestinal diseases while providing valuable fertilizer. This report describes an attempt to achieve similar benefits using a Guatemalan design and local materials. The authors indicate that significant local interest has led to latrine construction in at least 10 highland villages.

How to Build a Pit Latrine, MF 17-405, booklet, 46 pages, from UNICEF, P.O. Box 1187, Kathmandu, Nepal.

A well-illustrated booklet in Nepali and English, showing step-by-step construction of a very simple pit latrine made of local materials.

Sanitation Handbook (Nepal), MF 17-400, book, 59 pages, by Martin Strauss, 1982, Community Water Supply and Sanitation Program (SATA), Swiss Francs 10.00 from SKAT.

A reference book for latrine construction in Nepal, including a local version of the Zimbabwe ventilated spiral latrine. Describes the transmission of pathogens commonly found in Nepal.

<u>Slab from bamboo or timber support,</u> stone flooring and mortar

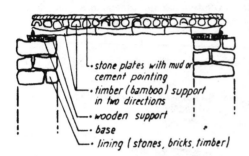

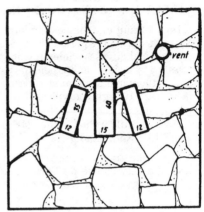

Compost Toilets: A Guide for Owner-Builders, MF 17-390, book, 51 pages, NCAT, 1979, $3.00 from National Center for Appropriate Technology, P.O. Box 3838, Butte, Montana 59701, USA.

The water-borne sewage system is the standard technology for safe disposal of human wastes in urban areas in the industrialized countries. These systems are extremely expensive to build and operate. By 1978, the capital investment necessary to connect one house to such a system in the U.S. was reported to be a minimum of $4000. A substantial amount of water, 25-60 gallons per person per day, is required to flush the toilets. Treatment of the sewage is also costly, energy-intensive, and represents the destruction of a potential resource.

In many areas both inside and outside the United States, a dry composting toilet appears to be a much more economically and environmentally-sound alternative. **Compost Toilets** is a well-organized introduction to the subject. It explains the composting problems associated with the major designs. Draining systems and simple jar fly traps are shown that have been successfully developed to overcome the common problems of liquid buildup and flies. There are three complete slant-bottom designs presented for owner-builders, with discussion of the pros and cons of each.

"A compost toilet...can be a safe and efficient, sanitary human waste treatment system. The main question facing owner/builders is whether they are prepared to take the time to manage the system efficiently." The right liquid and carbon/nitrogen balances must be kept or the toilet will not function properly. In most designs, the composted material must be removed approximately every 3 months after the initial start-up period.

Costs of commercially-made compost toilets are given as $850 to $2500. Systems built at the site are expected to cost about $450 for materials and $500 for labor. We recommend this book to U.S. readers. Readers in developing countries should refer to the excellent **Double Vault Composting Toilets: A State-of-the-Art Review** and the other books reviewed in this section.

Ventilated Improved Pit Latrines: Recent Developments in Zimbabwe,
MF 17-409, booklet, 39 pages, by Peter Morgan and D. Duncan Mara, December
1982, from Technology Advisory Group, World Bank, 1818 H Street N.W.,
Washington D.C. 20433, USA.

In Zimbabwe, 20,000 ventilated pit latrines have been built using an unusual
doorless design. The authors estimate that 20-35 years will be required before a
family of 6 manage to fill the pit. Urban designs of ferrocement or brick with
pipe vents cost about US$160. The rural versions of mud and wattle, thatch, ant-
hill soil, local bricks and timber are much cheaper, but require a minimum of 25
kg of cement. These designs are estimated to cost $8 for special materials plus
local materials and labor.

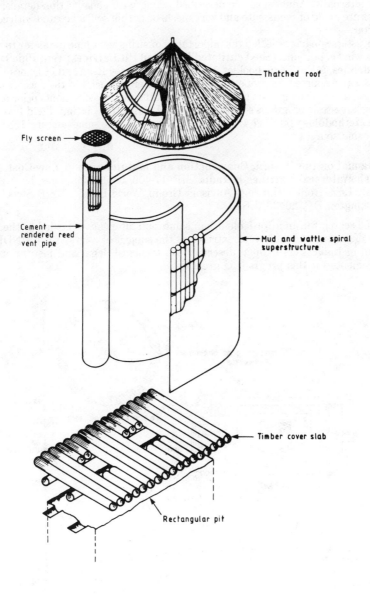

The Design of Ventilated Improved Pit Latrines, MF 17-402, booklet, 73 pages, by D. Duncan Mara, 1984, from Technology Advisory Group, World Bank, 1818 H Street N.W., Washington D.C. 20433, USA.

This summarizes the basic design considerations for building ventilated pit latrines out of a wide variety of materials. These latrines are claimed to have superior health benefits because they effectively control flies. They are relatively free of odors, making them more easily acceptable and perhaps more regularly used than conventional pit latrines. The design also eliminates squat plate covers, which have been a problematical element of many other latrine designs. Examples are given from a half dozen countries.

A central design feature of these latrines is a vent pipe which can be costly. Lower-cost alternative vent pipes are described, along with construction details; these pipes are made of reeds, jute and wire mesh, or anthill soil, all coated with cement mortar.

Investigation has revealed the importance of sizing vent pipe diameter to match local wind conditions. (See **Ventilated Improved Pit Latrines: Vent Pipe Design Guidelines**, MF 17-410, booklet, 16 pages, by Beverley Ryan and D. Duncan Mara, 1983, same source.) As proper vent pipe diameter is crucial to the success of this design, those wishing to do their own wind-ventilation measurements prior to launching large-scale programs should consult **Pit Latrine Ventilation: Field Investigation Methodology** (MF 17-407, booklet, 16 pages, by the same authors, 1983, from the same source).

Manual on the Design, Construction and Maintenance of Low-Cost, Pour-Flush Waterseal Latrines in India, MF 17-406, book, 109 pages, by A.K. Roy et. al., 1984, from Technology Advisory Group, World Bank, 1818 H Street N.W., Washington D.C. 20433, USA.

The search for an affordable urban sanitation alternative has led to the selection of waterseal double vault latrines as the subject of a large-scale UNDP program in India. This manual describes the technical, legal and institutional requirements for this program in great detail.

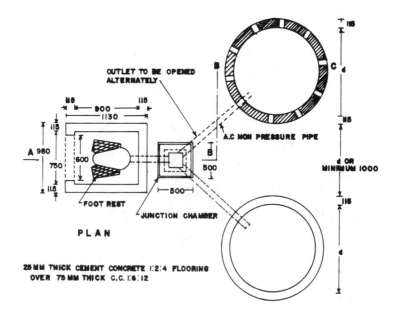

Septic Tank Practices, MF 17-398, book, 75 pages, by Peter Warshall, 1978, $4.95 from WEA.

Here is an excellent reference on septic tanks, emphasizing the natural ability of the soil to purify and absorb "waste water." This volume has very good sections on biology and maintenance, although it lacks the concise working details and plans of WHO's **Excreta Disposal for Rural Areas and Small Communities**.

"Homesite treatment is cheaper, pollutes less, recycles more, slows or controls urban sprawl, has fewer health hazards and remains personal and intimate with the necessities of water, nutrients, and the lives of other creatures. Centralized sewage disposal, shielded by public authorities, has kept citizens unaware of sewage costs, inadequate treatment and disposal as well as their own natural responsibility for recycling their own wastes and keeping other plants and animals productive and healthy."

The Design of Small Bore Sewer Systems, MF 17-401, book, 52 pages, by Richard Otis et. al., 1985, from Technology Advisory Group, World Bank, 1818 H Street N.W., Washington D.C. 20433, USA.

This unusual option for urban sewer systems consists of a small diameter pipe drawing off waste water only. All solids are caught in an "interceptor tank" at each house. The result is a system in which the costs of excavation, materials, pumping equipment, treatment, etc. are greatly reduced.

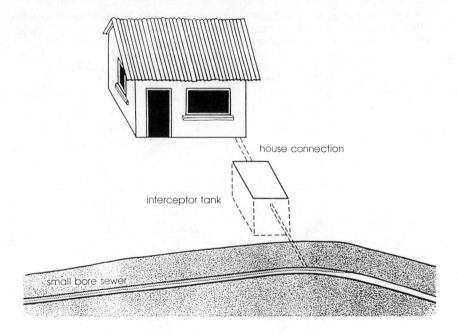

house connection

interceptor tank

small bore sewer

"Experience with the system is limited and mixed. Consequently, in spite of its obvious advantages it must be used judiciously and adopted only in situations where there is sufficient provision to ensure a strong organization for maintenance. This organization must also be able to exercise effective control over connections to the system. Special precautions should be taken to prevent illegal connections, since it is likely that interceptor tanks would not be installed in such connections, thereby introducing solids into a system which is not designed to handle solids. This could create serious operational problems."

Human Faeces, Urine, and Their Utilization, MF 17-394, book, 53 pages, translated by the ENSIC Translation Committee, 1981, $3.00 postpaid from the Environmental Sanitation Information Center, Asian Institute of Technology, P.O. Box 2754, Bangkok, Thailand.

Human wastes are high in nitrogen and other nutrients and can be a valuable source of fertilizer. But, in their raw state, human faeces may pose health hazards and the nutrients may not be available to crops. The Vietnamese original for this book was written to encourage local farmers to make use of simple composting methods for human faeces and urine in order to produce valuable and safe fertilizers. The nutrient requirements for various crops and nutrient content of fertilizers are presented, followed by several methods for collection and composting of human wastes. Proper application of the final product to various crops is also discussed. Emphasis throughout is placed upon maintenance of sanitary standards and maximization of the fertilizer's nutrient value. Exclusive use of locally available materials is assumed. Highly recommended.

Aquaculture: A Component of Low Cost Sanitation Technology, World Bank Technical Paper Number 36, MF 17-411, book, 45 pages, by Peter Edwards, 1985, available from Publications Office, World Bank, 1818 H Street N.W., Washington D.C. 20433, USA.

In a number of countries aquaculture ponds play a role in treating human waste. This volume describes the way this is done in China, India (Calcutta) and other countries. In outlining the feasibility of this technology for wider use, biological, public health, economic and sociological aspects are discussed.

The authors note that the expense of even a low-cost sanitation system is a large,

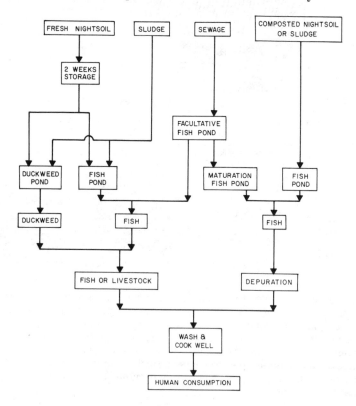

often overwhelming burden to governments and households. However, human excreta recycling in aquaculture is already done by millions of people in Asia, and the economic benefits can outweigh the costs. The result can be "a stronger motivation for further investments in sanitation."

Natural Sewage Recycling Systems, MF 17-395, report, 36 pages, by Maxwell Small, 1977, $8.50 (Accession No. BNL 50630/LL), price double outside U.S., add $3.00 postage for North America, $5.00 for postage outside North America, from NTIS.

"This paper reviews the work done at Brookhaven National Laboratory in the development of natural systems which produce potable water from sewage." A pond is constructed that is marsh at one end and open water at the other. Human wastes are pumped into this pond after passing through an aeration pond. The first pond adds oxygen to the sewage to reduce nitrogen levels and eliminate odors. "Conventional treatment plant hardware beyond aeration is not used . . . and no sludge is generated."

The marsh/pond system of natural treatment is much less costly than traditional Western systems of sewage treatment. Human wastes could be brought to the system in pipes, buckets or tanks. The aeration pond requires a floating aerator pump with .3 hp of capacity for each 1000 gallons per day of sewage passing through it. A pump is also recommended to move the aerated human wastes to the second pond.

"Experiments with two prototype systems are described and performance data are presented in detail for the marsh/pond. Empirical interpretations of results achieved to date are suggested for use in the design of marsh/ponds as natural sewage recycling systems."

Plants and aquatic life can be harvested to provide food, fiber and energy. The marsh plants are of great importance and must be harvested regularly to prevent overcrowding.

I. Water Re-use and Solid Waste Management

Residential Water Re-Use, California Water Resources Report No. 46, MF 18-401, book, 533 pages, by Murray Milne, 1979, $10.00 from Water Resources Center, University of California, Davis, California 95616, USA.

This is the best book available on the reuse of greywater (household waste water, not contaminated with human excreta). A good illustrated summary of proven and experimental household greywater reuse systems is followed by an explanation of the necessary components. The major recommended use for greywater is in garden and tree crop irrigation; a lengthy section on this topic summarizes the technical considerations involved. A limited amount of information is offered on developing sources of fresh groundwater and surface water for household use.

"The conclusion of this study is that residential on-site water reuse systems are already technically feasible and environmentally sound, and are becoming more economically attractive everyday, due primarily to the rapidly increasing cost of energy required for pumping and treatment by centralized water and sewage systems. The objective of this book is to help homeowners, builders, developers, architects, planners and lawmakers understand the design and installation of small on-site residential water reuse systems."

Two briefly treated topics of special interest are roof rainwater catchment tanks (some interesting ideas for filters) and a dry toilet called the "earth closet." This dry toilet worked "on the principle that powdered, dry earth, which contains clay

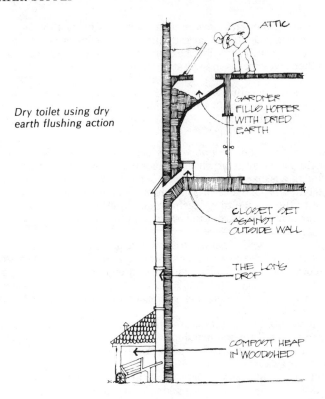

Dry toilet using dry earth flushing action

ATTIC

GARDNER FILLO HOPPER WITH DRIED EARTH

CLOSET SET AGAINST OUTSIDE WALL

THE LONG DROP

COMPOST HEAP IN WOODSHED

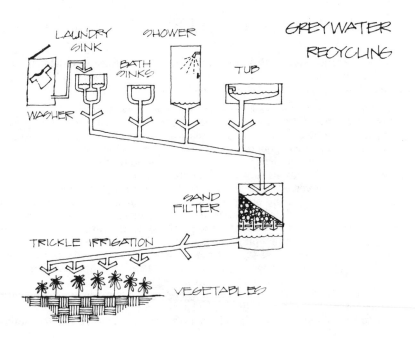

GREYWATER RECYCLING

LAUNDRY SINK

SHOWER

BATH SINKS

TUB

WASHER

SAND FILTER

TRICKLE IRRIGATION

VEGETABLES

and natural soil bacteria, will absorb and retain all offensive odors, fecal matter, and urine. It required a supply of dry and sifted earth, or a mixture of two parts earth and one part ashes. After the user got up from the seat a sufficient amount of dry earth was discharged to entirely cover the solid wastes and to absorb the urine. The wastes and the dry earth fell into a pail that was easily removed for emptying, or into an existing holding pit. The pit did not have to be emptied for up to a year." (See drawing.)

A directory of manufacturers of special equipment and an extensive annotated bibliography on greywater are also included. Though developed for conditions in the state of California, this book has much that will be of interest anywhere in the world.

Management of Solid Wastes in Developing Countries, MF 18-400, book, 242 pages, by Frank Flintoff, 1976, Swiss Francs 20.00 (US$12.00), half price to health workers and institutions other than commercial concerns within the South-East Asia Region of WHO, available from World Health Organization, Regional Office for South-East Asia, Indraprastha Estate, New Delhi 110 002, India.

"Wherever people live, wastes, both liquid and solid, are produced. While the disposal of liquid wastes more often receives priority attention, the management of solid wastes has generally been a neglected field. The aim in developing countries must not be to mimic the technology of the industrialized countries, but rather

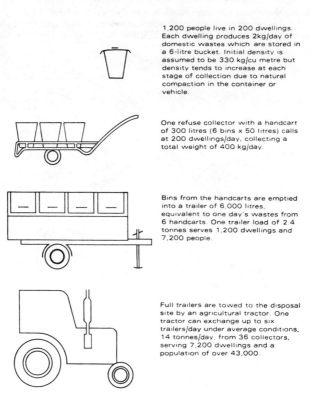

SHORT-RANGE TRANSFER
Flow diagram for handcart and trailer system.

1,200 people live in 200 dwellings. Each dwelling produces 2kg/day of domestic wastes which are stored in a 6-litre bucket. Initial density is assumed to be 330 kg/cu metre but density tends to increase at each stage of collection due to natural compaction in the container or vehicle.

One refuse collector with a handcart of 300 litres (6 bins x 50 litres) calls at 200 dwellings/day, collecting a total weight of 400 kg/day.

Bins from the handcarts are emptied into a trailer of 6,000 litres, equivalent to one day's wastes from 6 handcarts. One trailer load of 2.4 tonnes serves 1,200 dwellings and 7,200 people.

Full trailers are towed to the disposal site by an agricultural tractor. One tractor can exchange up to six trailers/day under average conditions, 14 tonnes/day, from 36 collectors, serving 7,200 dwellings and a population of over 43,000.

to employ the technology appropriate to their own situations, while still meeting the basic needs of public health."

This book covers methods for disposal and recycling of solid wastes (both household and commercial). It is intended "to provide a reference source for engineers, municipal officers, administrators and other interested persons, and to fill a need for a training manual for technicians in a field of universal and growing importance." Major topic areas include economic and other aspects of refuse collection and storage, sanitary landfills, and composting of urban wastes.

The coverage of composting programs is quite comprehensive. "Transport between the compost plant and the farm is an important cost element; in most situations this cost limits the marketing range to about 25 kms. diameter and if the plant is in a very large city, much of that circle will be occupied by urban areas; therefore, the larger the city the smaller the potential market for compost. The larger the city, however, the greater the quantity of wastes. Thus composting as a policy suffers from the paradox that the potential market is in inverse ratio to potential wastes production. . .The most successful composting plants have been those which serve small towns in agricultural areas."

Though this book is primarily devoted to large-scale solid waste operations, there is much that would be useful in small-scale projects.

ADDITIONAL REFERENCES ON WATER SUPPLY AND SANITATION

The use of human wastes in biogas plants is described in **Compost, Fertilizer, and Biogas Production from Human and Farm Wastes in the People's Republic of China**; see ENERGY: BIOGAS.

Simple Working Models of Historic Machines includes drawings of a variety of machines for pumping and raising water, including the Archimedes screw, chain pump, suction pump, and diaphragm pump; see GENERAL REFERENCE.

Energy: General

Energy: General

"It is the experience of most developing countries that energy produced through centralized thermal, hydroelectric and nuclear power stations rarely flows to rural areas where the bulk of the population lives. A typical distribution for such centralized power production is about 80% for urban industry (based on energy-intensive Western technology), about 10% for urban domestic consumption, and only about 10% for rural areas."
— **CERES: The FAO Review on Development**, March-April 1976

The use of alternative natural sources of energy is attractive because of the high price and limited availability of oil, the pollution that is associated with the burning of fossil fuels, the tremendous expense and dangers of nuclear power, and a variety of other reasons. In developing countries the first reason is of particular importance because their industrial development, coming at a time of low-cost plentiful oil supplies, has resulted in a greater reliance on this single source of energy than is true in the developed countries, despite the fact that the latter use tremendously larger quantities. For industrialized countries such as the United States, practical and economically-competitive alternative energy systems already exist that could replace the entire nuclear power contribution to U.S. energy supplies. (Editor's note: Wood space heating stoves [selling 1-2 million units a year] surpassed nuclear power in total contribution to U.S. energy supplies in 1980!)

For village level applications, there are many very promising existing technologies. The five sections which follow explore each of these in more depth: sun, wind, water, wood, and biogas. These technologies are small-scale and necessarily decentralized. This, rather than any other technical inferiority, is the primary reason earlier forms of these technologies were eventually passed over in the industrialized countries. While these systems cannot very effectively be used for the power needs of large industry, they can be well suited to the needs of villages and small communities. They can be low in cost, relatively simple in construction and maintenance, made of materials available in villages and small towns, and non-polluting.

With each price increase in the world's diminishing oil supply, renewable energy sources are made more attractive. The decentralized supply of these renewable energy sources — wind power, solar energy, water power and biofuels — matches the decentralized settlements of the rural Third World. Planners and program administrators are increasingly convinced that these technologies have a major role to play in the energy supplies of rural communities.

These same people, however, have been slower to accept the idea that urban communities could also be largely powered with renewable energy technologies. **Soft Energy Paths** *is for that reason a landmark document, making the case that a conservation-oriented, decentralized industrial society can be operated entirely with "soft" (renewable) energy technologies. Not only is this technically feasible, argues author Amory Lovins, but it is also necessary to avoid the disastrous political,* *economic, and environmental consequences of the alternative "hard" path, with its reliance on dangerous nuclear power stations, accelerating environmental disruption, and the nuclear weapons proliferation associated with nuclear power. Lovins has crafted probably the most tightly documented, academically respectable analysis of the political, economic, social and environmental consequences of energy technology choice, and in so doing has provided helpful direction and ammunition to appropriate technology advocates.*

Soft Energy Paths *and* **Rays of Hope** *together make the arguments that the exponential increases in energy consumption characteristic of industrial societies cannot continue, and therefore industrial development in all countries will have to shift towards decentralization, conservation, improved energy conversion efficiency, and a better matching of energy quality to end use needs.*

Other books in this section review the most attractive renewable energy technologies likely to fit the circumstances in the rural Third World. **Renewable Energy Resources and Rural Applications in the Developing World** *also notes the domestic and foreign policy implications that come with choice of energy strategy.* **Energy for Development: Third World Options** *points specifically to reforestation programs for fuelwood and soil conservation as high priorities in energy planning. A catalog of commercially available small-scale power generating equipment, entitled* **The Power Guide,** *has been introduced by ITDG. This book includes both renewable energy devices and diesel and gasoline engines.*

The increasing acceptance of an important role for renewable energy systems, noted earlier, has led to a proliferation of pilot projects. Economic feasibility has not been properly considered in many of these projects, a fault perhaps most common in the efforts of large international and bilateral aid agencies, who should know better. **The Economics of Renewable Energy Systems for Developing Countries** *offers three case studies illustrating this problem, and a methodology for evaluating the economic appeal of any renewable energy project. Author David French notes that, in particular, large agencies seem to have forgotten that most of the rural poor do not use commercial fuels and thus cannot simply switch cash payments towards the purchase of new equipment:*

"Most renewable energy devices now tend to be attractive primarily to people already using costly commercial power. Just as is happening in the United States, for example, some Third World city-dwellers are discovering that solar energy may be cheaper than electricity for heating water... Such systems will be of greatest use to the wealthy; there is little reason to suppose they will be of comparable interest to the poor."

In the rural Third World, most of the energy used is in the form of firewood and crop residues gathered and burned in cooking fires. Low-cost locally-built cooking stoves can greatly increase the efficiency of cooking, reducing the demand for firewood by up to 40%. This would both slow the rate of deforestation and lighten the burden of long-distance wood hauling. Technologies that use local materials and skills, such as improved stoves and village woodlots, are more likely to be immediately affordable than expensive devices such as solar pumps, photovoltaic systems, and biogas plants in almost all cases.

Other renewable energy technologies relevant to the rural Third World include locally-built waterpumping windmills (increasingly attractive for small plot irrigation and community water supplies) and windgenerators (more expensive but of interest where a small amount of electricity production has a high value); both can be found in the ENERGY: WIND chapter. Waterwheels and water turbines could play a greatly expanded role in rural crop processing and in supplying the energy needs of rural industries, as has been the case in China (see ENERGY: WATER chapter). Direct solar technologies for crop drying, currently probably the most important area for solar energy use, are examined in CROP DRYING,

PRESERVATION, AND STORAGE. Solar home heating and cooling, water heating, cooking, refrigeration, water pumping, and electricity production are all reviewed in the ENERGY: SOLAR chapter. The anaerobic fermentation of animal manures and crop residues to produce biogas and fertilizer is covered in the ENERGY: BIOGAS chapter, including two translations of manuals on the Chinese biogas plants.

A significant locally available energy source is animal power, which could be made more efficient through the design of better pumps, crop processing equipment, harnesses, carts, and agricultural implements. **The Management of Animal Energy Resources and the Modernization of the Bullock Cart System** *(see review in TRANSPORTATION chapter) examines this largely neglected topic, noting that for agricultural activities on the Indian farm, two-thirds of all energy is provided by animals, while humans contribute 23% and electricity and fossil fuels together amount to only 10%.*

Alcohol fuels have received a great deal of attention recently, bringing the hope that they could replace increasingly expensive and scarce gasoline. The technical requirements of alcohol production are presented in **Fuel from Farms** *and* **Makin' It On The Farm.** *Alcohol fuels can be made from crop residues and tree crops. However, large-scale alcohol fuel programs ignore these feedstocks in favor of more economically attractive grain, cassava, and sugar cane. In* **Food or Fuel: New Competition for the World's Croplands,** *Lester Brown argues that this will tend to reduce food supplies, as the major exporting nations could easily consume all their surplus crop in alcohol conversion programs. The first people to be affected will be the urban poor in developing countries.*

Pedal power offers some possibilities for use in small tasks that otherwise would require hand-cranking or high payments to the owners of engine-driven equipment. The small amount of power that a healthy person can produce (75 watts — ⅒ hp— continuously, 200 or more watts for brief periods) is best suited to short, intermittent tasks, such as the operation of small workshop equipment. While pedal-powered agricultural processing equipment, particularly pedal threshers, can be much more efficient in labor use than traditional techniques, larger quantities of crops require the power available from draft animals, waterwheels, or small engines. **The Use of Pedal Power in Agriculture and Transport in Developing Countries** *summarizes the potential applications, and is accompanied by books that present construction details for pedal-powered equipment.* **Bicycling Science** *(see review in TRANSPORTATION chapter) reviews the performance of human beings operating stationary pedal power units.*

Steam engines can be used for a wide variety of rural power requirements, and can be fired with agricultural residues; they are reportedly built in several small workshops in Bangkok. Five of the entries in this chapter are concerned with the design and construction of very small-scale steam engines and boilers, mostly in the range of 1-2 hp — equivalent to the pedalling power of 10-20 people. Steam engines are inefficient in conversion of fuel energy into work and they are heavier and require more materials and space than small gasoline or diesel engines of similar power. Yet they are less technically demanding to make, with larger acceptable tolerances when fitting parts. They are probably most commonly found in small sawmills in the Third World, where a ready supply of sawdust, bark, and wood scraps is available. (For repair and maintenance of small gasoline engines, see **How to Repair Briggs and Stratton Engines** *and* **Small Gas Engines,** *in the AGRICULTURAL TOOLS chapter.)*

The final two entries in this chapter are on electrical systems. One is a reference on installing electrical lines in small communities. The other describes synchronous inverters that allow the direct linking of windgenerators or small hydroelectric units to the electrical grid, thereby avoiding the need for costly battery systems.

The Economics of Renewable Energy Systems for Developing Countries, MF 19-407, report, 67 pages, by David French, 1979, available on request from Office of Development Information and Utilization, Development Support Bureau, USAID, Washington D.C. 20523, USA.

The author examines three projects employing some of the more sophisticated renewable energy technologies: solar pumps in Senegal, biogas plants in India, and solar-electric pumps in Chad. He presents a careful economic analysis and concludes that none of these technologies is now a good investment, nor does any of them appear likely to become a good investment in the next decade.

"Most renewable energy devices now tend to be attractive primarily to people already using costly commercial power. Just as is happening in the United States, for example, some Third World city-dwellers are discovering that solar energy may be cheaper than electricity for heating water. . . Such systems will be of greatest use to the wealthy; there is little reason to suppose they will be of comparable interest to the poor."

"Rather than concentrating on devices of the sort described above, organizations concerned with the poor might seek to meet basic energy needs through simpler systems: village woodlots, improved wood stoves, hand or pedal pumps and grinders, hydraulic ram pumps, and so on. Emphasis would be on systems whose benefits were likely to be commensurate with their costs, and whose costs were likely to be within reach of the poor. Given this approach, ways might be found to make energy widely available to people most in need of it."

In addition to pointing out the dubious appeal of the higher-cost group of alternative technologies, the methods of economic analysis clearly presented here can be used to help evaluate other renewable energy technologies. This report will also be helpful to people who need to understand the methods and concepts of analysis often used by major aid agencies.

Renewable Energy Resources and Rural Applications in the Developing World, MF 19-430, book, 168 pages, edited by Norman Brown, 1978, American Association for the Advancement of Science, $25.50 plus $1.50 postage and handling from Westview Press, 5500 Central Avenue, Boulder, Colorado 80301, USA.

This set of papers offers a valuable look at the potential for use of renewable energy resources in rural areas of developing countries. Norman Brown provides a thoughtful introduction to the topic:

"Choosing conventional large-scale capital-intensive technologies implies a priori decisions, conscious or not, about many important policies. These include the course of urban development, expanding industrialization, environmental impact, large-scale borrowing (or foreign investment) with long-term indebtedness and problems of debt servicing, and last but not least, the foreign policy stance dictated by these requirements."

"On the other hand, the choice of small-scale decentralized power systems (e.g. solar heating, cooling, and generation of electricity; windmills; small-scale hydroelectric plants) implies a different set of a priori decisions. These include, for example, de-emphasis of western-style industrialization as the sole or primary immediate goal of development; dispersal of industry and, perhaps, changes in financial mechanisms; and a shift from western agricultural techniques to emphasis on improvement of indigenous agricultural practices, with consequent reduced demand for energy-consuming nitrogenous fertilizers. All of these factors could contribute significantly to a slowing down of migration to the cities and urban growth, with important effects on the rate of growth of dependence on commercial energy supplies."

The other papers include a general introduction to rural energy requirements, a description of the U.S. photovoltaic program, a look at the potential for solar energy use, an evaluation of wood waste as an energy source in Ghana, a summary of the process of methane production, and discussion of a wide variety of alternative energy technologies in Brazil. An article on wind energy conversion in India argues that waterpumping windmills seem to be the most promising new energy technology in the rural areas. There is also a good historical summary of the development of waterwheels and water turbines, and their importance in the growth of the rural economies of the United States and Europe (and China today).

"The history of small scale hydro-power development provides sound suggestions of how to aid...rural areas of developing countries (that have water power potential) in achieving an improved standard of life...The major role in this development was played by the simple waterwheel...Later the small turbine provided more power at a given site than was feasible with the waterwheel...(In the rural areas of the United States water turbine production) was rapidly taken over by blacksmiths and foundrymen who found it easy to make, in great demand, and an extremely profitable business...By the middle of the 19th century the French turbine had been so radically altered by rural American craftsmen that American turbines began to take the names of their many improvers."

These mills showed the potential for rural industry based on decentralized power sources. They "turned out such household products as cutlery and edge tools, brooms and brushes...furniture, paper...pencil lead...needles and pins... watches and clocks, and even washing machines."

"For the farm they turned out fertilizers, gunpowder, axles, agricultural implements, barrels, ax handles, wheels, carriages. There were woolen, cotton, flax and linen mills;...tannery, boot and shoe mills...and mills turning out surgical appliances...and scientific instruments."

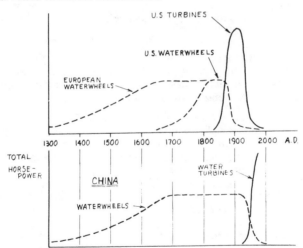

Comparison of the number of small waterwheels and water turbines in Europe, the United States, and China over time

Soft Energy Paths: Toward a Durable Peace, book, 231 pages, by Amory Lovins, 1977, reprinted by Harper and Row, 1979, $3.95 from Harper and Row Publishers, Inc., Keystone Industrial Park, Scranton, Pennsylvania 18512, USA.

In this book Amory Lovins demonstrates the feasibility of an advanced industrial society fueled entirely by renewable energy sources. Two strategies for energy development are compared and contrasted.

The conventional strategy or "hard path" is aimed at sustaining a high growth rate in energy consumption in the face of increasingly inaccessible and expensive petroleum supplies. This path would rely on massive expansion of coal and nuclear-based power generation. The latter in particular threatens world peace, as "nuclear power is considered by most informed observers today to be the main driving force behind the proliferation of nuclear weapons."

The "soft path," by contrast, would rely on a variety of sources carefully matched in scale and energy quality to specific tasks. "The laws of physics require, broadly speaking, that a power station change three units of fuel into two units of almost useless waste heat plus one unit of electricity. This electricity can do more difficult kinds of work than can the original fuel, but unless this extra quality and versatility are used to advantage, the costly process of upgrading the fuel – and losing two thirds of it – is all for naught...Where we want only to create temperature differences of tens of degrees, we should meet the need with sources whose potential is tens or hundreds of degrees, not with a flame temperature of thousands or a nuclear reaction temperature equivalent to trillions – like cutting butter with a chainsaw." This approach would allow conservation of scarce non-renewable fuels during a transition to renewable sources.

In his comparison of the hard and soft paths, Lovins argues that political and environmental considerations should lead us to choose a soft path. Furthermore, he shows that the hard path's centralized plant and distribution systems would require a huge percentage of all available investment capital.

In the United States, this book has helped to trigger a widespread re-evaluation of our energy strategies. The facts and arguments are also relevant to energy strategies in the Third World, particularly in urban-industrial areas.

This volume is probably the best synthesis of the technical, macroeconomic, and humanistic arguments for a serious political and social commitment to renewable energy alternatives.

Rays of Hope: The Transition to a Post-Petroleum World, MF 19-428, book, 233 pages, by Denis Hayes, 1977, $4.95 from W.W. Norton & Co., 500 Fifth Avenue, New York, New York 10110, USA.

Beginning with an overview of patterns of petroleum resources depletion, Denis Hayes shows that our planet cannot continue to support the way of life now characteristic of advanced industrial societies. With costs of delivering increasingly scarce petroleum skyrocketing, it will ultimately require more energy to deliver dispersed fuel in marginal deposits (e.g. tar sands and shales) than is available in the fuel itself. And while coal reserves are relatively plentiful, their use is limited by the capacity of the environment to process waste carbon dioxide. Public opposition to nuclear power is growing because of waste problems, rapidly rising capital costs, and vulnerability to accident and misuse (in weapons production around the world).

Following these arguments, most of this book explores more attractive, sustainable energy consumption patterns based upon direct solar, wind, water, and biomass resources. An analysis of energy use patterns in space heating and food and transportation systems shows that conservation efforts using technical approaches could save great quantities of energy: "A $500 billion investment in conservation would save the U.S. twice as much energy as a comparable investment in new supplies could produce." (In fact, since this book was published, another major oil price increase was followed by substantial investment in conservation in all of the industrial economies.)

Looking to the medium- and long-term future, Hayes also stresses the importance of policy and the pivotal nature of decisions made today: "Oil and natural gas are our principal means of bridging today and tomorrow, and we are burning our bridges. Twenty years ago, humankind had some flexibility; today, the options are more constrained. All our possible choices have long lead times...inefficient buildings constructed today will still be wasting fuel fifty years from now; over-sized cars sold today will still be wasting fuel ten years down the road. . ."

Energy: The Solar Prospect, Worldwatch Paper 11, MF 19-413, 40 pages, 1977, and **The Solar Energy Timetable**, Worldwatch Paper 19, MF 19-433, 78 pages, both booklets by Denis Hayes, $2.00 each from Worldwatch Institute, 1776 Massachusetts Avenue N.W., Washington D.C. 20036, USA.

In these two papers, Denis Hayes outlines possible strategies for a global tran-sition to a "solar-powered world" within 50 years, an ambitious goal. In discussing solar resources, he notes that the possibilities range from the simple to the com-plex, and from the decentralized to the centralized. This makes solar applications adaptable in many different societies, rich and poor, urban and rural.

The Power Guide: A Catalogue of Small Scale Power Equipment, MF 19-426, book, 240 pages, compiled by Peter Fraenkel, 1979, £9.95 from ITDG.

This is a guide to commercially available equipment. The authors list criteria for selection, but make no specific recommendations of equipment, as ITDG has no facilities for testing machinery. No prices are given, as they are rapidly chang-ing. Names and addresses are listed for manufacturers and their agents, informa-tion services, and organizations doing R&D work on small-scale power production.

Major topics are: solar electric cells, solar engines, solar space and water heaters, windgenerators, windpumps, hydroelectric units, hydraulic ram pumps, iron and steel cooking and heating stoves, methane digesters, steam boilers, wood gas pro-ducers, diesel engines, gasoline (petrol) engines, steam engines, alternators and generators, electric generating units, and batteries.

The lowest-cost small-scale energy devices, however, are rarely available from commercial sources, and cannot be found in this catalogue. Such devices are built within many developing countries. For more information on these, see the other reviews in this chapter and the other energy chapters of the **A.T. Sourcebook**.

Energy for Rural Development: Renewable Resources and Alternative Technologies for Developing Countries, MF 19-412, book, 301 pages, National Academy of Sciences, 1976, available free to developing countries from BOSTID, Rm. JH 217D, National Academy of Sciences, 2101 Constitution Avenue N.W., Washington D.C. 20418, USA.

A summary of what was the state of the art of manufactured or already-tested technologies frequently suggested as solutions to rural or individual family energy needs in developing countries. Covers direct uses of solar energy, wind power, hydropower, photosynthesis, microbiological conversion of plant materials to liquid fuels, geothermal energy and energy storage. The text is primarily a technical and economic evaluation of the applicability of these systems based on production by current methods in the industrialized countries. The authors do not include in their calculations the potentially very different forms such technologies might take in developing countries. Somewhat out of date in 1985, following 10 years of experi-mental work around the world.

Energy for Rural Development (Supplement): Renewable Resources and Alternative Technologies for Developing Countries, MF 19-411, book, 236 pages, 1981, free to developing countries from BOSTID, Rm. JH 217D, National Academy of Sciences, 2101 Constitution Avenue, Washington D.C. 20418, USA.

This is a supplement to the 1976 book by the same title. "Although there have been few remarkable new discoveries in the past five years, steady progress has been made in research and development on renewable energy resources and alternative technologies." This supplement includes information on new technologies developed during this period and on advances made in technologies described in the original volume. Like that volume, this report serves merely to direct the reader where to go for information, and is not intended to be a "how-to manual or detailed catalog."

Small Scale Renewable Energy Resources and Locally Feasible Technology in Nepal, MF 19-431, booklet, 60 pages, by Andreas Bachmann and Gyani Shakya, 1982, free from Swiss Association for Technical Assistance, P.O. Box 113, Kathmandu, Nepal.

A booklet filled with pictures of traditional and new technologies that can be seen in Nepal. Nearly 100 photos of stoves, solar dryers, watermills, microhydroelectric turbines, solar water heaters, biogas plants, and passive solar buildings.

Rural Energy and the Third World: A Review of Social Science Research and Technology Policy Problems, book, 214 pages, by Andrew Barnett, Martin Bell, Kurt Hoffman, 1982, $19.75 from Pergamon Press, Maxwell House, Fairview Park, Elmsford, New York 10523, USA.

The introductory chapters of this volume provide a valuable summary of lessons from the recent past, both about understanding energy needs of rural people and evaluating technologies that may have a role to play. These are followed by an interesting review of the literature (200 selected documents).

Energy for Africa, MF 19-409, book, 199 pages, edited by David French and Patricia Larson, 1980, limited number of copies available, send $2.00 for postage and handling to A.T. Project, V.I.A., Box 4543, Stanford, California 94305, USA.

"During 1979-80, the Africa Bureau of USAID worked to establish guidelines for its energy program. As part of this process, papers were commissioned on: the relationship of energy to African development, energy surveys, the economics of energy systems, technology transfer, community involvement in fuelwood activities, and the monitoring of energy projects. In order to reach a wider audience, these papers (condensed) are reproduced in this volume."

Martha Novick "raises the possibility that scarce, expensive energy may be a permanent condition in Africa..." which has major implications for development policy and priority programs in the region.

"Thomson notes that an African family has little incentive to protect or replace trees on the common land...The answer lies in either 'privatizing' land and trees or in strengthening the ability of local groups to manage common resources. Each of these solutions poses problems."

"Thomas Graham looks more broadly at the ways in which surveys can help governments know what to do in the face of changing energy conditions."

"Asif Shaikh looks in detail at the economics of energy systems... Shaikh introduces the idea of a 'dissemination cost ratio.' "

"Drawing on case studies of technology adoption in many parts of Africa, Cecil Cook argues that change is most likely to occur where...villagers feel that a new technology coincides with their self-interest and that the process of its adoption is under their control."

"Marilyn Hoskins examines this process in terms of the role of local groups in dealing with fuelwood problems...'it is increasingly apparent that the top-down approach is not working'...Hoskins proposes that fuelwood activities start with a 'project management agreement' to be prepared jointly by villagers, donors, and forest services (or other government agencies)."

In the final article, George Burrill proposes a set of questions to be asked of technologies undergoing village testing.

Proceedings of the Meeting of the Expert Working Group on the Use of Solar and Wind Energy, Energy Resources Development Series No. 16, MF 19-427, book, 147 pages, by the United Nations Economic and Social Commission for Asia and the Pacific, 1976, U.N. Publication Sales No. E.76.II.F.13, $11.00 from United Nations, Publications, Room A-3315, New York, New York 10017, USA.

This book contains reports and documents from a March 1976 conference in Bangkok.

Wind power: basic information and characteristics of different rotor types; pump characteristics; recommendations for activities in support of further development of wind power in the region; discussion of characteristics of Greek cloth sail windmills, industrially-produced wind pumps, and wind-generators; many drawings of simple low-cost windmills and pumps; use and potential use of wind energy in India, Thailand, New Zealand, Australia, Korea and Indonesia.

Solar energy: sample drawings and discussion of solar water heaters, stills, cookers, driers, and pumps; conversion to electrical and mechanical power; use and potential use of solar energy in India, Japan, Australia, Southeast Asia, and Pakistan.

For both topics there is a list of references and organizations worldwide.

Renewable Energy Research in India, MF 19-429, book, 269 pages, Tata Energy Research Institute, August 1981, out of print in 1985.

This compendium reports on the activities of 64 groups active in renewable energy research in India. Reports are organized alphabetically within categories: government departments, academic institutions and universities, research institutions and industry, and state government and community agencies.

Pedal Power: In Work, Leisure and Transportation, MF 19-424, book, 144 pages, edited by James McCullagh, 1977, Rodale Press, out of print in 1985.

This is the broadest collection of practical ideas for pedal-powered equipment. The authors feel that human energy can be most efficiently harnessed using pedal-powered machines, including but not limited to the bicycle, and that such machines can make significant contributions in any society: "At the time when the 'appropriateness' of technology is being questioned daily, the bicycle, perhaps the most appropriate and efficient machine ever invented, is making a comeback in many countries." These claims are backed up with a wealth of information on past and

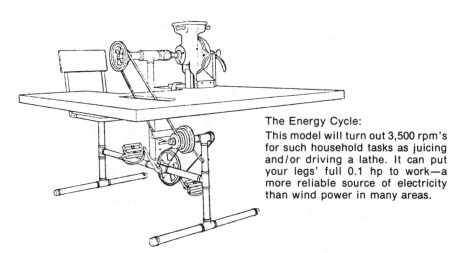

The Energy Cycle:
This model will turn out 3,500 rpm's for such household tasks as juicing and/or driving a lathe. It can put your legs' full 0.1 hp to work—a more reliable source of electricity than wind power in many areas.

present uses of bicycles and other pedal-powered machines, as well as potential future uses.

This volume contains most of the information found in the article entitled "Pedal Power" (reviewed in this section). An excellent chapter by Stuart Wilson is devoted to pedal-powered equipment currently in use or being developed in the Third World. Included are descriptions of various transportation machines, and stationary pedal machines, such as a two-person pedal-driven winch and a "dynapod," which uses a flywheel to smooth out power variations. Pedal-powered pumps shown include the traditional Chinese square pallet chain pump for irrigation and a two-person borehole pump capable of lifting water 100 meters. There are old catalog drawings of foot-powered cast iron workshop equipment, such as woodworking and metalworking lathes and jig saws. (Similar machines can be seen today in India and Sri Lanka.)

Another chapter gives a description and full set of building instructions for the Rodale Energy Cycle, as well as test results. The Cycle is a stationary pedal power unit which can be used to drive a variety of machines, from lathes and grinders to pumps, winches and a cable-plow. It uses a bicycle frame and various pieces of angle iron, bearings and pulleys. Some welding and drilling is required.

Construction details are provided for a rear wheel bicycle adapter to allow power to be taken from any ordinary bicycle. Both this and the Energy Cycle are straightforward and could easily be adapted to locally available materials.

With 72 photos and 65 illustrations, **Pedal Power** is an excellent idea book on the possibilities of using and/or designing pedal-powered machines.

Pedal Power, article, 18 pages, by Stuart Wilson, 1975, in **Introduction to Appropriate Technology**, MF 01-9 (see review).

A person on a bicycle is the most energy-efficient moving thing that exists (measured in calories per unit of weight per unit of distance). By measuring the energy output of a bicyclist, Wilson has found that "the normal cyclist has an expenditure of about 75 watts—roughly 0.1 horsepower...the fullest sustainable output of the human body, using the right muscles, right motions, and the right speed."

The author gives consideration to stationary pedal power, used to operate pumps, for example. A rotary pump is shown with pedal attachments. "It is such a simple type of pump and suitable for direct pedaling for heads of 3 to 8 meters that it is, I think, worth developing." Wilson notes that some traditional waterlifting devices

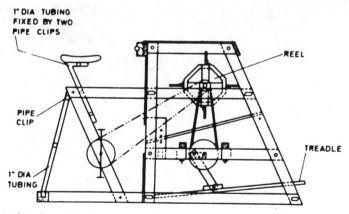

Peanut thresher showing options for either pedal-drive while seated or treadle-operation while standing

in India require 4 men to raise the same volume of water that one man on a pedal-power pump could lift.

An optimum stationary pedal power unit, called a "dynapod," is described. "It takes the drive forward and you can gear it down for something like a winch or gear it up for a winnowing fan...One of the requirements in a stationary application is a flywheel to steady out the torque, and here the flywheel is made from a bicycle wheel with cement filling in between the spokes."

Other pedal-powered machines shown are the traditional Chinese square pallet chain pump (also called the "water ladder"); a two-person powered milling machine; a hand-driven winnowing machine which could be adapted to use pedal power; a peanut thresher (see drawing); and a cassava grinder.

Notes on an improved cycle rickshaw (three-wheeled pedicab) are included, explaining how two bicycle "freewheels" are combined to form a differential — a device that allows a rickshaw with two rear wheels to turn corners with the two wheels rotating at different speeds. The author suggests a design for local production of bicycles in developing countries, relying on sheet steel and angle iron instead of imported steel tubes; he has built prototypes. The "Oxtrike," a rickshaw using these materials, also has a very low-cost 3-speed gearbox to allow easy starting and climbing hills.

Design for a Pedal Driven Power Unit for Transport and Machine Uses in Developing Countries, MF 19-405, report, 27 pages, by David Weightman for the ITDG Transport Panel, 1976, small charge for postage, from David Weightman, Faculty of Art and Design, Lanchester Polytechnic, Gosford Street, Coventry CV1 5RZ, England.

This report describes a proposed pedal-powered unit for use in rural areas of developing countries. The author discusses the need for and the desired characteristics of such a device, and the range of human power outputs that is possible. Ten photographs and a number of drawings are included.

An attached bicycle, an integral pedal drive mechanism, and a dynapod are compared as alternative ways to use pedal power efficiently for different machines and circumstances. The author lists a wide variety of agricultural and workshop equipment that is suitable for pedal power, including winnowers, threshers, grain mills, cassava grinders, maize shellers, winch plows, coffee pulpers, winches, blowers, air compressors, bandsaws, drills, grindstones, lathes, and potter's wheels.

For maximum utility and lowest cost, the author proposes a design for a one-wheeled basic unit. It could be used to power equipment, and could have a two-wheeled trailer attached to allow use as a tricycle for transport. It is not a proven design, but suggests an interesting avenue for further investigation.

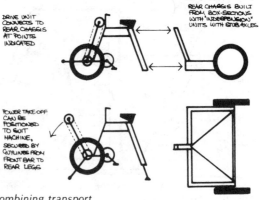

Pedal power concept combining transport and equipment operation

The Use of Pedal Power for Agriculture and Transport in Developing Countries, MF 19-436, report for ITDG Transport Panel, 22 pages, by David Weightman, May 1976, small charge for postage, from David Weightman, Faculty of Art and Design, Lanchester Polytechnic, Gosford Street, Coventry CV1 5RZ, England.

"This report examines the existing and potential applications of pedal power for simple agricultural machinery and transport devices in developing countries." For these uses, pedal power is compared to other power sources, such as draft animals, electric motors, biogas plants, wind machines, and internal combustion engines. Built-in pedal and treadle mechanisms, separate pedal drive units, and bicycle-connected drive systems are all compared.

"Both treadle and pedal actions are used to drive machinery. The treadle action is commonly operated by one leg, only using half the available power, but enabling the operator to support himself on the other leg and load the machine. Treadle mechanisms are commonly inefficient and much higher power outputs are obtained from the pedal crank arrangement." However, pedal drive systems restrict the operator's freedom of movement, making lathes, potter's wheels, and sewing machines better suited to a different foot-powered approach.

"If more widely used, the lower speeds and lower axle loadings (of pedal powered vehicles) could enable savings in rural road construction costs to be made. . . Certainly the Chinese transport system, being based on the bicycle rather than the car or lorry, indicates the particular suitability of pedal power to the transport requirements of developing countries."

No photos or drawings included.

Foot Power (Bike Generator Plans), MF 19-415, 4 pages, 1983, $10.00 postpaid from North Shore Ecology Center, 491 Madison Avenue, Glencoe, Illinois 60022, USA.

These are non-detailed drawings, with very little text. They show mechanical setup, and electrical wiring; the general idea of using a bike to run a generator. Three different designs.

The system provides a 12-volt power source and can be used to charge auto batteries. The bike can also be used to operate grinders and pumps.

Note: It is generally said that human beings can produce about 75 watts when pedaling at a comfortable speed that can be maintained for an hour or more. Also, 12-volt electricity requires very large diameter wires if carried over any distance; otherwise there will be large losses of electricity due to the resistance of the wire.

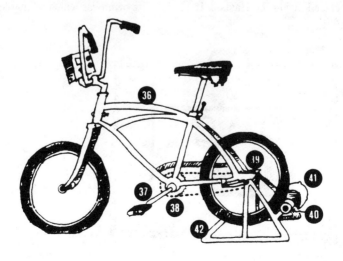

Manege: Animal-Driven Power Gear, MF 19-402, booklet with separate instructions for associated machinery, 30-page booklet, 8-page leaflet, U.N. Division of Narcotic Drugs, 1975, free from the U.N. Division of Narcotic Drugs, Vienna International Centre, P.O. Box 500, 1400 Vienna, Austria.

The manege is adapted to any task that can use mechanical power transmitted through a drive shaft — especially agricultural activities such as threshing grain. The booklet describes two sizes of the manege, along with five associated pieces of equipment that can be operated with it: thresher, chaff-cutting chopper, grinding mill, winnower, and root-cutter. All of the above pieces of equipment are on operating display at the Laboratoire de Techniques Agricoles et Horticoles de Chatelaine, near the U.N. office in Geneva.

"The animal-driven power gear works on the same principle as a bicycle...an arrangement of levers and gears that transforms slow leg movement into the speedy rotation of a wheel...Two wooden bars or levers, each about 4 meters long, are bolted to the center of the large horizontal input gear. They extend like two spokes of a large wheel." Speed of rotation is increased by a factor of 50. Equipment to be operated is located 10 meters away from the center of the power gear.

No complex or precision parts are necessary. The production of all the components in developing countries should not present serious problems. Gears are rough iron casting which can be made from scrap metal. Melting and pouring facilities are needed, as are sand molds. The gears are used just as they come from the mold — no finishing. Other metal parts could be forged by a reasonably-skilled blacksmith. Only machining requirement: a drill to cut holes for bolts to join the components. Animal fat can be used for occasional lubrication.

The instructions for use of the associated equipment give technical specifications and a description of the operation of each of these pieces of equipment.

Photos but no detailed plans are given for the manege and the associated equipment. With a great deal of imagination, only the manege could be constructed with this booklet alone. The U.N. Division of Narcotic Drugs may be willing to send technical drawings.

The Haybox, MF 19-419, pamphlet, 1977, Low Energy Systems, Ireland, out of print in 1985.

This describes the principles of a fireless cooker. Ideas for design and materials are given. For use with foods which can be cooked slowly (2-4 hours): beans, sauces, stews. The food is brought to a boil in a heavy pot, then removed from the heat and placed inside the Haybox. It cooks in its own heat which is unable to escape.

The Haybox

The Heat Generator, MF 19-437, book, 108 pages, by Reinhold Metzler, 1983, Swiss Francs 22.00 from SKAT.

The heat generator is essentially a fan turning in a closed box, converting mechanical power on the shaft into heat as it stirs up the air. In small waterpowered mills this may allow some very interesting possibilities for small industry applications for drying crops or boiling liquids. This book reviews some heat-using small industries in Nepal, discusses the economics of the heat generator as compared to several alternatives, and provides construction drawings of the equipment. The author concludes that under certain circumstances a heat generator would have the lowest unit cost of energy.

The technical attractiveness of this technology is unfortunately not matched by its financial appeal, at least for Nepal. To make his case that the heat generator would provide low-cost energy, Metzler assumes the following: it will be used with a turbine mill that is already installed and underutilized, full capacity utilization of the heat generator will be achieved, maintenance costs will be low (3.5%), fuelwood for small industries will all be purchased, and a low real interest rate (after inflation) of 5.5% can be achieved on the invested capital ($800 plus 30% of the mill investment — $2100 — for a 5kw output). He neglects the facts that local firewood-consuming units are often built at virtually no cash cost by family members, that in the rural areas firewood is usually gathered rather than purchased, that these small industries are usually seasonal and part-time, and that small investments in design improvements in small industry stoves and kilns can yield large fuel savings (e.g. 33%). When all of these factors are taken into account, the heat generator is likely to produce energy that costs at least twice as much and require an investment at least 10 times as much as the fuelwood alternatives.

In other countries and under other circumstances, there may be a place for this device, and therefore we include it here.

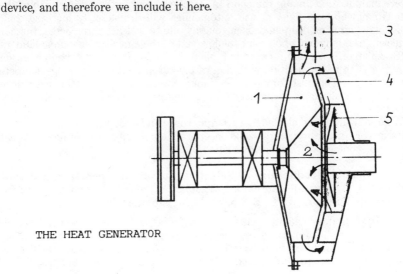

THE HEAT GENERATOR

Hot Water, MF 19-438, booklet, 31 pages, by S. and C. Morgan, D. and S. Taylor, 1974, out of print in 1981.

Drawings, materials lists, and step-by-step construction details are given for three kinds of solar collectors, hot water storage tank connections (pressure and drum), and water heater adaptations for wood- and coal-burning units. Drawings are not to scale.

"If you are running a pressure system you must use a storage tank built to operate under pressure. An oil drum and similar units do *not* qualify. They will deform and burst under pressure greater than 10 pounds per square inch...(However) a clean, 30-55 gallon drum will serve as a hot water storage tank for a *non-pressure* system."

The authors claim that "you can adapt any wood or coal burning unit to include a water heating device. Essentially this is a coil system. A tightly coiled copper tube is inserted into the chimney stack or stove pipe. The water feeds through the coil and into a storage tank." (Editor's note: The drawback to this kind of system is a large build-up of creosote condensation on the copper tubing, especially with inefficient stoves. This must be cleaned regularly; a heavy coating of creosote reduces the efficiency of heat transfer to the water, and increases the risk of a chimney fire.)

Food or Fuel: New Competition for the World's Cropland, Worldwatch Paper 35, MF 19-414, 43 pages, by Lester Brown, 1980, $2.00 from Worldwatch Institute, 1776 Massachusetts Avenue N.W., Washington D.C. 20036, USA.

This well-documented paper claims that if present trends continue, the world's alcohol fuel programs will be taking food away from the poor, especially the urban poor in developing countries. Full-scale national alcohol fuel programs could easily consume all of the surplus crops of the major grain exporting countries.

Operating a typical American car 10,000 miles/year at 15 mpg would require almost 8 acres of cropland for the alcohol fuel—enough to feed 39 people in the developing countries or 9 people in the United States. (These figures do not include the amount of liquid fuel needed to produce the grain in the first place.)

In Brazil, "the decision to turn to energy crops to fuel the country's rapidly growing fleet of automobiles is certain to drive food prices upward, thus leading to more severe malnutrition among the poor. In effect, the more affluent one-fifth of the population who own most of the automobiles will dramatically increase their individual claims on crop-land from roughly one to at least three acres, further squeezing the millions who are at the low end of the Brazilian economic ladder."

"Brazilian officials claim that the production of energy crops will be in addition to rather than in competition with that of food crops. Yet energy crops compete not only for land but also for agricultural investment capital, water, fertilizer, farm management skills, farm-to-market roads, agricultural credit, and technical advisory services."

"A carefully designed alcohol fuel program based on forest products and cellulosic materials of agricultural origin could become an important source of fuel, one that would not compete with food production."

Fuel Alcohol Production: A Selective Survey of Operating Systems, MF 19-416, booklet, 48 pages, 1981, $3.00 from the U.S. National Center for Appropriate Technology, P.O. Box 3838, Butte, Montana 59702, USA.

Surveys eight intermediate-scale fuel alcohol production operations in a brief yet pertinent and very informative overview. The plants covered demonstrate a cross-section of the available options, and the accompanying diagrams and charts make this a valuable resource for those considering going into fuel alcohol production.

Fuel from Farms — A Guide to Small Scale Ethanol Production, MF 19-417, book, 163 pages, by the Solar Energy Research Institute, 1980, $5.75 from NTIS, Overseas Development Assistance Division Office of International Affairs, 5285 Port Royal, Room 3064, Springfield, Virginia 22161, USA.

This Solar Energy Research Institute publication is a part of the Department of Energy's effort to encourage the production of alcohol for fuel in the United States. It "...presents the current status of on-farm fermentation ethanol production as well as an overview of some of the technical and economic factors. Tools such as decision and planning worksheets and a sample business plan for use in exploring whether or not to go into ethanol production are given. Specifics in production including information on the raw materials, system components, and operational requirements are also provided. Recommendation of any particular process is deliberately avoided because the choice must be tailored to the needs of each individual producer. The emphasis is on providing the facts necessary to make informed judgements."

This analysis is aimed at the American farmer, demonstrating how an ethanol plant can support and complement other farm activities. Surplus grains and spoiled or marginal crops can provide the feedstock base for ethanol production, which can then be mixed with gasoline or burned directly in farm vehicles. The remainder can be sold to blenders of "gasohol" (a commercially available fuel mixture composed of 90% gasoline and 10% ethanol). The solid byproduct can be fed directly to animals or mixed with other fodder as an animal feed supplement.

While ethanol can be produced from a wide variety of crops and agricultural byproducts and wastes, profitable production depends on many factors such as current prices of feedstocks, availability of a low-cost source of fuel for the distillery apparatus, and how much of the ethanol produced would be used directly by the farmer. Another key factor is high initial equipment investment for the cookers, wells, pumps, still, condensers, and storage tanks. The sample business plan includes a feasibility analysis of a 25-gallon/hour installation on a 1,200 acre farm and feedlot operation, and assumes an initial plant and equipment investment of nearly $125,000. This is hardly small-scale in most countries.

It is clear that farm-based production of ethanol is not the whole solution to increasing scarcity and cost of petroleum fuels. Even if all the crop land in the United States were devoted to cultivation of ethanol feedstocks, the fuel produced would not meet current demand from the transportation sector alone. A move toward renewable sources of energy is, however, crucial to a sustainable agriculture. Decentralized ethanol production may be a way for some American farmers to reduce their dependence on traditional fuel sources.

Makin' It On The Farm: Alcohol Fuel is the Road to Energy Independence, book, 87 pages, by Micki Nellis, 1979, $2.95 plus $0.75 postage from American Agriculture Movement, P.O. Box 100, Iredell, Texas 76649, USA.

This low-cost report has been published in the belief that small-scale ethanol production can be an important step toward viability for the American family farm. "Community size alcohol plants using locally grown farm products could make towns independent of Big Oil almost overnight. Alcohol fuel plants would. . .provide fuel, use up those 'burdensome surpluses' that are blamed for depressing farm prices, and provide a high-protein feed byproduct for local use that is oftentimes as valuable as the raw commodity that went into the alcohol. . .The farmer has the advantage over large alcohol plants because he can put up a small plant in a few weeks, compared to a two-year lead time on large plants. The farmer can use his own wastes when they are available. . .He can use the crops he grows best, produce as much fuel as he needs, adjust his livestock numbers for the amount of high-protein feed he will produce, and work at making fuel during slack times."

The core of this book is a discussion of how ethanol is produced by fermentation and distillation of mash made from grains and other crops. Several brief case studies document construction and performance of privately- and cooperatively-financed plants producing up to 30 gallons of fuel-grade alcohol per hour, fired with crop residues and/or steam injection. All the plants described involve an airtight vat or tank for fermentation of the grain mixture, a vertical column through which alcohol vapors rise, and a condensing apparatus. Drawings and parts lists are provided for construction of a plant with three fermentation tanks and distillation columns. (How to generate the dry steam which vaporizes the alcohol in the columns is not explained.) The authors claim that this plant can produce about 30 gallons/hour of 192 proof alcohol (96% ethanol, 4% water).

Other chapters briefly cover simple solar ethanol stills, ideas for using waste irrigation pump heat in alcohol plants, and modifications to improve performance of engines burning alcohol fuels. Appendices include lists of alcohol plant manufacturers, informative papers, farm products that can be used to make alcohol, and a glossary.

Fuel from Farms (see review) gives a better cost and technical analysis of ethanol plants which produce a relatively high volume of high-quality alcohol. **Makin' It On The Farm** stresses a low-investment, do-it-yourself approach. For this reason it should be a more useful resource for many family farmers and Third World groups interested in alcohol fuels. These are the only two alcohol fuel books we are aware of that are not simply high-priced booklets full of exaggerated claims.

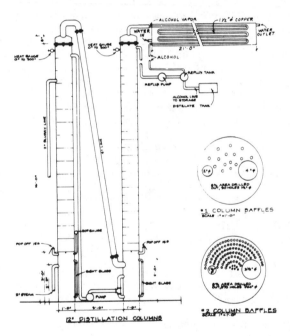

Some of the equipment used in farm-scale alcohol production

Steam Power, MF 19-435, quarterly magazine, 60 pages, $17.00 for one year, from Steam Power, 106A Derby Road, Loughborough, Leics., LE11 0AG, England.

This magazine reports on the latest advances and most useful technologies in steam power. It covers many different steam power topics, such as vehicles, boats, sawmills, engine plans, history, solar steam power, boilers, fuels, machine shop techniques for making equipment, and conferences.

Letters from interested individuals and many advertisements for kits and plans for fully functional steam engines help make this a useful magazine. Well-illustrated. Back issues are available.

Model Stationary and Marine Steam Engines, MF 19-423, book, 168 pages, by K.N. Harris, 1964, Model and Allied Publications, U.K., out of print in 1986.

A detailed treatment of the design of small steam engines for many different uses is provided in this book. Readers who would like to build small-scale steam engines should find it valuable. The model engines shown are 1 hp and smaller in rated power.

There are no steam engine construction plans contained in this book, but the design principles should be valuable when building a steam engine from plans acquired elsewhere. Knowledge of metalworking, including lathe techniques, is an important part of steam engine construction and necessary for effective use of this book. Many illustrations.

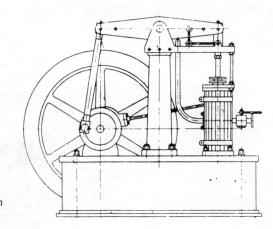

*Beam engine
driven by steam*

Live Steam Magazine, monthly, 68 pages average length, $24.00 per year in USA, $27.00 per year surface mail ($60.00 per year airmail) outside the USA, back issues $2.95, from Live Steam Magazine, P.O. Box 581, Traverse City, Michigan 49684, USA.

This magazine is primarily devoted to the building of model steam railroad engines. These devices are powerful enough to pull a dozen or more human passengers. While the tiny locomotives are far too small to be of practical use for transport, the detailed information presented can be applied to other small steam engine uses.

Live Steam is full of illustrations and plans for steam engines and boilers. The kind of metalworking techniques required to make efficient small steam machinery is a major topic. Construction of valves, descriptions of other types of steam power equipment (such as water pumps and steamboats) and news of steam railroading are among the other topics covered.

People actually building small steam power equipment will find many useful construction details and design ideas in this magazine. Back issues are also available.

Craftsmanship Catalog, 62 pages, $1.00 from Caldwell Industries, 603-909 E. Davis Street, Box 591, Luling, Texas 78648, USA.

This catalog includes kits and plans for a range of small steam engines, most of them models but some of them large enough to be used as a power source.

"The Clarkson 2×2 engines were designed to meet the demands for a larger more robust engine capable of real work...2" bore and 2" stroke cylinder. The bearings have been made stronger in proportion to the rest of the engine...The Vertical Compound is capable of about 2 horsepower...care has been taken in the design for the ease of construction in the home shop...These engines do take a lot of steam...The $2 \times 2H$ and the $2 \times 2V$ are robust, single cylinder, double acting steam engines fully capable of sustained high speed operation under load...fairly easy to make...The Vertical Compound is the engine for you if you have in mind something like a steam powered row boat or perhaps a motorcycle."

"The 5a engine...is rated at 1½ hp per cylinder...The steam boat crowd often use this engine on small boats, others have used it to pull electric generators at remote sites."

The kits of castings for these engines ranged from about US$90 to $200 in 1978. The buyer is expected to do a substantial amount of the work to finish the engines, before assembling them. Drawings can be purchased alone for $12 to $15. To operate these engines you will need small boilers; these could use agricultural residues to produce the steam.

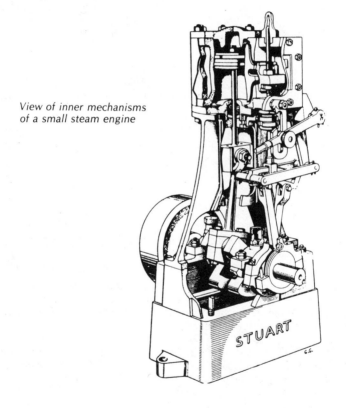

View of inner mechanisms of a small steam engine

Model Boilers and Boilermaking, MF 19-422, paperback book, 185 pages, by K.N. Harris, 1967, revised edition 1984, Model and Allied Publications, U.K., out of print in 1986.

Steam engines cannot operate without steam, and the steam boiler is where steam is produced and fuel is consumed. This book presents the theory and construction of small steam boilers. These boilers can be used to power engines of up to several horsepower. There are illustrations covering many types of boilers and fuel systems. Safety considerations are carefully outlined for both boiler construction and operation.

"Fig. 3-32 shows the Babcock, probably one of the most extensively used boilers in full-size pattern for both land and marine work."

A very useful book for anyone interested in producing steam boilers for steam engines or other uses such as heating.

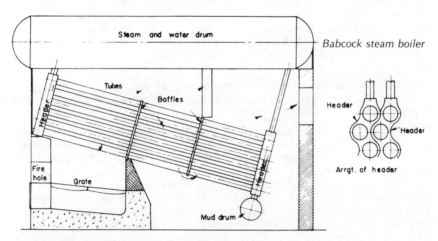

Babcock steam boiler

The Planning, Installation and Maintenance of Low-Voltage Rural Electrification Systems and Subsystems, MF 19-425, book, 151 pages, 1979, VITA, out of print in 1985.

Originally compiled in 1969 by American electricians, this manual was written for the training of Peace Corps volunteers who were to be assigned to rural electrification projects in developing countries. An introductory chapter provides a simplified introduction to electrical theory. Succeeding sections discuss wiring of houses, wiring for distributing power to houses, and connection of a village-scale electrification system to a generation plant or other power source.

Some attention is given to the differences between electrical installations in rural areas of developing countries and in the U.S. For example, the authors suggest that the trainees should wire two homes, one with standard techniques and one with "techniques applicable to mud construction." Yet in fact, the subsequent discussion assumes availability of commercial U.S. cable, connectors, meters, fuseboxes,

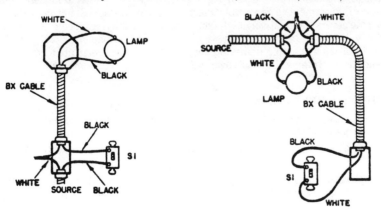

switches, and other components. And the reader is informed that "(convenience outlets) are normally located about 12" above floor level. They should be placed near (2 or 3 feet) corners of rooms rather than in the center of the wall to lessen the chance that they will be blocked by large pieces of furniture." With this perspective, the authors have missed an opportunity to present information on simpler systems (providing 50-100 watts per house) commonly found in developing countries.

A brief section on "Planning Requirements" explains how to calculate materials, labor, and overhead costs of an electrification project. There is no discussion of the needs for electricity in rural areas, how new electric installations might complement existing sources of power, or whether rural people will be able to afford their new electricity. Still, this manual provides a good overview and bibliography on the fundamentals of electricity and electrification.

Gemini Synchronous Inverter Systems, MF 19-418, booklet, 11 pages, on request from Windworks, Inc., Route 3, Box 44A, Mukwonago, Wisconsin 53149, USA.

A synchronous inverter is a device that allows the connection of small alternative energy systems to the large electric distribution networks (grids). All of the available power from the alternative energy system is converted to alternating current (AC) for normal use. Any extra electricity need is supplied by the grid, and any surplus electricity generated is fed back to the grid, where it can be used by other consumers on the same grid. In this way, the owner of a small windgenerator, microhydroelectric system, or solar photovoltaic array can use the grid in place of a costly battery storage system, or in place of no storage system at all. A synchronous inverter could be used with a combination 10 kw diesel generator set and windgenerator, for example, if the windgenerator never exceeds ⅓ the diesel generator capacity.

Windworks has a booklet and three similar papers describing the theory behind synchronous inverters and the possible applications. Synchronous inverters are available for single phase and three phase equipment, and cost (in early 1976) $160 per kw capacity for small units, down to $40 per kw capacity for 1000 kw installations.

Alternative Sources of Energy, MF 19-439, magazine, six issues each year, 60 pages average length, one year subscription in U.S. and Canada is $25.00, foreign subscriptions (airmail only) are $40.00, from Alternative Sources of Energy Magazine, Milaca, Minnesota 56353, USA.

"The magazine of the independent power production industry," ASE serves an audience of engineers and developers. U.S. government tax credits and other legislation requiring utilities to buy surplus electricity from private producers created a burst of investment in renewable energy systems in the U.S. in the 1980s. This magazine covers the relatively high technology, electricity-producing technologies: 200kw wind turbines in windfarms with thousands of machines, water turbines for installation in existing dams and old abandoned sites, solar photovoltaics, and cogeneration systems. Lots of coverage of equipment components.

ADDITIONAL REFERENCES ON ENERGY: GENERAL

More Other Homes and Garbage is an excellent reference book on most small-scale alternative energy systems; see GENERAL REFERENCES.

Two books on the maintenance and repair of small engines are reviewed in AGRICULTURAL TOOLS.

The Employment of Draft Animals in Agriculture reviews the power associated with draft animals and the use of animal power gears; see AGRICULTURAL TOOLS.

Energy: Improved Cookstoves and Charcoal Production

Energy: Improved Cookstoves and Charcoal Production

The world's forests are shrinking under tremendous pressure from agricultural and lumbering activities. In some areas the intensifying search for fuelwood, the primary cooking fuel for the Third World, is an important contributor to the problem. Most of this wood is burned in open fires or inefficient stoves. When wood is simply too expensive or too far away, animal manures and crop residues formerly returned to the soil as fertilizers frequently are burned as fuel instead. This practice, increasingly common in many parts of Africa and South Asia, adds to a downward spiral in soil fertility. Once the trees and vegetation on hillsides are removed, soil erosion proceeds rapidly with rain water runoff and flooding, and the land can be turned into a desert. Current patterns of daily firewood consumption around the world are thus important factors in an advancing environmental crisis.

Since the late 1970s, much work has been done on the design and dissemination of simple, low-cost improved cookstoves. Such stoves can save up to 40% of the wood fuel normally consumed in open fires, and 25-35% of the fuel consumed in typical traditional stoves. The collective experience of this work is described in **Burning Issues** *and a new forthcoming book by ITDG. After much enthusiastic pursuit of a variety of strategies to encourage owner-building of stoves, experienced observers are concluding that the small industry production of stoves is one of the most promising routes to take. The advantages of this approach include better quality control and therefore higher efficiency and longer stove life than can be achieved with owner-building. Costing $1-5 each, the stoves can often pay for themselves in fuel savings within 1-2 months if fuel is purchased. In rural areas where most fuel is gathered, very low-cost stoves can still be sold to some people, but the distribution problem is much more difficult, and clearly successful strategies have yet to be worked out.*

Fuel conservation through improved cookstoves appears to be the cheapest way for a nation to invest in new sources of energy. The typical artisan-produced cookstove conserving 35% of fuelwood costs less than $5. Three improved stoves have the same effect on the fuel supply as one family biogas plant (which would cost 40-50 times as much) — both mean that one additional family's cooking fuel needs can be supplied. The capital investment will be higher for electric or kerosene stoves, and one must also consider the cost of adding to the electrical generating capacity and extending the electrical distribution grid. Both electric and kerosene stoves have the added daily cost of fuel, which in the case of the improved stove is nil (because improved efficiency alone accounts for all of the gain). The common subsidies and the foreign exchange requirements make kerosene imports a burdensome one for the national economies of many countries.

The secondary effects of existing cooking systems must be understood before acceptable improvements can be made. In many places, smoke from indoor cooking fires is a significant contributor to lung and eye disease. Yet this smoke also serves to dry crops hung over the cooking area and to protect thatched roofs from insect damage. In highland regions and other colder areas, the space heating function of the indoor cooking fire may need to be included in cookstove design. Successful stove promotion efforts may depend on the availability of effective alternatives for these secondary functions of the cooking fire.

Experience has shown that despite the need for wood conservation on a massive scale, adoption of improved stoves cannot occur immediately for an entire nation or region. It will, instead, depend on involvement of local people in careful, systematic work which emphasizes testing and cooking methods. Existing stoves and new prototypes can be tested with a minimum of equipment. Testing techniques are covered by several of the books in this section.

Most knowledgeable people have revised their estimates of the fuel savings possible with the typical new stove. A 35% savings is now considered a realistic figure for the better stove designs. Similarly, most agree that the distribution of improved stoves alone is not going to greatly affect the rate of deforestation in most places. Nevertheless, improved cookstoves are now considered to be a cost-effective component in reforestation programs in some countries, and they clearly have a role to play in improving the quality of life by conserving family resources of cash and time, and reducing smoke in the cooking area.

Many of the entries in this section provide ideas and construction details for a variety of low-cost cookstove designs. **A Woodstove Compendium** *is a good introduction to the range of design choices and it nicely describes the physics of the cooking fire.*

In the affluent countries wood stoves for home heating are gaining popularity with the increasing prices of electricity and heating oil. The wood stove industry in the United States is now selling a remarkable 1-2 million units a year, a success story that unfortunately has brought air pollution problems with it. **Wood Burner's Encyclopedia** *is an excellent reference for North Americans interested in wood heating systems and the basic physics of woodburning.*

In the Third World, rice husks (or hulls) not consumed as fuel are usually returned to the soil or used as a binder in building materials such as bricks. **Rice Husk Conversion to Energy** *notes that most rice hulls are already being used in one way or another, and that only about half of the remainder could be used. There is much work to be done, though, in the search for more efficient rice hull burning methods. (See* **Rice Husks as a Fuel** *for 18 stoves and kilns from Southeast Asia.)*

Charcoal has a high energy content per unit of weight and is thus easier than wood to transport long distances. When fuel wood hauling becomes a serious problem in Third World communities, charcoal production tends to increase significantly, so that more fuel energy can be transported in a single load. Charcoal contains less energy than the wood from which it is made, because energy is required to fire the kiln and volatile gasses are removed. Included in this chapter are several publications on making and using improved kilns which produce more charcoal from the same amount of wood than most traditional kilns and pit-fired techniques.

Burning Issues: Implementing Pilot Stove Programmes, A Guide for Eastern Africa, MF 20-464, book, 184 pages, by Stephen Joseph and Philip Hassrick, 1984, £4.95 from ITDG.

Whereas much has been written elsewhere about the design, testing, and construction of improved cookstoves, there is little available on how to start up and manage a program to disseminate new stoves. This book fills the gap by drawing together the experiences of many stoves programs in Africa and Asia, and summarizing important management principles and options that have proven to be successful. Needs assessment, training workers, extension, marketing, monitoring and evaluation are all discussed. Although this was not intended to be a design guide, the material on options and matching stoves to needs and resources is good.

"In Kenya, successful market demonstrations have been held with the Ministry of Energy's pottery-lined charcoal jiko. Side by side with the traditional jiko, the two stoves simultaneously cook the same size pot of beans. The women watching determine when to open and close the doors, add fuel, and add water to the beans. The stoves start out with equivalent piles of charcoal and it becomes readily apparent that less charcoal is added to the improved jiko."

"It is important to have stoves available for sale at the time of inciting interest by offering such obvious proof of a good product. 'What good does this do for us?' people ask if you have no stoves for sale."

Recommended.

Helping People in Poor Countries Develop Fuel Saving Cookstoves, MF 20-448, book, 148 pages, by Aprovecho Institute, 1980, free to serious groups, from German Agency for Technical Cooperation (GTZ), P.O. Box 5180, 6236 Eschborn 1, Federal Republic of Germany.

Aprovecho's involvement in the development of fuel-saving stoves in Guatemala resulted in publication of **Lorena Owner Built Stoves** (see review). Since that experience, Aprovecho has carried out further research on how Lorena and other low-cost stoves might be improved, and continues to provide assistance to cookstove popularization efforts in other Third World countries.

This book is about such efforts, written for fieldworkers (such as volunteers and extension agents), administrators and planners (especially those responsible for forestry and soil conservation programs), and researchers. The purpose of the manual is not to present construction methods in detail for specific stoves. Instead, the emphasis is on how to encourage poor people to develop solutions to their problems, with the focus on cooking technologies. Topics covered include important background information on how deforestation, declining agricultural production, and stagnating rural economies are related; working with villagers to design stoves; and systems for spreading information and training stove builders.

"There are as many ways of going about dissemination as there are cultures, but (several points covered here are) raising public awareness; setting up an approach for dissemination; where to go for help in distributing information; promotion: ideas to try; where and how to start dissemination; setting up stove centers; training; involving women; evaluation and follow-up; use training; sponsoring and advising small businesses."

Three final chapters discuss how woodstoves work and how to design simple comparative stove testing procedures, and provide brief illustrated instructions for building a variety of Lorena, clay, metal, and other stoves.

Historically, efforts to introduce "appropriate technology" have relied on convincing people that they need a manufactured product. This valuable book is a down-to-earth discussion of how development workers can help people make use of their own ideas about what they need to develop an improved technology for themselves.

Woodstove Dissemination in the Sahel: Case Studies and a Few Suggestions, MF 20-463, booklet, 8 pages, by Timothy S. Wood, 1982, from VITA.

The author writes, "The experience of six West African woodstove programs illustrates some of the difficulties of dissemination. The importance of adequate training and follow-up and the dangers of subsidies are common themes. Usually it is difficult to identify short term indicators of success for stove dissemination projects. Special consideration should be given to: 1) stove durability and repair records; 2) suitability of stoves being promoted; 3) evidence of auto-diffusion; 4) the amount of wood actually being saved; and 5) the rate at which stoves are being built."

The Socio-Economic Context of Fuelwood Use in Small Communities, MF 20-475, book, 293 pages, by Dennis Wood et. al., 1980, publication number PNAAH747, $2.00 from Aid Document and Information Handling Facility, 7222 47th Street, Suite 100, Chevy Chase, Maryland 20815, USA.

"Community fuelwood programs should take into account the socio-economic organization and the environmental constraints and potentials of each community; usually little attention is paid to these critical village level aspects." This is a summary of the literature on these aspects of fuelwood use in developing countries, and the problems commonly encountered by fuelwood programs. It should be useful background reading for people involved in fuelwood, reforestation, and cookstove programs, to help better understand what is actually going on in rural areas and why.

Stoves and Trees, book, 92 pages, by Gerald Foley, Patricia Moss, and Lloyd Timberlake, 1984, £3.50 from Earthscan, 10 Percy Street, London, W1P 0DR, United Kingdom.

A review of the experiences of stoves programs around the world forms a valuable core to this book, which should be quite informative to people newly interested in working on this topic. The authors criticize the excessive claims of the 1970s stoves programs, review the progress to date, and conclude that improved stoves can have little impact in reducing deforestation. This final conclusion is probably more negative than the record would justify.

The technical and methodological criticisms presented here actually originate almost entirely from the stoves programs themselves, and are not new to those familiar with the field. The authors have not made allowances for the normal learning process associated with a new field, in which early working concepts are revised or abandoned and a more sophisticated understanding evolves over time.

Cookstove News Vol. 1:1-3, 1981; Vol. 2:1-4, 1982; Vol. 3:2, 1983; quarterly periodical, MF 20-442, $10.00 per year, free if you cannot afford $10.00, or in exchange for your publications, from the Aprovecho Institute, 442 Monroe Street, Eugene, Oregon 97402, USA.

"The increasing numbers of people designing, testing, and promoting cookstoves for poor countries indicates a need for a network linking us all together. **Cookstove News** is designed to encourage communication and cooperation among stove workers world wide." Regular columns include "News," for sharing successes and failures; "Cooperation," which prints requests from stove makers for needed information and tools; a pictorial "Catalogue," featuring state-of-the-art stove designs; and "Networking," with names and addresses of people, organizations, and institutions in cookstove development. An important forum for communication for those working in this changing field.

Testing the Efficiency of Wood-Burning Cookstoves: Provisional International Standards, MF 20-459, book, 75 pages, 1983, available in English, French and Spanish, $9.75 in U.S., $10.00 international surface mail, $13.25 international air mail, from VITA.

The procedures outlined in this manual were developed by a group of experienced stove workers with the hope of standardizing worldwide testing to the point where the efficiencies of stoves developed in different areas can be usefully compared. It is recognized that there is a tradeoff between tests which cover the widest possible range of cooking applications and those with the closest possible fit with local cooking practices. Three tests are presented with complete instructions, including forms for data collection and reporting. The authors stress that the tests are provisional, and that they seek feedback to help improve the standards.

Testing Timber for Moisture Content, booklet, 31 pages, CSIRO, 1974, publication C035, $6.00 from UNIPUB.

Some cookstove improvement programs use moisture meters to measure wood fuel moisture content before cookstove tests. This allows a more accurate comparison of tests of different stoves that take place at different times using wood

Cut a section.

Scrape the section.

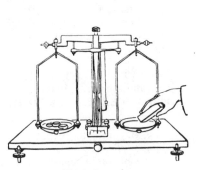

Weigh the section.

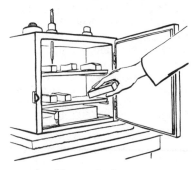

Place section in oven.

from different sources. This booklet explains the simple steps necessary to ensure that accurate readings of wood moisture content are obtained from proper use of the moisture meter. Instructions for proper testing by oven drying are also provided.

"Test the electrode circuit regularly by bridging the electrodes with your hand; the meter should then show an apparent high moisture content...Take several readings in different parts of a board to check evenness of drying."

This booklet will also be of interest to furniture and cabinet makers, who need to control swelling and shrinking of wood in their products.

Designing a Test Procedure for Domestic Woodburning Stoves, Interim Report No. 1, MF 20-443, booklet, 53 pages, by Stephen Joseph and Yvonne Shanahan, 1980, £2.50 from ITDG Stoves Program, ARS Shinfield, Shinfield Road, Reading R62-9VE, United Kingdom.

This report was written to help people develop procedures for testing woodburning stoves. Treatment of laboratory testing procedures for various measurements of efficiency is good but in some cases complicated. Most of the tests can be carried out with simple apparatus (thermometer, scale, watch, ruler). Useful appendices include "Standard Test Method," "Laboratory Test Data Sheets," "Example of Area Profile," and "Example of a Stove Checklist."

Guidelines on Evaluating the Fuel Consumption of Improved Cookstoves, MF 20-447, booklet, 30 pages, Aprovecho, publication number PN-AAJ-811, $4.82 from AID/DIHF, 722 47th Street, Chevy Chase, Maryland 20815, USA.

Evaluation is an important but often neglected component of programs which develop and disseminate improved cookstoves. Most published techniques for evaluation have focused on calculating "efficiencies" of the stove. This manual focuses instead upon how to evaluate stoves within the village or city setting in which they are being used. Information is collected at a household level, without complicated apparatus or calculations. Recommended.

Wood Burner's Encyclopedia, book, 155 pages, by Jay Shelton and Andrew Shapiro, 1976, Vermont Crossroads Press, $8.95 from WEA.

Here is an excellent reference book on "wood as energy." The chapter on energy, temperature and heat nicely provides an understanding of the basic physics involved in burning wood — in an open fire, a heater, or a cookstove. Although this book is primarily intended for use by North Americans wanting to use wood to heat their homes, the considerable amount of background discussion is often relevant to cookstove design. There are valuable sections on fuelwood, combustion, energy

Effect of a cold surface on a flame

efficiency (wood heating), safety considerations, and creosote and chimney fires.

There is a list of manufacturers and some product information (though no designs detail or efficiency claims) for 33 different cookstoves made by 12 different companies. While these stoves cost so much ($400-500) that they are not realistic models for developing countries, some lessons about the design of efficient cookstoves might be learned through careful analysis and testing.

Recommended for cookstove experimenters as a reference.

A Woodstove Compendium, MF 20-462, book, 379 pages, by G. DeLepeleire, K. Krishna Prasad, P. Verhaart, P. Visser, Wood-Burning Stove Group, 1981, $12.00 from the Eindhoven Institute of Technology, Wood-Burning Stove Group, Den Dolech 2, P.O. Box 513, 5600 MB Eindhoven, The Netherlands.

This compendium is the most complete work to date on woodburning cookstoves, and we highly recommend it. The authors begin with a clear and simple explanation of how food is cooked, how wood burns, and basic considerations affecting combustion, efficiency, and the structural integrity of woodburning cookstoves. This is followed by data on construction, fuel, testing results, etc. (depending upon available information) for over 100 new and traditional cookstoves. Diagrams of each are usually sufficient to convey the basic design characteristics, and references lead the reader to one or more of nearly 100 bibliographic entries (no ordering information, though). There is, however, no information from comparative tests of these stoves. The final third of the book takes a more technical and in-depth approach to design considerations, and is written with engineers, rather than generalists, in mind. Evaluation is briefly discussed, and useful forms for data collection are presented. Citing the importance of intricacies of design and quality control, the authors argue for stove development to be carried out by engineers and building to be done by trained specialists, rather than by the owner.

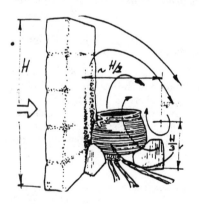

Modern Stoves for All, MF 20-453, book, 60 pages, by Waclaw Micuta, 1981, $12.00 from the Bellerive Foundation, Case Postal 6, CH-1211 Geneva 3, Switzerland.

This important manual begins with an easily understood discussion of combustion of wood and considerations for design of woodburning stoves. Part Two discusses different types of pots and alternative fuels such as briquettes pressed from materials such as dry weeds, husks, cotton waste, coconut fiber, sawdust, and municipal garbage. A simple diagram of a hand press for briquette production is included. Part Three presents 12 stove models from Africa, Europe, and Thailand, and methods for testing efficiency.

Wood Stoves: How to Make and Use Them, MF 20-461, book, 194 pages, by Ole Wik, 1977, $5.95 from Alaska Northwest Publishing Company, Box 4-EEE, Anchorage, Alaska 99509, USA.

Unlike most North American books on woodstoves, this one is concerned with making stoves. It also contains many ideas on design and construction of cooking stoves, which tend to be ignored in the literature. Those people experimenting with the design of improved-efficiency cookstoves will certainly want to read this book.

Only metal stoves, requiring purchased metal stovepipe and made primarily from discarded oil drums, are discussed. In the Third World, these stoves are expensive to build and corrode quickly. In addition, this book is based on years of experience in a very cold climate where wood is abundant and efficiency of combustion is not as important as in most semi-deforested regions. Also, protecting the cook and kitchen from excess heat is of little concern to the author. Designers using this book in the Third World will want to keep these differences in mind.

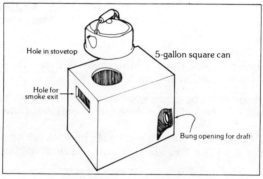

Cooking stove made from a can

Cookstove Handbook (Pilot Edition), MF 20-441, book, 247 pages, June 1982, write for exchange, N.K. Gopalakrishnan, Tata Energy Research Institute, Documentation Centre, Bombay House, 24 Homi Mody Street, Bombay 400 023, India.

This is primarily a compendium of more than 40 cookstoves. Several diagrams are presented for most stove models, with comments on fuel, materials, advantages, and disadvantages. This handbook is a survey of stoves and thus may provide new ideas for design, but it is not a construction manual. Many of the stove models are taken from other publications, which would be better sources for design details, as well as background information related to each stove. There is some discussion of design considerations and the principles of combustion, and 14 laboratory tests are presented in a standardized format.

Wood Conserving Cook Stoves: A Design Guide, MF20-460, book, 111 pages, 1980, $12.00 in U.S., $12.75 international by surface mail, $16.75 international by airmail, also available in French, Spanish and Arabic, from VITA.

The first half of this book gives construction and cooking procedures for four fuel-conserving cookstoves: a Lorena stove, a smokeless chula, a Singer stove, and a sawdust stove made from a rectangular 5-gallon can and sheet metal. Construction information is not detailed, but includes good drawings that can be followed by someone with good manual skills.

More detailed information on each of these stoves can be found in other publications. This book is valuable because it explains in non-technical English how fuel provides heat as it burns, and how traditional and improved stove designs contain this process and direct the transfer of heat for maximum cooking advantage. The chapter "How to make stoves efficient" explains how stoves lose heat energy and how these losses can be reduced by modifications in combustion chamber, chimney, damper, wall, and pothole design.

Clear and well-illustrated.

air flow pattern in insulated
single burner Thai "bucket" stove

Wood Conserving Cook Stoves Bibliography, MF 20-476, paper, 31 pages, VITA, November 1983, available from VITA.

200 articles, reports and books on wood stoves are listed, with a short description of each. Copies of half of the entries can be obtained from VITA.

New Nepali Cooking Stoves, MF 20-454, booklet, 19 pages, by Andreas Bachmann, free from UNICEF, P.O. Box 1187, Kathmandu, Nepal.

This booklet explains and diagrams a stove with prefabricated components which is being introduced in rural areas of Nepal. A potter who has received special train-

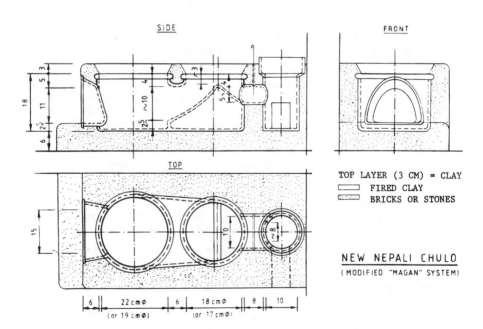

ing makes the stove body and pipes out of clay. These parts are fired and then assembled in the home. A rock or brick aggregate is packed around the fired parts to give the stove mass. This promising approach to cookstove dissemination has the potential to overcome problems of poor quality control experienced in many large mud stove dissemination projects. Other sources of information on improved and prefabricated cookstoves are listed at the end. Recommended.

From Lorena to a Mountain of Fire, MF 20-446, booklet, 52 pages, by Marcus Kaufman, 1983, $5.50 from Publication Section, Yayasan Dian Desa, P.O. Box 19, Bulaksumur, Yogyakarta, Indonesia.

Over the course of five years of improved woodstove dissemination in Central Java, Dian Desa—a local A.T. group—moved away from a monolithic lorena stove based on the Guatemalan model to progressively smaller and simpler stoves, better matched to local cooking patterns. The need for standardization and quality control of large numbers of stoves eventually led the project to adopt a simple pottery-liner approach, allowing for widespread dissemination without requiring a large number of highly-trained field workers. This is a case study, not a construction manual, and it is hoped people doing stove work elsewhere can learn from Dian Desa's experience. Recommended.

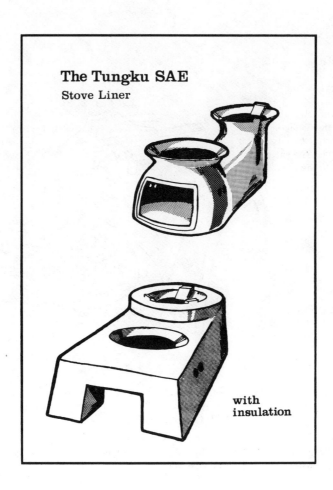

The Tungku SAE
Stove Liner

with insulation

One Pot, Two Pot...Jackpot: Some Suggestions for Future Directions for Woodburning Stoves in Sri Lanka, MF 20-473, book, 49 pages, by Simon Burne, 1985, available from ITDG Stoves Programme, Myson House, Railway Terrace, Rugby CV21 3HT, United Kingdom.

Burne presents an interesting discussion of the advantages of single piece two-pot ceramic stove liners as a design option in Sri Lanka. Training and marketing needs are explored. Many of the observations about economics and marketing have implications for stoves programs in other countries, particularly those involved with pottery stoves. Recommended.

Report on Training of District Extensionists, MF 20-474, book, 48 pages, ITDG Stoves Programme, 1985, available from ITDG Stoves Programme, Myson House, Railway Terrace, Rugby CV21 3HT, United Kingdom.

Large-scale stove promotion programs have substantial training needs for staff members and for potters or production workers. This report contains material used in training stove promoters who work with potters, as part of the Sarvodaya/CEB stove program in Sri Lanka. Advice is given on how to select potters and work with them, how the pottery stove production process works, and where there are likely to be problems.

Getting the Measurements Right

The templates:
use on wet stoves only
(as the stove is built)

The straight template measures the diameter of the firebox. Always use it on the inside. The cut shows us how wide the top should be.

The oval template is used 3 times. For the tunnel it should fit all the way in.

Lab Tests of Fired Clay Stoves, the Economics of Improved Stoves, and Steady State Heat Loss from Massive Stoves, MF 20-471, paper, 48 pages, by Georges Yameogo et. al., November 1982, CILSS/VITA, from VITA.

Five single-pot chimneyless ceramic stoves were laboratory tested and compared with the performance of an open fire. All the stoves saved at least 50% of the wood, while the best stove saved ⅔ of the wood. Cooking performance tests are not covered. Drawings and descriptions of the stoves are provided, along with the test data. The financial attractiveness of stoves is also explored, assuming various interest and discount rates. The authors conclude that very low cost stoves, even with a short lifetime, are the most financially attractive. A brief discussion of heat loss and stove wall thickness is included.

Single pot stove

Comparison of Improved Stoves: Lab, Controlled Cooking, and Family Compound Tests, MF 20-467, book, 67 pages, by Georges Yameogo et. al., 1983, IVE/THE/GTZ/CILSS/VITA, from VITA.

A team that tested a variety of stoves in the Sahel concluded that lightweight, single-pot, chimneyless metal and ceramic stoves had the greatest potential for fuel savings (40-50%), while the more massive 2-3 pot chimney stoves would use as much or more firewood than the open fire if the cook attempted to boil on the second pothole.

"Chimneyless stoves have A) more surface area of the pot exposed to the hot gases, B) a shape that also forces the hot gases close to the surface of the pot to improve convective heat transfer, C) grates to improve combustion and D) low mass to reduce the amount of energy needed to heat the stove body itself."

Test methodology and results, sample data sheets and drawings of all of the tested stoves are included.

PERSPECTIVE   **PERSPECTIVE**

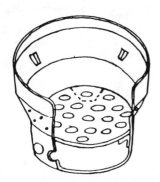   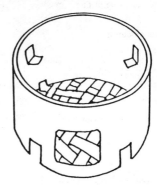

How to Make the Kenyan Ceramic Jiko, MF 20-470, booklet, 18 pages, by Maxwell Kinyanjui and Laurie Childers, 1983, available from Energy/Development International, P.O. Box 62360, Nairobi, Kenya.

The Kenyan ceramic jiko is an improved charcoal stove with design modifications taken in part from the bucket stoves common in Thailand. The stove has a metal exterior, a pottery liner, and a grate.

Field test results from 451 households indicate a 25-50% fuel savings with the

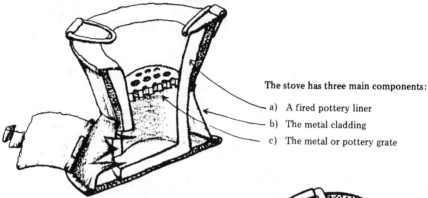

The stove has three main components:

a) A fired pottery liner

b) The metal cladding

c) The metal or pottery grate

The pottery liner is anchored inside the metal cladding with a mixture of cement (one part) and vermiculite or ash (three parts). The cladding protects the liner and supports the weight of the pot.

The standard household model weighs 5 kg and has the following dimensions:

Bottom and top diameter of cladding	31	cm
Overall height	23	cm
Top inside diameter of liner	22	cm
Basal diameter of liner	16	cm
Firebox depth	10	cm
Grate diameter	16	cm
Grate thickness	1.5	cm
Grate hole diameter	1.5	cm
Inlet air door	650	cm^2
Thickness of ceramic liner	2.5	cm

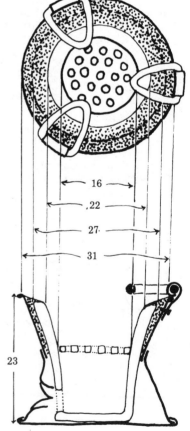

Fig. 2   The Kenyan Ceramic Jiko

new stove. The ceramic jiko appears to be well accepted by users. It requires less attendance and has less of a risk of burns than the traditional all-metal jiko.

This fuel-efficient, portable, chimneyless stove is sold in the market for a few dollars. The success of this experience suggests that other stoves with these traits may have an important role to play in other countries, particularly as a way to take advantage of skilled artisan construction and commercial markets as distribution channels.

This booklet describes the construction techniques required, especially to produce the ceramic liner.

Lorena Owner-Built Stoves, MF 20-452, book, 144 pages, by Ianto Evans and Michael Boutette, 1981, published by A.T. Project, Volunteers in Asia, out of print in 1986.

"What is the Lorena stove? It is a permanent cookstove made with a mixture of sand and clay. Almost anyone can build it, without special tools, at almost no

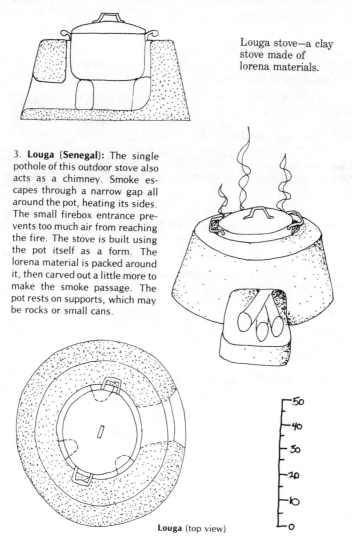

Louga stove—a clay stove made of lorena materials.

3. **Louga (Senegal):** The single pothole of this outdoor stove also acts as a chimney. Smoke escapes through a narrow gap all around the pot, heating its sides. The small firebox entrance prevents too much air from reaching the fire. The stove is built using the pot itself as a form. The lorena material is packed around it, then carved out a little more to make the smoke passage. The pot rests on supports, which may be rocks or small cans.

Louga (top view)

cost and with only this book or a few days training." This inexpensive stove, originally developed in highland Guatemala, was designed for improved fuel efficiency using a variety of organic waste fuels in addition to wood.

In illustrated step-by-step fashion, this manual explains Lorena stove construction: how to test for suitable sand-clay mixtures, design the stove, and build and carve out the sand-clay block. Cooking methods and possible design modifications are suggested. A final section describing research on acceptance and use of the stove by Guatemalans shows that builders continually alter the designs. These innovations improve (rather than reduce) fuel efficiency only when builders and users fully understand how the stoves work. Training courses must therefore communicate the operating principles in addition to the construction techniques.

The 1981 revised edition incorporates some designs from Java and an appendix on evaluating fuel savings and testing at the village level. Another appendix describes and illustrates rice hull burning stoves from Java.

After years of experimentation and field testing, in many countries the Lorena stove now represents an early prototype that has since been abandoned in favor of smaller ceramic or metal stoves made by craftsworkers in large numbers.

Laboratory and Field Testing of Monolithic Mud Stoves, Interim Report No. 3.2, MF 20-451, booklet, 50 pages, by Joseph and Y.J. Shanahan, £1.50 from ITDG Stoves Program, ARS Shinfield Road, Reading RG2-9VE, United Kingdom.

This report presents the conclusions of field tests on the Chula and Lorena stoves in Sri Lanka and Indonesia, along with details of testing and conclusions from laboratory tests. Procedures were based upon the ITDG report **Designing a Test Procedure for Domestic Stoves** (this section). Discussion includes effects upon performance of stove size, combustion chamber size and shape, and chimney design, length and shape of connection flues, pot hole size and shape, and chimney design. Useful design guidelines are presented. Also includes a discussion of three-stone fireplaces.

Cookstove Construction by the Terra-CETA Method, MF 20-440, booklet, 6 pages, by Robert Lou Ma, 1982, $2.00 from Centro de Experimentacion en Technologia Apropiada, 15 Avenida 14-61, zona 10, Guatemala City, Guatemala.

Recognizing the difficulty in disseminating large numbers of well-built cookstoves, CETA developed an adjustable mold design which will allow rapid production of clay/sand stoves, through a rammed-earth type method. The pot holes and firebox are formed by removable inserts. This seems to be a promising alternative to ceramic inserts (see **New Nepali Cooking Stoves**, this section) for those wishing to simplify or standardize stove construction.

Brief Notes on the Design and Construction of Woodburning Cookstoves, with Particular Reference to the CETA System, MF 20-437, booklet, 11 pages, by Robert Lou Ma, 1982, $2.00 from Centro de Experimentacion en Technologia Apropiada, 15 Avenida 14-61, zona 10, Guatemala City, Guatemala.

CETA, working in Guatemala, home of the original "Lorena" stove, has developed a method for cookstove construction which facilitates rapid construction through a modular design, with the critical components produced centrally by a local artisan. Although this approach may be of higher cost for materials, the on-site set-up of this stove would be simple and quick. Standardized production, the author points out, makes possible greater quality control. See also the more recent paper, **Cookstove Construction by the Terra-CETA Method**, this section.

A Cooking Place for Large-Sized Pots, MF 20-469, booklet, 28 pages, by Andreas Bachmann and Thondup D. Kongtsa, 1984, available from UNICEF, P.O. Box 1187, Kathmandu, Nepal.

Small cottage industries are often large users of firewood, for dyeing wool, paper-making, and many other kinds of processing. This fact has led some observers to propose alternative fuel sources (e.g. biogas, producer gas, water turbine-driven heat generators) that typically have high investment costs for the amount of wood fuel saved. Relatively simple, low-cost large stoves can significantly reduce fuel consumption. Such stoves are relatively familiar and require a much lower investment for the energy saved than does virtually any other alternative. The promotion of such stoves should be the first priority of programs to reduce cottage industry fuel use.

This booklet describes and provides drawings for one such stove that was designed for wool-dyeing in Nepal. The stove requires 2000 bricks, a cast-iron grate, and a brick or metal chimney.

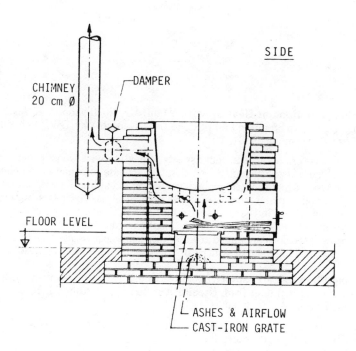

How to Build an Oil Barrel Stove, MF 20-449, booklet, 24 pages, by Ole Wik, $1.95 from Alaska Northwest Publishing Co., Box 4-EEE, Anchorage, Alaska 99509, USA.

This woodburning stove is primarily for cooking. Whereas most oil-drum stove designs retain the round shape of the drum, this design is a rectangular shape which provides the user with a fairly large cooking surface.

"The author has provided simple directions for making this stove. . .requiring shaping and assembling 12 pieces of metal cut from a discarded oil barrel, entirely without welding equipment or power tools." Very well-illustrated with photos and dimensional drawings.

The author is experienced at metalworking with simple tools, and includes many helpful suggestions, such as how to make a metal-cutting tool out of a scrap piece of metal. See also Ole Wik's other book **Wood Stoves: How to Make and Use Them**.

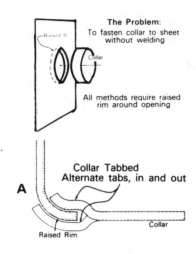

The Complete Book of Heating with Wood, MF 20-439, book, 123 pages, by Larry Gay, 1974, $5.85 plus $1.50 postage from Garden Way, GWP Schoolhouse Road, Pownal, Vermont 05261, USA.

The author covers many different aspects of heating with wood, concentrating on ways to burn wood efficiently. The chapters include information on choosing the proper type of fuelwood, log splitting, cutting enough wood without destroying forests, woodlot management, efficient stove designs, tips on ventilation, and using heat exchangers in the chimney to heat water. There are quite a few drawings of stoves, intended as ideas, not detailed designs.

Some parts of the book are aimed at American users, such as a section on choosing fuelwood that includes North American trees and climate considerations.

Splitting Firewood, MF 20-477, book, 142 pages, by David Tresemer, 1981, $4.50 plus postage and handling from Green River Tools, 5 Cotton Mill Hill, P.O. Box 1919, Brattleboro, Vermont 05301, USA.

North Americans who split their own firewood for heating stoves will find this to be an interesting and entertaining book.

"As we shall see in the section on modern splitting tools, helves (or handles) are made of several materials, including wood, steel, fiberglass, and new types of plastic-coated fiberglass. Comparing the performances of the different splitting devices makes it very clear what one wants in a handle. . .The helve must be firm but not stiff in order to absorb the vibration of impact without jarring the hands and arms, that is, it must have resilience, defined as 'the amount of strain energy which can be stored in a structure without causing permanent damage to it.' I prefer to carry the attitude of the old woodsman who bragged he had used the same ax for fifty years. 'Really?' inquired the listener. 'Yep,' said the woodsman, 'and it's had five new handles and two new heads.' "

Based on the author's painstaking research, this volume covers the art of splitting firewood in detail, with excellent illustrations, useful charts, and interesting historical quotations. Topics include the selection, care, and use of tools; proper procedures and techniques; and the spiritual dimensions of splitting.

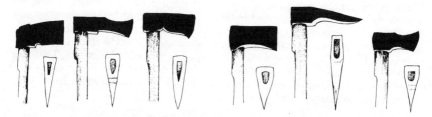

Some traditional splitting axes of Europe.

Less Smoky Rooms, MF 20-472, book, 104 pages, by Andreas Bachmann, 1984, available from UNICEF, P.O. Box 1187, Kathmandu, Nepal.

A collection of chimney and stove ideas from Bhutan and Nepal fill this book. Most unusual are the cement chimney blocks, the back-draft protection devices for the tops of chimneys, the small metal room heaters, the wood-fired water heaters, and several cast-iron stoves. The other material is covered in more detail in other books by the same author.

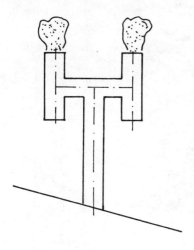

H - PIPE

The diameters of the pipes should be the same as that of the main chimney pipe, not smaller than 100 mm inside

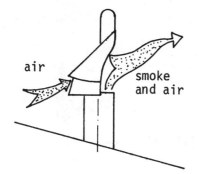

TURNING   CHIMNEY   HAT

This hat turns with the wind. It is designed to increase the draught, without back-flow to stoves.

Rice Husks as a Fuel, MF 20-456, book, 76 pages, by Craig Thorburn, P.T. Tekton Books, 1982, $4.50 from Volunteers in Asia, Appropriate Technology Project, P.O. Box 4543, Stanford, California 94305, USA.

Rice husks, usually regarded as a waste product of rice processing, can easily be used as a fuel for cooking or for firing bricks, tiles, or earthenware vessels, thus alleviating pressure upon rapidly diminishing sources of firewood. But burning unaided, rice husks smolder slowly, producing thick acrid smoke. This book documents 18 simple stoves and kilns developed by people in Indonesia, Thailand, and the Philippines to overcome these poor burning characteristics, and to take advantage of this plentiful and inexpensive fuel. Text in English and Indonesian with 60 illustrations.

Measurement / Ukuran : cm

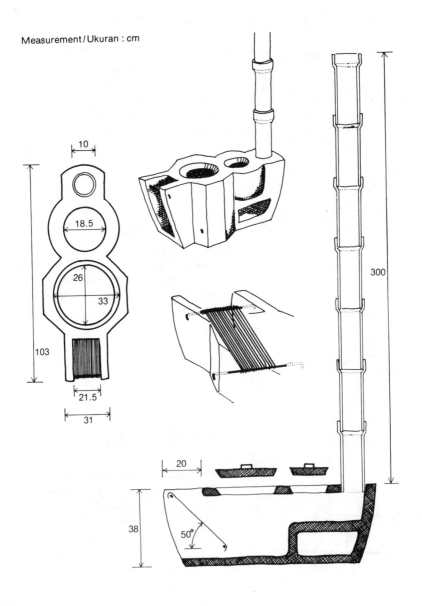

Rice Husk Conversion to Energy, FAO Agricultural Services Bulletin No. 31, MF 20-455, book, 175 pages, by E. Beagle, 1978, $10.00 from UNIPUB.

This is an extensive reference book on the enormous variety of energy applications for rice husks around the world. About half of the world's 60 million tons of rice husks produced annually are currently used; another 20% (12 million tons) apparently could be used as well.

The author discusses the general processes for converting rice husks into energy along with existing technologies for doing this. Steam engines, producer-gas engines, paddy dryers, and domestic cooking stoves are among the topics considered. Where parboiling is done, small steam engines can effectively be used to power the mills and provide heat for parboiling. Where parboiling is not done, the best power choice for small (less than 5 tons per hour) mills would be "an engine fueled by gas produced from rice husk...This system of 'producer gas' is of proven technology, having been in continuous use for over 75 years." The great range of technologies discussed is unfortunately not supported by enough drawings.

The format allows the reader to go on to find more detailed information when relevant. For example, it is noted that the standard rice mill in Thailand is driven by a rice hull fired steam engine. A 224-entry list of contacts includes makers of such equipment in Thailand, and the 264-entry bibliography leads to further information on a wide variety of other topics.

The author concludes that rice husks are used far more extensively as an energy source than is generally recognized, that manufacturing capabilities for the related equipment are greater than realized, and that difficulties in information exchange prevent wider progress in applications. This book is a major step in overcoming the information exchange problem.

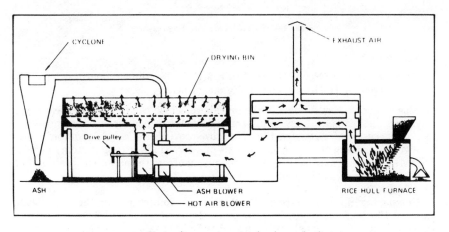

Grain dryer using rice husks as fuel

Double Drum Sawdust Stove (Research Note #NE-208 and Photo Story #30), MF 20-444, leaflet, 7 pages, by J. Wartluft, 1975, write Northeastern Forest Experiment Station, Forest Service, USDA, 370 Reed Road, Broomall, Pennsylvania 19008, USA.

This is a brief description of experiments done with a sawdust burning stove, which consists of an inner drum filled with packed sawdust, and an outer drum used to channel updrafts. Rice hulls could also be used as the fuel. Photos are included as well as a simple dimensional drawing of the original design (reproduced here). Installation and operation are also described.

These two papers are short but concise, providing enough information to enable someone to build a stove using this design. Although designed for space heating, this stove could be adapted for cooking as well.

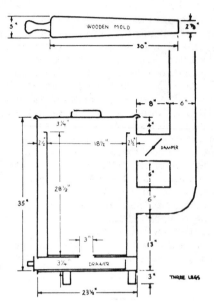

Figure 2.—Design of the experimental double-drum stove.

Sawdust-Burning Space Heater Stove, MF 20-457, dimensional drawings with text, 9 pages, by D. Huntington, 1975, out of print.

This is a stove very similar to the one above, which can be used for heating or cooking. The plans are easy to understand. Welding facilities are recommended but not necessary for construction. The stove provides a steady heat output. Ideas are given for using the stove as the basis of a forced air heating system in colder climates, where it may be placed in a room apart from the area to be heated. Rice hulls can be used as the fuel.

Comparing Simple Charcoal Production Technologies for the Caribbean, MF 20-466, book, 42 pages, by Jeffrey Wartluft and Stedford White, 1984, $8.75 in U.S., $9.00 international surface mail, $11.75 international air mail, from VITA.

Comparative testing of four charcoal kilns and retorts, and a traditional Caribbean method revealed some interesting results. "The traditional Montserratian coal pits can provide yields of charcoal that are comparable to the yields from larger metal kilns and retorts, and are superior in yield to single-drum kilns." The traditional pits are also by far the least expensive technology, with lowest initial investment, longest equipment life, and least time investment per unit of charcoal produced. Construction details are provided for the pit system and for each of the other technologies.

This report and independent results from Thailand provide evidence that well-made and -operated earth charcoal pits can be used to produce charcoal efficiently and at very low cost. This contradicts the general literature which portrays earth pits as quite inefficient.

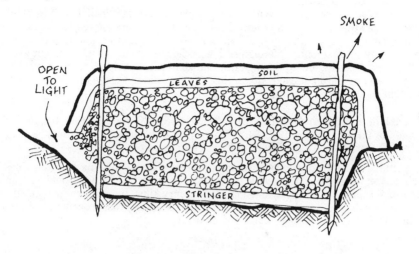

MONTSERRATIAN COAL PIT

The Development of the Subri Fosse Charcoal Kiln, paper, 28 pages, by J.M. Lejeune, FAO/Ghana, Field Document No. 28 from project GHA/74/013, 1983, from FAO.

This unusual charcoal kiln design was developed in a research project in Ghana, in an effort to minimize foreign exchange costs and total wood handling/labor costs. The application was in forest clearing operations, in which transportation was difficult and costly. Large fixed metal kilns resulted in high foreign exchange costs and high wood handling costs. Existing portable metal kiln designs also had high foreign exchange costs. The traditional earth pit/mound kilns could be constructed

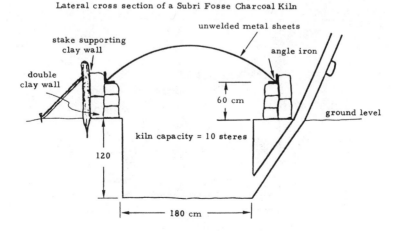

Longitudinal cross section of a Subri Fosse Charcoal Kiln

on the spot of use, but had high labor costs associated with covering the mounds with earth and sifting the charcoal from the top layer of dirt, which tended to collapse into the pit during or after firing.

The investigators came up with a compromise design that included an earth pit with loose steel sheets as a cover. This kiln could easily be moved from place to place, produced good quality charcoal at an economical price, and required only a relatively small amount of foreign exchange. The investigators solved the problem of the metal sheets being damaged by the charcoal by holding them in an arch with steel angle iron at each end; in this way they did not come into contact with the charcoal.

Cash in on Charcoal, AGRIX How To Series No. 26, Asia Edition, booklet, 39 pages, by Jose B. Blando, 1976, $1.25 from Agrix Publishing Corporation, 79 Dona Hemady cor. 13th Avenue, Quezon City, Philippines.

Pictures and scale drawings of several different charcoal kilns in the Philippines. These are: variations of the simple pit method, an oil drum kiln, a multiple oil drum kiln, a 4-drum vertical retort, and 3 larger masonry kilns. Instructions are provided for the construction and operation of each of these kilns. Wood, coconut shells and other materials are used to make the charcoal.

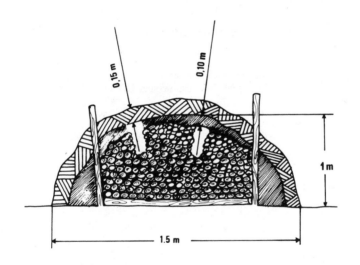

Earth kiln

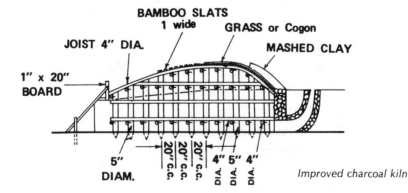

Improved charcoal kiln

Charcoal Production Using a Transportable Metal Kiln, Rural Technology Guide 12, MF 20-465, booklet, 18 pages, by A.R. Paddon and A.P. Harker, free to public bodies in countries eligible for British aid, £1.00 to others, from TDRI.

Photos and text show how to properly load and operate a lightweight sheet metal charcoal kiln that can be rolled from place to place. When properly operated, this kiln is more efficient than traditional pit systems. Production is ½ to ¾ ton of charcoal per batch. With two kilns, two people can produce 2-3 tons of charcoal per week. Construction details for the kiln have been published separately as Rural Technology Guide 13, **The Construction of a Transportable Charcoal Kiln** (MF 20-468, booklet, 19 pages, by W.D.J. Whitehead, 1980, same source).

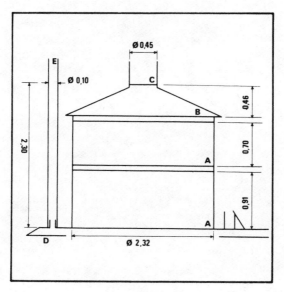

Portable steel charcoal kiln

Charcoal Making for Small Scale Enterprises: An Illustrated Training Manual, MF 20-438, 26 pages, International Labour Office, 1975, 6 Swiss Francs ($3.60) from International Labour Office, CH 1211 Geneva 32, Switzerland.

This short, large-format booklet is a good source of details of correct operation for two kinds of low-cost charcoal making kilns (most common and virtually no-cost) and small portable steel kilns (approximately $2000 each). "Earth kilns are simple to construct and operate, and produce good results when managed by experienced people."

The language is simple and there are many drawings and photos. Notes on the preparation of wood, tools required, calculation of production costs, marketing, and charcoal-making cooperatives are included. Unfortunately, there are no rules given for estimating efficiency of a kiln, nor is the end-use efficiency of charcoal vs. direct wood burning discussed.

Energy: Wind

Energy: Wind

The wind has been a significant source of power for centuries. Early windmills in China and Southeast Asia lifted water into rice fields. In Europe the windmill developed into an enormous structure, nearly the size of a small sailing ship, developing power in the range of 25 hp and higher, for use in grain grinding, drainage, and a multitude of small industrial tasks. The first windmills in North America and the Caribbean were of this type. In the late 19th century, waterpumping windmills were manufactured by the thousands, and several million machines were operating by the middle of this century. These were mostly lifting water for farmhouses and livestock.

Windgenerators for electricity spread by the hundreds of thousands across rural North America in the 1930s, supplying the farmhouses with small amounts of power for radios and a few lights. Both the waterpumping windmills and the windgenerators went into decline with the arrival of rural electrification, which offered cheap electricity for running electric pumps and many more household uses. With the energy crisis, however, sales of waterpumping windmills and windgenerators have greatly increased in the United States.

It is the waterpumping windmill that appears to be the most immediately relevant for rural energy needs in the developing countries, both for high-value community water supplies and for irrigation pumping. Irrigation is the biggest single factor in improving farm yields, and there are many places where low-lift irrigation on small plots could be accomplished with windmills. Thailand, Greece, Japan, Peru, and Portugal are among the nations where significant numbers of irrigation windmills have been used in recent times. In North America, farmers built thousands of scrap wood waterpumping windmills before the manufactured steel machines appeared. In all of these national experiences, local windmill designs were developed to fit pumping needs, wind conditions, and materials available. These machines were built in small workshops; this kept prices low and repair skills nearby. In other countries where manufactured windmills have been directly introduced, the high initial cost and lack of repair skills have greatly reduced their attractiveness. (South Africa and Australia may be exceptions. In these industrialized countries, variations of the American fan-bladed windmill have been widely used to water livestock and supply isolated farmhouses. These are expensive, high performance machines requiring infrequent but skilled maintenance and repair.)

*Thus the historical record suggests that successful windmill promotion programs in developing countries will need to focus initially on locally-adapted designs and craftsperson-based production using local materials, with a limited number of manufactured parts. Promotion programs might include credit mechanisms whereby the windmill itself is both loan and collateral. Also of interest is the Las Gaviotas approach in which the buyer assembles and installs a metal windmill from a kit (see **Un Molino de Viento Tropical**).*

Waterpumping windmills for irrigation purposes are most economically com-

petitive in areas that do not already have electricity for powering irrigation pumps. (Only 12% of the rural Third World has electricity.) Low-lift windmills for rice paddy irrigation appear to be economically attractive, compared to engine-driven pumps, for parts of South and Southeast Asia. Higher-lift applications for high-value vegetable farming may be economically competitive in many parts of the world. The economic appeal of locally-built windmills is even greater when the savings of scarce foreign exchange from reduced oil imports and the village-level economic multiplier effects are considered. Other advantages of locally-built windmills include the creation of village capital using local labor and materials, much lower initial cost, and avoidance of maintenance problems associated with engine-driven pumps. Such windmills appear to have more frequent but simpler maintenance requirements than manufactured windmills.

*A small number of people are working on waterpumping windmill designs in developing countries. These include versions of the Greek (Cretan) sail windmill (see, for example, **How to Build a Cretan Sail Windpump**). Even cheaper are the cloth and bamboo sail windmills of Thailand. The Thai designs in particular have the advantages of low cost and use of local materials and labor. They are well matched to the low-lift small volume pumping needs of small plot rice agriculture. For a comparative summary of waterpumping windmill costs, production requirements, and performance, see the U.N. Economic Commission for Asia and the Pacific (ESCAP) paper **Report on the Practical Application of Windpowered Waterpumps**.*

*In the United States, isolated houses have become a major market for wind-generators for electricity. **Wind Power for Farms, Homes and Small Industry** and **The Wind Power Book** are recommended for readers considering such an installation. Technical advances now also allow a windgenerator to feed surplus power back into a conventional electric grid, a practice which makes wind-generated electricity in urban and suburban settings much more attractive than before, as the substantial expense of a battery system can be avoided.*

For any windmachine, the choice of site is very important. Trees and buildings can greatly reduce the useful winds reaching a windmill. A small difference in wind speed can mean a big difference in power available, because the power in the wind varies with the cube of the wind speed. Thus a 12-mph wind has 8 times as much power as a 6-mph wind. Windgenerators operate in the highest range of wind-speeds, and the user will usually want to find the windiest spot possible for such an installation. Waterpumping windmills, on the other hand, need greater protection from the extremes of high winds, and are usually designed to operate in low and medium winds. We have included several publications on site selection for wind machines, including vegetative indicators of high average windspeeds at particular locations.

The Wind Power Book, MF 21-495, book, 255 pages, by Jack Park, 1981, $14.95 plus $1.50 postage (add $8.00 for airmail shipping) from Cheshire Books, 514 Bryant Street, Palo Alto, California 94301, USA.

This book incorporates many developments in the field of windpower since the author wrote **Simplified Wind Power Systems for Experimenters** and **Wind Power for Farms, Homes and Small Industry** (see reviews). As with **Simplified**, Jack Park has made his presentation simple and understandable in order to allow innovative people to adapt the basic concepts to fit their own situation. For example, he explains the necessary formulas for calculating windpower available, and what to expect from different types of machines. This is the best book available for an overview of the topic. Written for a North American audience, but useful for people in developing countries.

Wind Power for Farms, Homes and Small Industry, MF 21-497, book, 229 pages, by Jack Park and Dick Schwind, 1978, Document No. RFP 2841/1270/78/4, $20.00 (North America) from NTIS, overseas write Development Assistance Division, Office of International Affairs, NTIS.

This is a no-nonsense introduction to windpower and windmachines for the North American. It is not a design manual, but a book to help the reader understand how to decide whether to buy a windmachine, considering needs, wind conditions, and other power options. The author discusses the different kinds of wind measuring equipment, different electrical systems, possible legal problems, and the routine tasks that come with owning a wind system. Monthly wind data for most of the United States is included. If the reader decides to get a windmachine, the book will help him/her decide what kind, what size, and what kind of energy storage system to use. Windgenerators and waterpumpers are considered. Highly recommended for North Americans considering installing a wind system.

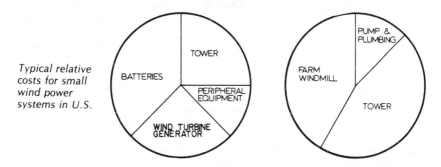

Typical relative costs for small wind power systems in U.S.

Wind Energy, Renewable Sources of Energy Volume III, MF 21-505, book, 263 pages, 1981, available from ECDC-TCDC Services, ESCAP Secretariat, U.N. Building, Rajadamnern Avenue, Bangkok 2, Thailand.

This survey briefly describes experimental windmachines and programs in Asian and Pacific countries, and provides very basic wind data for a few sites in these countries. Half the book consists of a list of individuals and institutions interested in the topic, and a 350-entry bibliography.

A Siting Handbook for Small Wind Energy Conversion Systems, MF 21-489, book, 120 pages, by Harry L. Wegley et. al., 1978, Accession No. PNL 2521, $13.00 (North America) from NTIS; overseas contact Development Assistance Division, Office of International Affairs, NTIS.

"The primary purpose of this handbook is to provide siting guidelines for laymen who are considering the use of small wind energy conversion systems." This kind of information is essential in promoting the effective use of windpower in the best locations.

The choice of a site for a windmachine is very important because: 1) the energy in the wind is proportional to the cube of the windspeed, and thus small differences in windspeed mean large differences in windpower available; 2) small obstacles on the ground in flat terrain can slow the wind considerably; and 3) wind patterns are greatly affected by hilly and mountainous terrain. This handbook will help identify the sites with the highest windpower potential. This is most important for windgenerators, which take advantage of the high range of winds at a site, for maximum electricity production. The manual will also be of value in choosing sites for waterpumping windmills, which need more protection from high winds and operate in the low range of windspeeds to allow more dependable water pumping.

Most of the information included can be used anywhere in the world. The core of this book is a well-illustrated presentation on the effects of trees (including wind-breaks), shrubs, and buildings in flat terrain, and the effects of ridges, passes, valleys and other features in mountainous or hilly terrain. Groups in other countries could substitute their own data for the section on special weather hazards of the United States (snow, hail, icing, tornadoes, thunderstorms, high winds and dust storms), with maps that identify affected areas. Most Third World countries do not have as firm a data base for these country maps, but some of the problems are avoided also.

"To understand and apply the siting principles discussed, the user needs no technical background in meteorology or engineering; he needs only a knowledge of basic arithmetic and the ability to understand simple graphs and tables."

"According to manufacturers. . .the greatest cause of dissatisfaction among owners has been improper siting. . .This handbook incorporates half a century of siting experience. . .as well as recently developed siting techniques."

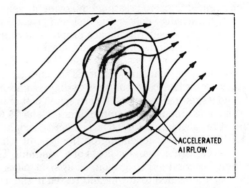

Airflow around an
isolated hill
(*top view*)

ACCELERATED
AIRFLOW

Report on the Practical Application of Wind-Powered Water Pumps, 26 pages, by Marcus Sherman, 1977, available on request from Natural Resources Division, U.N. Economic and Social Commission for Asia and the Pacific (ESCAP), United Nations Building, Sala Santiham, Bangkok 2, Thailand; also reproduced in "Proceedings of the workshop on biogas and other rural energy resources held at Suva, and the roving seminar on rural energy development, held at Bangkok, Manila, Tehran and Jakarta," Energy Resources Development Series No. 19, ESCAP, 1979, U.N. Sales No. E.79.II.F.10, $10.00 from U.N. Sales Section, Room LX 2300, New York, New York 10017, USA.

This short paper contains a unique and very useful set of tables comparing the operating characteristics, design features, and costs of a wide variety of water-pumping windmills. The author's intent is to "assist in the design and evaluation of future wind-powered water pumps projects for a wide range of environments. Water source, water use, local wind conditions, and availability of labor, capital, and materials are the major determinants of design selection."

Most windmill types are covered. These include Greek (Cretan) sail, multi-vane, Savonius, Chinese vertical axis, Thai cloth, Thai bamboo, medium speed cloth, medium speed metal, and high speed windmills. Categories for comparison include rotor diameter, blade material, pumping rates, starting and rated wind velocity, initial capital cost, expected lifetime, maintenance costs and cost per cubic meter of water lifted a standard distance. The format allows quick comparisons of different windmill types, though for some (e.g. Chinese vertical axis windmills) little performance information is available.

"It appears that local design and construction of wind-powered water pumps is generally feasible. . .The selection of low capital cost, low technology, high labor input designs is usually preferred for agricultural applications unless farmer credit schemes can be used. Higher cost is tolerable for public drinking water supply because the initial cost can be amortized through a long term community budget."

Feasibility Study of Windmills for Water Supply in Mara Region, Tanzania, book, 89 pages, by H. Beurskens, March 1978, $8.00 (single copies free to research institutes in developing countries), from CWD.

This is a very interesting example of a region-wide study of the potential for waterpumping windmills. A wide variety of "different sites were selected where water is needed for irrigation, domestic purposes or cattle farming. The water needs, heads and piping distances were determined for these sites...Only the lake was considered as a water source...Although a number of good sites to install windmills along riversides were noticed, they are not mentioned in this report."

The economics of diesel sets, central grid electricity use, commercial windmills and locally-built windmills are compared. Locally-built windmills appear to be most economical, in addition to creating employment, using locally available materials, saving foreign exchange, conserving fuel, and promoting self-reliance in the villages.

A set of design considerations are proposed for such locally built windmills to match the region's winds, water needs, local production capability, and available skills. The elements and costs of a pilot testing phase are briefly described.

The possibility of financing windmills through the gains from a single irrigated harvest are described based on an existing irrigation project: "In 1977 a group of 10 farmers grew onions on a diesel irrigated plot of 0.6 ha. (1.5 acres) at Mugubya. The net income amounted to approximately shs 11,000 for one harvest...Total investment for a windmill for 0.6 ha (1.5 acres) irrigation would vary roughly from shs 3,400 to shs 6,800, depending on the type of windmill...So the income per harvest is even higher than the costs of a windmill. This seems a very reasonable proposition for windmill irrigation, at least at plots with relatively low heads."

Highly recommended to anyone interested in the use of windmills for irrigation in the Third World.

Cost of Windmill Irrigation, booklet, 12 pages, by CWD, 1985, free from CWD.

A simplified economic comparison of windpumps and diesel pumps is presented, along with charts that allow various combinations of water depth, windspeed and

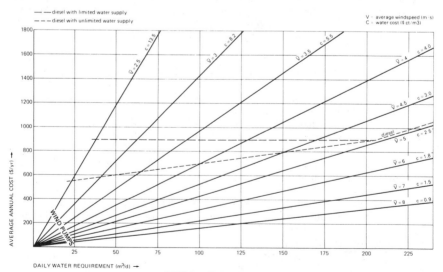

GRAPH 2: 7m STATIC LIFT; CWD WIND PUMPS AND DIESEL POWERED SUCTION PUMPS

water requirement to be examined. The assumptions that may be open to question are interest rates of 10% and diesel pump investment requirements of $1813 per kw of rated power.

"The analysis shows that, for farmers engaged in small-scale lift irrigation on areas of up to 1 ha (2.5 acres), CWD wind pumps are economically more attractive than diesel pumps for average wind speeds during the irrigation season of more than 3.5 m/s (7.8 mph). 'American' (U.S. manufactured) wind pumps are more attractive than diesel pumps for an average wind speed of more than 4.5 m/s (10.1 mph)."

Catalog of Windmachines, book, 100 pages, 1984, by D. Both and L.E.R. van der Stelt, WOT and CWD, $5.00 from TOOL.

A compilation of manufacturers' data on waterpumping windmills and windgenerators from around the world is presented here. Many of the waterpumping windmills are made in developing countries; nearly all of the windgenerators are made in industrialized countries. Approximately 200 manufacturers are listed.

A Survey of the Possible Use of Windpower in Thailand and the Philippines, MF 21-490, book, 74 pages plus appendix, by W. Heronemus, 1974, on request from Agency for International Development, Washington D.C. 20523, USA; or $14.50 in U.S. and $29.00 overseas, quote accession number PB-245 609 when ordering from NTIS.

This report answers favorably the question "could windpower be used by the peasant farmer in Thailand or the Philippines to improve the quality of his life?"

"Numbers of six-sail wind machines are currently in use in the salt works around the northern shore of the Gulf of Thailand. The machines are of about 6 meters diameter and use bamboo spars, rope and wire to form a wheel which carries 6 triangular sails, each woven from rush or split bamboo." These machines drive the paddles of the traditional water-ladder low-lift pumps. The author recognizes that while efficiency could be greatly improved, the current machines are "admirably sized to the task they are to perform" and the primary limiting factor is not in the machines but in the land available for salt evaporation.

For use in irrigation, the author makes some stimulating suggestions for improvements in the sail windmill design and for local adaptation of a wooden, 16-bladed fan mill. "The blades would be of molded plywood, made between matched concrete molds in the existing Bangkok plywood factories... Each laminated blade would be inserted into a wood spoke and the spokes would in turn be brought to an iron banded wood hub. The entire wheel would be a timber (plus glue) product, producible by native artisans possessing the same skills and tools required to build the water ladders."

Most of the report is focused on Thailand, but the contents are of general interest to people in any area where there is a need for low-lift pumps for irrigation. Photos of the sail windmill and water ladder are included.

Windmills in the Lift, booklet, 12 pages, CWD, 1984, available from Consultancy Services Wind Energy Developing Countries, P.O. Box 85, 3800 AB Amersfoort, The Netherlands.

This short booklet describes the windmill development program in Sri Lanka, in which a small (3-meter rotor), simple windmill was developed for irrigation of small farms of ¼ to ½ hectare (½ to 1 acre). The windmill is intended as a competitor to the small kerosene irrigation pumps commonly used. The cost of the windmill has been about $500; 200 were installed by the end of 1983. Work is proceeding on a simpler 2-meter windmill that will cost about $300.

Construction Manual for 12PU350 and 12PU500 Windmills and related books (see below), from TOOL.

These waterpumping windmills are the product of a 3½ year collaboration between Dutch engineers and some local organizations in India. The windmills were designed for irrigation pumping, and are manufactured in local metalworking shops. They still represent a relatively expensive investment, and the economic viability is not certain.

Four reports are available on the windmills themselves. **Technical Report 1982 (TOOL Windmill Projects)** (MF 21-504, book, 110 pages, by Niek Van de Ven, 1982, $4.00) describes the problems and design changes made, and testing equipment used, during the program. **Construction Manual for 12PU350 and 12PU500 Windmills** (MF 21-501, book, 80 pages, by Niek Van de Ven, 1982, $3.50) contains the necessary drawings, photos, and instructions to build these windmills. **Set of Construction Drawings for 12PU300 and 12PU500 Windmills** (MF 21-502, 14 large sheets, 1979, $2.25) contains many of the same technical drawings, but of a larger size for use in the workshop during fabrication. **Syllabus for Irrigation**

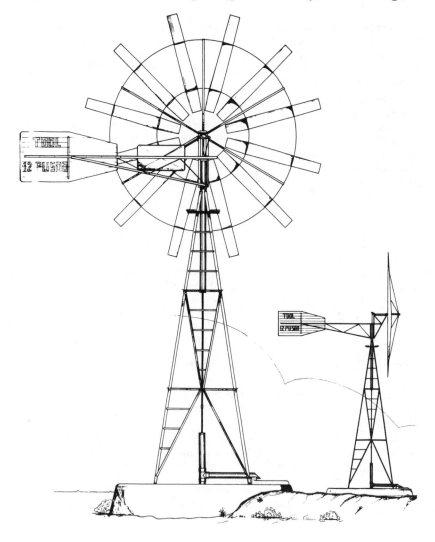

with Windmills: Technical Aspects (MF 21-503, book, 75 pages, by Willem Nijhoff, 1982, $3.50) is, despite the title, mostly concerned with the design calculations for this windmill, plus how to measure the windmill output.

A fifth report, **Aspects of Irrigation with Windmills** (MF 21-500, book, 100 pages, by A. van Vilsteren, 1981, $8.00) is a review of the agricultural and economic factors that affect the viability of windpowered irrigation. This material is certainly applicable to other windmill designs as well.

Un Molino de Viento Tropical Gaviotas, MF 21-479, booklet, in Spanish, 45 pages, by Centro Las Gaviotas, 1980, free to developing countries from Centro Las Gaviotas, Apartado Aereo 18261, Bogota, Colombia.

Presented in a popularized "foto-novela" (picture novel) format, this manual introduces a small waterpumping windmill designed by the Colombian appropriate technology center Las Gaviotas. The large number of photos and drawings are intended to allow the buyer of a windmill kit to assemble and install it him/herself.

The windmill described is the production version of the latest in a series of 56 prototypes built by Las Gaviotas in their attempt to develop a low-cost windmill that would operate in low windspeeds. This one is 1.9 meters in diameter, with a double-acting piston pump, able to pump to a depth of 25 meters. From a 10-meter depth, this windmill will pump 2 cubic meters of water per day in a light and sporadic wind, and 4-5 cubic meters of water per day in a moderate continuous wind. These windmills are made in a well-equipped large workshop.

Selecting Water Pumping Windmills, MF 21-487, booklet, 14 pages, 1978, free from Energy Institute, P.O. Box 3EI, New Mexico State University, Las Cruces, New Mexico 88003, USA.

This booklet is an introduction to the multi-blade windmill commonly seen on North American farms. It describes the parts of a windmill, tank sizes, and the

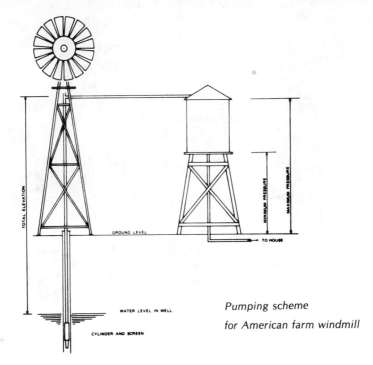

Pumping scheme for American farm windmill

lifting capacity of windmills of different sizes. "Selecting" in the title refers to the size (diameter), not the type of windmill.

Considerations for the Use of Wind Power for Borehole Pumping, MF 21-464, leaflet, 15 pages, by the Appropriate Technology Unit of the Christian Relief and Development Association, Ethiopia (out of print in June 1978).

An introduction to the basic considerations for the use of multi-bladed windmills for water pumping. Explains the importance of site selection, rotor design, and the other major components along with the criteria that affect these choices. No plans or detailed information given.

The Homemade Windmills of Nebraska, MF 21-472, book, 78 pages, by E. Barbour, 1898 (reprinted 1976), $3.50 from Farallones Institute, 15290 Coleman Valley Road, Occidental, California 95465, USA.

Sketches are provided of more than 60 different windmills. They appear roughly in order of efficiency, and the text explains the advantages and disadvantages of each. The book was written with the express purpose of providing good models to copy, so that builders would benefit from the experiences of others.

This is a great idea book: many of these designs could be adapted to use bamboo poles and woven bamboo mats for the blades or sails, along with wooden bearings

The homemade windmills of Nebraska

and power transmission arms. In fact, if combined with simple low-lift pumps, a waterpumping windmill could be put together for an extraordinarily small cash outlay in many developing countries. The designs are so simple that any carpenter could put one together just by looking at an existing machine. This is exactly how they spread all over the state of Nebraska in the United States.

The majority of the machines do not have the capability of turning to accept wind from any direction; they were designed for areas with a prevailing wind from a dependable direction. However, some of the machines do rotate to face the wind, and others are vertical-axis machines for which wind direction is not important.

"Labor, it is found, is contributed freely to such work, at times when more important work is practically at a standstill." Many of the farmers "put them to work in various ways to save hand labor, such as running the grindstone, the churn, the feed grinder, the corn sheller, the wood saw, and other farm machinery." It is also interesting to note that many of the farmers were wealthy and didn't purchase a shop-made mill (which was more efficient) because they could build a heavier-duty, cheaper mill themselves.

The text is full of "case studies" of the farmers and their mills.

Vertical Axis Sail Windmill Plans, MF 21-493, 16 pages, 1976, reprinted 1979, $4.00 from Low Energy Systems, 63 Greenlawns, Skerries Co., Dublin, Ireland.

This design combines some of the principles of sail and sailwing rotors. "The rotor consists of two or more sailwings mounted vertically at equal distance from a vertical axis. . .Each sailwing is formed from a rigid spar. . .at the leading edge of the sail. . .The surface of the sailwing is made from a cloth envelope. . .When

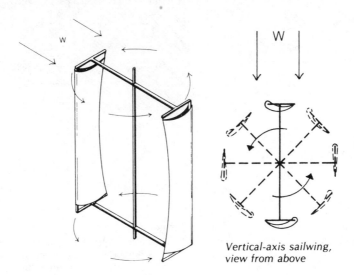

Vertical-axis sailwing,
view from above

the wind impinges on the sailwing it takes up an airfoil shape with a concave surface facing into the wind. . .During one complete revolution of the rotor the sailwing switches the concave surface from one side to the other automatically. . .It is self starting, unlike the Darrieus rotor, to which it is similar in some other respects."

This small lightweight windmill is used by its designers to grind grain. It develops a maximum power of about ¼ hp in a 20 mph wind.

(This design should not be confused with the traditional Cretan sail windmill, which has a horizontal axis, and is used for irrigation water pumping in Crete.)

Sahores Windmill Pump, MF 21-485, booklet, 80 pages, by J. Sahores, 1975, in French only, $6.00 (free to readers in developing countries) from CCPD, World Council of Churches, 150 Route de Ferney, 1211 Geneva 20, Switzerland.

French language edition only; however, the step-by-step construction plans are so detailed that the unit has been built without a translation of the text.

A group of French engineers has developed a light, simple windmill, mainly using bamboo sticks, cloth and string, which sets in motion a standard water pump (design not included). Only the welded transmission mechanism needs some sophistication for manufacture.

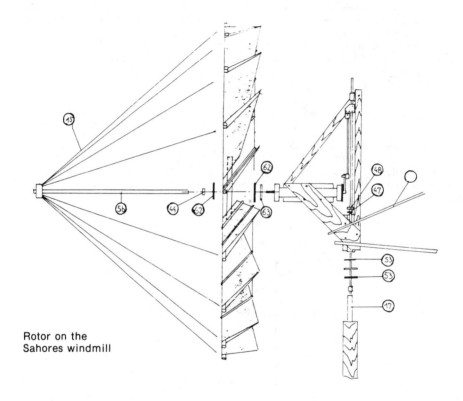

Rotor on the
Sahores windmill

There are three innovations of particular note: 1) The 3-meter diameter wheel is made of bamboo (or wood) with cloth sails in the shape of the American multi-blade design; its light weight and automatic feathering mechanism mean that the tower can consist only of a pole with 4 cord or steel guy wires rather than a large, expensive (usually steel) structure. 2) The automatic feathering system consists of pieces of inner tube attached so that the blades open more as the wind becomes stronger, thus protecting the windmill from damage while also allowing it to make use of light winds. 3) A counterweight system is employed which enables the pumping action to be adjusted by the owner, for operation at windspeeds from 2 m/sec up to strong winds.

The cost of materials in France was approximately US$85 (this included a purchased pump). The first prototypes worked for at least 3 years. 20 of these machines were built in 1974 and tested in Africa.

Low-Cost Windmill for Developing Nations, MF 21-477, booklet with dimensional drawings, 40 pages, by H. Bossel for Volunteers in Technical Assistance, $5.50 from VITA.

Despite the title, the need for a car axle and differential make this a design better suited to do-it-yourself construction in industrialized countries.

"Construction details for a low-cost windmill are presented. The windmill produces one horsepower in a wind of 6.4 m/sec (14.3 mph), or two horsepower in a wind of 8.1 m/sec (18.0 mph). No precision work or machining is required, and the design can be adapted to fit different materials or construction skills. The rotor blades feather automatically in high winds to prevent damage. A full-scale prototype has been built and tested successfully."

Performance data is included. The windmill is best used to transmit mechanical energy, but also can be connected to a generator.

Windpower in Eastern Crete, MF 21-499, booklet, 9 pages, by N. Calvert, 1971, 35 pence including postage, from The Society for the Protection of Ancient Buildings, 58 Great Ormond Street, London WC1, United Kingdom.

This booklet provides a good description of the techniques and materials used to build the Cretan sail windmill. It is not a construction manual, and it does not provide precise dimensions.

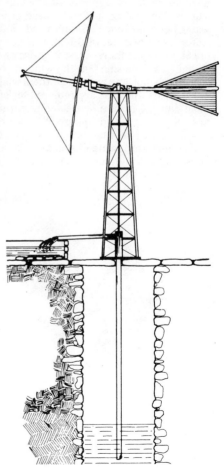

These machines, thousands of which still operate in the plain of Lassithi, were evidently mostly built during the period 1900 to 1950. Many of them were constructed partially from military debris from the two world wars. There seem to be three basic types: 1) those which could have been made by a blacksmith-wheelwright using wood and metal and fastened with wedges and rivets; 2) those which could have been built by mechanics, using mostly metal parts welded or bolted together; and 3) those which have a stone tower instead of a steel one.

"Observations were made on a number of machines in the fully rigged state and in rotation, at wind speeds commencing at 2.2 m/sec (5 mph). A useful output of water appeared at a wind speed of 2.75 m/sec (6 mph). When the wind rose to 3.5 m/sec (8 mph), a four meter diameter machine would run at a speed of up to 25 revolutions per minute (the highest observed)." The author later built a similar waterpumping windmill for testing in Britain, and notes that a four meter machine under full sail would develop power of 220 watts in a wind of 3.5 m/sec (8 mph). "There is no doubt that the Cretan Mill excels in its ability to utilize low windspeeds. This is consistent with the maximum number of operating hours per year and, in an irrigation context, is probably a criterion of excellence...The efficiency of 30% noted in the author's tests compares satisfactorily with that recorded for any other type of windmill."

The Cretan Mill "can hardly be improved for the efficient use of material. Aerodynamically, the low speed efficiency is high and it has an inherent stability against accidental overspeed."

Food from Windmills, MF 21-468, book, 75 pages, by Peter Fraenckel, 1975, £3.50 surface mail from ITDG.

Fraenckel describes adaptation of the Cretan sail windmill to fit the circumstances of an isolated area in Ethiopia. (For design improvements that double the efficiency of these machines, see review of **How to Build a Cretan Sail Windpump for Use in Low Speed Wind Conditions**.)

The report contains drawings and photos of the necessary components. Much of the text discusses the design, problems, and resulting modifications. By "racing" one design against another (rather than getting involved with expensive monitoring devices), the Presbyterian Mission was able to come up with a windmill that would pump at almost twice the rate of a commercial American Dempster multi-blade windmill. (This was partly because the sail windmill, due to its relatively light weight, was constructed so as to sweep a larger cross-sectional area.) The sail windmill also performed better than three Savonius rotor windmills. The most impressive design was a 16-foot diameter rotor, which when rigged with four sails and operating at a static head of 9 feet, was able to pump 1300 gallons of water per hour in a 14.5 mph wind. Water was pumped from a river that had a water level variation of 6 feet; a float was used on the intake system.

The experiments resulted in a design which has 8 arms. The number of sails actually used depends on the wind at the time. The owner/operators put up the sails in the morning and adjust them while the mill is in use; when work is finished in the fields, the sails are removed for safe-keeping (which also protects the mill from damage in case of a sudden storm and high winds). Thus these windmills are not taking full advantage of the 24-hour availability of wind, though in these circumstances the windmills are in operation during the peak wind velocity period.

The sails were made of donated Dacron sail cloth, which was both strong and resistant to the deterioration that comes from continuous exposure to strong sunlight. Cotton is claimed to be not generally strong and long-lasting enough; the kind of cloth sail used in Crete is not identified. Some experimentation was done with detachable aluminum sails, made from surplus roof cappings; these were

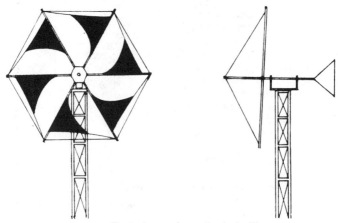

Two views of a sail windmill

claimed to be "readily available and cheaper than Dacron in most areas...more durable than locally-available textile."

By August 1975, 19 windmills of various types were being used by villagers, and another 5 were operating on the mission grounds. The 11-foot design has a cost estimate of US$250-350, almost all of which goes for the steel, the pvc pipe, and the commercially-produced pump. Costs might be significantly reduced in areas with a supply of strong bamboo and wood materials.

How to Build a "Cretan Sail" Windpump for Use in Low Speed Wind Conditions, MF 21-474, construction manual, 56 pages, by R.D. Mann, 1979, £4.95 from ITDG.

This waterpumping windmill design was based on the low-lift windmills which had been built on the Omo River in Ethiopia (see review of **Food from Windmills**), which had themselves evolved from the sail windmills of Crete. The author adapted the design for the lighter winds of the Gambia, and succeeded in nearly doubling the efficiency of the Omo River design. He reports on field testing done in 1978, and provides complete drawings and text for the construction of the windmill.

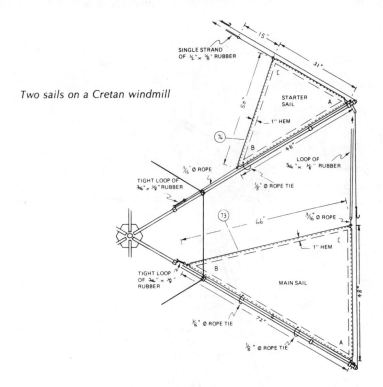

Two sails on a Cretan windmill

This machine was developed for irrigation use on small farms. In this region of the Gambia, there is no wind 31% of the time, wind of more than 12 mph only 6% of the time, and moderate winds to 12 mph 63% of the time. Needed is a windmill that will operate in winds of 5-10 mph. "The wind speed required to start the windpump from rest was calculated to be between 5.2 and 5.6 mph, and once started the windwheel continued to run in a steady wind down to 4.5 mph." During a series of 9-hour pumping trials spread over four months, the windmill lifted 1700 to 3400 gallons of water a height of 13′4″; windspeed averaged 5.1 mph at the low end and 6.75 mph at the high end of this range.

The windmill has 6 sails, three full-sized and three smaller sails that help in starting. There is a 23-foot tower. Estimated cost of the windmill is £750 ($1650). As of this report, the windmill had only been used to operate a lift pump, with a 14′ lift. Future tests will involve a force-pump and 45′ head (lift).

The drawings are separated from the text, making the book a bit awkward to use. However, the drawings can be clipped from the book and spread out separately, and with study they become clear to the reader. There are also 12 photos.

Construction Manual for a Cretan Windmill, MF 21-465, book, 59 pages, by N. Van de Ven, October 1977, available in English and Dutch, $5.00 (single copies free to research institutes in developing countries), from CWD, P.O. Box 85, 3800 AB Amersfoort, The Netherlands.

This is a construction manual for a waterpumping sail windmill similar to the ones found in Crete. This version was built at the Twente University of Technology in The Netherlands.

The low-cost design shown here could be built almost anywhere in the world with

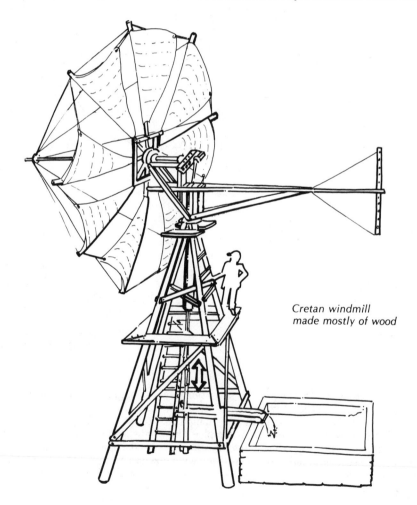

Cretan windmill
made mostly of wood

mostly local materials. It is best suited for low-lift pumping. The rotor diameter is 6 m, but could be made smaller. Sail windmills are especially interesting in areas where the winds are occasionally very high — the sails can be removed and the windmill protected under conditions that would destroy a commercial windmill.

Plans are also included for a pedal-powered woodworking lathe, which can be built with hand tools using wood and a few bicycle parts. The lathe is used in making some of the windmill parts. A shallow borehole, hand-drilling method using locally-made drill bits and augers is shown. A piston pump design is also provided. The manual is well-illustrated, with over 100 photos and drawings.

The Gaudgaon Village Sailwing Windmill, VITA Renewable Energy Series, MF 21-506, booklet, 94 pages, by William W. Smith III, 1982, $6.55 from VITA.

Aspects of erecting low-cost, labor-intensive windmills in rural India are covered in a thorough, if somewhat disjointed, manner. Includes checklists, appendices, scale plans, fabrication techniques, and construction tips that have proven relevant in the author's experience and should be useful for others engaged in similar work with local craftspeople in developing countries.

How to Construct a Cheap Wind Machine for Pumping Water, MF 21-475, leaflet, 13 pages, Brace Research Institute, 1965 (revised 1973), $1.75 from BRACE.

This device is a Savonius rotor, adapted to water pumping for irrigation where windspeeds are 8-12 mph or more, and water level is not more than 10-15 feet below ground.

Brace has tested the unit to find out its potential for low-cost water pumping. "From the tests the following conclusions can be drawn: the Savonius Rotor, although not as efficient as a windmill of comparable size, lends itself to water-pumping for irrigation due to its low initial cost, simplicity of materials and construction, and low maintenance cost...The only important points to be observed in erecting such a machine is the proper choice of the site and careful assessment of the average wind speeds. From this information, the proper pump size and stroke can be chosen from the graphs at the back of this pamphlet." Another graph is included which gives the output at various windspeeds. One pump designed to operate at 10 mph and lift water 15 feet will have an output of 181 Imperial gallons per hour at that windspeed.

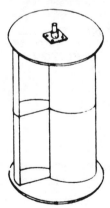

The rotor has been designed in this form for moderate windspeeds and waterlifting up to 30 feet. Brace reports that a fair amount of "experimentation was needed to determine the best location of the pump relative to both the source and the discharge." Design of a simple diaphragm pump is also included.

Performance Test of a Savonius Rotor, Technical Report T10, MF 21-481, technical report with charts and graphs of the test results, 17 pages, by M. Simonds and A. Bodek for Brace Research Institute, 1964, $2.55 from BRACE.

Performance tests were carried out using an 18 sq. ft. rotor on an open site. "It is concluded that a Savonius Rotor pumping system operates quite satisfactorily and is indeed a practical design of windmill. It is, however, only about half as efficient as the conventional fan mill" which costs 4 or more times as much.

Two rotors would thus have the same output as a conventional fan mill, but the total cost would be less than half that of the conventional machine.

"The system seems best suited for pumping in cases where the well-depth does not exceed 20 ft...the windmill should be designed to look after itself safely in storms."

This is clearly an important report for anyone who plans to experiment with Savonius rotors. Torque, power co-efficients, and tip speed ratios are examined.

Savonius Rotor Construction, Vertical Axis Machines From Oil Drums, MF 21-486, booklet, 53 pages, by Jozef Kozlowski, 1977, $5.50 from VITA.

The author "has built two Savonius rotors — one in Wales and the other in rural Zambia. This manual details the construction of these machines...puts the rotors in a perspective which allows potential builders to judge the applicability of such machines for meeting their needs and then provides effective guidelines for constructing each." One of the rotors is for pumping water, and one is for charging automobile batteries.

The rotors are not very effective compared to other low-cost windmills. For example, "The data from Bodek and Simonds' experimental S-rotor in the West Indies shows that the useful energy from a 12 mph wind...means that one can pump 75 Imperial gallons/hour up to 30' above the water level (341 liters/hour up to 9.14 m). In an 8 mph wind...only 25 Imperial gallons/hour (104 liters/hour) can be pumped to the same height." (This compares unfavorably to the 5.4 m Cretan sail windmill, which is reported to pump as much as 15 times this volume of water in an 8 mph wind. Low-cost sail or bamboo mat windmills in Thailand also appear to be considerably more productive.)

The summary of performance data on Savonius rotors and the reviews of other S-rotor publications are useful. The construction details are good, although many of the drawings are poorly reproduced.

THE ROTOR WILL TURN IN WIND FROM ANY DIRECTION

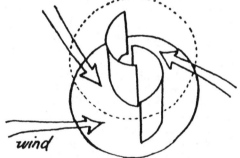

wind

Electric Power from the Wind, MF21-466, booklet, 40 pages, by Henry Clews, 1974, $3.00 from Enertech Corp., Box 420, Norwich, Vermont 05055, USA.

In readable non-technical language, this booklet contains the basics about producing electricity from the wind. Examples are given from Clews' own windgenerator (a commercial unit). A good place to start.

The Generation of Electricity by Wind Power, book, 323 pages, by E.W. Golding, first published in 1955, hardback only, £11.50 from E.F. Spon, North Way, Andover, Hampshire SP105BE, United Kingdom; or $25.00 from Methuen Inc., 733 3rd Avenue, New York, New York 10017, USA.

"First published in 1955...(this book) was soon recognized as the definitive account of the research on wind power undertaken up to that time." With the increasing interest in alternative sources of energy, this classic reference book has been reprinted. Included is an additional chapter outlining the research and technical developments since the book first appeared (brief).

Golding covers: 1) wind behavior and measurement; 2) windmachines (especially windgenerators); and 3) the economic use of wind power under different conditions. There is a chart of English, French and German terms.

Many of the conclusions from Golding's book have been widely accepted and reprinted. The part of this book that remains hard to find in other sources is probably the 135 pages given to wind characteristics and measurement (measuring devices have changed a bit).

Recommended for experimenters who want a more detailed reference book.

Harnessing the Wind for Home Energy, MF 21-469, book, 134 pages, by Dermot McGuigan, 1978, $6.95 from Garden Way Publishing, Schoolhouse Road, Pownal, Vermont 05261, USA.

Here is an introductory book on wind-electric systems, reviewing the basic factors that affect the practicality of such systems, and presenting a mix of experimental (including some large-scale) and proven designs; rapid changes in this field make these somewhat out of date. The book will give the reader an idea of the costs and problems involved in a small wind-electric system. (**Windpower for Farms, Homes and Small Industries** offers a much more thorough treatment of siting and other factors of interest to North Americans considering purchasing a windgenerator.) A list of manufacturers in the U.S., Europe and the U.K. is included.

Matching of Wind Rotors to Low Power Electrical Generators, MF 21-478, book, 85 pages, by H.J. Hengehold, E.H. Lysen, and L.M.M. Paulissen, December 1978, Serial Number SWD 78-3, free to research institutes in developing countries, $8.00 to others, from CWD, P.O. Box 85, AB Amersfoort, The Netherlands.

Here is a much-needed, good presentation of the design choices for the most likely application of windgenerators in the Third World: isolated, rural, low voltage, small capacity systems with battery storage. The text explains a number of design

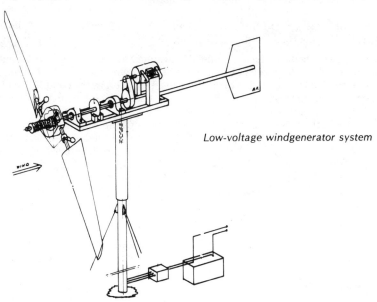

Low-voltage windgenerator system

"rules of thumb" for this kind of application, to maximize daily electricity output while minimizing cost. A good set of charts shows the important relationships between windspeed, power output, rotor diameter, and generator size. Readers will require some knowledge of basic physics, though an appendix explains the operation of a generator.

The authors begin by showing how to use information on the local wind conditions, and the computed energy demand, to calculate the necessary rotor diameter and rated power of the generator. "The emphasis (of the book) lies on the electrical part of the system and its optimum matching to the rotor. . . In the case of rural applications most windgenerators will be used to charge batteries for lighting purposes and to feed radio or TV equipment. Therefore we will limit ourselves here to DC loads, to avoid the complications of computing reactive loads." Particular attention is given to automobile generators and alternators. "These components are not the most suitable for our purpose, but since they are low priced and readily available they cannot be neglected."

Homemade 6-Volt Wind-Electric Plants, MF 21-471, booklet, 19 pages, by H. McColly (Ag. Eng.) and F. Buck (Elec. Eng.), North Dakota Agricultural College Extension Service, 1939 (reprinted 1975), $1.25 from Mother Earth News, 105 Stoney Mountain Road, Hendersonville, North Carolina 28791, USA.

"This publication deals entirely with a homemade wind-driven 6-volt battery charger system which may be used to generate energy to keep batteries charged for radios, autos, and small lighting systems for farm houses and other farm buildings where the energy consumption is not large." The booklet was written for small farmers in the U.S. in 1939, and reprinted in 1975 due to the large current interest in windgenerators.

Dimensional drawings (English units) with text, step-by-step instructions, and many useful hints are given. The blades are hand-fashioned out of wood. This low-cost system charges 2 6-volt batteries and powers several lights, radios, etc. It is designed to charge the storage batteries when the wind velocity is between 15 and 30 mph—probably too high for most situations. (Modification for charging during periods of lower windspeeds would involve either a gearing system, rewinding the generator, or using an alternator.)

The Homebuilt, Wind-Generated Electricity Handbook, MF21-470, book, 194 pages, by Michael Hackleman, 1975, Earthmind/Peace Press, out of print in 1986.

Much of this book is not on homebuilt systems at all, but on how to find and rebuild one of the hundreds of thousands of windgenerators that were manufactured in the United States between 1930 and 1950, before the completion of rural electrification. But there is a lot more to this book that is valuable to the person building his or her own windgenerator.

Potentially the most valuable are the 29 pages of simple explanations and drawings of the control box. "The point of this chapter is to detail the components of the wind-electric controls—how they work. . . If you're building a wind-electric system, this chapter will tell you what you must account for and protect, and how you can do it." Covers relays, voltage regulator, current regulator, and other components (ammeters, voltmeters, fuses, etc.) in non-technical language. There is a very simple design for a control box system for units producing less than 400 watts (see below) and a complete wiring diagram and explanation of the owner-built control box for higher wattage systems.

"Let's trace the path of current in this unit. The generator current goes through the heavy coil on the relay but is blocked by the open switch, so it goes through the smaller winding of wire on the relay. When the voltage from the generator is sufficient to begin charging, the current in this part of the relay will be sufficient to pull in the relay and close the contacts. Now the current will flow into the batteries through the ammeter. When the windspeed drops, the windplant will slow; when it's at a lower voltage than the battery voltage, current will flow in a reverse direction through the heavy wire winding and this will neutralize the magnetic field of the small wire winding portion of the relay and the contacts will open. If the wind is not present, and you want to be sure that all is okay with the windplant, you can hit the PTT (push to test) switch and this will short the batteries out to the generator and motor the windplant; if it starts turning up there, all is okay. If it doesn't, the batteries are dead or the windplant is frozen up or has a broken connection somewhere."

Also covered in this book is the art of tower-raising (57 pages). These are towers in the 40-foot and taller range, that are fully assembled on the ground. This is a rather delicate maneuver, and the text with photos and diagrams seems to cover the do-it-yourself methods nicely.

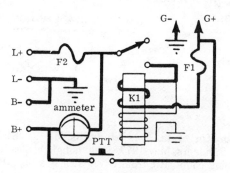

Control box for systems below 400 watts

Wind Power Digest, MF 21-496, quarterly journal, 65 pages average length, $12.00 for 4 issues ($30.00 outside the U.S. and Canada), from Wind Power Publishing, P.O. Box 700, Bascom, Ohio 44809, USA.

Tax credits for investors and legislation requiring electric utility companies to buy surplus power from independent producers led to the construction of thousands of windgenerators in "wind farms" in the period 1981-85 in the United States. **Wind Power Digest** is the journal of the U.S. small-scale windpower industry. In addition to articles primarily of interest to members of the industry, the contents have included how-we-did-it articles by people who use windmills or windgenerators as regular sources of power, ideas from experimenters and notes on new developments from among this informal network, experiences with various home-built and commercially-available windmachines, reviews of new publications and plans for home-built windmachines, and brief summaries of developments by the large scientific institutions.

Simplified Wind Power Systems for Experimenters, MF 21-488, book, 80 pages, by Jack Park, 1975, out of print in 1985.

Most of the windpower information available "requires engineering training or is not complete enough...It is hoped that (in this book) the reduction of complex mathematics into simple graphs and arithmetic problems will allow a greater segment of the innovative public to use the fundamentals an engineer has. To make this book as useful as possible, a page has been devoted to graph reading, and numerous examples are used to illustrate each step in the windmill design process."

Over 50 illustrations and photos of all kinds of windmachines and an equal number of simple graphs and minor drawings are included. This book comes close to reaching

Park's goal of providing "the reader with the engineering tools necessary to accomplish a respectable job of designing and planning the construction of windmills."

Major topics are power required, wind energy available, windmill efficiency, airfoils, windmill augmentation, structural design, and mechanical design. Very little is actually said about pumping water, electrical systems or direct mechanical conversion; you'll have to go elsewhere for this essential information. But for the design of the wind rotor itself, this is a good book to have.

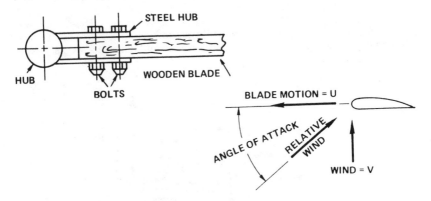

Rotor Design for Horizontal Axis Windmills, MF 21-484, book, 52 pages, by W. Jansen and P. Smulders, May 1977, $5.00 (single copies free to research institutes in developing countries), from CWD, P.O. Box 85, AB Amersfoort, The Netherlands.

"This publication was written for those persons who are interested in the application of wind energy and who want to know how to design the blade shape of a windmill rotor...a lot of attention is given to explaining lift, drag, rotor characteristics, etc...In the selection of a rotor type, in terms of design spread

airfoil name	geometrical description	$(c_d/c_l)_{min}$	α^o	c_l
sail and pole	c/10, c/3, c	0.1	5	0.8
flat steel plate		0.1	4	0.4
arched steel plate	f f/c=0.07	0.02	4	0.9
	f/c=0.1	0.02	3	1.25
arched steel plate with tube on concave side	d, d<0.1c f/c=0.07	0.05	5	0.9
	f/c=0.1	0.05	4	1.1
arched steel plate with tube on convex side	f/c=0.1	0.2	14	1.25
sail wing	cloth or sail, c/10, tube, steel cable	0.05	2	1.0
sail trouser	f/c=0.1, d_{tube}=0.6f, f, c/4, cloth or sail	0.1	4	1.0

Comparison of different blades

and radius, the load characteristics and wind availability must be taken into account...The availability of certain materials and technologies can be taken into account in the earliest stages of design. We therefore hope that, with this book, the reader will be able to design a rotor that can be manufactured with the means and technologies as are locally available."

The reader will need at least a good high school mathematics and physics background and familiarity with abstract technical presentations to be able to use this book.

Horizontal Axis Fast Running Wind Turbines for Developing Countries, MF 21-473, book, 91 pages, by W. Jansen, June 1976, $8.00 (single copies free to research institutes in developing countries), from CWD, P.O. Box 85, AB Amersfoort, The Netherlands.

This is a highly technical report of some work on the design of rotors for high-speed windmachines. The authors argue that "in contrast with airplane propeller design, a maximum energy extraction is reached by enlarging the chords of the blades near the tips."

"A simple method for manufacture of twisted, arched steel plates is given. Six rotors were built of blades that were manufactured with this method."

This report will be of value to readers with an engineering background. "Final conclusion is that with simple materials high power co-efficients are possible."

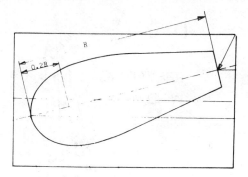

A blade cut from
curved steel plate

Optimization and Characteristics of a Sailwing Windmill Rotor, MF 21-480, report, 82 pages, by M. Maughmer of Princeton University, March 1976, $8.00 (accession no. PB259898) from NTIS.

This is the final report of the Princeton sailwing windmill project. "Through many years of extensive research, the sailwing has been found to provide a simple, light-weight and low-cost alternative to the conventional rigid wing, while not suffering any performance penalties throughout most low-speed applications."

This unusual wind rotor design uses a sail cloth sleeve over a spar and tension cable, instead of a solid blade.

Rapid evaluation of comparative performance of 8 different rotor shapes was made possible by using a test tower mounted on a jeep, and a homemade cup anemometer, demonstrating that effective testing can be carried out at low cost.

Many technical terms are used.

Low Cost Wind Speed Indicator, Publication No. T-113, MF 21-476, single page of blueprints, 1979, $2.50 from Brace Research Institute, MacDonald College of McGill University, Ste. Anne de Bellevue, Quebec, Canada H9X 1C0.

Plans for a simple tilting pointer windspeed indicator. Requires plastic tubing, aluminum sheet and aluminum rod, steel tubing, and a piece of wood.

Vegetation as an Indicator of High Wind Velocity, MF 21-492, and **Trees as an Indicator of Wind Power Potential**, MF 21-491, papers, 35 pages plus bibliography and 21 pages, by J. Wade, E. Hewson, and R. Baker, $2.00 and $1.50 respectively, from Dept. of Atmospheric Sciences, Oregon State University, Corvallis, Oregon 97331, USA.

These papers describe the development of a technique for using trees as indicators of the long-term average winds in a particular place. "Plants provide a quick, at a glance, indication of strong winds and when calibrated by the degree of wind shaping provide a rough, first-cut assessment of wind power potential...This technique could appropriately be used as a first stage in a wind survey prior to instrumentation with anemometers."

A widespread obstacle to the use of windgenerators is that the energy available — and therefore the economic feasibility — varies dramatically from site to site. The approach described here is intended to aid in the selection of sites for windgenerators, which require relatively high average windspeeds if they are to be economically feasible. The basic approach could also be used in identifying sites for waterpumping windmills, but they do not use — and in fact need protection from — the higher winds. New calibrators would be required for species of trees common to other areas, and a substantial amount of long-term windspeed data is needed in order to do such calibrations. Exposure and slope also affect the data.

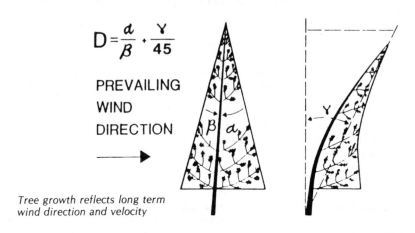

$$D = \frac{a}{\beta} \cdot \frac{Y}{45}$$

PREVAILING
WIND
DIRECTION

Tree growth reflects long term wind direction and velocity

Piston Water Pump, Publication No. T-114, MF 21-482, two pages of blueprints, 1977, $5.00 from Brace Research Institute, MacDonald College of McGill University, Ste. Anne de Bellevue, Quebec, Canada H9X 1CO.

The fabrication and assembly of a piston water pump for use with waterpumping windmills is shown. Materials required include galvanized water pipe and steel rod. Some welding is required.

Energy from the Wind: Annotated Bibliography, MF21-467, (first edition plus three supplements up to 1982), compiled by Barbara Burke, $45.00 in U.S., $50.00 overseas, from Publications Engineering Research Center, Foothills Campus, Colorado State University, Fort Collins, Colorado 80523, USA.

The literature described in this bibliography ranges from "a popular review to a technical aerodynamic study, from do-it-yourself homebuilt projects for house or farm to large scale commercial production for power networks." Some 6300 references are covered. Very few of the documents listed contain any practical construction information, and the index does not identify them for the reader. No addresses are provided for documents. For people with special topic interests and access to a university library, this bibliography will, however, provide very helpful access to a wide literature on the economic, policy and theoretical design aspects of wind power. The center that produced this bibliography is now offering low-cost computer searches of wind energy references.

ADDITIONAL REFERENCES ON ENERGY: WIND

More Other Homes and Garbage, especially for small-scale generation of electricity; see GENERAL REFERENCE.

Traditional Crafts of Persia has a vertical-axis windmill used for grinding grain; see GENERAL REFERENCE.

LeJay Manual has information on homebuilt windgenerators and how to rewind an automobile generator so that when used with a windmachine it will begin charging at a lower rpm; see THE WORKSHOP.

Proceedings of the Meeting of the Expert Working Group on the Use of Solar and Wind Energy has very good coverage of work in the Third World; see ENERGY: GENERAL.

Waterpumping windmills for India are discussed in articles in **Renewable Energy Resources and Rural Applications in the Developing World**; see ENERGY: GENERAL.

Locally-built waterpumping windmills in Peru are pictured in **MINKA**; see PERIODICALS.

Commercially available windgenerators and windpumps are listed in **The Power Guide**; see ENERGY: GENERAL.

Gemini Synchronous Inverter Systems describes an electronic device that allows a windgenerator to be linked directly to the electric grid, thereby eliminating the need for batteries; see ENERGY: GENERAL.

Energy: Water

Energy: Water

For 2000 years, waterpower has been harnessed to do useful work. Waterwheels played a vital role in early industrialization in Europe and North America, powering a wide variety of decentralized manufacturing and processing enterprises. The steel water turbine provided more power at a given site than the waterwheel, and in the U.S. many waterwheel-powered mills were converted to water turbines in the late 19th and early 20th centuries. Blacksmiths and foundrymen produced the turbines and modified the designs during this period of great innovation and profitable production. Water-powered mills produced

". . .such household products as cutlery and edge tools, brooms and brushes. . .furniture, paper. . .pencil lead. . .needles and pins. . .watches and clocks, and even washing machines. . .For the farm they turned out fertilizers, gunpowder, axles, agricultural implements, barrels, ax handles, wheels, carriages. There were woolen, cotton, flax and linen mills. . .tannery, boot and shoe mills. . .and mills turning out surgical appliances. . .and scientific instruments."
—**Renewable Energy Resources and Rural Applications in the Developing World**

The use of waterpower in the People's Republic of China has reflected the same pattern, with first waterwheels and then turbines being built in great numbers as power demands increased along with technical production capabilities. By 1976 an estimated 60,000 small hydroelectric turbines were in operation in south China alone, contributing a major share of the electricity used by rural communes for lighting, small industrial production, and water pumping.

With the rising costs of energy in the United States today, small hydroelectric units are returning in large numbers. Generating stations along New England rivers are being rehabilitated and put back into operation. The number of companies making small waterpower units has jumped. The U.S. Department of Energy has estimated that 50,000 existing agricultural, recreational, and municipal water supply reservoirs could be economically equipped with hydroelectric generating facilities.

In Third World countries, the potential for small hydropower installations has never been carefully measured. Past surveys of hydropower potential have focused on possible sites for large dams, as small hydroelectric units were considered uneconomical or ill-suited to the goal of providing large blocks of electric power for cities, industrial estates, or aluminum production. With the rapidly increasing costs of energy, however, the economics are now much more favorable for small hydroelectric units, which are also well-suited to the needs of rural small communities, and do not bring the degree of environmental disruption associated with large reservoirs. Many small units do not require reservoirs at all, and use small diversion canals instead.

The success of waterpower installations can be greatly affected by forestry conservation practices in the watershed above. Rapid deforestation brings high rates of soil erosion and subsequent rapid silt filling of reservoirs behind dams. At the same time, greater rain runoff causes increasingly violent floods that threaten hydropower installations. During the months following the floods, low water flows are likely to reduce generating capacity. A program to protect the watershed and the construction of a diversion canal may be necessary to prevent damage to a small waterpower installation.

The first requirement in estimating the potential for a small waterpower site is to measure the water flow in a stream during medium and low flow periods, and determine the high water level during flooding. **Low Cost Development of Small Water Power Sites** *is one of several publications that give good stream flow measurement instructions.*

For the construction of very small earth dams, the useful but out-of-print booklet **Small Earth Dams** *may be copied at an appropriate technology documentation center. Also of interest is the soil-cement sandbag technique for low dam construction employed by the Las Gaviotas appropriate technology group in Colombia.*

Waterwheels still have certain advantages for rural Third World communities. The best use of these slowly turning (about 20 rpm) devices is in direct mechanical applications. They can be constructed of locally available materials (e.g. wood and bamboo) by village craftspeople, and they can pump or lift water and perform a variety of important crop processing tasks. They are well suited to the small crop production of small farmers. Existing irrigation channel and small streams offer many potential sites at which the civil engineering works expenses can be minimized.

Industrial Archaeology of Watermills and Waterpower *is one of several publications that offer valuable insights into the design evolution of waterwheels.* **Design Manual for Waterwheels** *contains important figures for the design of overshot waterwheels.* **Overshot and Current Waterwheels** *and* **Water Power for the Farm** *are useful references that were used in rural extension efforts in the 1930s and 1940s and have been recently reprinted.* **Watermills with Horizontal Wheels** *and* **Waterpower in Central Crete** *describe in detail the vertical-axis, horizontal wheel, stone flour and corn mills once widely used in Europe and Asia, and still used in large numbers in mountainous countries such as Nepal.* **Multi-Purpose Power Unit with Horizontal Water Turbine** *gives details of a new Nepalese steel watermill that is proving to be very popular.*

The rapidly turning water turbine, made of steel or cast metals, can deliver a lot of power (e.g. 10-50 kw) from a very small unit, and is much better suited than the waterwheel to the task of producing electricity. Turbines can also be effectively used for direct mechanical applications; they are more efficient than waterwheels, but cannot be made with local materials. The reader interested in water turbines will find **Harnessing Water Power for Home Energy** *a good introduction to the subject, although the case studies are all from single homes in rich countries.* **A Pelton Micro Hydro Prototype Design** *contains an excellent example of a Pelton wheel installation in a village in Papua New Guinea. The Pelton wheel requires a small flow of water that drops 50 feet or more; installations can be built with plastic pipe and a small stream diversion ditch, for minimum environmental impact. Several reports and sets of engineering drawings are included on the cross-flow Banki turbine designs being successfully built in Nepal. These turbines are made of a standard diameter, with blades cut from steel pipe, and they can accommodate a range of flow and head conditions.*

The dissemination of large numbers of small waterpower devices is a challenging task. A very interesting successful experience in this regard is described in **Nepal: Private Sector Approach to Implementing Micro-Hydropower Schemes**.

Micro-Hydropower Sourcebook, book, approximately 250 pages, by Allen Inversin, 1986, $36.00 surface mail ($18.00 to students and volunteers) from NRECA International Foundation, Attn: Micro-Hydropower Sourcebook, 1800 Massachusetts Avenue N.W., Washington D.C. 20036, USA.

The most thorough reference available on small hydropower for developing countries, this book can be used as a primer for those wishing to undertake such projects. The author has personally visited and compiled the stories of many of the most successful small hydropower efforts.

"There are few publications available to serve as a guide to those implementing (microhydropower projects with a capacity of less than about 100kw). Some of these publications deal primarily with larger small-hydropower plants, leaving developers of micro-hydropower sites with few options but to reduce in scale the approaches and designs which are appropriate for large plants. Consequently, such publications tend to encourage the use of approaches and designs which do not take advantage of the unique factors encountered when implementing plants at the 'micro' end of the small-hydropower range, factors which must be considered if this resource is to be harnessed cost-effectively. Other publications are incomplete, leaving out, for example, any but cursory mention of power canals, while a survey of micro-hydropower plants around the world would indicate that such canals are used at a vast majority of sites.

"On the other hand, there is a wealth of experience in developing micro-hydropower sites which has been gained over the last several decades. But those implementing these schemes often have little time or inclination to document their efforts and, therefore, what they have learned cannot serve as a foundation on which others can build. By means of (this book, the author has gathered) information relevant to those implementing micro-hydropower schemes, preparing more complete descriptions of the many aspects of planning and implementation, and documenting some of the experiences around the world."

Included are good presentations of the measurement of head and flow, streamflow characteristics, site selection and layout. The civil works (canals, diversion and intake structures, etc.) are given considerable attention, as they can be very costly. Turbine types are reviewed, along with coupling options (direct, belt and chain drives, gearboxes). Electrical vs. mechanical power, load controllers and flow governors are also discussed.

"It is probably the experience of many individuals working in rural villages that electricity, especially for lighting, is a frequently sought-after amenity. But, at the

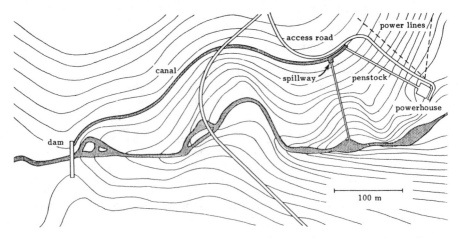

Contour map showing the major components of the 220 kw Buhiga site (Burundi).

same time, it is also clear that, unless the villagers are actually using kerosene for lighting, the financial resources to pay for this amenity are not available. The advantage of generating hydro*mechanical* power is that it forces a focus on mechanical uses of power which probably already exist in a rural community and which normally generate income. Such activities include the milling of grain, the hulling of rice, the expelling of oil from seed, the sawmilling of timber, ginning of cotton, the pulping of coffee berries, and the crushing of sugar cane. A plant generating mechanical power to directly drive agro-processing or workshop equipment has, therefore, a better chance of being viable as well as of being replicable elsewhere in the region."

Highly recommended for use in developing countries. Readers in industrialized countries will find this a valuable supplementary reference.

Micro Hydro Electric Power, Technical Paper #1, MF 22-531, book, 46 pages, by Ray Holland, 1983, £2.50 from ITDG.

This booklet contains a basic introduction to the technologies and economics of

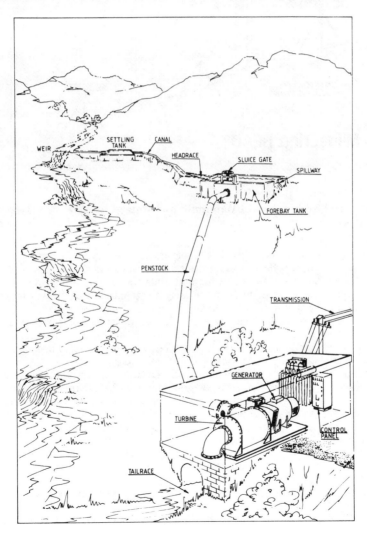

small-scale waterpower plants. Readers intending to build plants will need to refer to other entries in this section, especially the **Micro Hydropower Sourcebook**.

Micro-Hydro Power: Reviewing an Old Concept, MF 22-515, booklet, 43 pages, by Ron Alward, Sherry Eisenbart, John Volkman, 1979, $5.00 from the National Center for Appropriate Technology, P.O. Box 3838, Butte, Montana 59702, USA.

This technical manual, while aimed at those considering installing small hydroelectric systems in the U.S., presents the key considerations in so clear a step-by-step manner that it would be a useful resource for the individual or small community in any region. Most useful as a companion text to more technical reference works. Recommended.

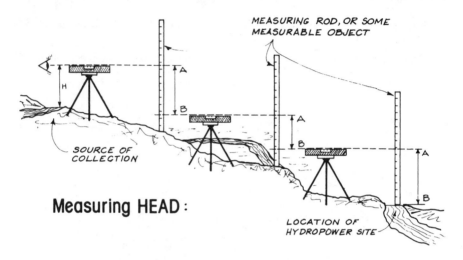

MEASURING ROD, OR SOME MEASURABLE OBJECT

SOURCE OF COLLECTION

Measuring HEAD:

LOCATION OF HYDROPOWER SITE

Industrial Archaeology of Watermills and Waterpower, MF 22-511, book, 100 pages, Schools Council, 1975, Heinemann Educational Books Ltd., out of print in 1985.

This well-illustrated book provides a very good summary of the history of waterwheel development. The reason for design improvements are discussed. This will allow the reader to better judge what materials and designs are needed for a particular application. For example, in the early nineteenth century, a very large slow-running waterwheel would develop high torque on the wooden main shaft, which might cause it to break. This was solved in two ways: by using iron shafts, and by using power drives off of the rim of the waterwheel (the main shaft then had only to be strong enough to support the wheel). Smaller waterwheels, for example, do not necessarily need these more expensive design elements.

By 1850, the British had built a number of very large industrial scale waterwheels, producing 65kw to 190kw of power, and ranging from 7m to 21m in diameter. Some of these waterwheels were kept in operation for 100 years. Such waterwheels would likely be very expensive to build today; but smaller wheels in the range of .3 to .5kw built locally in the rural Third World may be economically viable in many places.

Options for different installations are discussed: water course layout, types of wheel construction, bucket design, mechanisms for flow control, and gearing systems (belts, wooden teeth, iron gears) to take the power off the wheel and run it to the equipment.

The second half of the book is a guide for teaching students about waterwheels. This shows how to measure water flow in a stream, figuring torque on the waterwheel shaft assuming a certain wheel rpm, and calculating horsepower. Several working models can be used to illustrate principles. A brief but informative section on water turbines is included.

Those who want to design waterwheel installations will find this book helpful with its background information and 200 drawings and photos. However, the design formulas (for number of buckets, bucket depth, wheel width and diameter, etc.) that were well-developed by 1850 are not included, and will have to be found elsewhere (for example, in **Design Manual for Waterwheels**).

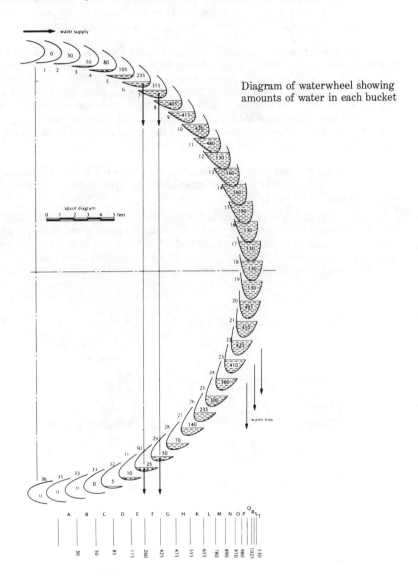

Diagram of waterwheel showing amounts of water in each bucket

Small Scale Hydropower Technologies, MF 22-540, book, 108 pages, by J.J. Tiemersma and N.A. Heeren, $3.50 from TOOL.

This is an introduction to the historical range of small waterpowered devices, including waterwheels, turbines, and other units. We prefer **Industrial Archaeology of Watermills and Waterpower** for the historical coverage.

Water Power for the Farm, Bulletin No. 197, MF 22-525, booklet, 42 pages, by O. Monson and A. Hill, Montana Agricultural Extension Service, 1941, $4.45 from Interlibrary Loan Service, Roland R. Renne Library, Montana State University, Bozeman, Montana 59717, USA.

"Information given here is intended to be helpful in the proper selection and installation of small water power equipment. Directions and specifications are included for the construction of some types of dams and water controls which are practical for use with water power plants." Discusses waterwheels and water turbines, how to estimate the power available in a stream, cost considerations, and methods of power transmission.

The water measurement section is inferior to **Low Cost Development of Small Water Power Sites** and the Popular Science article. But this booklet provides more than the others on electrical systems. There is brief information on switches and wiring, for people not familiar with electricity. A wiring chart gives sizes of wires needed for different transmission distances, voltages, and total capacity. However, it does refer to equipment that is out of date (32 volts) in the U.S.

Another useful chart shows power output at the wheel shaft and from a generator, given different heads and different waterwheels and turbines.

Low-Cost Development of Small Water-Power Sites, MF 22-513, booklet, 43 pages, by H. Hamm of VITA, 1971 (reprinted 1975), Spanish and French editions also available, $5.45 from VITA.

This important booklet is a guide to the desirability, selection, construction, and installation of a small waterpower plant. "The manual begins by describing in simple language the steps necessary to measure the head (the height of a body of water) and flow of the water supply, and gives data for computing the amount of power available. Next it describes the construction of a small dam and points out safety

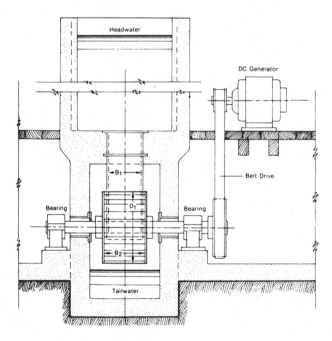

Arrangement for a Michell (Banki) turbine for low-head use without control.

precautions necessary. . . a discussion of turbines and water wheels. . . Guidelines are given for making the right choice for a particular site. . . The manual also describes in detail how to make a Michell (or Banki) turbine in a small machine shop with welding facilities, from usually available pipe and other stock material."

The booklet includes 32 drawings and sketches of different installations and pieces of equipment. The author recommends several companies that manufacture water-power equipment, cautioning that "the hazards accompanying the manufacture of so delicate a machine by do-it-yourself methods and the difficulty of achieving high efficiency should warn the ambitious amateur to consider the obvious alternative of securing advice from a reliable manufacturer before attempting to build his own."

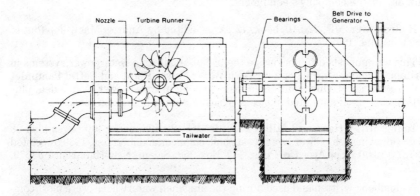

Two views of a Pelton wheel driving a generator. The water comes in under pressure through the pipe at the left, from a source higher than the wheel.

Your Own Water Power Plant, MF 22-510, article with drawings, 16 pages, by C. Basset in **Popular Science** magazine, 1947, reprinted in **Hydropower**.

This is a classic how-to article, written in simple language and covering much of what you need to know to build your own waterpower plant. Its usefulness is underlined by the fact that it has been reprinted so many times recently.

The article covers choice of location for a small dam, the measurement of flow and head with simple common tools, small dam construction, making a wooden flume and wooden overshot waterwheel, and fabricating a Pelton impulse wheel.

This article does not cover the final use of the power produced—neither electricity-generating equipment nor mechanical power are discussed.

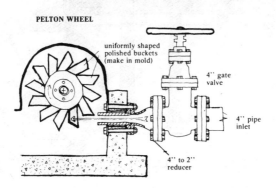

Hints on the Development of Small Water-Power — Leffel Pamphlet "A", MF 22-509, leaflet, 8 pages, free on request from James Leffel and Co., 426 East Street, Springfield, Ohio 45501, USA.

This pamphlet was prepared for those who are thinking of building small water-power plants on small streams to generate electricity. It is intended to give necessary information to people unfamiliar with the general rules and requirements of such developments. Explains the terms "fall" and "head," and how to measure the "head." Includes a simple table for measuring the quantity of water. Discusses the importance of ponds for water storage.

James Leffel and Co. have been manufacturing waterpower equipment for 115 years. The pamphlet is quite useful in itself, and does not require the reader to buy any of the company's equipment.

Hydropower, MF 22-510, book, 72 pages, edited by Andrew MacKillop (out of print in June 1978).

This was published to encourage the use of small-scale waterpower systems in Britain. Includes reprints of **Your Own Water Power Plant** and **Leffel Pamphlet "A"** (see reviews). One additional 6-page article on waterpower is included, plus articles on other unrelated subjects. Written with a humorous tone.

Young Mill-Wright and Miller's Guide, MF 22-528, book, 400 pages plus 28 plates (drawings), by Oliver Evans (watermill engineer and inventor), 1850 (reprinted 1972), $32.00 from Ayer Co. Pubs., P.O. Box 958, Salem, New Hampshire 03079, USA.

A handbook written and used during the era when waterwheels were most common. This is a remarkable, classic book on the use of waterwheels to grind grain into flour and to operate equipment such as saws. The entire book is oriented toward practical applications. The major subjects include the relevant principles of mechanics and hydraulics, descriptions of the different kinds of wheels including tables with proportions and power, descriptions of gears and cogs along with the additional equipment needed for grinding grain into flour, and information for building mills including the wheels and all auxiliary equipment. You can also find short discussions of the strength and durability of teeth of wheels, the bearings and shafts, constructing cogwheels, and mills for hulling and cleaning rice.

"The stones are to be dressed with a few deep furrows, with but little draught,

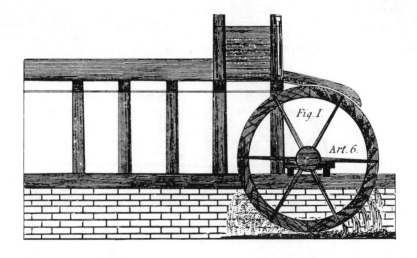

and picked full of large holes; they must be set more than the length of the grain apart. The hoop should be lined inside with strong sheet-iron, and this, if punched full of holes, will be thereby improved. The grain is to be kept under the stone as long as necessary...The principle by which the grains are hulled, is that of rubbing them against one another, between the stones with great force; by which means they hull one another without being much broken by the stones." (From description of "a mill for cleaning and hulling rice.")

The language used may well prove difficult at times for non-native English speakers; old forms are frequently used which may not appear in current two-language dictionaries. There are fewer drawings than we would like to see; they are grouped at the back instead of appearing with the corresponding text. On the other hand, this appears to be by far the most complete book still in print on large, powerful waterwheels.

Mill Drawings, MF 22-517, 30 large sheets, measurements and details, by W. Foreman, 1974, price unknown, from The Society for the Protection of Ancient Buildings, 58 Great Ormond Street, London WC1, England.

Each of these 30 sheets contains a set of perspective and scale drawings of a different old, large watermill installation. These are actual sites, and the drawings include lots of details of the wheels, machinery, and layout of each mill. Some of them are very unusual. There are overshot, undershot, and breast waterwheels shown. A possible source of ideas.

A Design Manual for Water Wheels, MF 22-501, booklet, 71 pages, by William Ovens, 1975, $5.50 from VITA.

This booklet is a result of a Papua New Guinea University of Technology project involving the development of low-cost machinery (waterwheels) to provide small amounts of mechanical power in remote locations. The manual is "for the selection of proper sizes required to meet a specific need and to set out design features based on sound engineering principles" in easily understood language. Wooden overshot wheels were selected as "the most likely choice to give maximum power output per dollar cost, or per pound of machine, or per manhour of construction time." The booklet covers the general principles of bucket design, calculating power output, bearing design (use of wooden bearings recommended), shafts, some information on construction techniques, and waterpumping applications. A set of sample calculations for the design of a village waterwheel/pump combination is given. No specific plans are provided. 2-page bibliography.

The slow speed of rotation of wooden waterwheels (5 to 30 rpm) "is advantageous when the wheel is utilized for driving certain types of machinery already in use and currently powered by hand. Coffee hullers and rice hullers are two which require only fractional horsepower, low speed input. Water pumping can be accomplished at virtually any speed...A usable water wheel can be built almost

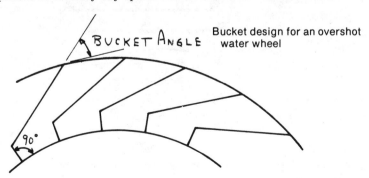

Bucket design for an overshot water wheel

anywhere that a stream will allow, with the crudest of tools, and elementary carpentry skills."

This leaflet's major weakness is the lack of illustrations. There are a variety of graphs, but only 7 drawings — only two of these have to do with the design of the wheel itself. There are 4 good drawings of mechanisms to convert the rotational motion of the wheel into the up and down stroke that a piston pump requires. The piston pump design provided is questionable — it must be cut open for inspection or repair.

Despite the lack of illustrations, we highly recommend this booklet to anyone considering the construction of overshot waterwheels. (See also **Oil Soaked Wooden Bearings**.)

Overshot and Current Water Wheels, Bulletin 398, MF 22-520, booklet, 30 pages, by O. Monson and A. Hill, reprinted September 1975, photocopies $1.85 from Interlibrary Loan Service, Roland R. Renne Library, Montana State University, Bozeman, Montana 59717, USA.

This 1920s booklet is a valuable supplement to others, such as the **Design Manual for Water Wheels** and **Low Cost Development of Small Water Power Sites**. It

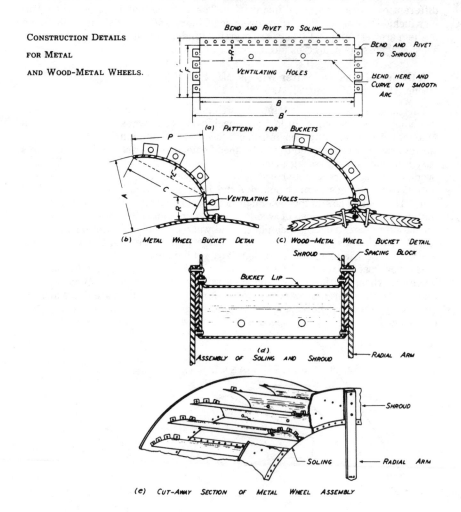

CONSTRUCTION DETAILS FOR METAL AND WOOD-METAL WHEELS.

(a) PATTERN FOR BUCKETS

(b) METAL WHEEL BUCKET DETAIL   (c) WOOD-METAL WHEEL BUCKET DETAIL

(d) ASSEMBLY OF SOLING AND SHROUD

(e) CUT-AWAY SECTION OF METAL WHEEL ASSEMBLY

gives details of bucket construction and mounting, hubs, and bracing for wide wheels. Useful hints are provided on bearings, wheel mountings, and assembly and balancing of the wheel. A chart compares steel shaft diameters to wooden shaft diameters for equal strength in twisting (shear). There is some discussion of the special problems presented by current (undershot) wheels.

This does not include the design formulas needed to design your own waterwheel if you know the available flow and head (height).

Watermills with Horizontal Wheels, MF 22-526, booklet, 22 pages, by Paul Wilson, 1960, 65 pence including postage, from The Society for the Protection of Ancient Buildings, 58 Great Ormond Street, London WC1, England.

This is a survey of the vertical-axis, small "horizontal stone" watermills widely used around the world for 1500 to 2000 years, and still in use today in isolated areas of countries like Nepal. A number of different installations around the world and six different mill wheel designs are shown. These machines are "not as efficient as an overshot or breast wheel, but they have the virtue of simplicity due to the absence of gearing," and they are very cheap to build. (Another book notes

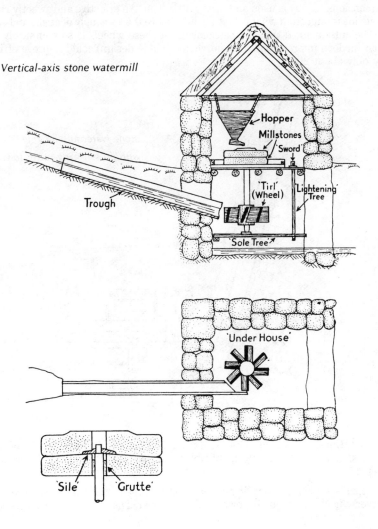

Vertical-axis stone watermill

that this type of mill is able to produce 40 to 50 pounds of cornmeal per hour; Nepalese watermills grind about 30-35 pounds per hour.)

Most of these watermills had a wooden trough bringing fast-moving water to strike the blades of the wheel, with a head of 4-10 feet. Two types of pressurized systems also evolved, one using wooden channels with nozzles, and the other using stone towers with nozzles. "The Aruba Penstock (water tower) was introduced (in Israel), giving much greater efficiency and enabling power to be obtained from quite small flows of water using heads up to 25 or even 30 feet."

On Watermills in Central Crete, MF 22-519, booklet, 8 pages, by N. Calvert, 1973, 40 pence including postage, from The Society for the Protection of Ancient Buildings, 58 Great Ormond Street, London WC1, England.

This is a look at two kinds of waterwheels in Crete. The most interesting one is a traditional vertical axis watermill, that has a stone tower and a pressurized jet with a deflector (almost like a modern high speed Pelton wheel). "The constructional materials are of the simplest and most local description. With one important exception (the millstone) stones are small and unworked, timber is of small dimensions...clay is used and a very little iron. An effective and sweetly running machine is built from what is literally little more than a supply of sticks and stones."

The author notes that the basic layout of these wheels is so technically sound that modern improvements (in nozzle and blade design) could improve efficiency by only about 20%.

Stone watermill in Crete
with pressurizing water tower

New Himalayan Water Wheels, MF 22-538, booklet, 84 pages, by A. Bachmann and Akkal Man Nakarmi, 1983, available from UNICEF, P.O. Box 1187, Kathmandu, Nepal.

Nepal is probably the leading country today in the installation of improved water-driven wheels and turbines for mechanical power. The many photos in this booklet illustrate details of traditional Nepalese watermills and a variety of newer alternatives, both well-established and experimental. The text summarizes the experimental work to late 1983.

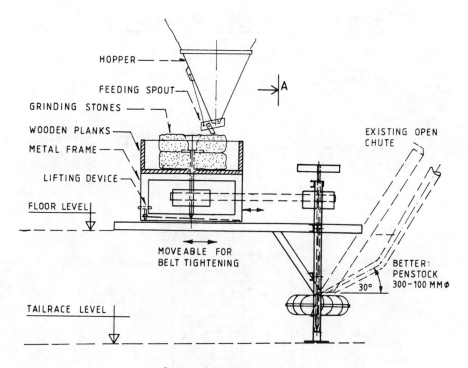

HOPPER

FEEDING SPOUT

GRINDING STONES

WOODEN PLANKS

METAL FRAME

LIFTING DEVICE

FLOOR LEVEL

EXISTING OPEN CHUTE

MOVEABLE FOR BELT TIGHTENING

BETTER: PENSTOCK 300-100 MM∅

30°

TAILRACE LEVEL

Improved Nepalese watermill

Multi-Purpose Power Unit with Horizontal Water Turbine: Basic Information,
MF 22-518, booklet, 60 pages, by A.M. Nakarmi and A. Bachmann, 1983, free from UNICEF, P.O. Box 1187, Kathmandu, Nepal.

An estimated 30,000 ghatta, a traditional water-powered mill, are in use in Nepal. This book describes the Multi-Purpose Power Unit (MPPU), a modular design mill which is based upon the traditional ghatta but is more efficient and can be used to power other machines such as a rice huller, oil expeller, or small dynamo for generation of electricity. Although the MPPU would not typically be constructed entirely on site and the MPPU is more expensive than a ghatta, it is produced in the country, and can be installed and operated under the same conditions as a ghatta. Its simple design makes local maintenance possible. Detailed plans for construction are not presented, but many diagrams and photographs are included so that the basic design concepts for the MPPU are easily understood.

Multi-Purpose Power Unit with Horizontal Water Turbine: Operation and Maintenance Manual, MF 22-536, booklet, 36 pages, by A.M. Nakarmi and Andreas Bachmann, 1984, available from UNICEF, P.O. Box 1187, Kathmandu, Nepal.

This second volume on the Multi-Purpose Power Unit is an operator's manual for the turbine and the milling equipment (small rice huller and oil expeller) commonly used with it in Nepal. Included is a trouble-shooting chart to help identify and solve mechanical problems.

MULTI - PURPOSE   POWER - UNIT

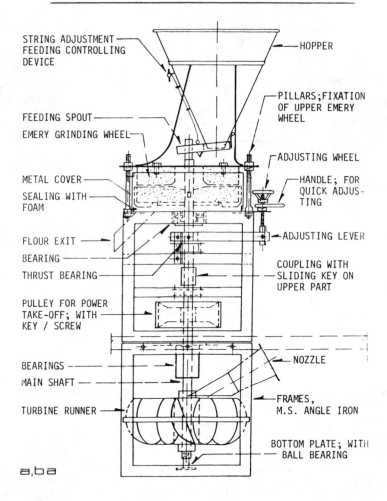

STRING ADJUSTMENT FEEDING CONTROLLING DEVICE

HOPPER

PILLARS; FIXATION OF UPPER EMERY WHEEL

FEEDING SPOUT

EMERY GRINDING WHEEL

ADJUSTING WHEEL

METAL COVER

SEALING WITH FOAM

HANDLE; FOR QUICK ADJUSTING

FLOUR EXIT

BEARING

THRUST BEARING

ADJUSTING LEVER

COUPLING WITH SLIDING KEY ON UPPER PART

PULLEY FOR POWER TAKE-OFF; WITH KEY / SCREW

BEARINGS

MAIN SHAFT

TURBINE RUNNER

NOZZLE

FRAMES, M.S. ANGLE IRON

BOTTOM PLATE; WITH BALL BEARING

a,ba

Nepal: Private Sector Approach to Implementing Micro-Hydropower Schemes, MF 22-537, booklet, 26 pages, by Allen Inversin, 1982, $4.00 surface mail from Small Decentralized Hydropower Program, International Programs Division, National Rural Electric Cooperative Association, 1800 Massachusetts Avenue N.W., Washington D.C. 20036, USA.

Possibly the most successful developing country experience with low-cost steel water turbines (outside of The People's Republic of China) has been in Nepal. Blades for the small turbines, which cost only a fraction of the cost of similar units in industrialized countries, are cut from steel water pipe and welded in place. Production is done in workshops in Kathmandu and Butwal, and the units are trucked and then hand-carried into the inaccessible middle hills. The turbines are sold to mill owners, who use them to drive grain grinders, paddy hullers, and oil presses.

This insightful case study describes the typical mill layout and the organizational structures that have been set up to work with customers, do site surveys and install the units.

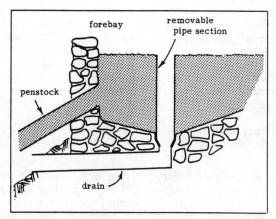

Fig. 25. A removable standpipe recently incorporated in the forebay design facilitates removing the sediment. It also serves as an overflow.

Small Water Turbine, book, 123 pages, by H. Scheurer, R. Metzler, B. Yoder, 1980, from German Appropriate Technology Exchange, Postfach 5180, D-6236 Eschborn 1, Federal Republic of Germany.

This book covers much of the same material as **Nepal: Private Sector Approach**. In addition, background information on the history of the Butwal water turbine program indicates the problems faced and why particular components and fabrication techniques were finally chosen. Technical drawings are provided.

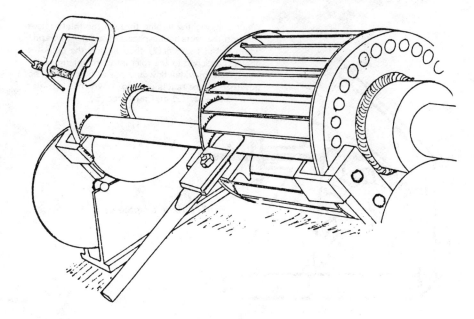

Micro-Hydropower Schemes in Pakistan, MF 22-532, booklet, 38 pages, by Allen Inversin, December 1981, $4.00 surface mail from Small Decentralized Hydropower Program, International Programs Division, National Rural Electric Cooperative Association, 1800 Massachusetts Avenue N.W., Washington D.C. 20036, USA.

Village electrification is being done in Pakistan using a variety of design simplifications, low-cost locally-made turbines, Chinese generators, and village materials and labor. This booklet describes 25 ATDO-sponsored installations in the range of 5-15 kw that attracted great interest and enthusiasm in the villages. The crossflow turbines have rudimentary governing systems. Penstock for water delivery from the canal to the turbine is made of wood or oil drums if the head is less than 6 meters. Costs were US$250-400/kw (1978 dollars).

Local Experience with Micro-Hydro Technology, SKAT Publication No. 11, Vol. 1, MF 22-512, book, 176 pages, by U. Meier, 1981, Swiss Francs 32.00 from SKAT.

A comprehensive examination of the potential for hydropower, particularly micro-hydro (installations producing less than 100 kw), in meeting the energy needs of developing countries. Considerations of technology choice emphasize in-country production and appropriate application of energy, relaxed standards for local manufacture of components, cooperative ownership, and on-the-job training to encourage adoption of this promising energy alternative. Includes case studies, some technical data, bibliography, and a list of institutions and organizations involved in hydropower development. Recommended.

Design of Cross-Flow Turbine BYS/T1, MF 22-502, booklet, 113 pages, edited by U. Meier, 1982, photocopy, Swiss Francs 30.00 from SKAT.

Engineering drawings and parts lists for construction of the BYS cross-flow turbine developed in Nepal, including housing and hand-operated flow control mechanisms. Steel plate and pipe are the construction materials, and a well-equipped metalworking shop is required.

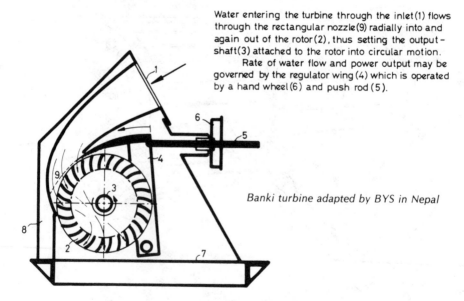

Water entering the turbine through the inlet(1) flows through the rectangular nozzle(9) radially into and again out of the rotor(2), thus setting the output-shaft(3) attached to the rotor into circular motion.
    Rate of water flow and power output may be governed by the regulator wing(4) which is operated by a hand wheel(6) and push rod(5).

Banki turbine adapted by BYS in Nepal

Design of Cross-Flow Turbine BYS/T3, MF 22-503, drawings, by U. Meier, 1982, photocopy, Swiss Francs 30.00 from SKAT.

Similar to **Cross-Flow Turbine BYS/T1**. Produces 10 kw to 20 kw with a 5-70 meter head.

The Banki (Michell) Water Turbine, MF 22-500, booklet, 27 pages, by Mockmore and Merryfield of the Engineering Experiment Station, Oregon State University, 1949, $1.50 in U.S., $2.00 foreign, from Engineering Experiment Station, Oregon State University, Corvallis, Oregon 97331, USA.

This booklet has lots of somewhat sophisticated mathematics and diagrams that explain the theory behind the Banki turbine, filling up most of the text. Oregon State University built an experimental version that worked quite well—a brief discussion of that unit is included.

Small Michell (Banki) Turbine: A Construction Manual, MF 22-524, booklet, 56 pages, by W.R. Breslin, 1979, $7.65 from VITA.

This is basically a reprint of the VITA booklet **Low Cost Development of Small Water Power Sites** (see review), with an expanded (15 page) section on construction of a Banki turbine.

Specifications are given for only one turbine diameter (30 cm), but turbine width can be varied to accommodate different volumes of water. The plans require 10 cm diameter steel water pipe for the turbine blades, and steel plate for the sides and nozzle. Welding, cutting and grinding tools are needed. The turbine can be used for direct drive of agricultural equipment or for producing electricity. (You will have to look elsewhere for the information to help you set up a proper electrical installation.)

A site with a head (total height water will fall) of 25 feet (7.6 m) and a flow of water of 2.8 cubic feet per second (81 liters per second) would produce about 6.3 hp (4.8 kw) of power at the turbine. Transmission losses or generator losses can be expected to cut this by ⅓ to ½.

Manual for the Design of a Simple Mechanical Water-Hydraulic Speed Governor, MF 22-514, booklet, 40 pages, by U. Meier, 1980, photocopies Swiss Francs 4.00 from SKAT.

This manual describes the mechanical speed governing system developed by Balaju Yantra Shala (BYS) in Nepal to control their cross-flow turbine. Schematic drawings help explain the operation of the unit, and detailed drawings provide information for construction of the key load-regulating valve.

"It is mostly cost that has stood in the way of speedy and large scale development of small hydro power potentials (in developing countries). Imported and sophisticated equipment becomes costlier and costlier and is in most cases not economically feasible. This applies mostly to hydraulic equipment such as water turbines, accessories and governing devices. The case is different for alternators and switchgear which are produced in great number in industrialized countries and are therefore relatively cheap."

"Experience in Nepal shows that it is possible to reduce costs of hydro electricity generation projects vastly by minimizing civil engineering and structural works and by producing hydraulic equipment in local workshops with simple designs and technology."

"Nonavailability of a simple mechanical governor has long been a major obstacle in implementing small hydro projects with acceptable standards of safety. The Swiss Association for Technical Assistance, Helvetas, in Zurich has sponsored a project to develop a simple governor that would be sufficiently accurate and reliable and could be manufactured by local workshops in Nepal . . . A prototype was built and tested in early 1979. The governor was designed for operating the gate of a cross-flow (Banki) turbine, but may in fact be utilized on the flow regulator of any turbine. . .this construction manual may enable other organizations and individuals to adapt this governor to their own needs and improve it further as a contribution to the design of simple but reliable hydraulic equipment for small electricity generation units."

The Dhading Micro-Hydropower Plant: 30kWe, MF 22-506, booklet, 29 pages, by U. Meier, 1983, $4.50 from SKAT.

This paper describes a micro-hydropower plant using a BYS MWH/P-governor and complements **Manual for the Design of a Simple Mechanical Water-Hydraulic Speed Governor**. Diagrams and photographs include a hydraulic profile of the turbine, a schematic of governor hydraulics, a proposed hydraulic damping arrangement, and photographs of equipment installed. General information presented includes technical specifications, plant performance and operation, plant safety, and a summary of the data collected.

The Segner Turbine: A Low-Cost Solution for Harnessing Water Power on a Very Small Scale, MF 22-522, booklet, 13 pages, by U. Meier, M. Eisenring, and A. Arter, 1983, $2.00 or Swiss Francs 4.00 from SKAT.

This very simple turbine is currently being produced in Nepal for US$670 (1983 prices). The history and operation of the turbine are presented along with basic

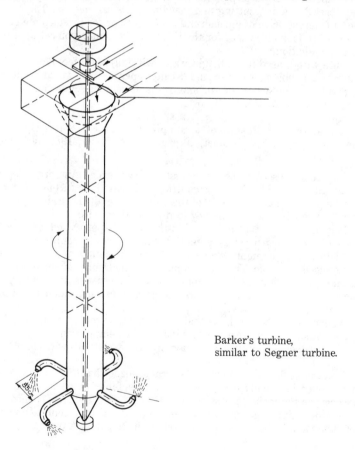

Barker's turbine,
similar to Segner turbine.

design details. The authors find that for Nepal the Segner turbine is only economical for certain functions such as oil extraction and rice hulling. The traditional ghatta was found to be more economical for milling of grains, and the Segner turbine cannot be scaled up sufficiently to replace the standard turbine for applications requiring a high power output.

Small Hydropower for Asian Rural Development, book, 353 pages, edited by Colin Elliott, 1981, $22.50 to developing countries, $30.00 to developed countries, from Renewable Energy Resources Information Center, Asian Institute of Technology, P.O. Box 2754, Bangkok, Thailand.

This well-matched set of conference papers provides a good introduction to the technical, environmental, and financial aspects of micro and mini (10 kw to one MW capacity) hydroelectric plant development. More extensive than **Small Hydroelectric Plants**, this volume also includes some case studies from Asia; most of the text would be relevant in any developing country. For readers interested in rural electrification using hydropower, this is a good place to start.

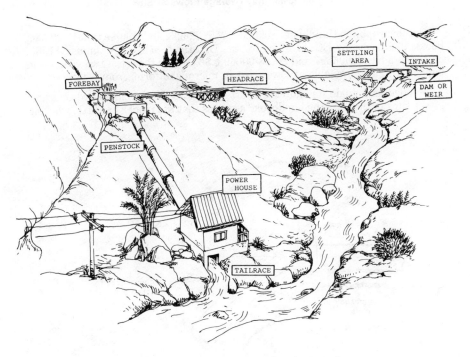

Typical installation with canal and penstock.

Small Hydroelectric Powerplants, MF 22-539, book, 333 pages, 1980, $20.00 surface mail (photocopies only) from Small Decentralized Hydropower Program, International Programs Division, National Rural Electric Cooperative Association, 1800 Massachusetts Avenue N.W., Washington D.C. 20036, USA.

The English and Spanish text side by side in this volume cover some of the same ground as **Small Hydropower for Asian Rural Development**, but with case studies from Latin America. This too is a compendium of conference papers. Typical installations are described. A glossary is included.

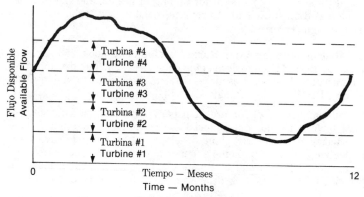

Figure 7. Monthly Average Flows at Site

Microhydropower Handbook, Volume 1, MF 22-533, and Volume II, MF 22-534, books, 920 pages, by EG&G Idaho for the U.S. Dept. of Energy, January 1983, documents DE83-006697 and DE83-006698, $69.90 for the set of two volumes in paper form, also available at lower cost in microfiche form, from NTIS.

Intended as a guide for individuals attempting to develop small hydroelectric power sites in the U.S., the handbook "assumes that the reader has little working

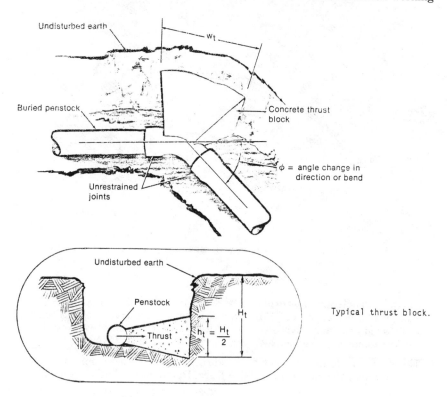

knowledge of hydropower or the engineering concepts behind the use of hydropower." The authors have attempted "to provide a mechanically proficient lay person with sufficient information to evaluate microhydropower site potential, lay out a site, select and install equipment, and finally, operate and maintain the complete system. The actual construction details of the site are not included; rather, pointers are given as to what help he should expect from a construction contractor, and general guidelines on construction details are provided. In addition, information about obtaining financing and permits is provided. To help offset the cost, the person performing the work, referred to as the 'developer', is encouraged to do as much of the work as possible."

This is probably a necessary book for people in the U.S. who wish to develop a microhydropower site and sell the power to the utilities. Where to get government streamflow data and the necessary permits are among the topics discussed that are essential in the U.S. but irrelevant elsewhere. The two volumes are lengthy and expensive, but probably represent the most accessible in-depth presentation of the technical considerations for anyone without a previous background in the field who is seriously interested in developing a site (e.g. of 100kw potential).

For Third World based projects, the **Microhydropower Sourcebook** by Inversin will be much more helpful than this book, as it concentrates on the different problems and opportunities found in these places.

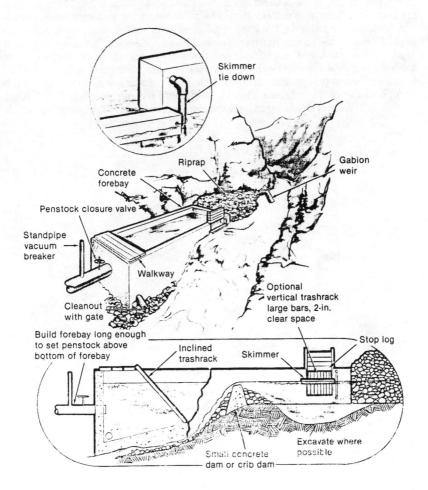

Mini Hydro Power Stations (A Manual for Decision Makers), MF 22-535, book, 163 pages, UNIDO, 1981, document #UNIDO/IS.225, available from UNIDO.

This manual provides project managers with an overview of the steps and considerations involved in the establishment of medium-scale ("mini") hydroelectric units, from prefeasibility studies to operation and maintenance. Common problems are noted, as are advantages and disadvantages of different materials and operational structures. For the intended audience, this should prove to be a useful reference. The reproduction quality of the text (particularly the charts which are often too small to read) is below average; this is likely to be corrected when this material is reissued as part of UNIDO's Development and Transfer of Technology series.

Directory of Manufacturers of Small Hydropower Equipment, MF 22-530, booklet, 71 pages, by Allen Inversin, 1984, $4.00 surface mail from Small Decentralized Hydropower Program, International Programs Division, National Rural Electric Cooperative Association, 1800 Massachusetts Avenue N.W., Washington D.C. 20036, USA.

A good summary of cost-saving strategies for small hydropower installations (1-1000 kw range) starts off this volume. This is followed by a description of manufacturers worldwide, some of them quite small, and some of them located in developing countries. This information should be quite helpful in obtaining price quotes.

A "method for reducing the cost of a hydropower installation which is gaining popularity is to use pumps in reverse as turbines...Because they are often massproduced by numerous manufacturers, costs are reduced. Since they are standardized and available off-the-shelf, delivery times are minimized...One major difference between pumps and turbines is that the former are designed to operate under a single set of conditions. There is no efficient way of controlling flow through a pump...(However) by using at least two pumps, preferably of different capacities,

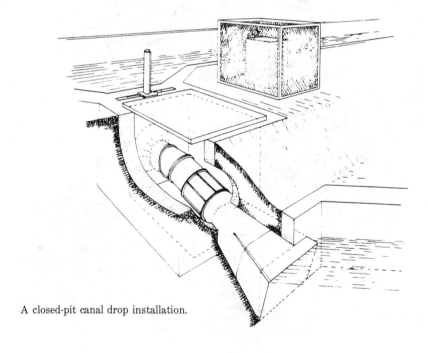

A closed-pit canal drop installation.

it is possible to harness a significant portion of the energy available in varying flows . . . the relatively low cost of pumps still permits the economical use of multiple units for power generation."

Cost Reduction Considerations in Small Hydropower Development, MF 22-529, paper, 12 pages, by D. Minott and R. Delisser, 1983, publication no. ID/WG.403/21 from UNIDO.

A useful summary of alternative materials for penstock construction is the unique feature of this brief paper. PVC, wood stave, fiberglass-reinforced polyester and asbestos cement penstocks are discussed.

"PVC pipes can be supplied to withstand heads of over 150 meters so long as an appropriate method of making joints is utilized to guarantee proper sealing. Although in many developing countries it is not possible to obtain PVC pipes in excess of 5 meters long with more than a 12 inch internal diameter, it is possible and even desirable where required to run two pipes in parallel in order to approximate a larger diameter penstock. But PVC has a low impact resistance and becomes fragile from prolonged exposure to sunlight ultraviolet radiation, so it is recommended that such penstocks be installed underground to increase the life of the installation."

Harnessing Water Power for Home Energy, MF 22-507, book, 112 pages, by Dermot McGuigan, 1978, $6.95 from Garden Way Publishing, Schoolhouse Road, Pownal, Vermont 05261, USA.

This is a good book for someone who wants to learn about the different small-scale water turbines that can be used to generate electricity. The Pelton wheel, Turgo impulse wheel, Banki (Ossberger) cross-flow turbine, and Francis turbine are shown in a total of 6 actual installations in England and the United States. Costs are provided for many of these examples. Only the Pelton wheel and Banki turbine are really suitable for construction in a small workshop. Manufacturers of turbines and whole systems are listed from around the world.

Useful notes are included on alternators, transmission drives, dams, and the electronic governor (a device which switches part of the electric current away from the main line — to heat water, for example — when the electric demand falls; this

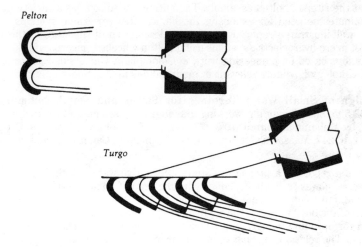

Fig. 12. Turgo and Pelton turbines contrasted. The jet on the Turgo strikes three buckets continuously, whereas on the Pelton it strikes only one. A similar speed increasing effect can be had on the Pelton by adding another jet or two.

eliminates the need for an expensive mechanical governor which regulates the amount of water flowing through the turbine).

There are many drawings and photos, but these are poorly explained. Electrical circuitry is not shown, and mechanical governors are not explained. Waterwheels are only briefly covered in a few pages. The examples are all single homes in rich countries, using large amounts of electricity. The language is relatively easy to understand, although a number of waterpower engineering terms are used without explanation.

You will not be able to build anything from the information contained in this book, but you can get a better idea of what would be required to install a small waterpowered electric system, on a useful scale for village electrification.

A Pelton Micro-Hydro Prototype Design, MF 22-521, report, 41 pages, by Allen R. Inversin, June 1980, exchange your publication with Appropriate Technology Development Unit, P.O. Box 793, Lae, Papua New Guinea.

"Is it possible that introducing electricity into rural villages could be one factor towards rejuvenating life in these villages? Can a technically and socially appropriate system with active villager participation in the planning, installation, management, and evolution of their own scheme have beneficial effects?"

"This report describes work to date on a modular design for a Pelton micro-hydro generating set with an electrical output up to. . .5 kVA and with a 'typical' installation cost of about K300/kVA ($400/kw) including penstock costs. . .This is less expensive than diesel generating sets, and, when recurring costs are included, less costly than both diesel and petrol. Also covered briefly are ideas on governing, bucket design and prototype performance, and cost/kw of PVC penstock pipe for different site configurations and pipe diameters."

Pelton wheels requiring a head of 50 feet or more were chosen, due to the mountainous terrain and small water flow required by these units. General design guidelines were to develop a low-cost but rugged design, which could be locally fabricated with a minimum of special skills, and which could be easily installed with little site preparation.

Notable design simplifications include: 1) a low-cost easily-made iron pipe cover for the main shaft, which prevents water from entering the bearings; 2) use of holes in steel plate to replace nozzles; 3) pulley substitution to adjust for actual head at the site; 4) bolted assembly. The author also discusses a variety of ways to eliminate the need for expensive mechanical flow governing systems.

This well-illustrated report is a valuable description of the state of the art of low-cost micro-hydroelectric systems using Pelton wheels. It incorporates ideas and suggestions based on pioneering work in Colombia at Universidad de los Andes. The technology is widely relevant in mountainous areas of developing countries.

Design of Small Water Turbines for Farms and Small Communities, MF 22-505, book (including working drawings for a selected water turbine), 163 pages, by Mohammad Durali, 1976, $7.00 from Technology Adaptation Program, Room E40-247, Massachusetts Institute of Technology, Cambridge, Massachusetts 02139, USA.

This is a report of a project "to study alternative water turbines producing 5 kw electric power from an available hydraulic head of 10 m and sufficient amount of flow, and to recommend one for manufacture," for use on Colombian coffee farms.

Much of the book presents the sophisticated mathematics and physics of turbine design for optimum performance. This requires some technical training to comprehend. The relationships between the various elements in the design are given in equations, allowing choice for simplicity in particular elements.

The design criteria included: simplicity of operation and maintenance (the machine is intended for use by farmers with little technical knowledge); and lower cost of electric power over the life of the machine when compared with transmitted power from the main electric grid. Choice of turbine would be determined in part by which of two production alternatives was selected: 1) use of a simple workshop capable of welding, drilling, and cutting steel parts (local farming area production); or 2) use of more sophisticated production methods like casting and molding with some plastic parts (industrial production at a centralized level).

"The work consisted of the preliminary design of different types of water turbine which could be used for this application. Then one was selected and designed completely. A complete set of working drawings was produced for the selected type."

"Four different types of water turbine were studied: a cross-flow (Banki); two types of axial-flow turbines; and a radial-flow turbine. Each one has some advantages and some disadvantages (explained in the text). One of the axial-flow turbines...was chosen for detailed design as presenting the optimum combination of simplicity and efficiency."

The materials range from riveted pieces of thin-wall steel tubing for the blades, wooden bearings, and bicycle sprocket/chain drive (Banki turbine) to molded, extruded, or cast plastic blades (axial-flow turbine).

"A big portion of the price of each of the units is the generator cost. The rest of the construction cost seems likely to be similar for all units for small scale production. For large scale production the cross-flow will be much more costly than the axial-flow types. This is because the material cost for the axial-flow machines is small but initial investments for molds and dyes are required."

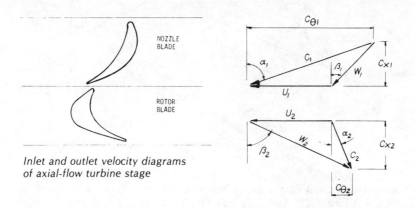

Inlet and outlet velocity diagrams
of axial-flow turbine stage

Design of Small Water Storage and Erosion Control Dams, MF 22-504, booklet, 79 pages, by A.D. Wood and E.V. Richardson, 1975, publication PN-AAB-118, $12.49 from AID/DIHF, 722 47th Street, Chevy Chase, Maryland 20815, USA.

Covers design criteria and construction methods (mechanical and manual) for small earth- and rock-filled dams. Includes discussion of several types of ponds, foundation conditions, and water uses, with special attention to outlet spillways. An appendix covers seepage and its influence upon design. The text is somewhat dense and a bit dry in style, but contains much useful information.

Small Earth Dams, Publication No. 2867, MF 22-523, booklet, 23 pages, by Lloyd Brown, 1965, U.S. Dept. of Agriculture, out of print 1980, contact an appropriate technology information center for a photocopy.

This introductory booklet has practical suggestions for those who want to build small dams to make ponds for irrigation or watering animals. Although the focus is on U.S. climate and methods, the booklet could be useful as a starting point for building low-head dams for micro-hydroelectric systems anywhere. The information is only for use in small (6 feet and under) dams and those dams that back up a limited amount of water. There are suggestions for selecting a site, a few hints on construction, and maintenance and management practices for the reservoir and spillway (water outlet).

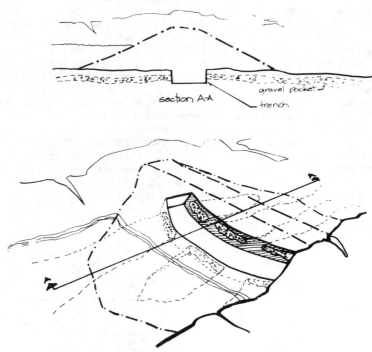

Trench dug and filled to prevent leaks
or failure of small earth dams

Micro-Hydro: Civil Engineering Aspects, MF 22-516, paper, 11 pages, by D. Mansell, G. Atkins and S. Kiek, free from Dr. Don Mansell, Appropriate Technology Section, Faculty of Engineering, University of Melbourne, Parkville, Australia 3052.

This paper identifies "some of the aspects of small hydro-electric schemes which are of particular concern to the civil engineer, and provides some guidance to non-engineers who wish to build such power sources . . . (includes) facts, problems and ideas which may be of interest to a person wishing to investigate the feasibility of a small scheme."

Discusses calculations for low flows, flumes and channels (earth, timber, concrete, and steel), and soil problems in small earth dams. The perspective is that of using local materials for small waterpower schemes in isolated rural areas.

"It is possible to build small dams with reasonable certainty of success with the use of a little simple technology. Such dams should not exceed 5 meters in height."

ADDITIONAL REFERENCES ON WATER POWER

Renewable Energy Resources and Rural Applications in the Developing World describes the evolution of the waterwheel and water turbine in rural industry in Europe, the United States, and present-day China; see ENERGY: GENERAL.

The Power Guide contains information on commercially available water turbines and a stream flow water pump; see ENERGY: GENERAL.

Hydraulic ram pumps are the subject of several publications reviewed in WATER SUPPLY.

More Other Homes and Garbage; see GENERAL REFERENCE.

Teknologi Kampungan includes several traditional Indonesian waterwheels; see GENERAL REFERENCE.

Energy: Solar

Energy: Solar

Increasingly, the term "solar technology" is being used to include any renewable energy system that directly or indirectly depends on the sun for energy. This includes waterpower, windpower, biogas, and wood fuels, for example, which we are covering in separate chapters. This chapter is therefore concerned with direct use of solar energy.

Probably the most significant direct solar technology for the Third World is that of crop drying, which is covered in the chapter CROP DRYING, PRESERVATION AND STORAGE. Solar distillation for water purification has been covered in the WATER SUPPLY chapter.

In this chapter you will therefore find materials on passive solar architecture for house heating, passive solar cooling for the tropics, solar greenhouses, water heaters, cookers, irrigation pumps, and photovoltaic cells. A good general survey of the technologies that may some day have relevance for the Third World can be found in **Technology for Solar Energy Utilization**; *most of these, however, are not economically competitive at present.*

Several publications on passive solar architecture, now a booming field in the United States, are included. Passive solar design involves careful choices of building orientation, layout, location of glass windows, and materials, to best take advantage of natural energy flows. Because they minimize the use of costly primary fuels for space heating and cooling, passive solar buildings will eventually dominate new construction in much of the United States. In North America and other parts of the temperate zones, heating is usually the primary design objective. This is also true in parts of the Himalayas, the Andes, and other mountainous regions, where indigenous structures often reflect certain passive solar principles. In these areas of the Third World there is the potential for new applications of recent advances in the field. By contrast, the cooling of living spaces is the primary object of passive solar design in the tropics. **Elements of Solar Architecture for Tropical Regions** *and* **Design for Climate: Guidelines for the Design of Low-Cost Houses for the Climates of Kenya** *introduce the basic design considerations for passive solar cooling.*

Conventional greenhouses consume large quantities of energy to control the climatic conditions inside. Solar greenhouses, on the other hand, are heated primarily by the sun, and are often attached to houses to provide home heating as well. Low-cost designs using plastic sheeting and local materials may be of relevance in the mountainous regions of the Third World for supplementary home heating and food production. In the tropics greenhouses are probably mainly of interest because the vegetables grown inside require less water. Several publications reviewed here offer a look at current U.S. solar greenhouses.

Solar water heaters for domestic hot water are becoming more widely used in industrialized nations as a response to the "energy crisis." They are well suited to temperate regions. A typical system consists of a flat plate collector and storage tank which holds water heated to about 140 degrees Fahrenheit (60 degrees Centigrade).

In tropical regions, solar water heating systems can provide hot water for bathing, washing clothes and other uses. (Water heated in a normal flat plate collector does not boil, however, so this is not directly suited to water purification schemes.) Solar water heating in these circumstances is probably best used in health centers and urban homes where there is already a demand for hot water. Kathmandu, Nepal is a good example of a Third World city with a well-established solar water heater industry.

For developing countries, the cost of materials for solar water heaters may make them rather expensive. There are more than a dozen ways to make a basic flat plate collector; there is some potential for very low-cost designs, particularly if a low-pressure (gravity-fed) system is being used. Such collectors can use metal other then copper, and even replace pipes altogether by using shallow tanks. The insulating material behind the collector plate can be local natural fiber such as coconut husks or rice hulls.

Solar cookers have been mentioned as a possible alternative in fuel-short and deforested regions. The 1962 publication **Evaluation of Solar Cookers** *offers a look at many designs, including most of those still being tested today. The high cost, awkward operation, slowness, and inconvenience of outdoor cooking have prevented this technology from finding a niche. Nevertheless, these devices remain a fixture at research centers and exhibitions, where they regularly amaze visitors. To our knowledge, despite two decades of scattered attempts, there are no examples of the successful introduction of solar cookers.*

The use of solar energy to drive engines for irrigation water pumps has recently received a great deal of attention. In this application, flat plate collectors provide hot water, which is used to heat liquid gas. The gas expands, and drives the engine. The gas then passes through a condenser, where it is cooled by the well water, and the cycle is then repeated. This appears to be one of those solar energy applications that is technically but not economically feasible in developing countries. Though the costs appear to be dropping below $25,000 per installed kw of capacity (the level of a few years ago) they are a long way from being affordable. Locally-built water-pumping windmills appear to be a far more cost-effective alternative in areas with even relatively low average windspeeds. In fact, the most thoroughly tested solar pump designs seem likely to remain technological deadends, built in poor countries only through the intervention of rich country aid programs. Some of the completely new concepts in solar pump designs may prove more fruitful.

Photovoltaic cells that produce electricity from sunlight may have a place in water-pumping in the future if their price comes down significantly. (For an economic analysis of several solar pumping projects, see "Economics of Renewable Energy Systems" *by David French.) Solar pumping systems can be designed without electrical storage equipment. Yet these will present considerable foreign exchange problems, as the very high technology production requirements will prevent domestic production in all but the most technically advanced developing countries. Solar cells seem less likely to be economically attractive for most rural uses. Whereas the decentralized energy production offered by solar cells is well matched to Third World settlement patterns, electricity is not an energy form well matched to the energy needs of these communities. A whole assortment of electrical equipment would be needed to store and make use of the solar electricity, and very little of this equipment could be produced or afforded in the villages. The exceptions to this are photovoltaic-powered remote communication equipment, slide projectors for extension work, and other small lighting devices, usually paid for by governments or development organizations.*

The sun's energy is "available" everywhere, yet it is also a diffuse or low-grade energy form. This means that while solar energy is an excellent, low-cost means of creating temperature differences of tens of degrees for drying and heating, it is inevitably difficult and expensive to collect and concentrate solar energy to generate electricity or perform mechanical work. For this reason, drying, heating, and cooling are today the most practicable solar applications for most Third World communities.

Technology for Solar Energy Utilization, Document No. ID/202, MF 23-563, 1977 conference report, 155 pages, 1978, in English, French, or Spanish, free to local groups in developing countries, $12.00 to others, Sales No. 78IIB, from United Nations Industrial Development Organization, P.O. Box 300, A-1400, Vienna, Austria.

This is a good overview of some solar energy technologies that may eventually have relevance for developing countries. Most of the solar technologies presented are technically feasible and proven. Because they are unusual they have attracted the attention of scientists and engineers looking for exciting new technologies to work on. Yet most of these technologies are far too expensive for the Third World. Indeed, probably the majority of the technologies presented would at present be reasonable only in an isolated desert region of a rich country. On the other hand, some of these technologies may one day prove economically attractive.

A good state-of-the-art review at the beginning of the book concludes that solar distillation, solar drying, and solar water heating (if needed) are currently attractive in some circumstances. Solar engines, solar water pumps, solar photocells for electricity, and solar refrigeration are labeled not yet attractive. Later, in the contributed articles, favorable evaluation is made of solar timber kilns for decentralized applications, and Tom Lawand provides a thoughtful examination of the potential for solar cookers and solar dryers. The rest of the articles (a solar electric power plant, conversion of solar into mechanical energy, water pumps, flat plate collectors, refrigeration and cooling, active space heating and cooling) review technologies which cost far more than the poor can afford.

UNIDO suggests the local manufacture of low temperature solar devices in the near future and applied research and development efforts for high temperature applications in the more distant future.

Recommended as a reference book for those active in the solar energy field in developing countries.

Solar Water Heaters in Nepal, MF 23-560, book, 27 pages, by Andreas Bachmann, 1977, from SATA, Box 113, Kathmandu, Nepal.

Here is a rare example of a book on solar water heating from a developing country. BYS (Balaju Yantra Shala) Plumbing Division has built systems in Nepal to supply

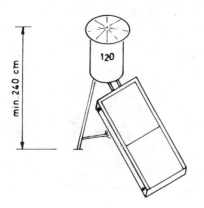

120 liter solar water heater in Nepal

hot water for bathing, washing clothes and cooking. While no detailed drawings are presented, the BYS designs are discussed, component by component. Specifications for the collector and storage tank are given, along with qualitative descriptions of construction and maintenance procedures.

Two systems are described: 1) a thermosiphon (natural circulation) system with separate collector and storage tank, and 2) a "flat tank" collector, where the collector also functions as the storage tank. This is less expensive, but only supplies a small amount of heated water at a time.

A Solar Water Heater Workshop Manual, MF 23-559, construction manual, 82 pages, 1979, $7.00 plus $0.75 postage from Ecotope Group, 2812 East Madison, Seattle, Washington 98112, USA.

This manual is designed to be used in a teaching situation, with an experienced leader who can provide background knowledge and teach construction techniques. Four pages are devoted to organizing a training workshop.

Ecotope Group and Rain Magazine staff have run these workshops in the Northwestern U.S. for several years, usually teaching 30 or more people from a community organization to build a solar water heater in a two day period. By teaching members of existing groups together, skills are transferred to a naturally supportive network, and more solar water heaters are likely to be eventually constructed. This approach could be used anywhere, with many different technologies.

The manual contains step-by-step instructions, with drawings, for building and installing a solar water heater. This includes siting the system, piping for natural circulation, and various open and closed loop storage alternatives.

Teaching solar water heater construction to a group

Bread Box Water Heater, MF 23-531, one large sheet of plans, $3.00 surface mail or $3.40 foreign airmail from Zomeworks, P.O. Box 25805, Albuquerque, New Mexico 87125, USA.

Drawings and a description of the principles, design, and construction of a simple and effective solar water heater are provided.

"Two tanks are painted black and placed in a glass-covered insulated box with insulated reflecting doors—the sun shines through the glass onto the tank and also bounces off the reflecting doors onto the tanks...The reflectors on the box serve to wrap the sun around the tanks rather than focus the sun on the tanks...The doors are opened during the day to receive the sun and then closed at night to conserve heat.

"The plans describe the construction of a solar hot water heater using two 30-gallon electric hot water tanks with electric back-up. (30-gallon drums can be substituted for the water heater tanks.) The plans also discuss the principles of the design so that an interested person can vary the construction and know generally what to expect. The plans stress the relative importance of different aspects of the design—where you must be very careful and where you need not be so careful."

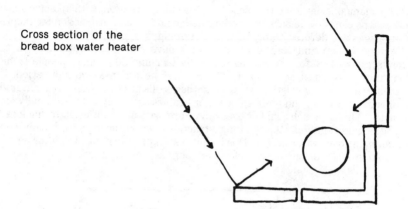

Cross section of the
bread box water heater

The Passive Solar Energy Book, MF 23-544, 448 pages, by Edward Mazria, 1979, $14.95 (paperback) and $17.95 (hardback) from RODALE.

This is now the best book available on the design of passive solar homes and buildings. ("Passive solar" space heating relies on direct solar energy, the orientation of the structure, and the natural heat storing capabilities of selected floor and wall materials.) The format was chosen to allow the reader to go through the book in about an hour, covering only the most important concepts, and then come back for more detailed technical information on each topic. The excellent illustrations also make this a valuable tool for teaching basic concepts in a classroom.

The author begins with the fundamentals of solar energy and heat theory. He then introduces the major successful design elements and strategies, such as masonry thermal storage, Trombe walls, attached greenhouses and roof ponds. His presentation on building orientation, north side protection, and location of different kinds of living spaces helps illustrate how crucial these factors are to successful passive solar design. The important contributions offered by movable insulation, reflectors, and shading devices, and the concepts behind summer cooling are also discussed.

The author notes that "more energy is consumed in the construction of a building than will be used in many years of operation," and recommends the use of relatively low-energy-consuming materials such as "adobe, soil-cement, brick, stone, concrete, and water in containers; for finish materials use wood, plywood, particle board and gypsum board."

A full third of this book contains the information needed for calculating solar angles, solar radiation falling on tilted and vertical surfaces, shading effects, space heat loss in winter, solar space heat gains, and auxiliary heating required. Data is included on the solar radiation (insolation) received and space heating needs for major U.S. cities and regions.

Highly recommended.

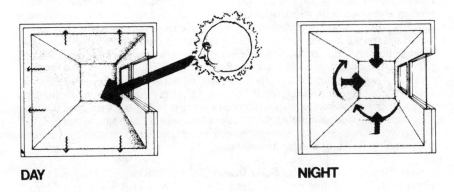

DAY   **NIGHT**

Masonry heat storage in a passive solar house

Homegrown Sundwellings, MF 23-537, book, 136 pages, by Peter van Dresser, 1977 and 1979, $7.95 from The Lightning Tree, P.O. Box 1837, Santa Fe, New Mexico 87501, USA.

Peter van Dresser, one of the pioneers of solar-heated houses, built his first one in 1958. His book summarizes a two-year program to develop low-cost, owner-built, solar-heated houses. It should be read for its sound observations on sensible solar construction based on local materials, and as an introduction to passive solar home design. More extensive information for designing passive solar homes can be found in **The Passive Solar Energy Book** and **The Solar Home Book**.

Although "the Sundwellings concept is firmly rooted in the living construction traditions as well as the socioeconomic circumstances of a natural ecological region—the uplands of northern New Mexico...it reveals principles of universal applicability...To construct using renewable resources is not a sentimental fad in an area without exportable products to pay for imports...In a low cash economy, it is the interactions of human resources with the immediate materials of the land that provide for the richness and fullness of life."

The total solar energy received in winter at sites in Montana, New Mexico and Arizona is greater than the requirement for home heating. The challenge is to store this energy effectively. "The basic strategy is to design the house so that its own masses—mainly walls and floors—are so placed, proportioned, and surfaced that they will receive and store a large measure of incoming solar energy during the daylight hours and will gently release this stored heat to the house interior during the succeeding night hours or cloudy days...A traditional New Mexican floor—either of treated and filled adobe clay or of brick or flagstone laid over sand—is very well suited...its sheer mass gives it great capacity to store this heat with a very slight rise in temperature. If we visualize such a floor 12 inches deep in a room 16 feet square with one exterior wall and an average window, warmed to a mere 72°F (22°C)...it will store 40,000 BTUs of heat which will be released into the room as it cools down to say, 65°F (18°C). This is sufficient heat to take care of a well-insulated room for 26 hours, with an outdoor temperature of, say, 20°F (-7°C)."

The Solar Home Book, MF 23-554, 293 pages, by Anderson and Riordan, 1976, $14.95 from Brick House Pub. Co., 34 Essex Street, Andover, Massachusetts 01810, USA; or WEA.

This is one of the best books that attempts to make the design principles of solar-heated homes understandable and usable for the average person. The emphasis is on passive systems (in which the building itself acts as a solar collector and storage unit, without special circulatory systems). Also covered are systems that can be added to existing homes. A chapter on do-it-yourself methods includes insulation, window box heaters, and attached greenhouses. Altogether, there are about 40 pages on the design of solar water heaters.

"Homes can be designed to respond to local climates . . . Simple low-technology methods are cheaper and more reliable than the many complex, high-technology devices being employed to harness the sun's energy. . . Anyone with good building skills and a knowledge of materials can take advantage of these simple methods . . ." Highly recommended for Americans and other people in temperate climates interested in building a solar-heated home.

Basic Principles of Passive Solar Design, MF 23-529, paper, 31 pages, by Fred Hopman, 1978, available from SATA, P.O. Box 113, Jawalakhel, Kathmandu, Nepal.

SATA has reprinted this paper from the Taos Solar Association of New Mexico, USA. The author presents operating principles and design considerations for passive space heating and cooling systems, including examples of direct gain designs, Trombe walls, roof ponds, attached greenhouses and water circulation systems. Although the examples use Western architectural styles, this excellent introduction to passive solar principles is relevant to building construction in cold climates throughout the world.

Direct gain—note difference between summer and winter sun

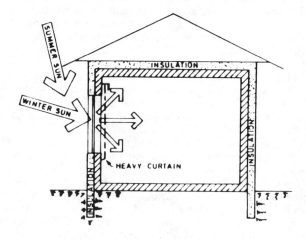

Elements of Solar Architecture for Tropical Regions, MF 23-534, booklet, 23 pages, by Roland Stulz, 1980, Swiss Francs 6.50 from SKAT.

One of only a few publications on the design of solar buildings in tropical regions, where cooling and protection from heat are the major objectives. This booklet concentrates on proper building orientation; cross ventilation; reflecting, absorbing, and insulating building materials; shading with trees, shutters, roof overhangs and other techniques; and evaporation of water (in arid climates) for cooling. Tables indicate some of the different considerations for buildings in humid vs. arid regions. A good illustrated introduction to the topic; many of these concepts have long been a part of indigenous architecture in different parts of the world, but have begun to disappear in the last few decades.

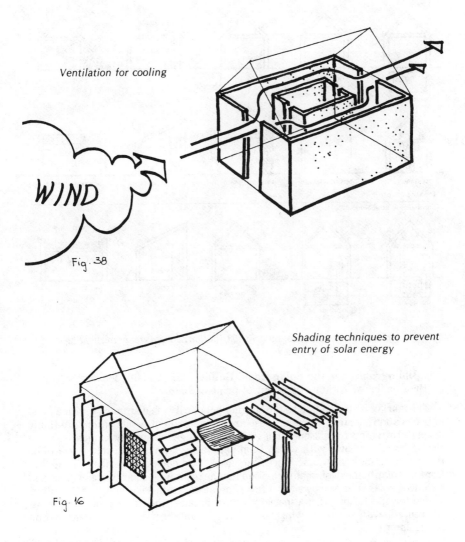

Ventilation for cooling

WIND

Fig. 38

Shading techniques to prevent entry of solar energy

Fig. 16

Solar Dwelling Design Concepts, MF 23-551, book, 146 pages, by American Institute of Architects Research Corporation, $2.30 (order Stock #023-000-00334-1) from U.S. Government Printing Office, Washington D.C. 20402, USA.

This volume presents principles in easy-to-understand terms for both passive and active solar heating and cooling of homes. Intended for architects, the emphasis is on the integration of solar concepts with traditional Western home designs. Factors influencing design are also covered, such as climate, comfort and choice of building site.

32 solar home designs are described, with architectural drawings, to show a variety of passive and active building concepts already in use. Although these designs are from the U.S., the concepts could be adapted by building designers in other temperate climates.

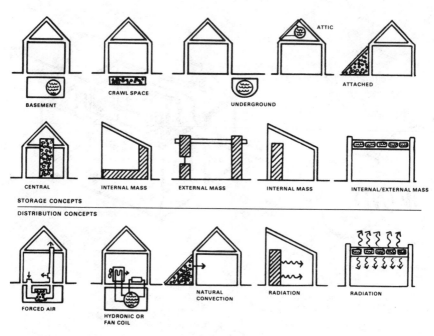

Common solar energy storage and distribution concepts for home heating

A Bibliography for the Solar Home Builder, MF 23-530, booklet, 38 pages, by Dr. Donald W. Aitken, 1979, out of print in 1986.

"The market is responding to the surging popularity of solar energy with a flood of books and reports... some of these are truly excellent, while others are thinly disguised attempts to sell something... the following bibliography summarizes only the books and reports with which I am personally familiar and that I feel to be the most useful, honest, and worth the cost." This booklet describes 71 publications on solar home design, information for the beginning solar home builder, and advanced solar studies as well as a few general works on solar energy as an alternative for the future. It is especially useful because the annotations are cross-referenced, with notes on which publications contain the most information on particular topics.

Also includes listings of solar energy societies and journals. A good "sourcebook" on solar home building, oriented toward applications for the West Coast of the USA.

The Food and Heat Producing Solar Greenhouse: Design, Construction, Operation, MF 23-565, book, 159 pages, by Bill Yanda and Rick Fisher, $9.25 postpaid from John Muir Publications, P.O. Box 613, New Mexico 87501, USA.

An excellent construction manual for a low-cost attached greenhouse that can provide both some house heating and fresh vegetable production in cold climates.

Many of these have been built by low-income families in the mountain regions of the western United States.

Although these designs come from a North American environment, it seems likely that they may be applied to the highlands of tropical countries and any colder areas of the globe where space heating is a priority. Attached greenhouses employ a "passive" solar heating concept. The structure acts as both a collector and a storage unit for solar energy, through the heat-absorbing combination of glass or plastic, concrete, adobe, stone and/or water-filled containers. During daylight hours, the last four of these substances store heat, and at night they radiate it to the living spaces. No expensive, complicated, or breakdown-prone devices such as pumps, heat exchangers, bulky collectors, or massive storage tanks are required. All that is needed is a good design and an active and alert person to regulate the vents, openings and natural energy flows in the dwelling.

An Attached Solar Greenhouse, MF 23-566, booklet, 18 pages, by Bill and Susan Yanda, 1976, $3.00 domestic and $3.50 foreign, from The Lightning Tree, P.O. Box 1837, Santa Fe, New Mexico 87501, USA.

"Solar greenhouses designed and built in northern New Mexico by the Solar Sustenance Project have proven that solar energy can be put to work now by low-income families," state the authors of this short but stimulating booklet. Included are sketches, photos and a bilingual text in English and Spanish (the working drawings lack an effective Spanish translation). This brief volume preceded the more extensive construction manual **The Food and Heat Producing Solar Greenhouse** (see review).

Attached
Solar
Greenhouse

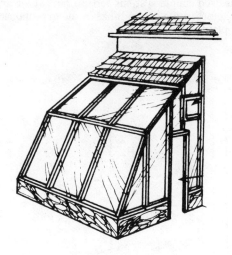

Low-Cost Passive Solar Greenhouses: A Design and Construction Guide, MF 23-541, book, 174 pages, by Ron Alward and Andy Shapiro, 1980, $8.50 from the National Center for Appropriate Technology, P.O. Box 3838, Butte, Montana 59702, USA.

Considerations for building passive solar greenhouses for space heating and food production are presented in a very clear and thorough manual. Includes a review of alternatives, siting, detailed construction pointers for a variety of designs, operation and management methods, etc. Highly recommended.

The Solar Greenhouse Book, MF 23-553, 344 pages, edited by James C. McCullagh, 1978, $11.95 from RODALE.

This book covers the design, siting, construction, use and maintenance of sun-heated greenhouses. Such structures can be used from temperate regions to highland areas of the sub-tropics. Plans are presented for a variety of greenhouses for North American readers; others may find the general presentation to be valuable as well.

The effectiveness of these "passive" solar-heated structures is dramatically shown by photos of greenhouses with snow outside and thriving plants inside. The appendix contains information on different types of glass and plastic window materials, suitable plants, available equipment, and a bibliography.

Proceedings of the Conference on Energy-Conserving, Solar-Heated Greenhouses, MF 23-545, book, 248 pages, edited by John Hayes and Drew Gillett, 1977, $9.00 ($7.50 to readers in developing countries), from Marlboro College Greenhouse Conference, John Hayes, Marlboro College, Marlboro, Vermont 05344, USA.

This is a collection of papers and reports, with some plans for solar greenhouse construction. The topics covered include the theory, planning, construction and operation of solar greenhouses for food, heat and shelter. The reuse of household water and human wastes is also covered. The language is sometimes difficult for non-native English speakers.

"The greenhouse must also be looked at in light of its water conservation over field crop conditions. Authorities report water usage for greenhouse crops to be $\frac{1}{10}$ to $\frac{1}{30}$ of the field crop...Tom Rolf of Silver City and the Chavez family of Anton Chico, devised simple systems to trap rain water and snow melt from the roofs of their homes, drain it into tanks in the greenhouse, and gravity feed the water to their plants."

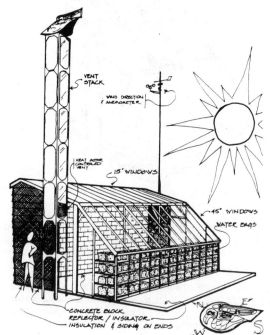

SOLAR GREENHOUSE
BOTHELL

No Heat, No Rent, MF 23-543, book, 90 pages, The Energy Task Force, 1977, limited supply of free copies are available, from Community Services Administration, Washington D.C. 20506, USA.

El Movimiento de la Calle Once (Eleventh Street Movement) is a group of tenants who have bought and renovated their old New York City apartment building. Energy conservation measures have been instituted and a domestic solar hot water system and windgenerator installed.

This manual describes the solar heating system, with instructions on how to install and maintain one in similar old urban apartments in the U.S. The authors hope this book can show others involved in tenant cooperatives how to approach self-help design, while recognizing that each housing situation will have different needs: "A careful reading and discussion of this manual can help people make preliminary decisions without the costly advice of an engineer or architect. However, this is a limited tool and licensed technical aid is required for actual design and construction."

Well-illustrated chapters cover energy conservation measures such as insulation and storm window, simple methods of determining if enough sun falls on your roof,

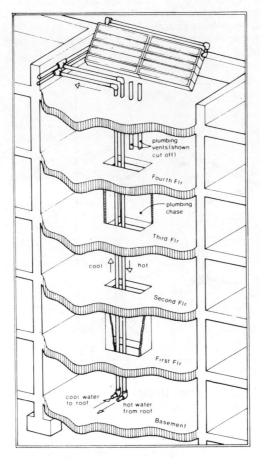

Eleventh St. Movement
solar water heating system

determining collector size needed, installation, solar plumbing, and maintenance and repair of solar systems. A glossary and an easy-to-understand economic analysis are included.

An important example of the application of appropriate technologies by a low-income group in the United States. The heavy costs involved, mostly borne by government agencies, suggest that in urban high-cost settings it will be very difficult indeed to overcome the problems of housing for the poor, even when using their own labor and appropriate technologies.

The Fuel Savers: A Kit of Solar Ideas for Existing Homes, MF 23-536, book, 60 pages, by Dan Scully, Don Prowler, and Bruce Anderson, 1976, $2.75 plus postage (discount to readers in developing countries) from Total Environmental Action, Church Hill, Harrisville, New Hampshire 03450, USA.

A collection of 20 energy-conserving passive and active solar ideas and projects to be used on existing buildings in cold climates. Although intended for North American homes, we have included this book because the projects do not require manufactured solar components, and can be easily completed by the owner.

Included are insulating curtains and shutters, window box air heaters, greenhouses and a thermosiphon (natural circulation) water heater. A drawing and description of each project are given, without exact construction details; the energy savings or each project are discussed.

Useful only in cold climates as examples of simple, do-it-yourself energy conservation measures.

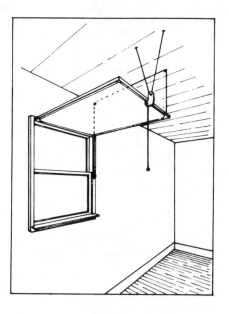

Insulating shutter for cold climates

Window Box Solar Collector Design, MF 23-564, construction plans with text, large blueprint, 1978, $2.50 from Small Farm Energy Project, Box 763, Hartington, Nebraska 68739, USA.

A window box solar collector will heat a room. Air moves by natural circulation, requiring no fan. The six dimensional drawings in this design are somewhat hard to follow, but the design principles are clear. Local materials could be substituted in the design where needed.

Reaching Up, Reaching Out: A Guide to Organizing Local Solar Events,
MF 23-548, book, 145 pages, 1979, by the Solar Energy Research Institute, $8.50
plus 25% for overseas, Stock No. 061-000-00345-2, from Superintendent of
Documents, U.S. Government Printing Office, Washington D.C. 20405, USA.

This "organizing manual" is designed to help groups and individuals organize
themselves to achieve awareness of and control over the energy they use. Thirteen
events are used as case studies, from solar water heater and solar greenhouse construction workshops to energy fairs and neighborhood energy conservation efforts.
Suggestions are made for planning and carrying out these kinds of community
events.

Half of the book is a bibliography on small-scale solar technologies (all U.S.),
general organizing, and a directory of solar groups in the U.S.

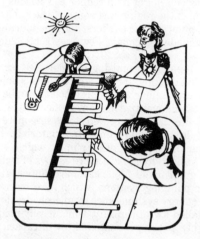

Making the collector
for a solar
water heater

The Solar Survey, MF 23-557, booklet, 21 pages, 1979, $1.35 postpaid from
Publications Section, National Center for Appropriate Technology (NCAT), Box
3838, Butte, Montana 59701, USA.

A collection of 31 solar designs from various community groups across the U.S.
The designs range from active water and air collectors to passive Trombe wall

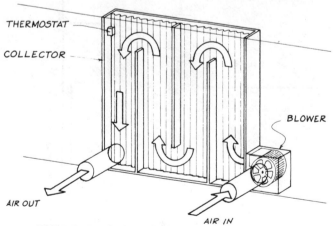

THERMOSTAT

COLLECTOR

BLOWER

AIR OUT

AIR IN

WEST CENTRAL MISSOURI—SYSTEM OPERATION

systems. For each entry, there is a short description and often a drawing (complete designs are not given). All were chosen as examples of low-cost, locally-built technologies.

The purpose of the survey is to exchange ideas and designs among community groups in the U.S. who work independently on similar projects. The specific technologies covered are not very relevant to developing countries.

A State of the Art Survey of Solar Powered Irrigation Pumps, Solar Cookers, and Wood Burning Stoves for Use in Sub-Saharan Africa, MF 23-562, book, 106 pages, by J. Walton, Jr., A. Roy, and S. Bomar, Jr., 1978, limited number of copies available free from Engineering Experiment Station, Georgia Institute of Technology, Atlanta, Georgia 30332, USA.

This is a survey of technologies which might help reduce the serious problems of deforestation and water shortage in the region just south of the Sahara Desert in Africa. Solar-powered irrigation pumps, solar cookers, and woodburning stoves are examined, and research recommendations made. Few construction details are provided.

Unfortunately, what seem to be the most promising technologies for carrying out the functions of lifting water and cooking are not treated in this volume. For example, low-cost, locally-made waterpumping windmills (such as can be found in Crete and Thailand) appear to be cost-competitive in many moderately windy locations and far cheaper than the solar alternative. Improved stoves save more firewood per dollar than solar cookers and do not require imported materials.

This is a useful reference on solar-thermal irrigation pumps, which, at $25,000 per installed kw of capacity, seem forever doomed to serve as toys of rich country aid programs, and may even divert government funds in some countries from more useful pursuits. Solar photovoltaic pumping systems, which have more promise, are not covered. (Other renewable energy systems such as microhydroelectric turbines cost $600 to $2000 per installed kw of capacity, while locally-made waterpumping windmills can cost roughly $2000 per installed kw of capacity.)

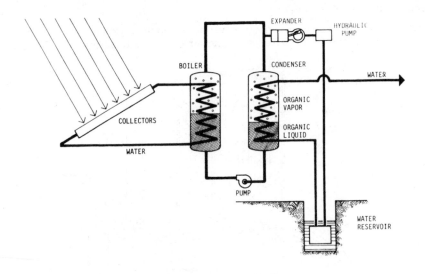

Schematic of a typical SOFRETES solar water pumping system

Evaluation of Solar Cookers, MF 23-535, booklet, 71 pages, by VITA, 1962 (reprinted 1977), out of print in 1985.

This 1962 report covers the early solar cooker designs, many of which are still being tried today. Cost (1962 prices), materials, cooking performance, and problems are presented for each of 12 parabolic reflector and 2 oven designs. Virtually all of the solar cookers that have been tested in recent years are based on designs already existing in 1962, or on ideas mentioned in this booklet.

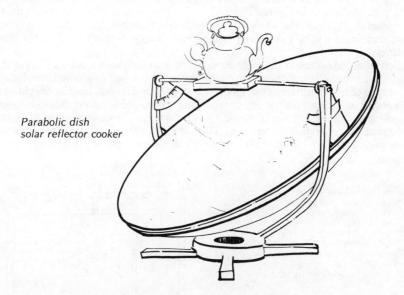

Parabolic dish solar reflector cooker

The Solar Cookery Book: Everything Under the Sun, MF 23-550, book, 122 pages, by Beth and Dan Halacy, 1978, $7.95 from Peace Press Inc., 3828 Willat Avenue, Culver City, California 90230, USA.

The first third of this book is a construction manual for two types of solar cookers: a solar oven and a solar parabolic reflector hot plate. Most of the rest of the book is devoted to detailed descriptions of solar cooking methods, with many recipes for foods that can be solar cooked.

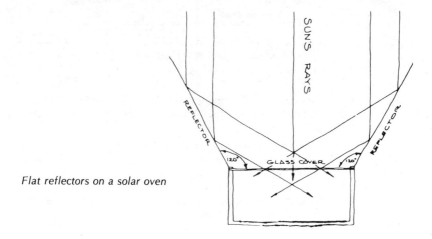

Flat reflectors on a solar oven

The Design and Development of a Solar Powered Refrigerator, MF 23-533, technical report, 74 pages, by R. Exell, S. Kornsakoo, D. Wijeratna, 1976, $8.00 in Thailand, $10.00 in developing countries, $15.00 in developed countries, from Library and Regional Documentation Center, Asian Institute of Technology, P.O. Box 2754, Bangkok, Thailand.

This report describes work on an experimental solar refrigerator designed to be a village-size ice maker or cold storage unit. The experimental version can make 1-2 kg of ice per day in Thailand; larger capacities will be possible in future designs. The cost of the unit is figured to be $750. Ice produced in this unit is calculated to cost about 11 times the wholesale price of ice in Bangkok. This makes it unlikely that such units will be considered "appropriate village technologies" in the near future.

Refrigeration occurs in the night by vaporizing an ammonia solution. During the day, a flat plate collector uses solar energy to pressurize and condense the solution. This type of non-continuous refrigeration, while less efficient, has the advantages of needing no compressor or electricity. Thus it is suited to decentralized applications (operation requires only turning a few valves in the morning and at night).

Most of the report is quite technical. There is also a review of other solar refrigeration work from the last 30 years. Work on these concepts is continuing.

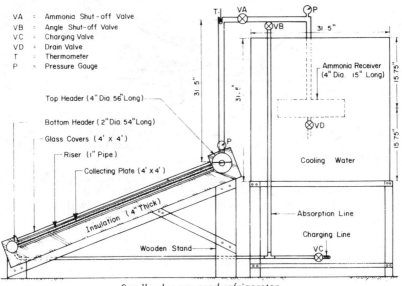

Small solar powered refrigerator

Solar Energy Books, MF 23-552, bibliography, 118 pages, $4.50 from National Solar Energy Education Campaign, 10762 Tucker Street, Beltsville, Maryland 20705, USA.

An extensive bibliography (almost 500 titles) of practical publications on solar energy. There are sections on solar, wind and biomass energy, as well as designs for the homeowner, energy conservation, policy and business. Most of the materials covered are relevant primarily in the U.S. and other rich countries.

A short description of each book is provided. All the publications can be ordered from the National Solar Energy Campaign.

ADDITIONAL REFERENCES ON ENERGY: SOLAR

Proceedings of the Expert Working Group on the Use of Solar and Wind Energy; see ENERGY: GENERAL.

More Other Homes and Garbage has a very good section on passive and active solar energy systems; see GENERAL REFERENCES.

The use of photovoltaic cells for water pumping is covered in **The Potential for Small-Scale Solar-Powered Irrigation in Pakistan, Small-Scale Solar-Powered Irrigation Pumping Systems**, and **Solar Photovoltaics for Irrigation Water Pumping**, all in AGRICULTURAL TOOLS.

Energy: Biogas

Energy: Biogas

The use of methane gas plants as a source of fuel and fertilizer is a practice only recently introduced in this century. The process of bacterial decomposition has occurred in nature since life began — plants and animals die and are recycled to sustain life on the planet. In the presence of oxygen, organic material "composts" (undergoes aerobic decomposition). When decomposition occurs in the absence of oxygen (anaerobic conditions), methane gas is produced, and the liquid remainder is rich in nitrogen and other nutrients.

The natural occurrence of methane (the bubbling gas seen in ponds where animal manures have been dumped) can be duplicated. Water- and air-tight containers (called "digesters") are built, either as pits lined with bricks, concrete or stabilized earth (if this can be waterproofed), or as steel, concrete, or brick tanks. Manures and other organic wastes (after being suitably diluted) can be stored and processed by either the "batch" or "continuous" methods. Premixing chambers, digestion tanks, and effluent discharge ponds are linked by pipes. The gas is collected in storage tanks and distributed by smaller gas pipes to serve as a fuel for cooking, lighting, or operating small engines. There are important factors to control in operating an effective methane plant — temperature, pH, detention time, loading rate, carbon/nitrogen ratio and other variables. Different designs and techniques based on local environmental factors and cultural practices have evolved over the last 30 years.

The term "biogas" is now used throughout the world rather than "methane gas" to describe the fuel produced through anaerobic fermentation of manures and vegetable matter in digesters. Biogas is generally between 40 and 70 percent methane (CH_4), with the remainder consisting of carbon dioxide, hydrogen sulfide (H_2S) and other trace gases.

While the prospect of generating fuel and fertilizer from organic wastes is an attractive one, significant problems and debate persist about the value of biogas in addressing the energy needs of poor villages in the Third World.

"Biogas technology represents one of a number of village-scale technologies that are currently enjoying a certain vogue among governments and aid agencies and that offer the technical possibility of more decentralized approaches to development. However, the technical and economic evaluation of these technologies has often been rudimentary. Therefore, there is a real danger that attempts are being made at wide-scale introduction of these techniques in the rural areas of the Third World before it is known whether they are in any sense appropriate to the problems of rural peoples."

—Biogas Technology in the Third World, IDRC

Some observers (see, for example, "The Economics of Renewable Energy Systems" by David French) conclude that the lifetime social and economic benefits of the heavily subsidized Indian family-scale biogas plants do not equal the costs of construction and maintenance. In Pakistan and Nepal, only prosperous farmers with adequate numbers of animals and significant amounts of capital have been able to afford to build biogas plants. Although the information on community-scale biogas plants is still very scanty, some results in Indian villages are not very promising. It appears that in terms of fuel and fertilizer, biogas may well be a poor proposition without good management, optimal resources, and a suitable social environment. In most villages it may be advisable to invest first in improved wood stoves and village woodlots rather than biogas systems. However, side benefits such as improved village health and increased productivity in associated enterprises (fish farming, livestock, agriculture, etc.) may tip the scales in favor of a biogas project. For example, just one small digester at a rural health clinic can power a refrigerator holding vaccines for thousands of people.

Spectacular successes have been claimed in the People's Republic of China. Up to 7 million family and community-scale biogas plants are reported to have been built there. Many people have talked about or actively tried to duplicate the Chinese successes in their own countries, and a number of new publications have arisen to report these trends and developments around the world.

In China, manure handling has much higher acceptance than in most other developing nations. The large number of pigs and the relatively even distribution of resources are significant factors as well. It appears that the Chinese designs are resource-conserving, compact, and adaptable to whatever building materials are locally available. Bricks and stones are used with locally-produced relatively low-cost cement, and in some areas digesters are even carved out of solid rock. Of particular interest are the built-in self-pressurizing mechanisms in the Chinese designs which eliminate the need for costly metal covers.

Recently some observers have questioned the applicability of the Chinese biogas experience. Attempts to replicate the Chinese results outside the PRC have yielded very uneven results. Building materials, such as cement, lime and quarried stones which are produced locally on Chinese communes are unavailable or very expensive in many other countries. Also, the Chinese skill and diligence in construction (particularly for the vaulted dome designs) and maintenance may be difficult to find or develop elsewhere. One observer notes that the Chinese digesters are very similar to septic tanks, and that their gas yields per unit volume may be only a fraction of large-scale sewage digesters — meaning the gas production may be significantly lower than commonly assumed. It should also be remembered that virtually all reports on the Chinese successes have come from the Chinese themselves, so that data on construction costs and gas yields need further confirmation.

Until recently, no clear and concise technical reports on the Chinese biogas technology were available outside China. The International Development Research Center (IDRC) and the Intermediate Technology Development Group (ITDG) have produced two fine translations of Chinese biogas manuals: **Compost, Fertilizer and Biogas Production from Human and Farm Wastes in the PRC** *(IDRC), and* **A Chinese Biogas Manual** *(ITDG). The former book covers health and sanitation aspects of biogas fully, while the latter presents more comprehensive information on building materials and construction techniques. IDRC's* **Biogas Technology in the Third World: A Multidisciplinary Review** *is an excellent review of the social, economic and technical aspects of this technology and the problems encountered in attempting to spread it outside of China. The authors of that publication conclude:*

"The viability of a particular biogas plant design depends on the particular environment in which it operates. Therefore, the research problem becomes one of providing a structure in which technologists, economists, and users of the technology can combine to produce both the appropriate hardware for various situations and the infrastructure that is necessary to ensure that the hardware is widely used."

Other Asian experiences, from Nepal, Pakistan, and the Economic and Social Commission for Asia and the Pacific (ESCAP) are also featured in the entries in this chapter. To our knowledge, widespread applications or experiments in the developing world have been concentrated in Asia. Interest and activities in other parts of the world have lagged behind to date.

Although methane digesters can offer a variety of potential benefits, they are often justified economically on the basis of the cooking fuel they produce. This justification, however, must be re-examined in view of the fact that in most rural areas of poor countries, existing cooking stoves are presently very inefficient, while more efficient designs can save 25-35% of the fuel and cost as little as $1 to $5. If fuel savings are the sole objective, locally-made efficient stoves appear to be a far more cost-effective investment than biogas plants.

Biogas Technology in the Third World: A Multidisciplinary Review,
MF 24-570, book, 132 pages, by Andrew Barnett, Leo Pyle, and S.K. Subramanian, 1978, IDRC, out of print in 1985.

"In response to the interest in biogas and other rural energy systems shown by a number of Asian researchers, the International Development Research Center (IDRC) commissioned this state-of-the-art review so that it might form a basis of further discussions concerning the direction of future biogas research. This book represents a multidisciplinary approach to the problem and attempts to review existing work rather than to champion particular solutions."

"Our objective is to stress the need to examine a wider range of technical and economic alternatives for meeting the energy and fertilizer needs of rural peoples. It is our hope that this survey contributes to this process by showing what has already been done, by pointing out pitfalls, and by indicating the major gaps that still remain."

The three chapters contain: 1) a broad overview of the energy options facing rural communities in the Third World, detailing what is already known about the technical aspects of biogas production; 2) an approach to social and economic appraisal of rural technologies, particularly successful biogas applications; and 3) a field survey of existing biogas systems and their supporting infrastructure in Asia. The authors are looking for the best uses of the waste material, including options other than biogas production. Estimated gas yields from various crop residues and animal manures are listed. Costs and performance of different digester designs are compared. The Chinese experience is not covered in great depth, due to the lack of information available at the time of publication.

This book can be read by non-technical people, and it deserves wide circulation among development planners, students, and technicians. A strong English vocabulary is required. Not a how-to-build-it book, this is nevertheless valuable to those designing, experimenting, and operating digester schemes.

Compost, Fertilizer, and Biogas Production from Human and Farm Wastes in the People's Republic of China, MF 24-573, book, 93 pages, edited by Michael McGarry and Jill Stainforth, 1978, IDRC, out of print in 1985.

"This collection of papers describes the design, construction, maintenance, and operation of Chinese technologies that enable the Chinese to treat human excreta, livestock manure, and farm wastes to produce liquid fertilizer, compost, and methane gas."

From a mere handful of experimental "marsh gas pits" during the Great Leap Forward in 1957, methane plants have proliferated to number 7-10 million at last report. Recent reports suggest that these biogas plants are cheap but inefficient gas producers, and are economically justified primarily by their fertilizer and health benefits. Most other developing country biogas programs, by contrast, have been primarily interested in the fuel production benefits.

The Chinese biogas technology appears promising for other developing countries, but its transfer to other places is probably unlikely without commitment on the part of the people or the support of the government of China.

"Since 1964 we have standardized the management and hygienic disposal of excreta and urine, expanded the sources and raised the efficiency of fertilizer, and collected and created a high-quality fertilizer by destroying the bacteria and parasitic eggs that existed in the human and domestic animal excreta and urine. As well, we lowered the morbidity of enteric pathogens, reduced the breeding areas of flies and mosquitoes, improved environmental health, promoted and increased food production, and increased the health standards of all the committee members. Between 1963 and 1971 food production per acre increased by 74%, enteric pathogen morbidity decreased by 80%, and the morbidity of pigs' disease dropped from 5 to 0.3%. Basically, the health profile of the villages was transformed."

The more recent book **A Chinese Biogas Manual** (see review in this section) provides more complete information on biogas plant construction and operation. Both books are recommended.

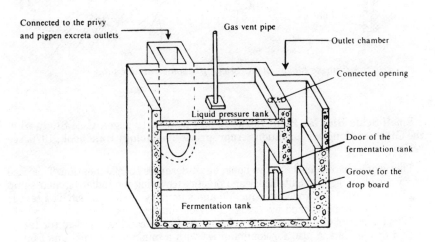

Enclosed three-stage biogas plant

A Chinese Biogas Manual, MF 24-572, book, 160 pages, by the Office of the Leading Group for the Propagation of Marshgas, Szechuan Province, English translation published 1979, £4.50 from ITDG.

This construction manual has been used widely since its original Chinese language publication in 1974. It shows how to plan, build, and care for low-cost pit-type digesters. Drawings and text explain the comparative design advantages and construction details of circular pits, rectangular pits and domed covers. Different combinations of stone, lime bricks, traditional cements and mortars, and commercial concrete are also discussed. Simple instructions include notes on why certain designs are suited to certain conditions: "A circular pit made from soft triple concrete with a large volume and a small opening is easy to seal and suitable for the areas where the earth is firm, the underground water level is low, and there is no water seepage. (It is) also quite suitable for plateau regions."

The manual also emphasizes the importance of careful prevention of leaks when the finished pit is filled and pressurized. A chapter on using biogas shows how to make burners for cooking and lighting, out of renewable and recycled materials such as bamboo, iron tubing, and discarded showerheads. An appendix gives an example of how this book has been used by the Shachio Commune of Guangdong Province to spread biogas technology.

A good technical reference, this construction manual is also an example of a tool for sharing skills and experience among rural communities.

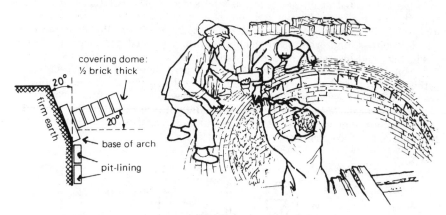

A Chinese biogas plant: bricking a dome without support

Small-Scale Bio-Gas Plant in India, MF 24-581, 19 pages, Case Study #6 in the Canadian Hunger Foundation's **Appropriate Technology Handbook**, 1976, see review.

This is one chapter in the above book, but it deserves special mention. This case study survey of biogas plant theory and practice (covering the Indian circular sump digester designs) is a good introduction and summary of the subject. The text is clearly worded and backed by straightforward illustrations.

"The bio-gas plants that were developed by this research were ideal for farms with 4 or 5 cows and also for communities with a minimum population of 50. A larger system simply requires larger numbers of the same basic unit. Construction of the plants is labor intensive, and almost all of the necessary skills and resources are available in rural areas. The local farmers own, manage, maintain and control their bio-gas plants."

"The initial capital outlay is relatively high. The plant described in more detail cost approximately Rs. 2000 (US$300) in 1973. However, study of the operation of bio-gas plants over the last 10 years indicates that the initial cost is recovered within 6 years in the form of fuel, fertilizer and improved crop yields. Maintenance and operating costs are negligible." (Editor's note: These claims have been disputed in recent years.)

Gobar Gas: An Alternate Way of Handling the Village Fuel Problem, MF 24-575, pamphlet, 16 pages, available free to serious groups in developing countries, from Appropriate Technology Development Organization, P.O. Box 1306, Islamabad, Pakistan.

"In China, a simple (biogas) plant has been developed which has gone a long way in relieving Chinese rural areas from fuel shortage. The plant developed by the Chinese is extremely simple, being a brick structure with a dome type roof. This has an added advantage on Indian type plants where a steel gas holder is the common method. The Chinese have been kind to us in sharing their technical know-how and having provided Pakistan with a complete set of working drawings."

In line with the Chinese philosophy of utilizing local material, skills, and labor, the Appropriate Technology Development Organization (ATDO) of Pakistan has built modified versions of the Chinese biogas plant in several locations. These experiments may prove to be very valuable in establishing whether or not this technology can also flourish under very different cultural, economic, and political conditions.

Fuel Gas from Cow Dung, MF 24-574, booklet, 104 pages, by B. Saubolle and A. Bachmann, revised 1983, free from UNICEF, P.O. Box 1187, Kathmandu, Nepal.

This concise booklet covers construction and operation of Nepali/Indian-style biogas plants. Diagrams are also presented for simple biogas burners and lamps. A local Nepali adaptation of the Chinese design is included, and Chinese and Indian technologies are compared for their strengths and weaknesses.

Nepal Bio-Gas Newsletter, MF 24-578, quarterly newsletter, 12 pages, available free to serious groups in developing nations, from Bio-Gas Committee, Energy Research and Development Group, Tribhuvan University, Kathmandu, Nepal.

Reports on biogas technology developments in Nepal and other Asian countries. Issue No. 2 reports on technical, social and economic problems of this technology in Nepal, and includes some articles on locally appropriate burners, lamps, and piping mechanisms. Also shown are some valuable details from the Chinese drumless biogas plants, such as an inexpensive device for pressure regulation.

This newsletter is a good model of a low-cost problem-solving and information-sharing channel. Those wishing to obtain this publication should plan to contribute or exchange something for it.

Burner for use with biogas

Biogas Systems in India, MF 24-569, book, 130 pages, by Robert Jon Lichtman, 1983, $19.25 in U.S., $19.50 international surface mail, $23.75 international air mail, from VITA.

"This study is an assessment of the 'appropriateness' of biogas technology in meeting some of the needs of India's rural population. Such an assessment is quite complicated, despite claims that a biogas system is a simple village-level technology. While there is evidence that biogas systems have great promise, they are subject to certain constraints. It is impossible to describe here all the factors that one might study to assess any technology. I only hope that the approach used in this study will help others." The author covers the potential of biogas to meet rural energy demands, digester designs, system operation, gas distribution, and the economics of a village biogas system. Particularly well-suited to planners.

Biogas and Waste Recycling: The Philippine Experience, MF 24-567, book, 230 pages, by Felix D. Maramba, 1978, from Liberty Flour Mills, Inc., Maya Farms Division, Liberty Building, Pasay Road, Legaspi Village, Makati, Metro Manila, The Philippines.

This book is primarily about the design of profitable biogas systems, rather than specific designs for biogas generators. Although it is based largely upon the experience of Maya Farms with its massive biogas plants, it has much to offer those designing a small community system. Of particular interest is the technique for conditioning of toxic sludge, rendering it safe for processing into high quality animal feed. "The value of the recoverable feed materials alone without considering the biogas, biofertilizer, and pollution control, makes the whole system a profitable venture." Recommended.

The Biogas/Biofertilizer Business Handbook: A Handbook for Volunteers, MF 24-571, book, 171 pages, by Michael Arnott, 1982, available to Peace Corps volunteers and development workers from Peace Corps, Information Collection and Exchange, Room 701, 806 Connecticut Avenue N.W., Washington D.C. 20526, USA.

"The purpose of this book is biogas systems, not biogas digesters. Biogas systems include raw material preparation, digesters, separate gas storage tanks, use of the gas to run engines, and the use of the sludge as fertilizer. In order to involve and benefit as much of the community as possible, new combinations of proven biogas concepts have been brought together and emphasis has been placed on several aspects of biogas technology that are often overlooked." Drawing heavily upon other publications and the experience of the author and others in the Philippines, this book is densely packed with information on a wide variety of topics related to biogas systems. Recommended.

Renewable Sources of Energy, Volume II: Biogas, MF 24-579, book, 280 pages, United Nations Economic and Social Commission for Asia and the Pacific, 1981, out of print in 1985.

A survey of biogas implementation in Asia and the Pacific concludes with a call for regional collaboration in the use of alternative energy technology. An Indian case study in cost benefit analysis and, at best, an uneven account of the current state of the technology is followed by a list of individuals and institutions engaged in the field. Includes comprehensive bibliography.

The Biogas Handbook, MF 24-568, book, 403 pages, by D. House, 1978, $8.00 ($9.00 outside the USA) from At Home Everywhere, c/o VAHID, Route 2, Box 259, Aurora, Oregon 97002, USA.

"This book makes no claim to startling originality or clever breakthroughs. Its usefulness comes mainly because here, gathered together in one place, is a great deal of information on biogas generation; what it is, where it comes from and how to make and use it. There are, however, only a few designs for biogas generators given in detail." Readers wanting specific digester designs should look elsewhere.
The author attempts to help the reader understand the complexities of biogas generation. The information covers nearly all problem areas, including safety features, compression ratios for engines, and sizing of effluent algae ponds, in a

detailed fashion. There are numerous charts, graphs, and equations to explain the chemical, biological and engineering aspects of biogas generation. The language varies from moderately technical to philosophical. Illustrations are crude, but helpful in understanding the text.

The oildrum digester designs presented in this book are of limited value due to their small size and costly corrosion problems. The rest of the book, however, would be valuable for trained village technology engineers and extension agents in developing nations, or biogas enthusiasts anywhere. A good knowledge of English is required to use this book.

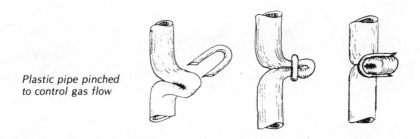

*Plastic pipe pinched
to control gas flow*

Report on the Design and Operation of a Full-Scale Anaerobic Dairy Manure Digester, MF 24-580, book, 77 pages, ECOTOPE Group, 1979, $10.00 from ECOTOPE Group, 2812 E. Madison, Seattle, Washington 98112, USA.

This is a thorough account of a large-scale digester project using dairy cow manure (now in operation). The system has two huge agricultural storage tanks of 378 cubic meter capacity, gas compressor, propane tanks to hold the compressed gas, heat exchangers between effluent and input lines, and a novel gas recirculation system which is claimed to eliminate the problem of scum accumulation, due to the agitation effect of the gas.

The project cost $70,000, a huge sum in most developing countries. Some of the information might still be useful for a dairy cooperative methane scheme.

The Anaerobic Digestion of Livestock Wastes to Produce Methane: 1946 to June 1975, A Bibliography with Abstracts, MF 24-565, 103 pages, by G. Shadduck and J. Moore, 1975, $3.50 from Department of Agricultural Engineering, University of Minnesota, St. Paul, Minnesota 55108, USA.

This annotated bibliography surveys the pre-1976 anaerobic digestion process literature. The authors have described the contents and evaluated each entry. Intended to give a broad overview of all available resources, so that readers' questions may be answered, as well as additional questions raised. Addresses are given only for the more popular books. There is an excellent scientific analysis of fuel and fertilizer results from different animal manures. Recommended for those already familiar with methane.

ADDITIONAL REFERENCES ON BIOGAS

The Economics of Renewable Energy Systems for Developing Countries examines a hypothetical village biogas plant in India, and concludes that it is not economically viable; see ENERGY: GENERAL.

Housing and Construction

Housing and Construction

"It is not so much 'how to build' as 'how to choose techniques and materials appropriate to a given situation.'"
—letter from a volunteer in Papua New Guinea

There are housing problems everywhere, in industrialized as well as developing countries. In Jakarta, Manila, Mexico City, and Calcutta millions of squatters camp indefinitely in structures made of cardboard, sheet plastic and flattened cans, on strips of land beside canals and railways, sometimes even in the shadows of high-rise "low-cost" housing. In the urban United States, the great majority of homeowners could not afford to purchase the homes they live in today if they had to do so at today's prices. In these and countless other urbanizing areas, the cost of a place to live is rapidly outstripping the ability of ordinary people to pay. Inflation of land values triggered by the growth of gigantic urban centers is one factor. The cost of energy-intensive manufactured building materials, which inevitably rises faster than the other costs of living, is another.

In developing countries, the amount of attention and resources that public works administrations and development assistance agencies devote to housing is probably second only to that devoted to water supply. And the history of housing projects, like that of water supply projects, is largely a history of disappointments worldwide. In **Housing by People** *(this section), John Turner notes that*

". . .it is common for public agencies to build houses or flats to standards which the majority cannot afford, nor can the country possibly subsidize them on a large scale. On top of this, it is not unusual for governments to prohibit private building of the type of housing the vast majority can afford and are satisfied with."

Turner argues that governments should not provide houses built to arbitrary specifications, but should instead make building codes more flexible and provide opportunities for secure access to land. An appropriate housing strategy would rely on a community's initiative, thrift, and ability to organize and turn local resources to advantage to meet the basic human need of shelter. Many of the entries in this section provide illustrations and documentation of the power and validity of this approach.

*Egyptian architect Hassan Fathy (***Architecture for the Poor***) helped to inspire a re-examination of traditional architecture and materials. Fathy and others emphasize the ingenuity contained in indigenous building systems, which have tended to evolve to fit local conditions. "Far from being backward or illogical as is often supposed, many traditions do in fact have an underlying rationale or system" which has developed in response to local climatic conditions and availability of materials, states Iran's Development Workshop. Appropriate technologies for housing should begin with and extend these indigenous systems. Self-help, owner-*

built housing, says John Turner, "is very much a process, intimately related to the user's needs and finances, and very much in the user's control. The idea of housing being the production and distribution of a number of units by the government or a private institution to a passive, recipient population is one of the misleading models set up by Western countries." The Development Workshop adds: "Control, participation and culture emerge more easily in an operation that uses local resources, is labor-intensive, is small-scale, and has continuity with local traditions."

Most of the entries in this chapter cover construction materials and techniques for building houses, other buildings, and bridges. The emphasis is on simple methods, whose principal advantages are twofold: they are inexpensive and they can be used by people to build their own homes. Wood-framed and stone structures are relatively low-cost in many areas. Earth is the most important building material, providing housing for the majority of the world's population. The thermal properties of earth also make it well-matched to passive solar design requirements in many climates. Several books in this section discuss construction of houses made with monolithic earth walls, soil-cement bricks, and adobe bricks. There are two sets of plans for the construction of hand-operated presses that can be used to make soil-cement blocks. Improved techniques for small-scale brickmaking is the topic of several books. Two more entries cover the principles of design of underground buildings; one of these presents an owner-builder approach.

Bamboo has a long history as a flexible, safe, low-cost building material, and is plentiful today in many parts of the tropics and subtropics. Three entries cover some recent innovations and results of research in structural uses for bamboo, as well as reinforcing applications in plaster, cement, and stucco roofs and walls.

Ferrocement — a strong, thin sheet of cement reinforced with mesh — is a more recent technology with potential applications wherever durable waterproof walls, roofs, or hulls are required. It is widely used in water tank and boat construction. The techniques are described in three entries in this chapter, and in books on water tank construction (WATER SUPPLY chapter) and boatbuilding (TRANSPORTATION chapter).

Housing by People: Towards Autonomy in Building Environments,

MF 25-604, paperback book, 169 pages, by John Turner, 1977, $5.95 from Pantheon, Random House Inc., 400 Hahn Road, Westminster, Maryland 21157, USA.

With many years of experience working in low-cost housing projects in developing as well as developed countries, Turner has written a penetrating analysis of the housing "problem," with broad implications for other kinds of appropriate technology work.

Turner proposes "a radical change of relations between people and government in which government ceases to persist in doing what it does badly or uneconomically — building and managing houses — and concentrates on what it has the authority to do: to ensure equitable access to resources which local communities and people cannot provide for themselves." Throughout the world, so-called "low-cost housing" projects have repeated the same mistakes by setting a material standard (including building codes) ill-suited and far too expensive for the poor majority. Backed by many case studies, Turner argues that within the constraints of poverty, the poor succeed rather well in providing for their housing needs when they have land tenure and access to materials. "The economy of housing is a matter of personal and local resourcefulness rather than centrally controlled, industrial productivity."

"Personal and local resources are imagination, initiative, commitment and responsibility, skill and muscle power, the capability for using specific and often irregular areas of land or locally available materials and tools; the ability to organize enterprises and local institutions; constructive competitiveness and the capacity to cooperate." The existence and vitality of "dense local communication and supply networks open to local residents" appears to be a key factor in the "material savings and human benefits of owner-building, rehabilitation, and improvement in the United States."

Government activities in housing often prevent or hamper the use of these resources and networks. Improved income opportunities, guaranteed land tenure, and building codes based on broad function rather than specific requirements would have more effect on housing for the poor than most direct housing projects.

In the Third World subsidized housing has proved a failure, for it usually is occupied by the relatively well-off and the ultimate costs of subsidized housing for all those who need it are far beyond the capability of governments to provide. Whereas, "By far the greatest financial resources are the actual savings of the population from their own earnings, and these are under their direct control. This probably represents between 10 and 15 percent of all personal incomes. It is roughly equivalent to all taxes obtained from incomes and retail sales in an economy such as that of Mexico."

Two non-monetary factors that play a very important role in housing for the urban poor are accessibility (to jobs) and security (of ownership, including the ability to sell so as to recoup the costs of improvements made). By concentrating solely on physical standards for dwellings, without reference to such factors, authorities cannot understand the decision-making context faced by the poor.

The author concludes with "an argument for the redefinition of housing problems as functions of mismatches between people's socio-economic and cultural situations and their housing processes and products; and as functions of the waste, misuse, or non-use of resources available for housing."

Architecture for the Poor, paperback book, 234 pages, by Hassan Fathy, 1973, $11.95 from University of Chicago Press, 11030 South Langley Avenue, Chicago, Illinois 60628, USA.

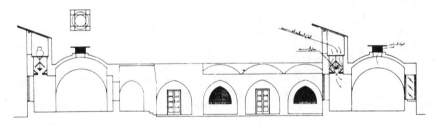

Ventilation system at girls' primary school

Hassan Fathy, an Egyptian architect, argues that housing should be based on traditional forms of architecture, not those forms imported from the West. The people themselves should be intimately involved with the design, building and ownership of their own housing. When the government or private contractors step in and build for the people, the result is often housing and planning which is vastly out of touch with local social, cultural, economic and environmental conditions.

"This book describes in detail Fathy's plan (during the 1940s) for building the village of New Gourna, Egypt, from mud bricks, employing almost exclusively such traditional Egyptian architectural designs as enclosed courtyards and domes and vaulted roofing. Fathy worked closely with the people to tailor his designs to their needs; he taught them how to work with the mud bricks, supervised the erection of the buildings, and encouraged the revival of such ancient crafts as claustra (lattice designs in the mudwork) to decorate the buildings...In addition, Fathy worked out an economic and organizational base, so that the production in the village derived from local crafts and organizational patterns."

Although bureaucratic and other problems prevented the completion of New Gourna, today Fathy's ideas are becoming more accepted as rural development becomes more of a priority throughout the world.

Self-Help Practices in Housing: Selected Case Studies, MF 25-633, book, 129 pages, 1973, U.N. Department of Economic and Social Affairs, out of print in 1985.

Adequate housing for the growing poor communities in urban areas of the Third World is the subject of this report. Case studies of self-help housing projects are included from cities in Colombia, El Salvador, Senegal, Ethiopia, and the Sudan. These projects were undertaken by local and national government agencies, sometimes in cooperation with private organizations. Timetables and size of project varied considerably. The Senegal project involved 90 white-collar and other middle-class family heads in training and construction over a period of four years. The dismantling and rebuilding of houses for 1000 families on new land in Port Sudan was accomplished within one month.

The studies show how certain key factors affect the outcome of any self-help housing scheme. An accurate assessment of loan repayment capability is one important consideration. Continued access to jobs, distribution of manual skills in construction work groups, kind of supervision, and timing of construction work periods are equally important factors that affect the success or failure of a project. The studies also show that communal activities essential to the success of the new neighborhoods, such as maintenance of waste disposal systems, depend on involvement of local leaders and groups from the earliest planning stages. An important reason for the success of the Port Sudan project, for example, was the fact that many people "had already organized themselves into teams which worked in the docks according to the arrival and departure of ships. In this way, the whole team would be free from work two or three times a week" and available to dismantle shacks and rebuild houses together. Other projects, which strictly screened participants according to need and eventual ability to repay, sacrificed these reservoirs of self-help potential by breaking them up in the selection process.

The sometimes difficult language used in this report may present problems for readers with limited English ability.

Chawama Self-Help Housing Project, Kafue, Zambia, MF 25-589, book, 80 pages, American Friends Service Committee, 1975, out of print in 1985.

"Between 1968 and 1973, a project to improve the conditions of life of squatters in Kafue was conducted jointly by the Government of Zambia, the Kafue Township Council and the American Friends Service Committee. The objective of the project was not only to provide acceptable housing with suitable amenities but also to develop patterns of cooperation among the residents which would create the conditions of a viable and harmonious community."

This well-illustrated report covers all aspects of the project design, planning, and construction. The successful effort in community-building at Chawama was the result of thorough surveys of the origins, nature and needs of the squatter settlement. Included is a good review of CINVA-Ram block construction, the building method the Chawama community finally chose.

"The project may be seen as an instance of productive collaboration between a foreign voluntary agency and an African government as they joined together to meet a pressing social need. The AFSC found that it could respond to the government's explicit request for assistance with a flexible and informed approach, as well as with a philosophical outlook in respect to self-reliance which was in harmony with the government's. Zambian participation in all aspects of the project, from planning to actual construction, was central to the philosophy underlying

the program's development. Thus the AFSC played a catalytic and facilitating role, not a controlling one."
Recommended.

House Form and Culture, MF 25-603, book, 135 pages, by Amos Rapoport, 1969, $16.95 from Prentice-Hall, Inc., Englewood Cliffs, New Jersey 07632, USA.

A thoughtful look at the way that cultural factors have influenced the form of houses. Although this is not intended to be a book on the practical side of building design, it is full of interesting examples of the ways different peoples have solved a wide variety of problems. Includes about 100 drawings.

"Construction and materials are best regarded as modifying factors...they do not determine form. They merely make possible forms which have been selected on other grounds...Given a certain climate, the availability of certain materials, and the constraints and capabilities of a given level of technology, what finally decides the form of a dwelling, and moulds the spaces and their relationships, is the vision that people have of the ideal life."

Recommended reading for those involved in low-cost housing. This book will hopefully dispel any lingering ideas that standardized box-shaped houses built of industrial materials should be imposed upon any people.

Design for Climate: Guidelines for the Design of Low-Cost Houses for the Climates of Kenya, book, 135 pages, by Charles Hooper, 1975, approximately US$6.00 (plus foreign bank charges and $2.50 overseas surface mail postage) from Housing Research and Development Unit, University of Nairobi, P.O. Box 30197, Nairobi, Kenya.

This is actually a manual on passive solar design. We include it here because, unlike other passive solar references, this one is relevant to housing design and policy in Africa. The analysis of design alternatives takes local customs, materials, and skills into account. "A well-developed, climatically appropriate, system of construction that fully utilizes local materials and skills, exists at the coast. Where regularly maintained this construction system has proven long-lasting and should not be scorned for use in publicly supported housing projects. The walls which consist of mangrove poles, mud, small stones, plaster and whitewash are relatively thin and have a reflective external surface. The makuti (palm thatch) roofs are thermally ideal"; they insulate well and have a low heat storage capacity.

Too many other plans for low-cost housing in the Third World have called for countrywide construction of one particular house design, without regard for variations in climate, culture, and other factors.

Guidelines for each of Kenya's six climatic zones are divided into subtopics: human comfort, site planning, house plan, structure and materials, and openings. Tables indicate month-by-month variation of windspeeds and directions, rainfall, sunshine, and temperature.

Shelter, MF 25-635, book, 176 pages, edited by Lloyd Kahn, 1973, $20.00 hardcover from Home Book Service, Box 650, Bolinas, California 94924, USA.

"This book is about simple homes, natural materials, and human resourcefulness. It is about discovery, hard work, the joys of self-sufficiency, and freedom. It is about shelter, which is more than a roof overhead."

Filled with photographs and drawings, **Shelter** is a tribute to native, traditional, rational, and recent innovative building styles. Included are articles on a variety of structures from animal dwellings to a survey of human habitats; from the so-called "primitive" to the futuristic.

The authors note that there is much to learn "from wisdom of the past: from structures shaped by imagination, not mathematics, and built of materials appearing

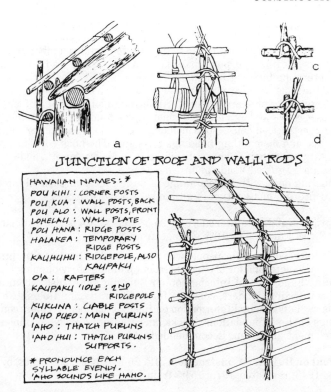

JUNCTION OF ROOF AND WALL RODS

HAWAIIAN NAMES : *
POU KIHI : CORNER POSTS
POU KUA : WALL POSTS, BACK
POU ALO : WALL POSTS, FRONT
LOHELAU : WALL PLATE
POU HANA : RIDGE POSTS
HALAKEA : TEMPORARY
             RIDGE POSTS
KAUHUHU : RIDGEPOLE, ALSO
             KAUPAKU
O'A : RAFTERS
KAUPAKU 'IOLE : 2ND
             RIDGEPOLE
KUKUNA : GABLE POSTS
'AHO PUEO : MAIN PURLINS
'AHO : THATCH PURLINS
'AHO HUI : THATCH PURLINS
             SUPPORTS.

* PRONOUNCE EACH
SYLLABLE EVENLY.
'AHO SOUNDS LIKE HAHO.

naturally on the earth."

A highly recommended and stimulating book, **Shelter** has some precise working drawings on basic designs, such as hipped, gabled, or shed roofs, concrete floors, wooden framing, windows and doors. At the back of the book, there happen to be some brief but very good drawings, photos, and text on sail windmills.

For those seeking design inspiration, **Shelter** is required reading.

Shelter II, MF 25-637, large paperback book, 224 pages, by Lloyd Kahn, 1978, $10.00 postpaid from Shelter Publications, P.O. Box 279, Bolinas, California 94924, USA.

Hundreds of photographs and drawings in **Shelter II** give an inspirational view of indigenous building styles and techniques, from Nebraskan sod houses to the thatched stick-dwellings of nomadic Kenyan shepherds. The author discusses the ways structure has related to culture, physical environment, and basic shelter requirements. The book emphasizes innovation and diversity among human dwell-

Turkmen (Northern Afghanistan)   *Kazakh*

ings, but the appropriateness of traditional building technologies is also a unifying theme. "Practical builders, wherever they live, work with simple techniques and what is most readily at hand: earth, thatch, stone milled lumber or abandoned city buildings. Weather, purpose, materials govern design. Tradition, experience, practice determine building technique."

Some of the most practical shelter alternatives for North America — stud-frame and adobe construction — are explored. An introduction to design of small single-family houses is followed by a guide for pouring the foundations, framing, and roofing a stud-construction house. Also included are sections on interiors, bungalows, yurts, cabins, and dismantling buildings for scrap. The book concludes with pictorial case studies of homeowner rehabilitation in Massachusetts and cooperative homesteading in gutted buildings in New York.

A fascinating book with a broad range of design ideas and useful information. Certain to fire the imagination of all kinds of owner-builders.

Appropriate Building Materials, MF 25-584, book, 324 pages, by Roland Stultz, 1981, 24 Swiss Francs plus 10% postage from SKAT.

A useful reference book for people who wish to research various traditional and promising new materials for use in construction of one-story buildings. The book begins with "Fundamental Information on Building Materials," which discusses soils and soil testing, binders, concrete fibrocement, natural fibers, bamboo and timber. Next, "Fundamental Information on Building Elements" covers components of buildings such as foundations, bricks, and roofing. Finally, examples of each building element are given. Recommended.

A Manual on Building Construction, MF 25-616, book, 360 pages, by the Rev. H. Dancy, 1948, reprinted 1973, £5.95 from ITDG.

Originally published by the Sudan Interior Mission in 1948, this book was reprinted by ITDG because it has "exceptional value as a practical field building manual." Written for missionaries as amateur builders/supervisors, the text occasionally reflects the paternalistic thinking of the time.

A comprehensive manual, it deals with the essential elements of permanent dwelling construction, relying on block, brick, adobe, or stone walls. The author makes

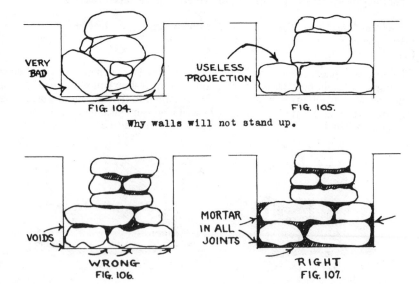

VERY BAD

USELESS PROJECTION

FIG. 104.   FIG. 105.

Why walls will not stand up.

VOIDS

MORTAR IN ALL JOINTS

WRONG
FIG. 106.

RIGHT
FIG. 107.

effective use of illustrations. The book does, however, reflect only Western ideas of proper house construction and design. It does not draw on the building methods, designs and experience of other cultures, nor does it touch on the innovative new building techniques such as ferrocement and the various methods for making stabilized earth blocks.

The Owner Built Home, MF 25-624, book, 367 pages, by Ken Kern, 1975, $6.95 from Owner Builder Publications, P.O. Box 817, North Fork, California 93643, USA.

"**The Owner Built Home** is intended to be a how-to-think-it book. Alternatives to the professionally executed, contractor built home are presented in text and through non-detailed sketches." It is mostly concerned with design considerations for all facets of home building.

The areas covered include heating and natural ventilation, living space design, floor, wall, and roof design. One-third of the book covers how to work with different kinds of building materials — adobe blocks, rammed earth, concrete, wood frames, pole frames, stone masonry. This is perhaps the most useful, practical information contained in the book; it gives a good view of the principles and techniques of building with rammed earth, for example.

The rest of the sections on general design are somewhat directed towards Americans building their own homes. However, the materials sections provide a very good practical overview.

This book does not tell you how to build a house — it tells you all the things to consider in designing a house.

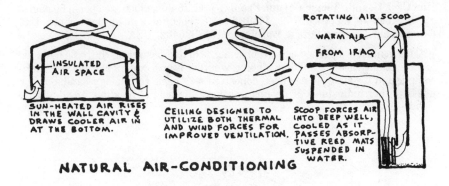

NATURAL AIR-CONDITIONING

The Owner Built Homestead, MF 25-625, book, 400 pages, by Ken Kern, 1975, $6.95 from Owner-Builder Publications, P.O. Box 817, North Fork, California 93643, USA.

This book is a supplement to **The Owner Built Home** (see review above). It covers how to develop the land around a home — a garden, orchard, pasture, woodlot, water supply, wells, fish-culture ponds, fencing, barn, shop and outbuildings. Also included are an oil drum stove design, an adobe barn and silo (for grain storage) design, animal shelter and feed management, waste disposal methods such as composting privies, and nutrition.

Like **The Owner Built Home**, this book is an overview of the great many topics included, and a broad compilation of skills and techniques. There is again a slant towards North American applications. For their value as very complete skills, ideas and methods guides, we feel Ken Kern's books are extremely useful, and lend themselves very well to use in other countries.

Construction Reference Manual, MF 25-652, book, 113 pages, by Donald Batchelder et. al., 1985, from The Experiment in International Living, Kipling Road, Brattleboro, Vermont 05301, USA.

This training manual, based on experiences in Uganda, covers a variety of Western and local construction techniques. These include, for example, poured perimeter foundations using concrete or a clay/ash/cowdung mixture, rough framing for doors and roofs, and anthill kilns for brick production.

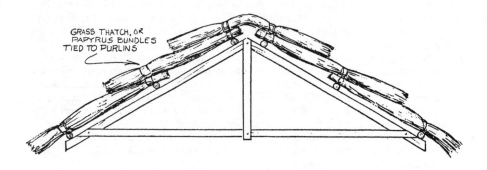

How to Build a House Using Self-Help Housing Techniques (Como Fabricar Una Casa Usando Tecnica Ayuda Propia), MF 25-605, illustrated book, 50 pages, 1974, Stock #023-000-00276-1, $1.40 from Superintendent of Documents, U.S. Government Printing Office, Washington D.C. 20402, USA.

"This manual is designed as a graphic means of demonstrating the basic methods and techniques used in building a home, whether it be a one room cabin or a more complicated dwelling. It has been conceived as a basic technology handbook for use by either individuals or groups who have the goal of building, or adding to,

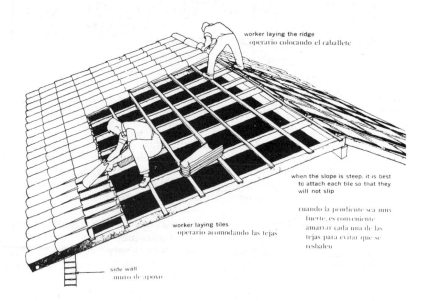

a home of their own, and for those involved in self-help home building projects."

Each of the many drawings presents a complete idea, so a knowledge of English or Spanish is not essential. The drawings are clear and simple.

This manual is intended to be an idea book, to show the reader different methods of constructing each part of a house. For example, there is a section which illustrates methods of making floors using either wood, concrete or stone. There are also sections on walls, roofs, windows and doors, water supply systems, sewage disposal systems, how to measure and lay a foundation, and a comparison of house designs appropriate to different climates: rainy, hot, hot and humid, and temperate areas. The designs are distinctly Western.

The Ecol Operation, MF 25-595, book, 128 pages, 1975, $5.00 from Center for Minimum Cost Housing, School of Architecture, McGill University, 3480 University Street, Montreal, Quebec H3A 2A7, Canada.

"This report describes the work done in the McGill program of Minimum Cost Housing . . . in which the main activity has been the construction of a self-sufficient, habitable low-cost house. This house was built as a test of ideas and a demonstration of how much can be done with unusual materials and methods of construction, and inexperienced builders."

Two structures were built: one from sulfur concrete blocks and the other from logs. The roofing was made of sections of asbestos cement (sewer) pipes.

The description of how to make sulfur concrete and then mold it into blocks is perhaps the most useful part of the report. The interesting characteristic of these blocks is that they are designed for mortarless, interlocking construction, so that walls can be built by anyone just by fitting the blocks together. This system is meant to simplify wall construction to encourage self-help building, and to be earthquake-resistant without the need for reinforced concrete.

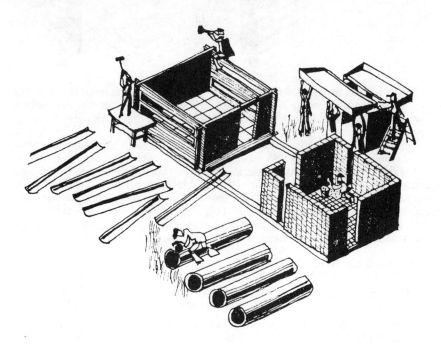

Self-Help Construction of 1-Story Buildings, Peace Corps Appropriate Technology for Development Series Manual M-6, MF 25-632, book, 235 pages, by Peter Gallant, 1980, available to Peace Corps volunteers and development workers from Peace Corps, Information Collection and Exchange, Room 701, 806 Connecticut Avenue N.W., Washington D.C. 20525, USA.

The author stresses the importance of involving the people who will use a building in the process of planning and design. The text balances basic concepts and techniques for planning with a more technical presentation of basic construction principles using low-cost materials available in most parts of the world. In particular, concrete, bamboo, and adobe are discussed, with separate chapters to deal specifically with latrines and construction in earthquake areas. Examples of cut-out "human measuring pieces" will help in arriving at room size and laying out of floor plans. Clearly illustrated.

Construire en Terre, MF 25-592, 265 pages, by Doat, Havs, Houben, Natuk and Vitoux (CRATERRE), 1979, 60F from Groupe de Recherche sur les Techniques Rurales (GRET), 34, rue Dumont d'Urville, 75116-Paris, France.

Mud brick
dome construction

Produced by a group of architects, this French language manual is one of the best books available on earth building construction. Rammed earth (pise), adobe, compressed blocks, soil analysis, soil stabilization, and earth roofs are the major topics.

This exceptional book contains hundreds of drawings and photos documenting a wide range of indigenous earth construction techniques from Sub-Saharan Africa, the Middle East, China, Latin America, North Africa and elsewhere. Use of local materials and owner or community labor in house construction has obvious advantages in the Third World; in fact, more than half the world's population is estimated to live in earth buildings. This volume may contribute to a cross-fertilization of ideas and thus better exploitation of the possibilities offered by earth construction in the Third World.

Handbook for Building Homes of Earth, MF 25-602, book, 158 pages, by L. Wolfskill, $16.00 in U.S., $32.00 overseas, accession no. PB-179 327, from NTIS; or free to serious groups in developing countries from Office of International Affairs, Dept. of Housing and Urban Development, Washington D.C. 20410, USA.

This is a very complete, all-purpose manual covering all types of earthen housing construction including adobe, rammed earth, and pressed blocks. The author also discusses different types of soils, testing soil, soil stabilizers, building site preparation, foundations, roofs, and preparing soil. There are detailed chapters on how to make different kinds of blocks, and how to build structures with them.

The contents will be useful in many different climates and regions — for example, there is information on soil cements applicable to humid, tropical climates where protecting earth structures from the rain is important. Photographs and illustrative drawings are included.

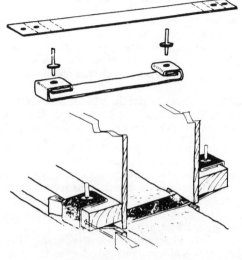

Thin metal strips such as these can be used instead of bolts to tie rammed earth forms together.

Earth for Homes, HUD Ideas and Methods Exchange #22, MF 25-593, book, 70 pages, available on microfiche only in 1981, free to serious groups in developing countries, from Office of International Affairs, HUD, Washington D.C. 20410, USA; others order publication no. PB 188 918/7, $11.50 in U.S., $23.00 overseas, from NTIS.

This book is very similar to **Handbook for Building Homes of Earth** (see review); it covers almost all of the same material but is not as detailed. For example, all

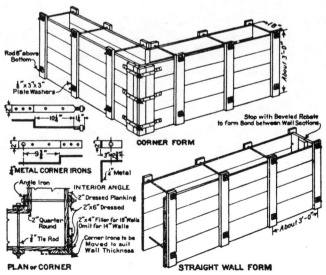

Corner and straight wall forms for rammed earth

the different methods of earth wall construction are covered in one chapter here. Soil stabilizers, earth floors and roofs, and general wall design considerations are discussed. There are only a few drawings and photographs. A good secondary reference book.

Mud, Mud: The Potential of Earth-Based Materials for Third World Housing, MF 25-620, book, 100 pages, by Anil Agarwal, 1981, £2.50 from Earthscan, 10 Percy Street, London W1P 0DR, United Kingdom.

The author argues that mud-based housing (such as adobe, earth bricks, soil cement, etc.) may provide the only answer to the need for low-cost housing throughout the developing world. Written primarily to influence people making planning and policy level decisions, the book also presents useful information for the designer/builder in its survey of mud-based housing in 25 countries.

Build Your House of Earth: A Manual of Earth Wall Construction, book, 130 pages, by G.F. Middleton, 1953, revised by Bob Young, 1975, $9.00 from Second Back Row Press, P.O. Box 197, North Sydney, NSW Australia 2060.

"The establishment of a well-tried technique for the identification of suitable earths, and a standard of practice for the methods of construction, should place earth wall construction, which has so much to commend it, high among the accepted building methods. Earth walls have adequate strength and durability to be practicable for building homes and other structures of any size. They can be attractive, hygienic, fire-resistant, dry and soundproof, and can provide good insulation against heat and cold."

Written from experience in Australia, the Middle East, Southeast Asia and elsewhere, this is an excellent introduction to the methods of pise (rammed earth) construction. This is both an idea book (with many photos, plans, and sketches of buildings and tools) and a well-organized step-by-step guide to building an earth wall dwelling. Site selection, design, soil requirements, estimation of cost and volume of materials, and building codes are also discussed. The author pays particular attention to the tools and forms needed for earth wall construction; many of these are to be made by the builder.

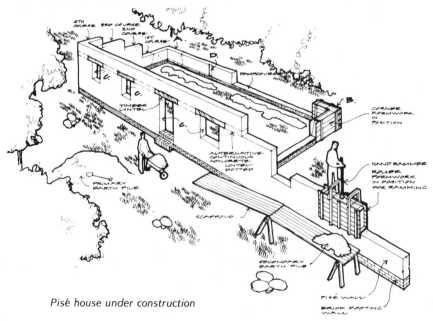

Pisé house under construction

Manual for Building a Rammed Earth Wall, MF 25-614, large illustrated booklet, 28 pages plus appendices, by Lydia A. and David J. Miller, $5.00 from Rammed Earth Homes, 2319 21st Avenue, Greeley, Colorado 80631, USA.

A concise book providing complete instructions for laying foundations, building and assembling form panels, and the earth tamping (ramming) process itself. Although the authors describe walls built for large homes in the U.S., the method has applications in many areas. Soil testing and stabilizing, making test blocks, and tamping tools are also covered.

"It is our experience that no concrete cap is needed on the wall. We recommend that you insert an eye bolt 12 inches long with a 12-inch piece of reinforcing rod through the eye of the bolt...We have not provided the specifications and plans (for a house). That is beyond our abilities. We urge you to consult one of the many good books on house construction."

Adobe as a Socially Appropriate Technology for the Southwest: Solar-Adobe Sundwellings, MF 25-582, report, 45 pages, by John Timothy Mackey, 1980, $5.00 from Center for Village Community Development, 220 Redwood Highway, Mill Valley, California 94941, USA.

Adobe construction (using sun-dried earthen bricks) has been an ecologically sound, low-cost building technique in many parts of the world for thousands of years. This paper examines the historical and current use of adobe in the southwestern U.S. Economic, social, and environmental considerations indicate that in this region, adobe is a truly "appropriate" technology: it is long-lasting, conserves energy, uses local building materials, creates jobs, requires little capital, and "fits" culturally. This last factor "also has a 'cost' component in the long term. For example, Indian reservations around the United States have many examples of run-down, poorly maintained modern woodframe constructed homes. These buildings last only a few years because they are not adapted to their environment and their Indian inhabitants refuse to maintain them."

Adobe brickmaking and basic construction techniques are discussed, along with the thermal properties of adobe which have made it ideally adapted to passive solar construction in the southwestern U.S. Mesa Verde, Colorado is an ancient Native

Steps in the adobe building process

American city where " 'massive stone buildings are clustered under a cliff which protects them from the heat of the summer sun. . . at Chaco Canyon (another ancient community in New Mexico). . . the buildings were terraced and the roofs of each succeeding unit provided a space outdoors to live and work in contact with nature. All day the sun's heat was buried in these massive walls, and in the great cliff to the north, which also protected them from winter winds.' "

Because it is low-cost and labor-intensive, adobe could be an important "self-help technology" today in some areas where families could not otherwise afford their own home. With recent developments in construction techniques, adobe dwellings may soon meet building codes even in earthquake zones.

While it does not provide much technical detail, this report is a convincing illustration of the potential of adobe as an appropriate building technology in the United States.

Making the Adobe Brick, MF 25-613, book, 88 pages, by Eugene Boudreau, 1972, $6.95 from Bookworks, Random House Inc., 400 Hahn Road, Westminster, Maryland 21157, USA.

Like several other books in this section, this one covers the basic operations in making adobe (mud) bricks. These include testing and choosing the proper soil, mixing the soil with a stabilizing agent (emulsified asphalt), and molding and drying the bricks using wood molds. Wall construction with the finished adobes is also discussed, as are Uniform Building Code requirements for construction with adobe in the United States.

Adobe Craft, MF 25-583, book, 72 pages, by Karl Schultz, 1974, out of print in 1985.

In addition to detailed information on brickmaking, this book describes the production of reinforced poured adobe, a process that eliminates the need for bricks. The appendix contains a very good explanation of adobe construction methods, as well as how to use oil drums to make both a soil sifter and a mixer.

Selection of Materials for Stabilized Brick Manufacture, Technical Bulletin #5, MF 25-631, photocopy of leaflet, 6 pages, by S. Mason and J. Kent of PNG Dept. of Works and Supply, 1970, limited supply, at cost to serious groups, from Librarian, DWS, P.O. Box 1108, Boroko, Papua New Guinea.

"The purpose of this bulletin is to provide instruction in the preliminary identification of suitable material for the manufacture of stabilized bricks." The soil combinations described are to be used with an earth-ramming machine, such as the CINVA-Ram. Tests to determine soil composition are described.

Soil Cement: Its Use in Building, MF 25-640, book, 126 pages, by Augusto A. Enteiche G., 1964, also available in Spanish and French editions, publication #E.64.IV.6, $7.00 from UNIPUB.

"The compound of soil, cement and water, mixed in the proper proportions and compacted to the proper degree, constitutes "soil-cement." This paper shows how soil-cement may be used at various stages in the construction of a house, together with a number of examples which may be helpful to anyone wishing to use this material for building purposes.

"**Soil Cement** is divided into chapters, dealing with basic facts and practical application on: knowing soils, soil as a construction material, the preparation of soil-cement, the use of soil-cement for housing, and accomplishments in soil-cement. The order of presentation, the terminology used, and the large number of illustrations, are all designed to make the instructions more readily understandable with

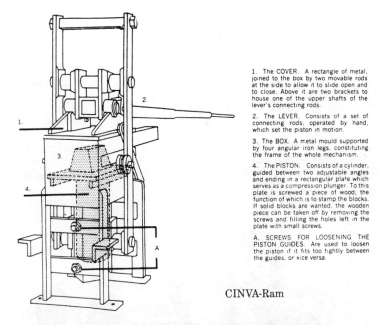

1. The COVER. A rectangle of metal, joined to the box by two movable rods at the side to allow it to slide open and to close. Above it are two brackets to house one of the upper shafts of the lever's connecting rods.

2. The LEVER. Consists of a set of connecting rods, operated by hand, which set the piston in motion.

3. The BOX. A metal mould supported by four angular iron legs, constituting the frame of the whole mechanism.

4. The PISTON. Consists of a cylinder, guided between two adjustable angles and ending in a rectangular plate which serves as a compression plunger. To this plate is screwed a piece of wood, the function of which is to stamp the blocks. If solid blocks are wanted, the wooden piece can be taken off by removing the screws and filling the holes left in the plate with small screws.

A. SCREWS FOR LOOSENING THE PISTON GUIDES. Are used to loosen the piston if it fits too tightly between the guides, or vice versa.

CINVA-Ram

a view to the greatest possible circulation and impact."

The author was a staff member of CINVA (Inter-American Housing and Planning Center) in Colombia, South America, where the CINVA-Ram was developed (see **Making Building Blocks with the CINVA-Ram**). **Soil Cement** also covers the use of the CINVA-Ram for making building blocks.

This book covers the subject of soils and soil-cement very completely; it is comparable to **Handbook for Building Homes of Earth** (see review) in the amount of useful information it has; the difference is that it concentrates on the use of cement as a soil stabilizer, rather than including all forms of stabilized soil construction.

Making Building Blocks with the CINVA-Ram, MF 25-612, instruction manual, 21 pages, 1966, Spanish edition available, $6.25 in U.S., $6.50 international surface mail, $8.50 international air mail, from VITA.

"The CINVA-Ram is a simple, low-cost, portable machine for making building blocks and tiles from common soil. The press, made entirely of steel, has a mold box in which a hand-operated piston compresses a slightly moistened mixture of soil and cement or lime." Blocks made with the CINVA-Ram are easier to make than concrete blocks, are low-cost, and can be made on a building site and so avoid transportation costs.

"This manual combines the experience of four people who used the CINVA-Ram and figured answers to the inevitable problems of detail as they came up day after day." It is intended as a manual for fieldworkers and supervisors, giving instructions on how to use the Ram, including: testing and mixing the soil, operating the Ram to make blocks, curing the blocks, and construction using pressed blocks.

Subtitled "A Supervisor's Manual," this book is intended as an instruction manual on how to use the CINVA-Ram. The Ram can be purchased for about US$250.00 (1976) from METALIBEC Ltda, Apartado Aereo 11798, Bogota, Colombia.

Two sets of plans for similar earth-block ramming machines are reviewed elsewhere (**Assembly Manual for the Tek-Block Press**, from Ghana, and **La CETA-Ram**, from Guatemala). See also review of **Soil Cement: Its Use in Building** and the accompanying drawing of the CINVA-Ram, in this section.

Soil Block Presses, MF 25-660, book, 128 pages, by Kiran Mukerji, 1986, available from German Appropriate Technology Exchange, Dag-Hammarskjold-Weg 1, 6236 Eschborn, Federal Republic of Germany.

Around the world there are quite a variety of hand-operated presses for the production of building blocks from compressed soil. This book is the only place to find a summary of the design options for such presses.

The manufacturer's address and the rate of block production are provided for each design. Rates of production are mostly 40-60 blocks per hour with 3 workers with the hand-operated equipment, although one design claims as much as 200 blocks/hour with 4 workers. The automated and semi-automated equipment generally produces from several hundred to as much as 1500-2500 blocks/hour with 3-4 workers. Much of the book consists of data sheets from the manufacturers.

Manufacture of Stabilized Bricks Using Ramming Action Brick Machine, Technical Bulletin #6, MF 25-618, photocopy of leaflet, 12 pages, by S. Mason and J. Kent of PNG Dept. of Works and Supply, limited supply, at cost to serious groups from Librarian, DWS, P.O. Box 1108, Boroko, Papua New Guinea.

"The purpose of this bulletin is to act as an instruction manual in the operation" of a brick ramming machine developed in Papua New Guinea, similar in principle to the CINVA-Ram. Basic steps in soil testing and preparation, and operation of the machine are provided, with photographs.

La CETA-Ram, MF 25-608, booklet, 14 pages, by Roberto E. Lou Ma, 1977, $2.00 postpaid from the author, Roberto E. Lou Ma, Centro de Experimentacion en Tecnologia Apropiada (CETA), 15 Avenida 14-61, zona 10, Guatemala City, Guatemala.

This Spanish language booklet (with English summary) provides drawings and photos of a machine for making pressed soil-cement blocks. This machine is unusual in that it makes two holes in each block so that reinforcing rods for earthquake protection can be used.

Only one of the drawings, showing only the block itself, includes dimensions. All other dimensions of the machine will have to be calculated from this. The thickness of steel to be used, and the precise positioning of the pivot points are not provided, which is likely to cause the reader some difficulty.

The construction details provided for the Tek-block press (see review) are much more complete. Readers may wish to combine the two designs, for use in earthquake areas.

Manual para la Construccion de la CETA-Ram, MF 25-617, booklet, 29 pages plus plans, by Roberto E. Lou Ma, CETA/USAC, 1981, $6.00, available only in Spanish from Centro de Experimentacion en Tecnologia Apropiada, 15 Avenida 14-61, zona 10, Guatemala City, Guatemala.

This manual, in Spanish, contains more detail and better diagrams (with dimensions) than **La CETA-Ram**. However, it lacks the English summary of the earlier version.

Assembly Manual for the Tek-Block Press, booklet of plans, 26 pages, by John Dye, $5.00 from Department of Housing and Planning Research, Faculty of Architecture, University of Science and Technology, Kumasi, Ghana.

This is a complete set of drawings for the production and assembly of a hand-operated press for making soil-cement building blocks. The blocks are about 4% cement and 96% soil. "These soil-cement blocks are nearly as strong and water resistant as sandcrete blocks, while containing about one-third as much cement." The blocks are made at the building site, greatly reducing the amount of materials that must be transported. The press can also be used to make sun-dried blocks (no cement added) for very low-cost construction.

These plans are for a simplified, strengthened version of the machine, which has been widely used in Ghana for more than 5 years. The basic concept is similar to the CINVA-Ram.

"Although a shaping machine, milling machine, and planing machine are all specified, it is possible to fabricate the machine if only one of these is available." The parts are all welded together.

The press can be operated by one person. Up to 10 people can be employed, at which point the machine is being operated continuously while digging and mixing of soil, and stacking of new blocks is going on. Output is 200 to 400 blocks per day with a 3 person crew.

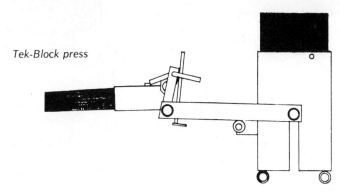

Tek-Block press

Technical Research Bulletin, MF 25-642, booklets, Volume 1: 29 pages, Volume 3: 48 pages, by the Dept. of Works and Supply in Papua New Guinea, limited supply, include return postage, from DWS.

Volume 1 has articles on stabilized bricks (including brickwork in earthquake areas), plain earth and stone construction, lime stabilization and production, and the treatment of organic materials against fire, decay and insect attack. In Volume 3, the emphasis is on the technical, rather than the practical, aspects of soil engineering. The contents are: a review of building foundation practice on swelling soils, cement requirements for soil cement bricks, and further notes on lime stabilization of soils.

Brickmaking in Developing Countries, MF 25-651, book, 88 pages, by John Parry, Building Research Establishment, United Kingdom, 1979, £6.35 from ITDG.

A very well-presented discussion of the technologies and economics of brickmaking, this book especially examines the advantages of traditional producers over modern mechanized brick plants. Some of these apply to other labor-intensive vs. capital-intensive technologies as well. The traditional producers have low fixed costs and low total costs, and are able to vary output with market demand without affecting their economic viability. The major disadvantage of the traditional producer has tended to be variable brick quality — the author explores simple tools and techniques that can overcome this problem.

Current practices in a range of developing countries are reviewed, and the scope for improvement is identified in each case. Well-illustrated and well-written. Recommended.

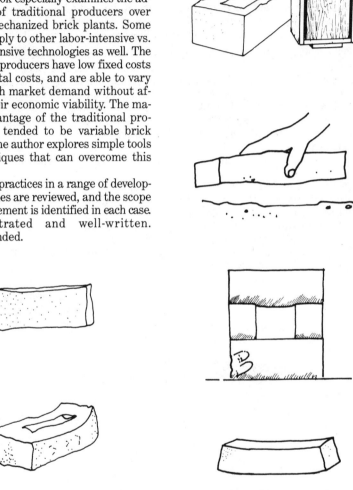

Selection of Materials for Burnt Clay Brick Manufacture, Technical Bulletin #7, MF 25-630, leaflet, 5 pages, by Papua New Guinea's Building Research Station, 1970, out of print in 1985.

"The purpose of this bulletin is to provide instruction in the preliminary identification of suitable materials for burnt clay products." Burnt clay bricks are made from clay, and then fired in a special oven (kiln). Simple tests to determine whether a material is suitable for use in burnt bricks are described.

Small Scale Brickmaking, MF 25-659, book, 210 pages, ILO, 1984, $14.25 from ILO.

This volume consists primarily of technical details on the various steps in brick production, and some possible improved technologies. There is more technical information here than in **Brickmaking in Developing Countries**, but the latter should be read first for its perspective on needed improvements in traditional production systems and its general observations on the economics of brickmaking.

The smallest production units of 1000 bricks per day capacity are the main concern of this book, but larger units are also described.

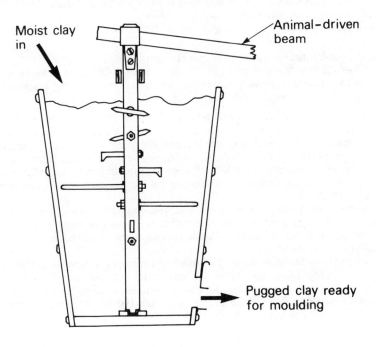

Moist clay in

Animal-driven beam

Pugged clay ready for moulding

Small-Scale Manufacture of Burned Building Brick, MF 25-639, booklet, 14 pages, by D. Thomas, also available in French and Spanish, $6.25 in U.S., $6.50 international surface mail, $7.50 international air mail, from VITA.

"The purpose of this manual is to outline, in as simple a manner as possible, the details of making and burning clay brick suitable for domestic building. The scope of the manual is confined to 'cottage industries'...the author has had personal contact with such brickmaking plants in both Central Mexico and Honduras."

The booklet "explores the establishment and operation of a building-brick plant wherein nothing but 'on-hand' materials and labor will be utilized."

This is a step-by-step guide that also covers important considerations such as the location of suitable clay deposits and the firing and cooling of the finished bricks. Includes illustrations of the kiln and the brick-loading patterns.

1000 to 3000 Capacity Brick Kiln, Technical Bulletin #12, MF 25-622, leaflet, 18 pages, by PWG Dept. of Works and Supply, 1973, limited supply, free to serious groups from DWS.

"A 1000 to 3000 capacity brick kiln has been devised by the Building Research Station, to meet the needs of small scale intermittent production of a durable material at the village level. The kiln is a rectangular construction with an internal dimension sufficient to stack to a predetermined pattern of a maximum of 3000 bricks within its walls."

According to the authors, "the design has been made as simple as possible, eliminating the need for skilled labor in its construction." Their design appears to be an efficient one capable of creating uniformly durable bricks; significant if this characteristic is an important one in the reader's area. This kiln is more complex than the one described in VITA's **Small Scale Manufacture of Burned Building Brick** (see review). Also, this design doesn't employ a flue system, and the firebox construction seems less flexible than in the VITA design (which could be easily enlarged to whatever capacity is desired).

A well-illustrated leaflet with a glossary of terms and detailed drawings.

The Owner-Builder's Guide to Stone Masonry, MF 25-623, book, 192 pages, by Ken Kern, Steve Magers, and Lou Penfield, 1976, $6.00 (two or more copies $5.00 each to readers in developing countries), from Owner-Builder Publications, P.O. Box 817, North Fork, California 93643, USA.

"The purpose of this book is threefold: 1) We show the inexperienced builder how to 'lay up' stone for various walls, how to 'face' building framework and how to 'cast' stone in a wall with a movable form; 2) . . .(we) acquaint readers with the native properties and the availability of usable building stone. Next to earth, there is no more universal nor less appreciated building resource than stone; 3) . . .(we) express the aesthetic satisfaction we three authors have experienced building with stone."

The authors carry out their purposes well: teaching the basics of building with stone. The only significant lack of information is on the coverage of earthquake problems. The book covers building with or without concrete, and there is a glossary of masonry technical terms.

"When you trowel mortar use only as much as necessary to provide the bed with sufficient covering. Too much mortar will only squish out and cover the stone face. Do not trowel smooth the mortar; let the stone mash it down. In this way gaps will more certainly be filled. Once a stone is in place try not to move it. Any movement will weaken the bond between stone and mortar."

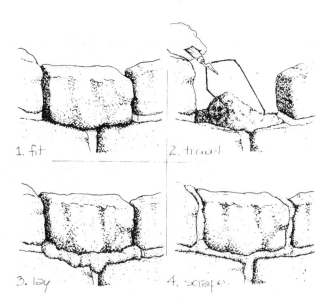

1. fit   2. trowel   3. lay   4. scrape

Fireplaces, MF 25-600, book, 192 pages, by Ken Kern and Steve Magers, 1978, $7.95 (two or more copies $5.00 each to readers in developing countries), from Owner-Builder Publications, Box 817, North Fork, California 93643, USA.

"The traditional fireplace not only sends some 80 percent of the fire's heat up the chimney but a goodly portion of the room's heat as well." This is a practical book on good fireplace design to overcome this basic disadvantage of fireplaces in home heating. Step-by-step construction techniques are presented. The authors discuss the qualities of different building materials: "Most stone cannot withstand intense heat; in a firebox it soon fragments...due to rapid surface expansion."

These specific skills and materials will be of most interest to readers in rich countries with cold climates. However, the general theory and principles presented are relevant in any setting. Another high-quality Owner-Builder book.

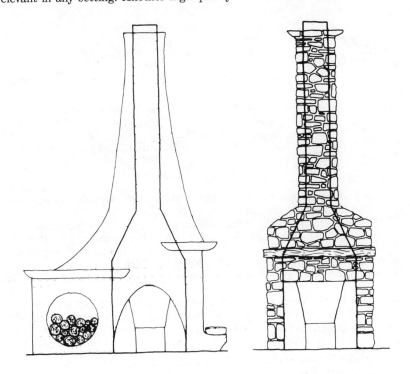

The Timber Framing Book, MF 25-643, paperback, 178 pages, by Stewart Elliott and Eugenie Wallas, 1977, $13.95 from Housesmith's Press, P.O. Box 157, Kittery Point, Maine 03905, USA.

Timber-framing is a method of housing construction using interlocking notches and grooves combined with wooden pegs to connect the major wooden beams. The method is labor-intensive and requires tools not common to modern Western carpentry but still common and inexpensive in many Third World countries: the adze, auger, draw knife, chisel, and axe.

"Timber-frame houses built in Europe as early as the fourteenth century stand proud and sturdy to this day. Compared to conventional construction, timber-frame structures can be 20 to 30 percent less expensive to build. Less energy is expended in both the milling and the construction of the frame...If you have some basic carpentry skills you and some helpers can frame a house using the information

Timber framing

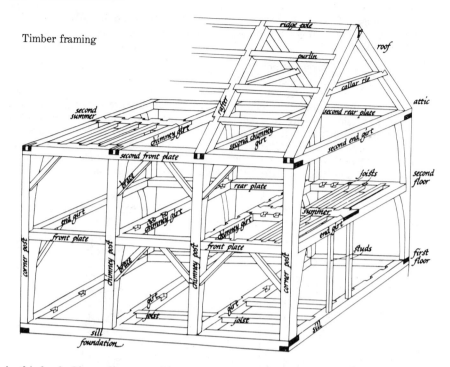

in this book. If you do not, and have a carpenter in mind who has not previously used timber framing, he can use this book to teach himself how."

Where wood is plentiful the timber-framing methods of housing construction can be used to build houses of great durability (but you will have to look elsewhere for preservation information). Where wood is scarce, soil-cement, adobe and other wood-conserving construction materials would be more appropriate.

There are illustrations and pictures on almost every page, and a thorough glossary.

Wood Handbook: Wood as an Engineering Material, Agriculture Handbook No. 72, MF 25-662, book, 432 pages, by Forest Products Laboratory, USDA, 1974, $15.00 from Superintendent of Documents, U.S. Government Printing Office, Washington D.C. 20402, USA.

An in-depth reference book on the physical properties and characteristics of wood, this covers North American and some other hardwood and softwood species. Shrinkage, working qualities, decay resistance and mechanical properties (e.g. shear

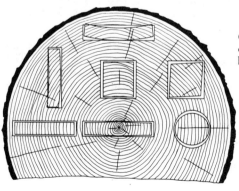

Characteristic shrinkage and distortion of flats, squares, and rounds as affected by the direction of the annual rings.

strength, modulus of elasticity) are discussed. Other topics include fasteners, beams and columns, glued-laminated timbers, plywood, and paint protection of wood. While the species listed here will not usually be the same as those encountered in the Third World, the reader can get an idea of the range of values within which local species can probably be placed (e.g. in the selection of timber beam sizes for short bridges). A good place to look when you need a few important, hard-to-find numbers.

Pole Buildings in Papua New Guinea, MF 25-627, booklet with design drawings, 41 pages, by Peter Lattey, 1974 (to be revised), US$3.00 from the Forest Products Research Centre, P.O. Box 1358, Papua New Guinea.

This book describes work with traditional designs from PNG using wooden poles to build houses, schools, and meeting centers. 12 designs are presented, with drawings and photos. Also covered are details of how to connect poles at joints, and how to join the poles to walls using galvanized iron strips.

The designs are based on the author's actual experience in building in PNG. He used traditional building techniques, updating and improving them. The methods and the designs should be applicable to many places where wood poles are available for housing, if an effort is being made to use low-cost local materials, local labor, and simple construction techniques.

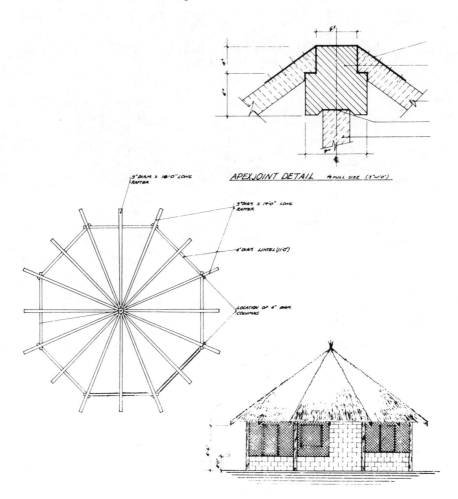

Wood-Frame House Construction, MF 25-663, book, 223 pages, by L.O. Anderson, Forest Products Laboratory, USDA, revised 1975, $7.50 from Superintendent of Documents, U.S. Government Printing Office, Washington D.C. 20402, USA.

Most houses in the United States are built using wood frame construction. This involves using wood 2" by 4" to build the structural portions that provide the strength, carry the weight of the roof, and hold the house together. Interior and exterior walls and the roof are then covered with other materials.

The technique requires an abundant supply of low-cost milled lumber, a condition not met in most developing countries. However, some elements common to wood frame construction can be usefully incorporated into other building systems. For this purpose, this is a useful reference.

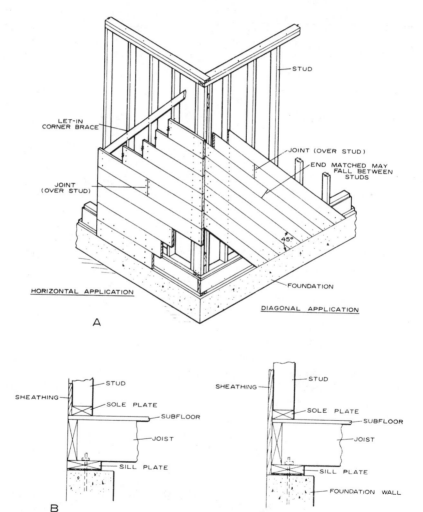

Figure 54.—Application of wood sheathing: A, Horizontal and diagonal; B, started at subfloor; C, started at foundation wall.

Popular Manual for Wooden House Construction, MF 25-656, book, 95 pages, by Instituto de Pesquisas Tecnologicas (IPT), Brazil, 1985, available to developing countries free from Editor, UNIDO Newsletter, P.O. Box 300, A-1400 Vienna, Austria.

Hundreds of cartoons and drawings illustrate the construction of low-cost wood frame houses in this manual based on designs originally used in Brazil. The construction system presented is an interesting simplification of Western platform frame construction, and may offer ideas to readers seeking the advantages of this technique for special structures. It does require a good supply of milled lumber of consistent dimensions. The cost (US$50-60 per square meter, $4.63-5.56 per square foot), while very low by industrial country standards, averaged $2000 (40 square meters) for the 40 houses built in 1982. The author does not consider the severe space constraints faced by urban slum dwellers, the piecemeal construction strategy they commonly use, the extreme difficulty they have in raising such sums of money, or the likelihood that "low income" families able to raise $2000 would probably choose to invest it in a small business rather than a house.

The manual is intended for people without construction experience. Local language translations can be substituted for the English text. Wood species appropriate for the different components are identified for different parts of the world.

Low Cost Country Home Building, MF 25-610, book, 119 pages, Department of Environment and Planning, Australia, 1981, Aust.$13.00 from Hale and Iremonger Ltd., G.P.O. Box 2552, Sydney, NSW Australia 2001.

A thorough and innovative guide for low-cost rural homebuilders in Australia, this text should be very useful in many other regions and applications as well. Of particular interest is the information on siting and landscaping to affect the climate of the area immediately surrounding the home. Also contains useful construction information for non-conventional, non-manufactured building materials. Recommended.

Low Cost Housing: Prefabricated Panel System, Technical Bulletin #14, MF 25-611, booklet, 39 pages, by D. Brett of Papua New Guinea's Dept. of Works and Supply, 1974, limited supply, include return postage, from DWS.

"To assist in providing accommodations for low income earners in PNG this bulletin outlines economies possible by using a prefabricated panel construction technique. Prefabricated building can maximize returns in material, labor and money. This bulletin explains a simple technique through which reductions in materials and construction time can significantly reduce other building costs."

Contains construction techniques using these prefabricated walls (made from wood), assembly drawings for making the panels themselves, and photographs. The panels can be made locally using only hand woodworking tools.

Painting Inside and Out, USDA Home and Garden Bulletin #222, MF 25-654, booklet, 26 pages, 1978, publication 203N, $1.50 payable to Superintendent of Documents, Consumer Information Center, Box 100, Pueblo, Colorado 81002, USA.

Wood and other construction materials need paint for protection against the sun and weather, to ensure a long life of service. General advice on painting is contained in this booklet written for a U.S. audience. The recommendations regarding such topics as surface preparation, use of primers, effects of temperature extremes, etc., also apply to other parts of the world, although the paints available will vary.

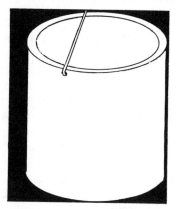

A wire across the top of the paint can or paint bucket is convenient for holding the brush.

Manual of Rural Wood Preservation, MF 25-615, booklet, 27 pages, Forest Products Research Centre, 1975, US$3.00 from Office of Forests, Forest Products Research Centre, P.O. Box 1358, Boroko, Papua New Guinea.

This is a practical manual for wood preservation techniques, useful in any tropical area where wood rots quickly or is eaten by termites. The areas covered include

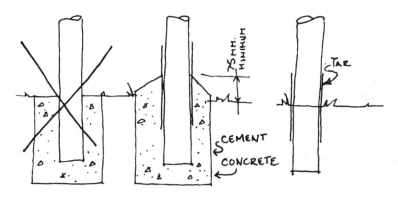

sections on: wood-destroying insects and fungi, building practice, materials (including poles and woven bamboo), treatment methods for rural areas (including sap replacement, use of C.C.A. and Octabor chemical preservatives). This last section outlines the various treatment methods in detail. The building techniques described will help in designing wooden structures to last longer.

Bambu—Su Cultivo y Aplicaciones, MF 25-586, book, 318 pages, by Oscar Hidalgo Lopez, 1974, in Spanish, $27.00 from Estudios Tecnicos Colombianos Ltda., P.O. Box 50085, Bogota, Colombia.

Available in Spanish only, this book contains a wealth of information about the cultivation and applications of bamboo in construction, engineering, paper processing, and handicrafts. Extensive illustrations and detailed graphs help present the biology and technology of this "wonderful weed" from throughout the world. Some of the more unusual examples include: a 225-meter bamboo bridge (with five supports) spanning the Min River in Szechuan Province, China; an experimental single engine airplane from the Philippines with wings and fuselage of bamboo; and a bamboo geodesic dome seating 2000 people built in Honolulu, Hawaii.

Many variations of bamboo construction joinery, appropriate hand tools, low-cost housing, bridge building, preservation techniques, and bamboo-reinforced concrete forms and formulas are described in this fascinating book. Even those unable to read Spanish will find many ideas and much inspiration through the illustrations alone.

Highly recommended.

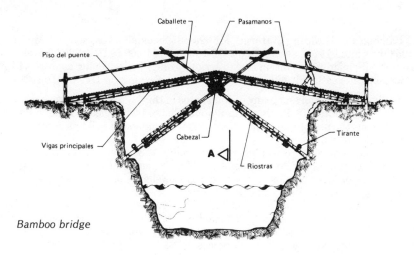

Bamboo bridge

Nuevas Tecnicas de Construccion con Bambu, MF 25-621, book, 137 pages, by Oscar Hidalgo Lopez, 1978, in Spanish, $9.00 airmail from Estudios Tecnicos Colombianos Ltda., P.O. Box 50085, Bogota, Colombia.

A companion to Oscar Hidalgo Lopez's epic **Bambu—Su Cultivo y Aplicaciones**, this volume provides information on cultivation of a valuable Colombian bamboo species, and several specific applications of bamboo in construction. Featured are A-frame structures for coffee processing and low-cost housing, and a soil-cement plaster on a split bamboo base as an innovative roofing material. Another application with a lot of potential is bamboo reinforcing of cement and concrete; here it is used in water containers, flat panels, and concrete beams (with technical information on strength).

The Book of Bamboo, MF 25-650, book, 332 pages, by David Farrelly, $17.45 postpaid from Sierra Club Books, P.O. Box 3886 from Rincon Annex, San Francisco, California 94115, USA.

An astonishing variety of bamboo uses for tools and structures are described in this book, along with a lengthy treatment of bamboo species and biology. The text knitting all of this together flows from fact to whimsy, from historical detail to philosophical wandering. English language readers now have something as voluminous and comprehensive as Oscar Hidalgo Lopez's Spanish language books on bamboo.

Gabions, an early and surviving mainstay of Chinese civil engineering, are essentially huge, loosely woven bamboo baskets full of rocks used to stabilize riverbanks and waterfronts. An empty gabion is pictured.

Bamboo as a Building Material, MF 25-585, booklet, 52 pages, by F. McClure, 1953 (reprinted 1972), accession no. PB-188 921, $10.00 in U.S., $20.00 overseas, from NTIS; microfiche edition free to serious groups in developing countries from Office of International Affairs, Dept. of HUD, Washington D.C. 20410, USA.

The how-to material and many of the photos in this booklet have been reprinted in the VITA **Village Technology Handbook**. Shows techniques of fastening bamboo without the use of nails, and various uses of bamboo in building construction around the world.

One section is given to bamboo reinforcement of concrete; this is a reprint of a technical summary of conclusions from tests on concrete beams. Problems included bond between bamboo and concrete, and swelling that occurs when seasoned bamboo absorbs moisture from wet concrete.

While many houses have been built with only a machete, more refined or elaborate structures might require some of the handtools briefly described (no illustrations). The booklet also includes a lengthy list of bamboo types used around the world, and a 60-entry list of selected references up to 1953.

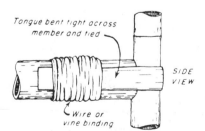

Tongue bent tight across member and tied

SIDE VIEW

Wire or vine binding

CONNECTION OF BAMBOO TO ROUND PINS, ETC.

The Use of Bamboo and Reeds in Building Construction, MF 25-645, book, 95 pages, U.N. Dept. of Economic and Social Affairs, 1972, out of print in 1985.

"Bamboos and reeds are the oldest and chief building materials in rural areas and villages throughout the world's tropical and subtropical regions...more people live in bamboo and reed buildings than in houses of any other material. Bamboo and reed construction is popular for good reasons: the material is plentiful and cheap, the villager can build his own house with simple tools, and there is a living tradition of skills and methods required for construction. This tradition has been augmented in recent years by experiments carried out principally in India, Indonesia, the Philippines and Colombia. The bamboo and reed housing is easily built, easily repaired, well-ventilated, sturdy and earthquake resistant."

"Deterioration by insects, rot fungi and fire is the chief drawback of bamboo and reeds as building materials."

This study was produced to inform government planners, extension officers, contractors and villagers of new or less well-known techniques of construction, and to stimulate additional research to improve the material properties and techniques of building construction with bamboo and reeds.

Included are descriptions with photos of common uses of bamboos and reeds, drawings of a wide variety of joints used in building with bamboo, a summary of research (now 25 years old) on concrete with bamboo and reed reinforcing, strength data on selected bamboo species used in construction, tools and species lists, and preservatives for different bamboo end uses. Some of the material was taken from **Bamboo as a Building Material** (see review).

A Series of Articles on the Use of Bamboo in Building Construction, MF 25-658, collected by Dr. Jules J.A. Janssen, 1982, 177 pages, £4.50 from ITDG.

This welcome collection assembles a variety of practical bamboo articles in one place. Preservation techniques are followed by sections on the use of bamboo in housing, bridges, water supply, and concrete reinforcement. One article explains how to calculate the strength of bamboos for construction purposes.

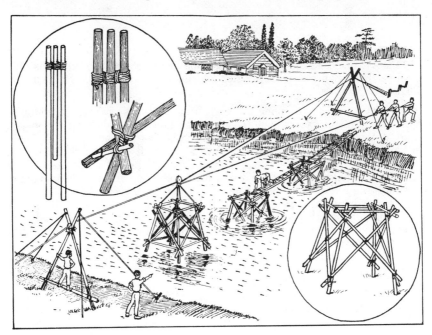

Plastic Sheeting: Its Use for Emergency and Other Purposes, MF 25-655, 18 pages, by Jim Howard and Ron Spice, 1973, 95p from OXFAM, 274 Banbury Road, Oxford OX2 7DZ, United Kingdom.

A basic introduction to polyethylene sheeting, its performance, and various means of fastening it on structures.

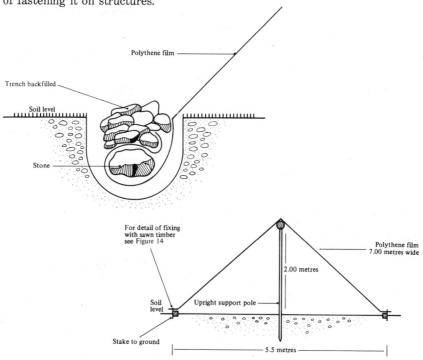

The Yurt, MF 25-649, 1 large sheet of plans, by W. Coperthwaite, specify 12- or 17-foot ($10.00), 32-foot ($20.00), or 54-foot diameter yurt ($25.00), ⅓ discount for developing countries, from the Yurt Foundation, Bucks Harbor, Maine 04618, USA.

The Yurt is a circular dwelling that originates in Mongolia "where the prototype has for thousands of years been found to withstand the severe cold and violent winds of the steppes...The purpose of this design is to reduce the skills needed in building to a minimum and still have a beautiful, inexpensive permanent shelter...The design of the contemporary Yurt is the result of 10 years' effort to develop techniques that make it possible for children and unskilled adults to participate in a major way in the creation of their own shelter."

Bill Coperthwaite created this particular design for North Americans. It remains simple in both materials and tools required, although some of the materials may be expensive in other parts of the world. It can be built by several people in just a couple of days.

The Yurt has a ten-sided plywood floor. The overlapping boards forming the exterior wall slope outward as they go up. They are held together at the top through the principle of the tension band (such as is often used in wooden buckets) with a ⅜-inch cable. The roof slopes gently to the center of the structure, where a steel band forming a skylight keeps the roof from collapsing inward. This structure is evidently strong, and requires no complicated, expensive supporting beams.

Build a Yurt, MF 25-587, book, 134 pages, by Len Charney, 1974, MacMillan Publishing Co., out of print in 1981.

Charney began with the Yurt Foundation's design, and incorporated many of the original elements from the Mongolian Yurt back into it. The walls and roof are made from 1×2 inch strips arranged in a lattice network, rather than the solid boards used by the Yurt Foundation. The positioning of the wood strips in combination with a ³⁄₁₆-inch steel cable provides for an extremely stable, strong structure.

The book has both text and drawings/photographs. The author describes in detail the construction steps, including building a wooden floor, using canvas, burlap, tarpaper and/or wood shingles to cover the framework. The explanations are clear and easy to follow. Another good design.

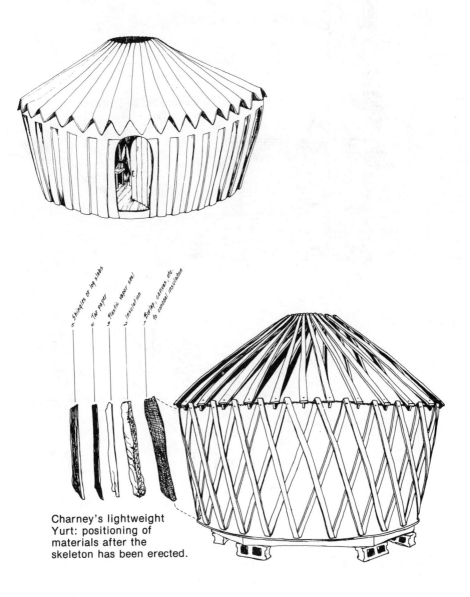

Charney's lightweight
Yurt: positioning of
materials after the
skeleton has been erected.

The $50 and Up Underground House Book, MF 25-599, large paperback, 112 pages, by Mike Oehler, 1978, $8.95 plus $1.00 postage (25% discount to **Sourcebook** readers), from Mole Publishing Co., Route 1, Box 618, Bonners Ferry, Idaho 83805, USA.

Low-cost underground dwellings are characteristically damp and somewhat dark. The houses described in this manual are designed such that the pitch of the roof coincides with the slope of a hillside, so that rainwater drains off and away. The

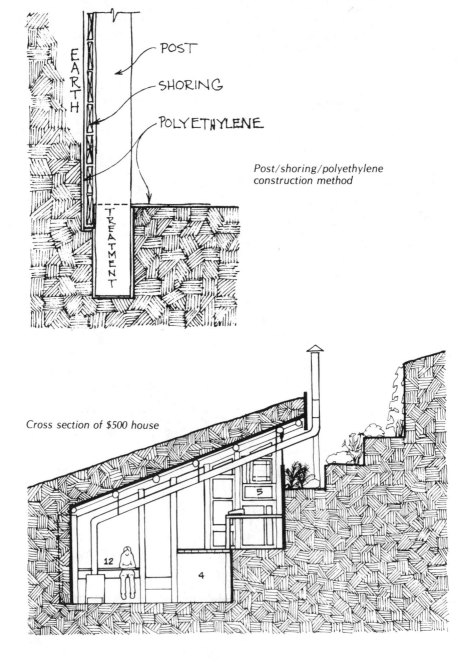

Post/shoring/polyethylene construction method

Cross section of $500 house

author's Post/Shoring/Polyethylene (PSP) construction method should result in a sealed, durable living space. "In the PSP system treated posts are set into the ground after excavation has been made. Beams for the roof are notched into these. Then a sheet of polyethylene is stretched around the outside of the wall. Shoring is placed between the posts and the polyethylene, one board at a time. The polyethylene is stretched snug, and earth is backfilled behind, pressing the polyethylene against the shoring and the shoring against the posts."

The author has lived in his PSP home for several years and made some adaptations — an uphill patio, a foyer, side-facing windows — which enhance its appeal. Photos and clear sketches show these and other possible modifications.

Underground housing has been used in many parts of the world for thousands of years. It offers, in particular, protection from extreme weather conditions. This book may calm some of those who accuse appropriate technologists of returning to the age of the caveman, with a nice look at the owner-built technology end of the underground housing spectrum.

Earth Sheltered Housing Design: Guidelines, Examples, and References, MF 25-594, book, 318 pages, by The Underground Space Center, University of Minnesota, 1979, $10.95 from Van Nostrand Reinhold Co., 135 West 50th Street, New York, New York 10020, USA.

"The intent of this study is to present information which will be useful in the architectural design of earth sheltered houses. Part A discusses design guidelines and includes pertinent factors to be considered. Part B gives plans, details and photographs of existing examples of earth sheltered houses from around the country. These serve to show a number of different ways in which the design constraints discussed in Part A have been dealt with in individual designs. Part C is intended to ease access to further detailed information and includes an annotated bibliography." This summary of design considerations for underground housing, compiled by North American building professionals, emphasizes conventional materials and approaches (e.g. reinforced concrete and planning for mass production). The authors plainly are not advocating independent design by owner-builders: "The provision of this design information should not be construed to mean that no outside assistance with design is necessary. In particular, the structural design for earth sheltered houses should not be treated lightly and professional assistance in

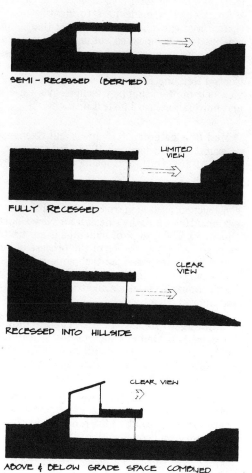

SEMI - RECESSED (BERMED)

FULLY RECESSED

RECESSED INTO HILLSIDE

ABOVE & BELOW GRADE SPACE COMBINED

this aspect should normally be sought." In fact, the kinds of earth-sheltered homes presented involve so much special architectural and construction expertise that they would be far too expensive for most families in rich countries.

Nevertheless, this book presents the best summary we've seen of factors influencing earth-sheltered housing design and siting. Sections discussing configuration and thickness of earth "blankets" covering wall and roof surfaces, and the cost vs. energy savings implied by these blankets are especially good. Also covered are basic strategies for heating, cooling, ventilation, drainage and waterproofing, and the fundamentals of passive solar design. Appendices discuss building codes and compare energy use in earth-sheltered vs. above-ground houses.

Recommended.

Roofing in Developing Countries — Research for New Technologies, MF 25-628, National Academy of Sciences report, 74 pages, 1974, $8.00 in U.S., $16.00 overseas, quote accession no. PB 234-503/1 when ordering from NTIS.

"The most serious obstacle to low-cost housing in the developing countries, regardless of setting or sophistication, is the lack of a low-cost roofing material that will provide satisfactory performance for a reasonable time under many adverse conditions... In many developing countries roofing alone represents more than 50% of the total construction cost of a low-cost house."

An attempt is made here to identify materials that would last longer than thatch/fired clay and yet be cheaper than imported corrugated iron. The use of plastics, foam composites, sulfur, carbonized plant materials, asphalt, hydraulic cement binders, agricultural and wood wastes, and ferrocement is discussed. The qualities and research needs for each of these are pointed out. The work of the Central Building Research Institute of India is briefly described. This is an overview only of promising new technologies — useful primarily to research institutions and universities. No illustrations.

Mud Brick Roofs, HUD Ideas and Exchange Series #42, MF 25-619, booklet, 16 pages, 1957 (reprinted 1978), free to serious groups, from Office of International Affairs, Dept. of Housing and Urban Development, Washington D.C. 20410, USA.

This short booklet describes the use of mud bricks for vaulted roof and dome construction, as used in traditional Egyptian architectural styles. It uses as a specific example Hassan Fathy's design for New Gourna (see review of **Architecture for the Poor**). The design of buildings using traditional vaulted arch construction is summarized; photographs of the process of building the arches are included. An appendix summarizes the technique for making mud bricks as done in Egypt.

The purpose of this booklet is to illustrate what can be done in housing using locally available materials and traditional construction techniques that are updated and improved.

Building to Resist the Effect of Wind: Volume 3, A Guide for Improved Masonry and Timber Connections in Buildings, MF 25-588, booklet, 48 pages, by S. Fattal, G. Sherwood, and T. Wilkinson, 1977, $4.75, stock number 003-003-01719-1, from Superintendent of Documents, U.S. Government Printing Office, Washington D.C. 20402, USA.

This report discusses the use of connectors in houses and other low-rise buildings to improve their strength under extreme wind conditions. Well-illustrated and clearly presented. One half of the report is devoted to detailed discussion of connectors in masonry wall construction. The other half illustrates fasteners used in timber wall construction.

Many of the solutions shown involve the use of manufactured metal parts (such

METAL ANCHORS:

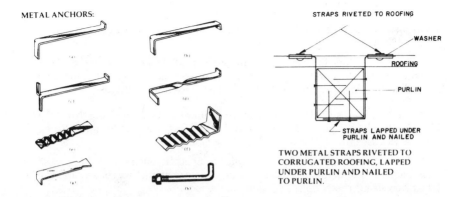

STRAPS RIVETED TO ROOFING

WASHER

ROOFING

PURLIN

STRAPS LAPPED UNDER
PURLIN AND NAILED

TWO METAL STRAPS RIVETED TO
CORRUGATED ROOFING, LAPPED
UNDER PURLIN AND NAILED
TO PURLIN.

as truss plates and sheet metal fasteners for timber construction or tiebars for masonry construction). These examples may provide ideas and patterns so that locally-produced fasteners could be used to strengthen buildings.

The report is particularly useful in that it identifies the parts of masonry and timber houses in need of greater strength in high wind areas. It is particularly in the rapidly growing urban slums, where people live in makeshift housing often in precarious locations, that damage from hurricanes and typhoons is increasing. This is of great concern in the Philippines and the Caribbean nations. The techniques described in this report could be part of a low-cost strategy to minimize that damage.

When You Build a House: A Manual of Construction Details for Caribbean Houses with Emphasis on Protection from Strong Winds, MF 25-648, booklet, 18 pages, by E.H. Robinson, $2.50 from Caribbean Appropriate Technology Centre, Caribbean Conference of Churches, P.O. Box 616, Bridgetown, Barbados.

Clear diagrams illustrate simple and useful methods for building better, more wind-resistant houses. This is not a complete construction manual, but is well worth looking over for ideas to incorporate into housing design.

Grasses—Their Use in Building, MF 25-601, leaflet, 5 pages, 1964, Dept. of Housing and Urban Development, Office of International Affairs, Washington D.C. 20410, USA; out of print in 1981.

This is a very brief survey of the worldwide uses of grasses, primarily for thatching. Scientific names for the grasses are given, along with the regions in which they are used. In addition, there is a discussion of the simple tools and methods generally needed to make thatched roofs.

Comparison of Alternative Design Wheelbarrows for Haulage in Civil Construction Tasks, World Bank Technical Memorandum No. 1, MF 25-590, booklet, 22 pages, 1975, from The World Bank, Transportation and Urban Projects Department, 1818 H Street N.W., Washington D.C. 20433, USA.

Wheelbarrows can, in many situations, be a very efficient means for transporting heavy materials. This study compares wheelbarrows with one or two wheels, with solid and pneumatic (air-filled) rubber tires, and with ball bearing and bushed (simple, smooth-surface to smooth-surface) bearings. The report concludes "...that a lightweight, single-wheel barrow with a scooter tire and ball bearing wheels is the most economical type of wheelbarrow for earth haulage." Includes diagrams of three models.

The Use of Wheelbarrows in Civil Construction, World Bank Technical Memorandum No. 13, MF 25-646, booklet, 26 pages, 1975, from The World Bank, Transportation and Urban Projects Department, 1818 H Street N.W., Washington D.C. 20433, USA.

This memorandum follows up on **Comparison of Alternative Design Wheelbarrows for Haulage in Civil Construction Tasks** (this section) with more discussion of design features relevant to civil construction applications.

The Jalousie — An All Wood Louvre Window, Technical Note No. 3/1975, MF 25-606, plans, 4 pages, $1.00 from Office of Forests, Forest Products Research Centre, P.O. Box 1358, Boroko, Papua New Guinea.

"For many years all-wood louvre windows called 'Jalousies' have been used to advantage in the Philippines. These windows...are attractive, secure, and can be fabricated using the simplest of tools and wood."

"The window is an arrangement of overlapping wooden boards or slats. The slats are nailed on side frames which are cut in half. Each board is nailed with two nails on each end, one nail on one half of the frame and the other nail on the other half. This allows free movement of the boards or slats to be in the closed or open position as desired."

Small-Scale Production of Cementitious Materials, MF 25-665, book, 49 pages, by R.J.S. Spence, 1980, £4.25 from ITDG.

Increasing demand for cement and related building materials (lime, pozzolana, gypsum, etc.) is an established fact for developing countries, and this clear, well-documented study illustrates the good sense — in terms of investment, employment, energy consumption resource utilization, multiplier effect, and local self-reliance — of moving towards plants of small-scale, i.e., 2-200 tons/day production. Draws primarily on the divergent examples of India and China to show how market distortion, monopolistic tendencies, and dependent attitudes have shaped past policies and how they can be improved. Includes good basic descriptions of the production of cementitious materials. Recommended for anyone involved in housing, construction, and related small industries in developing countries.

Lime and Alternative Cements, MF 25-609, book, 164 pages, compiled by Robin Spence, 1974, ITDG, photocopy available as publication no. PB 297-377/4, $16.00 in U.S., $32.00 overseas, from NTIS.

The proceedings of an ITDG seminar on low-cost materials having the properties of cement. Excellent reference book on small-scale manufacture of alternative cements. Photos, discussion, references, papers.

Shaft Lime Kiln, Technical Bulletin #13, MF 25-634, leaflet, 11 pages, by S. Mason, 1974, Papua New Guinea, limited supply, from DWS.

This kiln is appropriate "where only small quantities of lime are required for building purposes, stabilization of soils and lime washes."

"The shaft lime kiln is a vertical circular opening cut into the side of a hill. The lining can be large boulders of limestone, which are replaced as they burn out, or bricks made from clay in the area. The capacity of the kiln is three tons of hydrated lime per burn, which requires one week to produce."

Brief instructions are provided, covering testing for limestone, construction, and operation of the kiln. The lime that is treated in this kiln is usable as a stabilizing agent for soil construction. There are very clear, dimensional drawings with English measurements. Bricks are needed for construction.

Rice Husk Ash Cement, MF 25-657, book, 45 pages, by Ray Smith, 1984, £4.95 from ITDG.

This report documents some of the different methods for small-scale production of rice husk ash cement on the Indian sub-continent. Burnt rice husks are combined with lime to produce a cement that is cheaper and of lower strength than Portland cement, but still suitable for most rural requirements. The cost advantages of rice husk ash cement over Portland cement are not always as dramatic as might be hoped, particularly when similar strength mortar mixtures are produced, and quality control problems, government subsidies on Portland cement, and adulteration are taken into account.

Ferrocement: Applications in Developing Countries, MF 25-598, booklet, 89 pages, by a National Academy of Sciences panel, 1973, free to developing countries from BOSTID/NAS, 2101 Constitution Avenue N.W., Washington D.C. 20418, USA.

"Ferrocement is a highly versatile form of reinforced concrete made of wire mesh, sand, water, and cement, which possesses unique qualities of strength and serviceability. It can be constructed with a minimum of skilled labor and utilizes readily available materials. Proven suitable for boat-building, it has many other tested or potential applications in agriculture, industry, and housing.

"Ferrocement can be fabricated into almost any shape. . . is more durable than most woods and much cheaper than imported steel, and it can be used as a substitute for these materials in many applications. . . Ferrocement construction does not need heavy plants or machinery; it is labor-intensive."

The report examines the use of ferrocement for construction of boats in a Chinese commune, food storage silos in Thailand and Ethiopia, and water tanks in New Zealand. "The report considers the potential for further use of already discovered application, such as boats and silos, and identifies promising new application, such as roofs and food-processing equipment."

Ferrocement, a Versatile Construction Material: Its Increasing Use in Asia, MF 25-597, book, 108 pages, edited by R.P. Pama, Seng-Lip Lee and Noel D. Vietmeyer, 1976, $2.00 (add $2.00 for airmail) from International Ferrocement Information Center, Asian Institute of Technology, P.O. Box 2754, Bangkok, Thailand.

These are the proceedings of a workshop held in Bangkok in November 1974. It offers a general survey of ferrocement use and research in Asia, including activities in Korea, Fiji, Thailand, India, Sri Lanka, Malaysia, Singapore, Papua New

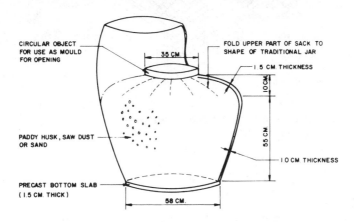

CIRCULAR OBJECT FOR USE AS MOULD FOR OPENING

FOLD UPPER PART OF SACK TO SHAPE OF TRADITIONAL JAR

35 CM.

1.5 CM. THICKNESS

10 CM

55 CM

PADDY HUSK, SAW DUST OR SAND

1.0 CM THICKNESS

PRECAST BOTTOM SLAB (1.5 CM. THICK)

58 CM.

Gunnysack water jar mold

Guinea and Bangladesh. The economics, labor and materials requirements, versatility and durability are explored. Specific construction details are not usually included, although some of the things described — for example, the water jars — could be built using only the instructions in this book.

"In India ferrocement is being introduced for silos in sizes to hold about 1 to 30 tonnes of grain. Methods developed for ferrocement boat building are being applied to these storage structures to obtain a structure of high quality."

Ferrocement products discussed include boats, housing, food and water storage silos and tanks, roofing, biogas plants, road surfaces and tube well casings.

Journal of Ferrocement, MF 25-607, quarterly, usually 80-100 pages, published by the International Ferrocement Information Center, subscriptions (includes surface mail postage) from USA, Europe, Canada, Australia, New Zealand and Japan are annually US$30.00 for individuals and US$60.00 for institutions; subscriptions from other countries are annually US$18.00 for individuals and US$36.00 for institutions, add $12.00 for airmail in North and South America, $10.00 for airmail in Africa in Europe, $6.00 for airmail in Asia and the Pacific, from Journal of Ferrocement, IFIC/AIT, P.O. Box 2754, Bangkok, Thailand.

"The purpose of the journal is to disseminate the latest research findings on ferrocement and other related materials and to encourage their practical applications especially in developing countries. The Journal is divided into three sections: (a) Proceedings (of conferences and workshops); (b) Technical notes (covering specific plans and construction methods); and (c) Annotated and indexed bibliography, current awareness service, news, etc."

Although the articles are thorough and detailed, many are very technical and use complex mathematics. This journal is therefore recommended primarily for serious researchers.

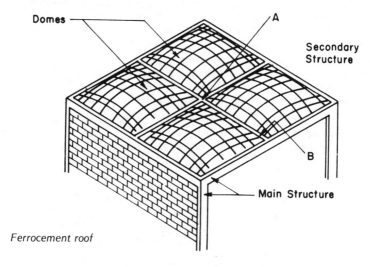

Ferrocement roof

Construction of Trail Suspended Bridges in Nepal: An Application of Traditional Technology, MF 25-666, paper, 21 pages, by Prachandra Pradhan, 1981, from the United Nations University, Toho Seimei Building, 15-1 Shibuya 2-chome, Shibuya-ku, Tokyo 150, Japan.

Traditional suspended foot bridges in some areas of Nepal are technically quite sophisticated and linked to cultural and economic aspects of village life in many fascinating ways. While modern suspension bridges being built by the government may be technically superior to the locally-built bridges, the local bridges are built at a fraction of the cost of the government ones, and they utilize broad community participation and locally available materials. Because they reuse cables which are purchased used, the traditional bridges may not be as strong as the government ones, but this seems to be offset by better maintenance by the community. This paper is a fine example of the important role of traditional and indigenous technology in community development.

Traditional Suspension Bridges in Taplejung District, MF 25-661, book, 100 pages, by Jim Rutherford, Max Leisibach, and Herbert Rice, December 1978, SATA, Swiss Francs 21.00 from SKAT.

Several traditional designs for effective suspended and suspension bridges have evolved in Nepal. This book contains the observations and conclusions of a study of 24 bridges built with one of these traditional bridge designs. The authors concluded that these bridges are structurally sound. Some suggestions are made regarding some of the minor disadvantages of these designs. Unfortunately, many of the photographs have reproduced poorly. Readers wishing to pursue the topic further are directed to sources of reports on post-1978 experiences of building improved versions of these bridges.

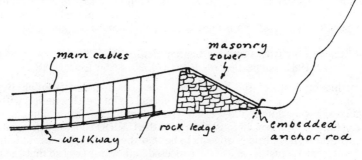

Standard Trail Suspended and Suspension Bridges, MF 25-641, 2 volumes, 400 pages, by Ministry of Works and Transport, Roads Department, H.M.G. of Nepal and the Swiss Association for Technical Assistance, 1977, out of print in 1985.

"This manual for construction of suspension bridges will be quite helpful to the engineers who will construct suspension bridges in Nepal. It contains the details of methods of surveying, calculations, and design procedures."

This set of books is specific to steel cable unstiffened suspension and suspended trail bridges. Spans described range from 40 to 170 meters. Includes bridge design, structural analysis, survey of bridge sites, cost estimates, construction practices, and maintenance. Most sections have examples of calculations, necessary engineering tables, and ample photos, plans or sketches. The manuals contain a wealth of information, but this is mostly in a form only useful to engineers. Poorly organized, these books may be very confusing to one without previous experience in the subject. The many sections have different formats and no continuous explanatory text.

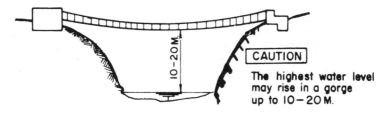

Traditional Bridges of Papua New Guinea, MF 25-644, book, 137 pages, by Jeff Siegel, 1982, $9.50 from the Appropriate Technology Development Institute, Papua New Guinea University of Technology, Box 793, Lae, Papua New Guinea.

Numerous photographs and diagrams show how traditional suspended foot bridges are made in Papua New Guinea using only locally available materials. The materials include wood, bamboo, tree bark, vines, cane, and stones. Construction details for specific bridges are given, including time and number of people required for construction, methods used, materials, and lifespan. The first of a series to be published by ATDI. Recommended.

Wooden Bridges: UNIDO's Prefabricated Modular System, MF 25-664, booklet, 16 pages, UNIDO, 1983, available from UNIDO.

This short booklet with color photos describes a simple road bridge design which can be prefabricated in 3-meter long wooden sections and hauled to the site. The span can be up to 30 meters, and the bridge can carry a live load of up to 40 tons. "The standardized components...do away with the need for expensive and scarce engineering design for each bridge. The components can be made in small workshops, transported without heavy lifting equipment and, once the abutments are built, erected in a few days using various tripod, cable and winch arrangements. The expected lifetime of the bridge is between 15 and 25 years."

The Kenyan Low Cost Modular Timber Bridge, MF 25-653, paper, 34 pages, by J.D. Parry, 1981, publication no. PB 1214595, $8.50 from NTIS.

Reporting on tests of the same bridge described above (**Wooden Bridges**, UNIDO), the author concludes that this is indeed an interesting design with some advantages, but assigns it a lower safe span (24m maximum vs. 30m) and lower safe load limit (20 tons vs. 40 tons) than does the UNIDO booklet. The main disadvantage of this type of bridge appears to be that the road approaches at both ends must be at least 2.5 meters above the expected high water level so that the bridge trusses will remain above water; this may involve extra costs. Detailed construction drawings of the bridge are provided; these are not included in the UNIDO booklet.

"There are also several comparatively low cost alternatives to this design that should not be overlooked. In countries where locally-grown timber is available in

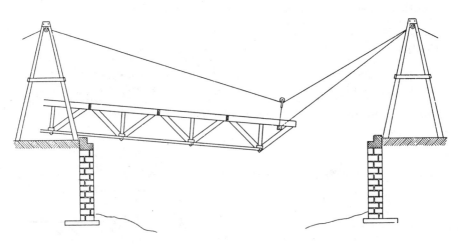

Fig. 11 LAUNCHING A PAIR OF TRUSSES

the requisite sizes, whole log or rectangular section timber beam bridges can be built at low cost over spans of up to 10m, or up to 15m if hardwoods are available. If the site conditions are favourable for the erection of piers, multispan bridges with timber beam decks will be the cheapest solution, as has been adopted in the Kenya Rural Access Roads Programme. . .Bridges constructed with other materials such as reinforced concrete, plain concrete (for arch bridges), rolled steel joists with timber or concrete decks, and prefabricated steel. . .will normally be the choice for spans greater than 12m where permanent or semi-permanent bridges are required. They are however likely to be between two and four times as expensive as the Kenya modular timber bridge. . .Simple reinforced concrete slab bridges are however very satisfactory for short spans and many are built on rural roads in Kenya each year, as in other developing countries."

Simple Bridge Structures, Project Technology Handbook No. 2, MF 25-638, book, 28 pages, by Project Technology/Schools Council, 1972, $8.50 from Heineman Educational Books Inc., 4 Front Street, Exeter, New Hampshire 03833, USA; or Heineman Educational Books Ltd., 22 Bedford Square, London WC1B 3HH, England.

This British book introduces students to basic bridge designs. Included are class activities to test models made of different kinds of wood. A well-illustrated set of experiments demonstrates the properties and functions of beams, frames, and columns in bridges and other structures. Simple methods for calculating the forces acting on the members of a framework are explained.

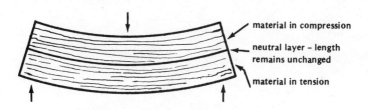

Effect of weight on wooden bridge model

ADDITIONAL REFERENCES ON HOUSING AND CONSTRUCTION

Design of Medical Buildings is a remarkable book on the use of local building techniques and architectural styles for low-cost medical buildings; see HEALTH CARE.

Small Farm Grain Storage also includes some information on ferrocement construction techniques; see CROP STORAGE.

The design of solar heated and cooled houses is the subject of books reviewed in ENERGY: SOLAR.

Small Scale Cement Plants describes the economics of small scale vertical shaft cement kilns in China; see LOCAL SELF-RELIANCE.

Transportation

Transportation

Readers investigating transportation alternatives in the light of appropriate technology principles will find that this topic area reflects many of the fundamental problems and issues of technology choice and development goals. In the Third World, traditional transport technologies (e.g. backpacks, bicycle-loading baskets and frames, bike trailers, animal packs, carts, pedicabs, push carts, wheelbarrows, and small boats) have been almost completely neglected in engineering design efforts.

Informed observers note that few modern vehicles fit the needs of the developing countries very well; in most cases the designs or the machines themselves are imported. These vehicles — trucks, busses, cars — bring with them high foreign exchange requirements for purchase and fuel costs, problems of maintenance and spare parts, and low durability when operated over rough terrain. Although busses are usually an effective means of transporting people (especially in heavily populated areas and for long distance travel), trucks are often ill-matched to the basic transport needs of small farms. Trucks also require heavy investments in high-quality road construction, without which they have even higher maintenance costs. Furthermore, World Bank studies in Kenya give evidence that the concentration of ownership of trucks significantly limits prices received by farmers for their produce.

The technologies of transport include not only the vehicles themselves, but also the roadbed and surface materials, as well as design speeds and road routes. In road-building, the technical choices reflect the goals of the programs themselves. Given the goals of most current road-building programs, once the route, design speed, and road surface and strength have been chosen, the most economical vehicle is likely to be the truck. Roads built with high strength roadbeds and high design speeds provide a hidden subsidy and competitive advantage for heavy-weight, high-speed trucks compared to other vehicles. The range, speed, and capacity of small motorized animal-drawn and pedal-powered vehicles would be served just as well by less expensive roads.

A peculiar characteristic of transportation systems is that the availability of higher speed transport technologies creates first a demand and then a dependence on long distance transport as settlement and industrial production patterns adjust. Increasing the speed of transportation increases the energy consumption at an even greater rate, because both wind resistance and weight of the vehicle increase. Thus one observer of transport in urban and rural Southeast Asia notes: "A shift in mobility from 2500 km to 5000 km in a 500 hour transport budget would increase energy requirements sevenfold through its greater emphasis on faster car-bus-rail-air modes at the expense of walk-cycle-subsidiary motor modes." (Peter Rimmer, in an article entitled "A Conceptual Framework for Examining Urban and Regional Transport Needs in Southeast Asia," 1978.) *The writings of Leopold Kohr on scale and velocity also contain a number of interesting observations on urban transportation dynamics (see* **The Breakdown of Nations***).*

There are also other negative effects that come with smoother, faster transporta-

tion links. Road-building is justified by arguments about the increased inputs that will be made available to small farmers, the increased market for farm surplusses that will be created, and the reduced running costs for the trucks that will operate over the better roads. Yet many observers have noted the classic pattern of destruction of crafts and cottage industries that also comes with the opening up of a road. Manufactured tools and household items trucked in from the towns and cities outsell the products of local potters and blacksmiths. The types of jobs available change, and the variety of income-producing activities in the community may be reduced. A whole chain of negative economic multiplier effects may be set in motion. The greater commercialization of agriculture is likely to also mean lower crop diversity and thus greater risks from pest attacks and global market fluctuations. Income in the community may shift significantly to land-owning farmers who sell their surplusses without being affected by higher rents.

There are reasons why national transport strategies dramatically affect the strength of local industry and decentralized development. In China, the development of the substantial rural small industry sector has brought with it a unique blossoming of managerial and technical skills among the rural population. One factor that seems to have greatly aided this process is the existence of protected markets that result from the commune system and the poor transportation infrastructure. (See, for example, the discussion of China's 2800 cement plants, in Small Scale Cement Plants.) It appears that there may be an optimum degree of transportation integration, beyond which damaging centralizing effects are felt.

The Transport Panel of the Intermediate Technology Development Group has done some of the most consistently thoughtful reevaluation of the transport problem and possible avenues for appropriate technology solutions. Transport Panel members give high priority to improvements in intermediate motorized vehicles, traditional vehicles, animal packs, and bicycle-powered units; these represent a better match of available capital to the transport needs of small farming communities.

The farm family needs to move small quantities of inputs to the farm, harvested crops from field to home (often over rough terrain), and small surplusses to market. Small vehicles travelling at low speed over simple roads and tracks seem to best match this need. In fact, the animal-drawn cart in most developing countries still dominates this activity. In India, it has been shown that the total national investment in bullock carts exceeds the investment in either the national railroads or the national road network, and the number of ton-miles of material moved is comparable. Recognizing that bullock carts are going to be part of the Indian transport network for many years to come, organizations such as the Indian Institute of Management have initiated work to improve cart designs through better bearings, lighter frames, and wheels less damaging to roadways. They are also developing harnesses that are not injurious to the draft animals (see **The Management of Animal Energy Resources and the Modernization of the Bullock Cart System***).*

The bicycle has often been cited as the most efficient machine for personal transport ever invented. It is also a major mover of goods in the Third World. Loads can be tied directly to bicycles or placed in special frames and baskets, and bike trailers and three-wheelers can be used to carry several hundred pounds of goods. **Bicycling Science** *offers the reader an excellent summary of the physics of bicycles and the human body as a power producer.* **Bicycles and Tricycles: An Elementary Treatise on Their Design and Construction** *provides an encyclopedic treatment of successful and unsuccessful design ideas.* **The Design of Cycle Trailers** *details the basic considerations in the design of two-wheeled trailers for hauling goods behind a bicycle, and includes design examples from around the world.*

Small engine-driven vehicles, including motorized bicycles, motorcycles, motorcycles with sidecars and other three-wheelers, and two-wheeled tractor-cart combinations have found a niche in many countries. These small vehicles with very low fuel requirements seem to have an almost unlimited number of possible applications. Discussion and examples can be found in many of the entries in this chapter (see, for example, ITDG's **Low Cost Vehicles***). Rough terrain vehicles produced in industrialized countries are catalogued in a World Bank report,* **Appropriate Technology in Rural Development: Vehicles for On and Off Farm Operations***. These are primarily expensive, relatively high speed vehicles with poor fuel economy, beyond the means of most farmers in developing countries.*

The kinds of roads needed by small vehicles can be built using labor-intensive road construction methods. Several of the books in this section discuss the requirements for labor-intensive programs that are economically competitive with those using heavy equipment in the construction of conventional roadways. The success of such labor-intensive road-building techniques has been demonstrated, but greater savings may be achieved if road standards are kept flexible, and labor-intensive programs are not required to always produce roads of equipment-intensive standards. Where transport needs are defined as including roadways for lightweight small vehicles to travel at moderate speeds, labor-intensive road construction methods are more likely to be the first choice. In any labor-intensive road construction program, good quality hand tools and simple equipment are essential to high productivity (see **Better Tools for the Job** *and* **Guide to Tools and Equipment for Labour Based Road Construction***).*

Small boats can be very economical to build and operate, taking advantage of existing inland waterways and coastal routes for quiet movement of heavy loads. In some areas inter-island communications and transport depend almost solely on small boats. Included are a variety of books on boatbuilding techniques that could in many cases be used to improve the safety, speed, and economic viability of traditional vessels.

A key consideration in vehicle choice and transportation strategy is, of course, fuel supply. Alcohol fuels, distilled from grains or crop residues, have been generating great interest as alternatives to gasoline. Brazil has taken the lead in alcohol fuel production, based on cassava and sugar cane. Several books reviewed in the ENERGY: GENERAL chapter offer plans and instructions for small-scale alcohol fuel-producing units. However, the author of **Food or Fuel: New Competition for the World's Croplands** *concludes that large national alcohol fuel programs are likely to greatly increase world hunger by diverting vast areas of agricultural land into fuel production for the relatively wealthy few. And the basic futility of such programs is indicated by the fact that the entire U.S. grain crop, if converted to alcohol fuels, would replace only about 30% of the gasoline currently consumed in the United States. The dramatic 1970s increases in oil prices hit the citizens of poor countries hardest, forcing them off the busses and away from kerosene cooking fuel. Despite the public outcry over higher gasoline prices in the United States, consumption dropped little, and one out of every 8 barrels of world oil production is burned as gasoline in U.S. automobiles. As long as 6% of the world's population continues to consume about ⅓ of the world's energy supply, the problems of conventional motorized transport in poor countries will intensify.*

Given the stiff buyer competition for scarce gasoline and the vast amounts of agricultural materials required for large volume alcohol fuels production, it can be reasonably predicted that there will never be enough fuel for more than a tiny part of the world's population to be driving automobiles. Decades of settlement patterns based on the daily use of the automobile in the United States have locked this country into a high fuel demand pattern that will be broken only through a very difficult and expensive process of great change. In Third World oil-importing countries, the decentralization of industrial production, along with increased emphasis on bicycles, improved carts, and small engine-driven vehicles appear to be important elements of a practical transport strategy for the future.

Rural Transport in Developing Countries, MF 26-683, book, 145 pages, by I. Barwell et. al., 1985, £7.95 from ITDG.

"Recent research has drawn attention to the fact that: 1) Few regular transport services operate away from all-weather road networks. However, many people live remote from such networks...2) In areas with all-weather road access, motor vehicles are beyond the financial means of the majority of people. Equally, many people cannot afford to use the transport services which do operate."

"There is unlikely to be a significant improvement in this situation for the foreseeable future given the limited resources available for expansion of road networks and motor vehicle fleets, and the problems of maintaining existing roads and operating conventional motor vehicles."

The nine case studies on the transport needs of rural people presented here provide some evidence that contradicts long-held notions about the nature of rural transport activities. Not only are footpaths and simple tracks the most used (though "invisible") part of the transport system, but rural people are more mobile than has been generally assumed.

This volume will aid in understanding the kinds of low-cost improvements in the transport system that would be most valuable to villagers.

Earth Roads: Their Construction and Maintenance, MF 26-675, book, 123 pages, by Jack Hindson, 1983, £4.95 from ITDG.

"In the early stages of development it is doubtful if modern high-cost roads are necessary: there is abundant evidence to show that the existence of a means of communication is more important than its quality...(Most so-called 'low-cost' roads described in other books involve construction methods that) presume the knowledge and skills of a graduate civil engineer and the use of complex equipment. The result is a technology largely incomprehensible to the layman, and a road that is not low-cost."

Based on 20 years' experience in northern Zambia, here is a well-illustrated, practical book on the construction of genuinely low-cost, relatively long-lasting earth roads. The key feature of this system is the primary attention given to soil conservation techniques that divert rain water flows away from the road at all times, and minimize erosion in drainage ditches. This manual was prepared for use by non-engineers for hand construction involving very little moving of materials; the author notes that even wheelbarrows will not be necessary for most of the work. Drainage techniques, road planning, construction and maintenance are all covered.

"The most important requirement on a village road, both in hilly and in flat country, is for slow, steady speeds in any weather and at any season of the year." The result is a slow speed road that is well suited to carts and bicycles, can handle up to 50 motorized vehicles/day, and that should remain passable.

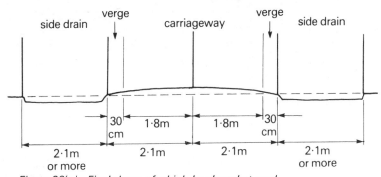

Figure 36(a). Final shape of a high-level market road.

The Rural Access Roads Programme, MF 26-682, book, 167 pages, by J.J. de Veen, 1980, $10.00 from International Labor Office, 1750 New York Avenue N.W., Washington D.C. 20006, USA.

The Rural Access Roads Programme in Kenya is widely regarded as an important achievement in demonstrating that labor-intensive road construction methods can provide good quality roads at relatively low cost, if a well-organized management structure can be created. This program succeeded in constructing thousands of kilometers of low-volume rural access roads, connecting farming areas with the existing road network.

This book is about the organizational structure and management experience of the program. A short appendix describes and illustrates the construction activities. Whereas most of the work was done by hand, tractors and trailers were used for gravelling. The technology unit of this program carried out some interesting work on the improvement of hand tools and wheelbarrows; this work is not described here, but is covered by two other books (see reviews of **Better Tools for the Job** and **Guide to Tools and Equipment for Labour Based Road Construction**).

Rural communities were involved in road selection. "In areas with average terrain conditions, the original target of 45 km/unit/year can be achieved with a labour force of 270 workers." Average costs were US$5600 per kilometer, including all overhead costs. Maintenance contracts were signed with individual workers to be responsible for each section (about 1.5 km) of road, after it was completed.

Manual on the Planning of Labour-Intensive Road Construction, MF 26-664, book, 253 pages, by M. Allal, G. Edmonds, and A. Bhalla of the International Labour Office, Geneva, 1977, $22.80 from International Labor Office, Washington Branch, 1750 New York Avenue N.W., Washington D.C. 20006, USA.

Not a how-to manual, this book is intended for use by planners who are responsible for national road programs, including people involved in evaluation and design

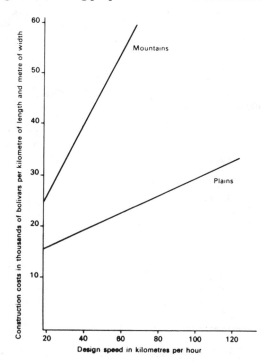

Example of the relationship between design speed and construction cost in different kinds of terrain

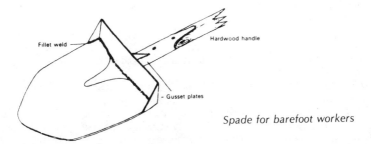

Spade for barefoot workers

of road construction projects. "They may fully agree with the notion of appropriate technology, but they must first be presented with viable alternatives to the technology they are using. They also need to be given the means of evaluating, assessing and taking advantage of these alternatives. The present manual constitutes an attempt to meet that need."

The authors note that an opening up of the spectrum of choice is required. Labor-intensive techniques should not be viewed as simply one way to achieve roads of equipment-intensive standards, but rather the design standards themselves should be flexible to allow for the most beneficial selection of technique, total road cost, user costs and maintenance costs.

There is a chapter (24 pages) on the range of labor-intensive techniques (mostly for hauling), including drawings, photos, and comments about relative costs and suitable applications. Included are headbaskets, stretchers, small trucks on rails, spades, pack animals, animal-drawn carts, animal-drawn scrapers, wheelbarrows, trailers, and small aerial ropeways.

"The planner of any labor-intensive scheme must bear in mind that the choice of the right sort of tool is as important as the choice of the right type of machinery in a capital-intensive project: given the right tools a worker's productivity can be enormously increased. A small research unit to consider the appropriate designs of small tools and equipment would be very useful."

"Earth roads are the most suitable for labor intensive construction... Also, earth roads are generally used to transport farm produce to market or to provide access to remote villages. Accordingly, they are of obvious and direct benefit to the local population."

Information is presented on the relationship between design speed and construction costs. Roads designed for vehicle speeds of 40 km/hour have substantially lower costs than those designed for vehicle speeds of 70 or 80 km/hour, because there is a larger acceptable range of curves and gradients.

The later chapters discuss cost-benefit analysis, problems of organization and management in labor-intensive works, and action to eliminate capital-intensive biases in policy and attitudes among engineers.

Roads and Resources: Appropriate Technology in Road Construction in Developing Countries, MF 26-668, book, 200 pages, edited by G. Edmonds and J. Howe, 1980, £6.95 from ITDG.

This study, prepared for the International Labor Organization, is about road construction programs. The authors note that "the use of more labor-intensive techniques can be technically and economically efficient." Part I, "Institutions and Issues of Implementation," is concerned with how to best organize labor-intensive programs and choose intermediate technologies. The special planning and administrative requirements of labor-intensive programs, and other institutional biases favoring equipment-intensive approaches are discussed. One chapter identifies a range of simple tools and equipment that, if given proper design attention, could multiply labor productivity by a factor of 3-6. These include Chinese wheelbarrows and animal-drawn carts on portable light rail systems.

Noting that road systems in many former colonies have been designed to move goods for export, one author urges that the emphasis should be "on providing inputs into the rural areas which will stimulate growth rather than access to ensure the maximum level of exportation."

Case studies in the second half of the book examine labor-intensive and construction programs in Mexico, Afghanistan, India and Iran.

"The use of labor-based methods would seem. . .to meet all the criteria upon which development planning is based. They serve the mass of the population, their implementation can involve popular participation in the decision-making process, they are an instrument of self-reliance, they can enhance the potential for rural development and they can, by providing income, serve to improve the standard of living of the mass of the population." Despite these claims, the authors have limited themselves to looking at how labor and good small tools and equipment can compete economically with heavy equipment. The goal of this strategy is twofold: income distribution and skill development on a broader scale.

There are a number of crucial questions that are beyond the scope of this book, such as: Who decides where a road will go? Who benefits from the road? Who loses? Who decides the road's design speed and strength (and hence costs and which vehicle owners will benefit)? What road-vehicle combinations go well together? Readers interested in these kinds of issues will find relevant material in other entries in this chapter.

Rural Roads Manual (Simple English Edition), MF 26-687, book, 128 pages. by the Papua New Guinea Dept. of Works and Supply, 1977, $3.00 plus return postage (or exchange your publications), from DWS.

Papua New Guinea's Dept. of Public Works, recognizing the importance of well-constructed and maintained roads, has published this manual in an attempt to promote self-help road construction all over PNG. Written purposely in very simple English (the national language), it is a complete guide to road design, construction and maintenance using low-cost local materials and tools, and local skills. Covers subjects such as surveying, laying out a road, drainage, building in swampy areas, maintenance and upgrading, plus information on building bridges, culverts and low-level crossings.

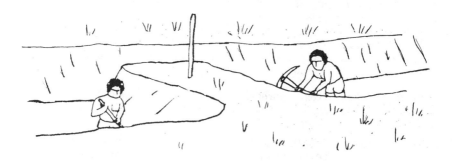

Illustrated with drawings on almost every page, this manual is intended for fieldworkers and local government councils in PNG, so that road building and maintenance can become a decentralized process. While specific to conditions in PNG, this manual is valuable as an example for adaptation to other areas.

Better Tools for the Job: Specifications for Hand Tools and Equipment, MF 26-652, booklet, 43 pages, by William Armstrong, 1980, £3.95 from ITDG.

Labor-intensive road construction projects need large quantities of good quality hand tools and carrying devices like wheelbarrows. Available tools are often of poor quality, due to the practice of seeking the lowest quoted price without specifying quality standards. A Kenyan technology unit has developed a set of specifications which have been successfully applied to tools for road projects in that country. By including these specifications with price requests, the tools may initially cost 30% more, but are likely to have a 500% longer working life.

Materials, strength and hardness, and construction specifications are provided along with detailed drawings for each tool and piece of equipment (shovel, hoe, wheelbarrow, forked hoe, crowbar, machete, mattock, axe, pickaxe, spreader, and rammer).

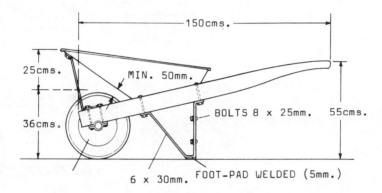

Specifications for a sturdy wheelbarrow

"A very large proportion of the problems encountered with hand tools in the field (on road, irrigation and construction projects, for example) arises from the use of handles made from cheap unseasoned softwood...The cost increase for a specified handle (of seasoned hardwood) as compared to a cheap handle is modest, and no other single step can return such high dividends in terms of cost effectiveness and productivity."

Steel strength and hardness depend on chemical composition and heat treatment. The author notes that by pressing a diamond or hardened steel ball into a small number of samples of the equipment, the buyer can perform a low-cost reliable test of hardness to insure that tools have been made to specification.

Guide to Tools and Equipment for Labour Based Road Construction, MF 26-677, approximately 30 pages, by International Labour Office, 1981, Swiss Francs 60.00 from ILO.

"So far as road construction is concerned studies by the International Labour Office and the World Bank have shown that it is feasible to use labour rather than machinery for many activities with a consequent increase in local employment possibilities. For labour-based road construction to be both technically and economically acceptable, it is necessary, among other things, to improve the tools and equipment available."

This guide contains manufacturing specifications for a wide variety of hand tools and animal-drawn equipment useful in road construction. The intention is to provide details on efficient, durable, safe, effective tools. Advice is given on testing and maintenance. Operations include surveying, excavation, rock crushing, hauling, spreading, and compaction.

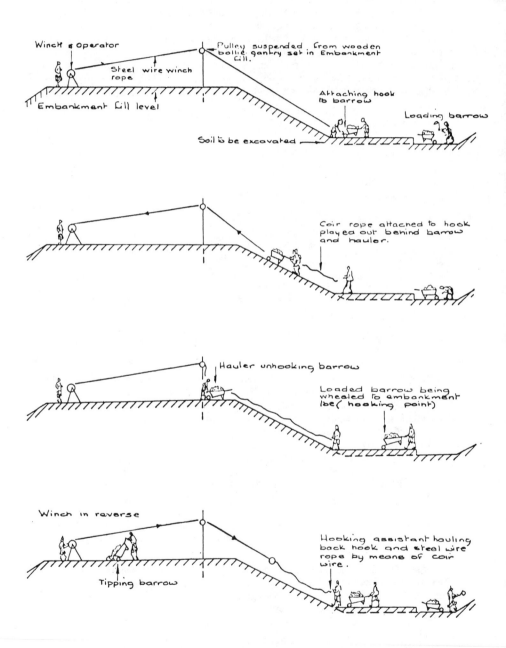

WINCH ASSISTED WHEELBARROW HAULAGE

DIMENSIONS OF CHINESE WHEELBARROW (mm)

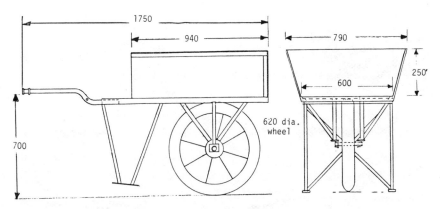

from Guide to Tools and Equipment for Labour Based Road Construction

Low Cost Vehicles: Options for Moving People and Goods, MF 26-680, book, 106 pages, by Gordon Hathway, 1985, £6.95 from ITDG.

Here is the only book that covers the full range of low-cost transport devices from around the world, from headstraps and backpacks to motorized three-wheelers and micro-trucks. This volume should prove valuable as a source of ideas for new vehicles to fit special transport needs. Many photos.

"The small farm transport vehicle (sftv) is a new type of wheelbarrow which has been designed and developed by IT Transport and ITDG. It is specifically intended to carry loads up to 150 kg for distances of up to 10 km, which are typical of the transport requirements of small farmers."

Low Cost Transportation, MF 26-679, book, 63 pages, by Gert Thoma, 1979, available from German Appropriate Technology Exchange, GTZ, Dag-Hammarskjold-Weg 1, D-6236 Eschborn 1, Federal Republic of Germany.

Here is a nice collection of designs from around the world for carts, tricycles, wheelbarrows and handcarts, and their associated wheels, bearings, brakes, steering mechanisms and other details. Many of the advantages and disadvantages of each are noted. Some good hints on the fabrication of strong joints are provided.

"The choice of appropriate wheels for carts influences their overall efficiency. For example, the rolling resistance of hard wheels is about 50% higher than that of pneumatic tires. On rough terrain the difference is less or zero. It is recommended to continue the use of hard wheels for transport on unprepared terrain with low speeds while giving priority to big diameters."

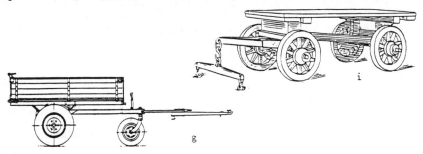

19th century carts in
Horse-Drawn Farm Vehicles

Horse-Drawn Farm Vehicles, MF 26-678, book, 78 pages, by John Thompson, 1980, £3.00 from John Thompson, 1 Fieldway, Fleet, Hampshire, United Kingdom.

This historical collection illustrates a wide variety of two-wheeled farm carts and four-wheeled wagons from the U.K. This should provide some useful ideas to people improving traditional carts or introducing new ones. For example, there is a two-wheeled cart that can be tilted to dump the load while the cart remains harnessed to the animals.

The Management of Animal Energy Resources and the Modernization of the Bullock Cart System, MF 26-686, book, 137 pages, by N.S. Ramaswamy, 1979, available on request to serious groups in the Third World, from Prof. N.S. Ramaswamy, Director, Indian Institute of Management, 33 Langford Road, Bangalore 560 027, India.

"For short hauls, small loads, versatile movement over any available surface and low freight charges, the cart has no peer either in the rural areas, or, for that matter, in the towns and cities. It is still cheap, readily available, and safe."

The author presents statistics to convincingly demonstrate the importance of animal power and carts in the Indian economy. Discussing deficiencies in design that need to be overcome, he offers evidence that the improvement of harnessing devices, agricultural implements, and carts should be given a high priority by the Indian government. To accomplish these objectives, he proposes the establishment of an Animal Energy Development Corporation, and outlines a program of activities. He also argues for less cruelty to the animals both in general use and through promotion of improved slaughterhouse facilities.

Animal power inputs on the Indian farm are even greater than in the transport sector. Two-thirds of all farm energy is provided by animals, while human energy provides 23% and electricity/fossil fuels only 10%.

Carts are used in moving 15-18 billion tonne-km of freight per year in India. But "the traditional cart is defective in design. The draught power of the animal is wasted due to friction resulting from rough bearings and crude and inefficient harnessing, etc. The wobbling rim cuts into the road surface and damages it...Weights run high. Traditional carts can be easily improved by: smooth bearings, lower weight, the introduction of a log-brake, better harnessing, the use of pneumatic tires on paved roads" and the use of hard rubber tires in rural areas.

As this is a compilation of papers, much of the text is repetitive. Photos of old and new cart designs are included.

Bicycling Science, MF 26-657, book, 243 pages, by Frank R. Whitt and David G. Wilson, second edition 1982, $9.95 plus postage from MIT Press, 28 Carleton Street, Cambridge, Massachusetts 02142, USA.

This very readable book describes the physics of bicycles and other human-powered machines, and the characteristics of the human body as a power generator. Topics include the power needed for movement on land, maximum performance of cyclists, optimum pedaling rates, comparison of human power with internal combustion machines and electric motors, bicycle design for rough roads, braking of bicycles, construction materials (including bamboo frames and plastic frames), water cycles, railway cycles, and possible future designing pedal-powered equipment or bicycle modifications for low-cost transport.

The authors note that tests of human energy production indicate that for prolonged periods (e.g. one hour) an ordinary college student would produce about

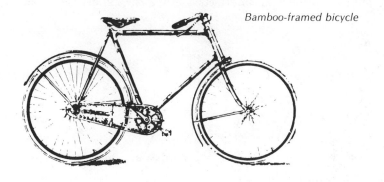

Bamboo-framed bicycle

The Garbien semienclosed bicycle. Springing of both wheels is provided in this design. Power to the rear wheel is through swinging constant-velocity cranks and an infinitely variable gear.

0.05 hp (37 watts). Other tests show highest power production for 1 minute of .54 hp (403 watts), and for 60 to 270 minutes, 0.28 to 0.19 hp (208 to 142 watts). Hand-cranking is not as efficient as pedaling. There is some evidence that screw-pedaled boats are more efficient than oar-driven boats. A gasoline engine added to a bicycle to give it the equivalent power of an extra human being would weigh 20 pounds. The same power using an electric motor would require adding the weight of one person, in the form of batteries and electric motor.

Some designs might be of particular interest in poor countries. Bamboo-framed bicycles were marketed prior to 1900. For rough roads, "some form of sprung wheel or sprung frame can greatly reduce the kinetic energy of momentum losses by reducing the unsprung mass and ensuring that the wheel more nearly maintains contact with the surface." (In developing countries, large diameter wide tires ensure an acceptably comfortable ride without a sprung frame.) Cycles with steel wheels developed for running on steel rails have less friction to overcome than the best bicycles on excellent roads.

The standard bicycle has seen few changes in design since 1890. The authors claim that this is partly because at about that time the automobile began monopolizing the attention of the inventive mechanics and mechanical engineers. There is certainly potential for new concepts and designs.

Bicycles and Tricycles: An Elementary Treatise on Their Design and Construction, MF 26-655, book, 536 pages, by Archibald Sharp, 1896 (reprinted 1979), $9.95 plus postage from MIT Press, 28 Carleton Street, Cambridge, Massachusetts 02142, USA.

This is a fascinating book on what is perhaps the most efficient machine ever created. A valuable reference for designers of bicycles, tricycles for hauling goods and people, bicycle trailers, and stationary pedal-power and treadle-power machines.

The first 140 pages contain an introduction to the physics and mechanical

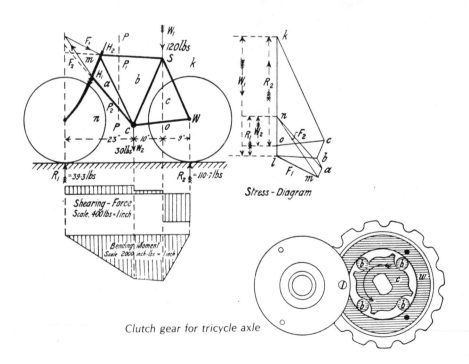

Clutch gear for tricycle axle

engineering of bicycles, essential to the design of successful machines. This would make a good text for design classes.

Part II reviews the history of the development of the bicycle, with the various improvements, when they were made, which ideas were dead ends and which ideas led to further refinements. The basic bicycle design we use today evolved by 1886.

The section on tricycle design may prove useful to those investigating design changes to make the pedicab more efficient and easier to operate. For example, the effects of different tricycle configurations on steering capability are explored. Several special gears for driving tricycle wheels at different speeds when rounding corners are discussed in detail (clutch gear and differential). The author notes that great accuracy is not needed in the production of the bevel gears for a differential; these gears only move slowly even when a tricycle turns a corner at 20 mph.

In the remaining chapters (300 pages) the author discusses motion over uneven surfaces, frames, stresses on frames, different kinds of spoked wheels, hubs, bearings, chains, chain gearing, toothed wheel gearing, lever and crank gearing, tires, pedals, cranks, bottom brackets, seats and brakes.

This is truly a classic and monumental work on bicycle design.

The Design of Cycle Trailers, MF 26-659, IT Transport, 44 pages, by Ian Barwell, 1977, £3.95 from Intermediate Technology Transport Ltd., 9 King Street, London WC2E 8HN, United Kingdom.

"The intention of this report is to provide basic design information for those people in developing countries who wish to build bicycle trailers." Detailed recommendations about the critical aspects of trailer design are made, to aid the reader in designing a trailer most suited to local circumstances. These design aspects include size of cargo space, center of gravity of the load, length of tow bar, hitch design, ground

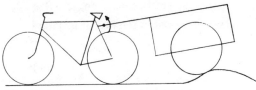

Side view

i) Rotation about lateral horizontal axis for traversing bumps

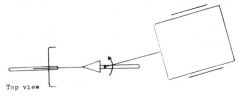

Top view

ii) Rotation about vertical axis for cornering

Movements required in a bike trailer hitch

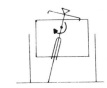

Front view

iii) Rotation about longitudinal horizontal axis for cornering

clearance, type and mounting of wheels, and chassis design. 15 bicycle trailers are described, along with photos and drawings of each.

"The trailer is a convenient way of extending the usefulness of bicycles. . . It is cheap to produce, suitable for small-scale manufacture by local industries and can, if designed for that purpose, also function as a hand cart. For these reasons the development of trailer designs which meet particular local requirements is to be encouraged."

A bicycle with a trailer can carry an amount of cargo almost as great as a tricycle (100 kg vs. 150 kg), yet the trailer can be quickly disconnected to allow use of the bicycle for personal transport. It should be possible to produce the trailers for not much more than ½ the cost of a bicycle.

An easy to read, valuable report.

The Bicycle Builder's Bible, MF 26-653, book, 376 pages, by Jack Wiley, 1980, out of print in 1985.

This is mainly a buying guide and maintenance manual for bicycles. Variations such as unicycles, tandems, and motocross bikes are also discussed. The author shows how to convert a regular bicycle to a folding bicycle, and how to make some of the other unusual variations from bicycle parts.

Three commercially sold adult tricycles (Schwinn Town and Country, AMF Courier, and Gobby), all with three speeds and rear wheel differentials, are pictured and briefly described. Also shown is an industrial tricycle, The Mover (manufactured by Industrial Cycles, Dayton, Ohio).

There are a few useful ideas included for rigging up pedal-powered equipment. Many of these seem to be taken from **Pedal Power in Work, Leisure and Transportation**, or from the work of S. Wilson in England.

Bicycles: A Case Study of Indian Experience, MF 26-656, book, 87 pages, by United Nations Industrial Development Organization, 1969, also available in French and Spanish, $1.00 (ID/SER. K/1, Sales No. E.69.II.B.30), from United Nations Industrial Development Organization, P.O. Box 300, A-1400 Vienna, Austria.

For anyone interested in the idea of making bicycles on a national or regional level, this is a fascinating book. Much of it is technical; for example, it lists the specifications of each of the different parts for the chosen model (a single speed, heavy-duty design). The book certainly does not provide all the information needed to begin bicycle manufacture, but it does give a good idea of what might be required.

There is a comparison of manufacturing requirements and costs in small- and large-scale production units in India. Describes tests made for each of the major components. Lists conventional equipment required and costs. Describes the manufacturing and assembly operations, including those for a small-scale plant producing 15,000 bicycles yearly. Discusses manufacturing of specialized components by small subcontractors.

The conclusions and recommendations include the following: a) A bicycle industry can be started with the manufacture of only a few simple parts and components and the rest imported. b) Complete bicycles can be manufactured by units making only a few parts themselves and obtaining the rest from cooperating small-scale units. c) Gradually imports can be reduced with a view to reaching self-sufficiency. Under a 3-phase program, the imports would be: Phase 1 — free-wheels, BB shells, hubs, rims, chains, spokes, nipples, tires and tubes, and steel balls; Phase 2 — only free-wheels, BB shells, hubs, tires and tubes, and steel balls would be imported; Phase 3 — only BB shells, tires and tubes, and steel balls would be imported. After this all components would be produced within the country.

If the reader were to combine what is provided here with S. Wilson's "Oxtrike" idea (making use of sheet steel and angle iron instead of tube steel for the frames), a much smaller-scale and lower-cost method of production might be possible.

Bicycle Resource Guide, MF 26-654, a series of bibliographies averaging 100+ pages, 1000+ entries, $5.00 to $15.00 each, from D.J. Luebbers, Editor, 78 South Jackson, Denver, Colorado 80209, USA.

This is a series of seven bibliographies. The 1976 bibliography, for example, has 106 pages, 1102 entries, an index, and costs $5.00 in the U.S. and $5.50 overseas. Entries include bikeway studies (both on existing roads and new separate pathways), accident studies, guides for local tours, bike laws, bike repair manuals, conference proceedings, 100 mail order catalogs, 290 newspaper articles, and 300 journal articles on medical, transportation, historical, legal, and industrial topics related to bicycles.

Of special interest to our readers in the 1976 bibliography are: repair and service manuals, case studies of bicycle/bus combinations as low-cost solutions to urban transport needs, articles describing new power packs for potential use with mopeds or bicycles, studies of "low-cost" bikeway pavement materials and design, publications presenting methods for using the bicycle in teaching certain principles of physics, and a document on transport planning incorporating bicycles in the city of Nairobi.

Maintaining Motorcycles: A Fieldworker's Manual, MF 26-663, booklet, 26 pages, by Russell Henning, 1982, $3.00 (add $1.15-$4.75 for airmail) from World Neighbors, 5116 North Portland Avenue, Oklahoma City, Oklahoma 73112, USA.

Basic considerations in preventative maintenance and selected "roadside" repair tips are combined in a common sense guide for keeping the small, simple beast of burden roadworthy. Includes rudimentary advice on commonly encountered maintenance problems such as battery and sparkplug malfunction; tire, chain, and air cleaner service; wheel alignment; and a service check schedule.

Automotive Operation and Maintenance, MF 26-688, large paperback manual, 200 pages, by E. Christopher Cone, 1973, $6.55 from VITA.

The author's experiences in Liberia, West Africa, of "experiment and occasional disaster" provided most of the material for this book.

"The intent is to offer suggestions to the driver or mechanic who operates in an area where service facilities and technical assistance are not readily available. In such areas he must be his own advisor on every problem which may arise.

"The first section concerns operation of a car in an area served by pioneer roads. The section is intended to assist the driver with temporary repairs to his vehicle so that he can get home in the event of mechanical trouble.

"The second major portion of the book is devoted to maintenance suggestions. These are intended for use in a frontier shop or repair center, no matter how ill-equipped this may be. This book should be used as a supplement to the vehicle's shop manual, and as a source of guidance. The shop manual will tell how to reline the brakes, for example, but this book is intended to indicate when relining is needed."

Chapter topics are: mechanical emergencies while driving, operating on pioneer roads, avoiding road hazards, extricating the vehicle, procedures when stranded, winches and towing, field expedients (on the spot temporary repair suggestions), check lists (for problem-locating and solving), tests and testing equipment, shop techniques, body repairs, a shop building, diesel engines, tools and equipment (for the car and shop), vehicle modification, parts and supplies, storage facilities, preventive maintenance, selecting a vehicle (a look at four-wheel-drive vehicles available), miscellaneous formulas, definitions, and an index.

The manual includes many large, simple drawings and diagrams that provide ingenious solutions (along with the text) to difficult problems; e.g. freeing a car stuck between logs on a bridge; extricating a vehicle stuck in mud or snow;

temporary repair of broken brake or fuel lines. There are diagrams for homemade hoists and tire removers as well as general shop hints and a very handy index. The language is not difficult; closer to standard English than almost any automobile shop manual. An excellent book.

The Backyard Mechanic, Volume One: MF 26-670, 57 pages; Volume Two: MF 26-671, 77 pages; Volume Three: MF 26-672, 92 pages; 1981, publication 104N, $7.00 for the set of three volumes, make checks payable to Superintendent of Documents, from Consumer Information Center, P.O. Box 100, Pueblo, Colorado 81002, USA.

Good illustrations and photos with clear instructions tell you how to do most car maintenance and repair activities. Brakes, cooling system, battery care, tune-up, body repair and painting and more topics are covered. The safe, permanent repair of tubeless tires is explained. Relevant to most automobiles.

Normal Combustion

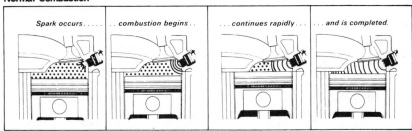

Detonation

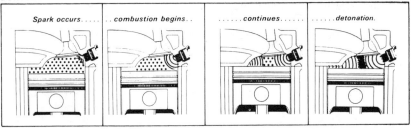

Preignition

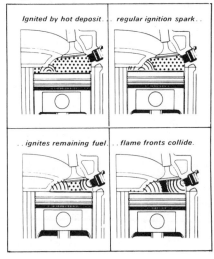

Gasoline Engine Tune-Up, MF 26-676, booklet, 18 pages, 1983, publication 105N, make checks payable to Superintendent of Documents, $1.50 from Consumer Information Center, P.O. Box 100, Pueblo, Colorado 81002, USA.

Many photos and clear instructions in this booklet provide a good introduction to the steps necessary in tuning up gasoline automobile engines. It is much better than typical workshop manuals, which usually provide needed specifications but little guidance for the inexperienced. Even the reader who has been tuning up his/her own cars for years will learn a few things from this booklet.

Notes on Simple Transport in Some Developing Countries, Information Paper No. 2, MF 26-666, ITDG Transport Panel, report, 26 pages, out of print in 1985.

"The report discusses intermediate transport in Papua New Guinea, the Philippines, China and India, and describes the simple vehicles, human-powered, animal-powered and motorized, which are used in those countries." 22 photos of simple vehicles are included.

In Manila, among the unusual vehicles is "a bicycle and sidecar with a 50cc two-stroke engine mounted in the cycle frame. This drives the rear wheel through an additional chain drive, the original pedal chain drive being retained so that the rider can augment the power of the engine when necessary."

In China "many of the minor roads and tracks in the rural areas are narrow and unsealed but are quite satisfactory for the types of vehicle which travel on them" (bicycles, handcarts, wheelbarrows, and two-wheeled tractors).

The Chinese have shown considerable innovation in the design of tricycles for proper gearing and effective braking, while the Indians have not. (This suggests that the subservient role of the tricycle driver in India may have led to neglect from designers.)

A 1974 commission in Papua New Guinea recommended that 1) private cars were inappropriate to PNG conditions, 2) use of bicycles and pedal drive car vehicles should be promoted, 3) a bicycle path system should be built in Port Moresby, 4) the feasibility of using electric vehicles powered by PNG's substantial hydro resources should be investigated, and 5) aerial ropeway systems for mountainous areas should be investigated.

"Simple vehicles can play an important role in the transport systems of all developing countries, yet their use is largely confined to the urban areas of Asia, and their design is often based on imported technology rather than on local requirements."

Proceedings of ITDG Seminar "Simple Vehicles for Developing Countries", Information Paper No. 3, MF 26-667, ITDG Transport Panel, report, 66 pages, 1977, out of print in 1985.

The papers included in this report cover "vehicles presently in use and prototypes currently being developed; the role of transport in agriculture; the use of simple vehicles in labor-intensive construction; manufacturing strategies for local production; and the transport needs and economic constraints in the rural areas of developing countries." The need for improved wheels and tires for rural dirt roads is noted as an important research priority. 36 photos are included.

One of the more interesting motorized vehicles discussed is the TRANTOR, a multi-purpose vehicle able to serve as a truck, tractor, and passenger vehicle. The TRANTOR has been designed to be economically produced in developing countries in very low quantities (1000 units a year). Simple machine tools and jigs are used in production, and components are grouped into similar categories to allow the benefits of a large batch production to be achieved without requiring the production of a large number of completed vehicles.

This report provides additional evidence that an appropriate technology approach to rural transport would be considerably different from the prevailing approaches. "It is a technical fact that the design of roads in developing countries is dictated by the characteristics of the private car and the lorry (truck). The 'desired' speed that it is assumed car drivers want dictates the overall horizontal and vertical alignment of the road, whilst the frequency and load carrying capacity of the lorries that will use it decide the strength of the road's structure. It has never been shown that either or both of these vehicles is in any sense necessary, much less optimum, for development to take place. The possibility that other, simpler and probably cheaper vehicles might be more appropriate to needs does not appear to have been given serious consideration...The simpler and thus most probably lighter, the vehicle, the cheaper the cost of having an adequate road."

Contributing to the above problem is the fact that in developed countries "there appears to be a misunderstanding about the nature of movement demands (in the developing countries). For passenger transport the existing buses and various forms of share taxis probably meet demands very well. But for goods transport the available evidence suggests that the fundamental demand is for the movement of small consignments over relatively short distances. Smallholder agriculture, almost by definition, gives rise to limited crop surpluses and farm inputs."

Intermediate Transport in Southeast Asian Cities: Three Case Studies, Information Paper No. 4, MF 26-662, ITDG Transport Panel, 30 pages, by A.K. Meier, 1977, out of print in 1985.

This report provides three case studies of intermediate transport technology in Asian cities (Penang, wartime Saigon, and Jakarta). The author "records the very rapid changes in intermediate forms of transport that have taken place in these cities, gives an account of the factors which have influenced this," and compares the three experiences. 12 photographs are included.

Among the examples discussed are: the motorized three-wheelers that were driver-owned in Saigon; the collapse of the Saigon government bus system in 1965 and the subsequent import of nearly one million small motorcycles to soak up the dollars flowing out of the American war effort; the becaks, bemos, opelets, helicaks, super helicaks and pickups of Jakarta; and the freight tricycles of Penang.

A widening zone of Jakarta is becoming off-limits for the becaks (3-wheeled pedicabs) to make way for faster vehicles with higher fares. "The implications of a ban on becaks are serious and serve as an example of the imposition of a technology on a society which is neither economically nor socially prepared. A large number of persons will become unemployed (or underemployed) while a much smaller number of new jobs will be created. Unless there is a substantial lowering of fares on the becak replacements, the ban will deprive the lower classes of their only means of individual transportation."

Freight tricycles in Penang have a large metal box between two front wheels, cost about $175, and number about 3,000. They "are ideally suited for Penang's narrow streets. They can efficiently carry loads of 5 to 200 kg for distances up to four kilometers. A number of tricycles travel much greater distances, leaving the city entirely to gather a crop of coconuts, sugar cane, or bananas, for use in the food stalls."

"Each city has several unique aspects due to its size, organization, social composition, climate and geography. The direct consequence of this is significantly different intermediate transport networks...There is a general tendency to shift into motorized vehicles, which, from (the owner's) viewpoint are almost always more efficient, especially in cities where a premium is associated with time." However, the foreign exchange burden created by fuel imports, the loss of jobs making and operating non-motorized vehicles, and the loss of transport for a segment of the population must be weighed against the gains provided by motorized vehicles.

Appropriate Industrial Technology for Low-Cost Transport for Rural Areas, MF26-650, booklet, 54 pages, UNIDO, 1979, document no. ID/232/2, available from Editor, UNIDO Newsletter, Industrial Information Section, UNIDO, P.O. Box 300, A-1400 Vienna, Austria.

A 24-page background paper entitled "Appropriate Transport Facilities for the Rural Sector in Developing Countries" by I.J. Barwell and J.D. Howe of the IT Transport Panel is the most valuable part of this booklet. It provides an insightful and thorough examination of the elements of appropriate rural transport technology (both equipment and roads), and what actions policymakers and R&D groups can take in support of such technology.

The authors note that crucial on-farm transport technology has been almost totally neglected, along with virtually all of the low-cost technologies of the traditional sector: backpacks, bicycles, hand-carts, wheelbarrows, animal packs, and animal carts. The road networks do not effectively serve the majority of the population, but in fact subsidize the privately-owned imported motor vehicles and can bring real disadvantages to the rural poor (e.g. by destroying local crafts through transport of manufactured goods into the area). "Few vehicles have ever been designed specifically to meet the needs of developing countries. Their use in developing countries indicates not that they best meet transport needs but rather that they are better than anything else currently available." The authors note a variety of existing basic traditional vehicles which should be improved and more widely used.

This background paper is an excellent summary of the issues involved, and the change in orientation that planners will have to make if rural transport technology is to serve the poor.

Three Wheeled Vehicles in Crete, MF 26-669, paper, 10 pages, by Alan Meier, Pub. No. UCID-3968, free from the author, Lawrence Berkeley Laboratory, University of California, Berkeley, California 94720, USA.

A three-wheeled vehicle has evolved in Crete, Greece, and reached widespread use in the rural areas in just 10 years. There are now 20 local factories producing these vehicles. Most have an 8-12 hp rope-started diesel engine. For many of these vehicles the engine can be converted in ½ hour to a rototiller for agricultural use.

"The vehicle appears to have been in part responsible for the economic revival of agriculture in Crete. The three-wheelers borrowed much of their early technology from two-wheeled rototillers but quickly evolved into a unique vehicle." The rapid

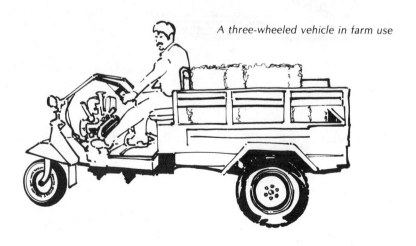

A three-wheeled vehicle in farm use

development and widespread use of these vehicles suggests they fill an important need for rural transport in less developed countries.

"A spectrum of transport alternatives seems to have developed. At the lower end is the cart pulled by the rototiller. . .The 3-wheeler comes next, providing greater speed and capacity. . . At the top is a group of light pick-up trucks which offer even higher speeds and slightly more capacity." 6 photos.

Appropriate Technology in Rural Development: Vehicles Designed for On and Off Farm Operations, MF 26-651, catalog, 150 pages, 1978, free to organizations involved in development work, from the Regional Development Unit, Transportation Department, World Bank, 1818 H Street N.W., Washington D.C. 20433, USA.

A catalog with brief descriptions of vehicles that are produced and sold commercially around the world, that could be used in rural areas of developing countries. The information comes from the manufacturers and has not been verified independently. There are more than 100 photos included.

Good as a summary of the range of rough terrain motorized vehicles designed in the industrialized countries: motorized tricycles and 3-wheeled vehicles, all-terrain vehicles, small tractors, small trucks, and hand tractors. Though a few animal-drawn carts and tricycles are shown, there is unfortunately little information included on the range of transport options affordable to the poor majority in developing countries.

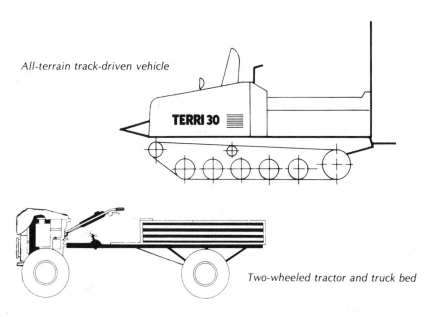

All-terrain track-driven vehicle

TERRI 30

Two-wheeled tractor and truck bed

The Manufacture of Low-Cost Vehicles in Developing Countries, MF 26-665, booklet, 31 pages, UNIDO, 1978, $3.00 (ID/193, Sales No. 78.II.B.8), from Sales Section, Room A-3315, United Nations, New York, New York 10017, USA; free to readers in developing countries from Editor, UNIDO Newsletter, UNIDO, P.O. Box 300, A-1400 Vienna, Austria.

This is a report of a meeting that discussed the obstacles to wider use of low-cost vehicles. An interesting variety of motorized vehicles are described, many of them from India and the Philippines. These include motorized bicycles, mopeds,

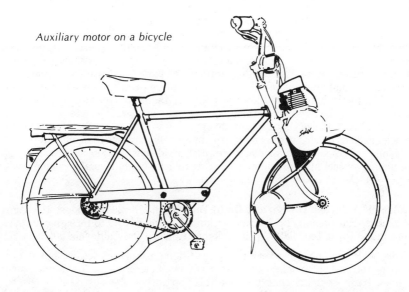

Auxiliary motor on a bicycle

motorcycles (often with a sidecar), three-wheelers (150 to 1200 cc engine) and small trucks (600 to 1600 cc engine).

Particularly for the 3- and 4-wheeled vehicles, the pattern has been first to import, then assemble, then partially produce vehicles locally. This has prevented radical innovation in design that might have led to vehicles more suitable to developing country circumstances.

A number of points are made in the report which suggest that perhaps the widespread use of small motors on existing non-motorized vehicles could provide additional power and speed where needed, while avoiding the need for enormous investment in high-speed, heavy vehicle roads. This might allow improved traditional vehicles to recapture some of the activity now monopolized by the imported high-speed cars and trucks. Transportation activities would thus remain in the hands of a broad section of the society.

In India there have "been moves to motorize cycle rickshaws, and at least two companies manufacture small two-stroke engines and conversion kits for fitting to rickshaws. One of these...uses a 35-cc, two-stroke general purpose engine developed for agricultural and other use. It is used to provide chain drive to only one of the back wheels, which makes a differential unnecessary." Power packs for bicycles are also manufactured in India.

In the Philippines "about 90 percent of the motorcycle population is fitted with side-cars." In the countryside these vehicles perform quite well on rough roads and paths.

"In terms of capital, space and economic volume, the requirements for making simple two-stroke engines are all only a fraction of those for manufacturing conventional four-cylinder engines. The technical requirements, although still exacting, are also much lower."

"In a world where high performance vehicles did not exist, the required road structure and system of traffic regulations would be considerably different from that of either an industrial or pre-industrial economy...Rigorous traffic separation reinforces the advantages of the more powerful vehicles."

Much of this report indicates that the traditional non-motorized transport vehicles have survived because they are better suited to existing needs for many tasks. Imported vehicles (and imported designs) suffer from high cost, difficulty of repair, lack of smooth supply of spare parts, high fuel consumption, and poor durability when operated over rough terrain. Thus there would appear to be an opportunity for low-cost motorized vehicles to replace many of the functions of the more expensive machines. Rather than argue for this, however, the expert group discusses ways to eliminate indigenous non-motorized vehicles: "The possibility of designing a motorized competitor for the rural bullock cart was discussed...Indeed, it is the extent that low-cost vehicles replace the more primitive means of transport that will effectively measure their success." The failure to consider vehicles in the light of who makes and owns them is a serious shortcoming here.

A different, more socially appropriate approach would defend the role of existing vehicles such as bullock carts, and try to improve them rather than eliminate them. If hidden subsidies (in the form of more costly road construction required for high-speed heavy vehicles) were removed, low-cost vehicles might favorably compete with larger vehicles in many activities.

Electric Vehicles: Design and Build Your Own, MF 26-660, book, 210 pages, by Michael Hackleman, 1977, $8.95 within USA and $10.00 to foreign countries, from Peace Press Inc., 3828 Willat Avenue, Culver City, California 90230, USA.

This book does not give very many specific construction details, but it does describe the basic principles of the design of small electric vehicles. You will need to know basic electrical theory to use this book.

Electric vehicles are not effective off of hard surfaced roads, and may require frequent battery recharging during a full day of use. The vehicles presented in this book can carry a couple of people but not heavy loads. Unless there are major future technological advances in battery efficiency, battery weight reduction, and solar generation of electricity, it seems clear that electric vehicles will remain too expensive and inefficient for transporting people or things (especially away from surfaced roads).

A better alternative for low-cost motorized vehicles and power packs for small vehicles and bicycles appears to be small internal combustion engines perhaps using fuels from biological processes (such as alcohol). But if you are interested in designing electric vehicles you should find this book useful. Many illustrations.

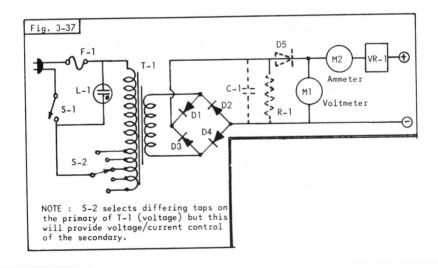

NOTE : S-2 selects differing taps on the primary of T-1 (voltage) but this will provide voltage/current control of the secondary.

A HOMEBUILT EV BATTERY CHARGER

Boatbuilding Manual, MF 26-673, book, 240 pages, by Robert M. Steward, second edition, 1980, $20.00 from International Marine Publishing Company, 21 Elm Street, Camden, Maine 04843, USA.

In this book traditional wooden boatbuilding is explained in a systematic, textbook style that employs abundant illustrations, tables and photographs. Boat construction is a field with a large number of unfamiliar technical terms, a fact that makes many books very difficult for the novice to use. Happily, this manual makes the entire subject, from choice of materials through detailed construction procedure, accessible to the careful reader without oversimplifying.

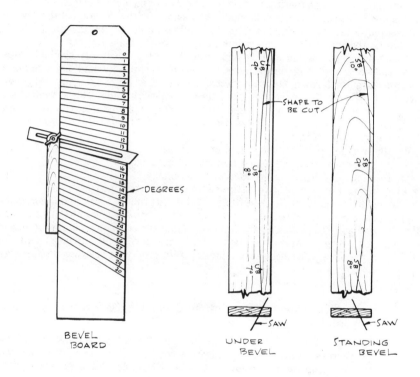

Figure 8-9(a) Making and using a simple bevel board

"Instead of using a protractor to measure a bevel each time you take one off, make yourself a simple bevel board as shown in Figure 8-9(a). Use a piece of plywood about 3½" wide and mark off angles from zero to about 30 degrees. Slide the adjustable bevel along the left edge of the bevel board until it lines up with one of the angles and read it off.

"When a bevel is marked on a piece of stock to be sawn, it must be designated as either 'under' or 'standing', marking the piece UB or SB. This is most important, and after you have ruined a few pieces, you will understand the principle."

There are not plans for a specific boat, but valuable information for completing a boat of virtually any design are provided. Alternative materials for hulls are covered briefly in the text and a list of recommended books on these and other aspects of boatbuilding is included.

New Working Watercraft, Special Report from the National Conference on Applications of Sail-Assisted Power Technology, MF 26-681, book, 94 pages, by James W. Brown, 1981, out of print. (For general information on the techniques described below, write to Kamberwood International Services Inc., P.O. Box 550, North, Virginia 23128, USA.)

This book presents the case for the role of low-cost, lightweight, sail-assisted boats in maintaining or revitalizing small scale fishing. Based on personal experience and consultancies in Africa, the Pacific and the Philippines, the author has adapted multi-hull design and cold-molding construction to create unique and ingenious craft. Many years of experimentation with new designs and alternative materials for high-performance sailing multi-hulls are apparent in the evolution of the designs presented. Most impressive is the resourcefulness and cultural insight shown in matching these designs to conditions in Third World fisheries.

Costs are kept low through maximizing the use of currently available local materials and reducing dependence on "alien" technology and petroleum. A patented system (termed "constant camber") is described for creating molded panels which can be sewn and glued together to create seaworthy hulls. This system alone, which circumvents exacting and tedious boatbuilding procedures, is high recommendation for the approach. Other features that distinguish the design(s):

a) human power can be used;
b) the working platforms are inherently stable;
c) small, non-marine, air-cooled motors can be used;
d) training time for local production is minimal;
e) prices can be competitive with existing indigenous craft.

This book does not include everything required to produce boats, and is currently out of print. However, a packet of materials termed the "Constant-Camber Info-Pak" is available for people interested in applying the technology in development projects or private enterprise. The contents are periodically updated and the US$25.00 purchase price includes a minimal patent royalty for licensing an introductory boatbuilding project.

Very worthwhile reading.

Fishing Boat Designs: 1—Flat Bottom Boats, MF 26-661, book, 46 pages, by Arne Fredrik Haug, 1974, $6.00 from UNIPUB.

"The paper contains a selection of designs of flat bottom boats suitable for fishing and transport work in lakes, rivers and protected coastal waters. The paper and the designs were prepared to provide detailed technical information to boatbuilders and fishery officers. . ."

The designs are intended to be built by people having basic carpentry skills and either some boatbuilding experience or a few weeks of training. Building procedures and timber selections are covered.

"The boat designs presented here are suitable where low cost, or ease of construction, are all-important factors and where a somewhat reduced sea-

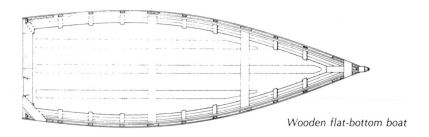

Wooden flat-bottom boat

MODERNIZED PROA ON LAMINATED HULL

Requiring a separate outrigger hull with daggerboard trunk, laminated cross-beams and tubular aluminum mast, this version is somewhat more costly than the "traditional" proa at right. The laminated main hulls are the same, but features are included to overcome the Tuvaluan's stated objections to their own boats; propensity to capsize, and difficult maneuvering.

Separate, elevated float on downwind side (behind sail) serves the function of a "pod" shown in the accompanying photographs; it effectively prevents capsize. When maneuvering, isosceles sail simply alternates tack and sheet from hull to "pod." Traditional version at right requires moving spars from one end to the other. Only trials in service will reveal which version works best, mechanically and economically.

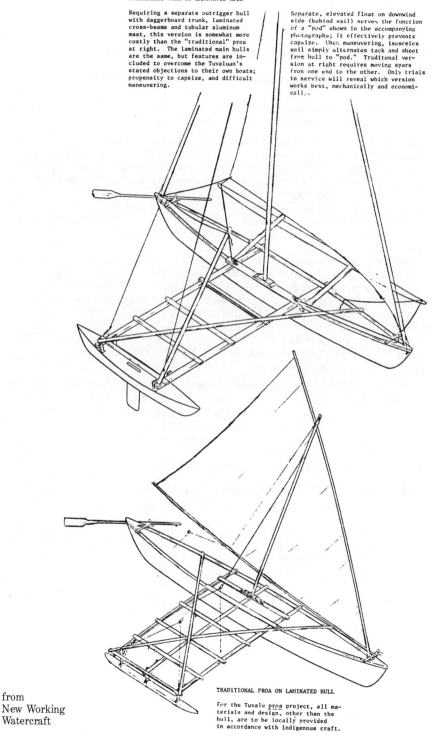

TRADITIONAL PROA ON LAMINATED HULL

For the Tuvalu proa project, all materials and design, other than the hull, are to be locally provided in accordance with indigenous craft.

from
New Working
Watercraft

worthiness...can be accepted, or where extreme shallow draft requirements are an over-riding consideration."

Materials needed for construction are wood, galvanized nails and screws, caulking compound, wood preservative and sealer, and caulking cotton. The boats could be built with only hand carpentry tools, but a table-saw and hand-held electric drill would be useful. The boats are powered by pole, oar or motor; some of the boats could be modified for sail power with the addition of side-mounted keel boards.

Handbook of Artisanal Boatbuilding, book, 131 pages, text in both English and French, by R. Lefebvre, 1975, FAO, $9.50 from UNIPUB.

This handbook sets down in a straightforward way the main points of establishing a small-scale boatbuilding industry where none formerly existed. Identifying and training capable local carpenters, establishing open-air workshops, and organizing for the production of very small rudimentary plank-built boats are among the topics covered. The text, presented in both English and French, is clear and systematic and closely matched to explanatory illustrations and photos.

The contents are based on an FAO project in Africa where fishing had previously been conducted in dug-out canoes. Though the circumstances of this project were unique, and such a simple approach will not always have as great an impact, there are valuable insights here for readers interested in establishing a cottage industry. The boat design presented is applicable for inland fisheries in other non-industrial areas. The emphasis is on full employment (hence the artisanal rather than industrial approach), low capital, and product quality, all of which make this a useful reference for project officers in small-scale economic development.

Boats from Ferrocement, MF 26-658, book, 131 pages, by UNIDO, 1972, ID/72, Sales No. 72.II.B, $2.50 from Sales Section, Room A-3315, United Nations, New York, New York 10017, USA.

"There is no doubt about the urgent need in most developing countries for fishing boats that will help solve their acute food problems and for boats that will facilitate transportation in areas where rivers and channels are the most commonly used communication routes...Ferro-cement boat-building is perfect for developing countries. It requires a minimum of qualified personnel, imported raw materials and capital equipment and the boats produced compare favourably with those made from other materials in terms of price, performance, maintenance costs and life span."

This book is a very detailed survey of the equipment, materials and methods used in ferrocement boatbuilding. Many sources of further information are mentioned.

"The basic qualities that make ferro-cement ideal for boat construction are the ease with which it can be moulded to any shape, and the unit weight per square foot."

Anyone building ferrocement boats will find many specific instructions in this book, but there are no complete boat plans.

Boatbuilding With Plywood, book, 278 pages, by Glen L. Witt and Ken Hankinson, 1978, $15.95 from Glen-L Marine Designs, 9152 Rosecrans, Bellflower, California 90706, USA.

Plywood has many advantages as a boatbuilding material for amateur and small-scale builders. The type of wood, and more importantly, the type of glue used to laminate the thin wood panels will determine if the plywood is suitable for marine applications. Plywood boats can be faster and easier to build and lighter than those made from alternative materials, but care must be exercised to benefit from these characteristics.

Where most boatbuilding books treat plywood as a material for interiors and

KEELS

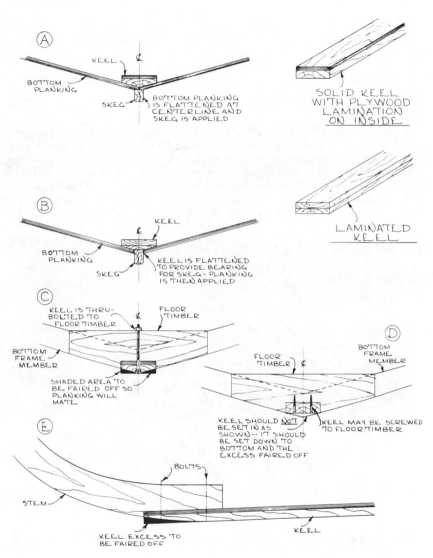

Keel types used in plywood boats

above-deck construction, this book gives detailed instruction for building boat hulls from plywood. Each step is illustrated with numerous photographs and clear two-dimensional drawings. The boat examples provided are mostly recreational craft with the high standards of construction for performance and appearance common in affluent areas. But quality construction (along with good maintenance) is more critical with plywood than with perhaps any other material, and this book provides the amateur builder with insights evidently gained through long experience. Not every design can be built with plywood, and not all plywood is suitable for boatbuilding, but when all the conditions are met this book should be useful.

The Dory Book, MF 26-674, book, 275 pages, by John Gardner, 1978, $25.00 from International Marine Publishing Co., 21 Elm Street, Camden, Maine 04843, USA.

"Of the simplest design, built from the most common materials, the dory has the ability to handle the most demanding tasks." Relative ease of construction, low cost, and legendary seaworthiness are the main advantages that have made this a popular design for small work-boats. Primarily distinguished by the use of wide planks (increasingly replaced by plywood) and the lack of a keel, dories have remained relatively unchanged for several centuries. Where conditions require seaworthiness and suitable building materials are available, this design may still find application.

This book begins by tracing the evolution of the dory with a scholarly, yet quite readable account of pre-industrial and early industrial boatbuilding. There is also a compendium of dory designs with construction details and text that provides guidance on the relative merits of each variation. But the most useful part (comprising about one-third of the book) is the section on layout and construction, aimed at the home or small-enterprise builder. The focus on one type of boat, and the abundant, clear three-dimensional drawings make the construction procedures much easier to understand here than in many boatbuilding books. A chapter on new materials could go into greater depth, but does provide helpful information for those with access to alternative building materials. First-time or amateur builders should find this book very useful either by itself or as a supplement to more technical boatbuilding books.

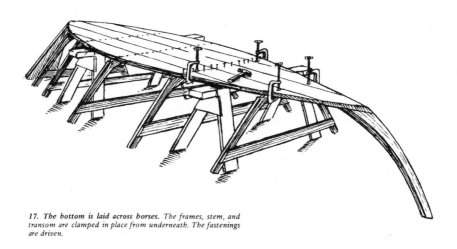

17. The bottom is laid across horses. The frames, stem, and transom are clamped in place from underneath. The fastenings are driven.

Wind-Power Vessels for Coastal and Inter-Island Use in the ESCAP Region, MF 26-685, paper, 18 pages, ESCAP, 1984, publication ID/WG.413/2 from UNIDO.

This is a brief review of the possibility of applying current technology to save fuel by making freight hauling vessels largely wind-powered. Some of the observations may be of interest in modifying existing small traditional vessels to make them faster and safer.

Small Boat Design, MF 26-684, book, 79 pages, edited by Johanna Reinhart, ICLARM, 1979, $12.00 from International Specialized Book Services, 10230 South West Parkway, Portland, Oregon 97225, USA.

A conference on small boat design held in New Caledonia in 1975 generated the 16 papers assembled in this book. Considerations for the design of work-boats are briefly covered by a variety of representatives of fishery development organizations and the marine industry. Many papers focus on the South Pacific, though the information is applicable elsewhere. While the new-found energy consciousness of the mid-70s is evident, a "small" boat is considered to be anything from a home-built craft powered by a recycled lawnmower engine up to a high-speed boat propelled by marine diesel motors costing several thousand dollars. This broad focus reflects the variety of conditions in which fishing is carried out, but may limit the usefulness of the book for many readers.

The collection begins to cover the complexity of matching small boat design to the needs of fishers in less developed regions. While not as comprehensive or systematic as it could be, it contains many important points for planners and builders in small-scale fisheries. Some of the topics are: engine selection, building materials, person-hour estimates for construction, design requirements for a "typical" village fishery, loan repayment calculations, etc. A list of addresses for the participants is included.

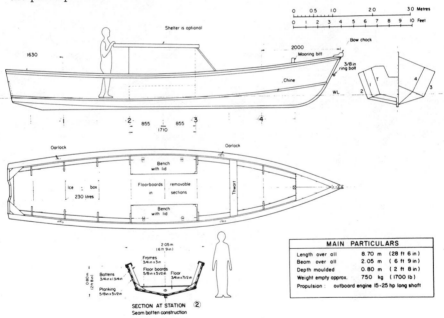

A 28-ft outboard powered boat suitable for village fishery operations.

ADDITIONAL REFERENCES ON TRANSPORTATION

"Technology for the Masses" contains an excellent article on the modernization of the bullock cart; see BACKGROUND READING.

A Landscape for Humans has some unusual and interesting recommendations for road building; see LOCAL SELF-RELIANCE.

Small Scale Cement Plants: A Study in Economics and **Rural Small Scale Industry in**

the People's Republic of China take a look at the relationship between transportation infrastructure and the development of small-scale industries in China; see LOCAL SELF-RELIANCE.

Bearing Design and Fitting should be a useful reference to people working on improved cart designs; see THE WORKSHOP.

Oil Soaked Wooden Bearings tells how to make durable bearings for slow-turning cart wheels and other applications; see AGRICULTURAL TOOLS.

Alcohol fuel production is covered by several items in ENERGY: GENERAL.

Small steam engines can be used on vehicles and in boats; see ENERGY: GENERAL.

The Handcart Handbook describes simple handcarts that can be used to transport small amounts of goods.

Books on bridge design and construction are in HOUSING AND CONSTRUCTION.

Health Care

Health Care

"Each month a civil servant dies in the capital because there is no penicillin. Each day a child in the country recovers from a fatal disease because of a plant growing in the forest."
— Benjamin Owuor, quoted by Aggrey Nyong'o

"We are dedicated to completely eradicating all anti-scientific attitudes and ideas."
— Cuban doctor

These contrasting views are common among people who are dedicated to improving the level of health among the world's poor. There is the romantic who unquestioningly believes in the general effectiveness of traditional remedies, and there is the crusading doctor who sees only superstition in native cures. Both perspectives are partly valid; traditional remedies range from the dramatically effective to the dangerous. The main weakness of traditional medicine has been the failure of its practitioners to question the validity of cures; due to coincidence and the power of suggestion, good and bad remedies are added uncritically to the medical kit of the indigenous healer. Nor has there been sufficient dispassionate review of what is effective, harmless, and dangerous within the drug arsenal of modern medicine. A major challenge in developing appropriate health practices and remedies is to draw together the effective, cheap, and safe treatments in both traditional and modern healing systems.

Equally important is the question of the kind of people and roles that are to be supported in a strategy for the development of a health care system or systems. Much has been written about why modern medical facilities cannot be extended to reach the entire population of most Third World nations. Among the many reasons for this, the great expense of elaborate facilities, the chronic shortage of professionals to work in rural areas, and the high cost of physician training programs are the most frequently cited. Because of these problems, health programs are increasingly involving lesser-trained health workers from the communities in which they work. These people have in many ways a more demanding role than the doctor, requiring a broader range of skills and knowledge to successfully offer basic curative care, lead preventive and health education programs, and take part in community organizing. A unique and significant advantage is that as members of their community they know it intimately. Schemes involving community level health workers are now operating all over the world.

The need for more "medical auxiliaries" is also acutely felt in the United States, a country which "imports" many thousands of graduates from the poor countries that can least afford it. This is no less than a national disgrace. We too need larger numbers of lesser-trained health workers to become self-sufficient in health care. Such people are quite capable of treating most common health problems. Doctors are probably universally over-worked, whether in the halls of "Mass. General" or in the rural areas of Central America. Even selfless service in a needy area, however, does not even begin to meet the longer-term health care needs of the people unless it involves training members of the community so that they can begin to tackle their own health care problems. In developing countries the vast majority of health problems are relatively simple ones, often avoidable through the application of basic principles of preventive medicine, and usually compounded by a poor level of nutrition and a lack of access to prompt treatment.

A villager whose main qualifications are the ability to read and write (3 to 6 years of primary education) and a sense of responsibility and compassion for his or her fellow human beings can be trained in two months to diagnose, treat and prevent 95% of the health problems commonly found in developing countries. Often these local health workers have proven themselves to be more effective in diagnosing and treating common local problems than a small, overburdened professional staff. They live among the people they treat and charge what people can afford. Because they have grown up in the community, they know the socio-economic and family history of their patients, and they are sensitive to local concepts of health, disease, and treatment. For these reasons, they frequently have insights into the causes of local health problems and their advice is more likely to be understood and followed.

Unfortunately, those who endorse the use of village health workers frequently pay only lip service to the depth and breadth of indigenous knowledge and skills. In health care, as in other related aspects of community development, outside agencies have often been quick to assert the absolute superiority of their (usually Western-based) methods. And people who have long been oppressed and belittled are sometimes also quick to accept what outside agencies offer, abandoning their own traditions. Making matters worse, the chief medical personnel in programs working with village health workers often have little faith in these people and allow them few responsibilities; too often the result has been the creation of little more than referral systems that continue to swamp understaffed clinics in towns and cities.

It appears that this situation is changing for the better. In the last ten years, a number of manuals for training village health workers (VHWs) have appeared which provide practical medical information while recognizing the validity of traditional health care roles and experience. The success of **Where There Is No Doctor**, with over a million copies in print and translations in more than 25 languages, is an indicator of the usefulness of and demand for this kind of reference material. **Helping Health Workers Learn**, by the same people, is a wonderful collection of ideas and insights; many of them could be modified for use in non-health programs as well. In addition to other manuals reviewed here, three bibliographies concentrate on materials written for trainers and program leaders.

The classics **Medical Care in Developing Countries** and **Pediatric Priorities in the Developing World** should be required reading for all expatriate medical personnel, and there is much in them to be recommended to nationals in developing countries. Half a dozen books are to be found on the Chinese experience with health care—of considerable relevance to other developing countries attempting to meet the health care needs of large dispersed populations under conditions of limited resources. The bibliography **Health Care in the People's Republic of China** identifies much of the literature on that nation's successful use of "barefoot doctors" in their decentralized health care system. It seems paradoxical but true that increased local self-reliance in health care depends greatly on supportive initiatives taken by the policy-making centers in government. A notable new strategy for health education and community participation in preventive and basic curative health care is described in **Child-to-Child**. Recognizing that small children are often cared for and taught by their older brothers and sisters, the child-to-child strategy is to develop activities in which older children teach younger children simple practices (like the use of homemade toothbrushes) and identify children with hearing, eyesight, and malnutrition problems. These activities make learning an *exciting adventure in which children discover for themselves how and why a problem exists, then together take action to do something about it. Where health workers and school teachers have conducted child-to-child activities, impressive gains have been made.*

In **Child-to-Child** *and the other manuals reviewed here, the words "child" and "children" appear again and again as the focus of rural health care programs. Especially vulnerable to disease below the age of five years, and often malnourished, children constitute the majority of the Third World's sick and dying people. Untreated infant diarrhea leading to severe dehydration in malnourished children is the leading cause of death in Third World communities. A simple rehydration solution that can be made in any village kitchen can save these lives. Through formal and nonformal education, including visits by village health workers, children and adults can be taught how to make this solution for early treatment at home before the dehydration becomes serious. The World Health Organization is now promoting the dissemination of pre-packaged powdered mixes that accomplish the same thing.*

In the long run, hygienic and public health measures, particularly the provision of a safe supply of water for washing and drinking, are critical steps in improving basic community health and reducing infant diarrhea and infant mortality. The control of communicable diseases (books on this subject are reviewed in this section) also depends heavily on a safe water supply and adequate waste disposal systems. Many of the references in the WATER SUPPLY AND SANITATION *chapter are relevant here.*

In addition to these factors which visibly influence the health of the community, land reform and agricultural development have major roles to play in improving the basic health of rural people. Some health care programs are now including agricultural development projects and pressure for land reform as part of a total effort to improve community health.

Health care equipment that can be locally produced is described in **Where There Is No Doctor, How to Make Basic Hospital Equipment,** *and* **Where There Is No Dentist.** *For physiotherapy and orthopaedic equipment, see* **Low Cost Physiotherapy Aids, Simple Orthopaedic Aids,** *and* **Rattan and Bamboo.** *The equipment needs and proper operation of basic medical laboratories are the subjects of* **A Medical Laboratory for Developing Countries** *and two other books reviewed after it.*

Where There Is No Doctor, MF 27-716, book, 458 pages, by David Werner, 1977, $8.50 ($6.00 to local groups in developing countries), plus $1.50 shipping in U.S., $2.00 shipping overseas, from the Hesperian Foundation, P.O. Box 1692, Palo Alto, California 94302, USA.

This famous medical handbook was written as a reference for literate village health workers. It is the product of more than 15 years' work in the creation of a villager-run health care network in the mountains of Mexico. The revised English and Spanish editions (**Donde No Hay Doctor,** MF 27-681, 430 pages, 1980, same price and source) have been translated into more than 20 languages around the world, including French, Portuguese, Swahili and Arabic. The foundation will provide addresses for local editions.

The text "takes into consideration local beliefs and customs, gives guidelines for determining the usefulness vs. hazard of different folk remedies, and discusses the common misuses as well as correct uses of medications commonly available. It starts with a discussion of traditional concepts of illness and healing, and from there leads into 'modern' concepts. The book, which has hundreds of simple but informative drawings, is also used by health workers to teach patients about their health problems, their causes and prevention." An interesting feature of this book is a colored index that tells the names and uses of drugs the villagers may come into contact with. (Many of these drugs are commonly used without any knowledge of their effects.)

HOW TO MOVE A BADLY INJURED PERSON

With great care, lift the injured person without bending him anywhere.

Have another person put the stretcher in place.

With the help of everyone, place the injured person carefully on the stretcher.

sand bags

If the neck is injured or broken, put bags of sand or tightly folded clothing on each side of the head to keep it from moving.

Health Care and Human Dignity, MF 27-684, paper, 25 pages, by David Werner, 1976, $2.00 from the Hesperian Foundation, P.O. Box 1692, Palo Alto, California 94302, USA.

Written by the author of **Where There Is No Doctor** (see review), this paper briefly summarizes the major insights gained from a study of nearly forty rural health projects in Central and South America. It is the clearest, most coherent discussion we have seen of the features of "community-supportive" rural health programs and the obstacles to be faced by people wishing to foster these programs on a broader scale. *"Community supportive* programs or functions are those which favorably influence the long-range welfare of the community, that help it stand on its own feet, that genuinely encourage responsibility, initiative, decision making and self-reliance at the community level, that build upon human dignity. . .the programs which in general we found to be more community supportive were small, private, or at least non-government programs, usually operating on a shoestring and with a more or less sub rosa (low-profile, unofficial) status."

Werner goes on to identify key factors tending to limit or slow the growth of community-supportive programs: paternalistic attitudes among those in charge of health care delivery programs, overemphasis on medical "safety," bureaucracy (or, the "superstructure overpowering the infrastructure"), commercialization, and government fear of the politically destabilizing potential of increased rural skills and abilities. The paper concludes with a list of steps that might be taken to implement a country-wide approach to community-supportive health care. Appendices compare and contrast the objectives, size, financing, and other characteristics of "community supportive" vs. "community oppressive" health programs.

An extremely useful combination of criticism and positive suggestions for future progress, of interest to anyone interested in health as part of community self-reliance. Highly recommended.

The Village Health Worker—Lackey or Liberator?, MF 27-714, paper with charts and drawings, 16 pages, by David Werner, 1977, $2.00 from the Hesperian Foundation, P.O. Box 1692, Palo Alto, California 94302, USA.

David Werner elaborates on points made in **Health Care and Human Dignity** (see review above), illustrating how socio-economic context and political objectives of program planners affect rural health programs. Werner and several co-workers visited some 40 health worker programs in Latin America. "In the majority of cases, we found that external factors, far more than intrinsic factors, proved to be the determinants of what the primary health worker could do. . .We concluded that *the great variation in range and type of skills performed by village health workers in different programs has less to do with the personal potentials, local conditions or available funding than it has to do with the preconceived attitudes and biases of health program planners, consultants, and instructors.* In spite of the often repeated eulogies about 'primary decision making by the communities themselves,' seldom do the villagers have much, if any, say in what their health worker is taught and told to do. The limitations and potentials of the village health worker—what he is permitted to do and, conversely, what he could do if permitted—can best be understood if we look at his role in its social and political context. In Latin America, as in many other parts of the world, poor nutrition, poor hygiene, low literacy and high fertility help account for the high morbidity and mortality of the impoverished masses. But as we all know, the underlying cause—or more exactly, the primary disease—is inequity: inequity of wealth, of land, of educational opportunity, of political representation and of basic human rights. . .As anyone who has broken bread with villagers or slum dwellers knows only too well: *health of the people is far more influenced by politics and power groups, by distribution of land and wealth, than it is by treatment or prevention of disease."*

Health by the People, MF 27-683, book, 202 pages, edited by Kenneth Newell, 1975, 36 Swiss Francs or US$18.00, from World Health Organization, Distribution and Sales Service, 1211 Geneva 27, Switzerland, or local WHO distributors.

These articles on 10 successful rural health programs in Indonesia, India, Guatemala, Venezuela, Niger, Iran, Tanzania, China and Cuba focus on community development and health services that use local people as health workers. The programs described range from national to village scale.

"There is no longer any doubt that a primary health worker can work effectively and in an acceptable manner and that he or she does not need to be a nurse or a doctor as we at present know them."

"The wider issues presented here include. . . self-sufficiency in all important matters and a reliance on outside resources only for emergencies; an understanding of the uniqueness of each community coupled with the individual and group pride and dignity associated with it; and lastly, the feeling that people have of a true unity between their land, their work and their household."

"Each country or area started with the formation, reinforcement, or recognition of a local community organization. This appeared to have five relevant functions: It laid down the priorities; it organized community action for problems that could not be resolved by individuals (e.g. water supply or basic sanitation); it 'controlled' the primary health care service by selecting, appointing, or 'legitimizing' the primary health worker; it assisted in financing services; and it linked health actions with wider community goals."

"In no example presented here is there a separation of the promotional, preventive, and curative actions at the primary health care level."

Written by planners, participants, and observers.

The Principles and Practices of Primary Health Care, **Contact** Special Series No. 1, MF 27-707, book, 112 pages, 1979, $2.00 from the Christian Medical Commission, World Council of Churches, 150 route de Ferney, CH-1211 Geneva 20, Switzerland.

This is the first book of the **Contact** Special Series, which reproduces articles on a single theme from the bimonthly periodical **Contact**. Includes 16 readings focusing on primary health care. Good background reading.

Health: The Human Factor, Readings in Health, Development and Community Participation, **Contact** Special Series No. 3, MF 27-688, book, 124 pages, edited by Susan B. Rifkin, 1980, $2.00 from the Christian Medical Commission, World Council of Churches, 150 route de Ferney, CH-1211 Geneva 20, Switzerland.

This book includes 11 readings on community participation in relation to health programs. Recommended.

Pediatric Priorities in the Developing World, MF 27-705, book, 429 pages, by Dr. David Morley, 1973, special ELBS edition available for £2.25 for those in or going to a developing country; Indonesian, Spanish, and Portuguese editions also available at £3.00, French edition £4.00, from TALC.

Dr. Morley "examines the problem facing child health services throughout the developing world: the urgent need to decide which of all the measures that may be taken to reduce the appalling levels of childhood mortality and morbidity should have the highest priorities when financial resources are so severely limited. . .The author is responsible for the innovation of the under-fives' clinic and for the design of a weight chart" to quickly identify and combat malnutrition. These two measures have subsequently been adopted by many developing countries.

"The author's objective is to orient the medical student or doctor towards the practical problems he will meet when involved in child care in a rural community. Careful emphasis is placed on the social, economic, cultural and ethical considerations which are ignored by most medical schools. Not only doctors but also nurses and other health workers. . .will benefit from this book. It is written for the doctor dissatisfied with the type of medical training which is based largely on European systems of health care, much of which may be inapplicable to his own country."

Morley emphasizes low-cost health services, within the means of the people involved, and the need to make extensive use of auxiliaries and villagers themselves. Primary focus is on rural societies because of the large numbers of children and the need for a different type of health care system than that suited to urban areas. Morley also stresses the need for the pediatrician to work on health education, and teach her/his own skills to her/his staff.

Morley worked for many years in a rural area of Nigeria. More recently he was instrumental in creating the Tropical Child Health Unit at the Institute of Child Health in London. He also helped create the group Teaching Aids at Low Cost.

Medical Care in Developing Countries, MF 27-694, book, 500 pages, edited by Maurice King, 1967, reprinted 1973, $13.95 from Oxford University Press, 16-00 Pollitt Drive, Fair Lawn, New Jersey 07410, USA; Spanish edition $8.50 from Editorial Pax Mexico, Libreria Carlos Cesarman, S.A., Avenida Cuauhtemoc 1434, Mexico 13 D.F., Mexico, 40% discount on Spanish edition to charitable groups.

"A primer on the medicine of poverty." This classic book evolved out of a WHO/UNICEF-supported conference on "Health Centres and Hospitals in Africa." In it, Maurice King, David Morley, Derrick Jellife and others come together under King's editorship to create a remarkable, comprehensive handbook for medical personnel. The slant is decidedly towards the doctor or other professional from the developed world who is working in the developing world. Material covered ranges from the organization of health services and the cross-cultural outlook in medicine to pediatrics, anaesthetics, and the laboratory. The recommendations are always realistically within the limits imposed by poverty and a commitment to get basic care to the largest number of people possible.

Primary Child Care: A Manual for Health Workers, book, 315 pages, by Maurice King, Felicity King, and Subagio Martodipoero, 1978, £2.00 from TALC.

Sponsored by the World Health Organization, this basic English text is intended to be adapted and translated for direct use by health workers everywhere. "It contains a selection of the most appropriate technologies for primary child care taken from all over the world."

The step-by-step approach, from the basics to the needed level of understanding, makes this a valuable book for people with only a limited knowledge of the field. For each major category of illness (e.g. "Coughs"), the authors begin with illustra-

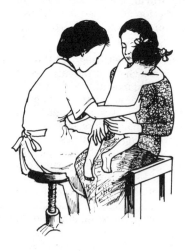

Examining the abdomen

tions and background information on the system or parts of the body affected (e.g. respiratory system). Then they discuss the different combinations of symptoms, diagnosis and treatment. They have included many effective diagrams that explain how infections and diseases spread.

More than 80 pages are devoted to community health problems, supplies and equipment, and procedures for examination, sterilization of equipment, and record-keeping. Dosage information is provided for all drugs mentioned. There is a glossary of 200 key scientific and medical terms, with which "you will probably be able to understand anything written in the rest of the book."

The three authors invested years of hard work in this wonderful book, undoubtedly the most valuable one that WHO has ever sponsored. This is an outstanding resource, which could become the basis for training programs for child health workers at many levels.

Standard First Aid and Personal Safety, book, 253 pages, 1979 (second edition), from American National Red Cross, 7401 Lockport Place, Lorton, Virginia 22079, USA.

A very good basic first aid book. Well-illustrated. A good value at the price.

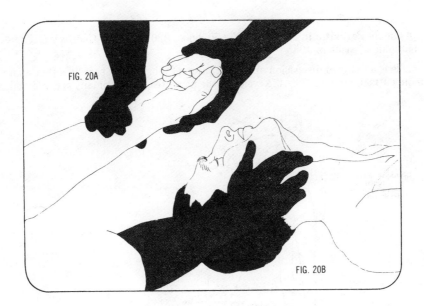

FIG. 20A

FIG. 20B

The Well Body Book, MF 27-715, large paperback book, 350 pages, by Mike Samuels, M.D., and Hal Bennett, 1973, $10.00 from WEA.

This book comes from the counterculture movement in the U.S., and is an attempt to demystify much of medicine as it is practiced here. The authors explain how to perform a simple, basic physical examination and how to take a systematic medical history, and describe the symptoms, causes and treatment of most common diseases found in the U.S. This enables the reader to do some self-diagnosis and treatment, but serves more to explain how the body works, what disease is, and how it progresses.

The more conventional sections of the book (on basic physical examination and diagnosis & treatment — 142 pages) are probably of more use outside the U.S. than the other, more culturally-bound sections. The simple language (some American slang, however) means that these more conventional sections might be adapted or serve as a model for manuals to be used with health auxiliaries. However, the lack of coverage of parasites and tropical diseases is a significant shortcoming in this regard.

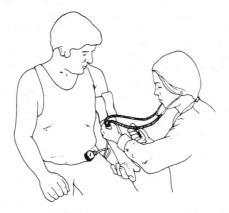

Animals Parasitic in Man, MF 27-670, book, 320 pages, by Geoffrey LaPage, 1963, out of print in 1985.

This is a detailed discussion and description of most of the parasites that commonly attack humans. The life cycles of the parasites, ways humans are infected,

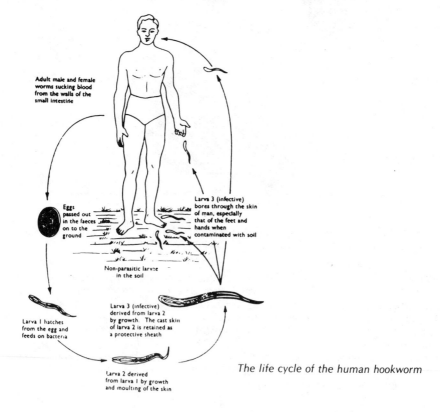

Adult male and female worms sucking blood from the walls of the small intestine

Eggs passed out in the faeces on to the ground

Larva 3 (infective) bores through the skin of man, especially that of the feet and hands when contaminated with soil

Non-parasitic larvae in the soil

Larva 1 hatches from the egg and feeds on bacteria

Larva 3 (infective) derived from larva 2 by growth. The cast skin of larva 2 is retained as a protective sheath

Larva 2 derived from larva 1 by growth and moulting of the skin

The life cycle of the human hookworm

prevention techniques and some medical treatments are discussed in detail.

"In any event each parasitic animal is limited to a certain range of hosts. It is, that is to say, *specific* to these hosts and cannot live in others. This *host-specificity* is an important feature of parasitism and it will be necessary to refer to it throughout this book. It will be evident, for instance, that if a particular host, such as man, is one of the usual hosts of a certain species of parasitic animal, it is necessary, if we wish to prevent the spread of this parasitic species, to know what its other usual hosts are, because all these hosts may be sources from which the parasitic animal may spread. These other hosts are reservoirs of the infection and they are called *reservoir hosts*."

Parasites are a problem in every part of the world that humans inhabit. Many of the parasites are so common in certain areas that it is quite unusual if an individual does not have them. Health campaigns to eliminate parasites must include education of the affected people about parasite hosts and requirements for preventing the spread of parasites. This book could be a useful reference in such an educational effort.

Communicable Diseases: A Manual for Rural Health Workers, MF 27-678, book, 349 pages, by Jan Eshuis and Peter Manschot, 1978, $3.50 from African Medical and Research Foundation, P.O Box 30125, Nairobi, Kenya.

A training and reference manual for Medical Assistants and Rural Medical Aides in Tanzania. "Most of the common diseases in Africa are environmental diseases due to infection by living organisms — viruses, bacteria, protozoa, or metazoa. These are called communicable diseases because they spread from person to person, or sometimes animals to people. Together with malnutrition they are today the major cause of illness in Africa. . . For the first time all the essential information on communicable diseases, from both clinical and public health aspects, has been collected in one volume, adequate for the training of paramedical staff."

This manual groups diseases by how they spread — by contact, by fecal contamination, by airborne germs, and so on. For each disease, information is provided on where it is found in Tanzania, causes, symptoms and diagnosis, and control. Much of the content is relevant in other regions. Most of the text is in simple English, although medical terms are also used. Drawings show sources and agents of disease in the African village environment. The authors discuss the kinds of public health measures which interrupt the transmission of diseases and prevent their spread.

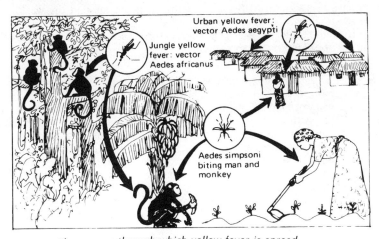

The process through which yellow fever is spread

Historically, adequate supplies of water and safe handling of human waste have been the most important factors in the prevention of communicable diseases.

The African Medical and Research Foundation has published a series of similar books on child health, health education, pharmacology, immunology, and other topics. More information on the series can be obtained from the Foundation at the address above.

Control of Communicable Diseases in Man, book, 418 pages, thirteenth edition, edited by Abram Benenson, 1975, revised 1980, $10.00 from American Public Health Association, 1015 Fifteenth Street N.W., Washington D.C. 20005, USA.

Communicable diseases and malnutrition are the major killers in the Third World. This is a good reference for teachers of health workers, and contains valuable ideas for program leaders who must cope with epidemics. The difficult language means that this book cannot be directly used in explaining the information to health workers. No attempt has been made to deal with the human, social, and cultural factors that must be considered before many of the recommendations can be followed. Some of the recommendations are not "affordable" in the Third World.

Helping Health Workers Learn: A Book of Methods, Aids and Ideas for Instructors at the Village Level, MF 27-689, book, 632 pages, by David Werner and Bill Bower, 1982, $8.50 from the Hesperian Foundation, P.O. Box 1692, Palo Alto, California 94302, USA.

This excellent book is the best of several new manuals on the training of village health workers. It is drawn primarily from more than 15 years' experience with an unusual community-based clinic and network of health workers operating in the tiny communities of mountainous Sinaloa in Mexico. Some of the material comes from visits and communications with health worker training programs in 35 countries.

Here is a wealth of good ideas for teaching about health and demonstrating health care practices, using simple materials and group participation. Some of these non-formal educational approaches can be effectively applied to disseminate information in other fields.

David Werner is the primary author of the widely-used and translated manual **Where There Is No Doctor** (see review). Bill Bower has contributed to the Spanish and English translations and revisions of **Where There Is No Doctor**, and has worked extensively in health worker training in Central America and Mexico. Both authors have visited many different training programs around the world.

Child-to-Child, book, 104 pages, by Audrey Aarons and Hugh Hawes, with Juliet Gayton, 1979, £2.50 from MacMillan Education, Houndmills, Basingstoke, RG 21 2XS, United Kingdom.

"We know a group of community workers who know every inch of the village in which they work, who are accepted by everyone, who want to help their community, who will work hard (for short periods of time) and cheerfully (all the time). Last month the health worker used them to collect information about which children had been vaccinated in the village. Next Tuesday some of them will help to remind the villagers that the baby clinic is coming and they will be at hand to play with the older children when mothers take their babies to see the nurse. Next month they plan to help the school teacher in a village clean-up campaign. These health workers are the boys and girls of the village. . .This book. . .calls on us to recognize what children already do towards helping each other and helping us. It suggests ways in which we can support them and in which we can make their contribution more effective, easier, and more fun."

This well-illustrated book was put together with ideas from around the world, from people who believe that development starts with local level action. It provides a selection of possible activities, such as organizing a survey, making a community health map, discovering common accident patterns and preventing them, treating children with diarrhea (including making a special salt and sugar spoon for the water mixture to treat diarrhea), caring for sick brothers and sisters, and finding out what younger children eat and whether it is nutritionally adequate.

Experience thus far suggests that this is an effective approach to health education. These examples of community-based learning and action (in which local resources, skills and problems are identified) are models of the kinds of steps essential for people's participation in any type of development effort.

Teaching Village Health Workers: A Guide to the Process, 2 books, 117 pages total plus several charts and visual aid cards, $3.00 to developing countries, $5.00 to developed countries, plus postage, from Voluntary Health Association of India, C-14, Community Centre, Safdarjung Development Area, New Delhi 110016, India.

Book I vividly illustrates how trainers of village health workers can approach communities in a sensitive manner. Diagrams, cartoons, and text give examples of how knowledge of the community helps village health workers deal with problems more effectively. "Don't be blinded to the social, political and economic forces which will play an important part in the shape and direction of the community health programme."

The first requirement is that the trainer be a "changed person." "Do you really feel that a little-educated, or illiterate woman or man knows more than you do about the village? Are you willing to learn from them and the other 'students' in your class of village health workers?" With this orientation, Book I offers guidelines for curriculum development, teaching methods, and simple communications media.

Book II (Lesson Plans and Curriculum Charts) describes how to teach a limited range of specific treatments and preventative measures to village health workers. Because the health workers in this program were mostly illiterate, the level of sophistication has been limited. Certainly literate health workers in many communities will be able to go far beyond this material, to use of more comprehensive manuals like **Where There Is No Doctor** or **Primary Child Care** (see reviews).

Low-Cost Rural Health Care and Health Manpower Training, MF 27-691, annotated bibliography, 164 pages, by Shahid Akhtar, 1975, free to libraries, researchers, institutions, etc. in less developed countries (others must pay Canadian $10.00), from the International Development Research Center, Box 8500, Ottawa, K1G 3H9 Canada. Volume One in a series. Also available are Volume Two (MF 27-692, 182 pages, by Frances Delaney, 1976, pub. no. IDRC-069e), and Volumes 3-15.

This is the most extensive of the annotated health bibliographies, with 700 entries. Publisher information is given where possible — no price information.

"This bibliography is an attempt to coordinate information of nontraditional health care delivery systems in remote regions of the world, especially in developing countries. The literature abstracted focuses primarily on new models of health care delivery, and on the training and utilization of auxiliary health workers. (Very little information is included on the economics of low-cost rural health care.) The bibliography is intended to be of use to: a) persons who are involved in planning, operating, and evaluating systems to provide rural health services; b) persons concerned with the training of auxiliary health workers to staff such systems; and c) organizations that are supporting research into the problems of organizing and staffing health care delivery systems."

The IDRC will attempt to supply a copy of any publication abstracted in the bibliography if it is impossible to find elsewhere.

Reference Material for Health Auxiliaries and Their Teachers, MF 27-709, annotated bibliography, 164 pages, 1982, publication #28, free from World Health Organization, 1211 Geneva 27, Switzerland.

This reference work is WHO's response to "the shortage of suitable reference material (textbooks, manuals, course guides, etc.) for health auxiliaries and their teachers and a nearly complete lack of such material in the local language spoken by these auxiliaries. In the delivery of health care the biggest need is for health auxiliaries working in rural and 'ultrarural' areas, i.e. medical assistants, auxiliary nurses, midwives, nurse-midwives and auxiliary sanitarians. Therefore REMEHA decided to concentrate its attention on reference material for these categories..."

"It was also agreed that by first giving priority to reference material suitable for the use of teachers — both groups, teachers and students, would be served. The main long-term objective however should be to promote production at national and local level of reference material for students — in other words to compose a kind of 'do-it-yourself kit' for teachers which should include a set of good examples of existing reference and source materials, a guide on the writing of manuals, and illustration material. This could enable them to undertake the local production of reference material for students which would meet the local requirements better and may be written in the local language."

540 references were selected from those gathered. The annotations are brief but concise. Publisher and price are given where possible.

Auxiliaries in Primary Health Care, MF 27-672, annotated bibliography, 126 pages, compiled by the Appropriate Health Resources and Technologies Action Group (AHRTAG), edited by Katherine Elliott, 1979, £4.95 from ITDG.

"Experience has shown that primary health services work most satisfactorily when they make use of local people, who remain part of the communities they serve but who have been given the right kind of technical and social training to enable them to respond effectively to local needs . . . New ways are being sought and found to train and to integrate increasing numbers of auxiliary health workers in systems which inevitably vary by country and by community according to the needs to be met and the human and material resources available for this purpose . . . This bibliography is intended to promote the greater exchange of know-how, of useful teaching materials and background information, and to encourage wider experimentation."

There are 357 entries (papers, articles and books), with 2-3 sentences describing each. Entries are indexed by subject and country. There is also a list of contacts by country, and an address list for journals and publishers to enable the reader to obtain the materials.

AHRTAG, an affiliate of ITDG, "acts as a clearinghouse for information about useful alternatives to high cost, high technology, hospital-based" medical care.

Medicine and Public Health in the People's Republic of China, MF 27-697, book, 333 pages, edited by Joseph Quinn for the Fogarty International Center, 1973, DHEW Publication No. (NIH) 73-63, single copies available free of charge, from FIC Publications Office, Building 38A, Room 609, Bethesda, Maryland 20205, USA.

Here is a collection of articles with information not found in the other books on China we've reviewed. The section "Chinese Medicine Throughout the Ages" includes articles on acupuncture, surgery, traditional medicine as a basis for medical practice and the role of the family in health care. The second section treats public health laws, health care in rural areas, and the training of medical workers and the Academy of Medical Sciences. The last group of articles describes the health problems that China is struggling to overcome today.

Health Care in China—An Introduction, MF 27-685, book, 140 pages, Christian Medical Commission, 1974, out of print in 1985.

The Christian Medical Commission gathered a group of medical and social scientists in Hong Kong (3 of whom then visited the People's Republic of China). This group was asked to try to answer the question "What in the Chinese experience of rebuilding a health care system might be of value to communities in other cultures and social systems?"

The resulting book was intended to "be of value to health workers both in the developing world and in the industrially developed countries where the failures in health care systems stand out so sharply against the technological and economic advancement."

The topics include: the relationship of health to national development goals, health care organization, epidemic disease control, population policies, traditional and Western medical practices, and humanpower for health care. At the end an interesting list of the contents of a barefoot doctor's bag is provided.

A good overview of the Chinese health care system by an impartial group.

A Barefoot Doctor's Manual, MF 27-674, book, 384 pages, translation of a 1970 Chinese manual by the United States Department of Health, Education and Welfare, Public Health Service, Cloudburst Press edition $14.95 from Madrona Pubs., Kampmann and Co., 9 East 40th Street, New York, New York 10016, USA.

This enormous paperback was translated by the U.S. Dept. of Health, Education and Welfare, from a manual originally published by the Institute of Traditional Chinese Medicine of Hunan Province, People's Republic of China, in September 1970. "It focuses on the improvement of medical and health care facilities in the rural villages. The purpose is to integrate the following areas: prevention and treatment; disease and symptoms, with stress on disease; traditional Chinese and Western medicine, with attention on traditional Chinese medicine; the native and the foreign, with focus on the native; and mass promotion and quality improvement, with mass production as the base, and quality treatment as the goal. By following these principles and adapting itself to actual conditions on the rural level, this manual aims to basically meet the working needs of the "barefoot doctors" serving the broad rural population.

The first six chapter headings are: Understanding the Human Body, Hygiene, Introduction to Diagnostic Techniques, Therapeutic Techniques (Chinese herbs, folk treatment, Western treatment), Birth Control, and Diagnosis and Treatment of Common Diseases. The seventh chapter is an extensive one (400 pages) on Chinese medicinal plants.

The successful integration of traditional with Western medicine serves as a useful model for many other societies.

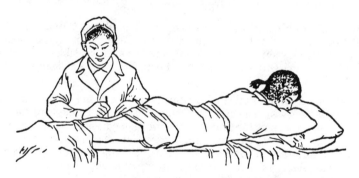

Acupuncture with the patient in the prone position

Health Care in the People's Republic of China: A Bibliography with Abstracts, MF 27-686, book, 182 pages, by Shahid Akhtar, 1975, publication IDRC-038e, free to local groups in developing countries, $15.00 to all others, from IDRC, Box 8500, Ottawa, Canada K1G 3H9.

"The material presented should prove useful to people concerned with providing health service and to those concerned with training auxiliary health workers. The literature concentrates on the now famous 'barefoot doctors' of China, and covers the period 1949-74."

Major topic areas include health care organization and planning (especially in the rural areas), functions and training of "barefoot doctors," and relationships between health care systems and other community organizations. This bibliography does not cover acupuncture and biomedical research.

There are 560 entries. Complete publisher information is listed for commercially available materials, but no addresses. IDRC will try to supply some of the limited circulation items to requesters from developing countries.

Better Child Care, MF 27-676, booklet, 52 pages, 1977, 50 cents plus postage to developing countries, $1.00 plus postage to developed countries, from Health Publications, Voluntary Health Association of India, C-14, Community Centre, Safdarjung Development Area, New Delhi 110016, India.

Good use of photos and a weatherproof plastic cover make this a model low-cost booklet on proper feeding and ensuring normal growth. Excellent color photos will be of great help in identifying anemia, which in 80% of cases is visually evident.

Nutrition for Developing Countries, MF 27-702, book, 300 pages, by Maurice King and others, 1972, £3.25 postpaid, special price to people in or going to developing countries from TALC; Spanish edition $10.00 from Editorial Pax Mexico, Libreria Carlos Cesarman, S.A., Avenida Cuauhtemoc 1434, Mexico 13 D.F., Mexico, 40% discount to charitable organizations for the Spanish edition.

"There are many reasons why children are malnourished. One of them is that people do not know enough about nutrition or how to feed children. This is why we have written this book. Some of the people who might read it have not been long in school, so we have tried to write it in easy English with as few new words as possible. We hope that it will be useful to everyone who can do anything to improve nutrition and especially to medical assistants, medical students, nurses, midwives, agricultural assistants, community development and homecraft workers and also to teachers in schools. All these people can teach other people. This, therefore, is mostly a book to teach what and how to teach."

Chapter headings include: Growth, When Growth Fails, Proteins, Energy Foods, Vitamins and Minerals, Non-Foods and Water, More About Food, The Need for Food and its Cost, Feeding the Family, Artificial Feeding, The Food-Path, Helping Families to Help Themselves, and Helping the Community to Help Itself. The appendix explains how this book can be used in class. There is also a vocabulary-index which explains the unusual terms.

The authors say that this is mostly a book for Malawi, Tanzania, Zambia, Botswana, Rhodesia, and Kenya. It certainly has much that would be of interest anywhere. Includes many drawings.

Nutrition Rehabilitation: Its Practical Application, MF 27-703, book, 130 pages, by Joan Koppert, 1977, out of print in 1985.

Nutrition information refers to care and dietary supervision for malnourished children and their mothers. It is an attractive alternative to hospital care for undernourishment. "In most developing countries around 1 percent of all children under the age of five years will be suffering from a severe degree of malnutrition at any one time, and in many countries the figure is far higher. In addition, there is a very much larger group of undernourished children. Admitting a tiny minority of the malnourished children to highly expensive hospital wards is almost irrelevant, particularly since studies have shown that a high proportion of such children die either in hospital or in the year subsequent to discharge. A more fundamental and realistic approach to the problem by promoting adequate growth — monitored by a weight chart held by every child — has been developed with the advent of the Under-Fives' Clinics. However, even in the few countries where such services are widely available, some children will develop a more severe malnutrition, and it is for these that nutrition rehabilitation centers are desperately needed."

This book is intended to be "an instruction manual with detailed information on the setting up of a center and its day-to-day running, a place where mothers would learn how to prepare balanced meals for their young, especially weaning children, on returning to their homes. Home economy, household budgeting, home gardening, food values, fathers' cooperation and ways and means of improving the family income have been included. Practical advice is given on the siting and construction of a center along with the financial implications...methods of adminstration and follow-up care are described."

Also included are helpful sections on community surveys and record-keeping. A useful, low-cost book summarizing a practical approach to an important problem in rural health care.

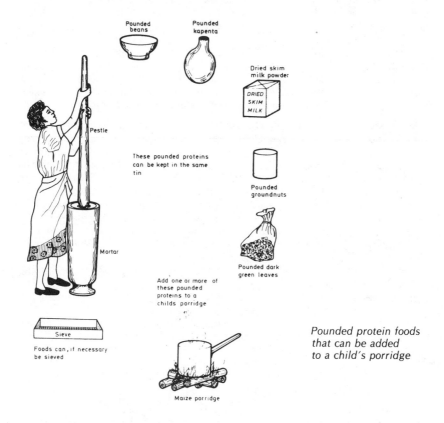

Pounded protein foods that can be added to a child's porridge

Health Care Publications from Teaching Aids at Low Cost, Institute of Child Health, 30 Guilford Street, London WC1N 1EH, England.

The following books and pamphlets are available from TALC. Ask for their latest publications list. (Most of the longer books we've reviewed separately.)

a) **Paediatric Out-Patient's Manual for Africa**, MF 27-704, booklet, 50 pages, by the staff of St. Luke's Hospital in Nigeria, 1975 (out of print in June 1978).

For use by senior staff nurses, student nurses and paramedical staff. Includes 5-year weight chart, immunization routine, intravenous fluids. Lists symptoms for common ailments and malaria, malnutrition, pneumonia, polio, anemia, cholera, urinary infections, tuberculosis, whooping cough, tetanus. Dosages of common drugs for newborn infants and young babies.

b) **Care of the Newborn Baby in Tanzania**, MF 27-677, booklet, 43 pages, by Dept. of Child Health at the University of Dar es Salaam, 1975 (out of print in June 1978).

"This manual was written for Tanzanian medical assistants, but nurses, rural medical aids, medical students and doctors should find it useful. It attempts to give an account of the most important aspects of care of newborn babies in this country."

Chapter headings: characteristics of the newborn baby, routine management and abnormalities during the newborn period, and the low birth-weight baby. Many illustrations.

c) **Memorandum on Tuberculosis Control in Developing Countries** (MF 27-699, out of print in 1985), and **Memorandum on Leprosy Control** (MF 27-698), 20 pages, £0.25.

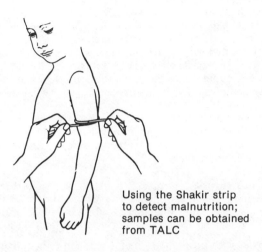

Using the Shakir strip to detect malnutrition; samples can be obtained from TALC

Mosquito Control—Some Perspectives for Developing Countries, MF 27-701, report, 63 pages, National Academy of Sciences, 1973, $8.00 in U.S., quote accession number PB 224-749 when ordering from NTIS; for overseas orders write Development Assistance Division, NTIS/Office of International Affairs, 5285 Port Royal Road, Room 306Y, Springfield, Virginia 22161, USA.

"Not a technical handbook, this report aims at arousing interest in some unusual but promising mosquito-control methods that might otherwise be ignored. It is written for administrators or program directors of agencies that fund mosquito-control research and application projects and for scientists working on neighboring topics."

The booklet deals exclusively with biological control of mosquitoes, though the need for simultaneous environmental control (e.g. drainage) is stressed. No pesticide approaches are discussed, in part because ". . . mosquito resistance to chemical pesticides has caused the failure of many vector-control campaigns."

Particularly successful seems to be the minnow Gambusia Affinis, which can destroy large numbers of mosquitoes by feeding on the larvae. This approach is "particularly appropriate for controlling mosquitoes in rice paddies and small water impoundments."

Handbook on the Prevention and Treatment of Schistosomiasis, MF 27-682, book, 1977, translation of a Chinese publication, DHEW Publication No. (NIH) 77-1290, single copies free of charge from the FIC Publications Office, Building 38A, Room 609, National Institutes of Health, Bethesda, Maryland 20205, USA.

This is an English translation of a Chinese handbook, originally published by the Shanghai Municipal Institute for Prevention and Treatment of Schistosomiasis (also known as bilharzia). China is perhaps the only developing country that appears to have been highly successful in controlling schistosomiasis. This book offers some valuable insights into how this can be accomplished.

There are five stages in the life cycle of the schistosome: 1) adult schistosomes, in humans and animals, produce eggs which 2) hatch in water, 3) enter snails and change form, 4) leave the snails, 5) re-enter humans and animals, and develop to adult size. If any of these stages can be eliminated, schistosomiasis can be stopped. Most control efforts concentrate on the destruction of the snails.

The snails in irrigation canals and rivers "are mostly distributed in a line on the water level...Snail elimination can be coordinated with dredging of riverbed soil as fertilizer...Build a dam and drain the water to lower the water level or utilize the dry season to expose the noninfested area of the base of the bank. Dig a ditch...The noninfested soil is piled on the side of the ditch near the center of the riverbed...Pare the soil 3 inches deep. First pare the heavily infested soil near the water level, and dump it into the ditch. Clean up the loose soil, and cover the whole ditch with noninfested soil...A five-inch layer of soil is used which is then pounded and hardened."

Other chapters in this handbook discuss frequently-used chemicals for killing snails (some of them very environmentally hazardous), personal protection, diagnostic procedures, treatment of patients, safe treatment of manure, and schistosomiasis in farm animals.

Better Care in Leprosy, MF 27-675, booklet, 64 pages, 1978, 50 cents plus postage to developing countries, $1.00 plus postage to developed countries, add $1.00 for airmail postage, from Voluntary Health Association of India, C-14, Community Centre, Safdarjung Development Area, New Delhi 110016, India.

A simple booklet with good photos and discussion to help distinguish leprosy from other skin problems that are similar in appearance.

Philippine Medicinal Plants in Common Use: Their Phytochemistry & Pharmacology, MF 27-706, book, by Michael L. Tan, 1978, revised 1980, $2.50 for overseas orders, from Alay Kapwa Kilusang Pangkalusugan (AKAP), 66 J.P. Rizal, Project 4, Quezon City, Philippines.

Covering the major medicinal plants of the Philippines, this book discusses their cultivation, harvest, storage and medicinal uses. The chemical composition of each plant is provided. Plants are indexed according to Latin names (family, genus, species).

"The present thrust of research into medicinal plants is geared towards the screening of plants for cardiovascular, anti-cancer and anti-fertility drugs. While this type of research has its value, it seems inappropriate in countries where available forms of treatment for widespread diseases such as tuberculosis, malaria, and schistosomiasis continue to be beyond the reach of the majority of the victims. In the Philippines, the situation is even more disturbing, with recent studies reveal-

Coconut water can be used intravenously for rehydration, but sterile methods should be used. As long as the shell is intact, the water inside is sterile. It is best to transfer the water to another container to filter out some of the sediments that may be in the water. Cut the ends of the nut 1 to 1½ inch into the soft meaty substance. Swab the cut surface with alcohol and allow it to evaporate. Insert a sterile hollow tube into the nut's cavity, and pass the water through a sterile glass funnel packed with sterile gauze, into a sterilized bottle. Use as soon as possible. (noted by Tan, from an article by H.S. Goldsmith, 1962.)

ing that 95% of the materials used to produce 'local' drugs are, in fact, imported."

There are sketches of many of the plants and the text is easy to read. Many of these plants are found or could be grown in other tropical, sub-tropical and mild temperate zones. The book also has a section on weights and measures, a guide to preparation of medicines using the plants mentioned, and a list of sources for further information.

Highly recommended.

Medicinal Plants, booklet, 39 pages, by I. & J. Lecup, available from Lecup, P.O. Box 3666, Kathmandu, Nepal, or UNICEF, P.O. Box 1187, Kathmandu, Nepal.

In northern Nepal, medicinal plants are collected by animal herders and sold in the towns. "They collect in one place everything they can with no regard to the reproduction of the plants for the following years. This uncontrolled gathering is followed by methods of drying unsuited to all kinds of plants. Such methods include direct sunrays, or over-fire hanging. Dried in this way, the medicinal herbs lose the major part of the medicinal value for which they are gathered. After prolonged storage in damp conditions, and following a long commercial circuit to the final destination, plants arrive in very poor quality, in insufficient and irregular quantity."

This booklet describes the growth stages of 6 different categories of plants, and how and when to harvest them to allow for future regrowth. Advice on drying and storage for better quality is also provided. The specific plants mentioned are all local Himalayan species, but the harvesting recommendations based on root and tuber growth etc. can be applied to other plants as well.

Schema 3: Collection of "Satavari type"

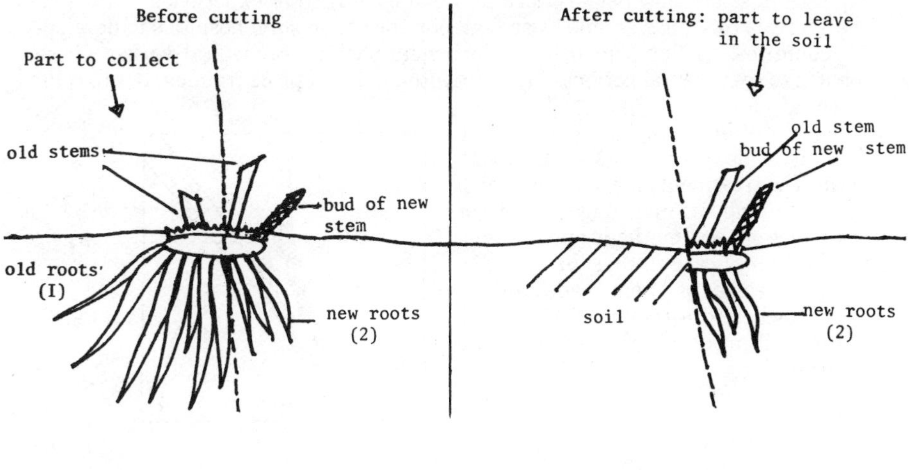

Where There Is No Dentist, MF 27-719, book, 188 pages, by Murray Dickson, 1983, $5.00 from the Hesperian Foundation, P.O. Box 1692, Palo Alto, California 94302, USA.

This book fills a gap in the literature on dental care, between materials that are too simple and those that are too complicated for use by village health workers. As was the case with **Where There Is No Doctor**, the author begins from the fact that most people in developing countries have no access to dentists, and the dental treatment they receive, if any, is provided by people with few skills. This volume attempts to remedy the situation, emphasizing preventative dental education, especially among children, and providing the details necessary to carry out simple curative work when needed.

Simple Dental Care for Rural Hospitals, MF 27-712, 26 pages, by D. Halestrap, £0.50 from Teaching Aids at Low Cost (TALC), Institute of Child Health, 30 Guilford Street, London WC1N 1EH, England.

This booklet came out of the author's experiences with dental workers in rural Africa. Extraction, sometimes without local anesthesia, was usually the only treatment provided in cases of severe toothache or advanced gum disease. "Consequently, it was considered that the dental workers in many of these hospitals would benefit from some further instruction in simple dental work, so the author arranged to provide this by re-visiting some eighteen of them. Any necessary instruments were supplied where needed and an experimental edition of this booklet was used during the work in order to provide a background to, and reminder of, what was being taught. It has now been revised in the light of further experience... Its aim, therefore, is to offer a simple basic textbook for use in rural hospitals in developing countries, it being primarily for the benefit of the para-medical worker whose job it is to treat dental patients." It is not intended to replace training, but to reinforce it.

There are simple explanations of tooth decay, gum disease, and how to keep teeth clean. The treatment shown is removal of tartar, locating and giving injections prior to extraction, and methods of extracting teeth. Complications are briefly discussed. Sketches of a homemade headrest that attaches to a regular chair are included. Simple English text, well illustrated.

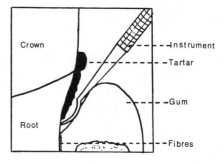

The Tooth Trip, MF 27-713, book, 232 pages, by Thomas McGuire (D.D.S.), 1972, $6.95 from Random House Inc., 400 Hahn Road, Westminster, Maryland 21157, USA.

Delightful and well-illustrated, this very readable book "tells how you can completely prevent cavities and gum disease through self-examinations and home care." It explains tooth decay and gum and mouth diseases, and provides enough information for the reader to determine the likely nature of any mouth problem he or she may have. The author explains the procedures and associated equipment so that the patient can understand what's happening and participate in decision-making about what treatment he or she will get for a particular dental problem.

Highly recommended for Americans. The illustrated simple explanations of preventive dental care will be of interest to health and dental programs in developing countries.

Simple Orthopaedic Aids, book, 45 pages, by Chris Dartnell, 1983, £4.50 postpaid from The Leonard Cheshire Foundation International, 26-29 Maunsel Street, London SW1 2QN, United Kingdom.

Handicapped people often need special orthopedic devices for rehabilitation and to help them walk and move around. This book provides designs for leg braces and other devices that can be made in a small workshop. In Khartoum, this ap-

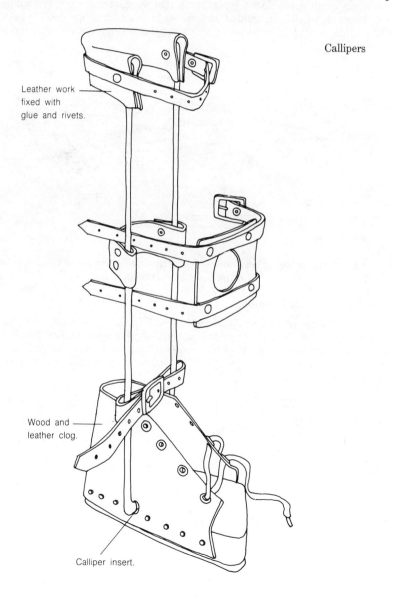

Callipers

Leather work fixed with glue and rivets.

Wood and leather clog.

Calliper insert.

proach meant great cost savings and rapid supply to the patients. The tools needed are handtools plus an electric hand drill and, for some designs, a welding machine. The materials are commonly available: 6 and 8 mm steel rod, flat steel and angle iron, leather and wood.

Low Cost Physiotherapy Aids, MF 27-718, booklet, 45 pages, by Don Caston, 1982, £1.00 from Appropriate Health Resources and Technologies Action Group (AHRTAG), 85 Marylebone High Street, London W1M 3DE, United Kingdom.

Physiotherapy involves rehabilitation of injuries through exercise and stretching. Needed are devices that can be pulled, pushed, lifted and twisted by the patient. These devices can be quite expensive to buy.

Here are self-explanatory drawings of a variety of simple aids that can be made of common locally available materials: bamboo or wood, string, cloth, and old bicycle inner tubes. A small workshop at a clinic could make these devices for patients, or they could be made by relatives by looking at the drawings. Few tools are needed.

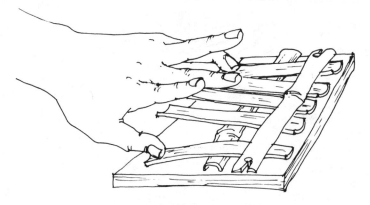

Rattan & Bamboo: Equipment for Physically Handicapped Children, MF 27-708, booklet with 13 large sheets of drawings, by J.K. Hutt, 1979, £2.00 postpaid from Disabilities Study Unit, Wildhanger, Amberley, Arundel, West Sussex BN18 9NR, United Kingdom.

Detailed designs of a variety of chairs and walking supports made of rattan and bamboo. The ready availability of the materials, good strength and durability in the tropics, and ease of repair make these designs attractive. All drawings use English measurements. There is no text to explain the particular use of each piece of equipment.

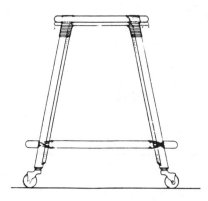

Bamboo walker

How to Make Basic Hospital Equipment, MF 27-690, book, 86 pages, compiled by Roger England, 1979, £4.50 from ITDG.

This booklet contains construction drawings for 22 different pieces of hospital equipment that can be produced in a small workshop. All dimensions and assembly instructions are given.

The larger equipment includes an invalid carriage with chain drive, an instrument trolley, a hospital wheelchair (not self-operated), a rough terrain wheelchair, a bicycle ambulance (essentially a wheelchair with a bicycle-pulled towbar), a blood transfusion drip stand and a patient's trolley. In addition, there are such things as folding beds, a bamboo walking frame, and other furniture. Of particular interest are a neo-natal suction pump, a premature baby incubator that uses standard electric light bulbs for heat, calipers, an exercising machine, a low pressure air bed, and thermoplastic aids made of plastic drainpipe.

All of the designs were developed in hospital workshops and the Zaria Intermediate Technology Workshop (Nigeria). The drawings have been reproduced with the hope that they will "provide ideas and stimulation to those interested in intermediate techniques."

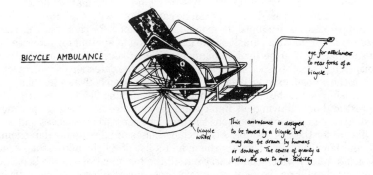

BICYCLE AMBULANCE

A Medical Laboratory for Developing Countries, MF 27-695, book, 330 pages, by Maurice King, 1973, $22.50 from Oxford University Press, 16-00 Pollitt Drive, Fair Lawn, New Jersey 07140, USA; Spanish edition $17.50 from Editorial Pax Mexico, Libreria Carlos Cesarman, S.A., Avenida Cuauhtemoc 1434, Mexico 13 D.F., Mexico, 40% discount on Spanish edition to charitable organizations.

"This book aims to bring the minimum level of laboratory services within the range of everyone in developing countries and is written especially for laboratory and medical assistants who work in health centres and district hospitals. Each piece of equipment needed in a medical laboratory is fully described and illustrated. (These drawings are not intended to be used for local production of the equipment.) Every step in the examination of specimens is simply explained and the method of performing it is illustrated; the methods chosen are those that give the greatest diagnostic value at the minimum cost. Ways of obtaining specimens are given, and where it might prove helpful some anatomy, physiology and a brief account of treatment is included. The last chapter contains a detailed equipment list (total cost about $500 in 1973)."

Users should have some basic laboratory science training, and a good knowledge of English. King attempts to present the material in "easy English," but this does not mean that beginning English speakers will be able to use this manual. Good drawings help to overcome some language problems.

King covers the following major topics: basic relevant chemistry, sterile technique, descriptions of equipment and chemicals, records and specimens, weighing and measuring, the microscope, blood, urine, cerebrospinal fluid, stools, blood transfusion, and other specimens. There are more than 100 clear color plates of commonly seen slide specimens (in the hardback edition).

This manual is focused on what are certainly "intermediate" technology and techniques for medical laboratories. Medical technology in the rich countries is rapidly becoming so capital-intensive that progressively fewer people can afford good quality care. Medical personnel are at the same time becoming increasingly dependent on expensive machines and tests to carry out their duties. Compared to this, King's book is a down-to-earth catalogue of relatively inexpensive equipment for basic laboratory tests. However, virtually all of the equipment King mentions would have to be imported (at a cost which in 1973 amounted to $500 per health center).

Manual of Basic Techniques for a Health Laboratory, MF 27-693, large paperback book, 487 pages, 1980, Swiss Francs 30.00 or $15.00, from World Health Organization, 1211 Geneva 27, Switzerland.

"(This) manual is intended for use mainly in medical laboratories in developing countries. It is designed particularly for use in. . . small or medium-sized laboratories attached to regional hospitals and in dispensaries and rural health centres where the laboratory technician often has to work alone. . .The manual describes only direct examination procedures that can be carried out with a microscope or other simple apparatus. For example: the examination of stools for parasites; the examination of blood for malaria parasites; the examination of sputum for tubercle bacilli; the examination of urine for bile pigments; the leukocyte type number fraction; the dispatch of stools to specialized laboratories for the detection of cholera vibrios."

This is the second, expanded edition of a book prepared both as a teaching manual and as a reference for health center laboratory technicians. Techniques are explained with text and line drawings in step-by-step fashion, from collecting specimens to recording results. Many photographs and drawings show what parasites and bacteria look like under the microscope. Also included: lists of all reagents (lab chemicals) used, and how to make or obtain them; and a list of all the apparatus needed to equip a laboratory which could carry out all the examinations in the book. An introductory chapter on "general laboratory procedures" gives detailed instructions on using and cleaning a microscope; sterilizing water and glassware; storage and preparation of materials and specimens; and simple plumbing and electrical repairs in a laboratory.

Medical Laboratory Manual for Tropical Countries, book, by Monica Cheesbrough, Volume I, 1981, £6.20 postpaid to developing countries, £9.15 postpaid to other countries; Volume II, 1984, £6.40 to developing countries, £9.95 to other countries; from Tropical Health Technology, 14 Bevills Close, Doddington, Cambridgeshire, England PE15 0TT.

Cheesbrough discusses laboratory techniques for regional hospitals and essential tests for community health centers. She includes sections on lab organization, anatomy and physiology, diagnosis of parasitic infections (with wall charts of important parasites), and clinical chemistry.

A Model Health Centre, MF 27-700, book, 167 pages, Conference of Missionary Societies in Great Britain and Ireland, 1975, £4.50 or US$10.00 surface mail from Publications Dept., British Council of Churches, 2 Eaton Gate, London SW1W 9BL, United Kingdom.

". . . A design primer and reference book for those engaged in planning, developing, and operating health services whether at a national or local level."

This manual offers some practical ideas on the architectural layout of a model health center, building dimensions, and cost of materials, with many detailed sketches and diagrams. It also discusses clinic schedules, record-keeping, number and type of staff, operational policies, programs in immunization, nutrition and maternal-child health, under-fives clinics, oral hygiene, school visits, latrine construction, and community involvement and support.

"Not only are the staff to go out into the community, but also the community is to have facilities within the centre; these facilities being the main new idea generated by this study." The need for medical auxiliaries is also identified, recognizing that they can do an "immensely valuable job extremely well" in promoting community-based preventive medicine. The center ideally would have a staff of eight: two nurses, midwives, or medical assistants working with 4 auxiliaries (with 1-2 years in-service training) and 2 local assistants. The center is expected to be able to refer patients to doctors in a district hospital when necessary, and to receive visits from doctors on a regular basis. The bibliography includes books recommended for the health center library.

Design for Medical Buildings, book, 146 pages, by Philip Mein and Thomas Jorgenson, 1975, reprinted 1980, $6.00 plus $2.50 surface mail plus $2.00 foreign bank charges, from The Director, Housing Research and Development Unit, University of Nairobi, P.O. Box 30197, Nairobi, Kenya.

"The manual contains design, construction and cost guidelines for the building of medical facilities with limited resources. It has been prepared primarily for the doctor and his staff who, in rural Africa, must often be their own architects. It should however also be of value to the architect who, perhaps for the first time, is confronted with the special problems associated with the provision of medical buildings in rural areas.

"Medical buildings at present tend to be excessively expensive, consuming funds which are sorely needed in other areas such as the primary health sector. The

FIGURE 16
x-ray unit

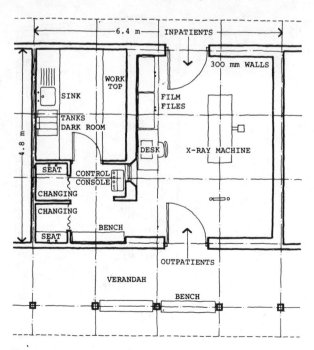

darkroom   The darkroom should be large enough to accommodate the developing, and fixing tanks and a large sink and work top area.

guiding principle of this book is that the expenditure of material, monetary and manpower resources (on buildings) should be reduced to the lowest level consistent with adequate and acceptable medical care."

The book covers everything from initial feasibility studies to supervision of the construction work. "Each building problem requires its own solution according to local needs." Design examples are given, but the emphasisis on "providing the tools and methodology for design in the form of standards and guidelines."

"The best guide to an appropriate type of construction is to study other buildings in the area, for example, their shape, whether they have flat or pitched roofs, and the materials from which they are made. It is generally true that the further one deviates from the local architecture, the more money and time will be used in building."

How to Look After a Refrigerator, MF 27-717, book, 58 pages, by Jonathan Elford, 1980, AHRTAG, £2.00 from ITDG.

"Vaccines need to stay cool all the time. If they are allowed to get hot they become useless. Refrigerators keep vaccines cold and safe. Therefore, they play a very important role in protecting children against infectious diseases. But refrigerators break down easily, so they must be carefully looked after to keep them working properly."

This volume includes information on simple maintenance and operation of kerosene absorption refrigerators (cleaning burners, trimming and adjusting the wick, cleaning the flue, etc.), and the regulation of gas and electric refrigerators. The author also discusses where to place different vaccines within the refrigerator, and how to pack cold boxes and vaccine carriers to protect vaccines as they are transported. An emergency action chart indicates how to identify and correct the problem if the refrigerator is too warm.

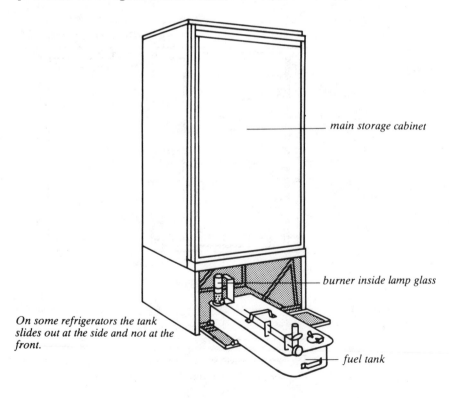

main storage cabinet

burner inside lamp glass

On some refrigerators the tank slides out at the side and not at the front.

fuel tank

Health Records Systems, MF 27-687, booklet, 20 pages, by C. Frost and G. Ellmers, VITA, out of print in 1985.

"The development of this manual grew out of a need for an easy and concise health record system that required little or no experience with filing methods. . . Because there are so many variables present in each medical application, this manual is not designed as a definitive answer to problems. Instead, it is hoped that the suggested methods can be adopted or modified to meet any situation."

The booklet stresses the need for simplicity and uniformity in a health records system — for easy implementation and local use by workers with minimal training. Several record systems are explained, and sample charts and cards are included for each one.

Salubritas: Information Exchange in Primary Health Care, MF 27-710, newsletter, 8 pages average length, published quarterly, $10.00/year from American Public Health Association, International Health Programs, 1015 Fifteenth Street N.W., Washington D.C. 20005, USA.

Combines short articles on participatory health and sanitation programs with good short reviews of related books. Also includes a "Readers' Exchange" where subscribers report on needs, successes, and failures of their projects. "Readers are encouraged to share their experiences with their colleagues by submitting articles, photographs and items regarding planning, implementing and evaluating health services in the developing world."

Contact, MF 27-679, journal, 6 times each year, about 15-20 pages in length, usually one article in each issue and some news notes, available in English, French and Spanish, free to readers in developing countries, $7.50/year to others, from Christian Medical Commission, World Council of Churches, 150 Route de Ferney, 1211 Geneva 20, Switzerland.

"The papers seek to report current innovative and courageous approaches to the promotion of health care. Individual copies are devoted to case studies of comprehensive health care projects, discussions on the churches' role in healing, and address many of the practical concerns and needs of health workers around the world."
Past issues have covered topics such as: community health care in rural Java, family planning to benefit whom?, primary health care and the village health worker, a need for change in medical education, health care and justice, and self-reliance and nutrition. Highly recommended.

Medical Self-Care: Access to Medical Tools, MF 27-696, quarterly magazine, average length 60-70 pages, 1-year subscription $15.00 in U.S., $17.00 Canada, $20.00 in other countries, from Medical Self-Care, P.O. Box 717, Inverness, California 94937, USA.

This journal was started by an American medical student as a thesis project. "Up until recently I was planning to go through a traditional internship and residency and become a family practitioner. But during my first year on the hospital wards, I realized that over half of my patients were suffering from a partially or totally preventable disease. . .somehow there was a whole area of health maintenance and preventive medicine that neither the doctor nor the patient was taking responsibility for. I got to feeling like a mechanic working on cars wrecked by people who had never learned to drive. What was needed was not more mechanics, but a little driver's education."
The magazine includes articles teaching basic paramedical skills and how to use medical texts, libraries, and bookstores as well as accounts of the growing self-

care/health consumerism movement in the U.S., and the ways American lifestyles affect health. Several pages in each issue are devoted to reviews of "popular" medical books.

Appropriate Technology for Health, MF 27-671, directory, 199 pages, WHO, August 1980, free from the ATH Programme, World Health Organization, 1211 Geneva 27, Switzerland.

A compilation of responses to a questionnaire, listing 382 organizations in 75 countries. The name and address of each organization are followed by a simple list of activities. No details on scale or scope of projects are provided. 183 listings from developing countries, 199 from industrialized countries.

ADDITIONAL REFERENCES ON HEALTH CARE

An Agromedical Approach to Pesticide Management; see AGRICULTURE.

Science Teaching

Science Teaching

It is a commonplace observation that people with little formal schooling are often quite adept at finding practical "hands-on" solutions to the problems of everyday life. In the rich countries, the educated live and consume in an artificial environment of technologies too complex to be understood, much less controlled, by individuals. For most, experience with natural phenomena and basic technical systems is very limited. Thus it is not at all surprising that relatively unschooled villagers in developing countries often demonstrate technical inventiveness and environmental understanding which astonish rich visitors. Farmers, for example, make complex decisions about which crops to plant and when, based on their knowledge of the soil and ecological interactions.

Most village-level technical innovation comes from trial and error and observation, often over many seasons. Village technology evolves as a result. But unsupported by systematic knowledge of natural science, the rate of village technology development is much slower than it could be.

Unfortunately, the science taught in Third World schools does not contribute to useful innovations in village technologies. Science studies should equip young people with an understanding of how to apply the basic principles of physics and biology to address a common problem (whether it be poor grain storage or a broken pump). Related skills — how to systematically control and vary a set of experimental trials, and how to carefully observe and record the results — are equally important. But educational methods and curricula that are based on repetition and memorization, or inherited from a colonial past, usually mean that science teaching in the Third World concentrates on phenomena that are beyond students' everyday experience, with little or no practical value.

Science education (and education in general) is, in fact, too often simply part of a sorting process through which a fortunate few may escape the rural areas and qualify for an urban job in government. Science teachers, themselves the products of such a system, do not expect the community to demand that they teach a practical curriculum relevant to local conditions. These teachers are, in any case, ill-equipped to do so; in most cases science is simply one of a number of subjects the teacher is covering each day.

As the science material taught is abstract and has little to do with local conditions, so it is natural that science teaching equipment for demonstrations is composed of what is by local standards expensive and exotic apparatus. The lucky teacher who succeeds in obtaining such apparatus from the education ministry is faced with two alternatives: to use it to demonstrate what are likely to be seen as peculiar and rather magical events, more a property of the equipment than the real world, or to lock it away in a closet to prevent damage to something so valuable. In either case it is rarely (if ever) used by the students themselves, who never get a chance to get excited about science and carry out their own simple experiments.

As the books in this chapter indicate, science teaching can be something quite different. **Towards Scientific Literacy** *makes the argument that if the aim of literacy is to enable men and women to better understand the world around them, then relevant science education should be considered a part of literacy, and should be included in non-formal education programs.* **The Production of School Science Equipment** *and related publications from the Commonwealth Secretariat review the problems and opportunities associated with the local production of science equipment. These educators from around the world recommend the use of objects, devices and tools from the community to illustrate scientific concepts whenever possible. Students are then more likely to see scientific principles at work in phenomena they encounter in their daily lives. Suitable curriculum development and teacher training will have to go with such equipment. The three-volume set* **Guidebook to Constructing Inexpensive Science Teaching Equipment** *presents construction details for a wide variety of easily-made yet sophisticated equipment that can be used to illustrate even some rather difficult scientific principles.* **A Method for Cutting Bottles, Light Bulbs, and Fluorescent Tubes** *provides instructions for making glassware for science class use.* **Adventures with a Hand Lens** *takes the science class outside, equipped with a magnifying glass, to study the natural world.* **Anti-Pollution Lab** *contains projects for students to measure the level and kind of pollutants in their community.* **The New UNESCO Sourcebook for Science Teaching,** *available in low-cost editions and in a large number of different languages, remains probably the best-known general science teaching reference volume.*

Many of the books reviewed in other chapters could be profitably used in practical science and technical classes. There are several that deserve a special note. **Minka,** *a Spanish-language magazine from the Peruvian highlands produced in a popular format, is dedicated to fostering scientific understanding and capabilities among the campesinos, building on a foundation of traditional wisdom. This magazine includes a special project for children in each issue.* **The Industrial Archaeology of Watermills and Waterpower** *examines the design evolution of waterwheels and turbines, and then presents small projects for schoolchildren, to allow them to confirm for themselves the operating principles involved.*

After decades of neglect, it may be that one of the best ways to improve village technology is through the strengthening of the scientific problem-solving capabilities of millions of rural farmers and craftspeople. Throughout the history of the United States, it has been the farmer-inventor who has most consistently contributed successful innovations in rural technology. Although circumstances in the Third World differ in some important ways, there are good reasons to believe that a similar high rate of technological improvement could be achieved, given the proper relevant science education support.

Towards Scientific Literacy, MF 28-724, book, 96 pages, by Frederick Thomas and Allan Kondo, 1978, $2.50 for postage and handling from Director, International Institute for Adult Literacy Methods, P.O. Box 1555, Tehran, Iran.

Towards Scientific Literacy "suggests a core curriculum of scientific ideas that should become part of the common human heritage...science can no longer be ignored if the aim of literacy is to enable men and women to understand better the world around them."

"Adults are *not* ignorant in science. They are already raising crops, raising children and managing their lives... Adult education should be designed to use and develop what adults already know. The purpose of teaching science is to enable learners to improve their ability to communicate in science with experts, with peers and with their apprentices."

"Everywhere in the world there are people who look carefully at the things around them and try to understand what they see. Any person who does this is a scientist, even if he or she never studied science from a book."

"People everywhere can do experiments. Anyone who has an idea on how to improve something should do an experiment to test the idea. Perhaps a tailor has an idea for a way to sew stronger seams. If he does, he should try the new way and compare it with the old way to see which is really stronger. If a woman has an idea for a better way to store her family's food without spoiling...she can do an experiment to see if the new idea is really better. She could store some food in the new way and some in the old way, and see for herself which stays fresher longer."

"By doing simple experiments, a farmer can learn for himself what methods are best. He can test different kinds of seed, and he can try different farming methods...All he needs is an idea about how he might improve his crops and a small plot of land on which to test the idea."

"Some people seem to believe that only new ideas are good. A scientist does not care whether an idea is old or new. He wants to see for himself which is better."

The authors discuss a variety of science subjects, using key concepts and key words, and proposing a set of activities for teaching science in non-formal educational settings (which could also be used in a regular classroom). Subjects include soil erosion, plant nutrition, a variety of health topics, energy sources, the internal combustion engine, and electricity. The content of many of these chapters is itself rather conventional, and not directly linked to appropriate technologies. (For example, when discussing herbicides and pesticides, no attention is given to the negative side effects of these and how the farmer might discover such side effects.)

"The learning experience should be related as closely as possible to the learner's life experience." A project method is presented, in which literacy workers help farmers to identify their problems, collect local data, seek out ideas from other sources, devise a procedure for testing of possible solutions, test them, and report the results to others.

Two case studies reveal some of the potential problems and solutions in training teachers. These case studies also "show that the facts of science and procedures based upon science can be taught successfully and usefully to unschooled adults, even though they are illiterate or semi-literate."

This kind of approach could be a very important element in appropriate technology strategy, by increasing the scientific skills of the poor, and thus strengthening their capacity to find their own technological solutions.

This book is intended for use by people preparing literacy materials or training literacy staff—not for direct use by adult learners or most field workers.

Highly recommended.

The New UNESCO Source Book for Science Teaching, MF 28-728, book, 254 pages, 1973, $13.75 from UNESCO (United Nations Educational, Scientific and Cultural Organization), 7 Place de Fontenoy, 75700 Paris, France; or UNESCO book distributors; or UNIPUB; or low-cost Asian edition available for $4.35 or 900 yen plus postage (only to countries in Asia) from Charles E. Tuttle Co., 2-6, Suido 1-chome, Bunkyo-ku, Tokyo, Japan 112.

This thorough book is intended for science teachers, for whom we recommend it highly. It will also be of considerable interest to others, because it describes how to make a whole range of simple equipment. There are hundreds of illustrations.

The principles of soldering are explained: you are told how to make solder and then how to use it in soldering. The composition by weight of the metals mixed to form bronze and casting brass is given, along with that of several low melting alloys.

Complete information is given on how to make the following things: simple weighing devices, a slide projector, a bunsen burner (which can illustrate the same principles to be considered when making a simple burner for biogas), several kinds of glues (including waterproof aquarium cement), soap, a dry cell battery, a simple thermometer, a model hydraulic ram, a model water wheel, and simple weather instruments such as a windspeed indicator.

Descriptions are given for the following processes: a method for depositing a bright silver mirror surface on glass; simple demonstrations of the comparative strengths of mud, clay, and sand bricks; the principles of heat transfer (important in the design of solar water heaters and insulated fireless cookers); and how to cut glass.

Another attractive feature of this book is that it suggests ways of avoiding the mold and rust on instruments associated with tropical conditions, particularly during the rainy season.

The authors' approach is to provide simple experiments or demonstrations to illustrate each scientific principle. As a science reference it is both thorough and broad in scope—covering chemistry, heat, magnetism and electricity (including circuits and fuses), wave motion, mechanics, fluids, biological sciences, rocks and minerals, astronomy and space science, and weather.

The book is intended as a guide for science teachers "for making simple equipment and for carrying out experiments using locally available materials." While it is successful in this for the most part, one possible limitation is that it does make greater use of gadgets normally found only in science labs: stands, beakers (you can make your own graduated cylinders if you have one already), two-holed rubber plugs, test tubes, and lenses. It has been translated into 30 languages (contact UNESCO at address given above for further information about this).

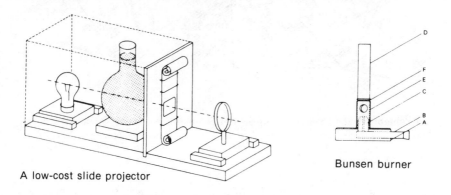

A low-cost slide projector

Bunsen burner

The Production of School Science Equipment: A Review of Developments, MF 28-727, book, 68 pages, by Keith Warren and Norman Lowe, 1975, Commonwealth Secretariat, out of print in 1985.

This is a review of the kinds of science teaching equipment that can be made domestically at lower cost than that imported from industrialized countries. Much of the book covers the work of organizations around the world and considerations for the development of appropriate science equipment.

The authors note that much beautifully designed imported equipment has suffered "because the price was totally out of reach of most schools in a developing country" and/or "it is not usable in the situation into which it has been put." Because of over-emphasis on such equipment, "the majority of the children are starved of relevant practical scientific experience."

"It is possible to avoid special manufacture if there is an object already available within the country which can illustrate a concept, or replace a chemistry beaker, and so on. Indeed, it may be an educational advantage to use an object which the children recognize rather than a foreign-looking object remote from their experience."

If local production is undertaken, there is a need for close collaboration between curriculum designers and apparatus designers. Also, it must be noted that if teachers are to be required to build their own apparatus, this represents a considerable time drain.

The book includes a review of activities in this field in the developing countries, along with 60 photographs of science teaching materials and kits.

Highly recommended.

Development and Production of School Science Equipment: Some Alternative Approaches, MF 28-725, booklet, 57 pages, by E. Apea and N. Lowe, 1979, £1.00 from Commonwealth Secretariat Publications, Marlborough House, London SW1Y 5HX, England.

This report offers a look at national curriculum and equipment development centers in India, Kenya and Turkey, and a regional center in Malaysia. The goals and organizational structure of each are described.

The most interesting of these, from the point of view of practical science education at the primary level, is the Kenya Primary Science Programme, in which a Science Equipment Production Unit has been formed. "The Programme has three basic aims: namely to encourage and assist children to: a) develop the manual and intellectual skills that are necessary to solve problems in a scientific way; b) preserve and acquire the attitudes that are necessary to apply those skills effectively; and c) acquire a deep understanding of the natural phenomena that take place in their environment. . . Activities in the classroom are made to relate directly to the pupils' environment. This is accomplished by helping children first to acquire problem-solving skills and then to apply the skills in solving problems based on their immediate environment."

"The use of locally available materials is important, not only in the name of economy and feasibility, but to help to prevent young children becoming alienated from their home community and background."

For the upper primary grades, "the topics for investigation will be concerned with applied science and technology, with the expectation that pupils will identify and solve problems of real and practical significance in areas such as agriculture, health and village technology."

The centers in India, Turkey, and Malaysia are primarily concerned with local production of science equipment for conventional science programs.

Low Cost Science Teaching Equipment, Report of a Commonwealth Regional Seminar/Workshop, Nassau, Bahamas, November 1976, MF 28-726, 98 pages, 1977, £1.00 from Commonwealth Secretariat Publications, Marlborough House, London SW1Y 5HX, England.

This report reviews the problems and progress being made in the development and production of low-cost science teaching equipment in the Caribbean, and includes recommendations for action by the governments of these nations.

"In the Caribbean, the traditional approach to science teaching — over-emphasis of teacher demonstration and learning by rote — is generally giving way to a new approach which involves inquiry, discovery, and the encouragement of pupil participation... Unfortunately, however, basic equipment needed for this approach to science learning is sparse, or, as in most cases, non-existent. Most primary school teachers have had little or no special training in teaching science at this level. As a result... teachers lack the confidence, knowledge and the skills that are necessary for effective science teaching, and are unable to identify potential sources in their environment that might be used in the classroom for teaching the subject." Teacher training is thus an important aspect of any strategy to develop low-cost science teaching equipment.

Experienced teachers are crucial to successful development of relevant equipment. In Kenya, "teachers formed the core of the committee that decided the original objectives; the consultant (a teacher) was a member of that committee... The field trials, the development of the accompanying teacher training programme, the evaluation, and all aspects of production required the involvement of teachers."

Low Cost Science Teaching Equipment: 2, Report of a Commonwealth Regional Seminar/Workshop, Dar es Salaam, Tanzania, September 1977, 55 pages, 1978, £1.00 from Commonwealth Secretariat Publications, Marlborough House, London SW1Y 5HX, England.

This report examines some of the experiences of African nations in tackling this subject, and includes recommendations for action by African governments.

"We are... presented with a dilemma: on the one hand it is educationally desirable to move towards student experimentation; on the other there are constraints imposed by meager school budgets and a lack of adequate numbers of qualified and experienced science teachers. This dilemma is of fundamental concern when one is considering strategies for the production and use of teaching equipment. Perhaps the best solution is to produce teachers' manuals to accompany the use of apparatus which provide adequate instructions both for work in small groups and for teacher demonstration exercises."

Guidebook to Constructing Inexpensive Science Teaching Equipment, MF 28-720, three volumes, 968 pages total, by the Inexpensive Science Teaching Equipment Project, 1972, $10.00 for the set of three books, from Science Teaching Center, University of Maryland, College Park, Maryland 20742, USA.

This is the final product of the Inexpensive Science Teaching Equipment Project at the University of Maryland. The project set out to: "1) identify laboratory equipment considered essential for student investigations in introductory biology, chemistry and physics courses in developing countries; 2) improvise, wherever possible, equivalent inexpensive science teaching equipment."

"In designing equipment for production by students and teachers, two factors have been kept in mind. One, project work in apparatus development can be extremely rewarding for students, bringing both students and teachers into close contact with the realities of science, and relating science and technology in the simplest of ways. Two, it is not difficult for cottage (or small scale) industries to adapt these designs to their own requirements."

All the designs have been tested at the University of Maryland, but at the time these books were printed the equipment had not been produced and tested under local conditions in developing countries. A draft edition was circulated for comments from science educators around the world before the current edition was produced. These materials should therefore be considered as ideas to be tried, adapted, and improved when needed.

Only handtools are needed to make this equipment. The drawings and instructions are very clear. Some of the basic materials required will be very expensive and/or hard to obtain in some circumstances: plastic lenses, glass test tubes, corks, and metal tubes. For the most part the equipment is made of simple materials, yet often it can be used to demonstrate rather sophisticated concepts. The emphasis is on qualitative, rather than precise quantitative, measurements.

Simple distillation apparatus

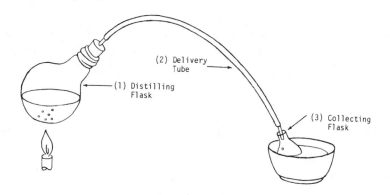

Notes on the use of the equipment are provided, but the reader will have to refer to other sources to learn how to best use some of it. Each volume has an index for all three volumes, which helps in locating equipment relevant to more than one subject area.

Volume 1: Biology

magnifying lens
microscopes
dissecting tools
tools for collecting: aquatic organisms, insects, soil organisms
traps for small animals and birds
plant press
aquarium
terrarium
cages

temperature-controlled cages
egg incubator
thermostat
apparatus for growing microorganisms
transfer pipette
kymography device
volumeter
manometer
chromatography apparatus
various uses of syringes

Volume 2: Chemistry

procedures for safely working with and cutting
   glass tubing, glass sheets, and glass jars
boring holes in corks
alcohol, charcoal, & gas burners
demonstration thermometer
bi-metal strip
burette
measuring glass
pipette
dropper
specific gravity bottle
supports, stands and clamps
glassware cut from lightbulbs
aspirator
mortar and pestle

sieves
distillation apparatus
electrolysis apparatus
hand drill centrifuge
hand operated centrifuge
gas generators
metalware
heaters and dryers
molecular models
kinetic molecular model
chromatography apparatus
variety of syringe uses

Volume 3: Physics

spring lever balance
rubber band balance
beam balance
extending spring balance
compression spring balance
pegboard balance
soda straw balance
micro balance
equal arm balance
single pan balance
sundial
water clock
pendulums
ticker tape timer
force and motion carts
ripple tank apparatus
stroboscope

uses of syringes
slit/aperture light box
reflection apparatus
optical board & refraction apparatus
light filter
lens apparatus
diffraction apparatus
transformers
rectifiers
simple batteries
circuit board
resistors
electric motors and generators
electromagnets
magnetic field apparatus
galvanometers
ammeter

Construction and Use of Simple Physics Apparatus, MF 28-719, book, 36 pages, by R.F. Simpson, 1972, US$3.00 surface mail from Swindon Book Company, 13-15 Lock Road, Kowloon, Hong Kong.

This delightful book includes dozens of ideas for simple equipment and illustrative experiments. Everything from the behavior of ping pong balls to the use of a polished half biscuit tin as a reflector for light experiments, to the construction of hand-held stroboscopes. Written by a former school teacher who has since been training science teachers at the University of Hong Kong.

"The use of simple apparatus constructed locally provides a magnificent oppor-

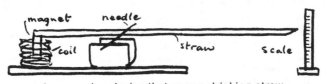

A measuring device that uses a drinking straw

tunity for educators in developing countries to extract the essence of a good science education without the expensive frills that have become associated with Western models."

In addition to the obvious advantages of very simple, inexpensive physics equipment made of commonly available objects, "pupils may become aware that scientific principles apply to everyday things and are not just associated with special apparatus, usually imported from abroad, and only found in laboratories."

A Method for Cutting Bottles, Light Bulbs, and Fluorescent Tubes, MF 28-722, 6 pages, by Allen Inversin, VITA, out of print in 1985.

These notes come from the author's efforts to find ways of making science equipment more accessible to the science teacher in developing countries. His initial use of this technique was for "cutting bottles and bulbs to make glassware for use in experiments." He has "cut hundreds of bottles of all sizes and in the process has refined the technique to the point where it should be fairly complete."

"Occasionally use can be made of cut incandescent light bulbs, as for example, beakers for boiling solutions in chemistry experiments, watch glasses, and glass chimneys for wick lamps." For this, a different technique is presented.

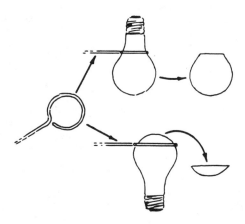

Adventures with a Hand Lens, MF 28-717, book, 220 pages, by Richard Headstrom, 1976, $3.00 from Dover Publications, Inc., 31 East 2nd Street, Mineola, New York 11501, USA.

This book consists of 50 explorations into the natural world using a magnifying glass, making the world outside the classroom the place where learning takes place. Basic natural principles can be taught using the simple experiments and observations. Many of the plants and insect examples are only found in temperate zones. In other regions the book could be a useful model for an approach that examines local plants and insects.

"If we look on cabbage leaves we would likely find conical, pale yellow eggs, and if we viewed them through our lens (magnifying glass) we would see that they are ribbed. The eggs are those of the imported cabbage worm...A little later, when squash leaves have developed, the squash bug, another common insect and rather injurious to squashes and other members of the squash family, appears and lays her eggs on the leaves. They are easy to find, for they are laid in clusters and are oval and pale yellow to brown."

Anti-Pollution Lab: Elementary Research, Experiments and Science Projects on Air, Water and Solid Pollution in Your Community, MF 28-718, book, 128 pages, by Elliott H. Blaustein, 1972, $2.25 plus $0.75 shipping from Arco Publishing Company, Inc., 219 Park Avenue South, New York, New York 10003, USA.

"The great merit of Elliott Blaustein's book is to demonstrate that we can use simple and practical scientific techniques to detect pollutants as well as their effects on the body, and also to develop action programs which will once more render our environment healthy and pleasurable." (From the Preface by Rene Dubos.)

Tests included are: vital capacity measurement (lung breath volume); maximum lung breath pressure; sulfur dioxide (SO2) air pollution; air dust particles; ozone testing; carbon dioxide (CO2); air visibility; water turbidity; water particles; algae; detergent in water; thermal pollution; salinity; and fiber decay resistance.

A user of this book should be familiar with simple chemistry. The problem of pollution is one which is increasingly found in all parts of the planet. Industrial manufacturing in Third World countries is increasingly developing and using technologies which are being banned or heavily regulated for pollution reasons in industrialized countries such as Japan and the USA. People in recently industrializing regions need information on effects of pollution and methods of pollution detection and control. This book provides a simple starting point in efforts to detect pollution.

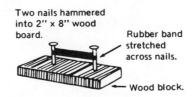

Stretching rubber band to test for ozone

Two nails hammered into 2" x 8" wood board.

Rubber band stretched across nails.

Wood block.

Preserving Food by Drying: A Math/Science Manual, Peace Corps ATFD Manual No. M 10, MF 28-723, book, 218 pages, by Cynthia Fahey with Carl Vogel and Per Christiansen, available to Peace Corps volunteers and development workers from Peace Corps, Information Collection and Exchange, Room 701, 806 Connecticut Avenue N.W., Washington D.C. 20525, USA.

This innovative manual forms a curriculum for math and science study in which the students learn basic scientific concepts by constructing simple apparatus and conducting experiments. Beginning with such basics as evaporation, determination of surface area, and measurements of the sun's angles, the students then move on to study, build, and test solar food dryers. Highly recommended both for use in teaching and as a model for curriculum development in other subjects.

How to Make Tools, Peace Corps Appropriate Technology for Development Series Reprint R-35, MF 28-721, booklet, 51 pages, by Per Christiansen and Bernard Zubrowski, 1980, available to Peace Corps volunteers and development workers from Peace Corps, Information Collection and Exchange, Room 701, 806 Connecticut Avenue N.W., Washington D.C. 20525, USA.

This is the companion volume to **Preserving Food by Drying** (see review). Simple, clever designs are presented for making tools such as a hammer, drill, saw, tongs, and tweezers, as well as for a balance to weigh things. These tools are intended for use in science classes. Although some may be sturdy enough for other applications, most would not be suitable for prolonged heavy use.

Nonformal Education
and Training

Nonformal Education
and Training

Development workers are increasingly recognizing the inadequacies of formal schooling systems in developing countries. Formal schooling inevitably depends on massive expenditures for schools, teacher training, and centralized administration, in addition to the continuing drain of government revenues to pay teachers' salaries. Typically, the shortage of revenues to devote to education has ensured a chronic shortfall in the number of teachers relative to ever-expanding numbers of pupils at all levels. Inadequately paid teachers cannot afford to devote all of their time to their teaching work, and teacher training based on foreign (often colonial) educational systems means that teachers inherit curricula and methods that have little to do with problems faced by students and their families. For these kinds of reasons, formal education systems are unable to provide relevant educational opportunities for many of the rural poor.

Given these inadequacies, there is a growing awareness among development workers that the rural poor are often their own best educational resource. Despite lack of formal schooling, they are the greatest source of background and insight on their own recurring problems. They also share, among themselves, a pool of locally-relevant skills and experience for tackling these problems. Recognizing this, many development workers now have two main objectives in their activities: to enable the poor to critically define their own problems and educational goals, and to help them find ways to mobilize the skills and resources to pursue these goals.

Such a strategy implies a belief in the capability of individuals and communities everywhere to define and control their destinies. One of the most powerful voices in this "humanistic" school of thought comes out of the Third World, that of Paulo Freire. His **Pedagogy of the Oppressed** tells how literacy can be a tool for describing and better understanding the world around the learner. This, in turn, is the first step towards useful action. An important part of Freire's method has been to involve illiterates in discussions about how words and pictures might describe or illustrate the troubling aspects of their lives. This methodology has sparked broad debate and has been adapted worldwide. It has influenced, for example, Latin America's liberation theologists, literacy workers in the ghettos of New York City, and field staff in bureaux of adult education from Thailand to Tanzania.

Successes in the application of Freire's methods, which rely on sharing of opinions and ideas in group settings, have triggered increasing interest in how the value of group insights is often greater than the sum of individual contributions. This well-known phenomenon of "synergy" is the focus of **Doing Things Together**, which offers a compelling theoretical illustration of how many individuals, each with different skills and information, pool their knowledge to solve a wide variety of community problems. **Appropriate Technology for Grain Storage** (see review in the STORAGE chapter) provides a concrete example of this effect. Tanzanian villagers — concerned with the drying and storage of their corn — knew more than the visiting team of specialists about the situation; they also collectively knew more *than any of them had guessed about what the real problems were, and how the problems might be solved.*

Key assumptions in this "problem posing/problem solving" approach are a free flow of facts and ideas among group participants, and leadership which is responsive to the group instead of "teaching" it predetermined solutions. "Culture Circles" in Latin America, "Family Life Education Groups" in Asia, and "Study Circles" in Africa are all approaches which rely on the increased creative and productive potential of participatory groups in which leadership is shared and not authoritarian. These Non-formal Education (NFE) programs, supported by a variety of public and private agencies, are efforts to reach and involve the young adults lacking formal schooling who are so numerous in the rural Third World. National NFE projects are often used by governments to channel and disseminate political programs and state ideology. Yet governments are now increasingly supporting the formation of adult groups based on some mutual interest in language learning, animal husbandry, tailoring, or some other income-generating skill. Examples of this "functional education" are found in a few parts of Indonesia, where members of "learning groups" (ranging in size from 10-25 participants) pool resources to capitalize projects ranging from chicken-raising to silk-screening T-shirts to installing a locally-built water pump at the community well. Soon the Indonesian NFE directorate plans to make available "learning funds," seed capital for the projects of learning groups.

This chapter includes several publications on NFE approaches and techniques. **Perspectives on Nonformal Adult Learning** *is a concise discussion of philosophical bases and practical approaches for NFE fieldworkers and trainers.* **Demystifying Evaluation** *is a manual on generating useful criticism, or "feedback," about NFE projects.*

The emphasis on local definition of learning needs, to be met with local resources, is essentially a strategy for educational self-reliance. One potential role for outside organizations is to share useful information and problem-identification techniques among various local groups. **Learning from the Rural Poor** *and* **Participatory Training for Development** *both describe training for leaders ("facilitators") and change agents aimed at improving their skills in working with participatory groups.* **From the Field** *is a compilation of exercises for NFE facilitators and their trainers, emphasizing increased group problem-solving power through broad participation and mutual trust.*

Because the success of any training or other educational project depends on a respectful awareness of the specific local situation, community surveys frequently are an initial step in the design of educational programs. Approaches to "needs assessment" vary a great deal. In this section we review two contrasting examples, **Community, Culture and Care** *and* **Assessing Rural Needs.** *Our experience suggests that objective, quantitative needs assessment techniques may do little more than confirm the survey designer's biases.*

Practitioners of non-formal, community-based education have always had mixed feelings about "higher" education in colleges, universities, and academies. On the one hand these institutions are a potential source of bright young people with perspectives and communication skills useful in villages. But on the other hand, in practice they often drain the rural areas of the most talented youth, conditioning them for new roles in urban settings; in this way these students are effectively lost as contributors to village progress. Many countries have established study-service schemes which require that college students live and work in a village before they graduate. However, the stay in the village is usually too brief, the student's work role is undefined, and there may be no practical objective which can be reached in a few weeks' or months' time. Some countries are deepening their study-service schemes and setting up volunteer service programs which place college graduates in villages for a year, two years, or more. These programs generate employment opportunities and provide a valuable educational experience for young people previously unfamiliar with the realities of life for their less-privileged fellow citizens. However, the volunteers almost always return to the city and their impact on village life is seldom a lasting one. FUNDAEC in Colombia has been developing a program that attempts an alternative strategy for linking higher education to village development (see **Rural University***). This program draws students from villages and is explicitly geared to dealing with village-level problems; traditional fields of knowledge are combined in a unique "cross-disciplinary" approach. (The experiences of "barefoot doctor" programs have shed some light on the requirements for successful efforts to develop new rural-based professionals. Health workers have proven to be most effective when they come from the communities in which they will work, and when they are genuinely selected by those communities. See review of the IDRC bibliographies* **Health Care in the People's Republic of China** *and* **Low Cost Rural Health Care and Health Manpower Training** *in the HEALTH chapter.)*

Both formal and non-formal community education should be based on local situations and challenges. Such an orientation is also crucial to health care and research-and-development programs (see the HEALTH and SCIENCE TEACHING chapters) which build on local skills instead of eroding them. Communities with these organizational tools for self-reliance will be in a much stronger position to innovate and to seek, adapt, and apply useful technologies from other places.

Pedagogy of the Oppressed, book, 186 pages, by Paulo Freire, 1970, $6.95 from Crossroads/Continuum Publishing Corporation, 370 Lexington Avenue, New York, New York 10017, USA.

In this pioneering book, Brazilian-born Freire outlines a humanistic theory of education which has become a cornerstone of people-centered development approaches. To be human is to both act and reflect upon the world; "To exist, humanly, is to name the world, to change it. Once named, the world in its turn reappears to the namers as a problem and requires of them a new naming. Men are not built in silence, but in word, in work, in action-reflection." In Freire's work with illiterates in Latin America, words and sentences became powerful tools with which peasants could symbolize and define the problems and contradictions in their own lives.

The most important consequence of this approach is that language and any educational content must be rooted in the world of the learner. "It is to the reality which mediates men, and to the perception of that reality held by educators and people, that we must go to find the program content of education. . .The starting point for organizing the program content of education or political action must be the present, existential, concrete situation, reflecting the aspirations of the people. Utilizing certain basic contradictions, we must pose this existential, concrete present situation to the people as a problem which challenges them and requires a response — not just at the intellectual level, but at the level of action."

In the Third World, Freire's work has helped initiate approaches to education and development which begin with local realities instead of planners' visions. For the "developed" world, **Pedagogy** stands as a warning against homogenized, mass-marketed language and culture which bury the human dialogue with the world in the conformity of products and slogans.

Perspectives on Nonformal Adult Learning, MF 29-730, book, 122 pages, by Lyra Srinivasan, 1977, $7.50 from World Education, c/o Ananth Narayan, P.O. Box 5066, Kendall Park, New Jersey 08824, USA.

The purpose of this book is to introduce the basic theory behind non-formal education (NFE) and to look closely at current NFE techniques. In Thailand, for example, "People in nonformal education programs, especially in the rural areas, are not students by profession: they are farmers and fishermen, mothers and marketwomen. They already have enough problems of their own: the water-pump does not work, the birds are all over the field eating the paddy, the baby is sick. So the approach selected by the Thai nonformal youth and adult education programs focuses on the real and immediate needs of the learners." Thais apply this "problem-centered approach" by using sequences of photographs to illustrate and spark discussion about community problems. Another approach, "self-actualizing education," emphasizes the capacity of individuals to creatively identify their own problems and goals: "...the pace of development will remain restricted if the full creative and visualizing power of rural communities is not turned on...it is not the out-siders as much as the insiders whose imagination holds the key to a major breakthrough in rural development."

Appendices contain exercises to encourage learner participation in groups.

Non-formal education is an important strategy for self-reliant rural development. This book is an excellent introduction to the field.

Demystifying Evaluation, MF 29-727, book, 69 pages, by Noreen Clark and James McCaffery, 1979, $6.50 from World Education, c/o Ananth Narayan, P.O. Box 5066, Kendall Park, New Jersey 08824, USA.

An important task for the staff of any village-level development effort is to ask whether or not the project or program is achieving its objectives and addressing villagers' needs. This short book describes a low-cost, flexible approach to program evaluation. It provides a detailed outline of a practical seminar concentrating on "1) helping program administrators and field staff become aware of the need for evaluation to improve decision making and 2) assisting them to ask the right evalua-tion questions about their projects. The seminar is not designed to produce experts in evaluation; it is intended to assist administrators to identify and initiate evalua-tion approaches to improve the operation of their organizations."

The seminar includes small-group discussions exploring the reasons for evalua-tion, developing common-sense evaluation questions, and collecting data. The greatest amount of time in the one-week seminar is devoted to visits to the "case project," in which teams of participants try out and refine their evaluation strategies in the field. Instructions for leading or "facilitating" the sequence of activities are clear and complete. Emphasis is on getting work done in groups, with authority and responsibility shared among members; the group problem-solving techniques included could be adapted for use in a wide variety of cultural situations.

Recommended as a guide to help project staff develop experience in evaluation techniques. Easy to read and well-illustrated.

From the Field: Tested Participatory Activities for Trainers, MF 29-729, three-ring binder, 148 pages, compiled by Catherine Crone and Carman St. John Hunter, 1980, $8.00 from World Education, c/o Ananth Narayan, P.O. Box 5066, Kendall Park, New Jersey 08824, USA.

Non-formal education practitioners have, in recent years, reached an important conclusion about their "target" groups of rural people without traditional schooling. While their needs for information and skills are many and varied, their own pooled experience is the most important source of knowledge relevant to solving local problems. Thus horizontal or community-wide sharing and exchange of ideas is a crucial key to meeting local needs. Non-formal educators believe that this kind of communication is most likely to occur in a group of people with a mutual interest, in an atmosphere in which all members share authority and submit ideas.

Many teachers and other leaders have never experienced such a "participatory" atmosphere. This collection of group activities is intended to help them learn about this approach. "(Participatory education) emphasizes mutual learning rather than teaching. In this kind of process, the teachers or leaders or trainers take on some roles that may be different from those they are used to. What they are learning is not so much how to teach nutrition or family planning or moral values. What they are learning, rather, is to work with particular groups of people who are affected by their own unique circumstances."

Most of the exercises require less than two hours. Many involve large and small group discussions, demonstrations, role-playing, interviewing, and eliciting ideas with photos and pictures. Each exercise is presented in the context of a particular training session (most of which were held in developing countries): "We introduced this activity to enable the group to identify important facts they should know about the rural people with whom they work, and how they can collect the information they need to develop effective learning experiences...The trainers wanted to discover whether village-level facilitators could invent and use games in their own educational activities...The trainer wanted a group of materials developers to become adept at selecting pictures that stimulate active learning, and to discuss and establish criteria for choosing such pictures. He hoped that this three-part mini-course would help to extend the group's use of visual learning materials."

A sequence of exercises on developing and testing learning activities is included. An appendix contains an excellent outline for an introductory planning workshop on simplified PERT (Program Evaluation and Review Technique).

Recognizing the unique value of every individual contribution to a group effort, participatory learning approaches are an important tool in mobilizing local human resources. This manual provides practical material to accompany the introductory book **Perspectives in Nonformal Adult Learning** (see review in this section).

A PERT chart

Learning from the Rural Poor: Shared Experiences of the Mobile Orientation and Training Team, book, 114 pages, by Henry Volken, Ajoy Kumar, and Sara Kaithathara, 1982, Rs. 15 in India, $3.00 overseas, from Indian Social Institute, Lodi Road, New Delhi 110 003, India.

Practical insights for supporting grass-roots-based development are compiled in this report by a mobile training team. The four-member team has spent 2 years in the villages of India, working among the poor and offering training to other voluntary organizations. The group notes that the major task for voluntary organizations is a difficult one: "to shift the emphasis from a predominantly *managing* role in development to a new role of *facilitating* educational processes" and helping the poor create their own organizations.

"The rural poor are 'voiceless' not because they have nothing to say, but...because they have no 'say' in the decision-making structures of society. In this perspective it is legitimate tó say that development begins with listening to the people...Unless we begin with an attitude of respect for traditional knowledge we will never be able to make an objective assessment of traditional practices."

The team reports on their goals and methods, the experiences of one member in agriculture, and the training of illiterate women as basic health workers.

"Often we were surprised to see that the rural poor are not even aware of the resources they have...Our agriculturalist...has been able to concretely point out the many possibilities people had in each place we went, to develop their local resources...there is scope for a mutual give and take."

In agriculture, training began with and built upon existing agricultural practices. The team always emphasized working with the marginal and small farmer groups who form the poorest half of the population; the others tend to know how to tap available credit and information resources. Special attention was given to low-cost and no-cost ideas that, once introduced, would spread by themselves. One of the goals of the team was to create locally-based teaching material, using the ideas and images of the people themselves.

"Today there is much talk about 'total revolution' and radical transformation of society. But what really matters are the changes taking place in the socio-economic reality of the villages where poverty crushes the poor. In this stark reality of life the rural poor can hardly envisage more than creating for themselves some free space in society where they can breathe more freely and begin to stretch themselves. What is crucial at the moment is to create a base for joint action which is relatively free from control of the locally powerful. Wherever this has been achieved, people begin to move."

"What does expanding the space of freedom concretely mean? It can mean the ability to reduce maternal and child mortality, to double agricultural production by a scheme of dry farming, to get goats for all the families, to get rid of bondage to money-lenders."

These new experiences can convince the poor "of their capacities and new possibilities of collective action. By analyzing the obstacles they encounter in these endeavors they come to understand gradually the working of society and the deeper issues of a more just society."

Highly recommended.

Bridging the Gap: A Participatory Approach to Health and Nutrition Education, MF 29-726, book, 103 pages, edited by Martha Keehn, 1982, available in English and Spanish, free from Save the Children, 54 Wilton Road, Westport, Connecticut 06880, USA.

"This manual is addressed to nutrition and health educators who are interested in trying out new participatory ways of working at the community level. Its purpose is to describe simple techniques by which field staff can be trained to approach local communities more sensitively and to involve them more fully in achieving better health." Topics include planning and carrying out workshops for community health workers, methods and materials for non-directive assessment of villagers' needs, creating learning activities, and techniques for planning and evaluation which involve the villagers. Full of practical material which can be adapted to local situations.

Doing Things Together: Report on an Experience in Communicating Appropriate Technology, MF 29-728, book, 108 pages, by Andreas Fuglesang, 1977, $9.00 surface mail or $11.00 airmail from the Dag Hammarskjold Foundation, Ovre Slottsgatan 2, S-752 20, Uppsala, Sweden.

In this report on a workshop on A.T. in village development, the author makes some contributions towards a new theory of communication compatible with appropriate technology principles. Among the key issues he identifies: Who chooses what is appropriate? What is leadership in a context of people's participation?

Because individuals have different skills and information "the mass (community) can carry and handle an information burden far beyond any individual's" capability. "The mass (community) is a perfect communication system. . .It covers all fields of importance to our society's life. It adapts continuously to changes. . .The communication flow in the mass is controlled by the interests of the individuals." This observation has interesting implications for the way in which problems are identified and solutions proposed in development projects.

"Leadership is a communication problem. Decisions must be based on information from the mass. Otherwise they are non-responsive to social realities. . .The ideal leader is an individual in the mass whose perceptions of the need for social change are ahead of the mass, but who recognizes that the ideas originate in the mass itself."

"It has been commonly assumed among information specialists that an information intervention follows a two-step flow, from mass media through opinion leaders to a number of individuals. This idea offers intriguing opportunities for those who have a manipulative outlook, but it is fortunately not borne out by experience. The opinion-leader theory is probably little more than a superimposition of outmoded authoritarianism on modern sociology."

Participatory Training for Development, book, 59 pages, by Kamla Bhasin, 1977, available from Freedom From Hunger Campaign/Action for Development Liaison Officer, Regional Office for Asia and the Far East, Phra Atit Road, Bangkok 2, Thailand.

This is the story of a training program for a new kind of "change agent" who can facilitate full community participation in solving local problems. Nine people took part in a traveling field level training process that included visits to 50 groups in 3 countries of Southeast Asia, to compare approaches and establish links. The program emphasized self-training and group learning through field visits and dialogue — all approaches that would be important later in the community work of the participants. "The best way to teach about 'bottom-up planning,' people's participation and decentralization is by practicing these very ideas in a training program."

"Gradually it dawned on the change agents in the program that field workers like them should develop a capacity and knack to write about their work and their observations of village life and its problems. . .to feed the higher-ups and sympathizers with genuine accounts of issues related to the mobilization of people, cadre-building, rural power relationships, exploitation, injustice, etc. . .To reverse the flow of information, it is necessary that change agents function also as field level researchers. By learning simple techniques of research they can gather valuable information on the basis of which realistic and sensible decisions and policies can be made by the higher-ups."

"The participatory approach to development emphasizes the need for people to become aware of their own conditions, their socio-economic-political interrelationships with others (like money lenders, landlords, government officials, etc.). It also emphasizes the need for people to be able to analyze their own situation and to take action to attain self-defined goals. In this approach the responsibility to direct change lies with the people, and not with outside agencies...Change agents must encourage the people to work in groups, because it is only through group action that the poor stand a chance of increasing their bargaining power."

This book provides a useful variety of down-to-earth views on participation, with good ideas on roles for change agents in village-level development efforts.

Highly recommended.

Community, Culture and Care, book, 297 pages, by Ann Templeton Brownlee, 1978, free to Peace Corps volunteers from the Office of Multilateral and Special Programs, Peace Corps, Washington D.C., USA; others $12.95 from the C.V. Mosby Company, 11830 Westline Industrial Drive, St. Louis, Missouri 63146, USA.

" 'Once upon a time a monkey and a fish were caught up in a great flood. The monkey, agile and experienced, had the good fortune to scramble up a tree to safety. As he looked down into the raging waters, he saw a fish struggling against the swift current. Filled with a humanitarian desire to help his less fortunate fellow, he reached down and scooped the fish from the water. To the monkey's surprise, the fish was not very grateful for this aid...' " (from the Introduction).

For a cross-cultural health program to be successful, the outsiders involved must understand what is needed and what is possible. This book will help an outsider to develop that understanding by investigating the various aspects of community life which influence health care. The book consists of a series of questions about the community, and strategies for answering them. The questions are grouped into topics for inquiry (e.g. income, attitudes toward work) and broader subject areas (e.g. economics). Quotes from health workers in the southwestern U.S. and Africa are included to illustrate important points. Concerning the Muslim fast (Ramadan) in North Africa: "When community people had their Ramadan, they wouldn't come to the dispensary. They wouldn't eat during the whole day, and for the same religious reasons they didn't want any ointment in their eyes, they didn't want anything in their bodies..."

This book does not give answers. Instead, it emphasizes the best ways of asking good questions. The author stresses the importance of "low-profile" roles for health care planners and workers, and the value of learning by living close to the people. Thus the book is a kind of cross-cultural study guide useful to a wide variety of people (such as extension workers and volunteers).

While it is essential that outsiders approach communities with sensitivity and a keen desire to learn, this should be only part of a process in which local people are supported in their own efforts to address their own problems.

ADDITIONAL REFERENCES ON NONFORMAL EDUCATION AND TRAINING

A Solar Water Heater Workshop Manual describes a weekend training course given to a community group; see ENERGY: SOLAR.

Rural Small Scale Industries in the People's Republic of China notes that these industries have contributed to the "scientification" of the rural population; see LOCAL SELF-RELIANCE.

Small Enterprises and Cooperatives: Organization and Management

Small Enterprises and Cooperatives: Organization and Management

In the Third World, small producers and farmers must overcome the high cost of capital (interest rates of 10-20% per month are common in the rural areas) and must survive market fluctuations caused by influences beyond their control. Penetration of local markets by cheap goods manufactured in the modern industrial sector, inconsistent governmental tax and import/export quotas and restrictions, and seasonal price cycles in agricultural produce are only a few of the difficulties faced by the small business enterprise.

But because a viable local economy depends on preventing the drain of resources out of the community, small manufacturing and other commercial units seem to be an especially "appropriate" form of business organization. Small businesses channel investments which improve local capital stocks; they develop local skills and increase job opportunities while using local materials; and they allow the diversity which is crucial to a healthy, stable local economy. Significantly, locally-owned small businesses are unlikely to abandon a community in search of lower wages elsewhere.

A relative neglect of institutional support for small businesses, worker-owned enterprises, and cooperatives is found in both the United States and the Third World. On the whole, small enterprises give a better return on investment (risks are higher, gains are higher) and create more jobs per unit of capital than large enterprises. Yet small enterprises have great difficulty in obtaining capital, due to the poor match between their capital needs and the operating rules of the capital markets. Compounding the problem is the fact that small enterprises in rich and poor countries are often failing to make best use of what capital and human resources they do have, and they face substantial difficulties in obtaining technical assistance to change this situation. **Small Business in the Third World** *is an insightful review of the problems and opportunities faced by small enterprises; this book is a must for people involved in related activities.* **Consultancy for Small Businesses** *presents an innovative means for improving management skills in Third World small enterprises through a low-cost system of consulting. In rich and poor countries, a variety of governmental and non-governmental efforts are being initiated to stimulate the growth of small businesses and other enterprises.*

Entrepreneurs are the people who take risks in order to create and sell new products and provide new services. The most lucrative business opportunities in developing countries are usually urban and/or import-oriented, and these usually attract the most experienced entrepreneurs with the greatest financial resources and the best political connections. However, there are often some individuals with a real interest in establishing businesses that could help the rural areas. These people, if exposed to the right opportunities to produce and market innovative agricultural tools, can be much better at these activities than government or NGOs. Entrepreneurs can also positively influence R&D work sponsored by NGOs and governments, due to their concerns for the commercial and economic viability of innovations. **The**

Entrepreneur's Handbook *is an excellent resource for Third World entrepreneurs and would-be entrepreneurs.*

One promising type of small enterprise is the cooperative. By pooling resources and functioning as a unit, a group of producers or consumers can operate at a more efficient scale and share the benefits. They may be able to buy in quantity, or store and ship produce to more profitable markets, for example. The cooperative also has great potential as a mechanism for increased capital investment in the rural Third World. Groups of individuals pooling small monthly surpluses have been able to finance community improvement projects, and establish credit funds. Clearly cooperatives have great potential as tools to help break vicious circles of poverty and lack of opportunity, yet they have seen only limited success. Especially in the poor countries, cooperatives fall prey to distrust among members, unskilled or corrupt management, domination by ruling local interests, and manipulation by governments intent on using them for political purposes. Cooperatives have generally been unable to help those most in need. Often farmers must own land to qualify for membership in Third World agricultural co-ops; this excludes tenants and laborers.

Like any tool or technique, the cooperative will be an appropriate organizational form only when it grows out of the aspirations of the people who will be members. The great mass of the literature, however, treats the co-op as a fixed organizational structure that extension agents should promote. Case studies in the **Handbook for Cooperative Field Workers in Developing Countries** *show how this approach is bound to fail. There are, however, a flourishing variety of informal cooperative organizations in the Third World. The "arisan" is an Indonesian capital-formation club in which each individual contributes the same small amount to a monthly "pot," all of which goes to a different member each month. Other Indonesian villagers form savings associations to provide revolving loan opportunities to members. Interest is collected on small loans and paid on savings, at moderate rates. This is, in effect, an alternative to the commercial banks which are unable to respond to most village credit needs. Many experts view effective government support (in the form of training, facilities, consulting, etc.) as essential to a cooperative's success. Yet these Indonesian associations are informally organized, and avoid registration with the government ministry for cooperatives.*

In the promotion of cooperatives and small business enterprises, as in so many other activities, it appears that government agencies and NGOs have been too quick to supply answers and promote adoption of fixed organizational structures, and have failed to support local initiatives or strengthen existing organizational forms. Certainly a process may be set in motion by carrying out a dialogue with a community about the many forms a cooperative might take. But it appears that best use is made of training and other "inputs" when these are provided only in response to requests from businesses or cooperatives which have already defined their own activities. While traditional extension programs do not operate in this way, there are certainly other, more participatory approaches. Non-formal education, in particular, puts increasing emphasis on supporting group-defined educational and vocational goals. Small-scale non-formal education programs might provide one of the best mechanisms for successful support of cooperatives and other small enterprises in the Third World.

This chapter concludes with entries that discuss the principles of running a small business and simple accounting systems. The authors have attempted to meet "a real and widespread need for a (bookkeeping) system which is both effective and straightforward enough to be taught to rural-based people in a relatively short period of time."

Small Business in the Third World, MF 30-762, book, 211 pages, by Malcolm Harper, 1984, £6.95 from ITDG.

Here is an outstanding review of the factors that help and hinder small enterprises in developing countries, richly illustrated with real examples. The ("Capital") chapter on interest rates and bank lending practices is particularly insightful and illuminating. Harper challenges a number of widely believed myths about small business, and identifies some key issues to be addressed by those who wish to aid such enterprises.

Small businesses are the most promising means for the production and distribution of appropriate technologies. This book should therefore be required reading for most people working to develop successful dissemination systems for new technologies, as well as those involved more directly in small business promotion.

"Everyone in Government and in particular those responsible for employment and small enterprise promotion must be persuaded to appreciate the economic significance of the smallest enterprises; they are the most difficult to assist, but their problems usually arise more from an excess of regulation than from too little official assistance, and the most effective and simple way of helping them, even if it is not too attractive to the institution builder who wishes to enhance his authority, is to modify and withdraw existing legislation or programmes which actively damage the interests of the smallest enterprises."

"Moneylenders and other sources of so-called 'informal credit' are as ready to serve small non-farm enterprises as they are to lend money to small farmers. These 'loan sharks,' as they are sometimes called, are in fact providing a service which is needed by other businesses. Those who complain about their apparently extortionate behavior would be better to examine the reasons why so many small enterprises find it necessary to borrow from these sources, and should encourage competition rather than attempting to forbid unofficial moneylending. . . Because of what are effectively local monopolies, however, borrowers from moneylenders may fall totally under their control."

"Since the supply of capital is the means by which. . . the financier. . . secures his control over the small business, this problem is often seen as a symptom of a shortage of capital, which can be remedied by providing it. It is hardly surprising that attempts to remedy this problem by providing alternative sources of finance have not generally been successful. People who have never had the opportunity or the need actually to run a business are not likely to acquire the necessary skills or attitudes just because somebody lends them money on reasonable terms. . ."

"A large scale knitting factory could never be economic. . . if it had to depend on occasional deliveries of wool, but a small-scale enterprise, with two or three knitting machines costing perhaps $200 each, can still earn enough money to pay for the machines and make some profit if raw material is only available for three or four months every year. Labor is also often available only for part of the year, since people are fully occupied in their farms during the seasons for planting, weeding and harvest."

"There are. . . powerful arguments against subsidized interest rates. . . capital is of course needed, but if its price is artificially lowered below the prevailing market figure this will tend to encourage borrowers to use more of it than they would if it was more expensive. Demand will also be increased; the effect of low interest will thus be to attract a larger number of applicants, but to satisfy very few of them. The tendency will be towards a small number of relatively capital intensive enterprises, and a larger number of frustrated applicants who receive no help at all." Highly recommended.

Entrepreneur's Handbook, MF 30-757, book, 282 pages, by UP Institute of Small Scale Industries, 1981, Swiss Francs 72.00 from SKAT.

Entrepreneurs can play a very important role in technology development and marketing in the Third World, by finding ways to make and sell tools and equipment that buyers want.

Developing country entrepreneurs are the intended audience for this valuable book. A discussion of the personal traits common to successful entrepreneurs is followed by much good advice about starting and operating a business. Emphasis is given to the importance of marketing — central to any successful business and often given too little attention in developing countries.

"The ability of an entrepreneur to perceive and identify business opportunities is proportionate to the degree to which he is aware of the economic, political, sociocultural and technological developments in his environment...Remember that people are special in every organization. Do not take your people for granted for they can make or unmake your organization. Outstanding people can make even a poor organization operate successfully, while poorly-motivated people can impair the performance of the soundest organization."

A much-needed, well-written book on a very important subject. Recommended.

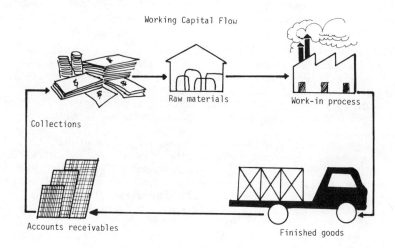

Working Capital Flow

Raw materials
Work-in process
Collections
Accounts receivables
Finished goods

Training Village Entrepreneurs, MF 30-764, book, 135 pages, available from Xavier Institute of Social Service, Post Box 7, Purulia Road, Ranchi 834001, India.

Village-level entrepreneurs are much needed to create new enterprises, jobs, and economic growth in the villages. In many villages, the perceived lack of opportunities drives young people to the towns and cities in search of employment, draining away some of the most energetic and creative individuals.

This book is based on years of experience selecting, motivating and training young people to start their own businesses. This is a difficult task indeed. The authors identify many of the prime causes of failure, and suggest ways to improve the odds of success. An outline of the curriculum and some of the materials used in candidate selection and training activities are included. Candidates "should have a capacity to take risk. A person who lives from hand to mouth undergoes risk but cannot take it...stands with back against the wall, and can hardly be expected to become an entrepreneur."

This practical, village-oriented volume is at the opposite end of the spectrum from the theoretical book **The Practice of Entrepreneurship** (see review). The program described in **Training** appears to be a very good attempt to translate entrepreneurial thinking into village-based action. Voluntary agencies interested in developing their own programs using this approach should be sure to have at least one person with extensive business experience on their team.

The Practice of Entrepreneurship, MF 30-760, book, 196 pages, by Geoffrey Meredith et. al., 1982, $11.40 from ILO.

This volume is for individuals who would like to develop their entrepreneurial skills systematically. It is not written in simple language, nor does it specifically address the special problems faced by Third World entrepreneurs. It does provide a good exposure to entrepreneurship as it is understood in the United States.

"Some of the most important risks are those in which you learn something new about yourself. Situations which involve personal risks should challenge your abilities and capacities to the fullest extent. . .You must be a planner in the sense that you can visualise how your creative ideas might be used. However, you must also have the risk-taking ability to be able to implement your ideas and carry them to successful conclusions."

Size, Efficiency and Community Enterprise, MF 30-747, book, 129 pages, by Barry Stein, 1974, $5.00 from Center for Community Economic Development, 1320 19th Street N.W., Mezzanine Level, Washington D.C. 20036, USA.

The purpose of Barry Stein's well-written book seems to be to make a case and sketch the economic context for community-owned and -operated enterprises. Realizing that his greatest dogmatic obstacle lies in the notion of economies of scale, he spends the bulk of his book reviewing the economies of scale literature, and discussing the factors that determine firm efficiency. Simply stated, his general conclusion is that economically optimal plant size for many industries is quite modest.

Proceeding from the economies of scale discussion, Stein examines the rationale and proper role for community enterprise. He points out that firms actively seek, through advertising and packaging, to differentiate their product from the competition, thus achieving a monopoly position. Stein maintains that price competition is not significant for mass-produced differentiated products. He further maintains that for many staples, competing products are fundamentally the same so that firms spend large amounts to promote product identity. Thus he argues that these products can be the outputs of successful community enterprises, particularly in poor areas. The rationale is that community enterprises would not need to spend on product differentiation.

Although there is little treatment of practical problems such as capital formation, Stein's book should be useful to community organizers and others concerned with community economic development within a capitalistic consumer economy. Although his review of the economies of scale literature would be enlightening, most residents of developing countries may find the rest of the book somewhat outside their interest.

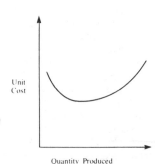

U-shaped curve:
Diseconomies of scale begin
to appear as plant size
continues to increase

Unit Cost

Quantity Produced

Small Enterprises in Developing Countries: Case Studies and Conclusions, MF 30-748, book, 115 pages, by Malcolm Harper and Tan Thiam Soon, 1979, £4.95 from ITDG.

"The A&B Soap Manufacturing Enterprise was established by two brothers in 1973...A small factory which produces candy is located in Marcato, Addis Ababa...Mr. Qhoqhome manufactures leather belts at his home in Katlehong Village...During 1971 a Mr. Zabuli, who was a very experienced businessman, applied to the Ministry of Planning to set up a factory to produce Coca Cola, Fanta and Sprite..." These are the opening phrases from some of the case studies in this intriguing little book. Each of these short summaries provides background details and describes problems faced by a particular small business. Each case study is then followed by "a brief note summarizing some of the issues which were raised...including some suggestions as to what a small business promotion agency ought to do in the situation described." This book covers much of the same ground as **Small Business in the Third World**, by one of the same authors.

"It is perhaps surprising, in view of its importance, that small-scale business, and ways in which governments can help or hinder it, have not been more intensively studied. A great deal of information is available about various types of appropriate technology, and some work has been done on systems of financing, treated from the point of view of a bank, a trainer, or perhaps a technologist, but very little information has been published on the ways in which the various methods of assistance actually impinge on their 'target'..." The authors note that variations in economic circumstances make it impossible to lay down absolute rules for promoting indigenous enterprise. Still, the cases illustrate certain truths and key factors. Entrepreneurial talent is a human resource found everywhere. On the other hand, small-scale business promotion officers, whose task is to help businesses become profitable, are often faced by businesspeople content to operate at little profit or even at a loss. Small-scale enterprises can be established with relatively little capital investment; yet because of their limited resources they are especially vulnerable to supply and demand cycles, shifting import restrictions, price competition from larger enterprises, and innovations which make production techniques obsolete. In a section devoted to analysis of the cases, the authors discuss ways in which governments might help: "The first priority should be...to examine carefully the ways in which all its activities impinge on small business, and to make whatever changes are possible in order to avoid the unintentional discrimination which often arises when regulations, which are basically conceived for larger businesses or transferred from industrialized economies, are applied to small enterprises."

"The case studies demonstrate the need for well-planned assistance programmes...Staff responsible for implementing the programmes must appreciate that the manager of a small business is usually responsible for all the details of finance, production, marketing and personnel, as well as the long-term direction of the enterprise itself. The manager may not distinguish between these functions in his own mind, but any outside intervention is bound to affect the business as a whole, even if it is nominally concerned only with credit, markets or technology."

The book concludes with a short synopsis of how intermediate technologies are a vital part of strategies for small-scale industrialization, and a review of policy suggestions to encourage indigenous enterprise.

Developing Small-Scale Industries in India: An Integrated Approach, MF 30-741, book, 96 pages, by Marilyn Carr, 1981, £5.50 from ITDG.

Several case studies of small industry development in India illustrate the viability of a progressive scheme for decentralized rural industrialization. Started by students at the Birla Institute of Technology, which is set in an undeveloped region, the approach has proven successful in starting technical financial assistance, infrastructure, marketing, etc. Most notable is the achievement of applying the resources of an institution of higher learning, in concert with government and banking, to the needs and realities of the surrounding area; a lesson pertinent to both industrialized and nonindustrialized regions alike. This is more detailed than necessary, but worthwhile for planners, technical trainers, and those concerned with employment development.

Blacksmith, Baker, Roofing Sheet Maker, MF 30-754, book, 144 pages, by Marilyn Carr, 1984, £5.95 from ITDG.

There is a great need for viable income-generating activities for women in developing countries. Especially needed are activities that produce goods and services for local markets, and go beyond handicraft production for uncertain export markets. This collection of 55 short case studies provides lots of ideas, and will serve as great encouragement to those responsible for developing and supporting such programs. The examples include the production of special foods for sale, cloth manufacture, rice milling, and bus operation. References and sources for further information are provided.

Josbarko Enterprise, Case Study No. 2, MF 30-758, booklet, 37 pages, by J. Powell and J. Quansah, Technology Consultancy Centre, 1981, £1.95 from ITDG.

A fascinating account of the successful establishment of a steel bolt manufacturing enterprise by a Ghanaian entrepreneur, with technical assistance from the TCC. The entrepreneur overcame a wide range of problems typical to developing countries.

Manual for Commercial Analysis of Small Scale Projects, book, 90 pages, by Henry Jackelen, 1983, from A.T. International, 1331 H Street N.W., Washington D.C. 20005, USA.

Small-scale enterprises must be commercially viable if they are to survive without subsidies. This manual presents the basic steps in evaluating the likely financial health of a proposed (or existing) enterprise, under various assumptions about costs and selling prices. This kind of analysis is an important piece of homework that must be done by aspiring entrepreneurs and technical or community development groups that wish to aid entrepreneurs in using new technologies or producing new products.

Consultancy for Small Businesses, MF 30-739, book, 254 pages, by Malcolm Harper, 1976, £9.95 from ITDG.

"It is generally realized that small businesses have a particularly important role to play in the development of employment opportunities and economic progress because they are in a far better position than large organizations to make use of 'intermediate technology'. It is not enough, however, for business people to be encouraged to use appropriate technology; they must learn how to decide what is right for their particular business, how to calculate costs and selling prices, how to sell their products and generally how to operate a successful and profitable enterprise. The system described in this manual is, in a sense, a way of conveying 'intermediate management' to small enterprises — the method itself is also labour intensive and may therefore be considered as an example of 'appropriate training'. "

"Small businesses are widely scattered...competitive with one another...different from one another...vulnerable. Small business owners are usually not well educated...speak a variety of different languages and dialects...busy, often running their business singlehandedly." Because assistance to businesspeople involves teaching analysis skills and affecting attitudes and behavior, advice should be available on an individual consultancy basis. Yet "the cost and scarcity of suitable candidates usually means that individual advisory services are impossible. . .There is clearly a need, therefore, for some system which would enable less qualified and quite inexperienced staff to provide useful advice for small business people."

Part One of this manual explores the potential for low-cost small business consultancy in developing countries, and outlines a service in consultancy training which could be provided by government and/or development agencies, banks, or voluntary organizations. Topics covered include selection of consultant trainees (six or seven is probably a suitable number to start out with), the training period (approximately 21 days of instruction), supervision, administration, financing and evaluating the service. "One of the most common problems of small business people is that they think they need more money but are in fact using the money that they do have in the wrong way. The first object of any diagnosis must therefore be to discover how the businessman is using his capital."

Part Two of the manual is the training course itself, nearly 200 pages of detailed outlines of lectures and discussions, role-playing exercises, field assignments, and tests. Hand-out exercises for each training session are also included.

Here is a carefully-assembled learning resource aimed at sharing and developing important skills on a decentralized basis. Highly recommended.

Small Business Promotion, MF 30-761, book, 118 pages, edited by Malcolm Harper and Kavil Ramachandran, 1984, £5.95 from ITDG.

This very readable book contains 28 case studies by different authors, examining small businesses in 17 countries. It provides a good sampling of the problems faced by small enterprises, and the positive and negative effects of interventions by official agencies. This volume is similar to **Small Enterprises in Developing Countries** (see review).

"The owner or manager of a small enterprise must be a generalist, and he cannot consider marketing, finance, technology or anything else in isolation. The same applies to those working with small enterprises. They may eventually identify particular problems which require particular attention, but they must initially look at the business as a whole."

Guidelines for Management Consulting Programs for Small-Scale Enterprises, Peace Corps Appropriate Technology for Development Series, MF 30-742, book, 212 pages, by Gary L. Vaughan, 1981, available to Peace Corps volunteers and development workers from Peace Corps, Information Collection and Exchange, Room 701, 806 Connecticut Avenue N.W., Washington D.C. 20525, USA.

This manual was written to assist management consultants working with small-scale entrepreneurs in developing countries. The author defines a "small-scale enterprise" as one which employs 10-15 people, serves a regional market, and has a adequate equity base. This contrasts with a "micro-enterprise," which employs one to three people, markets locally, and has marginal resources. The manual addresses ". . .three basic areas: the problems of small-scale enterprises and their role in Third World development, various kinds of management consulting programs which might address such problems, and specific tools and techniques which the management consultant can employ in assisting the small entrepreneurs." Appendices include aids in consulting and teaching small entrepreneurs, and references to other publications and information resources. A very practical manual written for a specific audience.

Management Workbooks for Self-Employed People, 5 volumes, books, by Gerard R. Dodd and friends of The Maine Idea, 1984, $18.00 for the set of five, from Dodd-Blair and Associates, P.O. Box 644, Rangeley, Maine 04970, USA.

Written for small-businesspeople and those who would like to start a small business, this series of five booklets reviews the basic elements of good business management. Lots of good advice is presented in an easy-to-read format. Much of this material could be well used in developing countries.

The Business Review (MF 30-756, 58 pages) takes a look at the entire business: what it is, its best products and customers, distribution, employees, production, finances and a yearly plan. "Before you manage your business, you must understand how it works. The purpose of the Business Review is to help you analyze your business as a whole, or to assess any specific part of it. Our objective is to get you thinking and excited about your business. When you have completed the Business Review, you should be better informed about how your business operates, and therefore in a much better position to guide its operation."

The Business Plan (MF 30-755, 60 pages) suggests the use of 1-3 year goals for the business and describes the elements of a written plan. "The process of setting goals helps you to analyze your problems and sort through options. A well-prepared business plan is the best way of presenting your ideas to others; it's indispensable if you're looking for credit. The business plan is proof that you are seriously managing your business and the operation is a viable one."

Basic Finances (MF 30-752, 46 pages) discusses bookkeeping systems, balance sheets, profit and loss statements, and cash flow projections. "Sound management is based on facts, not guesswork. Before you can know where you're going, you need to know where you've been! Effective recordkeeping (when combined with conscientious monthly analysis) will give you the information needed to make decisions about the future of your business. It will help you plan, organize and control what has to be done. It will help you trim costs, save on income taxes, keep track of payroll records, sales tax, etc. It is only by taking firm control of the financial aspect that you will be able to turn a high quality product or service into a thriving, stable business. The simple discipline of recordkeeping will make you a more cost-conscious and effective manager."

RECORDKEEPING IS THE BEST WAY TO CUT EXPENSES

Basic Marketing (MF 30-753, 44 pages) emphasizes satisfying customers' needs and targetting the market. "Ask your customers what they want to see in your store; talk to them informally or ask them to fill out a simple questionnaire, in return for a special discount or small gift. This kind of direct feedback from your customers is invaluable in planning your marketing strategy."

Managing Time and Personnel (MF 30-759, 48 pages) presents steps for selecting and managing employees and making best use of the manager's time. "Learn to distribute the load and encourage others to take the responsibility to think for themselves. Motivate them! Encourage them to identify with and be a part of your business undertaking. . .You may be able to purchase someone's time and labor, but loyalty, cooperation, and enthusiasm must be carefully nurtured."

Highly recommended.

How to Grow a Shop (MF 30-744) and **A Complete Cash-Analysis Accounts System for Businessmen** (MF 30-738), booklets, 55 and 36 pages, by G.H. Barker, limited number of copies available to local groups in developing countries, small charge for postage, from the author, c/o Diani Beachalets, P.O. Box 26, Ukunda, Mombasa, Kenya.

"Most Africans will happily admit that they know better how to grow a crop than a shop." **How to Grow a Shop** is an imaginative discussion of the principles of operating a small retail, wholesale, or industrial business, relating the essential factors of successful trade to farming practices. We begin with "two seeds (capital and human resources). . .what crop? (trade specialization). . .rain (buying). . .sunshine (selling). . .weeding (dead stock, credit sales). . .growth (accounting and using the bank)." Contains many practical hints on facilities, equipment, and strategies for the small businessperson.

A Complete Accounts System is a companion workbook, explaining and giving examples of how to do bookkeeping so that each different kind of income and expense can be easily identified. "Few African businessmen of today were 'born behind the counter'. Economic independence can be hastened if a simple and practical introduction to commerce and accounts is encouraged in schools. . .and more directly relevant study material made available to budding businessmen."

A Handbook for Cooperative Fieldworkers in Developing Nations, MF 30-743, packet P5, seven booklets, 408 pages total, edited by Mark S. Ogden, 1978, free to Peace Corps volunteers and development organizations in developing countries, from Peace Corps, Information Collection and Exchange, Room 701, 806 Connecticut Avenue N.W., Washington D.C. 20525, USA.

Produced to supplement the training of Peace Corps volunteers, this handbook is a compilation of excerpts from publications of international cooperative development groups, university cooperatives extension services, and Peace Corps volunteers (PCV) reports. "The resulting anthology is by no means 'the complete guide' for PCVs. . .individual variances from country to country and from program to program, make it difficult to arrive at. . .all-inclusive guidelines." The seven parts of the handbook include an introductory section using case studies of cooperative projects in Bangladesh and Peru, and a directory of organizations active in cooperative work in developing countries. Another section on cooperative organization uses a case history from a Guatemalan regional cooperative scheme to illustrate how indigenous ideas about debt and membership are important to a successful cooperative. A chapter entitled "Determining the Economic and Social Feasibility of a Cooperative" lists key questions for evaluating the potential of marketing, purchasing, and service cooperatives. "Cooperative Education and Training" provides interesting material on participatory group learning approaches (e.g. study circles, role-playing case histories of hypothetical cooperatives). Other useful sections discuss simplified accounting methods, cooperative forms of group credit, and a case history of a Nigerian handicraft marketing cooperative.

Some parts of this handbook are taken from books written about cooperatives in the United States; these sections are less directly relevant to conditions in developing countries. Still, the handbook is the best compendium we've seen of on-the-ground experience and insights as to why cooperatives do and don't work. Frequent quotes from PCV field reports show how difficult it is for a foreigner to sensitively enter a community and introduce a new organizational technology: "Recently a volunteer terminated and returned to school. He was well experienced in agricultural technology and a bona fide expert in hog production. He like all PCVs who are well trained, knew that Guatemalan farmers need more money, more protein for their diets, and product diversification. He deduced that his hog knowledge was well suited to meeting the needs of the people. One month after he left, the hog co-op with which he had worked for two years held a meeting to consider what it could do without their expert-in-residence. The result was an immediate dissolution of the co-op, distribution of the 30 hogs to the members and a sale of the assets (purchase price with AID assistance: $5,000) for $500. Each member received more money, ate a little pork, and briefly experienced diversification of production. Is this developing Guatemala?... Another volunteer, dedicated to patterning Guatemalan co-ops after his father's group in Iowa, arranged the purchase of a tractor for his co-op and happily left knowing he had effected progress. Today the co-op has a $200 debt and the implement company has the tractor. The members aren't sure why they couldn't make enough with the tractor to meet payments but are certain that they want no further heavy equipment. They wish the volunteer had not pushed the tractor purchase because now it is difficult to get new members interested in joining a cooperative with a substantial debt."

A useful document for cooperatives extension, non-formal education, and other community development workers.

Cooperative Organization, MF 30-736, booklet, 34 pages, by B.A. Youngjohns, 1977, £1.95 from ITDG.

A short, clear summary of cooperative principles emphasizing their potential application in developing countries. Cooperative organization allows individuals to combine their resources for greater economic strength, but experience shows that this pooling of resources cannot be done haphazardly. Democratic control, open membership, limited ownership of shares, and commitment to the cooperative through realization of common economic interest, are generally key factors in the success or failure of cooperative groups.

The advantages of each of the most important types of cooperative (agricultural and farming, credit, supply and marketing, industrial production, housing) are outlined. Multi-purpose and linked cooperatives are discussed briefly.

The cooperative, as a source of credit and framework for education and innovation, often plays an important role in development schemes. "Comprehensive development projects are becoming more and more common... a typical development project provides a comprehensive package including roads and communications, agricultural extension, credit, supply and marketing services. Sometimes, all the services and control are provided by the project. Inputs are supplied direct, on loan, from the project to the farmer. Increasingly, however, it has come to be realized that this is an expensive way of doing things. Furthermore, there is often no provision for continuity after the project itself has come to an end, and the experts have gone home. Cooperatives are, therefore, being introduced into these projects..."

The booklet concludes with an appraisal of the most common of problems facing cooperatives in developing countries: "The ordinary members know little if anything about the way the cooperative is supposed to work...comparatively large sums of money are handled by people whose own income is relatively small...(domination by) a few wealthy or influential people, who direct the affairs of the cooperative in their own interest."

A brief but well-rounded overview of cooperatives.

Cooperative Organization Papers, MF 30-740, booklet, 18 pages, by D.A. Huntington, 1975, out of print.

"Written as an informational resource for groups (in the United States) that wish to conduct a business under that form of legal organization known as a Cooperative...a special kind of corporation in which members usually contribute the same amount of investment for their shares, always have an equal voice in the direction of the business, and are limited in their liability...by the monetary value of their shares...if you are devoted to a one person-one vote-one monetary share philosophy, then a cooperative corporation is the way to go."

The required legal procedures for incorporation vary somewhat from state to state in the U.S., but often the process is simple enough to do by yourself. The author discusses pros and cons of incorporating on a for-profit or non-profit basis, and how to obtain necessary information on tax status and legal forms. Also included are sample articles of incorporation and by-laws. "Articles of Incorporation...are the papers that must be registered and filed with the powers that be. They give life to that legal individual called the Corporation...Your job in writing the Articles for your co-op is to adapt the general format accepted by the law to the needs and goals of your group. It pays here to be as farsighted as possible. Don't limit your co-op's future activities or possible areas of future interest by being too specific in the Articles, at least in the sections dealing with goals and powers. The best Articles are those that can be lived with no matter what direction your group turns in later years."

Stock-Taking, MF 30-763, booklet, 42 pages, MATCOM/ILO, 1979, $2.85 from ILO.

A simple well-illustrated guide for staff of consumer cooperatives or other small stores, this volume describes the importance of counting inventory (stock-taking) on a regular basis. This is an important management technique to quickly identify thefts or other losses, and establish good control over what is happening with the store's stock and assets. Some of the recommendations (e.g. marking down and getting rid of damaged stock immediately after it is discovered) could be particularly beneficial to small family-run stores.

Basic Control of Assets: A Manual on Prevention of Losses in Small Co-operatives, MF 30-751, book, 53 pages, by Co-operative Education Materials Advisory Service, 1979, £4.95 from ITDG.

"Studies of the development of the co-operative movement in many countries tend to reveal that losses of assets — money and merchandise in particular — are a very serious problem. Losses often render co-operatives incapable of bringing about the expected and potential benefits and they are quite often the cause of complete failure. Closer studies of this specific problem tend, again, to show that one very frequent reason for losses is the inefficiency of the existing control systems...There are many doors to be closed, and some of them might easily be overlooked."

This manual is a teaching guide for training cooperatives' managers in techniques for minimizing losses through theft, error, and maintenance failure. It includes sample forms for records of stock movements, cash transactions, and so forth.

EXAMPLE 5:   A CASH RECONCILIATION

```
              Cash Reconciliation of No. 2 Cash Account
                   at 9.15 a.m. on 23rd January 1980

                                                              LC

Balance of No. 2 Cash account 21st January 1980             32.61
     ADD:    Cash sales receipts on 22nd January 1980,
             not yet recorded (Cash Sale Receipts
             Nos. 123 - 132)                               128.20
                                                           160.81

     LESS:   Unrecorded Cash Payments 22nd January 1980.
             Share withdrawals (Payment Voucher 761)        12.50
                                                           148.31


Cash counted:                      LC

   LC  10  Notes               110.00

   LC   5    "                   10.00

   LC   1    "                   10.00

             Coins                6.71

   Cheque                         8.50                     145.21

Shortage requiring explanation                               3.10
```

Business Arithmetic for Cooperatives and Other Small Businesses, MF 30-731, book, 87 pages, ITDG, 1977, out of print in 1985.

"This manual deals with...business calculations. A good book-keeping system is no good unless the calculations on which it is based are accurate, and it is hoped that this manual will help those many of us whose arithmetic was not very advanced or has gone rusty." In fact, most of the book is arithmetic; a section on calculating interest, mark-up and margin, and gross and net profit, accompanies the basic arithmetic review.

None of the mathematics presented goes beyond what primary school students learn. The explanations and exercises using business calculations might be adapted for use in cooperatives education programs.

Co-operative Book-keeping: 1—Marketing Co-operatives, 2—Consumer Co-operatives, 3—Savings and Credit Co-operatives, 4—Industrial Co-operatives, MF 30-735, set of four large booklets, 27 to 51 pages each, by the Co-operative Education Materials Advisory Service, £1.50 each from ITDG.

"It is a common complaint that, in many primary cooperatives, the standard of book-keeping is poor. The need has long been recognized for a basic, simplified system of book-keeping, for use in...developing countries, in order to help improve that situation." This system, originally introduced in Botswana, uses a double-entry method: both a credit and a debit are written down for every transaction. Thus, when the accounts of the cooperative are accurate, the sum of credits equals the sum of debits and the accounts "balance." Each of these booklets includes examples and explanations of each type of ledger, deposit, and slip used in the cooperatives' transactions, as well as sample budgets and monthly reports. Exercises require the reader to transform lists of incomes and expenditures into a main ledger.

The importance of accurate, understandable accounts to the success of new cooperatives cannot be overemphasized. "The members are the owners of the society (cooperative). They need to know how their business is doing and how their funds are being used...the book-keeping system must therefore show:

a. How much the society owes. These are its liabilities and indicate the source of the funds in use in the society.

b. How much the society owns. These are its assets and show the use being made of these funds.

c. Whether the society has financial stability and is able to pay its debts as they arise.

d. Whether the society is operating efficiently, covering its costs and providing a net surplus."

Clearly and thoughtfully written, these materials could be adapted for use by a wide variety of cooperative and small business education programs.

Co-operative Accounting #1, Thrift and Credit Co-operatives, MF 30-732, 20 pages, ITDG, 1970, out of print in June 1978.

This is a booklet for small thrift and credit cooperatives that do not yet have an efficiently working accounting system. In addition, it can be used to form such cooperatives. Such organizations serve to encourage members to save, and provide a locally-controlled mechanism to grant loans to members.

Co-operative Accounting #2, Consumer Co-operative Societies, MF 30-733, 38 pages, ITDG, 1971, out of print in June 1978.

"The main function of a consumer co-operative is to buy goods and re-sell them to its members. It raises capital from its members" for rent and an original stock of goods, by selling shares to them.

Co-operative Accounting #3, Marketing Co-operative Societies, MF 30-734, 31 pages, ITDG, 1972, out of print in June 1978.

This booklet is for any small group marketing the same product, especially produce. "A marketing co-operative is primarily concerned with marketing the goods that its members produce. Cattle, coffee, cotton, fish, handicrafts, rice, and wheat are examples. These goods can be sold in many different ways: to a marketing board, to wholesalers, through co-operative unions, direct to individual retailers or consumers, or by auction." The advantages of a marketing co-op are: members can get a better price for their goods than as individuals, they can often sell directly to consumers, they can spread the transport costs, and they can establish a reputation for grading and reliability.

A Single-Entry Bookkeeping System for Small-Scale Manufacturing Businesses, MF 30-746, booklet, 54 pages, by Derry Caye, 1977, $7.25 in U.S., $7.50 international surface mail, $10.25 international air mail, from VITA.

"VITA publishes this manual in the belief that it can help support efforts to increase local self-reliance and to create job opportunities in developing areas by serving as a valuable tool for use by small business managers and advisors...This manual describes a bookkeeping system which is contained in a kit, or carrying case, of some kind. There are suggestions in this manual for building one kind of kit, but the system could be used as well in different containers. The important thing is to package the system in some way so that important records are all in one place." The uses of entry books, record-keeping, and files are explained step-by-step. The booklet includes an annex on business letters and a glossary of business terms, as well as a section on how to use inventory and monthly summaries to pinpoint strengths and weaknesses of a business.

The record-keeping forms explained in this booklet could be stenciled or mimeographed and bound at very low cost. In this way this bookkeeping system would be simplified or adapted to the needs of cooperatives, learning groups, and other group enterprises.

An Initial Course in Tropical Agriculture for the Staff of Cooperatives, MF 30-745, book, 54 pages, by Peter Yeo, 1976, £1.95 from ITDG.

This is a self-guided learning text presenting very basic information on soils, fertilizers and plant nourishment, controlling infestations, and animal husbandry. Each part is followed by a progress test.

"If you are a Co-operative officer or otherwise concerned with rural development programmes in a tropical country...(you) ought to know in outline the conditions under which the products co-operatives market for farmers can flourish...The idea that 'agriculture is the job of another department and, therefore, does not concern the cooperative officer' is indefensible."

"The course should help you to cooperate better with people who know more about agriculture than you do...It certainly doesn't justify any feeling of superiority over those who make their living by using traditional methods of agriculture."

The fact that there is a need for a book like this is itself an alarming commentary on the way in which cooperatives are often structured. It seems clear that those people responsible for administration of agricultural cooperatives should have intimate knowledge of the local agricultural situation; certainly the manager of a farming cooperative should be a farmer. Unfortunately, the people who implement cooperatives programs often have had more experience in bureaucratic work than in the productive activities of the cooperatives they supervise. It is partly because of this that cooperatives programs can be seen by farmers as an intervention from outside, willed upon them by a government agency.

Local Communications

Local Communications

Grass-roots A.T. groups and other community organizations wishing to share their successful ideas with a larger audience will be faced with the problem of how to make this information available in a low-cost, understandable form. The books reviewed in this chapter should be helpful in choosing ways to present information effectively and at low cost. **Experiences in Visual Thinking** *shows how most people can use sketching as a tool for developing ideas in the problem-solving process.* **Visual Literacy in Communication** *and* **Communicating with Pictures** *are concerned with finding drawings and pictures, especially those based on common local images, that can be effectively used to communicate ideas from one community to another and among illiterates.* **Illustrations for Development** *provides lessons for improving drawing skills.* **Visual Communication Handbook** *and* **Screen Printing** *offer many ideas on low-cost visual communications media that can be produced in small communities.* **Rural Mimeo Newspapers** *looks at one particularly promising low-cost print technology.* **Print: How You Can Do It Yourself** *gives an overview of the low-cost print technologies as they now exist in the developed countries.* **Basic Bookbinding** *provides the necessary information for small-scale hand bookbinding; also useful to a library or information center.* **How to Do Leaflets, Newsletters and Newspapers** *gives some valuable guidelines for newspaper writing, editing, and organization. (***Rural Mimeo Newspapers** *also does this well). And* **The Organization of the Small Public Library** *can be valuable for any group with an information center or local appropriate technology library.* **Grass Roots Radio** *provides the basic outlines for the low-cost production of radio programs in rural communities, for broadcast throughout a region. Here is an approach for two-way communication, in which rural people can seek technical help and discuss their own successful technological innovations.*

The techniques described in this section are but a few of the possible tools of a grass-roots-based communications strategy. Such an approach will also involve close collaboration between researchers and beneficiaries, and mechanisms to ensure that technical suport for problem-solving can be provided when requested by villagers. Visits by individuals from one community to another, technical databanks responsive to rural requests, and low-cost catalogs covering a broad range of topics (like the **Liklik Buk***) also have a place.*

Experiences in Visual Thinking, MF 31-752, book, 171 pages, by Robert McKim, second edition 1980, $16.95 from Brooks/Cole Engineering Division, 555 Abayo Street, Monterey, California 93940, USA.

" 'Visual Thinking' is used to describe the interaction of seeing, imagining and idea-sketching." This is a book on thinking about design, and how sketches and other representations of design ideas can be a great aid to releasing the creativity of the reader as a designer. The reader is taken through a series of small problems to develop the understanding of many different ways in which "visual thinking" can aid in design work. The author has drawn from a wide literature on creativity, mental processes, and the history of great inventions.

"Unlearn the stereotype that places drawing in the category of Art...Drawing, most of all, stimulates seeing...Almost everyone learns to read and write in our society; almost everyone can also learn to draw."

"Graphic ideation is not to be confused with graphic communication. The former is concerned with conceiving and nurturing ideas; the latter is concerned with presenting fully formed ideas to others. Graphic ideation is visually talking to oneself; graphic communication is visually talking to others...The graphic ideator...can sketch freehand, quickly and spontaneously, leaving out details that he already understands...he feels free to fail many times on the way to obtain a solution."

This is a valuable tool for strengthening the design and problem-solving abilities of individuals and groups. It could be used for a short course for members of an appropriate technology unit.

Highly recommended.

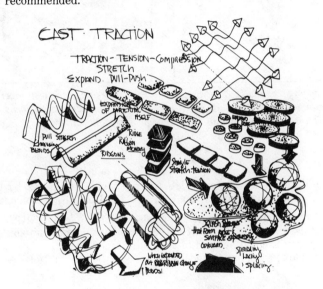

Visually working out ideas with drawings

Visual Literacy in Communication: Designing for Development, MF 31-760, book, 144 pages, by Anne Zimmer and Fred Zimmer, 1978, free of charge except $2.50 for postage and handling, from the International Institute for Adult Literacy Methods, P.O. Box 1555, Tehran, Iran.

This is about how to communicate effectively with drawings and pictures. It is intended for use by artists and most development workers (good English language ability required). The author presents a systematic strategy for improving the effectiveness of drawings, with a lot of examples.

Many posters and drawings fail to communicate what is intended. Partly this is because "most communication theory as we know it today was developed in the industrialized West...it takes little notice of the kinds of communication — visual and otherwise — that have been important in spreading and maintaining tradi-tional...cultures." Foreign methods of visual presentation can be as hard to understand as a foreign language.

"The first job of the visual communicator is not to draw pictures. It is to find out what visual communication is already going on among the people he wants to reach, and to get the other information he needs in order to design materials that communicate properly. To do this, he makes a collection, called a 'visual inventory'. Instead of putting together elegant designs from all over the world, he samples the visual communication his intended audience already sees. Then he finds out how — and whether — these examples communicate by asking questions..."

"The message is: read your own culture and understand your own visual language as you design visual messages for use in your particular cultural setting."

Improving realistic drawings. Before: viewing angle does not make the important action clear. Details are confusing and contrast is weak.

After: new composition, stronger contrast, and details all focus on the important activity.

Communicating with Pictures, MF 31-751, booklet, 56 pages, by UNICEF-Nepal, 1975, available on request from UNICEF, P.O. Box 1187, Kathmandu, Nepal.

This booklet is a summary of a full report also obtainable from UNICEF in Nepal. The booklet describes the results of a study that was undertaken to discover how effectively pictures could be used in communication.

"Is it possible to communicate ideas and information to villagers by using pic-

tures only? Probably not. In the course of the study, over 20 pictures intended to convey ideas (rather than just to represent objects) were shown to villagers. Many (but not all) of the villagers could recognize the objects shown in the pictures. But the ideas behind the pictures were almost never conveyed to the villagers. For example, one picture was intended to convey the idea that people who drink polluted water are likely to get diarrhea. It was shown to 89 villagers, and only one of them understood the message behind the picture."

The reasons for the failure of pictures to convey ideas are thoroughly discussed. Many different types of pictures (illustrations, sketches, photos, and other graphics) were used: the disadvantages and advantages of each type are covered. The effects of colors are mentioned too.

"People are interested and attracted to pictures, even though they may need help to interpret them . . . During the study one picture was taken to six villages and shown to over 100 people. In five villages, none of the villagers who saw the picture could understand it. But in the sixth village, many villagers could explain exactly what the picture meant. They could understand it because five months before, some health workers had visited their village and talked about TB, and had shown them this picture."

Anyone attempting to use pictures to communicate ideas and information would find this booklet useful. Highly recommended.

Illustrations for Development, MF 31-762, book, 69 pages, edited by George McBean, 1980, from Afrolit Society, P.O. Box 72511, Nairobi, Kenya.

Artists, would-be artists, and the people who publish drawings to communicate with village people will find this a valuable manual. The authors summarize recent findings from research about how drawings are perceived by rural people, and go on to provide lessons to improve drawing skills. Basic drawing tools are presented along with some good advice about pursuing a career as an illustrator.

"Close up illustrations which cut off any part of the body (e.g. head or hands) are difficult to comprehend. Full-figure drawings are usually understood, and pro-

vide a useful starting point for educating and introducing an audience with a low visual literacy level to picture communication."

Visual Communication Handbook, MF 31-759, book, 127 pages, by Denys J. Saunders, 1974, £2.95 from TALC.

The author does an excellent job of explaining how to use a great variety of inexpensive visual aids, including paper pictures, posters, flannel boards, and puppets. This book would be useful to anyone trying to carry out an education program as cheaply as possible.

A simple device (a pantograph) is shown which can be used "to make enlargements up to eight times the size of the original. By means of a screw you fix the pantograph to the table or the drawing board. With the pointer you trace the lines of the original picture and a-pencil draws the enlarged picture on another sheet of paper."

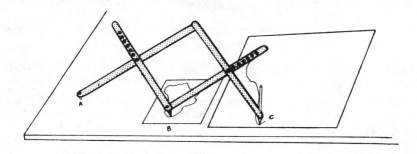

A pantograph can make accurate enlargements easily

How to do Leaflets, Newsletters, and Newspapers, MF 31-755, booklet, 100 pages, by Nancy Brigham, 1982, $7.95 plus $0.53 postage from PEP Publishers, P.O. Box 289, Essex Station, Boston, Massachusetts 02112, USA.

This booklet provides guidelines for the small community or neighborhood newspaper. Includes suggestions for the effective design of leaflets, the scheduling of a newsletter or newspaper, how to determine the "look" of the newspaper, the techniques of layout and paste-up, obtaining and presenting information, and editing. Briefly covers the low-cost print technologies.

While this booklet is intended for use in the United States, the language is quite easy to understand and it may be useful in other areas.

Women and Graphics: A Beginner's Kit, in **The Tribune**, Newsletter No. 21, MF 31-761, 60 pages, 1982, free to women in the Third World from International Women's Tribune Center, Inc., 305 East 46th Street, 6th Floor, New York, New York 10017, USA.

Though directed at, and most applicable to, women's groups, this packet of techniques for media outreach and education is an informative and stimulating resource for community groups and organizers. Includes tips for lettering, graphics, and communicating by simple yet effective means. With bibliography. Other issues of this newsletter, covering a wide variety of topics related to women in development, are available from IWTC.

Plain Talk: Clear Communication for International Development, MF 31-766, book, 75 pages, by David Jarmul, 1981, $6.55 from VITA.

Much of what is published about development is hard to understand, especially for anyone reading in a foreign language. This book has twelve rules for simple writing that will help you write more clearly. A system for measuring the difficulty of text is described. The effective use of drawings is also discussed.

Rural Mimeo Newspapers, MF 31-758, booklet, 42 pages, by Robert de T. Lawrence, 1965, UNESCO, 7 Place de Fontenov, 75700 Paris, France; out of print in 1981.

This is a low-cost printing scheme for small communities in developing areas. Describes a successful project in Liberia, in which 30 mimeo papers grew up within a year, a number of them spontaneously. Small mimeograph machines are lightweight and easy to repair. They can be purchased for as little as US$40-50. "On the basis of the Liberian experience, it is estimated that a paper could be

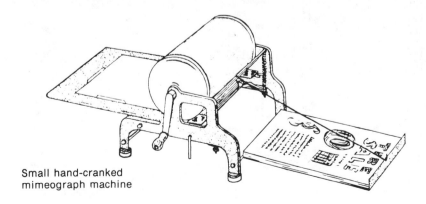

Small hand-cranked
mimeograph machine

established with an initial outlay of as little as $100, and that it could provide a living for its owner/editor from the outset."

Part II, on organizing a rural newspaper program, gives suggestions on how to plan, staff, publish, and assist low-cost newspapers in rural communities of developing countries.

Part III, on how to publish a low-cost community newspaper, gives hints on writing, editing, printing, and distributing a rural newspaper. It is suggested that sponsoring agencies adapt this section to fit local conditions and publish it in pamphlet form.

Low Cost Printing for Development, MF 31-763, in four booklets, 104 pages total, by Jonathan Zeitlyn, 1982, available from Jonathan Zeitlyn, 51 Chetwynd Road, London NW5, United Kingdom.

To minimize the costs of printing posters, flyers, community newspapers and booklets, it is important to understand the various simple printing technologies available, and the appropriate uses for each in terms of quality, numbers of copies and cost. The author of these four booklets has summarized this information and provided additional details to allow readers to make their own simple printing devices and deal more economically with printers. The final volume discusses the requirements for setting up a small printshop. These volumes have more of a developing country focus, but are otherwise similar in purpose and scope to **Print: How You Can Do It Yourself** and **How to Do Leaflets, Newsletters and Newspapers**.

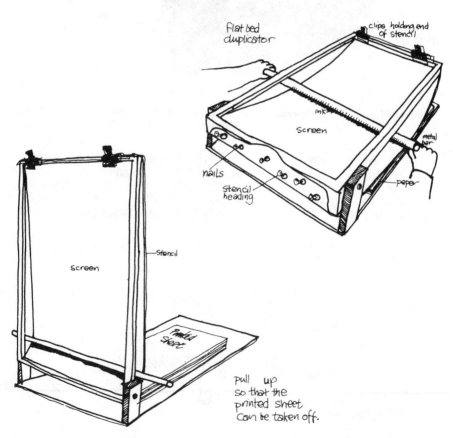

The Photonovel: A Tool for Development, MF 31-765, booklet, 105 pages, by Daniel Weaks, 1976, available to Peace Corps volunteers and development workers from Peace Corps, Office of Information Collection and Exchange, Room 701, 806 Connecticut Avenue N.W., Washington D.C. 20525, USA.

The photonovel is similar to the comic book, but with pictures in place of drawings. It "fills a special need felt by those who lack reading material written at a level that they understand. To fill this demand, photonovels are found in every country of Latin America and many cities of the U.S."

This is a good introduction to the production of photonovels.

Print: How You Can Do It Yourself, MF 31-757, booklet, 96 pages, by J. Zeitlyn, 1975, £2.95 plus postage or US$5.00 from Interaction Trust Ltd., 15 Wilkin Street, London NW5, United Kingdom.

This is a good overview of low-cost community-level print technologies. While most relevant to groups in developed countries, it does give a good idea of the operation of spirit and stencil duplicators, offset presses, and silkscreen techniques.

57 How-to-do-it Charts on Materials & Equipment & Techniques for Screen Printing, MF31-753, paperback book, 63 pages, by Harry L. Hiett, 1980, $6.50 from Signs of the Times Pub. Co., 407 Gilbert Avenue, Cincinnati, Ohio 45202, USA.

Screen printing (also called "silk screen printing") is an excellent way to print pictures and words on leaflets, posters, clothing and other materials. The methods of screen printing are thoroughly described in this book. There are a large number of illustrations.

Highly recommended to anyone looking for information on screen printing as a means of cheaply and efficiently producing high quality graphics.

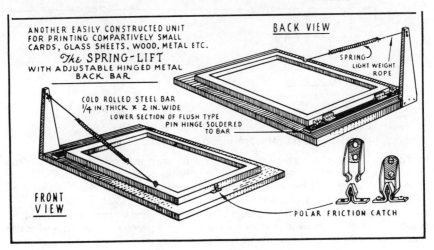

A spring lift on a silk screen printer

The Sten-Screen: Making and Using a Low-Cost Printing Process, MF 31-767, booklet, 13 pages, by Ian McLaren, 1983, £2.50 from ITDG.

"The Sten-Screen process is a hybrid duplicating and printing technique. Basically it combines stencil duplicator stencils with the screen process. This enables one to create legible and compact printed matter, using equipment which one can make oneself out of readily available items. The process does not require electricity. These instructions give guidance on how to build and use the equipment. The screen uses a simple rectangular frame with textile stretched across it. This is used as a support for stencil duplicatory stencils. The text and images which are required to be reproduced may be either typed, handwritten or drawn upon these." Photographs can be reproduced if an electronic stencil cutter is available to produce the stencil.

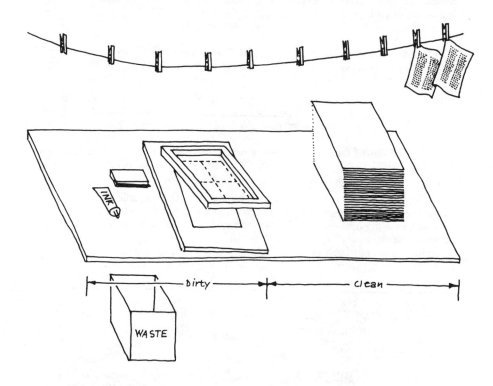

Basic Bookbinding, book, 136 pages, by A. Lewis, 1957, $2.75 from Dover Publications, 31 East 2nd Street, Mineola, New York 11501, USA.

This book provides step-by-step instructions with many illustrations for the essential operations involved in the binding of books by hand in cloth and in library style. "Sufficient detailed information is given to enable a student, working on his own, to do so with success."

Materials used are carefully explained. All the tools necessary are relatively simple ones. The descriptions and illustrations of the tools needed are sufficient for the craftsperson to make them him or herself.

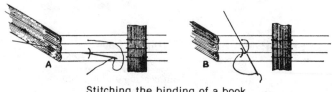

Stitching the binding of a book

The Low-Cost Wooden Duplicator, MF 31-764, booklet, 19 pages, by David Elcock, 1984, £2.50 from ITDG.

Detailed construction drawings and step-by-step instructions are provided for a hand-operated stencil duplicator made mostly of wood.

"From one inking you can, with practice, produce over 200 copies of good quality print. The quality of the print is nearly as good as that from much more expensive machines."

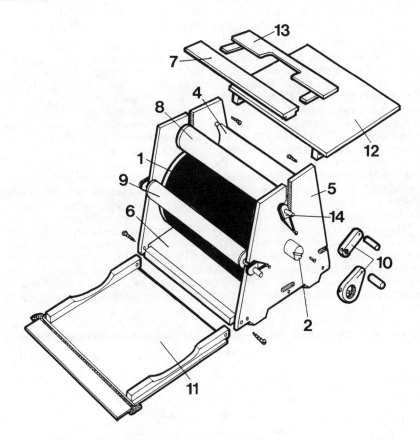

Small Technical Libraries, MF 31-768, booklet, 40 pages, by D.J. Campbell, 1973, reprinted 1980, UNESCO, $6.00 from UNIPUB, out of print in 1984.

In this valuable little book you will find lots of good ideas that will prove very helpful in organizing and effectively operating a small technical library to support the work of a small research institute or a technical information clearinghouse. The author emphasizes frequent meetings with the research staff to better understand and provide for their information needs, and make them aware of newly arrived reference materials of possible interest. Recommended.

The Organization of the Small Public Library, MF 31-756, booklet, 66 pages, by I. Heintze, 1963, out of print in 1985.

This booklet "has been written specifically for people without previous training in librarianship who are faced with the task of running small public libraries and need guidance. . .in a simple and practical way, with many illustrations, it gives the reader the basic information he needs. . .Intended primarily for the rapidly developing countries" but the principles are universally applicable. May be useful in the organization of a library of A.T. materials.

Grass Roots Radio: A Manual for Fieldworkers in Family Planning and Other Areas of Social and Economic Development, MF 31-754, book, 66 pages, by Rex Keating, 1977, $6.50 (contact if currency difficulties prevent you from paying for this), from Distribution Department, International Planned Parenthood Federation Publications, 18-20, Lower Regent Street, London SW1Y 4PW, England.

"Rural broadcasting, as practiced in most developing countries, is a one-way line of communication, the specialist or government official instructing farmers and other members of the rural community. . .But any form of adult education yields its best results when the communication is two-way and this is the secret of the Farm Forum success. . ." By 1974, most villages in Senegal were listening to farm forum broadcasts, many of them holding organized discussion groups. Members of the broadcasting team "are always on the move, systematically covering the countryside, and in each village they hand over their microphone to anyone willing to use it. The program's producers insist that ¾ of the time on the air, in the three weekly programs, is devoted to what the villagers have to say. . .The broadcasts embrace all aspects of the rural scene, from animal husbandry and crop production to public health and prevailing market conditions. (This broadcast) has brought about a better mutual understanding between farmers and the officials who run the technical services of the countryside."

This manual is intended to introduce the techniques of successful low-cost production in rural areas of taped interviews and scripts for broadcasts. The reader is expected to be a development fieldworker who through the use of this book will be able to produce good quality tapes on topics in his or her area of activity. Written primarily as a guide for use by family planning workers, it has a bias towards information dissemination from a central authority rather than grass-roots information sharing.

Central to the production of low-cost grass-roots radio programs is the use of cassette recorders, which are now available at reasonable prices and capable of

Cassette recorder for making
grass roots radio programs

electret
microphone

excellent performance. Steps for the operation of these recorders for best results are presented.

The author offers some ideas that will help the fieldworker make interviews and scripts appealing to the listeners. He suggests how to organize discussions and news shows.

The language used in this book is sometimes difficult, and will pose problems to fieldworkers. Some of the suggestions for script writing and interviewing are relevant primarily in the English language.

Beekeeping

Beekeeping

Beekeeping — the controlled raising of bees in hives to obtain honey — has a very long history. In the industrialized countries, beekeeping is a solid income-generating venture for many people, and a hobby for many others, both in rural and semi-urban areas. The basic piece of equipment in these countries is the rectangular wooden hive with interchangeable parts, including movable frames into which commercially-made wax honeycomb foundation can be inserted, to control and accelerate honey production. **The Beekeeper's Handbook** *provides a practical summary and guide to the tools and techniques of beekeeping as it is practiced in the rich countries.*

One major problem with the practical literature on beekeeping is that most of it was written for developed countries. It is assumed that such specialty items as prepared comb foundations can be purchased (not made) by the beekeeper. These foundations, fitted into the frames, assure that there will be a "beespace" of ⁵⁄₁₆-inch between frames, which bees will leave as a passageway. Comb foundations are important, as they reduce the amount of beeswax required for building comb, enable the beekeeper to control where the comb will be constructed, and are usually made of worker-cell bases, which reduces the number of unwanted drone cells.

Several options are available to prospective beekeepers in areas where the equipment to make the comb foundations is not available. These were recommended to us by Ken's grandfather, an experienced beekeeper who began long before the time of commercially-made comb foundations. One approach uses comb cut from a natural hive, tied in place in the frames with string. The bees will extend the comb to fill each frame. The string should be cut within the first few days as soon as it is no longer necessary, or the bees will waste considerable effort in cutting it themselves. A technique for making wax honeycomb foundation is described in **Home Honey Production**. *This should be of interest in tropical countries where distance, cost and high temperatures make it difficult (or impossible) to get commercially-made wax foundation in good condition.*

Tree trunks, hanging logs, baskets, and jars are among the simpler hives traditionally used by beekeepers in the Third World. Beekeeping could play a greater role in supplementing rural incomes in these countries. A number of valuable books with a developing country perspective have appeared in the 1980s. **The Golden Insect** *and* **Small Scale Beekeeping** *are two welcome new practical manuals.* **Beekeeping in Rural Development** *and* **Apiculture in Tropical Climates** *are efforts by apiculturists and rural development agents to share knowledge about many different traditional beekeeping systems. Improved "hybrid" methods should result, some of them "intermediate" between indigenous and manufactured technologies.*

An excellent example of a promising "hybrid" is a modification of the Tanzanian top bar hive. **A Beekeeping Handbook** *provides step-by-step instructions for making a low-cost cowdung and cardboard version of this simple hive. Several other simple, low-technology hive designs are presented in* **A Beekeeping Guide**.

Apiculture in Tropical Climates, large paperback book, 208 pages, edited by Eva Crane, 1976, £15.00 or US$28.00 from International Bee Research Association, Hill House, Gerrards Cross, Bucks. SL9 0NR, England.

This large volume is the full report of the First Conference on Apiculture (beekeeping) in Tropical Climates. The twenty-six papers presented to the conference describe apiculture popularization and development programs in several Asian, African, and Latin American countries.

"The Senegalese authorities began to take an interest in beekeeping development and rationalization in 1962...A transitional stage was undertaken to get beekeepers accustomed to intermediate hives (with frameless movable combs). The Rivka hive, of wood, has rope slings so that it can be hung in trees like a traditional hive, the David hive is made of straw, bamboo and reeds...These two hives are not so very different from the traditional hives but make better management possible: examination of bees and combs; honey harvesting without destroying colony; and a real increase in production."

Other papers cover traditional bee management practices (using log hives) in Africa, honey and wax quality and processing, the various species of honeybees in the tropics and subtropics, and crop pollination.

The editor notes: "In reading the papers...several points have struck me especially. One is the immense variety of conditions in the tropical regions where beekeeping could be extended, usefully on an economic basis, and with reasonable safety on an environmental one. A second is the immense size of the tropical regions...they must represent at least 40% of the earth's total land area where beekeeping would be viable. The movable-frame hive was first developed and promulgated in 1851, and...an intensely inventive phase of beekeeping came in the fifty years that followed. I think that in the tropics beekeeping is now at the threshold of a similar phase of innovation and expansion."

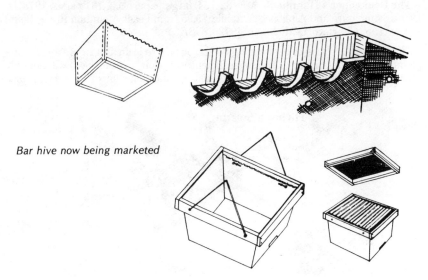

Bar hive now being marketed

Beekeeping in Rural Development, MF 32-766, large paperback book, 196 pages, £2.50 from Commonwealth Secretariat Publications, Marlborough House, London SW1Y 5HX, United Kingdom.

This collection of 20 papers reviews beekeeping practices and potential in developing countries of the Commonwealth. Though there is some overlap in content with

Apiculture in Tropical Climates (see review in this section), this book deals specifically and extensively with traditional practices and the introduction of adapted or new methods. Indigenous techniques and current development programs are discussed for 9 African nations, India, Sri Lanka, the Guianas, Belize, Panama, and the Pacific islands. Photographs of Kenyan log hives and Tanzanian pegged-bark hives are included.

An introductory article presents a valuable summary of geographical distribution of colony-forming honeybee species, honey production and trade, and traditional vs. modern equipment and methods. "Traditional hives are simple containers made of whatever material is used locally for other containers; hollowed logs, bark, woven twigs or reeds, coiled straw, baked or unbaked clay, plant stems and leaves, or fruits such as gourds. In the tropics and subtropics almost all these hives lie or hang horizontally. In the most primitive form of beekeeping the bees are killed or driven out once or twice a year when the honey and wax are taken, the colony being destroyed in the process. . . At the other end of the scale are the movable-frame hives used in modern apiaries throughout the world, which consist of a tier of accurately manufactured wooden boxes. . . Between these two extremes — each irreplaceable in its appropriate context — there are various 'intermediate' hives that provide some of the benefits of moveable-frame beekeeping with a much reduced need for precision. . . In movable-comb frameless hives, used successfully in development programs in East Africa. . . the rectangular frame fitted with foundation wax is replaced by a top-bar only, rounded on the under side and smeared with wax (or perhaps supplied with a narrow strip of wax). The top-bars must be at the correct distance apart to give the bees' natural intercomb distance (beespace) but that is the only precision measurement."

A useful overview of beekeeping's potential as a low-cost, appropriate technology for supplementing rural incomes in many parts of the developing world.

The Beekeeper's Handbook, MF 32-764, large paperback, 131 pages, 1978, by Diana Sammataro and Alphonse Avitabile, $5.95 from Peach Mountain Press, Route 2, Box 195, Charlevoix, Michigan 49720, USA.

"There are hundreds of beekeeping books, but there is an almost universal complaint that beginners' books are not sufficiently explicit. . .(this book) will not only give you good understanding of the life history and behavior of bees, but it also

Hiving a Swarm

cut away excess leaves, branches, flowers, etc.

cut main branch

spray bees with medicated syrup or water

shake swarm in front of prepared hive

tells you how to manage bees, how to control their diseases, how to remove and process honey, and many other 'how-to-do-it' aspects." Especially useful for its simple, clear discussions of bee behavior and various methods of locating, starting, feeding and maintaining hives. The authors assume that beekeepers will buy commercial hive parts, but line drawings and text may provide enough information to improvise some equipment.

A clear, comprehensive introduction to beekeeping.

A Beekeeping Handbook, MF 32-763, 65 pages, by B. Clauss and L. Tiernan, price unknown, write to Ephraim Kilon, Beekeeper, KRDA, P/Bag 7, Molepolole, Botswana.

Here is an excellent combination: a primer on honeybees and a manual for setting up and keeping colonies using simple low-cost equipment. "On a small scale the prospects of beekeeping in Botswana are good...(it) can be completely home based; the hives are made in Kanye and Molepolole or the individual can try constructing his own, from a cardboard box and cowdung." Both the simple manufactured hive and the cowdung hive (a cardboard box strengthened and protected with a plaster of cowdung and sand) are of the top-bar type, and do not require frames or commercial comb foundation. A smoker made from a tin can and a feather (for brushing bees off combs) are the key accessories. The handbook gives detailed instructions on starting a colony from a swarm or capturing an existing wild colony. Appendices discuss problems and pests, costs of hives and materials, and honey production as a source of income.

Photographs show children doing all of the handling operations. Clear, convincing; a welcome document on low-cost beekeeping methods. Highly recommended.

The Golden Insect: A Handbook on Beekeeping for Beginners, MF 32-772, book, 112 pages, by Stephen Adjare, 1984, £5.50 from ITDG.

Written as a training manual for beekeepers in Ghana, this is a basic introduction to tropical beekeeping by a man with several years of practical experience. "The aim is to put into the hands of the Ghanaian and African beekeeper information that he can readily understand and put to immediate use." Very readable, with numerous photographs.

"After the first bee sting you must run away. The bee may chase you but do not be afraid of it because it cannot sting a second time. You may catch and crush it because once it has stung it will die later. Killing it may save you as it will have no chance to go back to the hive and inform others to chase you."

Bee Population of West Africa

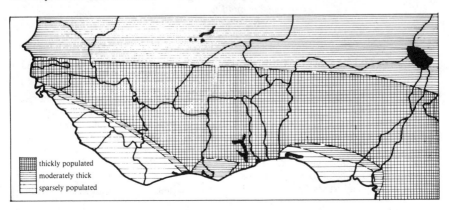

thickly populated
moderately thick
sparsely populated

Small Scale Beekeeping, Peace Corps Appropriate Technology for Development Series Manual M-17, MF 32-771, book, 211 pages, by Curtis Gentry, 1982, from Peace Corps, Information Collection and Exchange, Room 701, 806 Connecticut Avenue N.W., Washington D.C. 20525, USA.

The basics of beekeeping are covered with the author advocating an "intermediate" level of technology in this manual written for Peace Corps volunteers. More advanced techniques are also discussed. Information is offered on project planning, characteristics and needs of honeybees, hive products, diseases and pest control. Includes plans for building most of the needed equipment.

Home Honey Production, MF 32-767, book, 72 pages, 1977, by W.B. Bielby, £1.45 from EP Publishing Ltd., East Ardsley, Wakefield, West Yorkshire WF3 2JN, United Kingdom; write for addresses of local distributors in India, Philippines, Kenya, Malaysia, Singapore, and West Indies.

A "do-it-yourself" manual for the beginning beekeeper, less complete than **The Beekeeper's Handbook** (see review). This book, however, includes drawings and instructions for making hives, plaster molds for wax foundations (the patterned surface on which bees build honeycombs), a solar wax extractor, and candles. Dimensional drawings and a list of materials are included for the catenary hive, which is shaped so that bees will build their combs on a homemade foundation hanging from a single strip of wood. This design eliminates the rectangular frames and beespaces of a conventional hive.

One step in making a plaster mold for wax foundations

The ABC and XYZ of Bee Culture, MF 32-762, book, 726 pages, reprinted 1983, $13.80 from A.I. Root and Co., P.O. Box 706, Medina, Ohio 44256, USA.

This is a complete encyclopedia on the art and science of beekeeping, arranged alphabetically and well-illustrated. A.I. Root and Company are pioneers in beekeeping enterprises in the United States, and have enjoyed an international reputation since the first edition of this volume was published in 1877. They cover the innovations in the U.S. up to the present, and an extensive glossary helps the reader to understand the more technical portions of the book. Recommended to those interested in large-scale bee cultivation.

"Some cover of boards or other shade material (trees, bushes) should be provided to protect the hives from the severe heat of the summer sun. In very hot climates, sheds are built to shelter the hives. It is not uncommmon in hot climates for the combs to melt from excessive heat." (Under such circumstances the bees do their own airconditioning of the hive. They gather small droplets of water to be evaporated inside the hive, cooling it down. The beekeeper can cooperate by placing nearby a pan of water filled with pebbles, so that the bees can land without falling in and drowning — Editors.)

The Hive and the Honey Bee, book, 740 pages, Dadant & Sons, Inc., 1974, $13.60 from Dadant & Sons, Inc., Hamilton, Illinois 62341, USA.

"Twenty-two chapters cover all the aspects of beekeeping from history of beekeeping through equipment, management, anatomy and behavior, pollination, disease, honey and honey processing, honey plants, beeswax and pesticide poisoning."

Those willing to make the major investment in this expensive text will not be disappointed. The format is more readable than **The ABC and XYZ of Bee Culture**, although the content is essentially the same.

A Beekeeping Guide, Technical Bulletin No. 9, MF 32-765, booklet, 34 pages, by Harlan Attfield, illustrated by Marina Maspero, $7.25 in U.S., $7.50 international surface mail, $10.25 international air mail, from VITA.

This booklet presents construction details for beehives made of wood, tree trunks, clay jars, woven bamboo/reeds/straw, and empty kerosene tins. A honey extractor and several smokers are also included, along with guidelines for selecting sites, caring for hives, and choosing proper clothing. This booklet was originally published in Bangladesh by the Appropriate Agricultural Technology Cell.

Bellows smoker

A Homemade Honey Extractor, MF 32-768, plans, 3 pages, by Larry McWilliams, 1974, in **Countryside Journal**, out of print in 1985.

This is a simple unit made mostly of wood, which holds honeycombs in wire baskets and spins them with the use of a hand crank. This motion forces the honey out of the comb, and it flows down to a drain at the bottom of the barrel or wooden box in which the spinning unit is housed. You get clear honey with a minimum of effort. The empty wax honeycombs can be reused by the bees, who will concentrate on filling them with honey rather than having to build them again.

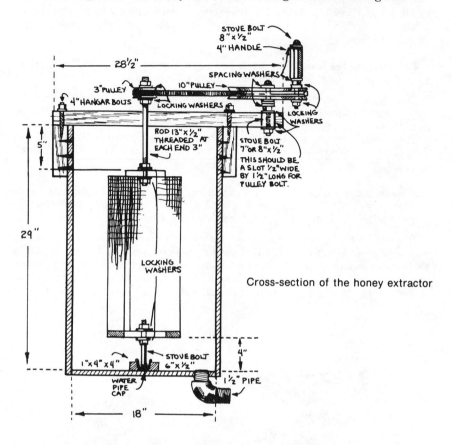

Cross-section of the honey extractor

Plans for a Complete Beekeeping System, MF 32-770, dimensional drawings, 20 pages, 1975, Garden Way Publishing, out of print in 1981.

This is a full set of plans for small-scale honey production. Included are the beehive with all components, honey extractor, smoker, gloves, and protective veil. The equipment can be easily made of locally available materials in most places.

Smoker for temporarily driving the bees out of the hive

Directory of Important World Honey Sources, book, 384 pages, by Eva Crane et. al., 1984, £27.50 or US$44.00 from International Bee Research Association, Hill House, Gerrards Cross, Bucks. SL9 0NR, United Kingdom.

A list with data on each of 467 plants that are reported to be major honey sources somewhere in the world. Special lists of drought-tolerant and salt-tolerant entries are included.

"Each entry contains information (as available) on the plant and its economic uses, its flowering period, its nectar or honeydew flow, honey and pollen production, and the chemical composition and physical properties of its honey, including flavor, aroma and granulation."

The Impact of Pest Management on Bees and Pollination, book, 207 pages, by Eva Crane and Penelope Walker, 1983, £15.00 or US$27.00 from International Bee Research Association, Hill House, Gerrards Cross, Bucks. SL9 0NR, United Kingdom.

The authors explore the pesticide killing of bees in developing countries—which crops and poisons it tends to be associated with, and how to determine whether poisoning is in fact taking place. Three bibliographies are appended: 1) pesticides and bees, 2) bee pollination of crops in the tropics and subtropics, and 3) laws and regulations to prevent bee poisoning.

Making and Using a Solar Wax Melter, MF 32-769, leaflet no. 2788, plans, 3 pages, 1975, one copy free from Publications, University of California, Division of Agricultural Sciences, 1422 Harbour Way South, Richmond, California 94804, USA.

This glass-covered box uses solar heat, collected in a black metal pan, to melt and recover beeswax from old combs and hive scrapings. Drawings showing construction details are very clear. A metal pan measuring 24 inches by 36 inches can recover wax from up to 60 hives. The size can be varied. This melter can be closed during operation, protecting the wax from robber bees.

Solar wax melter

Small Industries

Small Industries

Small industries which produce goods for local consumption play an important role in a healthy economy. Many of the tools and equipment found in other chapters of this book could be the products of or could be used in small enterprises.

This chapter includes publications on the production of pottery, leather, soap, candles, paper, shoes, glassware, rattan furniture, hand looms, natural dyes, dairy and soy products, sewing machine maintenance and other topics. Among the activities that could form the basis of innovative businesses are the recycling of plastics and the production of single-strand barbed wire.

For books on the management of small businesses, see the chapter entitled SMALL ENTERPRISES.

A Potter's Book, book, 383 pages, by Bernard Leach, 1940 (reprinted 1973), $10.00 from Transatlantic Arts, P.O. Box 6086, Albuquerque, New Mexico 87197, USA.

Leach has written what many potters consider to be the best reference book on ceramics. This is a book on "the workshop traditions which have been handed down by Koreans and Japanese from the greatest period of Chinese ceramics in the Sung Dynasty. It deals with four types of pottery: Japanese raku, English slip-ware, stoneware, and Oriental porcelain. The student of pottery learns how to adapt recipes of pigments and glazes, and designs of kilns, to local conditions. A vivid workshop picture is given of the making of a kiln-load of pots from start to finish . . ."

Includes basic recipes for glazes and descriptions of different kinds of kilns and firing methods. Many illustrations. There is a glossary of pottery terms.

Highly recommended.

Pioneer Pottery, book, 327 pages, by Michael Cardew, 1969, $6.95 from St. Martin's Press, 175 Fifth Avenue, New York, New York 10010, USA.

A book to help the potter working in a remote place find and "use intelligently the rocks, clays, ashes and oxides with which high temperature pots are made."

The author notes that when he first went to West Africa, he found "a land where the potter's art had been flourishing for centuries without the use of wheels, kilns, or glazes. When I started on a modest scale to introduce these things, and to make glazed stoneware there, I soon discovered the inadequacy of all my previous knowledge and experience. Yet at that time I had already been a potter for nearly 20 years, during which I had . . . acquired a reasonably wide and fundamental experience of the craft." Cardew filled in many of the gaps in his knowledge during his 23 years in West Africa, and has recorded much of that material here, supplemented with approximately 100 photos and drawings.

He begins with chapters on the geological formation and location of clays. Then he discusses looking for clays, preparation of clays, making pots with and without a wheel, glazes and how to make them with raw materials, and how to build and operate wood-fired kilns. Appendices cover clay testing, kiln brickmaking, and the design of simple ball mills for clay preparation.

Highly recommended for use in efforts to improve traditional techniques; also relevant to people working on improved ceramic cooking stoves.

The Kiln Book, book, 291 pages, by Frederick L. Olsen, second edition 1985, $24.95 from Chilton Book Company, 201 King of Prussia Road, Radner, Pennsylvania 19089, USA.

In this well-illustrated manual the design, construction and operation of kilns for ceramic production is presented with uncommon clarity and attention to detail. Kilns currently in use in diverse cultures are thoroughly examined, offering the student or potter a variety of options to utilize available materials or achieve special effects. The text is quite readable for the amount of technical information contained and provides interesting background and observations on kiln construction and use in South and East Asia, North America, and Europe. Plans, photographs and drawings, along with numerous tables and formulas, are abundant and well-coordinated with the text.

With this book and some masonry skills the reader should be able to construct and fire a kiln from available materials. A sample of the unique and/or noteworthy information provided here:

— the characteristics of various refractory brick types;
— basic design considerations and plans for specific kilns of the updraft, downdraft, crossdraft, and electric (no draft) type;
— instructions for building arched roofs, curved walls, and other brickwork;
— calculations for fuel requirements and burner layout for gas-fired kilns;
— comprehensive conversion tables;

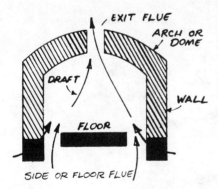

Fig. 6–1
The flow of air through an updraft kiln.

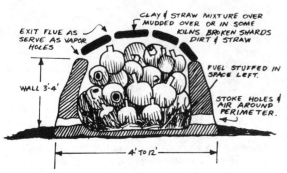

Fig. 6–2
Improved pit kiln with air-supply holes around the perimeter.

—firing schedules for woodburning kilns;
—materials lists for kilns of different configurations.

Examples are drawn from a range of small commercial pottery enterprises with facilities that range from the quite primitive to the modern. Some of these options are in use for their artistic rather than strictly practical value. Nevertheless, the broad range of options presented and the straightforward design and construction advice should make this book useful wherever optimal use of local resources for pottery production is a goal.

Kilns: Design, Construction, and Operation, MF 33-782, book, 256 pages, by Daniel Rhodes, revised 1981, $25.00 from Chilton, Schl., Library Services, Chilton Way, Radnor, Pennsylvania 19089, USA.

"This book is written from the point of view of one who has built and fired kilns, rather than that of a theorist. . .The principles and methods involved in kiln design and construction receive a thorough and authoritative treatment. The information which applies to the structure and size of any kiln, be it gas-fired, oil-fired, wood burning, or electric, updraft or downdraft, is the basis for discussion of methods and procedures required by specific kilns. Thus, all aspects—masonry construction, fuels, burners, combustion, refractory materials, heat retention, and transfer—are covered."

Thoroughly illustrated and detailed with photographs and drawings, this book is written in easily understandable English. Included are various original designs, accompanied by step-by-step instructions and diagrams, enabling the reader to construct a kiln with confidence. Firing theory and techniques, temperature measurement and control, and safety precautions are presented effectively for proper maintenance.

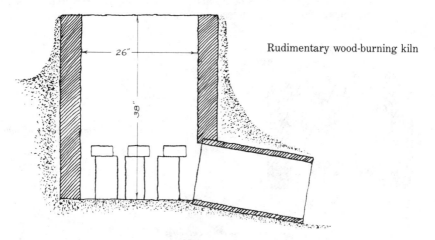

Rudimentary wood-burning kiln

Rural Tanning Techniques, FAO Development Paper #68, MF 33-785, book, 250 pages, 1974, $8.50 from FAO or UNIPUB.

This is a very detailed, thorough book on rural tanning techniques. It covers the preparation of hides and skins for tanning, various tanning methods and processes for different types of hides and skins. There is a section on setting up a rural tannery and checking for suitable water supplies, and a section on the tanning process as performed in rural India, using improved techniques from the Central Leather Research Institute in Madras. Very labor-intensive techniques are presented with extensive examples and illustrations from Kenya. Many photos are included.

This book was written for less developed areas where all of the materials and chemical compounds commonly used in tanning processes might not be readily available. Thus, there is discussion of how to obtain the ingredients and make these different compounds, such as vegetable tannins, from barks, trees, and nuts.

Tanning of Hides and Skins, MF 33-802, book, 225 pages, ILO, 1981, $14.25 from ILO.

Intended for use by tanners in developing countries, to help in the selection and use of tanning processes. A general description of the steps involved in tanning is followed by more detailed information on four different scales of production, ranging from 2 to 200 hides per day.

Home Tanning and Leather Making Guide, book, 176 pages, by A.B. Farnham, 1950, $3.00 from Fur-Fish-Game, 2878 East Main Street, Columbus, Ohio 43209, USA.

It has been said that this book "contains absolutely everything you need to know — old time techniques." In fact, that's not quite true, and **Rural Tanning Techniques** has several advantages over this book. Farnham covers the various aspects of tanning, including how to skin an animal, curing the hides, preparing hides for tanning and the actual tanning and leather-making process. Also included are descriptions and illustrations of the simple sharp tools that are needed, and other considerations such as how to check for hard water, which tanning chemicals to use, etc. The author assumes that the tanner will be able to obtain the necessary potash and other solutions, and does not cover how to make these materials locally (see **Rural Tanning Techniques**).

The last three chapters of the book deal with the marketing of hides. Much of the information is directed at rural American towns, but there is good information on the preparation of hides for shipping and marketing, as well as how to make hides into leather in this section.

This book would be useful in teaching tanning techniques, or as a reference for someone who is already familiar with the processes.

Introduction to Soap Making, VITA Technical Bulletin #3, MF 33-781, leaflet, 23 pages, by Marietta Ellis, $2.50 from VITA; also available in French.

An excellent description of the process of home or village-level soap-making. Provides recipes for a variety of soaps made of different materials and with different uses. Explains how to make your own lye from hardwood ashes, and how to measure the strength of this lye solution. (For example, the author notes that the proper strength of lye leached from wood ashes is reached when an egg will float in it.)

We think this is the best paper available on soap-making in village circumstances. Recommended.

The Preparation of Soap, MF 33-784, leaflet, 13 pages, by Ir. S.P. Bertram et. al., $1.60 from TOOL.

This leaflet includes a method for determining the concentration of lye through the use of a float; it also covers vegetable oils other than coconut oil, which are mixed with lye in different proportions. Sometimes a bit confusing.

How to Make Soap, Reprint #628, MF 33-780, 4 pages, $1.00 from Mother Earth News Reprints, P.O. Box 70, Hendersonville, North Carolina 28791, USA.

This is quite good; it tells both how to obtain lye from hardwood ashes and general soap-making hints when using purchased commercial lye. It does have a recipe that uses coconut oil instead of animal fat (mineral oil cannot be used to make soap).

Soap Pilot Plant, Case Study No. 3, MF 33-801, booklet, 32 pages, by Peter Donkor, 1981, Technology Consultancy Centre, £1.00 from ITDG.

"To many people in Ghana the Technology Consultancy Centre is synonymous with soap...The work programme has resulted in some twenty small scale soap plants in Ghana and others in Guinea Bissau, Mali, Sierra Leone, and Togo. It has also led to many of the soap plants producing their own caustic soda and has stimulated the establishment of some twenty small rural oil mills to supplement existing palm oil supplies."

"Now Peter Donkor has been persuaded to pause in his labours to put on paper the story of eight years work and to record the experience gained. It is hoped that many will be encouraged to do what he has done: to apply the knowledge gained from a university education to solve the real grass roots problems of small-scale craftsmen and industrialists in a developing country."

The case histories included also make fascinating reading.

Making Homemade Soaps and Candles, MF 33-783, book, 46 pages, by Phyllis Hobson, new edition 1984, $2.95 from Garden Way Publishing, Charlotte, Vermont 05445, USA.

Lots of recipes for making soap with animal fat and leftover kitchen grease, and for making candles out of animal fat, wax or paraffin. Includes instructions for making lye out of wood ashes (needed in soap-making).

*Cutting soap
with a wire tool*

Simple Methods of Candle Manufacture, MF 33-786, compiled by the Industrial Liaison Unit of ITDG, 19 pages, 1975, £1.65 from ITDG.

"The technology of candle making is very old and despite the introduction of mass production methods, candles can still be made by well-established methods which require only simple equipment. Much of this equipment can be made by rural craftsmen." Different waxes and wicks are discussed. Illustrations and descriptions are given for each of four methods of small-scale production.

Small Scale Papermaking, MF 33-798, book, 325 pages, by A.W. Western, 1979, £26.00 from ITDG.

This is a description and evaluation of Indian small-scale industrial paper mills of 5 to 30 tons per day capacity. The author presents considerable evidence to support the claim that such mills are more economically attractive for developing countries than the larger-scale mills usually established with imported equipment. In particular, the smaller Indian mills can be located next to sources of supply and cost ⅔ less per unit capacity for the capital equipment. Such mills could mean substantial savings in imported paper and equipment costs for many developing countries, while providing greater employment and learning opportunities for local people.

Case studies with cost details are provided for plants ranging from 1-30 tons per day. Average return on investment for these plants was 27%.

Small Scale Manufacture of Footwear, MF 33-797, International Labour Organization, 204 pages, 1982, $11.40 from ILO.

This ILO book provides ". . .technical and economic details on alternative footwear manufacture technologies used in scales of production ranging from 8 pairs per day to 1,000 pairs per day." The document is intended to assist entrepreneurs who wish to either make their equipment locally or minimize the amount of imported equipment necessary. The various operations in the production of footwear of various types are described, along with equipment alternatives. Few drawings are included, and there is much technical vocabulary (explained in the glossary); consequently, this may be difficult reading for the shoemaker who is not familiar with these terms and procedures.

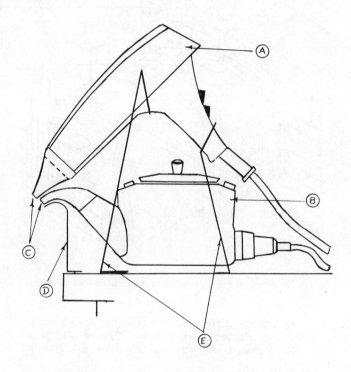

A simply made hot treeing unit for small volume production

A. Domestic electric hair dryer stapled to bench on both sides.

B. Domestic electric kettle with handle removed

C. Lengths of copper or steel tube flattened into slits at one end to form fish tails for dryer outlet and kettle spout.

D. Short metal strip bent to remove drips.

E. Two lengths of bent wires for supporting dryer.

Note: It is very dangerous to let hair dryers get wet.

Glassware Manufacture for Developing Countries, MF 33-792, book, 45 pages, by Garry Whitby, 1983, £2.50 from ITDG.

Here is good introduction to the materials, techniques, fuels and equipment used in small-scale production of glass jars, bottles and other containers. Some existing glass factories produce as little as 250 kg/day, using a few pieces of equipment and a handful of employees. Many photos from factories in Asia are included. Sample calculations for investment and production costs for a 5 tons/day unit are presented.

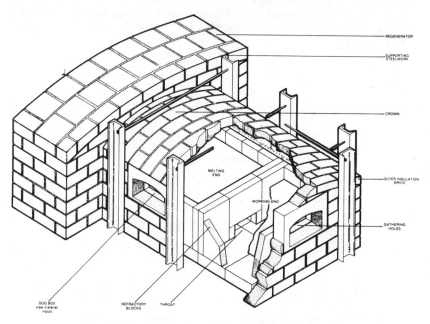

A typical oil or gas fired continuous furnace (not to scale).

Barbs, Prongs, Points, Prickers, & Stickers: A Complete Illustrated Catalogue of Antique Barbed Wire, MF 33-790, book, 418 pages, by Robert Clifton, 1970, $12.95 from University of Oklahoma Press, Norman, Oklahoma 73019, USA.

In many places there is a need for low-cost fencing (e.g. to protect reforestation areas and control grazing), but wood and stone are not readily available, and living hedges cannot be easily grown. Hundreds of different designs of barbed wire were originally developed to fit the same need in the western United States. Single strand barbed wire could be produced in developing countries at a cost far lower than that of the double strand barbed wire currently used in these countries.

In industrialized countries, the cost of barbed wire is only a very small part of the cost of erecting a fence, and with high labor costs, maintenance must be avoided. Two strand barbed wire is somewhat more durable than single strand wire, and

Dodge–Washburn's Barb

Two-strand wire with four-point wire barb. Barb is double wrapped around one strand. Patented [252746] January 24, 1882, by Thomas H. Dodge and Charles G. Washburn of Worcester, Mass.

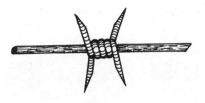

147 Merrill's Brads
Single-strand wire with four-point wire barb. Body of barb is tightly coiled to hold barb in position. Patented [155538] September 29, 1874, by Luther and John C. Merrill of Turkey River Station, Iowa.

74 Glidden's Barb, One-strand Variation
Single-strand wire with two-point wire barb. Variation of patent 157124.

73 Glidden's Coils, Flattened-strand Variation
Flattened single-wire strand with two-point wire barb. Variation of reissue patent 6913.

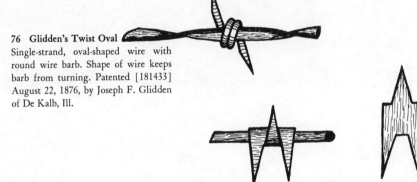

76 Glidden's Twist Oval
Single-strand, oval-shaped wire with round wire barb. Shape of wire keeps barb from turning. Patented [181433] August 22, 1876, by Joseph F. Glidden of De Kalb, Ill.

Knickerbocker's Barb   213
three-point sheet metal barb. Patented

145
Glidden's Coils, One-strand Military Concertina Variation
One-strand high tensile strength wire with four-point wire barbs. Variation of patent reissue 6914.

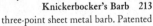

thus has become the standard form of barbed wire produced all over the world. However, in developing countries, the cost of barbed wire is a much larger part of the cost of erecting a fence. In these places, a fence made with single strand barbed wire would be much cheaper, but would require a small amount of additional long-term maintenance. It should be possible to manufacture single strand barbed wire at a cost of 50-60% of the cost (per linear foot) of double strand wire. Production of single strand barbed wire (from plain wire) could be done on a cottage industry basis, using simple tools.

This volume shows hundreds of different designs, including more than 150 types of single strand barbed wire.

Manual on the Production of Rattan Furniture, MF 33-794, UNIDO, 1983, 108 pages, publication no. ID/299 from UNIDO.

A good look at rattan furniture production using small industry techniques. The equipment shown includes a variety of machines and locally-made devices for different production steps. The large number of photos and drawings of the production process are supplemented by drawings of furniture designs.

Methods of binding rattan joints

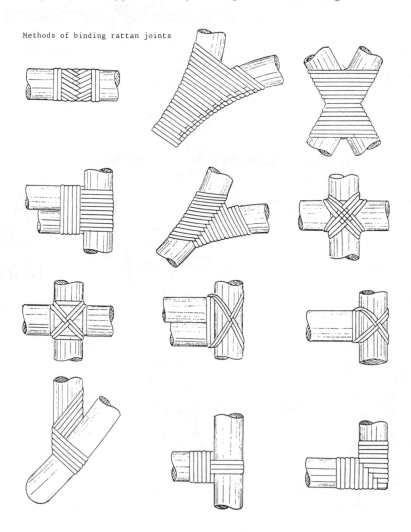

Basic Sewing Machine Repair, MF 33-774, book, 63 pages, by K. Kiri and S. Kalmakoff, March 1979, K4.00 PNG Kina in South Pacific region, K8.00 PNG Kina to the rest of the world, from South Pacific Appropriate Technology Foundation, P.O. Box 6937, Boroko, Papua New Guinea.

A well-illustrated book on the proper adjustment and care of several common varieties of sewing machines. Oiling the machine, adjusting and fixing the stitch regulator, replacing broken springs, and adjusting needle timing are among the topics presented. A trouble-shooting chart helps in identifying the likely source of specific problems. Very simple language is used along with the 200 drawings.

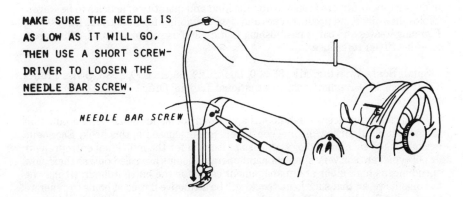

MAKE SURE THE NEEDLE IS AS LOW AS IT WILL GO, THEN USE A SHORT SCREW-DRIVER TO LOOSEN THE NEEDLE BAR SCREW.

NEEDLE BAR SCREW

Handloom Construction: A Practical Guide for the Non-Expert, MF 33-778, looseleaf manual, 163 pages, by Joan Koster, 1979, $9.75 in U.S., $10.50 international surface mail, $14.50 international surface mail, from VITA.

"With inexpensive machine-made cloth increasingly available almost everywhere, it seems likely that fewer and fewer people will be interested in producing their own cloth...Yet weaving can be done in one's spare time using free or inexpensive fibers available locally, and simple, efficient looms can be built from local materials

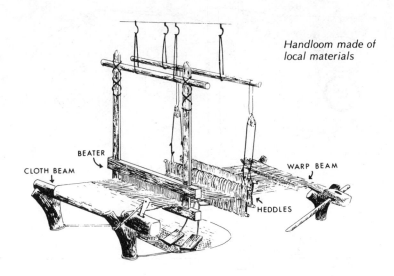

Handloom made of local materials

BEATER

CLOTH BEAM

WARP BEAM

HEDDLES

at little cost. Therefore, as long as the loom and fibers cost little, the finished cloth requires an investment in time rather than money. . . Because people all over the world have been weaving since the very earliest times, there are many styles and varieties of looms. This is a book about building and using some of these. Three types of looms, including two variations of a foot-powered loom, are presented here. The book gives 1) detailed directions for building each kind of loom, 2) the advantages and disadvantages of each, and 3) instructions for weaving."

Large, clear line drawings show materials, construction sequences, and weaving techniques for frame looms, pit and freestanding footpowered looms, and the Inkle loom (a small loom for rapid weaving of strong strips of cloth). All the looms are made from low-cost, commonly available materials. The choice of loom will depend upon the types of fibers available and the kind and quantity of articles to be woven. Tables show fiber and product types and their suitability for the various loom styles. Planning weaves and patterns, finishing fabrics, and use of colors are also discussed. A well-written reference.

Small Scale Weaving, MF 33-800, book, 129 pages, ILO, 1983, Swiss Francs 17.50 from ILO Publications, International Labour Office, CH-1211 Geneva 22, Switzerland.

The different choices of handlooms and power looms for small-scale production of low-cost cloth for low-income consumers are discussed in this book. Economic evaluations of each technology are also presented for the individual entrepreneur or policymaker. The very simplest hand-operated looms are ruled out, as their slow speed means high labor and management costs for the entrepreneur. (It may be the case, however, that such looms could still be attractive if used at home to generate income for families during spare hours.)

This book identifies the important technical and related productivity differences

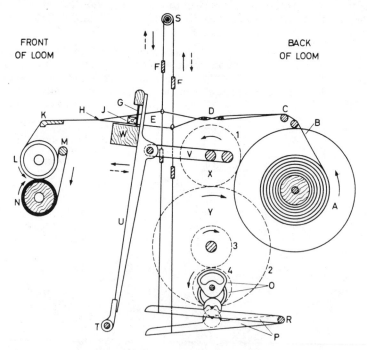

Sectional diagram of a power-loom for the weaving of plain cloth

between looms, and should prove of value to anyone involved or interested in weaving projects.

"When the weft is inserted by hand-thrown shuttle in the weaving of cotton-type fabrics of nominally 1 metre width, picking speeds are most unlikely to exceed 20 picks/min and, more usually, are appreciably less than this. Weaving similar cloths on looms with a fly-shuttle. . .could enable the weaver, if sufficiently skilled, to operate at speeds of up to 40 picks/min. . . If the take-up and let-off are mechanically linked to the primary motions, the (entire) loom can be foot-pedal operated. These features, if incorporated in a loom of improved structure and with good bearings, enable the loom to be operated at speeds which are claimed to be in excess of 80 picks/min."

Vegetable Dyeing: 151 Color Recipes for Dyeing Yarns and Fabrics with Natural Materials, MF 33-787, book, 146 pages, by Alma Leach, 1970, out of print in 1985.

This book is about dyes from vegetable and other natural sources (such as clay and insects). A large number of the dyes are from tropical and subtropical plants in addition to temperate zone plants. The simple recipes and techniques can be used by a beginner. Sources for dyeing equipment and materials are listed. General principles of dyeing are covered, along with specific instructions for particular dyes.

The author notes that different readers will produce slightly different shades when following the same recipe, due to water composition, timing, temperature and other factors. "Time of year when the dyestuff is collected perhaps most influences the final color. The amount of moisture during a season, the number of daylight hours, and the type of soil where the plant grows are also factors that will affect its dye properties. Generally, parts of the plant above ground need a lot of sunshine to produce strong dyes. Barks may be an exception."

A dye substance information chart lists the common name (but not the Latin name) of each plant, the part of the plant required, the time of year for harvesting (in northern hemisphere temperate zones), and methods of preservation. A color information chart lists the proper cloth to use, the color, the proper mordant (a chemical added to prevent fading), and the relative performance of the dye. There is a bibliography and an index.

Natural Plant Dyeing, MF 33-795, 64 pages, by Brooklyn Botanic Gardens, 1973, $3.05 postpaid from Brooklyn Botanic Gardens, 1000 Washington Avenue, Brooklyn, New York 11225, USA.

A collection of short articles on natural dyeing in different parts of the world. Most directly useful are the color pages showing a simple test for color fastness, and the color effects of using different mordants with a single plant dyestuff. The discussion of the chemistry of dyeing provides some helpful insights, and the material on classroom dyeing will be useful for science classes.

Dye Plants and Dyeing, MF 33-791, 100 pages, by Brooklyn Botanic Gardens, 1964, $3.05 postpaid from Brooklyn Botanic Gardens, 1000 Washington Avenue, Brooklyn, New York 11225, USA.

Here are a general introduction, 35 recipes, and details on plants used for dyeing in 20 countries around the world.

Tintes Naturales, book, 90 pages, by Hugo Zumbuhl, 1984, $8.00 from Kamaq Maki, Apartado 609, Huancayo, Peru; or $12.00 from SKAT.

Written in Spanish, this well-illustrated natural wool dyeing manual is a remarkable attempt to better communicate with the campesinos of the Peruvian Andes. Samples are included of chemicals used to make the plant dyes more permanent; there are also drawings and real samples of native plants and insects along with small tufts of the dyed wool that give a clear indication of the colors achieved. The quantity of plant material and the recommended method of dyeing are given for each plant/color combination. Wool preparation before dyeing is also discussed.

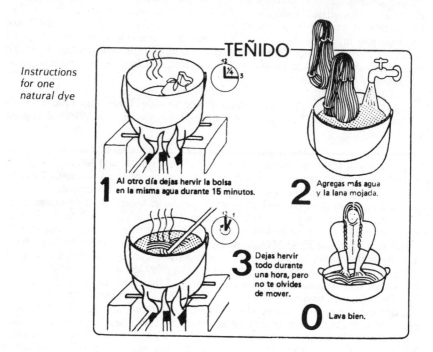

Instructions for one natural dye

TEÑIDO

1 Al otro día dejas hervir la bolsa en la misma agua durante 15 minutos.

2 Agregas más agua y la lana mojada.

3 Dejas hervir todo durante una hora, pero no te olvides de mover.

0 Lava bien.

Yay, Soybeans!, MF 33-789, pamphlet, 36 pages, The Farm, 1976, out of print in 1985.

Soybeans are converted into a wide array of nutritious and exotic foods in the recipes of this stimulating booklet: soymilk, soycheese, soy ice cream, soy yogurt, and many others. Recipes and techniques are detailed, delicious, and simple. The information comes straight from the mouths and stomachs of The Farm, a rural community of young American vegetarians living on a solid rice and beans diet in Tennessee.

The Book of Tempeh, MF 33-775, book, 160 pages, by William Shurtleff and Akiko Aoyagi, 1979, $6.95 from WEA.

Tempeh is a high-protein Indonesian food made from soybeans through a 24-48 hour fermentation process. The bean patties formed are fried until crisp and golden brown; the flavor and texture has been compared to fried chicken and fish. Soy tempeh contains approximately 19.5% protein (this compares to beef at 20% and eggs at 13%). Tempeh is also the "world's richest known vegetarian source of vitamin B12, one of the ingredients most often lacking in vegetarian diets." This book contains illustrated instructions for making tempeh and tempeh starter, including adaptations to fit U.S. conditions (e.g. use of an electric light bulb inside a styrofoam cooler for an incubator). Also described are the techniques used in an Indonesian tempeh shop. Only simple kitchen equipment, soybeans, and some home-made starter are needed. 130 recipes.

Full Fat Soy Flour by a Simple Process for Villagers, MF 33-777, leaflet, 11 pages, 1975, free (request pub. USDA#225) from Agricultural Research Service, U.S. Dept. of Agriculture, Northern Regional Research Center, Peoria, Illinois 61604, USA.

This useful leaflet presents all the needed information for converting raw soybeans into flour with a high nutritional value.

"One part of this research was to find a simple hand process for villagers where skilled labor, electric power, and steam cannot be had. A process that uses only simple equipment was developed. With this equipment six men can make 136 kg. (300 lbs.) of soy flour in an 8-hour day. Operation can be changed from hand to mechanical by wind, water, animal, or other available power source. A production of 136 kg. per day will supply half the daily need for protein of more than 1,600 adults."

The equipment required appears to be available in a village setting, or easily manufactured locally, such as a hand grain winnower and a hand grinder (usually commercially available). This process could be used in many circumstances.

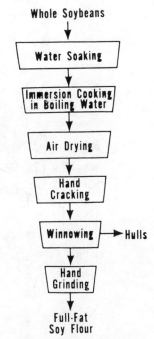

The Backyard Dairy Book, MF 33-773, 128 pages, by Street and Singer, 1975, £2.95 from Prism Press, Stable Court, Chalmington, Dorchester, Dorset DT2 0HB, United Kingdom.

This book was written to encourage small-scale home dairy production in England, using goats and cows. Briefly looks at breeds, feed and housing requirements, and milking. Most of the book is on home production of dairy products from milk: cream, butter, cheese and yogurt.

The Village Texturizer, MF 33-788, booklet, 76 pages, Meals for Millions Foundation, 1977, $6.25 in U.S., $6.50 international surface mail, $8.50 international air mail, from VITA.

This hand-operated device was adapted from a Korean design used by street vendors to make snacks from sweet potato pellets. This modified version created texturized food products from high-protein, low-fat flours (from legumes such as soy, peanut, or chickpea), seeds, and dried vegetables. The products do not spoil quickly and are easily digested, especially by children. A variety of foods with different protein and calorie levels and suitable flavoring can be produced.

There are good construction drawings and detailed sections on operational costs and nutritional composition of raw materials and end products.

"The machine described in this manual is an excellent example of an intermediate technology: construction costs are low (it can be built with pieces of metal and old auto parts for roughly $50); operation is labor-intensive; it requires no special knowledge (only experience) to operate and a minimum of maintenance; it can produce a wide variety of products which are both highly nutritious and tasty; and it can be used in a variety of situations—from home to small business."

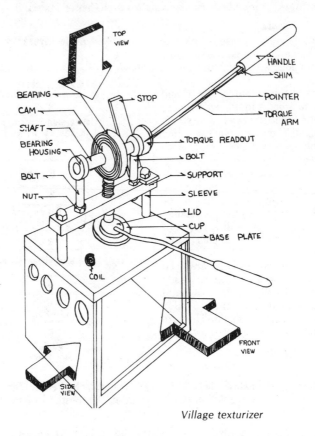

Village texturizer

Community Canning Centers: A Project Profile in Community Economic Development, MF 33-803, report, 54 pages, by Stephen Klein, 1977, $2.50 from Center for Community Economic Development, Mezzanine Level, 1320 19th Street N.W., Washington D.C. 20036, USA.

Small-scale community canning enterprises, many of them owned on a cooperative basis, have existed in the United States for most of this century. Canning (the preserving of foods in tightly sealed tins or jars) has long been a part of rural self-reliance, as farm families saved their own harvest-time surplus for consumption through the rest of the year. Relatively low-cost community-scale canning technology was developed in the 1930s, and thousands of government-subsidized canning centers were established in the effort to increase food supplies during World War II.

This report is a comparative survey of 16 community canning centers, most of which are cooperatively owned, producing from 7,000 to 12,000 quarts of food per year. The centers use glass jars and/or tin cans, and most of the equipment is hand-operated. Users are involved in the canning process, and locally-grown produce is processed for local consumption.

Whether or not a community canning center is a viable proposition in the U.S. depends on local conditions and initiative, as well as cost and availability of different types of equipment. Key choices for any center include production for personal use or for commercial sales, use of tins or jars, and self-service or staff-service food processing. The author discusses the different combinations of these variables and finds a surprising variety of strategies. "The combination (jars, self-service processing, commercial sale) occurs in upper New England at the Gardens for All Community Canning Center in Shelburne, Vermont. Small farmers utilized a noncommercial, self-service canning center to process products for sale at their roadside stands, taking advantage of the center to can specialty items. Through direct marketing at their stands, they were able to charge a price that was sufficient to cover costs and still leave a fair profit."

Charts of projected monetary costs and savings for hypothetical canning centers are included, along with appendices on regulatory and technical considerations, and how to calculate project costs (at 1977 prices).

Most community canning centers are unable to cover their investment and overhead costs with proceeds from processing and sales. Government and other agencies often provide subsidies, and membership fees are charged. "In reviewing the costs and benefits of community canning we find ourselves asking why it is that towns, counties, states, and various funding agencies continue to build and support community canneries in increasing numbers despite the need for subsidization . . . (but) those whose support sustains community canning centers understand that in community economics, profits involve more than a direct dollar inflow. The benefits of community interaction, increased self-reliance, better quality food, and skill-building, plus monetary savings for families and added stability for area growers, are vital enough social reasons to far outweigh the costs of the initial investment and the ongoing subsidization."

Due to the costs of processing equipment and glass or tin containers for the food, community canning centers are not likely to be feasible and appropriate in the poorest countries.

Small-Scale Gold Mining, MF 33-796, book, 51 pages, by E.H. Dahlberg, 1984, £4.95 from ITDG.

With the great increase in the price of gold in recent decades, the economic viability of small-scale mining has greatly improved. This volume discusses placer mining with a sluice box in stream beds, a technique that can be carried out by a single worker with a minimum of equipment. Methods for systematically exploring an area are described. It is assumed that these activities will take place in a location in which gold mining historically was practiced.

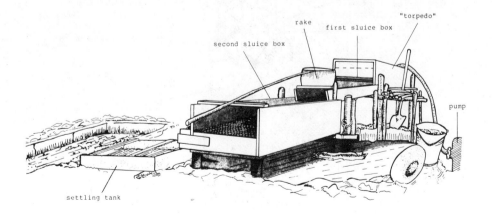

Fig. 9 Arrangement of sluicebox as used by GMD

Work from Wastes: Recycling Wastes to Create Employment, MF 33-804, book, 396 pages, by John Vogler, Oxfam/Intermediate Technology Publications, Ltd., 1981, £11.95 from ITDG.

This book contains "details of appropriate technologies being employed all over the world to recycle paper, iron and steel, tin, non-ferrous metals, plastics, textiles, rubber, minerals, chemicals, oil, and human and household wastes. All these materials are suitable for labour-intensive processing, often requiring little capital and providing a cash income plus other environmental and community benefits." Also describes how to set up a small waste recycling business. No coverage of organic wastes, or the simple clever "reuse" of materials commonly found in developing countries.

Small Scale Recycling of Plastics, MF 33-799, book, 94 pages, by Jon Vogler, 1984, £10.00 from ITDG.

Jon Vogler presents a good introduction to the different plastics commonly used and the basic economic evaluation necessary to determine which materials can be profitably recycled. He then provides advice as to which materials are likely to be economically handled, testing procedures to help identify each type of plastic, and processing equipment to transform the material into a form acceptable to the manufacturers of plastic goods. He also describes the chemistry of plastics.

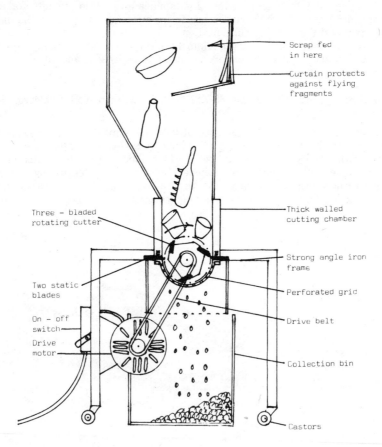

FIGURE 16:   Granulator - (horizontal axis).

Periodicals

Periodicals

Magazines, journals, and newsletters are important tools for documenting appropriate technology developments and discussing other issues related to community self-reliance. Some of these items are published using few sophisticated processes or equipment, and as such are interesting attempts to disseminate information regionally at low cost. Other periodicals that focus on topics within one of the chapter divisions can be found in the relevant chapters.

Appropriate Technology, journal, 4 issues per year, £10.00 per year to developed countries, £8.00 per year to less developed countries, from ITDG.

If you are working in a developing country and can afford only one journal, this is the one to get. The journal of the Intermediate Technology Development Group is dedicated to communication among people involved in developing and disseminating appropriate technologies in developing countries. Problems, ideas, and solutions are shared. Readers are encouraged to contribute. Each issue includes news, notes, and book reviews. There are typically thirteen 2-page articles on a wide range of subjects in each issue. Highly recommended.

TRANET (Transnational Network for Appropriate/Alternative Technologies), MF 34-808, newsletter, $15.00 for four issues (one year), from TRANET, P.O. Box 567, Rangeley, Maine 04970, USA.

The TRANET newsletter is a quarterly directory which gives descriptions of A.T. centers around the world, along with the activities of many related groups and individuals active in specific topic areas such as low-cost housing and bicycle transportation. Some literature is reviewed. **TRANET** is intended to aid the flow of information within the developing network of appropriate technology groups. TRANET has 25 board members from A.T. groups on 5 continents, and is developing other networking support activities in addition to the newsletter. Send a donation or trade for a sample newsletter.

New Internationalist, MF 34-801, magazine, monthly, 30 pages average length, about US$22.00 per year depending on location; for Australia and Papua New Guinea: P.O. Box 82, Fitzroy 3065, Victoria; for New Zealand: P.O. Box 1905, Christchurch; for U.S. and Canada: 113 Atlantic Avenue, Brooklyn, New York 11201; for U.K. and rest of the world: Montagu House, High Street, Huntingdon, PE18 6EP, Cambridgeshire, United Kingdom.

"The New Internationalist exists to report on the issue of world poverty; to focus attention on the unjust relationship between rich and poor worlds; to debate and campaign for the radical changes necessary within and between nations if the basic needs of all are to be met; and to bring to life the people, the ideas and the action in the fight for world development." Each issue discusses a particular topic or theme (e.g. "The Struggle for Control of Third World Farming," "The Rich World's Poor," "Women and World Development"). Articles relate individual human poverty and oppression to exploitative national and international structures.

A good educational resource with a liberal perspective on a broad range of development topics. Includes a section of book reviews.

ADAB News, MF 34-790, development journal, bimonthly, 48 pages average length, annual subscription TK 35 in Bangladesh, $5.00 in other countries ($10.00 airmail), from ADAB, 46A, Road 6A, Dhanmondi, Dacca-9, Bangladesh.

Information for and about appropriate agricultural development in Bangladesh, of interest throughout the humid tropics. Issues contain articles and case studies within one general topic area, such as rural women's organizations, livestock, integrated pest management, or grain storage. There are also articles on specific pests or crops. Some issues are devoted entirely to one subject, offering opposing viewpoints.

Ap-Tech Newsletter, MF 34-792, edited by M.M. Hoda, published 6 times a year, average length 14 pages, subscriptions $3.00 per year plus postage from ATDA, Post Box 311, Gandhi Bhawan, Lucknow 226 001, India.

This is a collection of "concepts, views, news, research and development reports, practices, and techniques related to appropriate technology," published by the Indian partner and affiliate of ITDG, the Appropriate Technology Development Association. Most items are short summaries of Indian training courses and projects, although some articles deal with developments in other countries. Also includes a section of annotated book reviews.

Reading Rural Development Communications Bulletin, MF 34-805, newsletter, 36 pages average length, published 3 times yearly, £5.00 per four issues, available from University of Reading Agricultural Extension and Rural Development Centre, London Road, Reading RG1 5AQ, United Kingdom.

Not a technical bulletin, this magazine contains in-depth critical essays and case studies exploring the philosophy and politics of Third World rural development and appropriate technology. Up to half of the bulletin is devoted to long and thoughtful book reviews, including information to help the more isolated reader obtain hard-to-find volumes.

Impact, magazine, 36-48 pages average length, approximately $6.00 per year to subscribers in Asia; $10.00 in Australia, PNG, New Zealand; $12.00 in Africa and Latin America; $15.00 in North America and Europe. For nearest distribution outlet write IMPACT, P.O. Box 2950, Manila, Philippines.

Subtitled "a monthly Asian magazine for human development," **Impact** presents a combination of Asian current events and feature articles on the lot of Asia's rural and urban poor. With correspondents and outlets in many of the countries in the region, this publication may reach more development workers at the grass-roots level in Asia than any other of its kind.

An effective link among voluntary and humanitarian organizations, available at low cost. Highly recommended.

Tarik, MF 34-807, small magazine, published once or twice a year, average length about 30 pages, write to Publications Unit, Project Dian Desa, P.O. Box 19, Bulaksumur, Yogyakarta, Indonesia.

A journal aimed at documenting and sharing information on appropriate technologies being developed by Indonesian community development groups. Each of the first two issues has described a technique in enough detail for readers to attempt construction themselves. (These include building a Lorena stove and fabricating 9-cubic-meter ferrocement and bamboo-cement water storage tanks for use with rooftop catchments.) Photos and drawings are mostly self-explanatory for those unfamiliar with Indonesian or Malay languages.

R.E.D., MF 34-803, bimonthly newsletter published in English, French and Spanish, 12 pages average length, yearly subscriptions $3.00 in Guatemala; $4.00 in Central America, Panama and North America; $4.50 in South America; $6.50 in Europe, Africa, Asia, Australia, Oceania; and $7.00 in the Philippines and Hong Kong; from CEMAT/R.E.D., Apartado Postal 1160, Guatemala City, Guatemala, Central America.

Reports compiled by the Mesoamerican Center for Studies of Appropriate Technology (CEMAT) on experiments in agriculture/nutrition, non-conventional sources of energy, rural health, alternative construction, and non-formal education. "The newsletter's main function is to be informative and a link between groups that are working in rural development with appropriate technologies in the Mesoamerican region...For the preparation of the newsletter we are mainly interested in experiences of campesino groups that have experimented directly with an appropriate technology, that has solved some problem in the community and has generated a certain amount of approval by the groups that have known of its existence. We would like to take advantage of this opportunity to invite appropriate technology groups of the Mesoamerican region to share with us their experiences and accomplishments."

Articles are short and non-technical.

Asian Action: Newsletter of the Asian Cultural Forum on Development, bimonthly, 20 pages average length, $15.00 per year in developed countries, $9.00 per year in undeveloped countries, from ACFOD, 232/9 Nares Road, Bangkok 10501, Thailand.

"**Asian Action**...attempts to reflect Asian initiatives in development; to provide information on regional trends and to pin-point the effects...of current development strategies being followed by many governments and institutions." The newsletter reports on the plight of Asia's rural poor, and discusses the kinds of helping initiatives that might be undertaken by non-governmental organizations (NGOs). Also included are reports of ACFOD's conferences, seminars, and training sessions for development workers aimed at building cooperation among such organizations in the region.

The International Foundation for Development Alternatives (IFDA) Dossier, MF 34-795, journal, published bimonthly, $30.00 (15.00 to developing countries), available from IFDA Secretariat, 2, Place du Marche, CH-1260 Nyon, Switzerland.

This publication presents papers in French or English with abstracts in both languages, on a wide variety of general subjects. Some titles from the Jan.—Feb. 1980 issue: "Third World Commodity Policy at the Crossroads: Some Fundamental Issues," "Another Development for Japan." Language is scholarly, and may be difficult for non-native speakers of French or English.

The Ecologist, MF 34-794, magazine, six to ten issues per year, average length about 60 pages, £2.00 per issue, subscriptions from Maria Parsons, Managing Editor, Worthyvale Manor Farm, Camelford, Wadebridge, Cornwall, United Kingdom.

Subtitled "journal of the post-industrial age," this magazine presents broadranging articles on humankind's changing place in the environment. Contributions are from scholars, technologists, scientists, and authors from around the world. The contents reflect a belief that an understanding of worldwide ecological problems should affect choices made by individuals.

Includes editorials, letters, and a section of book reviews.

Mazingira, bimonthly journal, published in English, French and Spanish, about 100 pages average length, subscriptions $25.00 or £15.00 per year ($15.00 per year for individuals in Africa, Asia and Latin America), from Tycooly International Publishing Ltd., 6 Crofton Terrace, Dun Laoghaire, Co. Dublin, Ireland.

Mazingira, which means "environment" in Swahili, is a forum on environmental issues in development, started with the support of the United Nations Environment Programme. The focus is on problems in the Third World, but the context is global; the linkage of all development issues to the planet's carrying capacity is a central theme. Articles by contributors from all over the world are some of the most thoughtful in all the development literature related to appropriate technology. Each issue contains a short section surveying potentially important applications of appropriate technologies.

Ecodevelopment News, journal published biannually in English and French, average length about 130 pages, subscriptions 100 FF Europe, 50 FF less developed countries, 150 FF other countries, from C.I.R.E.D., 54, Boulevard Raspail, Room 309, 75270 Paris CEDEX 06, France.

Like **Mazingira**, this was started with the support of the United Nations Environment Programme. Articles discuss the emerging concept of ecodevelopment and examine village development efforts in light of the concept. An "Ecodevelopment at Work" section in each issue reviews projects and literature on promising tools and techniques for environmentally sound development. Also included are brief reports of international conferences and seminars on the topic.

A good networking tool; may be difficult reading for non-native speakers of English or French.

RAIN Magazine, MF 34-804, 6 issues a year for $15.00, institutional rate $25.00, living lightly rate $9.50, from RAIN, 3116 North Williams Avenue, Portland, Oregon 97227, USA.

This journal serves to encourage communications among groups in the Pacific Northwest of the United States. Includes news and notes on groups, books, and other publications along with a few articles on subjects of broader American interest. The staff is committed to unearthing the best, serious documentation supporting arguments for environmentally-sound, decentralized, human-scale technology in the U.S. Not directly relevant to developing countries. The magazine has a "living lightly" subscription rate for people with low incomes.

CoEvolution Quarterly, MF 34-793, journal, 4 issues per year, $14.00 ($16.00 overseas), from CoEvolution Quarterly, P.O. Box 428, Sausalito, California 94966, USA.

Launched to cover much of the same material as **The Whole Earth Catalog** (see review), this journal includes a section on soft technology and a wide variety of articles. It was recently merged with a computer software magazine published by the same people.

Undercurrents Magazine, 10 issues per year, subscriptions £10.00 for individuals, £12.00 for institutions, overseas by surface mail, from Undercurrents Subscriptions, 27 Clerkenwell Close, London EC1R 0AT, England.

A journal of people's technology in the United Kingdom, full of news notes on groups and events, and information on small-scale "alternative" technology that fits conditions in that country. They are continually pointing out how intermediate technology can be taken over by the powerful members of the community unless the poorer members are somehow organized politically. While most of the subject matter is not of direct interest to people in developing countries, this magazine should prove to be of considerable interest to alternative technologists within other developed countries. A delightful, humorous, irreverent style.

The Mother Earth News, MF 34-800, magazine, 6 issues per year, $18.00 per year in U.S., $21.00 all foreign subscriptions, article reprints available $1.00 each, from The Mother Earth News, P.O. Box 70, Hendersonville, North Carolina 28701, USA.

This magazine has articles on farming, organic gardening, alternative sources of energy, and a variety of simple techniques and equipment. There are many ideas and personal stories by people who have designed, built, and used a variety of equipment and techniques in North American rural settings; but the articles are rarely in depth and tend to overlook the problems encountered.

The limitations (as we see them) of this magazine for readers in developing countries are the following: 1) the text is often not in standard English, 2) few thorough detailed plans are presented — most articles are short idea pieces and brief descriptions, 3) the vast amount of other information (such as classified ads and specifically U.S.-oriented articles) tends to overwhelm the one or two items of relevance to developing countries that appear in each issue.

Home Farm, magazine, bimonthly, average length 68 pages, from Broad Leys Publishing Company, Widdington, Saffron Walden, Essex CB11 3SP, United Kingdom.

A journal of the "back-to-the-land" movement in England, aimed at an audience interested in small-scale farming and reducing dependency on government institutions. Articles are mostly of the how-to-do-it variety: poultry keeping, beginning beekeeping, cutting and laying hedges, and so forth. There are active reader correspondence and classified advertising sections. This magazine is relevant mainly in the U.K. and other industrial nations.

ADDITIONAL REFERENCES FOR PERIODICALS

World Neighbors Newsletter; see GENERAL REFERENCE.

Disaster Preparedness
and Relief

Disaster Preparedness and Relief

Natural and human-caused disasters continue to be regular events in developing countries. Some of the original damage is avoidable; several of the items included here discuss low-cost ways to minimize damage to houses from earthquakes and hurricanes, for example. Some of the damage comes after the initial disaster, as water supplies are polluted and perhaps food supplies are interrupted. The relief efforts themselves can cause additional damage. This may happen if the basic food supply was not affected by the original disaster, and a sudden inflow of donated food distorts the agricultural produce markets. This kind of common event means a second economic disaster for the farmers.

The items reviewed here provide experienced management guidelines for maximizing the positive effects of disaster relief operations while minimizing the negative side effects. Public health measures, control of medical supplies, and housing reconstruction are major topic areas.

Shelter After Disaster, MF 35-833, book, 127 pages, by Ian Davis, 1978, £5.50 from Oxford Polytechnic Press, Headington, Oxford OX3 0BP, England.

This fascinating book points out many of the myths about disaster relief that continue to shape aid responses around the world. The author presents the elements of successful shelter rebuilding programs in the light of historical experience over the past 300 years.

Worldwide the frequency and death tolls of disasters are rising, reflecting the increasing vulnerability of the poor primarily in the rapidly growing urban centers of the Third World. This is mostly because they are living in precarious circumstances on hillsides and waterfronts, where damage is likely to be greatest. The author notes that while there is an enormous quantity of post-disaster relief shelter design ideas, most of them are conceived without an understanding of the realities of post-disaster shelter needs. "The vast majority of these concepts mercifully have never left the drawing board or filing cabinet, but this seems no deterrent to the ingenuity and persistence of designers."

Following disasters around the world, local people using their own ingenuity and initiative have accomplished more than 80% of the reconstruction themselves, even in this age of rapid transport and communications. This matches the normal circumstances of the world's poor, where "development projects" are but a tiny part of local activity. The challenge to national and international agencies is thus quite similar in both cases: to make a genuine contribution by doing something that strengthens and extends what the people are going to do anyway on their own.

"Housing using low technology is more likely to come within the price range of disaster victims, it is probably better suited to local cultural patterns and climate, and it will probably generate local employment." Rubble from collapsed homes should not be cleared, except from roadways, as it is a primary source of building materials. Rebuilding begins almost immediately, and officially provided shelter (particularly oddly shaped houses) will be the least appealing to the people.

Although there are many examples of indigenous housing well-suited to resist the effects of typhoons and earthquakes, for example, these appear to have evolved over an extended time period. Rebuilding following a disaster is usually done in response to everyday needs — not the possibility of a repeat of the disaster in the far distant future. One of the most interesting housing projects in Guatemala is a retraining program that promotes "earthquake-proof construction techniques that use traditional materials and existing (though developed) construction skills. The result is that the traditional character of the houses is retained while the structure is made safe."

An important book, with implications for appropriate technology efforts. Well-illustrated.

Shelter After Disaster:

A page from a comic book in use in Guatemala providing guidance on the correct siting of houses

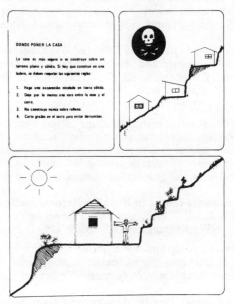

Building to Resist the Effect of Wind, Volume 1: Overview, MF 35-810, booklet, 28 pages, by Richard D. Marshall, Noel J. Raufaste, Jr., and Stephen A. Kliment, U.S. National Bureau of Standards, 1977, $1.75, ask for publication number C13.29/2:100-1 from Superintendent of Documents, U.S. Government Printing Office, Washington D.C. 20402, USA.

First in a five-part series detailing the findings of a research project in wind-resistant housing, this overview summarizes the background, establishment, and activities of the project. Results of tests conducted in cyclone-prone areas in Jamaica, Bangladesh, and the Philippines over a three and a half year project are reported in the companion volumes. Thorough appendices of relevant organizations and references are included.

Building to Resist the Effect of Wind, Volume 2: Estimation of Extreme Wind Speeds and Guide to the Determination of Wind Forces, MF 35-811, booklet, 23 pages, by Emil Simiu and Richard D. Marshall, U.S. National Bureau of Standards, 1977, $1.30, ask for stock number 003-003-01718-3 from Superintendent of Documents, U.S. Government Printing Office, Washington D.C. 20402, USA.

This discussion of wind loads on buildings — including equations, tables, and diagrams — is sufficiently clear to be usable by people with only a moderate technical background. This is due, in part, to the summaries and conclusions in non-technical language. Does not include wind measurement techniques, but does contain an example which illustrates the application of this material.

Building to Resist the Effect of Wind, Volume 4: Forecasting the Economics of Housing Needs: A Methodological Guide, MF 35-812, booklet, 30 pages, by Joseph G. Kowalski, U.S. National Bureau of Standards, 1977, $1.85, ask for publication number C13.29/2:100-4 from Superintendent of Documents, U.S. Government Printing Office, Washington D.C. 20402, USA.

Following up emergency response shelter programs with well-considered reconstruction schemes requires thorough assessment of unmet housing needs. This volume offers a methodology for the analysis of factors contributing to housing shortfalls, including population growth, urbanization trends, cultural patterns, etc. Useful for planners in government and the major international organizations.

Building to Resist the Effect of Wind, Volume 5: Housing in Extreme Winds: Socio-Economic and Architectural Considerations, MF 35-813, booklet, 31 pages, by Stephen A. Kliment, U.S. National Bureau of Standards, 1977, $1.85, ask for publication number C13.29/2:100-5 from Superintendent of Documents, U.S. Government Printing Office, Washington D.C. 20402, USA.

A discussion of relevant cultural patterns and building practices in three cyclone-prone regions (Jamaica, Bangladesh, and the Philippines) is integrated with architectural and planning considerations to present a very readable and interesting analysis of shelter in less developed countries. This last volume serves well as an overview of the process, as distinct from the product, of emergency shelter.

Economic Issues in Housing Reconstruction, MF 35-814, booklet, 11 pages, by Frederick C. Cuny and Paul Thompson, 1981, from Intertect, 1789 Columbia Road N.W., Washington D.C. 20009, USA.

Issues and options for orderly recovery from disaster, avoiding undue disruption of development goals and additional market distortions, are presented in clear, non-technical terms. Very useful for project planners.

Emergency Health Management after Natural Disaster, Scientific Publication #407, MF 35-815, booklet, 67 pages, 1981, $6.00 plus shipping, 50% discount to government agencies, from Pan American Health Organization, World Health Organization, 525 Twenty-third Street N.W., Washington D.C. 20037, USA.

Sound advice for managing disaster relief efforts of large agencies is presented in a clear, easily accessible text. Though claiming to be only an overview of general application, much detailed, specific advice on many topics ranging from management of mass casualties to food and nutrition, and training of non-professional health personnel (and much more) is included in this very useful guide to disaster response. With annexes. Recommended.

Emergency Vector Control after Natural Disaster, Scientific Publication #419, MF 35-816, booklet, 98 pages, 1982, $6.00 plus shipping, 50% discount to government agencies, from Pan American Health Organization, World Health Organization, 525 Twenty-third Street N.W., Washington D.C. 20037, USA.

This companion text to the previous manual combines specific advice on controlling disease agents commonly encountered in disaster relief programs (particularly in tropical developing countries) with advice on program management and interagency collaboration. Annexes include a bibliography, sources for control substances, insecticide and rodenticide application regimes, and lots of required equipment.

Environmental Health Management after Natural Disaster, Scientific Publication #430, MF 35-817, booklet, 58 pages, 1982, $6.00 plus shipping, 50% discount to government agencies, from Pan American Health Organization, World Health Organization, 525 Twenty-third Street N.W., Washington D.C. 20037, USA.

This manual provides planners and administrators of disaster relief health services with specific advice for establishing procedures and setting priorities for sanitation and water supply. The measures suggested involve the use of health professionals and non-professionals alike, and make use of widely available disinfectant chemicals.

Establishing Needs After a Disaster: Assessment, MF 35-818, booklet, 12 pages, 1981, from Intertect, 1789 Columbia Road N.W., Washington D.C. 20009, USA.

Guidelines for setting priorities in emergency response, including survey techniques (sample forms provided), a list of relevant international agencies, and a list of further references. A quick-access resource for field staff and administrators.

How to Build a House of Modern Adobe, MF 35-819, booklet, 46 pages, $2.50 from Oficina de Investigacion y Normalizacion, Ministerio de Vivienda y Construccion, Panamericana Norte Km 17, Previ, Sn. Martin De Porres, Apartado 31-056, Lima 31, Peru.

This step-by-step guide to adobe home construction is an excellent resource for improving the product of indigenous builders. Includes design considerations for earthquake and high wind resistance. Used together with **Improving Building Skills** (reviewed in this section), this pamphlet is a valuable resource for optimizing structure strength, life-span, and resistance to natural disasters. Recommended.

Improving Building Skills, MF 35-820, booklet, 33 pages, by A. Andia and A. James Viets, $2.00 from Oficina de Investigacion y Normalizacion, Ministerio de Vivienda y Construccion, Panamericana Norte Km 17, Previ, Sn. Martin De Porres, Apartado 31-056, Lima 31, Peru.

A clear and well-illustrated presentation of salient points of low-cost housing using block construction (adobe, brick, stabilized earth, etc.) on stone foundations with timber truss roofs. Considerations for earthquake and high wind resistance are included in a format suited to non-formal education. Highly recommended for regions where block construction is a practical option.

The Management of Nutritional Emergencies in Large Populations, MF 35-821, book, 98 pages, by C. de Ville de Goyet, J. Seaman, U. Geijer, 1978, from the World Health Organization, CH-1211 Geneva 27, Switzerland.

Emergency nutritional care, while closely allied with emergency medical efforts, is often carried out by non-professionals. This booklet contains practical guidelines which are to the point. It should be a valuable resource for volunteers and fieldworkers in disaster response. The text is not intended for long-term nutritional care, reconstruction policy following disasters, or preventative measures. Rather, it is focused on the immediate response following a disaster, with an emphasis on adaptability and improvisation. Very useful.

Medical Supply Management after Natural Disaster, Scientific Publication #438, MF 35-822, book, 135 pages, 1983, $6.00 plus shipping, 50% discount to government agencies, from Pan American Health Organization, World Health Organization, 525 Twenty-third Street N.W., Washington D.C. 20037, USA.

Detailed, specific advice for top-level administrators of disaster relief efforts primarily in the area of medical supply management. Includes treatment schedules, a brand name cross-index of common pharmaceuticals, storage requirements, sample management and order forms, international symbols, and a list of essential drugs. With references. Very useful.

Minimum Standards for Cyclone Resistant Housing Utilizing Traditional Materials, MF 35-823, booklet, 44 pages, 1981, from Intertect, 1789 Columbia Road N.W., Washington D.C. 20009, USA.

Considerations for siting, design, and construction of cyclone-resistant single family housing in a number of common building materials are presented in a clear, non-technical manner. Applicable to earthquake-resistant construction as well. Recommended.

Minimum Standards for Earthquake Resistant Housing Utilizing Traditional Materials, MF 35-824, booklet, 23 pages, 1981, from Intertect, 1789 Columbia Road N.W., Washington D.C. 20009, USA.

Design criteria for building earthquake- and wind-resistant housing in a variety of traditional materials is presented in clear, non-technical text. While intended for the staff of housing reconstruction programs, the information should prove useful in a number of applications where optimum strength and durability of structures using traditional construction materials is desired.

Program Planning Guide, MF 35-825, booklet, 20 pages, from Intertect, 1789 Columbia Road N.W., Washington D.C. 20009, USA.

The considerations for establishing a successful relief or reconstruction program — including strategies, management, policy, staffing, budgeting, monitoring, evaluation, etc. — are followed by a discussion of commonly encountered problems and failures in the field. Includes sample forms for emergency operations monitoring.

Program Planning Options for the Reconstruction of Disaster Resistant Housing, MF 35-826, booklet, 10 pages, from Intertect, 1789 Columbia Road N.W., Washington D.C. 20009, USA.

Advantages and disadvantages of six options for emergency shelter are covered in clear and concise terms, providing a valuable and accessible decision-making resource for fieldworkers and disaster relief administrators.

Resource Index: Refugee Relief Operations, MF 35-827, booklet, 26 pages, 1981, from Intertect, 1789 Columbia Road N.W., Washington D.C. 20009, USA.

Bibliographical listings of resources for disaster relief including brief explanations of the materials. Followed by a compilation of agencies involved in the field.

Shelter after Disaster: Guidelines for Assistance, MF 35-828, book, 82 pages, 1982, from UNDRO, United Nations, New York, New York 10017, USA.

This guide for relief organizations and governmental agencies sets down principles and offers advice on procedures for providing shelter for emergency victims. Most notable is the emphasis on self-help and the observation that housing is a process inseparable from local custom and not a product to be dispensed without regard to local conditions, cost effectiveness, and its effect on the long-term development efforts of the recipient country or national group. Each chapter/topic concludes with explicit policy guidelines that, with the numerous examples cited, should prove very useful for fieldworkers and administrators of disaster relief. With appendices and reference lists. Recommended.

United Nations High Commissioner for Refugees Handbook for Emergencies, Part I: Field Operations, MF 35-829, book, 194 pages, 1982, available also in French and Spanish, free from Emergency Unit, United Nations High Commissioner for Refugees, Palais des Nations, CH-1211 Geneva 10, Switzerland.

Long experience in managing the influx of refugees resulting from emergencies is apparent in this manager's guide for relief work. Several chapters relevant to inter- and intra-agency protocol are followed by very thorough, practical discussions of refugee management, especially the establishment of camps, which is considered an option of last resort. Involvement of the refugees in decision-making and implementation is stressed throughout, as is the need to preserve past social arrangements, use local skill and materials, respect local cultural patterns, and plan for a worst case scenario, e.g. long-term detention in a "temporary" refugee camp. Topics include: supplies and logistics, site selection and shelter, health, food and nutrition, water, social services and education, etc. The need to call in expert assistance is often cited in place of detailed information on certain topics, which, like the pointers on common mistakes in camp management and the advice to encourage self-reliance and discourage dependency, appears to have been learned through hard experience. Further reference listings follow each chapter. Recommended.

What is a Hurricane?, MF 35-830, booklet, 5 pages, from Intertect, 1789 Columbia Road N.W., Washington D.C. 20009, USA.

A brief, step-by-step, practical discussion of the nature of hurricanes and recommended measures to minimize damage and loss of life. Useful as an educational tool.

What is a Tidal Wave?, MF 35-831, booklet, 8 pages, from Intertect, 1789 Columbia Road N.W., Washington D.C. 20009, USA.

The nature and destructive capability of tidal waves are covered in a brief, straightforward manner, with specific recommendations for minimizing damage and loss of life.

Wind Resistant Block Houses: Basic Rules, MF 35-832, booklet, 8 pages, from Intertect, 1789 Columbia Road N.W., Washington D.C. 20009, USA.

A brief, illustrated guide to wind- and earthquake-resistant construction for basic housing clarifies the principles and vocabulary of other more technical publications.

How to use the
A.T. Microfiche Library

How to use the A.T. Microfiche Library

Using the Appropriate Technology Microfiche Library

This Sourcebook serves as an index to a low cost library on appropriate technology. More than 90% of the books reviewed in the Sourcebook appear in the Appropriate Technology Microfiche Library.

Books in the A.T. Microfiche Library are reproduced on 11 cm x 15 cm (4"x6") cards of durable plastic film, called microfiche. Each microfiche card contains up to 133 pages of text. The pages on microfiche are read using a microfiche reader, a device similar to a slide projector. The microfiche library offers several advantages over paper libraries. Most importantly, it costs 1/20th of the paper library price. This allows small development groups to have an excellent library in their offices. The microfiche library comes organized and indexed, and is fully portable. A full list of the books in the microfiche library appears at the back of this appendix. *(Further information on the microfiche library can be obtained by writing to the Appropriate Technology Project, Microfiche Library Division, PO Box 4543, Stanford, California 94305 U.S.A.)*

How to Find Information in the Microfiche Library

There are several different ways to find information in the microfiche library. The three most common ways are to a) start with the book reviews in the Sourcebook, looking through the appropriate chapter, b) start with the index to the Sourcebook and look up the topic, and c) start with the title of the book.

A. Starting with the book reviews in the Sourcebook:

1. Find the right chapter by looking in the table of contents of the Sourcebook. (The table of contents is in the front of the Sourcebook. It lists the chapter names.)

2. Read the book reviews in the chapter you have selected. Select a book you want to look at.

3. Find the microfiche number for that book. The microfiche number begins with the letters MF. It is listed directly after the book title at the top of the review.

4. Use the microfiche number to find the card or cards you want to see. On the microfiche cards, the microfiche numbers appear in the upper left corner. The microfiche cards are arranged within the microfiche library in numerical order. (Users of microfiche libraries produced before September 1986 should see the special note which appears at the end of this section.)

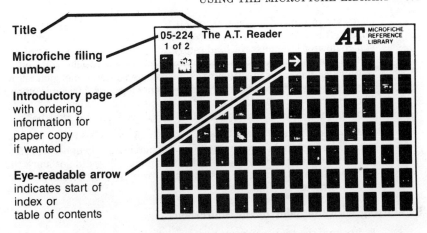

Title

Microfiche filing number

Introductory page with ordering information for paper copy if wanted

Eye-readable arrow indicates start of index or table of contents

5. Each microfiche card contains up to 98 or 133 pages of text. Books longer than 98 pages usually are produced on two or more microfiche cards. You can find out how many cards a book uses by looking at the numbers listed below the microfiche number. There will be 2 numbers separated by the word "of" (e.g. "2 of 3") or by a slash (e.g. "2/3"). The second of these numbers tells how many microfiche cards the book is reproduced on. The first number tells which of those cards you are looking at. For example, the first book in the microfiche library is Appropriate Technology for African Women. It is about 110 pages long and uses two microfiche cards. The first microfiche card shows the numbers "1 of 2" (which can be read "one of two"). This indicates that it is the first of two cards which cover this title. The second card for this title shows the numbers "2 of 2", indicating that it is the second in a set of two cards. On some sets this is marked "1/2" and "2/2".

6. Use the colored index card labeled "Out" to mark the spot in the microfiche library where you found the microfiche card or cards which you want to look at. Then remove the

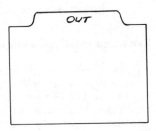

microfiche cards you have selected from the library. The "Out" card will allow you to easily return the microfiche cards to their proper place when you are finished with them.

7. To read the microfiche, you will need to use a "microfiche reader". The exact procedure for using the microfiche reader depends upon what kind of reader you have. As you look at the microfiche card, notice that most of it is covered with small boxes. Each of these is a page of a book. The

pages are organized in rows, from left to right. The first page is in the upper left hand corner. When you reach the right edge of the microfiche, you go down to the next row and return to the left side of the microfiche to find the next page. Some of the boxes on the microfiche contain arrows which you can see without the microfiche reader. (One such arrow appears in the fifth box of Appropriate Technology for African Women.) These arrows indicate the start of the book's index or table of contents. You can use them to quickly find the index materials for that book.

8. When you have finished reading the book on microfiche, put the microfiche back in its proper place. Use the number in the upper left hand corner (for example, 02-21) to file the microfiche if you did not mark the place with the 'Out' card. Be careful—an incorrectly filed microfiche book is very difficult to find!

B. Starting with the index of the Sourcebook:

1. Look up the topic you want to reseach in the index at the back of the Sourcebook. Two kinds of numbers are listed in the index. The numbers that begin with **MF, in bold face type**, are microfiche numbers for the books that cover this topic. The numbers in regular type are the page numbers of reviews of these books.

2. Use the page numbers from the index listing to locate the reviews of books on your topic.

3. Read the book reviews and select a book that you want to look at.

4. Locate and read the book on microfiche by following the instructions in part A above, beginning with step 3.

C. Starting with the titles of a book:

1. If you already know the title of a book you are looking for, look up the title in the index at the back of the Sourcebook. The microfiche number will be in **boldface**, and will begin with the letters 'MF'. Or, for faster access, check the alphabetical listing of titles at the end of this appendix.

2. Locate and read the book on microfiche by following the instructions in part A above, beginning with step 3.

Can't find what you want in the Index?

In any library, the subject index (or card catalog) is always incomplete. This is because there is an endless number of different ways to index materials, and at some point the index gets too big to use, and is too expensive to produce. In this microfiche library, as in any library, you may have to search for a while before you find what you need. If you cannot find what you want through the index, try reading the reviews, as outlined in section B above. If this doesn't yield results, check the table of contents or index of any books on microfiche that seem likely to cover the topic you are looking for.

Maintenance of the microfiche library

If the microfiche library gets heavy use, you will need to occasionally scan the microfiche numbers to see that they are in the proper sequence. Unless this is done, microfiche that have been filed in the wrong place will be effectively "lost". Start at the front of the microfiche library, beginning with the number 01-1, and work your way back through all the microfiche until you reach the last one. When you find a microfiche card that is out of order, pull it out and file it in the correct place. (This same procedure is used in a regular paper library, where books are also filed incorrectly at times.)

There are some gaps in the microfiche numbers. If you want to check whether a book is missing, refer to the list of titles organized by microfiche number, at the back of this appendix.

Special note for microfiche libraries produced before September 1986

Microfiche libraries produced before September 1986 use a slightly different numbering format on the microfiche cards than that outlined above. These earlier editions of the library list the microfiche number as two separate numbers. For example, the first book in the set is Appropriate Technology for African Women. The microfiche number for this book is 01-1. In the pre-September 1986 sets, this number appears on the microfiche cards as "01" on the top, with "1" just below it. This change does not affect the sequence of the microfiche. The microfiche numbers given in this Sourcebook correspond with the numbers in the pre-1986 microfiche library when the top two numbers on the microfiche card are treated as a single hyphenated number.

A second change is that in the earlier edition the numbering system of the different microfiche cards for one book uses a slash in place of the word "of" (for example "1/2", "2/2" instead of "1 of 2","2 of 2").

Finally, the September 1986 edition of the microfiche library includes over 200 new books which were not in the earlier edition of the library. Those holding the earlier edition of the library can purchase an "expansion kit" which contains the new titles. for more information on this, write to us at the address listed at the beginning of this set of instructions. A small number of books in the earlier edition of the library have been dropped from the 1986 edition and are therefore not listed in this Sourcebook. The dropped books have been replaced by better, more recent references.

Books in the Microfiche Library
Listed by Chapter

Books in the Microfiche Library Listed by Chapter

Local Self-Reliance

Workshop

•

Agriculture

Agricultural Tools

Crop Preservation

Forestry

Water Supply: Pumps

Water Supply: Tanks

Water Supply: Treatment

Water Supply: Sanitation

Water Supply: Solid Wastes

Energy: General

Energy: Cookstoves

Energy: Wind

Energy: Water

Energy: Solar

Energy: Biogas

Housing and Construction

Science Teaching

Nonformal Education

Small Enterprises

Local Communications

Beekeeping

Small Industries

Glossary

Glossary

The following words are defined as they are used in the text.

a priori — at the beginning; given.

abdomen — the part of the body containing the stomach and intestines.

abolition — the banning of something.

abrasives — substances used for grinding, polishing, sanding, etc., such as sandpaper.

abundant — plentiful; available in large quantities.

accessible — easily reached or obtained.

accommodate — to adjust.

accumulated — gathered or saved (up).

acetate plastic — a clear plastic sheet that can easily be marked with a pen or other writing instrument.

acidity — the degree to which a substance has the properties of an acid.

acupuncture — the ancient Chinese practice of piercing parts of the body with needles to treat disease or relieve pain.

acute — severe, serious.

adept — skillful.

adhesive (solder, glue) — a substance used to permanently join two objects.

adobe — unburnt sundried brick.

adverse — unfavorable.

adze — a metal cutting tool like an axe, but with a blade at right angles at the handle.

aeration — the process of mixing with air or oxygen.

aerial ropeway system — a transport system using a permanent set of ropes or cables to carry goods over rough terrain.

aerobic composting — process of decomposition while oxygen is present.

aerodynamics — the study of the motion of air and the forces acting on bodies in motion (such as windmill blades).

aesthetic — related to taste or beauty.

afforestation — the process of planting trees in an area that does not have them.

agile — quick; able to move quickly.

agitator-type washing machine — a machine in which the dirt is loosened from clothing through the up-and-down motion of one or more pistons or other parts, which serve to move the water.

agribusiness — a term describing highly-centralized agriculture operations in developed countries, where agriculture is a business rather than a way of life.

agronomist — a person who is trained in the science and economics of crop production and the management of farm land.

ailment — illness; health problem.

airfoil — the shape of an airplane wing or a windgenerator blade; designed for high-speed movement through air.

algae — small water plants, valuable as a protein source and animal feed or raw material for a methane digester.

algae bloom — the uncontrolled growth of algae in a pond.

alien — foreign.

alienating — causing loss of sense of purpose.

alkaline — having a high level of soluble salts; this can make agriculture difficult.

alkali-puddled clay — a building material; clay is mixed with water and lime to create an easily-shaped material that is durable.

alleviate — to make less hard to bear; to lighten or relieve.

allied — joined together for a common purpose.

all-inclusive — complete; covering all parts or aspects.

allocation — the amount of something set aside for a particular purpose.

alloy — a metal made of a mixture of two or more common metals.

alternator — a machine for changing mechanical energy into electrical energy; a kind of generator that initially produces alternating current.

all-terrain vehicle — a heavy-duty vehicle especially designed to operate in rough and wet terrain (including hills, swamps, and creeks).

aluminized Mylar — a very strong thin sheet of plastic material coated with aluminum.

amateur — a person who is not a professional.

ambient — surrounding, on all sides.

ambitious — demanding great effort, skill or enterprise.

ambivalent — undecided.

amenities — comforts.

amenities in the workshop — special tools in the workshop.

ammeter — an instrument which measures the strength of an electric current in the form of amperes (amps).

amortize — to gradually pay off a debt.

ample — plenty.

anaerobic fermentation — fermentation in the absence of air or oxygen.

analysis — breaking a problem or question down into parts.

ancestral — of anything regarded as prior to a later thing.

anecdote — a short account of some happening.

anemia — a condition in which there is a reduction in the number of red blood cells or of the total amount of hemoglobin in the blood stream, resulting in weakness.

anemometer — a simple device that is used to measure windspeed.

angle iron — pieces of iron or steel with a cross-sectional shape like the letter "L".

animal husbandry — a branch of agriculture concerned with the raising of animals.

animal power gear — a gear that converts the power of a horse or other animal walking in a circle into the high-speed motion of a drive shaft, used to operate equipment (such as a thresher).

anodize — to coat with a protective film using electric current.

antecedent — any happening or thing prior to another.

anvil — a heavy steel block on which metal is pounded for shaping (blacksmith's tool).

aperture — the opening in a camera or telescope through which light passes into the lens.

apiary — a place where bees are kept.

apparatus — equipment.

appliance — a small device for performing a specific task; in the U.S., especially household devices that use electricity.

aquaculture — the raising of fish and other marine organisms.

aquarium — a glass-walled container for fish and other animals and plants, which allows careful observation of their behavior.

aquatic — having to do with water (ponds, streams, oceans).

arable land — land which can be farmed.

arbitrary (arbitrarily) — without reason.

arc welder — a kind of welding machine that uses an electric current passing across a gap to produce the necessary heat.

Archimedes' screw — a waterlifting device that has a screw-shaped rotating blade and axle inside a cylinder.

arid — dry.

armature — the iron core with wire wound around it, in a generator, alternator, or electric motor.

array — a regular arrangement or series.

artisan — craftsperson, artist.

aspirations — hopes, desires for the future.

aspirator — a device for moving air or fluids by suction.

assimilation — the process of becoming part of something.

astute — accurate; showing a clever mind.

attached greenhouse — a solar greenhouse attached to a house, where it helps in heating by acting as a solar collector.

attributable to — due to, caused by.

auger — a tool for boring holes.

authoritarian — characterized by unquestioning obedience to authority, as that of a dictator, rather than individual freedom of action.

auxiliary — extra, reserve.

auxiliary generating equipment — additional electric generating equipment; for example, a unit that can be used during periods when there is no wind to operate a windgenerator.

axial-flow turbine — a turbine in which water flows parallel to the axis.

backlash — a strong political reaction resulting from fear or resentment of a movement.

backslide — to slide backwards, failing to fully implement a political promise.

backward — from earlier times, not modern.

bacteriological — related to the study of tiny life forms present in all organic matter.

bagasse — the part of sugar cane that is left after the cane has been crushed and the juice has been removed.

baled hay — hay that has been compressed into bundles and tied.

ballyhoo — noise and hollering.

band saw — a saw that has a long narrow continuous band for a blade; the band travels in one direction only, rotating around several wheels.

banish — to send away permanently.

barefoot doctors — local health workers doing preventive medicine and basic health care without lengthy medical training or expensive equipment; originated as a description of local health workers in China.

barometer — an instrument for measuring atmospheric pressure; anything that indicates change.

barrel staves — narrow, curved strips of wood which form the sides of a wooden barrel.

baseboard heating — a space heating system which radiates heat from panels on the wall near the floor.

batch process (methane digester) — a system in which the digester is loaded only at the beginning of a digestion cycle; gas production varies considerably during the digestion period.

BB shells — pieces of metal which serve as a case for steel balls in ball bearings.

beaker — a glass container used in scientific experiments.

bearing — any part of a machine on which another part revolves.

becak — pedicab; three-wheeled taxi (Indonesia).

bellows — a blacksmith's device for forcing air into a fire to increase the rate of fuel consumption and thus the temperature.

belt sander — a machine with a long abrasive belt that travels around two or more rotating cylinders; the belt is used for sanding and smoothing rough pieces of wood.

bemo — small transport vehicle in Indonesia.

benign — not dangerous; not causing damage or hurt.

bevel gear — a gear wheel meshed with another so that their shafts are at an angle of less than 180 degrees.

biased — unfairly affected or directed; not fair, prejudiced.

bicycle caliper brake — a bicycle hand-operated brake that has two arms that can be forced to rub on the rim of the wheel to slow the bicycle.

bicycle hub — the center of the wheel which revolves around the axle.

bicycle sprocket — a gear.

bikeway — path or lane reserved for bicycle use only.

bilharzia — see schistosomiasis.

bi-metal strip — a device made of two strips of different metals that expand at different rates when heated; the strip bends or curls when heated.

biodegradable — capable of being decomposed by bacterial action.

biogas — see methane gas.

biogas plant — see methane digester.

biological control — control of insects and other pests using natural means (predators, competitors, bacteria); non-chemical methods.

biomass — the total amount of living organisms in a particular area or volume.

biomass energy — energy from biological sources.

biotic — of life, or caused by living organisms.

bit — the cutting edge of a tool.

bloat — to swell.

block and tackle — a set of pulleys and ropes for hauling and lifting.

blueprint — a large set of detailed plans.

board feet — a unit of measure of lumber equal to a board one foot in length on two sides and one inch thick.

bona fide — real; made in good faith.

borehole — hole drilled in the earth to make a well.

borne out — proved to be true or accurate.

botany — a branch of biology that deals with plants.

bow saw — a saw operated by a foot treadle with an overhead bow which acts as a spring mechanism; together they pull the saw blade up and down.

brace — a support; also a tool into which a drill bit or auger is inserted for drilling.

brackish — water with a heavy salt content, such as in inland seas.

brazing — to bond two pieces of metal using a metal rod with a lower melting temperature than either of the pieces to be connected; usually uses copper wire, and can be done with a small propane torch.

breastshot (breast) water wheel — a water wheel driven by water entering near the midpoint of the wheel.

bridle — a head harness for guiding a horse.

brittle — easily broken.

broadcast sower — a device which spreads seeds over a small area by throwing them through the air.

brunt — the major portion of negative consequences.

BTU — British Thermal Unit, a measure of heat energy; specifically, the amount of heat required to raise the temperature of one pound of water one degree Fahrenheit.

buffer — a machine for polishing metal.

bulk — greatest part.

bungalow — a small house with a porch.

bunsen burner — a simple gas burner.

burlap — coarse material used to make sacks and bags, usually made out of jute; also called "gunny sacks."

bushing — a round lining for an opening, used to limit the size of the opening, resist wear, or serve as a guide.

butyl rubber basin liner — a kind of plastic sheet used to prevent liquid from leaking through a basin.

byproduct — other or additional product.

cable plow — a plowing system in which a lightweight plow is pulled across a field by cable instead of by a tractor or draft animal.

cadre — a local-level leader and motivator.

calcium chloride — $CaCl_2$.

calculus — calculation; estimation.

calibrated — carefully and correctly adjusted.

cam — a bump on a turning shaft which lifts or pushes.

campesinos — rural people (Spanish).

canning — the preservation of foods in tightly sealed cans or jars.

capital — money; or equipment that represents an investment in money.

capital formation — gathering resources and buying or making tools, equipment or buildings to be used in production.

capital-intensive — techniques that have a high equipment-to-labor ratio to accomplish a particular task; an automobile is a much more capital-intensive form of transportation than is a bicycle.

carbonized plant material — dry plant matter high in carbon content that will make a building material; straw, thatch, palm leaves.

carbon/nitrogen ratio — the proportion of carbon to nitrogen in the material being placed in a methane digester; there is a proper ratio that allows maximum gas production and a proper chemical reaction.

carburetor — that part of an engine in which air and fuel are mixed.

carding machine — a machine used to prepare cotton or wool for spinning.

cardiovascular — of the heart and the blood vessels.

carnivorous — meat-eating.

carrying capacity — amount of life or activity that the ecosystem can support.

caseharden — to harden the outer layer of a piece of metal.

cash crop — a crop that is produced for sale rather than for consumption by the farm family.

casting (verb) — the process of making products from a mold, usually using hot molten (liquid) metal.

casting (noun) — a product made from a mold; the result of the above process.

catalyst — something which acts to help a process take place.

catalyze — to act as a stimulus in causing something.

caulking (caulking compound) — a filling material used to make a boat or other object "watertight" so that water cannot enter or escape.

cellulose — the bulky or fibrous part of plants, consisting of natural sugars.

centralize — to concentrate the power or authority of a central organization; to gather together; to focus on a center.

centrifuge — a spinning machine used to separate particles of different density.

certified — having a license issued by an authority, proving the ability to do something.

chaff — the seed coverings and other material separated from the grain during threshing.

chaff cutter — a tool which is used to chop dry vegetative materials such as straw into small pieces.

chain pump — a pump with an endless chain passing over a wheel at the top and entering a pipe below the water; it is fitted with discs which lift the water through the pipe.

chainsaw — a portable power saw that has teeth linked together to form an endless chain.

channel iron — pieces of iron or steel which have the cross-sectional shape of a channel.

charitable — kind and generous in giving money or help to those in need.

chassis — the part of a motor vehicle that includes the frame, suspension system, wheels, steering mechanism and so forth, but not the body or engine.

chemical coagulation — bringing together suspended particles in water by adding a chemical.

chisel — a tool for cutting grooves or shavings from wood or metal.

chlorination — purifying water by adding tiny amounts of the chemical chlorine to it.

chromatography — the process of separating the elements in a mixture by having a solution flow through a column of absorbent material on which the different substances are separated into distinct bands.

chronic — happening again and again.

churn — a container in which milk or cream is beaten to form butter.

circuit board — an electrical system laid out on a board for use in teaching.

circuitry — the elements of an electrical system.

circular sump — a circular pit lined with bricks, cement, or other material to hold wet material without losing the moisture.

cited — noted, identified.

clarify — make clear.

clear-cutting — cutting down all of the trees and plants.

climatology — the study of weather patterns.

clods — large dried pieces of soil that must be broken up before planting.

clogged — blocked or stopped flow.

closed loop — in a solar energy system, using water or another liquid to move heat from a collector to a storage area, and then returning the same liquid to the collector.

coalition — a group of organizations that agree to cooperate.

coefficients of transmission of heat — generally accepted statistics about the rate at which heat will move through different materials.

coercive — based on the use of force.

cogs — the teeth on the rim of a wheel, for transmitting or receiving motion by fitting between the teeth of another wheel.

coherent — fitting together well; making sense.

collaboration — working together.

collaborative — from working together.

collateral — something of value owned by a borrower, such as a house or land, used as a guarantee to a lender that a debt will be paid; if the debt is not paid, the lender takes the collateral as payment.

colleague — a fellow worker in the same profession.

color patina — surface color of metal, caused by the hardening process in blacksmithing, or long exposure to air.

combat — fight.

combustion — the process of burning.

commencing — beginning.

commend — to praise; to favorably point to.

commutator — in a generator or electric motor, a revolving part that collects the electric current from, or distributes it to, the brushes.

compacted — compressed and packed firmly together.

companion planting — a strategy used in intensive gardening in which different plants are raised next to each other to take advantage of nitrogen-fixation, insect-repelling properties, shade, etc.

compatible — going together well; fitting together well.

compelling — convincing, persuasive.

compensated — paid.

compendium — collection, compilation, summary.

composting — a method for breaking down organic solids (such as leaves, straw and manure) into easily used fertilizer.

compost toilet — a waste disposal system in which wastes break down to become fertilizer.

compounding — adding to.

comprehensive — including all aspects.

compression — being pushed or squeezed together.

compulsory — required.

computing — figuring out using numbers.

concave — curved inward, like a bowl.

concerted — concentrated, deliberate, vigorous.

concientizacion — a group discussion process aimed at creating an expanded awareness of the factors that keep people poor, and stimulating action for change.

condensation — the process whereby water vapor or another gas changes into a liquid as its temperature drops.

condenser — a device for converting a gas into a liquid.

conduit tube — lightweight metal tube usually used for protecting electrical wires.

configuration — arrangement of parts.

congealed — become solid or firm.

conical — shaped like a cone.

connecting rod — a rod connecting by back and forth motion two or more moving parts of a machine; for example, the connecting rod between the crankshaft and piston in an automobile engine.

conscientious — very careful and consistent.

consensus — decision-making by a group in which all members participate and are satisfied with the outcome.

constraints — limits; problems.

construed — understood, interpreted.

contacts (electricity) — metal points which when touching allow electricity to flow through a circuit.

containment — where animals are held inside.

contamination — dirtying or poisoning.

continuous process (methane digester) — a system in which the digester has a small amount of material added each day; gas production remains fairly constant.

continuity — the act of proceeding smoothly over time; ongoing.

contour — an imaginary line around the side of a hill that maintains the same elevation.

convergence — combining; coming or flowing together.

converter — a device employing mechanical rotation for changing electrical energy from one form to another.

convey — communicate.

conveying — communicating, showing.

cooper — someone who makes or repairs wooden barrels.

cope — to deal with problems effectively.

coppicing — the controlled production of small trees repeatedly from the same stumps (root systems).

copra — coconut meat dried for storage and transport; used to produce coconut oil.

corn (maize) sheller — a tool used to remove the kernels (seeds) from pieces of corn.

corollary — a proposition related to one that has been proven correct.

corrode — to eat into or wear away gradually, as by rusting or the action of chemicals.

corrosive — causing the wearing away of metal or other material by rusting or the action of chemicals.

corrugated — having parallel grooves and ridges.

corrupt — dishonest in handling money; using influence unfairly.

counter-sink — a tool used to drive a nail or screw below the surface of a piece of wood.

counterweight — a weight equal to another, used to balance it.

crankshaft — a shaft used to transfer rotational motion into up-and-down motion; or the reverse.

crannies — small cracks.

creativity — the ability to use the imagination and invent.

creosote — unburned gas from a wood fire, that has condensed to form a sticky, dark substance.

crop diversification — the practice of growing a variety of plant crops within a particular area; opposite of "monoculture."

crop duster — a device for spreading pesticides or herbicides in the form of dust or spray.

crop-lien system — a system in which a future crop is sold at a low price to store owners or other middlepeople, in order to acquire credit for essential purchases by a farm family.

crop rotation — a system of growing successive crops that have different nutrient requirements, thereby preventing soil depletion, and breaking disease cycles.

cross fertilization — stimulation and improvement through exchange (of ideas).

cross-flow turbine — a wheel with curved vanes driven by the pressure of water flowing through it, and in which the water acts on the vanes twice, once while entering and once while leaving the turbine.

crucible — a container used to hold metal while it is being melted.

cube (math) — the product of multiplying a number by itself three times. The cube of the number 2 is 8 ($2 \times 2 \times 2 = 8$).

culmination — the highest point, the climax.

cultivator — an implement to loosen the soil and remove weeds while crops are growing.

cultivating — the process of loosening the soil and removing weeds while crops are growing.

culture plates — glass microscope slide plates used to observe blood samples and other very tiny materials.

culvert — a drain that passes under a road, railroad, footpath, etc.

curing (cement) — physical processing with water to help the cement reach its maximum strength.

curing (fish) — to preserve by chemical or physical processing.

curing (hides or skins) — to preserve by chemical or physical processing for future use.

current regulator — an electrical device which controls the level of current (amperes) passing through an electrical circuit.

curricula — plural of curriculum.

curriculum — the set of concepts being taught in a class.

currier — a worker who treats leather.

cutical (insect) — skin or covering of an insect.

cutlery — knives; tools used for eating.

cutout — a switch which cuts the electric

circuit to a windgenerator under two conditions: 1) windspeed too low to charge the batteries, and 2) windspeed so high that electrical output threatens to damage the system.

cycle rickshaw — pedicab, three-wheeled taxi.

cyclist — a person riding a bicycle.

cynical — antisocial; believing that all people's actions are based on selfishness, and thus basing one's own actions on selfishness as well.

cyst — a growth in the skin.

damper — a piece of metal used to control the flow of air and hot gases in a stove.

Darrieus rotor — a vertical-axis windmachine that has long thin blades in the shape of loops, connected at the top and bottom of the axle; often called the "eggbeater" windmill because of its appearance.

data bank — a place where information is collected and stored for later use.

data processing — a method for evaluating and using information, usually by means of a computer.

dawn on — become clear to.

debilitating — making weak.

debit — amount to be subtracted.

debris — rough, broken bits of material left after a war or other disaster.

debt servicing — interest paid on a loan.

decentralization — a shift in the patterns of decision-making and production so that these activities go on in many more places than before.

decentralize — to break up a concentration of governmental decision-making, industry, or population, and distribute it more evenly.

decomposition (bacterial) — the chemical breakdown of organic matter by micro-organisms.

decorative — of interest due to its appearance only.

decoy — a plant which attracts insects away from other, more valuable plants.

deduced — realized; understood.

deep litter bedding — straw, leaves, or wood shavings used in a deep layer to cover the bottom of a chicken coop.

defecation — the act of passing human waste out of the body.

deficit — the amount by which a sum of money is less than the required amount.

deflector — a device that can be used to change the direction of a flow of water in a turbine to reduce the power produced.

deforestation — the destruction of forests.

degradation — making worse; becoming less usable.

dehydrate — to remove water from fruits and vegetables for preservation (drying).

dehydration — the draining of fluids from the body through diarrhea or perspiration; dangerous if the fluids are not replaced.

demoralizing — discouraging.

demystify — to remove the mystery from; to make something understandable.

depletion — using up.

deplore — to regard as unfortunate.

derive — obtain, get.

desertification — the creation of deserts.

destitute — very poor.

detention time — the time period that incoming material is retained in a methane digester for processing.

deterioration — the process of becoming worse.

determinant — cause.

detract — undermine, reduce, subtract.

devastated — having suffered great destruction.

diagnosis — the process of deciding the nature of a diseased condition by examination of the symptoms.

dialects — different forms of a language; local languages.

dialogue — conversation; talking between two people or groups.

diaphragm pump — a pump which moves water through the alternating expansion and contraction of a chamber.

diarrhea — excessive looseness and frequency of bowel movements.

diatribe — a bitter, abusive criticism.

die — a metalworking cutting tool, e.g. for cutting screw-threads in a steel rod.

diesel set — an electric generator driven by a diesel engine.

dietary — related to what a person eats.

differential — an arrangement of gears connecting two axles in the same line and dividing the driving force between them, but allowing one axle to turn faster than the other when necessary; it is used in the rear axles of automobiles to permit a difference in the speeds of the two wheels while turning corners; also has the characteristic that the shaft comes in at a 90-degree angle to the axle, and does not turn at the same rpm.

differentiate — show difference among or between; separate.

diffraction — the breaking up of a ray of light into the colors of the spectrum.

diffusionist — an approach to technological change in which new techniques chosen by central agencies are spread, concentrating on community leaders.

digestion — the process by which organic materials are decomposed by the action of bacteria, producing gas and fertilizer.

digression — a wandering from the main subject.

dilemma — problem for which a solution is not evident.

diligence — hard working, responsibility.

direct gain — solar energy that enters a building without the use of collectors.

discharge — release.

discredit — to show reasons for disbelief.

disinfectant — a substance which cleans and kills disease-causing organisms.

dismantle — take apart.

dispel — remove, clear away.

dispersed — spread out.

disposable income — that portion of an income which can be spent.

dissecting tool — a tool used in separating the parts of an animal or plant.

dissemination — spread.

dissolution — breaking apart; breakdown.

distill — carefully select the essential elements of; evaporate and condense.

distilled water — water that has been evaporated and condensed so that all chemicals and salts have been removed; pure H2O.

diversified — having many different activities or components.

divert — to move water or resources away from their normal channels.

dogmatic — closely following the rules; unwilling to listen to other ideas.

donor — a group that provides funds.

dosage — the exact amount of a medicine to be given at one time.

double-acting pump — a pump designed so that water is lifted during both the up and down strokes of a piston or diaphragm.

double-digging — a technique used in intensive gardening in which the topsoil is removed, the subsoil is loosened, and the topsoil is then replaced.

dowel — a round length of wood used to join two other pieces of wood.

drag (aerodynamics) — the slowing force acting on a blade or wing moving through air.

drainage — the removal of surface water.

draught — British spelling of draft.

draught chain — a heavy chain used to pull objects, such as harrows.

draw-knife — a two-handled knife used in making precise cuts in wood.

drill press — a machine for drilling holes in metal or wood.

drive shaft — a shaft that transmits motion or power, as from the transmission to the rear axle of an automobile.

dropper — a glass or plastic tube used to pick up and transfer drops of liquid.

drought — an abnormally long period of time with lower than normal annual rainfall.

drudgery — hard, boring work.

dry cell battery — a battery that uses dry chemical activity for storage of electricity; cannot be recharged.

dry steam — high-temperature steam which contains little moisture.

dubious — doubtful; uncertain.

dung — animal waste, manure, shit, excreta.

duplicate — to copy; to do again.

dynamic — moving, changing.

dynamo — see generator.

dynapod — a basic pedal-power unit that can be attached to small machines.

dwindles — gets smaller quickly.

earth auger — a device for drilling narrow diameter holes for wells.

earthen — made of earth.

ecologically-sound — any approach which fully considers and does not affect the natural balance of the environment and ecosystem.

economies of scale — savings that come with increasing size of a business or activity.

ecosystem — a system made up of a community of people, animals, plants and bacteria, and the physical and chemical environment with which it is connected.

edible — that which can be eaten.

effluent — material or waste flowing out.

eke out — scrape together.

electrical conduit pipe — lightweight metal tubing used to protect electrical wires.

electric grid — system of electric lines which distribute and regulate electricity in a community.

electrolysis — the process of changing an

electrolyte by passing an electric current through it.

electrolyte — a liquid or solution which conducts electricity and deposits a metal coating; used in electroplating.

electro-magnet — a core of material that becomes a magnet when electricity is passed through a coil of wire around it.

electro-magnetic device — a core of magnetic material surrounded by a coil or wire through which an electric current is passed to magnetize the core; used in switches.

electronic governor — a device which switches part of the electric current produced by a turbine away from the main line (for example, to heat water) when the electric demand falls; this allows the turbine to be run at a constant speed, avoiding the need for an expensive governor to regulate the amount of water flowing through the turbine as electric demand changes.

electroplate — to coat with metal using electricity passed through a solution.

elicit — to draw out (a response).

emery stone — a stone for grinding the edges of tools to sharpen them.

empirical — based on practical experience and observation rather than theory.

emulsified asphalt — asphalt in liquid form, containing some kind of solvent which breaks it into tiny drops.

endeavors — efforts, projects.

endorse — recommend.

energy-gobbling American homes — homes built in North America that consume enormous amounts of energy in the form of gas and electricity.

enhance — improve, make better.

enteric pathogens — organisms causing disease in the intestine.

entrepreneur — someone who sees an opportunity to start a new enterprise or activity; businessperson.

entrepreneurial — related to undertaking the risks and management of a new enterprise or activity.

environment — the physical and biological surroundings.

environmentally-sound — see ecologically-sound.

envisage — imagine.

epidemic — a disease that is spreading rapidly among many individuals in a community at the same time.

epoxy — liquid material which hardens in the air, used in glues.

equate — to consider the same.

equitable — fair, equal for all.

erosion — the wearing away of land, soil, and other earth formations by wind, water, or ice.

escalating — rising, increasing.

escapement mechanism (clock) — the special gearing inside a clock that allows a sprocket to turn one notch at a time.

ethanol — alcohol made from grain or other vegetable.

euphemistically called — given a nice name.

evaporation — the process whereby water changes from a liquid to a vapor and disappears into the air.

exacerbate — make worse.

excerpt — a piece taken from a longer article or book.

exclusion — the leaving out of something.

excreta — human or animal waste matter; shit.

existential — involving awareness of being a free individual.

exotic — highly unusual; not part of daily life.

expediting — to speed up.

explicit — directly, obviously.

exponential — rapidly increasing.

extraction — the process of taking something out.

extractive — something that is drawn out or removed.

extrapolation — a conclusion reached by estimating beyond a known range.

extruded — to be forced out.

eyebolt — a bolt which has one circular end through which a piece of wire or rope can be passed.

fabricate — make, construct.

facilitate — enable, help to happen.

fad — a temporarily popular activity.

fall prey — become a victim; be taken advantage of.

fallible — possibly wrong; capable of making mistakes.

fallow land — land not planted in a crop for a growing season, to allow improvement in soil fertility.

farrier — a blacksmith who makes horseshoes (metal bands) and attaches them to horses' hooves.

feasible — possible, practical.

feathering mechanism — a mechanism on

a windmill which in strong winds turns the blades increasingly out of the wind; this slows the windmill and protects it from damage.

fecal coliform bacteria — microscopic (tiny) organisms in human waste which can cause sickness.

fecal matter — solid human waste; shit.

feed grinder — a tool used to grind food into very small pieces so that fish or other animals can eat it.

fencerow — a row of bushes forming a fence.

fermentation — the breakdown of complex molecules in an organic material, caused by a bacteria; action of yeast making vinegar or alcohol.

ferrocement — cement-sand concrete reinforced by wire mesh.

fiber — any substance that can be separated into threads for spinning, weaving.

fiberglass — glass in the form of small fibers (similar to hairs), used in making insulation and harder structures such as boats.

fibrous insulation (local) — insulation made of local plant or animal materials such as coconut husks or animal hair.

field (electricity) — magnetic forces created by an electric current; important in the operation of a generator or alternator.

field wash — soil erosion caused by the flow of water.

firebreak — a strip of land on which trees and other plants have been removed, to prevent the spread of forest fires.

firebrick — special brick that will not break at high temperatures.

flagstone — a hard stone that splits into flat pieces.

flametrap device — a unit to prevent the flame from backing up along a gas pipeline towards the source.

flange — a rim for attachment to another part, usually on a pipe or a wheel.

flannel board — a board on which scenes and processes can be illustrated for an audience; the flannel holds the movable pieces in place.

flap valve pump — a simple lowlift hand pump with a valve on top but no piston; same as inertia pump.

flat plate collector — a glass- or plastic-covered metal panel which traps the solar energy that falls on it; this heat is then transferred by a water or air system for hot water heating or home heating.

flaws — mistakes.

flow — the amount of water that moves past a point in a given amount of time; often measured in liters per second.

flow regulator — a device that controls the amount of water flowing through a turbine, to match the power needed at any moment.

fluctuations — variations.

flue — a pipe through which smoke or hot air passes.

flue duct — an opening to a flue which can be regulated to affect the amount of air passing through; this has an effect of regulating the rate of fuel consumption and the temperature in a fireplace or kiln.

fluorescent tube — an electric light bulb that uses a tube of fluoride gas instead of a wire filament; usually 2½ times as efficient as a standard electric light bulb — this means that a 40-watt fluorescent tube provides as much light as a 100-watt electric bulb.

flywheel — a heavy, rotating wheel used to moderate any variations in the speed of the machinery with which it revolves.

foam composite — an industrialized lightweight material.

focal point — the central point at which activities are directed and effects are felt.

fodder — plant food for animals, such as leaves and straw.

foliage — plant growth.

forage — food for domestic animals; to search for this food.

forage crops — crops valuable as animal feed.

foreign exchange — money in the form of foreign currency that can be used to buy things from outside the country.

forerunner — one which came before.

forge — a blacksmith's furnace for heating iron or steel hot enough so that it can be shaped by pounding.

format — general arrangement.

formica — rigid plastic product.

formulation — a theory or plan.

forum — a place where discussion and exchange of ideas can take place.

fossil fuel — coal, oil, natural gas.

foundation (building) — the base on which a structure rests; usually made of concrete, stone, or blocks, and positioned partially underground.

foundry (iron) — a workshop where iron is melted and poured into molds to make tools.

foundryman (foundryperson) — a person who operates a foundry.

foyer — entryway, entry room.

fragile — delicate, easily broken.

fragments — breaks apart; small pieces.

freewheel (bicycle) — an arrangement in the rear hub which allows the rear gear to either drive the wheel or rotate freely when not being pedaled.

fringe areas — margin; edges.

frugal — economical; not wasteful.

fry — young fish.

fungicide — a substance used to kill fungus.

funnel — a device with a large opening on one end and a smaller opening on the other; used to pour liquid into a bottle, for example.

furrow — a shallow channel made in a field by a plow.

fuse — a wire or strip of easily melted metal placed in an electrical circuit; if the current becomes too strong, the metal melts, cutting the circuit before the entire wiring system is destroyed.

gabled roof — a roof with two sloping surfaces that meet at a line along the top in an inverted "V" shape.

galvanized — coated with zinc for protection from rust and corrosion.

galvanometer — an instrument for detecting and measuring a small electric current.

gas compression — the process of pressurizing gas so that it can be burned effectively.

gasogen — a stove-like device carried by a vehicle, producing gas through the partial burning of charcoal or wood.

gauze — a very thin, loosely-woven piece of cotton or silk.

gear down — to arrange gears or pulleys so that the original speed of rotation of a pedal-power unit, windmill, or water wheel is decreased; for example, to operate a winch.

gear up — to arrange gears or pulleys so that the original speed of rotation of a pedal-power unit, windmill, or water wheel is increased; for example, this would be necessary to generate electricity.

generator — a machine for changing mechanical energy (such as the rotation of a windmill rotor) into electrical energy; has a stationary field and rotating armature, and produces direct current electricity.

genetics — the branch of biology that deals with heredity and variation in similar or related plants and animals.

germination — the process of starting to grow or sprout.

germplasm — the portion of the reproductive cells of an organism involved in heredity.

gestation — a development, as of a plan in the mind.

glaze — in ceramics, the coating given before the final firing (placement in the kiln for heat treatment); helps to seal the clay and adds color to the object.

glazing — the plastic or glass covering on a flat plate collector for solar water heating.

gleaned — picked out of.

gobar gas — methane gas (CH_4).

gouge — a tool like a chisel used to remove chunks of wood.

governor — a device that controls the amount of water flowing through a turbine, to match the power needed at any moment.

grain silo — a long-term storage chamber for grains; usually watertight and airtight to prevent spoilage and insect damage.

graphic ideation — the use of drawings to express and develop ideas.

grass-roots — local communities; where people live and work.

grass wilderness — a name for rain forest land which has had all of the trees and cover vegetation removed — the soil can only support the growth of hardy grasses, and is very difficult to restore to fertility; sometimes called a "green desert."

green manure — a crop which is plowed back under into the soil while still green, for its beneficial nitrogen-adding effect on the soil.

greenhouse — a glass- or plastic-covered building used to trap solar energy and protect plants from bugs, wind, rain, cold, evaporation, of moisture; allows a controlled environment.

greenhouse effect — the effect when heat from sunlight is trapped inside any closed container with a glass or plastic cover.

greywater — waste water from sinks or washing machines.

grindstone — a hard stone for grinding grain; or revolving stone for sharpening tools or shaping and polishing objects.

groundwater — water found underground, for example, in a well.

gutted — destroyed by fire.

guy wires — wires attached to a tower, for example, so that it cannot move or shake due to the wind.

gypsum board — a thin board formed of layers of gypsum plaster and paper, used on interior walls of buildings.

hacksaw — a handtool used to cut metal.

halter — a rope or strap for tying or leading an animal.

hamper — to make difficult; to hinder.

hands-on — practical.

handyman (handyperson) skills — general maintenance and repair skills.

haphazardly — in a disorganized way; carelessly.

hard-pressed — faced with a very difficult task.

hardware store — a kind of store in the United States which sells small tools, nuts and bolts, wire, plumbing parts, and miscellaneous metal parts with a wide variety of uses.

harnessing — using to advantage.

harrowing — using an agricultural implement with spikes or discs to break up and level plowed ground.

hatchery — place where fish are raised from eggs to small but viable size before being released to feed and grow larger.

have-nots — those who don't have enough wealth and income to live at an acceptable standard of living.

haves — those who have enough wealth and income to live relatively comfortably.

head — the total usable height water falls when used in a water wheel, turbine or hydraulic ram pump; or the distance water is lifted by a pump.

health auxiliaries — health workers who have undergone a short training period, but are not among the categories normally thought of as "professionals."

heat exchanger — any unit which is designed to pass heat from one fluid or material to another.

heat pump — a device that extracts heat from one location and distributes it to another, by expanding and contracting a fluid; one unit of energy used to operate the pump can allow four units of heat energy to be captured. Due to the unique characteristics of this kind of a pump, heat energy can actually be extracted from a cold area (such as the inside of a refrigerator) and distributed to a warmer area (which seems to defy the normal laws governing the movement of heat energy).

heater duct tape — a wide, strong variety of tape that serves to prevent heat loss in hot air pipes.

hedgerow — a row of bushes forming a boundary or fence.

helicak — motorized three-wheeled taxi (Indonesia).

helical — winding or circling around a center or pole while getting smaller and smaller; spiral.

hence — therefore, thus.

herbicide — a chemical substance used to kill or control weeds or other undesirable plants.

herbivores — animals that eat only plants.

heritage — something handed down from one's ancestors or the past.

hermetic storage — airtight storage.

hierarchical — having people arranged in order of rank.

high carbon steel — steel that has a relatively high carbon content and can be hardened for this reason.

high-tech — complicated technology that requires a specialized industrial base to produce and service it.

hinges — metal pieces that connect doors and windows to walls.

hipped roof — a roof with four sloping surfaces coming to a point at the top.

hitch — a connecting device.

hock, in — in debt, with house or land or other asset as collateral.

hoist — a device for raising another object; a kind of winch.

holdover — something staying on from an earlier period.

hollow block mold — a mold used to make hollow building blocks that maintain the strength of solid blocks but are lighter in weight.

honey extractor — a device that removes honey from honeycomb, usually by spinning.

hookworm — any of a number of small parasitic roundworms with hooks around the mouth, that infest the small intestine of humans, especially in tropical areas.

horticulture — the science and art of growing fruits, vegetables, shrubs, and flowers.

horticulturist — one who works with horticulture, especially in gardens or orchards.

host — a plant or animal that has a parasite living on or in it.

huller — a machine used to remove the outer coverings (hulls) from rice, peanuts or other agricultural products.

humidity — dampness or wetness in the air.

humility — humble attitude or approach; the opposite of pride or arrogance.

humus — black or brown decomposed organic matter.

hurdle — a portable frame made of branches, used as a temporary fence or enclosure.

hybrid — a new variety created by plant breeding, often producing higher yields but genetically sterile (the crop cannot be used for seed).

hydraulic — using water or other liquid.

hydraulic ram pump — a device used to pump water with no other power source; uses the impact of the water itself to pump a small portion of the water to a higher level than the original source.

hydraulics — the study of the properties of water and other liquids within engineering.

hydroelectric unit — a unit that generates electricity from falling water.

hydrology — the study of where water is and how it behaves.

hydroponics — the cultivation of plants without the use of soil.

hydropower — energy generated by falling water.

hypothesis — an unproved theory or proposition.

hypothetical — for example; imaginary.

ideologically-tainted — associated with an ideology and therefore appearing biased.

illiterate — unable to read or write.

illiterates — people who cannot read and/or write a language.

immunology — the branch of medicine dealing with immunity to disease and biological reactions such as allergies.

impacted soil — soil which has been compressed to make it firmer.

impaled — pierced through with something pointed.

impenetrable — cannot be entered.

imperative — the evidence that some action must be taken; an urge; necessity.

impinge — affect.

implicit — suggested or understood though not plainly stated.

imposition — hardship or burden forced from outside.

imprinting — a learning mechanism operating very early in the life of an animal in which a stimulus creates a behavior pattern that is remembered.

improvisation — something made with the tools and materials at hand to fill an immediate need.

improvise — to solve a problem using what is available.

inadequacy — not enough; not good enough.

incandescent light bulb — a light bulb that glows due to intense heat caused by electricity passing through a special wire coil.

incentive — something that stimulates one to take action or work harder.

income disparity — the difference or gap between high and low incomes.

income stratification — the division of a community or nation into several very different income levels.

incremental — involving small changes or improvements.

incubator — a special compartment used to keep chicken eggs or premature babies at a warm temperature.

indigenous — native; originally from an area.

indispensable — something that cannot be left out.

inertia pump — see flap valve pump.

infestation — attack by insects or other pests causing damage to crops.

infuse — to fill with something.

ingenuity — creative ability.

inherent(ly) — by itself; existing in someone or something as a natural quality.

inhibition — a mental process that restrains or suppresses an action.

injurious — harmful.

in kind — with goods or food, not money.

innumerable — too many to count.

inoculant bacteria — nitrogen-fixing bacteria that are spread on seeds to aid in later plant growth.

inoculation — the spreading of bacteria or other life forms into soil or water for beneficial growth; the injection of a disease agent into an animal or plant to build up an immunity to it.

input — what is put in.

insecticides — chemicals used to kill insects and therefore protect crops.

insolation — the amount of solar energy falling on an area, usually measured in BTUs per unit of area.

insulation — material used to reduce the transfer of heat through a wall, a roof, the back of a solar water heater, or the walls of a fireless cooker.

intake — the place where water enters the pump.

integrate — to mix together, to combine.

intensive methods — gardening techniques used on small plots to obtain high yields; the productive potential of the soil is increased through composting, aeration, and other techniques.

intercropping — planting two or more crops together.

intergranular spaces — the air spaces between the kernels in a pile of grain.

interlocking — linked together.

intermittent — an activity that starts and stops irregularly.

internal combustion engine — an engine in which the fuel is burned inside the chambers in which expansion takes place and moves the pistons.

inter-row cultivator — a tool that is used to remove weeds in several rows at once.

intertwining — interconnecting; linked.

intervening — entering and altering the normal flow of activities in a community.

intervention — a project begun by an outside agent or agency.

intolerable — unbearable; too painful to be endured.

intravenous — directly into a vein.

inventive — skilled in creating processes or mechanisms.

inventory — a detailed list.

invertebrates — spineless organisms.

inverter (electricity) — a device for converting direct current into alternating current by mechanical or electronic means.

invoked — referred to with reverence.

jacks and lifts — devices for raising objects using teeth or threads or a hydraulic system.

jargon — special words used and understood only within a particular field of activity.

jig — a guide for a tool that allows the repeated production of the same cut or part.

judicious — careful; well-placed.

juvenile — young.

keel — the primary timber or piece of steel that extends along the length of the bottom of a boat or ship.

keen — eager, strong.

kernel — a grain or seed, as of corn, wheat, or peanut.

khadi — a word used by Mahatma Gandhi, referring to hand-spun cloth made by small cottage industries or individuals; also used to describe a policy based on village self-reliance stressing local production of food, clothing and other things to meet local needs.

kiln — a structure for the high-temperature treatment of bricks or pottery for hardening; or for the conversion of limestone to lime, used as a cement-like material in building; or for the reduction of wood to charcoal; or for the drying of wood.

kinetic energy — the energy of a body that results from its motion.

kink — a short twist, curl or bend in a rope, wire or chain.

knack — talent, ability.

Ku Klux Klan — a secret society of white men created in the United States following the Civil War in 1865, to re-establish and maintain white supremacy.

kymography — the study of wavelike motions or variations.

labor bottleneck — a period during the season when total output is limited by the fact that all available labor is being used; under these circumstances, labor-saving equipment will not destroy any jobs.

labor-intensive — techniques or projects that have a low capital-to-labor ratio.

laminated blade — a blade made of thin sheets of wood glued and pressed together.

landfill — area that has been filled in with a mixture of soil and solid waste.

landmark — something that marks an important place.

land reform — the redistribution of agricultural land by breaking up large landholdings and spreading them among all of the rural population.

larvae — the young worm-like form of an animal that changes structurally when it becomes an adult (e.g., caterpillars to butterflies).

laterite soil — a red soil formed by the decomposition of many kinds of rocks, and found especially in tropical rain forests.

lathe — a machine which turns wood or metal while it is being cut by a tool.

latitude — a distance measured in degrees, north or south of the equator.

lattice — pieces of wood interwoven together with spaces in between.

latrine — a device for depositing and isolating human waste.

leaching — the draining away of important nutrients by water action.

leap-frog — to jump over.

ledger — list of amounts of money.

legumes — plants that add nitrogen to the soil, such as soybeans or any other beans.

leguminous — of the family of plants that produce pods, to which peas and beans belong; legumes.

leprosy — a chronic and infectious disease caused by a bacterium that attacks the skin, flesh, nerves, etc.; characterized by white scaly scabs and wasting of body parts.

lever — a bar for prying or lifting.

liabilities — debts.

lift (aerodynamics) — the part of the total aerodynamic force acting in a direction perpendicular to the relative wind; opposes gravity in an airplane.

lift (waterpumping) — the height water is raised by a pump.

lime — calcium oxide; a cement-like substance used in building (for mortars and plasters).

lime kiln — a furnace used to make lime from coral or limestone.

limestone — a rock that is formed mainly by the accumulation of organic remains (such as shells or coral); consists mainly of calcium carbonate and is used extensively in building; yields lime when burned.

linkage mechanisms — connecting devices.

litmus paper — paper which is used in a simple chemical test for acidity or alkalinity of water or soil.

load (electricity) — the amount of power moving through an electrical circuit at any moment; or the device which is using this power; or the amount of power that a generator is producing.

loading rate — the amount and timing of loads of material being placed in a methane digester; important in obtaining an optimum concentration of solids.

lorry — truck.

low-impact technology — technology that fits into the human and biological environment with very little disruption or consumption of resources.

Luddites — a group of workers in England (1811-1816) who smashed new labor-saving textile equipment in protest against reduced wages and unemployment.

lunar — having to do with the moon.

lye (caustic soda) — a strong alkaline solution rich in potassium carbonate, leached from wood ashes; used in making soap.

machete — a large knife, used for chopping brush and other heavy cutting.

machining — precision work on metal.

magnifying lens — a hand lens used to enlarge an image for closer inspection.

magnitude — size; amount.

malnutrition — inadequate nutrition.

manipulative — affecting events or other people without consulting them.

manometer — an instrument for measuring the pressure of gases.

manure — animal excreta; shit; dung.

manure spreader — a specially equipped wagon used to spread barnyard manure around the fields.

marine borers — small animals that live in sea water and eat holes in the hulls of ships and in the posts of docks.

mash — mixture of grain or other vegetable, yeast, and water.

masonite — thin board made from compressed wood fibers.

masonry — the fitting together of cut or formed blocks, bricks, or stones.

master — completely understand.

mattock — a tool for loosening the soil.

meager — very small.

mechanization — replacing handtools with machines.

media — various means of communication.

mediate — to act as a communication channel and intermediary between two people or groups.

medicated — containing drugs.

metabolizable energy — food energy which can be converted for use.

metal primer — a first protective layer of paint; usually to combat rust and build a base for additional layers of paint.

metal spinning — the technique of bending and shaping metal by pressing on it while it is turned on a lathe.

metaphorically — using words to create an image in the mind to illustrate an idea.

metazoa — any of a group of very small animals that have cells for different functions; many of these are parasites.

methane (biogas) digester — a device which through biological activity produces methane gas and fertilizer from animal manures and crop residues (such as straw and leaves).

methane gas (biogas) — a naturally-occurring gas (CH_4) that can be produced using a methane gas digester; this gas burns with about 2/3 the level of BTU's of natural gas.

methane (biogas) plant — see methane digester.

methanol — alcohol made from wood.

methodology — a system of methods.

Michell water turbine — a turbine with curved vanes and hollow center; water passing through it propels the turbine both when entering and leaving; considered by many people to be the most practical easily-constructed water turbine; operates well under a range of head and flow rates.

microbe — a microscopic organism.

microbiological action — activity by tiny organisms; for example, decomposition in the soil.

microhydroelectric turbines — small power systems with generators that use falling water to produce electricity; usually in the range of 1-40 kw of power.

micro-organism — a very tiny organism that can only be viewed through a microscope.

midwife — a woman who assists women in childbirth.

migrant — a farm worker who moves from place to place with the agricultural calendar.

mild steel — low carbon steel; easily shaped but cannot be hardened.

millenia — thousands of years.

milling machine — a metal-cutting machine in which the surface of the work is shaped by being moved past revolving toothed cutters.

mimeoed — printed on a low-cost machine called a "mimeograph" machine.

minimum tillage — an agricultural strategy in which plowing and cultivating is kept to a minimum to reduce soil erosion and encourage micro-organisms.

misconception — mistaken idea.

mitigate — reduce the negative effects of; make less bad or serious.

mocking — showing scorn, contempt or defiance.

mode — method, way of operating.

modes of transport — types of transport; bicycles, cars and buses are all different modes of transport.

modular — made in small units which can be combined as needed.

mold — a container in the shape of a desired product, used to form building blocks or for casting metal parts.

molecular model — a visible model of the structure of molecules, used in teaching.

momentum — the quantity of motion of a moving object, equal to mass times velocity.

monetary — involving money.

monitor — carefully observe.

monoculture — the practice of using only one crop variety in a given area; the crop tends to be more vulnerable to attack by pests and diseases than in a diversified crop area.

monolithic — solid, the same throughout; all of one kind.

moped — a motor-assisted bicycle.

moratorium — temporary halt.

morbidity — the level (incidence) of disease among a population; how many people are sick.

mordant — dye preservative to prevent fading.

mortar and pestle — a very hard bowl (mortar) in which softer substances are ground or pounded to a powder with a hard tool (pestle).

motive power — power to move something, as an engine.

motocross bikes — a heavy-duty bicycle popular among children in the United States, in imitation of motorcycles used in racing over hilly terrain on dirt tracks.

mowing machine — a farm machine with a reciprocating blade that cuts standing grain or grass.

mulch — a top covering of the soil consisting of organic materials (grass, compost, dead weeds) that serves to keep moisture in the soil and reduce weed growth.

multi-blade (fan) windmill — a windmill design, common on American farms, which has a large number of blades and is usually used for waterpumping.

multiple cropping — involving more than one crop.

mundane — common, unexciting, normal.

mutual — involving both or all sides.

Mylar — see aluminized Mylar.

mystification — the process of making something deliberately hard to understand.

natural calamity — a disaster such as a hurricane, flood, or forest fire.

natural phenomena — processes and events that occur normally in nature.

naught — nothing.

needs assessment — technique for deciding what people need.

networking — the process of making people with similar interests aware of each other, to increase communication and cooperation.

neutralize (magnetic field) — to stop the action of a magnetic field.

niche — place.

night soil — human excreta.

nipples (bicycle) — small threaded pieces of metal which serve to attach the spokes to the rim of a bicycle.

nitriding — a process used in hardening forged steel.

nitrogenous fertilizer — fertilizer that contains nitrogen.

nodule — a small knot on a root that contains nitrogen-fixing bacteria.

nonconformist — one who does not do things in the way in which they are normally done.

nonviability — inability to be sustained.

nooks — small hidden places.

novice — beginner.

nozzle — a device at the end of a hose or pipe with which a stream of water can be controlled and directed.

nuisance — a person or thing causing trouble or inconvenience.

nurture — to raise or promote the development of.

nutrient — substance vital for growth and development of organisms, such as vitamins, fertilizers, protein, etc.

nutrient cycling — the process of moving nutrients through the agricultural system, from fodder to manure to fertilizer to additional plant growth, for maximum production and continued fertility.

nutritive — promoting health through a balanced diet.

obscure — relatively unknown.

obsolescence — the process of going out of use.

obtainable — available.

oil press — a tool used to crush oil-bearing vegetable material to extract the oil.

oilseed — any of a number of plants grown for the oil contained within their seeds.

oligarchy — a form of government in which the ruling power belongs to a few people, families, or groups.

opelet — small transport vehicle in Indonesia.

open loop — in solar energy systems, heating water or air by passing it through or over a collecting surface and then moving it to where it is needed.

opt — choose.

optical — having to do with the sense of sight.

optics — having to do with the properties of light.

optimize — to obtain the most efficient or maximum use of.

optimum — best.

organic — of, related to, or coming from living organisms.

organic agriculture — a form of agriculture that uses only natural materials and techniques.

organic gardening — a form of gardening that uses only natural materials and techniques.

organic manures — waste material from natural sources, such as animal dung and decaying plants.

organic solvent — liquid distilled from vegetable matter that can be used in cleaning.

outmoded — out of date; no longer useful.

output — what is produced.

outstripping — surpassing, increasing at a greater rate.

ova — eggs.

overhaul — to check thoroughly and make needed repairs.

overhead functions — tasks performed which enable other more basic activities to go on.

overriding — extremely important.

overshot water wheel — a water wheel driven by water entering near the top.

overuse — too much use.

oxy-acetylene welding — a welding system that uses compressed oxygen and acetylene gas to supply heat.

paddy weeder — a handtool used to remove weeds between the rows of rice plants in a paddy.

panacea — a cure for all problems.

papier-mache — a material made of paper and glue or flour that is easily shaped when wet, but dries hard.

parabola — a shape commonly used in solar cookers to focus sunlight on a small area so that it becomes very hot.

parabolic cylinder — a solar energy device with a cross-sectional shape of a parabola; sunlight is focused all along the length of a pipe or tube.

parabolic dish — a solar energy device shaped like a dish or bowl, having the characteristics of a parabola and focusing sunlight on a point or very small area.

paradigmatic — showing a model or pattern.

paramedical — of auxiliary medical personnel.

parasite — a plant or animal that lives on or in an organism of another species (the host) while usually doing harm.

parboiling (para-boiling) — a preliminary cooking process which serves to seal the outer surface of a grain such as rice.

parcelization — dividing up into small pieces.

pare — to cut away the outer covering of something.

particle board — board made of small pieces of wood or other material compressed together.

passive solar — any solar technology that uses natural energy flows in the materials and orientation of a building for heating, without the use of special collectors, pipes, and pumps.

patent — a license giving the inventor or patent owner the exclusive right to make, use, or sell a particular invention for a period of years.

paternalistic — resembling the relationship a father has with his children.

pathogens — dangerous and harmful micro-organisms, such as bacteria and viruses; found in human and other wastes, responsible for spreading diseases.

pathological growth — growth or increase in size which is unhealthy, or which is not good for people.

peak power — the highest level of power that can be provided at any time.

pedal thresher — a lightweight machine operated by foot power, that is designed to be carried easily into the fields for use in threshing; mainly a wooden drum revolving at about 450 rpm, driven by a pedal and gearing system.

pedicab — a three-wheeled pedal-powered taxi.

peers — people who do the same work, or are of the same social status or age.

pelton impulse wheel — a kind of water-power device which is driven by the impact of a jet of water; can be used to generate electricity.

pendulum — a weight hung from a fixed point so as to swing freely under the combined forces of gravity and momentum.

perennial — any plant that produces from the same root structure year after year; important in soil conservation.

perennial crops — crops in which individual plants continue to produce each season for a period of years.

perforated — having holes.

perseverance — continued, patient effort.

pertinent — significant, important.

pesticide — a chemical substance which kills plant pests (insects and rodents).

pesticide persistence — the tendency for pesticides to remain in the soil and water supply after use.

pharmaceuticals — drugs.

pharmacological — having to do with the science of study of the effects of drugs on living organisms.

phenomenally — amazingly.

philanthropic — showing a desire to help humankind by gifts to charitable institutions.

photovoltaic array — a set of photovoltaic cells.

photovoltaic cells — solar energy devices that directly convert solar energy into electricity.

physiologically — having to do with the functions and vital processes of living things.

pickling — a process for canning or bottling vegetables using vinegar.

pictorial — using pictures.

piecemeal — bit by bit; not organized very well.

pioneers — early workers in a new field.

pipe nipple — a pipe connector with threaded fittings.

pise — rammed earth; a construction technique in which earth is pounded inside movable forms to make walls.

piston pump — a pump which raises water by the up-and-down motion of a rod with a valve, on the inside of a cylinder.

pit latrine — a toilet in which human waste accumulates and is buried in a hole in the ground.

pivotal — most important.

plankton — microscopic animal and plant life found in water, used by fish for food.

planned obsolescence — a deliberate attempt by manufacturers to produce an item that will be rapidly out of style or no longer used.

plateau — a high flat or level place.

plight — a sad or dangerous situation.

plowshare — the cutting blade of a plow.

plumbing float control valve — a valve commonly used in flush toilets, which allows water to slowly fill a tank until the floating ball reaches the desired water level and the valve is closed; can also be used in a variety of other systems such as an oil-drum storage tank for a solar water heating unit.

pneumatic tires — air-filled tires.

pole saw — a saw operated by a foot treadle with an overhead pole which acts as a spring mechanism; together they pull the saw blade up and down.

pollination — the act of transferring pollen between the parts of a flower, important in the production of fruits and vegetables, carried out by bees and other insects.

polyethylene — a plastic material used in sheets and waterpipes.

poly-phase electric motor — a motor driven by more than one alternating current.

polythene — British spelling of poly-ethylene, a plastic used in sheeting.

polyvinylchloride — a plastic material used in waterpipes.

porridge — a soft food made of cereal grains boiled in water or milk until thick.

potable water — safe drinking water.

potter's kick wheel (potter's wheel) — a tool used to form cups, bowls and other round objects; a heavy flywheel on the bottom allows smooth work on the clay.

poultry — chickens and similar birds raised for meat.

power co-efficient — the percentage of the total available power in the wind that a windmachine can capture at any specific windspeed.

power drive — the system of spinning shafts and gears used in transmitting mechanical energy.

power output — the amount of mechanical or electrical power produced.

power tiller — a small engine-driven machine for plowing or breaking the soil; usually has two wheels.

pragmatic — practical, taking into account organizational constraints and capabilities; for example, when deciding a path of action; taken too far, being "pragmatic" can mean taking the easier path so that fundamental problems are never addressed.

precarious — dangerous, insecure.

precision file guide — a tool that aids in sharpening chainsaw blades.

predators — animals that eat other animals.

prejudice — an opinion held in disregard of facts that contradict it.

preliminary — introductory; coming before or leading up to the main action.

privy — a kind of latrine; usually a platform with a hole over a pit, for isolation of human waste.

producer-gas engine — an engine which runs on gas produced in a charcoal-making process.

product differentiation — marketing technique of making products appear to be different from other similar products with the same function.

production version — the final form of a product to be made in large quantities for the market.

productivity — the amount of product created or work accomplished per unit of something (usually labor time) invested.

proliferation — spread, increase.

prolific — producing a large amount.

propagandistic — involving the uncritical promotion of particular ideas and doctrines.

propagation — the reproduction or multiplication of a plant or animal.

propane torch — a hand-held torch that burns propane gas; used for workshop activities.

propeller — a device with two or more twisted blades that rotate with the hub in which they are mounted.

protective canopy — a plant cover, in the form of shrubs or trees, which protects the soil from the harsh effect of sun, wind and rain; particularly important in tropical forests that receive heavy rainfall.

prototype — an experimental version for testing.

protozoa — any of a group of microscopic animals made up of a single cell or group of identical cells; many of these are parasites.

protracted — extended.

prudent — wise.

pulp — a mixture of ground-up wood from which paper is made.

pulse — any member of the legume family (peas, beans, lentils, etc.).

punch — a tool for making holes.

punitive legislation — laws that declare certain activities illegal and create punishments for these activities.

pvc pipe — polyvinyl chloride (plastic) pipe, made from petroleum products.

qualitative — not numerical; involving kind or type.

quantitative — numerical; involving numbers or quantities.

quarried stones — pieces of rock cut out from under the earth.

quasi- — somewhat; to a certain extent.

radial-flow turbine — a turbine in which water flows around the axis.

radiating plate — a metal plate which serves to pass the heat from a fire underneath to the area or substance being heated; prevents direct contact with the flames and smoke of the fire.

rammed earth — a technique of building construction in which earth is pounded inside movable forms to make walls.

rapacious — taking by force, greedy.

rarity — a very unusual thing or event.

rasp — coarse file for removing wood or metal.

rationale — reasons used to support a decision or conclusion.

rattan — a long slender tough stem that comes from a climbing palm and is used in making furniture.

ravine — a small narrow valley with steep sides, created by a stream.

reallocation — spending in a different place, or for a different purpose.

realm — area.

reamer — a tool used to smooth out or enlarge the inside of a pipe.

reaming — work using a reamer to smooth out or enlarge the inside or a pipe.

reap — to harvest.

reaping machine — a machine that cuts grain in the fields.

rearing — raising.

reclamation — a reclaiming; especially the recovery of wasteland or desert by irrigation, drainage, replanting, etc.

recoup — make up for something lost; recover.

rectifier — a device that converts alternating current into direct current.

recurring — happening again and again.

recycling — reusing; processing in order to reuse material.

reforestation — the process of planting trees in an area that once had them.

refraction — the bending of a ray of light as it passes from one medium to another.

refractory cement — cement that will survive high temperatures.

refractory materials — heat-resistant materials.

reinforcing rod (rebar) — metal rod used to increase the strength of concrete.

refuge — a place of protection against storms, etc.

rehabilitation — repair or rebuilding.

rehydration — the process of restoring the body to its natural balance of fluids.

rejuvenate — to revive.

relay — an electro-magnetic device for automatic control that is operated by variation in conditions of an electric current; used to operate other devices (such as switches).

remote — far away.

render — make.

rendering fat — melting fat until it becomes a liquid.

renewable energy — energy from sunlight, wind, falling water, or biological sources that is continually recharged by the sun.

renovation — the process of repairing and rebuilding.

repatriated — sent back to the country from which it came.

repudiate — to deny; to refuse to accept or support.

reputable — respectable.

reservoir — a body of water held behind a dam.

resin — a solid or honey-like substance from plants.

resistor — a coil of wire used in an electrical system to provide resistance and thus heat.

respiratory system — the system of organs, including the lungs, involved in the exchange of oxygen and carbon dioxide with the environment.

restoration — a putting back into a former, normal condition.

retort — a container in which a material is heated to extract gases.

retrogression — a return to a less complex or worse condition.

revegetation — the process of replanting in an area that has lost most of its plant life.

rhetorical — having unnecessary, exaggerated language or style in making a point.

riddled — filled; filled with holes.

rigorous — very strict, thoroughly accurate.

ripping chain — a tool used on a chainsaw for cutting along the length of a log, instead of across it.

ripple tank apparatus — a device made of

glass and filled with water, used to show wave motion.

rivals — is similar to.

rivet — a metal pin used to bind two pieces of metal together.

riveting — binding of metal to metal using rivets pounded on both sides.

roadbed — the foundation of a road.

romantic — without a basis in fact.

roof pond — a shallow reservoir of water on a roof used to collect, store, and release energy to heat or cool a building.

root crops — crops in which the roots are the parts that are eaten; for example, potatoes and carrots.

rotating wooden drum washing machine — a machine that loosens the dirt in clothing by the rotating action of a drum or barrel inside a tub of water.

rote — (to memorize) mechanically and unthinkingly.

rototiller — a small motorized hand-tractor or cultivator usually with rotating blades.

routine — normal, regular, common.

rpm — revolutions per minute.

rubble — damaged building material.

rudimentary — primitive, simple.

rudiments — the elementary steps or information.

runoff agriculture — a form of cultivation totally dependent upon water which can be channelled onto the field during and immediately following rains.

sail cloth — cloth normally used on sailing ships.

sail windmill — a kind of windmill that uses removable cloth sails (usually 4 to 8) as the blades.

sailwing windmill — a kind of windmill that has a small number (usually 2 or 3) of blades that are generally made of cloth and are shaped like an airfoil (the shape of an airplane wing).

saline water — water with a high level of salts.

salinity — level of salt content.

sandcrete blocks — building blocks made of sand and cement.

sanitation — the use of hygienic measures such as the drainage and disposal of sewage.

savannah — a treeless plain found in tropical and subtropical regions; a transition zone between rain forest and desert.

Savonius rotor — a windmachine with a

vertical axis, usually made from split oil drums.

sawyer — someone whose job is to saw wood.

scanty — too little, not enough.

schematic drawings — drawings that show the complete layout of a system with all of its connecting parts.

schistosome — a parasite that causes schistosomiasis when it enters and lives in the human body; spends part of its life in the body of a snail.

schistosomiasis — a tropical disease that involves problems in the liver, nervous system, urinary bladder, or lungs; spread by a parasite.

scholarly — showing much knowledge, accuracy, and critical ability; presented in standard form acceptable to professors and other academics.

screen printing — a method of printing through a piece of silk or other fine cloth on which all parts not to be printed have been coated with film that prevents ink from passing through.

scrutiny — careful examination.

scum controlling device — a mechanism that is used to break up the thick layer of materials that rises to the surface in a methane digester; this layer tends to prevent the production of gas.

scythe — a handtool with a long handle and metal blade, used to cut grain or grass.

sealant — a substance such as wax, plastic or silicone used for sealing, to make a substance airtight or watertight.

seam — the line formed by sewing together two pieces of material.

seasonal — taking place only during certain seasons of the year.

sedimentation — accumulation of mud, sand, and gravel carried by water.

seedbed — the earth in which seeds are planted in a garden.

seed dressing drum — a rotating drum in which seeds are mixed with fertilizers or pesticides.

seed drill — a tool which places seeds into the ground, usually by dropping them through a tube.

seed propagation — the production of seeds for future use.

segregate — keep divided.

self-actualizing — helping people to know themselves better.

semantic — related to meaning in language, the relationship between words and the concepts they represent.

sentimental — romantic, unrealistic, emotional.

septic tanks — large tanks for settling and decomposing human waste.

sewage — human waste material carried away by water.

shanty — substandard crude shelter.

shearing force — a force tending to cause a piece of metal tubing, for example, to separate in a direction perpendicular to the tubing.

shears — heavy scissors for cutting sheet metal.

shelterbelt — a barrier zone of trees or shrubs planted to protect crops and soil from strong winds and erosion.

shingles — overlapping pieces of wood or other material used in roofing.

shoot — a new growth, sprout or twig.

shop tools — tools that are commonly found only in small workshops; usually mechanized.

short out (electricity) — to allow the electric current to go in a shorter path, thus preventing the normal action of a circuit, by connecting two wires that are not normally connected.

shrouded windmill — a windmill with a funnel around the outside edge of the swept area which forces wind from a larger area to pass through the blades.

sickle — a handtool with a curved metal blade for cutting grain or grass.

sieve — a device with small holes or screen to separate out larger particles while allowing smaller ones to pass through.

silhouette — outline against a light.

silicone sealant — a plastic compound used to seal a container so that water cannot enter or escape from it.

silk-screen printing — see screen printing.

silt — small particles of soil intermediate in size between sand and clay.

simultaneous — at the same time.

siting — choosing the location for.

sizing — determining the proper size; or separating according to size (for example, "sizing peanuts").

skewed — distorted in one direction.

skilsaw — a hand-held electric saw with a circular blade.

skylight — a glass or plastic piece of a roof which allows light to enter a house or a room.

slang — popular words not found in dictionaries.

slash and burn shifting cultivation — the practice of cutting and burning forest vegetation to open land for subsistence agriculture in tropical countries; usually by small farmers; the soil is exhausted within five years and the farmers must move on to clear more forest.

slit — a narrow cut or crack through which light can pass.

sludge — the outflow of a digester or sewage treatment plant.

sludge treatment ponds — basins in which sewage, animal manures, and other wastes are broken down.

slurry — diluted waste material as it is placed into a digester.

smallholder — someone who owns only a small amount of land or some product.

smoker — a device used in beekeeping; a hand-bellows with some burning material which produces smoke to force the bees to move out of or into the hive.

soakway — a place for waste water to sink into the ground.

social account — the net economic effects of an investment or other action, measured as they affect an entire community or nation; which investments and policy measures appear wise may be different in social account than when only individual investment-profit effects are considered.

sod houses — houses with roofs or walls made from strips of soil still containing the roots of grass.

soil amendment — a substance that aids plant growth indirectly by improving the condition of the soil.

soil cement — a mixture of soil and a small amount of cement used in making blocks without sand for construction purposes.

soil conservation — a policy of maintaining and promoting the health and fertility of the soil; for example, by planting trees to prevent erosion.

solar distillation — a process in which solar energy is trapped and used to evaporate water, which then condenses as pure water that can be used for drinking.

solar greenhouse — a greenhouse that depends primarily on solar energy for heating; differs from a conventional greenhouse that uses fossil fuel energy to control the inside temperature.

solar radiation — energy from the sun.

soldering — a technique of lightweight metal bonding, by melting a soft metal at a lower temperature than in brazing.

soldering iron — a small tool used in

lightweight metal bonding.

Solomon — a very wise king and judge in the Bible.

solvent — a liquid substance capable of dissolving or dispersing another substance.

sowing — planting seed, especially by throwing (broadcast sowing) or use of a mechanical metered device.

space heating — heating the air in a house, room or small area.

spar — long pole which supports a sail.

sparingly — in small quantity.

sparse — not common; few.

spawning — producing or depositing eggs, sperm or young.

species diversity — the number of different species in an area.

specific gravity — the ratio of the weight or mass of a given volume of a substance to that of an equal volume of water (liquids and solids) or air (gases).

spectrum — range.

spinning wheel — a device used to make cloth thread.

spinoff — a secondary development.

spokes — the bars or wires extending between the hub and rim of a bicycle or cart wheel.

spontaneous — happening suddenly or without an obvious cause.

spoon-tilt hammer — a device that has a hammer at one end, a balancing point, and a bucket-shaped (spoon-shaped) hollow at the other end; the bucket is slowly filled by a continuous flow of water from a pipe or stream; as the water fills this end it begins to drop down, which raises the hammer end; the water is able to escape when the bucket tilts too far, and the hammer then falls; the hammer can be used in a blacksmith's shop, and the same principle has been used to pound rice to remove the hulls.

sporadic — occasional, irregular.

spring leaf — high carbon steel, tempered to be very hard and respond like a spring; used in automobile springs.

sprung frame — a frame mounted on springs.

squatters — people who have built shelters and houses on land they do not own.

squatter settlements — areas where poor people have moved in to live on previously unoccupied land.

stabilized soil — soil that has had emulsified asphalt, cement or other material added to make it resist erosion; used to make blocks for construction.

stabilizing agent — a substance that binds or makes firm, such as cement or lime; usually used in making building blocks.

stagnant — unchanging; lifeless.

staples — basic foods such as grains, beans, and tubers.

state-of-the-art — latest, most current, most technically advanced.

static — unmoving.

stator — the fixed outside part of an electric motor or generator.

staves — see barrel staves.

stereotype — a fixed concept about a group of people or an idea.

sterile — free from living germs.

stewardship — taking care of in a responsible manner to preserve quality and benefits over the long term.

stratification — the division into groups of different rank, status, or income.

stricken — affected by something painful or sickening.

striving — attempting; trying hard.

stroboscope — a revolving disc with holes around the edge which allow flashes of light to pass through it at regular intervals.

stucco — a coating for the outside walls of buildings, applied like plaster.

styrofoam — an industrially-created material that is used for insulation, floating objects, and packaging.

subscribe (to an opinion) — believe.

subservient — humbly submissive.

subsidy — a grant of money.

subsistence agriculture — a system of farming in which a family produces all or almost all of their own goods, including food, tools, cloths, etc.; there is usually not a significant surplus for sale.

subtropics — regions bordering on the tropics, having a nearly tropical climate.

suction pump — a pump which lifts liquids only by creating a vacuum above the liquid level; used to lift water but only to about 20-25 feet (33 feet is the theoretical maximum).

sugar cane crusher — a tool used to flatten sugar cane stalks and extract the juice which contains the sugar.

sundial — a clock that indicates the time of day using the shadows caused by the sun.

super helicak — small taxi (Indonesia).

superimpose — to place on top of.

superphosphate — a synthetic chemical fertilizer, made by treating bone or phosphate rock with sulfuric acid.

surging — rapidly increasing.

surpass — to be better than.

suspension bridge — a bridge that is hung from cables.

sustainable — that which can be continued indefinitely into the future.

swab — to clean with a small piece of cotton.

swampy areas — land that is always wet.

swell — increase greatly.

swelling soils — soils that expand and shrink under conditions of changing pressure, water content, or temperature.

swine — pigs.

symptoms — evidence of disease.

synchronous inverter — device for changing direct current.

synergy — parts or ideas working together.

synthetic — human-made; non-natural.

synthetic fertilizer — an artificial substance which helps plants grow and develop.

syringe — a medical device used with a needle to give injections.

table saw — a saw with a rotating circular blade that has a flat surface built around it like a table.

tabular — arranged in a table or chart.

tandem — a two-wheeled bicycle tht has seats and pedals for two riders.

tanner — someone who tans (preserves) animal hides and skins.

tannery — a place where animal hides and skins are preserved.

tapered — becoming smaller at one end.

tap-root — a large main root found on many plants.

tarpaper — a thick paper product soaked in asphalt; used for waterproofing in roofs and walls.

technical fix — an attempt to solve a social, political or economic problem through a purely technical change, which may simply postpone the problem.

technocratic — of government in which all economic resources and the social system are controlled by scientists and engineers.

technological determinism — a theoretical point of view which holds that technological change is the primary cause of political and social change.

tempeh — an Indonesian food made from soybeans inoculated with bacteria.

temper — harden.

temperate zone — either of two zones of the earth between the tropics and the polar regions.

tenant — someone who pays rent to use a house or piece of land.

tension — being pulled apart.

tenure — the act of holding property.

tenurial — related to holding property.

terminology — words from a particular field of activity.

terracing — the building of flat areas along contour lines of a hillside, to prevent soil erosion while allowing productive use of the land.

terrain — the surface of the land.

terrarium — a glass-walled container for small animals that allows careful observation of their behavior.

therapeutic — serving to cure, heal, or improve health.

thermal pollution — heat from a power plant or other source that can disturb the ecological balance.

thermal storage — heat storage during the warm or sunny parts of the day, for use during the colder parts of the night.

thermosiphon principle — the principle that heated liquids tend to rise; in a solar water heater, this principle can be used to enable circulation of water from a flat plate collector to a storage tank located above it, without the use of a pump.

thresher — a machine used to separate grain or beans from the unwanted straw or other plant material.

thriving — growing very well.

tiebars — strips of metal for securely fastening roofing pieces.

tie-ridging — a technique of field preparation in Africa, in which channels between ridges are periodically blocked by earth, to trap rainwater and prevent drainage.

tier — level.

tillage — the plowing of land.

tiller — a device for plowing the soil; a cultivator.

timescale — period of time during which an activity is planned or expected to take place.

tines — the teeth of a rake, harrow or cultivator.

tinkerer — a person who likes to make gadgets and inventions, but not in a serious manner.

tin snips — a tool similar to scissors, for cutting sheet metal.

tip-speed ratio — the ratio of the speed of

the tip of a windmachine blade to the speed of the wind; a low tip-speed ratio (such as 1:1 in the Savonius rotor) at a moderate windspeed means the windmachine is better adapted to mechanical applications such as waterpumping; a high tip-speed ratio (such as 5:1 in a two-bladed windgenerator) at a moderate windspeed means the windmachine is better adapted to generating electricity.

tolerance — the amount of variation in the dimensions of parts that is acceptable when constructing a machine.

tongs — a tool used by blacksmiths to pick up hot pieces of metal.

toolbar — a frame to which different tools can be attached for various land preparation activities, such as plowing or cultivating.

topography — the surface features of a region.

torque — the force that acts to produce rotation.

torrid — very hot.

torsion — the act of turning or twisting.

totalitarian regime — a government in which one group maintains complete control under a dictatorship.

toxic chemicals — poisons which may be harmful to plants, animals and humans.

tragedy of the commons — the phenomenon that land, water, air and other things owned in common are frequently abused, polluted, or otherwise damaged, to the disadvantage of all.

trailer chassis — the frame of a trailer.

transaction — exchange of something for something else.

transfer pipette — a tube of glass or plastic used to move liquid from one container to another.

transformer — a device containing two or more coils of insulated wire that is used to change the voltage and amperage levels of an electric current.

transit level — an instrument for identifying a horizontal line or plane.

transmission loss — the amount of power lost between a turbine and the machinery it is operating; or electricity lost between the generator and the point of use.

trap — a plant which can eliminate harmful insects.

treadle — a foot-powered mechanism that converts an up-and-down motion of the foot on a board into a rotating motion on a machine; commonly seen on sewing machines.

trip-hammer — a heavy mechanical hammer that is regularly lifted and dropped; used in blacksmithing.

Trombe wall — a space heating system that involves a wall covered with glass that traps solar energy and circulates the heat through vents into the building.

tropics — the region of the earth lying between the Tropic of Cancer and the Tropic of Capricorn, marking the limits of the apparent north and south journey of the sun.

troubleshooting — seeking the source of a problem in a piece of equipment.

trowel (verb) — to apply mortar using a trowel (a flat handtool).

truss — a rigid framework of beams or bars for supporting a roof or bridge.

truss plates — metal plates attached to the beams that support a roof.

T-square — an instrument for drawing or cutting 90-degree angles.

tuberculosis — an infectious disease that affects the lungs.

tubers — plants such as sweet potatoes which can be reproduced by planting pieces of the roots.

tuft — a small piece of wool.

turbidity — cloudiness.

turbine — a wheel with curved vanes on a shaft, driven by the pressure of water.

turbulence (wind) — wildly irregular motion of air.

turnbuckle — a metal sleeve with opposite internal threads at each end; by turning it, one can tighten or loosen two threaded rods coming together at that point.

twist bit — the cutting edge of a wood drill; has a twisted blade.

typhoon — hurricane.

u-bolt — a bolt shaped like the letter "u".

undermining — removing the justification for.

undershot water wheel — a water wheel that is turned by water flowing underneath it; for example, by a small river.

unduly — unnecessarily.

unfettered — without restrictions.

unforeseen — unexpected.

unhampered — not restricted.

unicycle — a pedalled cycle having only one wheel.

unsubstantiated — undocumented.

updraft and downdraft kilns — the adjective refers to the direction of air movement through the kiln.

urea — a high nitrogen fertilizer made from animal wastes or natural gas using a high-technology, energy-intensive process.

urine — liquid human waste.

vaccinate — to give an injection that produces immunity to a specific disease by causing the formation of antibodies.

validity — truth, accuracy.

vane — a thin flat or curved object that is rotated about an axis by a flow of water or wind; for example, in a windmill or water turbine.

vaporizing — converting from a liquid to a gas by heating.

vaulted roof — a roof in the shape of an arc.

veil — to hide.

velocity — speed.

ventilation — the circulation of air through a room or enclosed space.

verbiage — an excess of words beyond those needed to say what is meant.

verging on — bordering, approaching.

versatile — can function or be used in many different ways.

vertical axis — an axle or axis which runs in a vertical (up and down) motion.

vertical-axis water wheel — a water wheel driven by water coming through a channel and hitting in on one side; has a vertical axis instead of the usual horizontal axis found on water wheels.

vertical-axis windmill — a windmill such as the Savonius rotor which always faces the wind, regardless of what direction it comes from; this differs from the more common horizontal-axis windmills which must turn to face the wind.

vertical shaft kilns — relatively small kilns used in the production of cement, having a vertical main shaft, differing from the more capital-intensive rotary kilns.

viable — successful, possible, practical.

virus — any of a group of extremely small infective agents that cause disease in animals, people and plants.

vise — a workshop device used to clamp or hold objects.

vogue — popularity or fashion.

volatile gas — unburned, energy-containing gases in the smoke of a fire.

voltage — the electric potential between two points, expressed in volts; can be understood as the "pressure" forcing electricity through the lines similar to pressure in a water system.

voltage regulator — a simple electrical instrument that controls the voltage level of the current from generator to battery (as in an automobile or windgenerator system).

voltmeter — an instrument for measuring voltage.

volumeter — an instrument used to measure the volume of liquids and gases directly, and of solids by the amount of liquid they displace.

vulnerability — the state of being open to attack or damage.

vulnerable — easily hurt.

water-borne — carried by water.

water catchment — an apparatus for collecting and storing water.

water hammer — see spoon-tilt hammer.

waterproofing — applying a substance to protect an object from contact with water.

water seal privy (water seal toilet) — a human waste disposal system that has a passageway filled with water which prevents odors, gases, and disease organisms from returning through the passageway.

water turbine — a device powered by the reaction or impulse of a current of water subject to pressure; usually has curved blades; is used to generate electricity because it has a higher rpm than a water wheel.

water wheel — a wheel with buckets or paddles which allow it to be turned by falling water or water moving underneath.

weaning — the process of causing a young child to eat other foods than mother's milk.

weatherization — the process of sealing air leaks and insulating a house to reduce heat loss.

wed — join.

welding — high-temperature heavy-duty metal bonding; arc-welding uses heat created as an electric current passes across a small gap; oxy-acetylene (carbide) welding uses the heat created by burning a mixture of oxygen and acetylene gas.

welding jig — a device used to hold metal that is being welded.

well rings — metal or concrete cylinders placed inside a well to prevent material from the walls from collapsing inward.

well-tuned — well-matched.

wheelwright — someone whose job is the making or repair of wheels or wheeled vehicles.

whole-heartedly — enthusiastically.

winch — a device for hauling, pulling, or

raising another object, that allows the operator to slowly move something that he or she would normally not be able to move at all.

winch plow — a plow pulled across the field by a cable attached to a winch.

windbreak — a hedge, fence, or row of trees that serves as protection from wind.

windgenerator — a machine which uses wind power to generate electricity.

winding (wire) — a coil of wire; when electricity is passed through this coil a magnetic field is created, which can be used to operate switches.

windmachine — any kind of machine which gets its motion from the wind.

windmill — originally a machine which uses the wind to drive the grinding stones of a mill to make flour from grain; often used to refer to any kind of windmachine, particularly wind-powered machines for waterpumping.

windwheel — any kind of windmachine which has blades or arms in the shape of the spokes of a wheel.

winnower — a machine used to separate grain from hulls or straw.

wire mesh — wire or steel reinforcing bars in a woven pattern; used as reinforcement in ferrocement construction.

wither — to dry up.

wobbling — unsteady; unstable.

woodlot — land planted with trees grown for fuelwood.

workplace — the site of a job, in this context including a calculation of all supporting capital costs for tools.

yurt — a traditional Mongolian dwelling.

Index

Index

MF = microfiche number; p. = page number of review

MF = microfiche number; p. = page number of review

MF = microfiche number; p. = page number of review

MF = microfiche number;   p. = page number of review

MF = microfiche number;   p. = page number of review

MF = microfiche number;   p. = page number of review

MF = microfiche number; p. = page number of review

MF = microfiche number; p. = page number of review

MF = microfiche number;   p. = page number of review

MF = microfiche number; p. = page number of review

MF = microfiche number; p. = page number of review

MF = microfiche number; p. = page number of review

MF = microfiche number; p. = page number of review

MF = microfiche number; p. = page number of review

MF = microfiche number; p. = page number of review

MF = microfiche number;   p. = page number of review

MF = microfiche number;   p. = page number of review

MF = microfiche number; p. = page number of review

MF = microfiche number;   p. = page number of review

MF = microfiche number; p. = page number of review

MF = microfiche number;   p. = page number of review

MF = microfiche number; p. = page number of review

MF = microfiche number; p. = page number of review

MF = microfiche number; p. = page number of review

MF = microfiche number; p. = page number of review

MF = microfiche number; p. = page number of review

MF = microfiche number; p. = page number of review

MF = microfiche number; p. = page number of review

MF = microfiche number; p. = page number of review

MF = microfiche number;   p. = page number of review

MF = microfiche number;   p. = page number of review

MF = microfiche number; p. = page number of review

MF = microfiche number; p. = page number of review

MF = microfiche number; p. = page number of review

MF = microfiche number;   p. = page number of review

Notes

Notes

Notes

Notes

Notes

Notes

Introducing
the most powerful tool
for appropriate technology
work:

The expanded
Appropriate
Technology
Microfiche Library

The most comprehensive... practical... economical A.T. reference collection ever compiled.

You can now get your own copy of one of the world's best libraries on appropriate technology, for 5% of its original cost! People in more than 100 countries are using these portable libraries to answer 50,000 technical questions yearly.

Speed your access to technical information

With your own complete library at your fingertips, you can get the information you need much faster than ever before. The wide variety of options covered in the microfiche library will enable you to effectively evaluate choices and make better decisions. The detailed practical information in these books will allow your work to proceed immediately.

"The library is a great aid toward speeding projects along without waiting for info."
—R.D., Bolivia

138,650 Pages of Text—Organized and Indexed

The Appropriate Technology Microfiche Library includes every page of text from 1000 books and documents reviewed in the new Appropriate Technology Sourcebook, a total of 138,650 pages. In a few minutes you can learn to use this fully organized and indexed collection.

Covering a Full Range of Information Needs

With the new A.T. Microfiche Library on your desk you can find the information you need on agricultural tools and techniques, workshop tools and equipment, crop storage systems, water supply systems, forestry, aquaculture, improved cookstoves, solar/wind/water power, biogas, transportation, health care, science teaching, communications, small industries, small enterprise management, nonformal education techniques, and all other small scale technology topics.

This library collection includes all kinds of information, from how-to-do-it instructions to performance figures, from approximate costs to engineering considerations.

For example, in the water supply topic area you can use the library to 1) estimate water flow and demand, 2) design or select a pump, 3) evaluate the appropriateness of a slow sand filter for a specific application, 4) build tanks of many different materials, 5) work with plastic and metal pipe, 6) estimate costs, 7) train maintenance workers, and carry out any other activity related to water supply.

You'll find needed information to plan, design, evaluate, build and maintain almost anything related to small scale technology in the hundreds of major topic areas covered by the library.

"Select and valuable references."
—R.P., Wm. Carey Univ., USA

"Thanks. . . You do a lot of work for us by evaluating and choosing the books, that would take so much time and money to organize."
—D.E., VTIS, Lesotho

Information When You Need It

During project work in developing countries, most technical questions never get answered. Access to good information is limited by the high cost of books, the lack of good library facilities, and the difficulty of communications.

Ordering single books, as the need arises, is the most common solution to the problem of finding necessary technical information. However, this can be difficult and time-consuming, and the cost per book is usually high. Also, the 2–6 months' wait for book delivery means that most projects must proceed without the needed information or be delayed. Most technical questions are therefore set aside and forgotten. Unfortunately, projects run without good technical information frequently fail.

With easy, daily access to the practical technical information you need, you will choose better projects, with lower costs and greater chances of success. By doing your homework more thoroughly before taking action, you will be able to eliminate dead ends and to concentrate your efforts on the most productive opportunities.

The most valuable information tool you can have is a good library. Until recently, few really good libraries on village technology existed, despite the existence of thousands of organizations carrying out small scale development projects. A library of sufficient size to answer most questions was far too expensive to buy and too time-consuming to organize. Now, however, these problems have been solved by the Appropriate Technology Microfiche Library. At a cost of US$0.70 per book (about 5% of the cost of the books in paper form), the microfiche library costs no more than a small motorcycle for a field worker. The library is fully organized, with indexing and reviews of each book.

Thousands of people are now using these microfiche libraries to do research in their own offices, homes, workshops, and field projects. The result: better choices of project activities and greater success in achieving goals.

> *". . . how incredibly useful the microfiche library has been to us. It has provided invaluable research information in our development of a Banki turbine and hydraulic ram pump for use in Bolivia."*
> *—D.B., La Paz, Bolivia*

> *"It has been a tremendous resource for volunteer projects, lending technical support and generating new ideas."*
> *—D.H., Asst. Dir., Peace Corps, Papua New Guinea*

A Cost-Effective Investment

Most organizations cannot afford to work *without* such a reference tool to support their activities. If you can avoid one mistake in project activities or the use of one foreign consultant, the library will pay for itself. Better planned, more successful projects generate more benefits, and these benefits will quickly exceed the cost of the library. Many donor agencies have sponsored the purchase of these microfiche library sets for local organizations that cannot find the funds themselves.

> *"It will more than pay for itself in a short time."*
> *—P.P., Kamagambo H.S., Kenya*

Develop Staff Skills and Make Better Use of Consultants

The microfiche library allows you to do your own homework first before asking other people for help. This gives you and your staff members the chance to look at a broader range of options and learn more. If outside assistance is still needed, you can ask more specific, informed questions. This results in faster, better answers that can be more quickly implemented. You will find that you need fewer consultants and that you make better use of the consultants you do use.

"It has increased our confidence and helps us to promote better nutrition through kitchen farming, assist villagers to repair other civil engineering structures (suspension bridges, irrigation channels), etc."
—H.H., Pokhara, Nepal

What are microfiche?

Microfiche are 4″ × 6″ (11cm × 16cm) plastic cards on which photographic images are made. Each card of microfiche in this library set can hold 98 or 133 pages of text (depending upon the size of the original pages). The microfiche is used with a microfiche "reader," which magnifies the image on the card back to its original size.

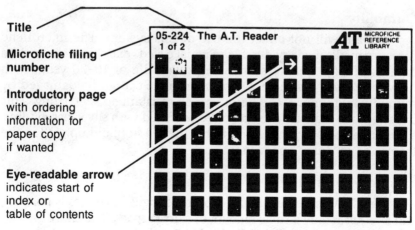

Sample microfiche card (one-half actual size)

Easy to Use

Several features make this microfiche set easy to use. The top strip of each plastic card lists the title of the book, along with indexing numbers for easy location of the card within the set. The index and table of contents of each book are marked by large "eye-readable" arrows, making them easy for you to find. Within the storage container, the microfiche are organized into topic categories according to the chapters in the **Appropriate Technology Sourcebook**. A new user can become familiar with the system in about 15 minutes.

"Easy access, simple to use, well organized."
—A.D., Univ. of N. Sumatera, Indonesia

Index and Book Reviews

A complete index on paper makes it easy to find what you are looking for in this large microfiche collection. A hardcover copy of the new **Appropriate Technology Sourcebook** contains a 10,000 entry index to the microfiche library, and reviews of each microfiche book. You can read the **Sourcebook** reviews to get a good feel for the contents of each book in the microfiche library, and identify specific books with needed information before using the microfiche. Additional paperback copies of the **Appropriate Technology Sourcebook** can be distributed among staff members working in different locations, so that they will know what is contained in the microfiche library.

"If you work overseas, you need this book and the library. Spread the word."
—J.B., Whole Earth Catalog

Durability

Climate will not affect the use of this system. The microfiche cards are made of a very durable material called "diazo," which provides excellent image quality and has a proven life of 10–20 years with heavy use in any climate. Diazo microfiche cannot be damaged by humidity and fungus, and has a scratch resistant epoxy coating. This durable diazo material should not be confused with silver-based films, sometimes used in other microfiche, that do not hold up well in the tropics or in dusty conditions.

Size and Portability

The A.T. Microfiche Library system is designed to be easily portable, and it requires only a small amount of storage space. The entire system, including 1785 microfiche cards, and the **A.T. Sourcebook** (which serves as the index), weighs 16 pounds (7 kg.). Together with the portable Cube II microfiche reader (the most portable reader we sell), the total system weight is 25 pounds (11 kg.). The microfiche cards are packed in a rugged plastic file box, with a built-in handle, designed specifically for this system. The microfiche library and the Cube II microfiche reader can be transported on foot or by bicycle, motorcycle, bus, car or any other mode of transportation. You can lend the whole library to a co-worker. The small physical size and light weight of this collection allow us to send it by airfreight to any major city in the world.

"We find our microfiche library to be an amazingly powerful yet compact reference center."

—T.B., Madagascar

Additional Reference Materials

The acquisition of a microfiche reader will open up a large range of additional low-cost reference materials on microfiche that can be ordered on a title-by-title basis. The best sources of these materials are noted in the **Appropriate Technology Sourcebook.**

New Publications

Among the 1000 publications reviewed in the **Appropriate Technology Sourcebook** that are included in this set, we have added more than 200 new titles this year, including the best new books

A COMPARISON OF PAPER COPIES AND MICROFICHE		
	Original Paper Copies of Books and Reports	**A.T. Microfiche Library and Micro Design 425 Reader**
1. Cost of a 1000-volume reference library	$14,000	$695 for microfiche (plus $225 for reader); total, $920
2. Storage space required	one large room	one desk drawer, plus one small cupboard for reader
3. Cost of shipping library overseas	$2000 by surface mail	$100 to $300 by airfreight
4. Shipping weight	750 pounds	35 pounds
5. Delivery time	4–8 months	1–3 weeks
6. Staff time required for locating, ordering, and picking up materials	1000 hours	2 hours
7. Staff time required for cataloguing materials	1000 hours	none (materials come indexed to the **A.T. Sourcebook**)
8. Durability in tropical conditions	quick deterioration due to humidity and fungus	10–20 year life with heavy use; no damage from humidity or fungus

from such groups as ITDG, ILO, IDRC, GTZ, and VITA. The library is the only source for more than 100 out-of-print but sought-after materials, such as the comprehensive **Farmer's Guide** (Jamaican Agricultural Society), and **Small Earth Dams** (USDA). A list of all 1000 publications included is available upon request. Periodic updating with new materials will ensure that the A.T. Microfiche Library stays up-to-date. Updating kits will be available in the future for everyone already holding the A.T. Microfiche Library. This edition of the library incorporates the September 1986 update package.

"In a country where books are scarce, this library is an important resource indeed. Already it has some readers' minds whirling as they realize 'we can do that technology here.'"

—L.F., MCC, Laos

"Where there is interest in appropriate technology, this collection will be warmly received and readily employed."
—CHOICE, American Library Association

Other Sources of Microfiche

The following groups are distributing publications on microfiche:

IDRC — International Development Research Centre. This Canadian aid organization has consistently produced valuable books on subjects of interest to village technology workers. Their publications in both paper and microfiche form are free to local people in developing countries. For others, IDRC publications are available in microfiche form for $1.00. Microfiche publications should be ordered from the Communications Division, IDRC, Box 8500, Ottawa, Canada K1G 3H9.

I.T. Publications — Back issues of ITDG's excellent journal **Appropriate Technology** are available in microfiche form (see review page 656.) Four quarterly issues make up each volume, and sell for £3.00 per complete volume (postage included.) A free paper index from the publishers will help you locate the volumes you need.

UNIPUB — This U.S. company handles a large number of United Nations publications, along with those of other international organizations such as FAO and IDRC. All FAO publications are available in microfiche. The price for each publication is $4.00 for the first microfiche card and $1.50 for each additional card for that publication. Each microfiche card contains 60 pages of text if released before 1981, and 98 pages if released in 1981 or later. The minimum charge per order is $7.50. Write to UNIPUB for information on the availability of microfiche from other sources. UNIPUB, 205 East 42nd St., New York, New York 10017, USA.

NTIS — National Technical Information Service. This U.S. government organization reprints many of the publications other government agencies have originally produced. This is where things can be found when they have gone out of print at the National Academy of Sciences. Most of this material is available on microfiche ($4-8 per title), but unfortunately the original filming is not of high quality. NTIS is represented by local sales agents in about 20 different countries. Orders from developing countries should be sent to Development Assistance Division, NTIS, Office of International Affairs, 5285 Port Royal Rd., Rm 306 Y, Springfield, Virginia 22161, USA. All other orders should be sent to NTIS, Springfield, Virginia 22161, USA.

PIP — The Postharvest Institute for Perishables operates a large information clearinghouse for postharvest food loss reduction of fruits, vegetables, roots, tubers and nuts. Virtually all documents are available on microfiche. Postharvest Institute for Perishables, University of Idaho, College of Agriculture, Moscow, Idaho 83843 USA.

U.N. Publications — Some publications from the United Nations are available in microfiche form. Write for a microfiche price list. United Nations Publications, Room A-3315, New York, NY 10017 USA; or, Palais des Nations, CH-1211 Geneva 10, Switzerland.

UNU — All UNU publications are available in microfiche. Write: Publications Section, Academic Services, The United Nations University, Toho Seimei Building, 15-1, Shibuya 2-chome, Shibuya-ku, Tokyo 150, Japan.

Harvester — The Harvester Project has been developing a portable audiovisual package for non-literates using microfiche projected on a screen (like a filmstrip.) The Harvester Project, 14275 Gayhead Road, Apple Valley, California, 92307 USA.

Also available from the publishers:

The Appropriate Technology Microfiche Library.

In addition to serving as a guide to the best references on small scale technology, this book can be used as an index to the **Appropriate Technology Microfiche Library**. The microfiche library has been designed to contain the best selected references available on small-scale and village-level technology, and includes over 1000 of the books and documents reviewed here in the **A.T. Sourcebook**. The very low cost of the microfiche library makes it affordable for small organizations and individuals. People are using these portable libraries in more than 100 countries, often in remote areas.

Having your own complete library makes it far easier and faster to get the information you need. It allows you to immediately research possible solutions to problems and identify opportunities. The easy access to information on a wide variety of possible options enables you to rapidly evaluate choices and make better decisions when planning programs. And the detailed practical information in these books allows work to proceed immediately.

We put our appropriate technology library in a box...

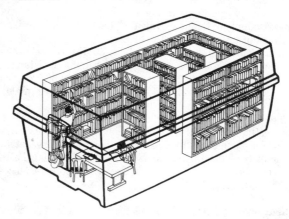

The microfiche library is compact, lightweight and portable. It contains more than 138,500 pages of text. See pages 792–798 of this book for a more complete description of the microfiche library. A list of the 1000 books in the microfiche library can be found on pages 676–696. Instructions for the use of the microfiche library are included on pages 670–673.

For more information, write to: Appropriate Technology Project, Microfiche Library, Volunteers in Asia, P.O. Box 4543, Stanford, California 94305, USA.

DATE DUE

MR 7 '04			

#47-0108 Peel Off Pressure Sensitive